CANADA
1896-1921

ROBERT CRAIG BROWN
AND RAMSAY COOK

CANADA
1896-1921

A Nation Transformed

The Canadian Centenary Series

© Robert Craig Brown
and Ramsay Cook, 1974

Reprinted 1988

CANADIAN CATALOGUING IN PUBLICATION DATA

Brown, Robert Craig, 1935.
  Canada, 1896-1921

(The Canadian centenary series; 14)
Bibliography: p.
ISBN 0-7710-2269-7

1. Canada–History–1867-1914.   2. Canada–
History–1914-1918.   I. Cook, Ramsay, 1931-
II. Title.   III. Series.

FC540.B76   971.05'6   C74-3619-X
F1033.B76

McClelland and Stewart
The Canadian Publishers
481 University Avenue
Toronto, Ontario
M5G 2E9

Manufactured in Canada by Webcom Limited

To Professor D. J. McDougall

A History of Canada

W. L. Morton, *EXECUTIVE EDITOR*
D. G. Creighton, *ADVISORY EDITOR*
Ramsay Cook, *EXECUTIVE EDITOR, 1983*

†ALSO AVAILABLE IN PAPERBACK
Volumes I, III, VII, and XII of The Canadian Centenary
Series were published with the help of grants from the
Humanities Research Council of Canada.

CONTENTS

Canada 1896-1921

The Canadian Centenary Series

Half a century has elapsed since *Canada and Its Provinces,* the first large-scale co-operative history of Canada, was published. During that time, new historical materials have been made available in archives and libraries; new research has been carried out, and its results published; new interpretations have been advanced and tested. In these same years Canada itself has greatly grown and changed. These facts, together with the centenary of Confederation, justify the publication of a new co-operative history of Canada.

The form chosen for this enterprise was that of a series of volumes. The series was planned by the editors, but each volume will be designed and executed by a single author. The general theme of the work is the development of those regional communities which have for the past century made up the Canadian nation; and the series will be composed of a number of volumes sufficiently large to permit adequate treatment of all the phases of the theme in the light of modern knowledge.

The Centenary History, then, was planned as a series to have a certain common character and to follow a common method but to be written by individual authors, specialists in their fields. As a whole, it will be a work of specialized knowledge, the great advantage of scholarly co-operation, and at the same time each volume will have the unity and distinctive character of individual authorship. It was agreed that a general narrative treatment was necessary and that each author should deal in a balanced way with economic, political, and social history. The result, it is hoped, will be an interpretative, varied, and comprehensive account, at once useful to the student and interesting to the general reader.

The difficulties of organizing and executing such a series are apparent: the overlapping of separate narratives, the risk of omissions, the imposition of divisions which are relevant to some themes but not to others. Not so apparent, but quite as troublesome, are the problems of scale, perspective, and scope, problems which perplex the writer of a one-volume history and are magnified in a series. It is by deliberate choice that certain parts of the history are told twice, in different volumes from different points of view, in the belief that the benefits gained outweigh the unavoidable disadvantages.

In their joint, well-knit history of the events and changes in Canada from 1896 to 1921 the authors have made a critical analysis of the transformation the country experienced during those years. They do not merely retell but re-interpret and re-state our understanding of a period which saw Canada tested as it was and reshaped as it was to be. Here is a scholarly accomplishment of rare merit, both in its re-structuring of the period and in its perception of its significance. Readers of *A Nation Transformed,* we feel, will better understand both those years of industrial boom, urban growth, and all-demanding war, and the changes Canada has since undergone.

W. L. MORTON,
Executive Editor.
D. G. CREIGHTON,
Advisory Editor.

A Nation Transformed

The period of Canadian history surveyed in this book is one that has attracted much interest in recent years. Our footnotes reveal, imperfectly, the extent to which we have relied upon the exciting work that has been accomplished, though often not yet published, by a new generation of Canadian historians. In a sense, then, this book is a progress report on Canadian scholarship, our own and that of others. We hope that we have fairly reflected what has been done, and, at least by implication, that we suggest new questions that might be asked of old evidence and new areas that need further examination. Since this book is an attempt at synthesis, we wish, first of all, to express our gratitude to all those writers whose research has made our effort easier.

We have many other important debts. The first is to the general editors, W.L. Morton and Donald Creighton. They have constantly encouraged us, tolerated our tardiness (particularly that of one of the authors), and, finally, read and criticized the manuscript with the same intelligence and perception that appear in their own writing. Carl Berger and Blair Neatby both made a sacrifice beyond the call of friendship in devoting a Christmas vacation to reading our book. Perhaps the season explains their generosity. Their criticisms were both helpful and encouraging. C.P. Stacey, Robert Bothwell, Richard Clippingdale, Ian Drummond, Viv Nelles, and Paul Rutherford read various sections of the book. We very much appreciate the willingness of these busy people to assist us with their expert knowledge. Naturally none of our debtors is responsible for the shortcomings that remain in the book.

Particular thanks is due to various archives and libraries throughout Canada. They have given us indispensable help at each stage of our research. While every one of these institutions is important, none is more so than that haven of scholarship and friendship, the Public Archives of Canada in Ottawa. We are especially grateful to Wilfred Smith and his staff for the unlimited cooperation which they so cheerfully gave to us. Jack Saywell, in his usual generous way, opened up his splendid collection of illustrations and photographs to us. Henry Borden, Q.C., gave us full use of his uncle's diary. There are many more people who deserve our appreciation. Matt Bray and Jim Pitsula worked very hard to collect and collate an extraordinary bibliography, which we have had to drop for reasons of space. Karen Huhn typed the final manuscript carefully and with good humour.

Our publisher has waited a long time for this book, and in the end he has accepted an overlength manuscript. In these days when Canadian publishing is experiencing difficulties, we want to record our deep appreciation for the generous fashion in which McClelland and Stewart has treated us.

Finally, and most important, we wish to thank Eleanor Cook. She managed, miraculously, to find a month in a schedule that included wifing, mothering, teaching, and completing a book of her own, to edit this entire manuscript. She brought order to the footnotes, ruthlessness to the verbiage, and clarity to confused sentences. Her most important contribution to the completion of this book, and that of Gail Brown, remain unmentioned. A preface must be short.

RAMSAY COOK
ROBERT CRAIG BROWN

CHAPTER 1

The Great Transformation

Canada, in the twenty-five years between the election of Sir Wilfrid Laurier and the resignation of Sir Robert Borden, was a country being transformed. The population increased by more than three million. Two new provinces were created in the prairie west. The northern regions of the two central provinces and of British Columbia opened up, revealing vast new sources of mineral wealth and energy. Foreign trade and foreign investment rose to unprecedented levels. Wheat, the gold of the prairie, flowed into the bakeries of Europe, as western Canada produced a new staple to replace the fur and lumber of her earlier history. Two new transcontinental railways were chartered and, with the era of the automobile, highways and roads began to slice up the landscape more systematically than in the day of the horse, the buggy, the carriage, and the sleigh.

But the transformation must be measured by more than number and size. The new Canada that emerged from the Laurier period, continued to grow, and faced the grim test of world war in the Borden years, was not just a bigger edition of the old Canada. It was new in quality and spirit. It grew, of course, from seeds planted in previous decades, even centuries. But there was more than the process of growing up – the analogy which contemporaries loved to use in describing the process in which they perceived themselves participating. To begin with, another two million and more new Canadians added a new ethnic dimension to Canadian life. They were too numerous to be rapidly absorbed into a Canadian melting pot. And since almost one-third of them came from outside the English-speaking world, or the French-speaking for that matter, they did not simply reinforce old Canada. Indeed, they often challenged it.

Many of these new settlers took up homes and homesteads in the prairie west. They were going to build a new society. And that society would not follow the rigid patterns of their numerous homelands. It would be new. Nor would it necessarily follow the patterns of settled Canada, which had already two centuries or more of history. The new society would be part

1

of Canada, of course; but it would be a part with its own sectional identity. The growth of the western prairies, exuding their own brand of Canadianism, altered and made significantly more difficult that balancing act which characterizes political leadership in Canada. To linguistic and religious differences was added sectional conflict. That had always existed of course, but force of numbers now gave it greater significance.

But the peopling of the prairie west was not the only change in the structure of Canadian society after 1896. The altering balance between city and rural dweller was just as striking and more significant in its long-run effects. Though the Laurier years were the age of the wheat boom and the pageant of western settlement, none the less the percentage of Canadians who lived on farms declined continually during the twenty-five years of the Laurier-Borden regimes. Canada was becoming an urbanized country where people's livelihoods depended increasingly on industry, natural resources, and service occupations. The dividing line was 1921: in that year the rural-urban balance was nearly equal.[1] But more important, the two largest provinces, Ontario and Quebec, had already passed that threshold by the outbreak of the Great War in 1914.

The effect of advancing industrial and urban growth on the character of Canada was profound. Indeed, the Laurier-Borden years should be seen as the history of a people attempting to bring its institutions into conformity with the demands of a new, unfamiliar kind of society. For the farmers the adjustment was traumatic, bursting into full blown, but belated, revolt in 1921. For the industrial classes the adjustment took place through the growth of trade unions and sporadic efforts at political action. There was labour revolt, too: most startlingly in Winnipeg in the late spring of 1919. For investors and businessmen, members of the upper economic classes, it marked a period of enormous expansion of total investment and output, of profits and wages, and of the size of business organization. The large corporation, the monopoly, and the trust became the characteristic form of business organization in these years. Business became national in scope. And it became even more international in its sources of support than ever before. It was in the prosperous Laurier years that Canada offered immensely attractive opportunities for investment – especially for investors with a willingness to risk large sums in the expectation of heavy returns. Such investors came, most often, from the United States. As the Laurier period advanced, American money began to rise toward the levels already occupied by British investment. But a significant difference existed between the type of investment provided by Canada's two closest neighbours. British investment took portfolio form for the most part in bonds that did not carry ownership and control. American investors, almost from the outset, showed strong preference for direct investment, and for the ownership and control that went with it.[2]

Foreign capital was necessary to Canada's growth and welcomed by nearly everyone. Its impact, of course, was uneven, being greatest in Ontario, British Columbia, and Quebec, least in the maritimes and prairies. This, too, was a cause for regional friction. In Quebec, the industrial and urban growth that followed investment had a peculiar dual effect. Most positively, of course, it provided jobs. And the demand for labour in the home market solved a problem which had beset Quebec throughout the latter three-quarters of the nineteenth century: emigration. The stream of French-speaking Canadians that had flowed south with such intensity in the 1880s and 1890s as to make some predict the conquest of Puritan New England for Rome, dried up. Instead the surplus sons and daughters went into the factories, pulp mills, and mines of Montreal, Sherbrooke, Trois-Rivières, or Lac St-Jean.

But if the problem of emigration was thus solved, others were created. Could the traditionally rural French Canadian preserve his distinctive way of life in the increasingly urban milieu? In one sense this was the same question farmers were asking everywhere in Canada by 1910. But in Quebec it had an ethnic connotation lacking in rural Ontario or the prairie west. And the ethnic quality was given a special edge because the new wielders of economic power in Quebec were not merely urban capitalists; they were also, almost always, English-speaking capitalists. That made the industrial and urban transformation of Quebec all the more foreboding. The impact of industrial and urban life was thus the central concern of French-Canadian social thinkers in the Laurier and Borden years.

So it was for social thinkers elsewhere in Canada. The development of the urban proletariat, the urban slum, and the vices of city life was a growing preoccupation of the country's churches. The social gospel in its many forms was the most obvious response. But even when the churches devoted their attention to rural Canada – usually to sing the virtues of the family farm – it was because of worries about the decline of agriculture resulting from urban growth. What was true of organizations like the churches was true of those scattered individuals who thought and wrote about social problems in Canada: a J.S. Woodsworth, concerned for the immigrant and the labourer of the city; a W.C. Good, frightened by the evidence of rural depopulation; a Henri Bourassa, fearful for the future of his culture; a Stephen Leacock, satirically remorseful about the disappearance of old values. All were aware, if sometimes only vaguely, that a great transformation was in progress, that a new Canada was being born and only partly out of the old. They sought to understand that transformation, to ease its impact or to slacken its speed. These were the voices that pointed to the problems and dislocations of the period. They were, of course, a small minority.

For the majority, optimism was the ruling passion, even after signs of collapse had begun to appear in the Edwardian world. Material expansion became, for most, the measure of national and moral progress. The potential of Canada seemed unlimited. The vast, empty spaces of the land would welcome millions of settlers, giving Canada a population that would challenge the United States and surpass Great Britain. That population would exploit the untold resources of the country, providing a standard of living envied by the remainder of the world. The twentieth century would belong to Canada.

This confidence, this boom mentality swept away all the deep doubts about the future that had hung over the early 1890s like a pall. The fears of so many that Canada was doomed to collapse into the arms of the United States either from internal bickering or economic failure disappeared. Few people anticipated, and even fewer advocated, annexation to the Great Republic. With the disappearance of that debate, advocates of the other prominent panaceas for the Canadian question also trimmed their sails. The supporters of complete Canadian independence seemed willing to accept quietly a slowly evolving autonomy. The proud proponents of imperial federation seemed satisfied with British-Canadian sentiment that ensured a close, harmonious, and equal partnership with Britain. In times of crisis, real differences could emerge among the heirs of these old schools, but all were united in one conviction: Canada, as a nation, had an unbounded and assured future.

Yet that layer of confidence, founded upon an expanding economy, had a brittleness that could easily crack. Prosperity might sooth sectional frictions, calm class conflicts, and temper ethnic hostilities, but by itself it could not remove them. Indeed, the very process of change, at certain critical points, intensified these disharmonies. The control which central Canada appeared to exercise over national economic policies and national organizations, such as the trade unions and the churches, sharpened conflict between east and west in Canada. So, too, the unequal division of prosperity between workers and employers, and that between farmers and grain handlers, provided a new edge to class conflict, an edge that took on new cutting power as each boatload of immigrants swelled the ranks of the farm and urban workers. Then there was the eternal French-English conflict, and its awkwardly related Catholic-Protestant partner. Industrial and urban growth produced internal tensions within the Quebec community that helped to increase the selfconscious sensitivity of French Canadians. There was another factor, however, for the settling of the west by a vast new influx of non-French-speaking Canadians gave the French Canadian a new consciousness of his minority status. Most immediately it raised again the question of the rights of French Canadians who lived outside the province of Quebec. But equally significant, western settlement marked a shift in the delicate population balance of Canada. Immigration was the high card which the English Canadians held in the Canadian poker game. Little of it came from France, with the result that the French Canadian was left only with his admittedly extraordinary fecundity to stave off extinction. These circumstances were well suited to create tension – especially when many of the new immigrants were Catholics unwilling to leave the French-Canadian ascendancy in the Church unchallenged.

Left alone, Canadians would have had a difficult enough time shaping a recognizable community out of the new and historic elements that had to be combined. But the age of Laurier and Borden was not an age of watertight compartments. The transformation of Canada took place against a backdrop of global change. The forces of industrial and urban growth had already had a profound impact upon much of western Europe and the United States when the twentieth century opened, and several nations were jockeying for position in the world balance of power. Each, and especially Britain, Germany, France, and the United States, exhibited a new national confidence often called the "new imperialism." In various combinations and permutations, these nations tested each other's strength around the world – Pago-Pago, the Transvaal, Cuba, Venezuela, Alaska, and Tripoli. New alliances were in the making and old friendships facing strains.

In the world balance Canada exerted little weight. Yet Canada was closely related to two of the world's great powers, Great Britain and the United States, and tenuously related to a third, France. What was more, the immigrants who poured into her vacant spaces in the years before 1914 came from all the trouble spots of Europe, as well as from Great Britain and the United States. Canadians were thus extremely sensitive to European affairs especially if Britain, with whom they had close constitutional, military, economic, and social ties, was involved. There were also economic, social, and geographic ties, strong and growing more so, with the United States. But most significant, yet most difficult either to manage or to measure, were the emotional ties which Canadians maintained with the outside world. Britain, the United States, and France each had complex roles to play in the emotions that Canadians had about their country and its place in the world. To English-speaking Canadians, France was just another foreign country. To French-speaking Canadians such a neutral attitude was impossible: France was the mother country which had deserted her American colony, and which later had committed the blasphemy of revolution; but it was the source of French culture. Britain created even more confused emotional counter-currents. Britain was the home of English Canada's culture and institutions and for many it was the home of close relatives. Few English Canadians would question the benefits of the British connection in the past, though there were deep differences over what that connection should be in the future. For French Canadians, Britain was a conqueror who had, after many struggles, recognized French Canada's right to its peculiar institutions. For that French Canadians were grateful, but not to the extent of believing they owed any debt to their conqueror beyond the shores of Canada. The United States attracted an equal variety of attitudes from Canadians. In one sense, the U.S. was what most Canadians were striving for: wealth, power, and at least approximate equality of opportunity. Yet, in another sense, the U.S. was everything many Canadians abhorred: imperialism, lack of discipline, and moral relativism. Canadians feared and envied the United States. But they knew that probably no country, not even Great Britain, was as important to them as their immense, frequently turbulent neighbour. The task for Canadians was somehow to obtain the benefits of American society without its faults, while at the same time assuring that Canadian society remained distinct from the nation to the south.

As these great powers shifted and manoeuvred on the checkerboard of world diplomacy, Canadians watched eagerly. Both their interests and their emotions were touched each time Britain and the United States moved closer, or fell apart. To a lesser extent, the same was true of Britain's and France's friendship. So to the sectional, class, and ethnic relations of Canada's great age of growth, was added an international climate that affected Canada in infinitely more ways than she could hope to affect it. That is why the age of Laurier and Borden was one of high excitement politically as well as one of profound change materially.

CHAPTER 2

The Laurier Style

For nearly thirty years after Confederation most Canadians had given their confidence to the Liberal-Conservative party. Only once, in 1873, had the Liberals won a chance to display their talents, and on that occasion economic depression had ensured that the result fell far short of brilliance. Now, in the autumn of 1896, Wilfrid Laurier had an opportunity to prove that his Liberal party was worthy of the support given it once more by the voters. A peaceful revolution had taken place at the ballot boxes; a normally Conservative Canada had voted, and voted by a clear margin, for the Liberal party. Quebec had led the way, though in that province the Liberals had already replaced the Conservatives as the majority party in 1891. But in 1896 Quebeckers provided the margin of victory by giving 49 of 65 seats to their native son. But Ontario gave Laurier nearly as many seats, 43, though an equal number remained with Sir Charles Tupper's Conservatives, while two Patrons, two McCarthyites, and an Independent waited to be wooed by the new government. British Columbia sent the government a majority of its six seats, Nova Scotia divided exactly, while New Brunswick, Prince Edward Island and Manitoba remained with the Conservatives. [1]

Wilfrid Laurier was the man the Governor General, Lord Aberdeen, called upon to form the new government. A French Canadian, the first to lead the country since Confederation, he was a lawyer by profession and a man of culture, perhaps even of two cultures. In his younger years his health had been uncertain and his interests bookish; only gradually had his political activities taken precedence over his profession. Though active in *rouge* politics and an opponent of Confederation in the 1860's, Laurier's views had moderated and his ambitions grown. His legal training at McGill University and his later absorption in the classics of English political writing had provided him with both skill in a second language and an admiration for the traditions of parliamentary government. After reluctantly succeeding Edward Blake as party leader in 1887, Laurier had quickly learned that a successful Canadian politician – he carefully watched the old master, Sir John A. Macdonald – required endurance, organizing skill, the ability to manage men and, not least of all, a talent for compromise. To temporize, to blunt divisive issues, might not be heroic, but it could ensure peace – and power.[2]

Endowed with a gracious manner and skilled in the arts of oratory, Laurier had mastered the methods of working with men as wilful, and different, as Joseph Israel Tarte and Sir Richard Cartwright. And he was also learning the ways of calming the doubts and suspicions of protectionist Ontario businessmen and determined Quebec bishops. Once a free trader in economics and perhaps a free thinker, or at least a mild anticlerical, in religion, he had hardened into a practical politician anxious to use and to hold the power that had at last come to him. Soon he would be telling those who had once admired his eloquently articulated idealism that "in politics, the question seldom arises to do the ideal right. The best that is generally to be expected, is to attain a certain object, and for the accomplishment of this object, many things have to be done which are questionable, and many things have to be submitted to which, if rigorously investigated, could not be approved of."[3]

At fifty-five he was near the height of his powers in 1896. Balding at the front, his hair – not yet the silver plumage of later years – flowed back fashionably to touch his high Victorian collar. Frock-coated suits and double-breasted vests set him off stylishly, even somewhat romantically, and he wore a top hat, and sometimes a cloth cap, with elegance. His strong, distinctive face broke easily into a smile when he greeted a political friend, and even when he skilfully admonished an erring foe. A friendly, if carefully controlled personality, he attracted genuine affection from adulators and critics alike. It was his deep-set eyes, perhaps, that best revealed the will and determination that were an important part of this politician's make-up. Even his most powerful colleagues would soon realize that "despite his courtesy and gracious charm," Laurier was "a masterful man set on having his own way, and equally resolute that his colleagues shall not have their way unless this is quite agreeable to him."[4]

Laurier's talent for persuasion, for careful political assessment and for ruthless decision were all to be tested now that he had won the right to lead a government. The country had just come through a vigorously fought election whose backdrop was a gradually improving, but still depressed economy, as well as the cultural and religious animosities that centred on the separate school question. This was enough to make every decision crucial for any prime minister. But Wilfrid Laurier was not just any prime minister. He was a man determined to prove to his party and his people, French and English-speaking, that a French Canadian could succeed as the Queen's first Canadian Minister.

I

The first test of the new Prime Minister's skill, and the initial hint of the policies that might be forthcoming, came with the formation of the cabinet. A party which had been in opposition for eighteen years naturally suffered from a lack of administrative experience. Laurier's own tenure of office in the Mackenzie administration had lasted scarcely a year. The only other hold-over from that earlier Liberal ministry was Sir Richard Cartwright. His record as Minister of Finance for five years, and his subsequent advocacy of unrestricted reciprocity between Canada and the United States, were viewed by many as an obvious example of experience being a poor guide to cabinet qualifications.

But if the parliamentary party was short on experience, the provincial Liberal parties, several of which had long terms of office behind them, provided a wealth of talent. No less than three provincial premiers, W.S. Fielding of Nova Scotia, A.G. Blair of New Brunswick, and wise old Oliver Mowat of Ontario, were drawn into federal service by Laurier. And from the Manitoba cabinet, after a slight but important delay, came a man probably more powerful than that province's premier: the ambitious young Attorney General, Clifford Sifton. These four men received the major positions in the new government. Each in his own way brought administrative talent and, more important, respectability to the new government. These men gave proof that the Liberal party had turned its back on its free trade past, had come to terms with the Canadian business community, and would soon begin to write new, vibrant chapters in the long history of the national policies of tariffs, railways, and settlement.

Mowat's appointment as Minister of Justice had perhaps more symbolic than real significance. He had already served for twenty-four years as Premier of Ontario and his career stretched back far enough to make him a father of Confederation. Obviously he was not expected to assume heavy administrative, or even less, political duties in the new government. Yet Mowat had the confidence of the Canadian business community and his presence in the cabinet gave assurance to those who suspected that Laurier was less than loyal to the British connection.[5] Moreover, by giving Mowat such a prominent position, Laurier doubtless found it easier to pass over another Ontarian in making his choice for the key position of Minister of Finance. On grounds of administrative experience and loyalty to the party, the post rightfully belonged to Sir Richard Cartwright. It was given to W.S. Fielding. George H. Bertram, a prominent Toronto Liberal businessman gave Laurier some advice on the subject shortly after the election: "It is of the greatest importance that the Finance Minister of a Liberal Administration should be an exceptionally strong man having the confidence of all classes, but more particularly of the business community. The name of Premier Fielding which you mentioned to me, I have since learned is an exceptionally strong one. I trust you will secure him. . . . I do not wish to write one unkind word regarding Sir Richard Cartwright, but the interests of the country and the party are paramount to all others and I am sure that Liberals generally *do not on any account* desire to see Sir Richard back into his old position of Finance Minister."[6]

By 1896 it is doubtful that Laurier needed the advice. Ever since the Convention of 1893 the Liberal party had been attempting to redeem itself from its free trade past. Moreover, since at least 1894 Laurier had been trying to entice Premier W.S. Fielding to Ottawa. Though Fielding, too, had a dubious past both as a Nova Scotia separatist and a free trader, his ten years as Premier had been characterized by sound administration, cautious policies, and a growing awareness of the importance of the tariff to the Nova Scotia coal industry. In all this, Fielding symbolized neatly the evolution of the federal Liberal party.[7] Cartwright, loyal old workhorse, accepted a secondary post as Minister of Trade and Commerce – perhaps in the knowledge that there were those who wanted him totally excluded from cabinet office.[8] But he had to sit beside William Paterson, an Ontario manufacturer, who was put in charge of the Ministry of Customs.

Laurier's choices from Quebec showed a similar circumspection. No one better represented the new tone of Quebec Liberalism than Joseph Israel Tarte, who began and ended his life a Conservative and never ceased during his six years in the Laurier government to call himself one. Tarte was an ingenious political organizer who had given Laurier enormous assistance in the 1896 campaign. His position as Minister of Public Works ensured his continued effectiveness as party organizer in Quebec. But he also had close connections with the business community, exhibited a deep interest in economic policy and adhered firmly to the protectionist faith.[9] None of Laurier's old *rouge* associates entered the cabinet except Sir Henri Joly de Lotbinière, though an offer was probably made to C.A. Geoffrion. Richard Dobell, a former Conservative, Sydney Fisher, and Charles Fitzpatrick represented various elements of the English-speaking minority in Quebec. There can be little doubt that Laurier was anxious, in the selection of his Quebec colleagues, to avoid creating unnecessary difficulties with the ecclesiastical authorities with whom he knew he would soon have to discuss the settlement of the school problem in Manitoba. The same objective was served when, a few months after the election, Tarte purchased the Montreal *rouge* paper *La Patrie* and replaced its two anticlerical directors, Henri Beaugrand and Godfrey Langlois, by the young Henri Bourassa, a Liberal in politics but an ultramontane in religion.[10] Plainly Laurier's new liberalism was in the process of shedding much of its past Grit and *rouge* heritage as it moved to fill that centre position in the political spectrum so long occupied by Macdonald's Conservatives.

No one in western Canada better represented that centrist spirit than the man Laurier wanted to fill the Ministry of the Interior: Clifford Sifton. In 1896 Sifton was only thirty-five. Yet he had already gained a good education in Ontario and the beginnings of a fair fortune in the west. At thirty he had been appointed Attorney General of Manitoba, a post that placed him at the centre of the quarrel with Ottawa over the Manitoba school question. He joined the Laurier cabinet late, having first played a large role in working out a compromise school settlement. Yet the important fact about Sifton was that he was less a lawyer than a businessman. His faith in the potential of the west was nearly limitless as was his frustration with the failure of successive Conservative governments to develop it. But he never looked upon the west as a section separate from the rest of the country. Rather it was an integral part of the national economy to be developed in an orderly, businesslike fashion. That Sifton fitted easily into the Laurier cabinet is well illustrated in a letter he sent off to a Manitoba free trader shortly after taking office. "I not only would not retire from the Government because they refused to eliminate the principle of protection from the tariff, but I would not remain in the Government if they did eliminate the principle of protection from the tariff. I would consider that to so construct the tariff as to wantonly destroy the industries that have been built up under it, would be utterly unjustifiable from any possible standpoint of reason. I may say that on principle I am a very strong freetrader. I have been fed and educated on free trade doctrines, but doctrines do not always apply to facts."[11] These were hardly the sentiments of a prairie radical, but they fitted well into the perspective on the "facts" held by most of Sifton's new colleagues.

These, then, were the elements that combined to form Laurier's first cabinet. It was a remarkably, if unevenly, talented group. It was characterized by a determination to adopt practical measures which would quicken the development of the country and ensure the renewed election of the party. The problems both of finding the formula to get the economy moving, and of restoring religious and ethnic peace were very large. Yet the very newness of the government was, in itself, something to inspire the country. At the centre of the administration, from its first months, was the new Prime Minister, Wilfrid Laurier. Both his warm Gallic charm and his steel Gallic will had passed the test of political leadership during nearly nine hard years in opposition. His shrewd political judgment as well as his determination to succeed was clearly illustrated in his well-constructed cabinet. He had a mind that was sharp and subtle; a voice that in French or English could sonorously summon both his party and his people to action. By mid–1896 this frail but tough politician had proven his mettle as a campaigner and party leader. As he turned to face the issues, as summer changed to autumn, he had laid a sound basis for his premiership.[12]

II

"What a disaster! What a pirate's hands we have fallen into! Is it the Quebec French Canadians who are going to prevent us from having a federal remedial law; whether we like it or not we will be reduced to accepting a few crumbs that Greenway will throw at us disdainfully. . . . The Liberals want to beg from Rome with their accustomed cheek and their diabolical hypocrisy, a muzzle for the hierarchy. When they have succeeded in closing the Bishop's mouths, then they will attack the Pope himself. *Progenies viperarum.*"[13] Bishop Langevin's concern was couched in extreme language, but it was hardly untypical of the attitude of many members of the Catholic Church in Quebec toward the newly elected Liberals. Forty years of intermittent quarrels between cleric and *rouge* had left deep scars. Some of these had been reopened, almost brutally, in the campaign of 1896, for though the Church hierarchy had adopted a moderate collective position during the election, its suspicion of the Liberals was far from erased.[14] Once in office Laurier had to face squarely the immediate test of finding a solution to the six-year-old school dispute in Manitoba. Over and above that pressing problem was the larger one of the relations between the Liberal party and the leaders of the Quebec Church. Unless peace could be made, the party would never be able to free both hands to fight the Tories. Here was a challenge for the new government and, above all, for its leader. If it could be successfully met, other problems, more normal political and economic problems, could then be faced with confidence.

The Manitoba school dispute was one of extreme delicacy, not least because Laurier had never committed himself to any single position on the matter. On the one hand he had argued that provincial rights had to be respected and that, therefore, a negotiated settlement would be preferable to remedial legislation forced on Manitoba by Ottawa. This was a view applauded by English-Canadian followers. On the other hand he had never denied that remedial legislation would be necessary if his "sunny ways" negotiations failed. His Quebec supporters had emphasized this position in the election.[15] Once in office Laurier had to find a means of satisfying both these viewpoints without, he hoped, further antagonizing the leaders of the Catholic Church in Quebec. This was not a small assignment.

The new Liberal government at Ottawa did, however, have certain advantages not enjoyed by its predecessor. Most significant, in an age of intense partisanship, was the common political colour of the governments of Thomas Greenway in Winnipeg and Wilfrid Laurier in Ottawa. Then, too, there was the ambition of Clifford Sifton. He wanted to transfer from Manitoba to Ottawa, a change Laurier entirely favoured. But before he came, he had the task of working out a school settlement with his future colleagues. Finally, and ironically, Laurier had yet another advantage: the electors of Manitoba had returned a majority of Conservatives to Ottawa in 1896. Thus, as one correspondent put it to Laurier, "It can no longer be said that province is unitedly and unanimously opposed to separate schools."[16] In these moderately hopeful circumstances, Laurier quickly set in motion a series of actions directed toward reaching a negotiated settlement. Judge A.B. Routhier, a former Castor, now a supporter of Laurier and compromise, set out for Manitoba and talks with Archbishop Langevin, hoping to persuade him to accept something less than remedial legislation.[17] Routhier had little success with the unbending prelate and, like most French Canadians, developed deep reservations about the prospect of getting much satisfaction from Sifton.[18]

Laurier was more optimistic. Negotiations with Sifton by mail opened the discussions, and Joseph Israel Tarte and Henri Bourassa were dispatched to Winnipeg to conclude the pact. By November the major elements of the agreement had been decided upon. Of course, there was no suggestion that state-financed separate schools would be restored. No realist ever believed that possible, though Mgr Langevin continued to insist that nothing less was acceptable. But religious teaching in the public schools would be allowed for half an hour at the conclusion of each day. Moreover, Catholic teachers could be employed in urban schools with forty Catholic pupils or in rural districts with twenty-five. Finally, "when ten of the pupils in any school speak the French language or any language other than English, as their native language, the teaching of such pupils shall be conducted in French, or such other language, and English upon the bilingual system."[19]

The Laurier-Greenway compromise was a politicians' agreement: each apparently believed it could be acceptable to his supporters and their constituents. Greenway had preserved a single, public school system. Laurier had gained some concessions for the Catholic minority and for the French language. But there was no disguising the fact that the provisions of the Manitoba Act for a bicultural province had been permanently annulled: Catholics were not to gain a separate but equal school system, French was not to be a language with a status equal to English, but rather second to English and more significant, equal to "any language other than English." The 1870 Manitoba Act had attempted to make Manitoba the last of the old provinces; the 1890 Manitoba School Act made it the first of the new. The Laurier-Greenway agreement did very little to alter that decision; it merely made the decision slightly more palatable to the minority.

Having achieved agreement with Manitoba, Laurier next tested the reaction of the public at large and, more particularly, the leaders of the

Catholic Church. Ontario offered no problem. John Willison, editor of the *Globe* and close confidant of several leading federal Liberals, carried out a broad survey of sensitive areas of Protestant opinion and was able to pronounce the proposed arrangements acceptable.[20] A similarly encouraging view came from the Catholic segment of Ontario's population.[21] Quebec was more sensitive and Laurier set his newspaper allies the task of getting the message across to the public – doubtless anticipating an ecclesiastical attack on the agreement.[22] A dissident Liberal M.P. complained that the settlement was a step toward assimilation since it gave the French and Catholic minority no guarantee of autonomous development. Laurier's reply, while skirting the particular accusation, was an effective statement of his views on French-English relations in Canada. "For me," he wrote, "the salvation of the French race is not in isolation, but in struggle. Give our children the best education possible, put them on an equal footing with those of the other race, and give them the legitimate pride which they will have in such a struggle. There is salvation. There is autonomy."[23]

It was easy enough to gain the support of the politicians. The Church was another matter, and unless the prelates were at least neutralized it would be difficult to hold the support of the people and the politicians. Even before the Manitoba settlement had been made public, Laurier had sent off two carefully chosen emissaries to the Vatican: Abbé Proulx, and a former Papal Zouave, Gustave Drolet. Laurier armed Proulx with the argument which he, and later representatives, were to press with boring repetition in Rome. "The population is with us," Laurier maintained. "We will have a strong government. A Catholic is Prime Minister. If the extremists wish to precipitate a struggle on this point, and draw the clergy into a struggle against the government – and that is just what they are going to do, I am already informed of it – it is not difficult to see what perturbation there will be in the country. The Catholics in this country are a minority. With tact, with firmness, they can always make themselves respected, but the moment they use violence, the consequences of their act will only be disastrous."[24]

At the Vatican Proulx and Drolet performed like two innocents abroad, proving no match for the counter emissaries from Quebec – the Bishops of St. Boniface, Quebec City, Nicolet, and Chicoutimi. Proulx remarked, perhaps unintentionally going to the heart of the matter, that "almost the whole of Canada is going to be transported to Rome; it would be much simpler if a single person, in Rome's name, were transported to Canada."[25] As the Quebec bishops – at the behest of Mgr Langevin of St. Boniface – began to mount a growing attack on the Manitoba settlement and the Liberals, Laurier concluded that the only way to avert a "holy war" like the one that had raged in the seventies, was to appoint a papal delegate to Canada. The bishops were certainly beginning to throw their weight around. L.O. David's rather mild criticism of the political activities of the Church in his pamphlet, *Le Clergé Canadien,*[26] suffered condemnation, and the book was placed on the Index in January 1897. *L'Électeur,* Laurier's mouthpiece in Quebec City, was declared forbidden reading for having published excerpts from David's pamphlet. When Ernest Pacaud brought out the paper under the title *Le Soleil,* the day after the condemnation, it was banned in the diocese of Chicoutimi, though no other bishop followed the example.[27]

If Rome was to be convinced of the need to dispatch a special envoy to Canada, Laurier would have to send more effective spokesmen to the Vatican. When Bishop Emard of Valleyfield, a man very sympathetic to the Liberals' position, found it impossible to accept the mission,[28] Laurier decided to send his Solicitor General, Charles Fitzpatrick. Fitzpatrick, an Irish Catholic with a great talent for behind-the-scenes negotiations, would during subsequent years perform many similar tasks for Laurier. But none would be so difficult or significant as his trip to Rome early in 1897.

Fitzpatrick travelled first to London where he armed himself with letters of introduction and support from Cardinal Vaughan, the Duke of Norfolk, Chief Justice Russell (the latter two being leading English Catholics), and Joseph Chamberlain, the British Colonial Secretary. From Edward Blake he obtained a legal statement explaining the constitutional problems involved in restoring the separate school system in Manitoba.[29] Once in Rome Fitzpatrick recruited the assistance of Charles Russell, son of the British Chief Justice, a young man of considerable diplomatic skill, knowledgeable in the ways of Vatican politics, and blessed with a sense of humour that must frequently have been needed in the weeks of going the Roman rounds. In any event it was Russell who, through his friend Mgr Merry del Val, one of the Pope's closest advisers, opened all the necessary Vatican doors for Fitzpatrick. The latter, despite what Russell felt were undue displays of piety and faithful submission, was able to press his case for the appointment of a papal delegate.[30]

The Papacy, of course, was under strong pressure from the Quebec bishops to give its approval of their position. The Vatican authorities were thus in a ticklish position and Fitzpatrick had made it plain that the bishops' demands were politically impossible. On the other hand, the appointment of a papal delegate might have the appearance of a reproach to the Quebec hierarchy. Nevertheless the appointment was made. The man who arrived in Canada in March 1897 was not an Englishman, as Laurier had hoped,[31] but nevertheless the appointee must have been entirely acceptable to the Ottawa authorities: Mgr Merry del Val.[32]

Del Val insisted to Laurier that he had not come to discuss or approve the Laurier-Greenway agreement, but rather to establish the facts of the case.[33] In reality the task was far more demanding. To establish the facts of this intricate case was one thing, to re-establish peace within a divided hierarchy was another. But most pressing was the need to return to Rome with advice that would make it possible for Church leaders to save face, while accepting the reality of the political position of the Catholic minority in Canada. After lengthy discussions with all parties involved, del Val apparently concluded that the principle of the Laurier-Greenway settlement would be exceedingly difficult to alter. No doubt, too, he quickly satisfied himself that Laurier's political position was secure and unshakable. The defeat of the Conservative government in the Province of Quebec by Marchand's Liberals in May of 1897 must have convinced him that, whatever the Quebec bishops might hope, the Quebec electorate had other expectations. Merry del Val therefore decided that his best course would be to obtain as many administrative charges in the Manitoba school arrangements as possible. These should include the appointment of a member of the Board of Education and an inspector acceptable to Mgr Langevin, the adoption of acceptable text books and certification of members of religious orders as teachers.[34]

Laurier and Sifton accepted these proposals and set to work in an effort to squeeze them out of Greenway. By July Greenway was evidently in a mood to accept – a mood encouraged by the federal government's promise that $300,000 would be transferred to Manitoba from the sale of school lands for which Ottawa was responsible. But the agreement broke down. Once back in Winnipeg Greenway apparently judged changes in the school law politically dangerous. In retaliation the Catholic Members of Parliament prevented passage of the resolution providing for the transfer of the school lands fund. At this juncture, with Laurier off in Britain at the Imperial Conference, the papal delegate returned to Rome.[35] Del Val apparently had been won over to Laurier's side. At the Vatican he set out to combat the pressure now brought directly by the newly appointed Archbishop of Montreal, Mgr Bruchési, and the machinations of the Canadian College against the settlement.[36] In December, Pope Leo XIII issued his encyclical *Affari Vos* condemning the Manitoba School Act of 1890, describing the Laurier-Greenway agreement as inadequate but calling on Catholics to accept it as a basis from which to work toward a full restoration of their rights.[37]

Laurier's response was to proclaim the encyclical "on the whole very satisfactory."[38] Not surprisingly Mgr Langevin felt differently. "I do not insist on protecting souls more than the Pope himself," he told Mgr Bégin,

and if the way of concessions, after having lightened the burden on us for some time, leads us to the abyss, I will not be responsible for it before God and before my conscience. I want very much to continue the struggle in poverty, in humiliation and without the least encouragement from Rome; but

I do not wish to say a word nor take a step against the wish of our supreme leader.[39]

Laurier had thus won another major battle in the struggle to settle the school problems of Manitoba, and to diminish, as far as possible, the threat of the Church hierarchy's disfavour to the Liberal party in Quebec.[40]

There remained a few skirmishes before the matter finally disappeared from national politics. Laurier continued to make strenuous efforts to gain further concessions for the minority in Manitoba, and to use the school lands money as an inducement.[41] He obtained the appointment of Thomas Rochon, one time classmate of Mgr Langevin and later an Ontario Inspector of Schools, to the inspectorate in Manitoba.[42] Rochon worked hard and was convinced that, if properly operated, the Laurier-Greenway agreement could provide highly satisfactory results. But everywhere he turned he faced the adamant opposition of Archbishop Langevin who remained determined to have nothing less than a completely separate system. "I have studied my man," Rochon wrote in despair in 1899, "and I am convinced now that as long as Mgr Langevin is Archbishop of St. Boniface, we will be able to do nothing; everything will always have to begin again."[43] Though Laurier never totally ceased his efforts to obtain better conditions for Manitoba's French Canadian and Catholic population, the defeat of Greenway in 1899 meant that subsequent efforts had to be more circumspect for fear of political repercussions.

Elsewhere too, there were a few loose ends to tie up. Small though the matter was, Laurier made a strong and ultimately successful effort to persuade the Ontario provincial Liberal government to elect a Franco-Ontarian speaker of the Ontario Legislative Assembly. That would counteract any negative influence that the Laurier-Greenway settlement might have on French-speaking voters.[44] Much more telling, however, was the pressure Laurier brought on the new Liberal administration in Quebec in the matter of educational reform. Premier F.G. Marchand had been elected on a platform of educational reform, including a promise to appoint a Ministry of Education. Archbishop Bruchési of Montreal fought hard against the proposal, attempting to enlist the support of both Rome and Ottawa.[45] In 1897 a bill establishing a Ministry of Education passed the Quebec Assembly, but was rejected by the Legislative Council. At the next session of the Quebec Legislature, the education bill passed, but this time it did not include the provision for a ministry. Both Tarte and Fitzpatrick worked for the amicable settlement "in the interests of the peace that we have concluded" with Mgr Bruchési.[46] Doubtless Laurier, too, had played his part in assuring that no new causes of religious-political war would be allowed to emerge – though the price may have been an educational system in Quebec ill-suited to the needs of a new scientific century.[47]

In fact Laurier was developing a close and friendly relationship with Archbishop Bruchési, and far from proving the young firebrand that he had appeared when first consecrated, the Montreal prelate was soon aiding Laurier in working toward a better school settlement and religious peace in Manitoba.[48] The suspicion existing between the Liberals and the Church in Quebec was by no means totally ended; there were still those who insisted the Liberals aimed at "the destruction of Catholicism to the profit of rationalism."[49] But the atmosphere was changing. In June 1899, on Laurier's prompting, Mgr A. Falconio was appointed as permanent Apostolic Delegate to Canada.[50] In short, Laurier had gradually convinced the Church that his way was the right way – or at least, the only realistic way. And there was even some evidence that Laurier himself, the old *rouge,* was moving closer to the Church in his personal beliefs.[51] In any event, Laurier knew full well that whatever his personal beliefs, a good relationship with the Church hierarchy made the Liberal party's political ascendancy more secure. Mgr Merry del Val, who was as shrewd a politician as Laurier himself, wrote the epitaph on these years when he told the Prime Minister, "It is undeniable that in finally ruling on the school question in Manitoba, you have gained the recognition of the Holy See, and strong in this support it will be much easier for you to realize other projects in our programme to the moral, material and political advantage of your country."[52] Obviously Ottawa was worth a Mass.

III

Just as the Liberals, prior to 1896, had been suspect in the eyes of the Catholic hierarchy in Quebec, so too their trade and tariff policy had left much of the Canadian business community hostile, or at least unenthusiastic. After all, under Laurier the party had adopted the policy of unrestricted reciprocity with the United States, a policy seen not only as dangerous to Canadian business, which feared equal competition from the American enterprises, but also as anti-imperial, continentalist, or even annexationist.

By 1893 the Liberals had set about modifying their trade and tariff views, and offering various signs to the business community that business had little to fear from a Liberal victory. Colonel George T. Denison, who could smell a continentalist more than a mile away, told Lord Salisbury shortly before the 1896 election of the changed attitude. "The Liberals," he wrote, "have seen the great mistake they made in 1890-91 and are now very careful not to squint towards the United States. In fact they remind one of the Indian's tree that stood so upright that it leaned a little the other way."[53] On the whole the Liberals seem to have been successful by 1896 in their efforts to win the confidence of the business community. A further step in that direction was the appointment of W.S. Fielding as Minister of Finance. In his campaign for election that autumn Fielding stated his views emphatically: "It would be the duty of the present government," he said, "while guarding to a reasonable extent the interests of the manufacturers, to frame the tariff into the interests of the masses. That . . . did not mean that manufacturing interests were to be sacrificed . . . But care must be taken that, while aiming at the carrying out of these views, NO RASH OR ILL CONSIDERED MEASURES should be adopted."[54] If the business community was at all jittery about the new government's policy, it had only slight need to be. Laurier was certainly convinced that no tariff change should be made "except after ample discussions with the businessmen."[55] So, too, he was adequately aware that in Ontario, at least, "a preferential tariff in favour of Great Britain as against the United States"[56] would receive widespread approval. Nor was he left uninformed about the farmers' hope that the tariff would be reduced immediately.[57]

Faced with these competing pressures and requiring time to assess them before presenting a policy, the government chose the obvious course: conduct investigations. Unofficial probes were sent out to Washington to see if there was any possibility of arriving at a mutually advantageous arrangement between the two countries. In November a new administration, led by the Republican William McKinley, had been elected, and that made the prospects of any easing of trading relations very slight. Or did Laurier expect any real progress on the United States front? Could it not have been that he merely sent the old Ontario freetrader, John Charlton, to satisfy the rural Ontario wing of the party that the effort had at least been made? In any event, before long Laurier was telling his emissary that "whilst I am strongly impressed with the view that our relations with our neighbours should be friendly, at the same time I am equally strong in the opinion that we may have to take the American tariff – if conceived in hostility to Canada – and make it the Canadian tariff."[58] To the old commercial unionist, Erastus Wiman, Laurier was even more blunt, telling him that he was not really at all anxious for reciprocity, except on a few articles. "The feeling in Canada on the subject of reciprocity," he wrote, "is very far from what it was some years ago. Since our American neighbours will not trade with us, we have come to the conclusion that we will have to do without it and I think we can do without it very successfully."[59] The new Dingley tariff in the United States made reciprocity a virtual impossibility, and Ottawa was now also moving in a new direction – a direction which a despairing Charlton, still in Washington, summed up: "We may as well tell a Yankee to go to Hades and we will go to England."[60]

The Laurier government's second probe was much more productive. This took the form of a three-man tariff commission appointed to hear the opinions of the country. It was headed by Fielding, flanked by the protectionist Paterson and the freetrader Cartwright. The commission heard from various groups, chiefly representing business and agriculture. Since the agricultural community had as yet no strong national organization, its pressure was ineffective. The manufacturers, on the other hand, made their views loud and clear. After the hearings, the cabinet began to draw up its proposals for the 1897 budget. On Easter Sunday, Sydney Fisher, Minister of Agriculture, was able to inform his colleague, Frederick Borden, Minister of the Militia, of the direction of discussion: "The tarif [*sic*] is pretty well in shape as good as we can hope for tho' not what we tarif [*sic*] reform men would want. The fear of closing down industries is overshadowing everything else and the jingo spirit attendant on the Dingley bill monstrosity of the U.S. enables those views to obtain. I hope this spirit will be constant enough to hold out but I expect that it will soon pass and we will be held responsible for its effects."[61]

On April 23, 1897, W.S. Fielding rose in the House of Commons to deliver his first budget statement. He did his best to please all his listeners by claiming that the government was determined to reject the "mistaken policy" of the past, the protective tariff, but without moving to free trade. He then proceeded to announce the novel feature of the policy. The Dingley tariff had destroyed all hope of freer trading relations with the United States. Therefore the government had decided it would adopt a two-tiered tariff: one tier would be, in effect, the existing rates to be applied to those countries whose tariff was protectionist against Canada. The second tier would offer an immediate $12\frac{1}{2}$ per cent preference, to be raised to 25 per cent the following year, to any country which admitted Canadian goods at a rate equivalent to the minimum Canadian tariff. Though it was not stated in the resolution, Fielding made it plain that Great Britain would be the major beneficiary of the proposal.[62]

The Fielding tariff was a brilliant coup. In the first place it maintained the protective principle and the essential features of the national policy. Indeed, where the tariff was lowered, the reductions were almost invariably offset by a substantially broadened schedule of bounties. Consequently one form of protection was replaced by another.[63] But the idea of preference, itself borrowed from Conservative tariff reformers, saved the Liberals from the charge of totally deserting their principles. It was not free trade but, at least in the case of Great Britain, it would be 25 per cent freer than previously. Moreover, for those who still yearned for a continental market, it could accurately be claimed that it was the Dingley tariff, not the Canadian government, that stood in the path of the free flow of goods, north and south. Fielding made it abundantly clear that the onus for freeing world trade now rested with other countries, not with Canada.[64] The preference might worry the businessmen a little, but it provided some small satisfaction for the agricultural community. That was one of its virtues.

But its greatest virtue was political rather than commercial. Since a free trade Great Britain automatically qualified for the preference, it was viewed by those Canadians with strong affection for the Empire as an act of loyalty and generous gratitude on Canada's part. As the Liberals' record in imperial matters had always been somewhat suspect, the British preference, as it came to be called, was doubly welcomed as a sign of imperial solidarity and as evidence of Liberal loyalty. Colonel Denison bubbled with enthusiasm. The Liberals, he told Lord Salisbury, "had come out straight in favour of the Imperial idea, and have wrapped themselves in the old flag to the satisfaction of all parties except the extreme partisans in the Conservative ranks, and their only objection is that they see their opponents receiving universal support."[65] It was true, of course, that the preference actually caused the British a certain embarrassment because of their most favoured nation treaties with Belgium and Germany. But the new spirit of imperial brotherhood that Joseph Chamberlain was determined to foster settled that complication. On the unanimous advice of the participants at the Colonial Conference of 1897, Britain announced that the agreements with Belgium and Germany would be terminated.[66]

It was the preference which won Laurier the favour of numerous Empire enthusiasts in Canada. It was the preference which, in large measure, ensured Laurier a rousing welcome at the Colonial Conference called in conjunction with Queen Victoria's Diamond Jubilee in the summer of 1897. But, finest irony of all, it was the preference which won for Laurier an unexpected honour: the Cobden medal. Poor Richard Cobden would surely have shuddered, for no one who had gone beyond the rhetoric of the preference to the reality of the tariff could doubt that Laurier had fully embraced Sifton's Macdonald-like hope that "the free trade theory, which has already been shattered, will not be permitted to stand in the way when it is plainly not in our business interests."[67]

Thus, well before the end of the first term of office the major characteristics of the new Laurier liberalism had begun clearly to emerge. Laurier, or Sir Wilfrid as he was known after his return from London in 1897, was plainly in control. His government had acted promptly in the two areas which had dominated the politics of the 1890s: the separate school question and the tariff. The results were plain, if a little surprising: the *rouges* had made peace with the Church and the freetraders had entered the temple of protectionism. The Laurier style was rapidly defining itself.

IV

Prohibition, like the tariff and the separate school question, was another sensitive problem which the Liberal government inherited when it took office. It was also a very divisive issue and, again like the school question, one in which Canadians expressed their religious convictions with intensity.

Both political parties, in the early nineties, had difficulty working out a policy on the alcohol question that would unite their supporters. The Conservative government had chosen to gain time through investigation. A Royal Commission was appointed, which brought in its report in 1895.[68] For their part the Liberals were forced to confront the question at their convention in 1893. They found that party unity could best be assured by returning the question to the people. If elected, they promised a plebiscite on prohibition and pledged themselves to act quickly to implement the people's will.[69]

In the 1896 election, members of the leading prohibitionist organizations, the Dominion Alliance and the Woman's Christian Temperance Union, exerted strong pressure on individual candidates and party leaders in an effort to make their special interest a major national issue. It now seemed especially important to get action, since the Judicial Committee in the "Local Prohibition Case" had just handed down another of its decisions on the liquor question, this time making it plain that only the Dominion parliament could enforce total prohibition.[70] Laurier and his party, when confronted by the prohibitionists, felt secure in merely repeating the 1893 promise of a plebiscite. The returns were hardly tabulated when the Dominion Alliance sent a delegation to the new Prime Minister, and once again Laurier reiterated his promise to consult the people directly. The 1897 Speech from the Throne announced the plebiscite, and it was held, after some delay caused by Laurier's absence at the Imperial Conference, in September 1898.

Earlier plebiscites in several provinces had resulted in majorities for restrictive liquor legislation, and the prohibitionists now entered the new campaign optimistically. From the outset both the "dry" forces and the Laurier government recognized that the Province of Quebec was crucial in the campaign. In that province the Catholic Church, though entirely favourable to campaigns for moderation and temperance, refused to join the other churches, most notably the Methodists, Baptists, and Presbyterians, in demanding enforced total abstinence. The Dominion Alliance, an almost completely Protestant body, experienced insurmountable difficulties in appointing organizers for the 1898 plebiscite in Quebec, and strongly suspected that the Liberals were working against them.[71] Laurier denied the charge, but there can be no doubt that he and his advisers were worried about the prospect of a plebiscite which would divide the country on cultural and religious lines.

That was exactly the division which the returns revealed on September 29. Every province except Quebec voted affirmatively on the "dry" side. Quebec remained overwhelmingly "wet." But the majority for prohibition was only about 13,000 out of a total vote of 543,058. Wherever there were strong Roman Catholic and French Canadian concentrations in the country the vote was negative.[72] Equally striking – and this would permit Laurier to avoid a decision – was the relatively small total vote. As the Returning Officer emphasized, only about 44 per cent of the electorate had bothered to register an opinion. That figure was substantially below a normal vote in a general election.[73] The prohibitionists insisted that this was really a very large turnout given the lack of party machinery and patronage that would be available in a regular election.

Laurier disagreed. He immediately recognized that the low electoral return was his avenue of escape from enacting legislation that was obviously unpopular in the Province of Quebec. "Only a trifle over one fifth affirmed their conviction of the principles of prohibition," he informed F. S. Spence of the Dominion Alliance. "I venture to submit to your consideration, and to the consideration of the members of the Dominion Alliance, who believe in prohibition as the most efficient means of suppressing the evils of intemperance, that no good purpose would be served by forcing upon the people a measure which is shown by the vote to have the support of less than twenty-three percent of the electorate."[74] The reasoning was logical enough, though it hardly conformed to Laurier's earlier statements in which he had plighted his faith to the will of the majority without suggesting that any particular percentage of the electorate would have to vote. The fact was, of course, that he did not wish to set Quebec against the rest of Canada over the prohibition question any more than he did over the school question. Inaction seemed the best way to avoid difficulty. The prohibitionists, of course, saw matters in an entirely different light. They believed they had won in a fair fight only to have victory snatched away from them by wily politicians, some of whom were no doubt the lackeys of the liquor interests. There were also those who viewed Laurier's inaction as yet another sign of the undue influence of Quebec and the Catholic Church on the Liberal government, which now stood in the path of Christian progress.

The prohibitionists now had little choice but to turn their attention to the provinces where majorities had been registered in an effort to choke off the vile traffic bit by bit, awaiting the day for a more sympathetic government to take office in Ottawa. In almost every province the liquor question now became an issue of great importance. By 1907 every province, except British Columbia, had enacted local option laws of greater or lesser stringency. The fight for the total prohibition of alcoholic beverages was to be a long and hard one, but no prohibitionist ever doubted that righteousness would prevail over evil liquor interests. As one Manitoba "dry" put it after a defeat in 1902: "The cause on behalf of which we labour is the cause of righteousness, the cause of humanity, and must ultimately triumph. The act may be killed, but the cause is not dead: Phoenix-like it will rise purified and strengthened from the tribulations through which it has passed."[75]

There were various reasons for the growth of prohibitionist sentiment, at least among the Anglo-Saxon Protestant middle classes. One concern of these people was the impact which the vast new population of foreigners would have upon Canadian society. As the number of immigrants increased, often coming from backgrounds which lacked moralistic attitudes to alcohol, the temperance cause seemed to gain greater urgency. "Many of the foreigners have yet to be taught the A.B.C.'s of temperance," one reformer announced. "Beastly drunkenness has been banished from our social life. With some foreigners they do not consider they are having a good time unless they get uproariously drunk."[76]

Teaching those A.B.C.'s was to become an important activity for many high-minded reformers in the new century. Nellie McClung, beginning her career as so many women reformers did in the W.C.T.U., described one such lesson she and her co-workers taught in the schools. "They explained the circulation of the blood, and the effect of alcohol on the stomach, and showed why athletes do not drink even mild intoxicants, and had the children figure out how many pairs of boots and little red sleighs a man could buy with the money he spends on a daily glass of beer. At the Band of Hope [a W.C.T.U. children's group] they gave badges and pins and taught the children a marching song of which the refrain was: *Tremble, King Alcohol, We Will Grow Up.*"[77] Mrs. McClung, the Protestant middle-class suffragist and prohibitionist, epitomized a new force that was to gain strength in Laurier's growing Canada. Many people, dissatisfied with mere material progress, hoped to see the country grow morally too. Women would help if they had the vote. Certainly they would help banish the bar and the bottle. It was often in organizations like the Woman's Christian Temperance Union, the Social and Moral Reform Council of Manitoba, the Dominion Alliance, and the People's Prohibition Association of British Columbia, that women first cut their political teeth, before joining the suffrage cause and other reform groups.[78]

Thus the movement to control the liquor traffic not only grew in strength, but also changed in character. No longer was the "demon rum" viewed merely as a matter of personal sin. In the new century, under the impact of liberal optimism and the Christian social gospel, alcohol comsumption became part of a wider social problem to be excised in a more general reform of society. Drinking came to be judged not only as a threat to individual health and the stability of family life, but also as a cause of poverty, prostitution, industrial indiscipline, disease, and accidents.[79]

Prohibition would lead to extensive social betterment. Spearheading this new reformist front were the Protestant Churches, which were increasingly under the influence of those social gospellers who taught that Christ was a social reformer whose programme was set out in the Sermon on the Mount and the Ten Commandments.[80] Rev. H.R. Grant, the leader of the Nova Scotia prohibition forces, put this view succinctly when he told the Synod of the Presbyterian Church in 1907: "Public affairs, the social and political business of the country must be brought under the Commandments and the Sermon on the Mount . . . the pulpit must have an outlook on the everyday life of men . . . the state as well as the individual has a character and the social and political life of the state must obey the . . . teachings of Christ . . . temperance [is] but one of the social, we might say, national questions which the Church must consider. . . . Abuses must not only be discovered but reformed as well."[81]

Prohibition was thus only a part of a generous reform impulse, which sought ways of ameliorating the injustices, inequalities, and sufferings of a society undergoing rapid change. In 1898 Laurier had turned the prohibition forces aside for the moment. But the developmental policies of his government ensured that both the crusade for prohibition, and the broader currents of social criticism, would continue to grow as the country moved into a period of accelerated expansion.

CHAPTER 3

Canada and the New Imperialism

Wilfrid Laurier's government took office at a time when profound changes were in the making in world politics. These changes, particularly since they affected the outlook and actions of both Great Britain and the United States, were certain to have a critical impact upon Canadian life. As the nineteenth century drew to a close, a new age of imperialism was reaching full flood. The sources of this aggressive new sentiment were many and varied, as John Hobson explained in his influential book, *Imperialism*, published in 1902.[1] Certainly, as the English writer had stressed, economics was fundamental: the industrial revolution in Europe and the United States had reached a point that required new outlets for products and investment capital, and new sources of raw materials. But there was a good deal more to it than that.[2] Again, as Hobson realized, there was a psychology of imperialism born in nearly every European country, a psychology which stressed the superiority of one "race" over another, and attributed "missions" and "burdens" to the white man's nations. A rising young British politician named Joseph Chamberlain had caught that spirit when he told a Toronto audience in 1887 of "the greatness and importance of the destiny which is reserved for the Anglo-Saxon race . . . infallibly predestined to be the predominating force in the future history and civilization of the world."[3]

This "new imperialism" struck a sympathetic chord at almost every level of the new industrial societies, perhaps providing a sense of adventure and challenge amid the drabness and routine of factory and slum. "Jingoism," that chest-thumping spirit of the age, was a word which originated in a popular music hall song. And the new popular press in Great Britain, the United States, and Canada found that jingoism could be made the basis for enormous circulations. Moreover, the new imperial spirit could be linked with the cause of social change. A successful overseas empire could provide an outlet for growing populations, and the spirit of patriotism, sacrifice, and enterprise might galvanize those who stayed at home into building a better society.[4] "The democracy," Austin Chamberlain observed early in the new century, "wants two things: imperialism and social reform."[5] In the United States, as in Great Britain, "progessive" reformers were often exponents of the imperial mission of the republic, none more so than Theodore Roosevelt.[6] These conditions combined, at a time when the world balance of power was shifting and relative stability giving way to change and conflict, to stimulate a "new imperialism." It manifested itself in the scramble for Africa and the Spanish American and South African wars at the turn of the century; in a series of international incidents and growing military rivalry between Great Britain and Germany in the first decade; and finally in world war in 1914.[7]

This "new imperialism" had a direct impact upon Canada. That spirit of Anglo-Saxon superiority and mission, celebrated wherever the members of that "race" lived, naturally influenced English Canadians. It made them part of a great enterprise, and was often used as justification for the way they treated people of other nationalities who lived in Canada. But it also created problems for English-speaking Canadians. Anglo-Saxonism drew English-speaking people together.[8] But, while closer unity with Britain was one thing, it was quite another when the partner was the United States. Good relations with the southern neighbour were obviously desirable, but "manifest destiny" had always to be kept under close watch. Consequently, in the new imperialist age, Canadians had to tread a treacherous path between the glories of Anglo-Saxondom and the dangers of becoming the object of imperialist thrusts. On the whole, most English Canadians rejoiced in the new imperialism of Great Britain. Their sense of national identity could even find expression in it. Indeed, in the optimistic years of Laurier's government, many English-Canadian nationalists foresaw the day when Canada would be number one in the Empire.[9] As Rudyard Kipling observed, many Canadians had "a certain crude faith in the Empire, of which they naturally conceive themselves to be the belly-button."[10] But there were other Canadians, especially those who spoke French, who were far from enthusiastic about visions of Anglo-Saxon greatness.

The emergence of the "new imperialism," because it divided and threatened Canada, ensured that Laurier's government would devote more attention to foreign affairs than any of its predecessors. During his first two years of office he participated in the first and most spectacular of a series of Colonial and Imperial Conferences, and in major negotiations with the United States. During his first two terms of office his government met, and survived, major crises in both imperial and Canadian-American relations. Both proved to be preludes of things to come.

I

During the late 1880s and early 1890s Canadians, in a mood of pessimism and failure, debated the future of their country. Almost every option was considered: commercial union and even annexation to the United States, imperial federation, independence, and the possible collapse of the federal union of 1867.[11] By the turn of the century, with the return of prosperity and self-confidence, that debate lost its urgency and even appeared somewhat academic. For most Canadians the future pointed to a growing Canada working in close co-operation with Britain and the Empire. The specific nature of that partnership remained undefined and became the subject of extensive debate. But the fact of partnership was accepted. French-Canadian nationalists were at least temporarily quieted, and annexationism was dead. Indeed, economic prosperity, combined with the rumblings of the new imperialism in the United States, served to stimulate the feeling that, as Principal Grant of Queen's University put it, "we are Canadian, and in order to be Canadian we must be British."[12] That sense of Canadianism also manifested itself in suspicion toward the United States. Lord Minto, not long after his appointment as Governor General, summed up the mood neatly for his brother:

> There is a general dislike of the Yankees here and I do not wonder at it. It's all very well for people in England to romance about the sentimental love of his [sic] Anglo-Saxon Race on either side of the Atlantic but mercifully England has an ocean between him and his love. . . . What the Canadian sees and hears is constant Yankee bluff and swagger & that eventually he means to possess Canada for himself. And he reads with wonder of the so-called rapprochement of the old country with a people with which he, the Canadian, has no sympathy and whom he thoroughly distrusts.[13]

"A general dislike of the Yankees" may have put too sharp an edge on Canadian sentiment toward the United States at the turn of the century, but not by much. Certainly with a return of prosperity came a renewal of confidence in Canada's ability and will to maintain a separate political posture in North America. With it too came an increasing awareness, reinforced by continual re-statement of the point, of the distinctiveness of Canada and of the desire to protect and enhance the peculiar characteristics of the nation. These attributes, regarded as particularly virtuous in a great age of nationalism, largely motivated Canadian reluctance to bargain away their heritage to the Americans at the diplomatic table. That sentiment was echoed in the Minister of Railway's assertion, unquestioned by other members of the House of Commons, when he introduced the abortive Yukon Railway Bill providing for an "all Canadian" route into the Yukon, that "the importance of securing that trade and preserving it to

Canada becomes a national question. . . . It is ours, it is within our own borders and of right belongs to us."[14]

But more important than any discreet policy decisions or statements was Minto's point. Nationalism is a sentiment, an attitude, growing out of a set of postulates, coherent or otherwise, rational and irrational, fixed upon the protection and development of the citizen's identity with his nation. It is communal; it is defensive. In Canada there could be only one real focus for its defensiveness, the United States. Doubtless not all Canadians disliked the United States; nor, for that matter, were all Canadians nationalists. But for all Canadian nationalists a central article of faith was fear of the real or imagined potential of the United States to absorb Canada. Hence a profound distrust of the neighbour to the south, and of individual Americans. Contacts between Canadians and Americans, personal, commercial, social, intellectual, and official, increased enormously at the turn of the century. So too did the harshness of the Canadian image of America and Americans. The increasing intimacy of neighbourhood bred some friendship but more rivalry.[15] As important to the faith of Canadian nationalists as the distrust of the United States was the conviction of the superiority of monarchical over republican institutions. The "Kingly function," as Charles Mair called it, established the foundations of Canadian life, dictated the tone and the style of the Canadian community. Maintenance of the "British connection," then, had manifold implications.

Some points were rather quickly established. In commercial policy the "imperial preference" gave a great boost to imperial sentiment. Though some hoped that the bond would be even closer with the granting of reciprocal preference by the mother country, that was not to be. More important, with the exception of some strong-minded imperialists, the Canadians were as hardheaded about the preference, as nationalistic about it, as were the British. The leader of the opposition, Robert Borden, asserted in 1902 that "our interests must sometimes give way to imperial interests; but any system or policy which closes out industries, causes our machinery and plants to be idle, and sends our operatives to the United States is not a policy which is advantageous to Canada or to the empire, merely because it gives an increased output to some manufacturing industry in Great Britain."[16] In short, if it came to a choice between Canadian industrial development and strengthening the imperial bond, the latter would be sacrificed. Increased profits and wages for a factory in Yorkshire made no contribution to the Canadian economy. As Adam Shortt put it in a pamphlet on the preference, "We cannot undertake to reserve any portion of our market for [Britain's] benefit. On the contrary, we propose to produce anything that we can for our own use, and for any other markets that are in want of them."[17] John Willison, who had close connections with politicians and businessmen alike, was even more blunt in his explanation of the politics of "imperial preference." "This country is greatly influenced by proximity to the United States," he told the Governor General in 1903, "and we shall not readily forego the ambition to make this a great manufacturing community, somewhat on the lines of the Republic. The Canadian manufacturers who profess to want preferential trade with the Mother country are not very frank. They are really hostile to the existing British preference and look for a movement toward protection in Great Britain rather than to further advance toward free trade in Canada. Both parties here fear the manufacturers, and properly so, for they have been the controlling factor in every election since 1878."[18]

The Laurier government knew the facts of Canadian political life. The main effect of the 1897–98 preference was to enable British manufacturers to keep a diminishing portion of the Canadian market. By 1912 British imports had slipped from one-third to one-fifth of Canadian totals; without the benefit of a preference, but through deliberately constructed holes in the tariff to aid Canadian industrial growth, American imports jumped from one-half to two-thirds of the whole. Without the preference British manufacturers would have lost an even greater share, but that was small consolation to sentimental imperialists. Beneath their gaze and to their despair, and in no small measure because of quiet but effective government policy, both federal and provincial, Liberal and Conservative, the great prosperity of the first decade of the century was largely financed and developed by United States capital and technology. British manufacturing representatives in Canada were smug, complacent, and poor. American business firms were aggressive and prosperous. British investors shied away from Canadian development schemes because they were so notoriously speculative; American capitalists, urged on by the Canadian business and political community, gobbled them up.[19]

Still, the British connection stood for much more than monarchial institutions and a tariff preference. For some Canadians, who styled themselves imperialists, it was a way of life and an avocation. Men like Colonel Denison, Toronto police magistrate, historian, militia officer, and professional imperialist, had participated in the heady campaign against Commercial Union in the 1880s. In the mid-nineties their goal of imperial union seemed to take on new life. The decade was replete with imperial rivalry and expansionism resulting in German, French, and American threats to Britain's imperial supremacy. In 1895 Joseph Chamberlain, an aggressive Birmingham industrialist and politician, accepted the minor cabinet post of Secretary of State for the Colonies and determined to make it a major office in Lord Salisbury's administration. Chamberlain was a tireless propagandist and schemer for imperial unity as a counterweight to the growing colonial ambitions of France and Germany. He was inclined to read more optimism into his plans than they warranted; the 1897

Colonial Conference, he said at its conclusion, was "the beginning of a Federal conference."[20] Nevertheless, Canadian imperialists were greatly encouraged by his presence at the Colonial Office. He was a man who talked their language and sympathized with their deepest desires. It was true that as an identifiable group, Canadian imperialists were as nationalist as any other Canadians, more so than most. Like other nationalists, they knew and used the history of their country to support their cause. Like other nationalists, they too understood their history as a steady progression of self-government to national maturity. But what set them apart, what made them "imperialists," was their belief, as Carl Berger argues, "that there was as much inevitability in the movement from colony to nation through the imperial alliance as the advocates of complete Canadian independence, like John Norris or John Ewart, found in the evolution to autonomous nationhood."[21]

One expression of the growth of imperialist, or perhaps better, British-Canadian, nationalist sentiment, was the establishment of "Empire Day." In origin this celebration was designed to provide an opportunity to use the public schools for the promotion of patriotic sentiments. The idea was first discussed by the members of the Wentworth Historical Society in Hamilton in 1896. It soon won the support of George Ross, the Liberal Minister of Education in Ontario, who suggested to the Dominion Education Association at its 1897 meeting in Halifax that a day be set aside to celebrate Canada's place in the Empire. May 23, 1898, the day before "the Queen's Birthday," was declared "Empire Day" in the schools of Ontario, Nova Scotia, and the Protestant schools of Quebec. The form of the celebrations varied from school to school: street parades of children carrying flags and maple leaves; patriotic songs and poetry, and essay-writing contests. The spirit of the day, with its intertwining of imperial and Canadian sentiment, was well expressed in a directive sent by the Ontario Minister of Education to all school inspectors:

Part of the forenoon might be occupied with a familiar talk by the teacher on the British Empire, its extent and resources; the relation of Canada to the Empire; the unity of the Empire and its advantages; the privileges which, as British subjects, we enjoy; the extent of Canada and its resources; readings from Canadian and British authors by the teacher; interesting historical incidents in connection with our own country. The aim of the teacher in all of his references to Canada and the Empire should be, to make Canadian patriotism intelligent, comprehensive and strong. The afternoon, commencing at 2:30 p.m., might be occupied with patriotic recitations, songs and readings by the pupils, and speeches by trustees, clergymen and such other persons as may be available. The trustees and public generally should be invited to be present at the exercises. During the day the British Flag or Canadian Ensign should be hoisted over the school building.[22]

It was sentiments such as those expressed at Empire Day parades that were put to the test in the next twenty-five years.

No doubt the Empire Day movement was given an enormous boost by the pomp and circumstance of Queen Victoria's Diamond Jubilee celebrations in July 1897. Pageantry, parades, banquets, and balls, interspersed with music, poetry, and oratory — every event was flashed to the most remote corners of the Empire. Canadians were daily treated to news of their new Prime Minister's latest success, for he was looked upon as a prize jewel in the imperial diadem. And he responded accordingly.

But the Jubilee was more than a mere anniversary party. It provided the backdrop'for one of a series of Colonial Conferences at which the leaders of Britain and the dominions could discuss the state of the world and the future of the imperial partnership. In 1897 Joseph Chamberlain certainly had high hopes that his idea about imperial reorganization would be welcomed by the visiting prime ministers. He had done his best to put them in the right mood. All had been wined and dined, and some, including Laurier, had been awarded knighthoods. Nevertheless, Chamberlain showed remarkable restraint. His invitation merely said that the Jubilee would provide an opportunity for an "informal discussion of many questions of greatest imperial interest."[23] Canada's response to the suggestion must certainly have gratified, and later confused, the Colonial Secretary for it bubbled with enthusiasm. The celebration, the Canadian government hoped, "would tend powerfully to cement the union between the Mother Country and her Colonies, both socially and politically."[24]

Laurier's speeches in Britain, before the Conference opened, further underscored Canada's warm regard for the Empire: "It would be the proudest moment of my life if I could see a Canadian of French descent affirming the principles of freedom in the parliament of Great Britain."[25] Was that a plea for imperial federation, or merely a diplomatic remark made to encourage the British to look favourably on Canada in trade matters? Whatever its intent, it gave Chamberlain reason to share the view of many British newspapers that the Canadian Prime Minister was "the strongest imperialist and one of the most clear-sighted statesmen of the Empire."[26]

Chamberlain, in his opening speech to the Conference, set out modestly, but clearly, his hopes for a closer imperial union. He proposed consideration of a "great council of Empire" where imperial problems could be discussed and decisions taken. He spoke of a "true partnership" based upon a sharing of both rights and responsibilities in matters of defence. He hoped that there would be serious consideration of an imperial free trade. These matters, he emphasized, were suggestions for discussion only. He knew that the time might not yet be ripe.[27] Then in turn, the Premiers rose to respond.

Laurier's attitude now seemed more ambiguous. Certainly the existing relationship needed to be looked at, and would one day have to be changed. But the time had not yet arrived. He would support a motion declaring the "the relations between the United Kingdom and the self-governing colonies are generally satisfactory under the existing condition of things." That was to become his permanent view. Moreover, he fully acquiesced in the opinion that some day the Dominions would want a voice in imperial decisions, but since that would be accompanied by a contribution to imperial defence, that day could be put off for a while.[28] He was still prepared to rise to the oratorical occasion. "Let the bugle sound, let the fires be lit on the hill," he proclaimed,[29] but he had no wish, and certainly no expectation, that the call should come in a hurry. That is not to say that Laurier's enthusiasm for British institutions, and even the Empire, was all rhetorical flourish. It was that, but it was also a sincere belief in the value of British political traditions, and a recognition of Canada's need for Britain's military support. His speeches in Britain reflected, and were probably aimed at, that British-Canadian nationalism evident in English-speaking Canada. But he also knew, and sympathized with, his French-Canadian compatriots' traditional reluctance to assume imperial responsibilities. It was safest to preserve a careful ambiguity.

That ambiguity fairly reflected Canadian public opinion, and consequently suited Laurier's political needs. But he came as close as he could to defining his essential position when he spoke in Paris on his way home. "If, as the price of imperial representation," he told his audience of British businessmen, "we had to renounce our autonomy, our legislative independence, we would have none of it. If imperial representation is to be the solution, it can only be as the complement and not as the negation of that which exists today."[30] Obviously Laurier, in his own mind, was completely clear about the nature of the imperial constitution problem.

Returning to Canada, late that summer, the Canadian Prime Minister was doubtless exhilarated by the warm welcome he had received in London. That would help him with those voters who were still sceptical about the loyalty of a French Canadian. Moreover, the preference was a reality now, since the Mother Country had decided to denounce those most-favoured nation treaties that had stood as an obstacle to accepting Canada's gesture of imperial economic unity. Relations with Britain were perfectly amicable. That was important, for the next diplomatic event was the opening of serious negotiations with the United States.

II

The Fielding tariff was as much a symbolic expression of the state of Canada's relations with the United States as it was a partial concession to imperial sentiment in Canada and Britain. It was all very well to place the onus for unsatisfactory trade relations with the United States upon the supposedly hostile intent of the Dingley tariff and to reply in kind with an equally protectionist – and nationalistic – schedule of customs rates. But there was no denying the fact that Canada's relations with the United States were generally in bad repair. It was clear to Laurier and his colleagues that this dangerous state of affairs should not be allowed to drag on indefinitely.

Thus, in the fall of 1897, Laurier and Sir Louis Davies quietly slipped off to Washington for exploratory talks with State Department officials. They urgently pressed for the appointment of an Anglo-American joint commission to consider all outstanding problems. The American response was cool and conditional and led to a series of exchanges and proposals throughout the fall and winter. Then, suddenly, for reasons quite unrelated to Canada, the United States warmly accepted the Canadian suggestion. In March, with his government on the brink of war with Spain and faced with hostility from nearly every major power save Great Britain, President McKinley, reported the British Ambassador, "expressed the most earnest desire to facilitate the settlement of all those questions."[31]

When the Joint High Commission of 1898-9 opened its sittings in Quebec City in August, many items on the agenda were of minor international importance. Agreements on alien labour legislation,[32] and on the conveyance of prisoners, and mutual legislation on the wreckage and salvage of ships, among other points, were, in essence, housekeeping diplomacy common to the amiable relations of most neighbouring states. But also open for discussion were a number of major problems of long standing in Anglo-American diplomacy. Not only were vital Canadian commerical interests at stake here; even more important, the survival of Canada was heavily dependent upon Anglo-American friendship.

The oldest of the major disputes evolved out of the Anglo-American Convention of 1818 regulating the use of inshore waters of the North Atlantic fishery. The provisions of the Convention barred American fishing vessels from access to British North American inshore waters except in cases where their survival was in question. At various times during the previous eighty years the restrictions had been relaxed under temporary Anglo-American agreements, often, ironically, to the benefit of Canadians in the fishing industry. And for the last decade the restrictions had been waived under another temporary licensing agreement for American vessels. The 1888 *modus vivendi* was a temporary solution at best. In addition, the whole complex problem raised serious questions of international law, which needed a final settlement.

The Bering Sea dispute originated in the mid-1880's from the rival claims of the Canadian and American fur seal industries. The American interests exploited the seals on their breeding grounds on the American-owned Pribilof Islands; Canadian pelagic sealers, shipping from British Columbia, captured the seals in the open waters of Bering Sea as the animals went to and from the islands. On the ground that Canadian sealers were destroying American property (the seals) and threatening the herd with extinction, in 1886 United States revenue cruisers began to seize Canadian vessels on the high seas and to bring their masters to trial for violation of United States municipal law. By so doing the United States implicitly claimed the Bering Sea as a *mare clausum.* That claim was summarily dismissed by an international tribunal in 1893 and the British (Canadian) legal case in the dispute was upheld. But the tribunal also established regulations governing pelagic sealing in the vicinity of the Pribilofs, which were due for periodic revision in 1898.

When Ambassador Pauncefote saw the President in March, 1898, McKinley indicated that he was "especially" anxious to resolve the questions "which related to the development of the gold mining industry of the Valley of the Yukon."[33] Various attempts to determine the boundary between Canada and Alaska had been made since the United States purchase of Alaska in 1867. Indeed, by 1898 the boundary was well established except south of Mount St. Elias in the panhandle. But that was just the problem. Since the discovery of gold in the Klondike, the boundary question had taken on a totally new and especially dangerous perspective. At two places in the panhandle, Lynn Canal and Observatory Inlet, especially at the former, Canadian and American interests were in conflict. The panhandle boundary itself was supposedly defined in the confusing provisions of the Anglo-Russian Treaty of 1825, and Canadians believed that a correct implementation of the Treaty would give them control of the headwaters of Lynn Canal, one of the two principal routes to the gold fields. But whatever the Treaty said, the fact was that the United States was in *de facto* control of the headwaters of Lynn Canal and, hence, of all the trade to and from the Yukon. Laurier candidly explained the Canadian dilemma to the House of Commons in March 1898.

> . . . the fact is . . . that possession is nine points of the law; and even though by the letter of the treaty, Dyea is in Canadian territory, the fact remains that from time immemorial Dyea was in possession of the Russians, and in 1867 it passed into the hands of the Americans, and it has been in their hands ever since . . . . At this moment we cannot dispute their possession, and . . . before their possession can be disputed, the question must be determined by a settlement of the questions involved in the treaty . . . [34]

At stake in 1898 was more than a boundary line, though even that might determine whether the next anticipated strike was in Canadian or Ameri-

can territory. Most important was the control, and thereby in large measure the origin of supply, of the enormous trade in goods and gold into
and out of the Yukon. The United States controlled the access routes to
the gold fields and dominated the Yukon trade. The Canadians were
determined to get their share – if not all – of the lucrative business in the
vicinity of the undetermined boundary.

The final major question before the Joint High Commission was Canadian-American reciprocal trade relations. Like the other issues, it too was of
long duration; but there the similarity ended. The North Atlantic fisheries
and Bering Sea disputes were largely determined by questions of international law and were open to either final or long-term solutions. The Alaska
Boundary question, again, was capable of final determination. But not so
trade relations with the United States. Canadian-American trade, whether
characterized by reciprocally protective tariffs or by reciprocity, was in its
very nature everchanging, with the increasing industrialization of both
economies and the varying demands of North American consumers. Thus,
what might have been a most significant concession at mid-century could
be of minor importance in 1898. And as both national economies grew
in sophistication, so too did the vested interest components in them
become more varied and interrelated. Consequently, negotiators would
find that their scope for bargaining was considerably circumscribed by
their mutually protective national development policies.

Of almost as much importance to Canada as the agenda of the Joint
High Commission was the decision as to whom the negotiators for Canada
would be. Clearly the Governor General, with or without the British
Ambassador in Washington, could not act for Canada as Lord Elgin had
done in 1854. Since Confederation, members of Canadian governments
had played increasingly influential roles in Canada's negotiations with the
United States. This was, in part, a recognition of Canada's developing
national stature. By 1898, it was clear to the British government that
Canadians were more intimately acquainted with the intricacies of Canadian-American disputes than were the officials of the Foreign Office. As Lord
Salisbury put it, "Several of the questions included in the list . . . for
discussion are of a purely local character, about which this Department,
at least, is without information on which any instructions to the British
Representatives . . . could be usefully framed." It followed, he suggested,
that the British government should nominate only one representative, the
Canadians the remainder, and that all "should take their instructions from
the Dominion Government."[35] In short, the British government would
retain its formal responsibility for the negotiations, but the Canadian
government would determine the actual conduct of the bargaining.

Just before the Commission met, a strong protest was made by Sir James
Winter, Premier of Newfoundland, against the exclusion of his colony

from the proceedings. Winter had a good point. The omission of New-foundland from a resolution of the North Atlantic fisheries dispute would make it worthless, and could also compromise talks on reciprocity. Winter was therefore added to Lord Herschell from Britain and Laurier, Cart-wright, Davies, and Charlton from Canada, on the British side of the table, facing an equal number of American delegates. The inclusion of New-foundland had the advantage for Canada of joining the interests of the two colonies together. One of Laurier's colleagues was enthusiastic about the potential results: "This will pave the way for their admission into the Dominion and complete our area."[36]

The meetings started auspiciously enough – "the Yankees are in a proper frame of mind," said Joseph Pope[37] – and some of the minor difficulties were easily resolved. Indeed, the Bering Sea question was also virtually solved when the Canadians reversed their position and agreed the pelagic sealing was leading to extinction of the seal herd. In return for a cessation of all pelagic sealing they were ready to accept a compensatory payment for their sealers based on a percentage of the receipts from American exploitation of the herd on the Pribilof Islands. Then too, the North Atlantic fisheries dispute, which Lord Herschell had initially con-sidered the most difficult item, was found susceptible of resolution, de-pendent only upon the conclusion of satisfactory trade agreements with the United States for both Newfoundland and Canada.

The reciprocity negotiations gave the first hint of a serious hitch in the talks. The Canadians opened cautiously, proposing a "pretty full free list . . . on raw materials." Representative Dingley responded with the aston-ishing suggestion "to make a complete zollverein between the U.S. & Canada." In fact, such ambitious schemes were never seriously discussed. "The Americans will grant tariff concessions very grudgingly," John Charlton noted with despair.[38] But that was only half the story. Canadian manufacturers and Boards of Trade bombarded Laurier's colleagues in Ottawa with tales of woe and threats of political disaster if their interests were compromised in a trade agreement with the United States. "The members of the Canadian Government who are my colleagues on the Commission have exhibited a very reasonable position," Lord Herschell reported, "but from what I have heard from themselves, as well as from conversations I have had with other members of the Dominion Govern-ment, . . . all the members of that Government are not actuated by an equally reasonable spirit."[39]

Gradually it became clear that the success or failure of the Commission's deliberations would stand or fall on the Alaska boundary talks. For some time it appeared that all would be well; the United States was willing to lease a strip of territory at the head of Lynn Canal to Canada, providing access into the Yukon Territory. But news of the deal leaked to the press,

President McKinley was subjected to violent protests from the Pacific Northwest and the Americans were forced to withdraw the offer. Both sides then fell back on various proprosals for arbitration, only to find that the built-in guarantees of their interests made their positions irreconcilable. The Americans, in a last desperate effort to salvage the Commission, offered to go back to final consideration of other problems, but the British stood firm for all or nothing. On February 20, 1899, the Commission "adjourned" until August. It never met again. "The Americans were certainly in the wrong," Laurier self-righteously told Willison at the height of the crisis, and "I am not to be either bulldozed or bamboozled by them."[40]

In retrospect it is apparent that the failure of the Commission was in some measure due to its own structure. It tried to do too much too quickly. Success depended upon a complex series of interrelated bargains and counter-bargains that would have been, at best, difficult to achieve. But more important were the conflicting aims of all the governments involved, especially Laurier's. The Prime Minister was generally praised by the Canadian press when he came home empty-handed. He had not accepted, or been forced to accept, in Sifton's words, "a jug-handled" treaty. Laurier, instead, had to choose between amiable relations with the Americans, a strategic necessity, and keeping himself and his government in office, a political necessity. He chose the latter, partly in the sure knowledge that British power would protect him from the more extreme excesses of American wrath. But he also made the precarious choice because he was aware that that was what Canadians wanted.

III

With Canadian-American relations in a state of limbo by the spring of 1899, Laurier doubtless hoped that he would now have a respite from these weighty international issues. But as summer arrived it became increasingly apparent that the hope was false. Serious trouble was brewing in South Africa. Canadian newspapers were filled with news of the faraway continent – often news supplied by an agent of the Imperial South African Association, a front organization for Cecil Rhodes' interests.[41] There were also growing signs in English Canada of sympathy for the English-speaking Uitlanders who were being denied their political rights in Kruger's republic. That sentiment found expression in a resolution passed by the House of Commons at the end of July. Sympathy was free; no one seemed to anticipate any more direct involvement. No one except Henri Bourassa, who warned Laurier that the resolution was the first step down the path to involvement. The Prime Minister was unimpressed.[42] But events now began to move rapidly and Laurier soon realized that the fires were being lit on the hills.

On October 3, 1899, nine days before official hostilities broke out in South Africa, the Canadian *Military Gazette* announced that in the event of war the Canadian government would offer troops for overseas service. The Prime Minister immediately dismissed the report as "pure invention." It was true that for some months the government had been aware of an offer of a volunteer force made to the British and Canadian governments by Lieutenant-Colonel Sam Hughes, M.P. But that idea had been effectively killed by General Hutton, the General Officer Commanding the Canadian Militia, who had ambitious plans for leading an "official" force himself. Laurier was quite clear about where the government stood: the Militia Act would not permit the automatic dispatch of Canadian troops overseas. And in words that were later to haunt him, he told reporters: "There is no menace to Canada, and, although we may be willing to contribute troops, I do not see how we can do so. Then again, how could we do so without Parliament's granting us the money? We simply could not do anything. In other words we should have to summon Parliament."[43] That seemed a safe enough position. What it ignored was the growing agitation in English-speaking Canada for a policy of participation. Constitutional niceties would hardly satisfy the nationalist sentiments of English Canada. And that Laurier could not ignore for long, especially as he began to receive letters like the one that read, "French Canadian loyalty is now on trial. I hope it won't be found lacking."[44]

Other reminders came even sooner. On the very day that Laurier explained his position, the *Montreal Star* published a report, released by Chamberlain in London, that the British government would accept an offer of troops from Canada. The Colonial Secretary's official cable, which reached Ottawa two days later, expressed "high appreciation of signal exhibition of patriotic spirit of people of Canada shown by offers to serve in South Africa." The implication was that an offer had been made, or if it were to be made, it would certainly be accepted.[45] Quickly a popular campaign, headed by Hugh Graham, the *Star*'s flamboyant publisher and Canada's most successful practioner of the jingoistic penny-press journalism that was flowering in both Britain and the United States, was developed to force the government to send a contingent. The campaign met a ready audience among English Canadians anxious to show the Mother Country that a new nation had been born.[46]

Enthusiasm for participation in English-speaking Canada was matched by firm opposition in French Canada. The French-language press was virtually unanimous in seeing the war as an example of imperial aggression. Certainly it had nothing to do with Canada. Where most English Canadians sympathized with the Uitlanders' demand for political rights and admired Cecil Rhodes, many French Canadians were concerned about the Boers' "national" rights and preferred Kruger to Rhodes.[47] Tarte's paper, *La Patrie,* was ambiguous; Canada should only participate in British wars if she had a voice in British policy. That sounded like a plea for imperial federation but, in fact, it meant opposition to Canadian participation in the war. The leading Liberal journal, *La Presse,* did not equivocate: it totally opposed participation. An unpleasant note was obvious in the paper's sarcastic comment: "20,000 Canadians are leaving to make themselves Kaffirs, and, in exchange, 25,000 Doukhobors are brought to us to make themselves Canadians. That is a beautiful imperialist policy."[48]

That same division was present in Laurier's party and cabinet. Postmaster General Mulock led the interventionists, knowing what his constituency wanted; Tarte spoke for the isolationists, equally concerned about the sentiments of his province. Laurier knew immediately that he would be damned if he did, and damned if he did not. Was there a way to escape between the horns of that dilemma? After heated cabinet meetings, and caucuses with his French-Canadian supporters, Laurier hit upon a way out that seemed to meet the demands of almost everyone. On October 18, the government announced that "in view of the well known desire of a great many Canadians who are ready to take service under such conditions," the government would equip and transport a volunteer force of 1000 men for service at Britain's side. Once the men reached South Africa the British government would assume financial responsibility. That, it was hoped, should satisfy those English Canadians clamouring for action. As for the opponents, the government had something a little less tangible. The Order-in-Council enunciating the policy contained the statement that the action "cannot be regarded as a departure from the well-known principles of constitutional government and colonial practice, nor construed as a precedent for future action."[49] And what of the need to have Parliament decide? To avoid a public display of division in the country, and in the Liberal party, Laurier conveniently forgot his constitutional qualms of October 4.

The essence of Laurier's policy was simplicity itself. In Quebec the tactic was to deny that there was any real departure from the past – participation was purely voluntary with the government doing the minimum to assist. That was hardly a high price to pay to assuage English Canada.[50] In English Canada the line was to insist that Canada had done exactly what Chamberlain wanted. How could a policy be more loyal? "The jingoes & tories would have us plunge into heavy & unfathomable expenditures," Laurier told the editor of the *Globe.* "You know my objections to such a course. . . . To all the attacks of the tories we have an easy answer, in the fact that we have just complied with the request of the home authorities which is so moderate that we could deal with it without having the previous sanction of parliament."[51] The strategy was superb, and apparently satisfied most Canadians. Only the nationalists rejected it as abject colonialism. English-Canadian nationalists like John Willison wanted Canada to participate as an equal in the war, and to prove that equality by assuming full responsibility for Canadian troops in South Africa.[52] French-Canadian nationalists wanted Canada to prove her equality of nationhood by refusing to participate at all. That was the essence of Henri Bourassa's view, and he was to resign his seat in Parliament to display the strength of his convictions. His quarrel with Laurier was that, despite all disclaimers to the contrary, the dispatch of troops was a precedent which was contrary to the past relations of Canada and the Empire. "The precedent, Sir, is the accomplished fact," he wrote with that logic which made him both a brilliant journalist and a poor politician. "The principle at stake is the axiom *par excellence* of English liberalism, resting at the base of the parliamentary regime: NO TAXATION WITHOUT REPRESENTATION."[53]

But the decision had been made. The first contingent, commanded by Lieutenant-Colonel Otter, sailed at the end of October. A second contingent was offered a week later and accepted during "black week" in December. Lord Strathcona, the High Commissioner in London, raised a unit of mounted rifles, and other Canadians were enlisted through the Militia Department for the British government. In all, more than seven thousand Canadians fought in the Boer War, about a third of them in official contingents.[54] And while the war raged in South Africa, another battle was in progress at home.

French and English Canada had decisively split on a critical issue and Laurier had compromised in the interest, he argued, of national unity. The Prime Minister sincerely believed that the British cause in South Africa was just and was willing to have Canada support the Mother Country as a loyal colony.[55] But he did not deny that the imperialist pressure of English Canada had precipitated the sending of the first contingent. "If we had refused our imperative duty," he told the House of Commons in May 1900, "the most dangerous agitation would have arisen, an agitation which, according to all human probability, would have ended in a cleavage in the population of this country upon racial lines. A greater calamity could never take place in Canada."[56]

Henri Bourassa, returned to Parliament by acclamation, remained implacably opposed to sending troops. He rejected Laurier's claim to have acted in the best interests of national unity. Pandering to racial differences, he thought, would increase, not diminish them. "Here is a liberal government," he told Goldwin Smith,

> brought to power under the flag of national pacification and harmony. They are now going back on the oldest, the soundest, the most respectable principle of constitutional liberalism and playing in [to] the hands of Mr. Chamberlain

and other megalomanic imperialists – and this, because they are afraid of
being called a french dominated and priest ridden government. Don't you
think it is a direct premium offered to racial appeals?[57]

Smith was sympathetic; if anything he was more opposed to Laurier's
policy than Bourassa. During the war the two fought a lonely battle against
Laurier, who, Smith said, was "spoiled by the Jubilee . . . and by his
knighthood." Smith campaigned valiantly in Ontario, using his *Weekly Sun*
to bring the views of Bourassa from Quebec, Morley from England, and
Merriman from South Africa before the province. But all in vain. When
queried by Bourassa about an anti-imperialist campaign in the province
during the 1900 election, Smith discouraged the idea as futile.[58]

Bourassa's plight in Quebec was no better. Anti-war sentiment ran high
in the province and in March there had been student riots in Montreal.
On the thirteenth, Bourassa proposed in the House of Commons that
"parliament insist on its sovereignty and independence, refuse to consider
the government's action a precedent of the future." Only nine Quebec
members, from both parties, supported him. A year later his support
dwindled to two other members when he moved a resolution for peace
on the basis of South African independence. Even more telling had been
the general election of 1900. In Ontario the Liberals had lost fourteen
seats but in Quebec only seven Conservatives had been returned. "In spite
of favourable popular feeling," Bourassa conceded that he was unable to
organize any effective campaign against Laurier. He bitterly remarked that
Laurier's

> followers and his organs will shout that Laurier is more of a patriot and of
> a Canadian than ever and will thus induce the people to believe that Laurier
> is an anti-imperialist. They will thus prevent the electors to realize that, whilst
> Sir Wilfrid is opposed to an impossible form of Federation, he is leading them
> to the real practical military imperialism. You know how hard it is to bring
> the masses and even the supposed educated men to appreciate future events
> and yet unapplied theories.

A sceptical Goldwin Smith was probably closer to the mark when he
observed that Quebec's opposition to the war had to be "balanced by
affection for a [French] Canadian Premier and his meal bag."[59]

Bourassa's disaffection would ultimately cause great trouble for Laurier,
but for the moment the Prime Minister was master of Quebec. Imperial
sentiment ran at high tide elsewhere. One result was the founding of the
Imperial Order of the Daughters of the Empire in Montreal in February
1900 by Mrs. Clark Murray, wife of a McGill professor, and other "prominent women." "For the encouragement of Patriotism," Children of the
Empire groups were simultaneously formed. The I.O.D.E. stated its aims
to be stimulation of patriotism binding women and children of the Empire

to the throne, the creation of an association for prompt and efficient action by imperial women and children should it be required, promotion of the study of imperial questions, care of the dependants of British military personnel and the direction of "women's influence to the bettering of all things connected with our great Empire."[60]

Joseph Chamberlain quickly sought to turn to practical account the surge of imperial enthusiasm in Canada and elsewhere. As early as March 1900, he suggested to Minto that something "might be done towards that closer union we have constantly kept in view." First, he wondered if the colonies might be consulted regarding the settlement of the war. But more important was his proposal for "something in the nature of an Imperial Council, sitting permanently in London and acting as permanent advisers to the Secretary of State for the Colonies." At the beginning the Council might concern itself with common problems of imperial defence; in time it might even have a voice in problems "arising with any other Power which were likely to lead to war. . . ."[61] Minto, after consulting key members of both the government and opposition and such influential imperialists as Principal Grant, advised Chamberlain to go slow. He had found some half-hearted support for consultation on peace terms but both Tupper and Laurier shied away from any plan for an imperial council.

Nor was Laurier encouraging about schemes for imperial defence. Canada's commitment to national development was large and expensive. "In case of need," the Prime Minister told Minto, Canada had shown that "she may be relied upon to afford loyal assistance to the Mother Country. But is not this assistance more likely to be given voluntarily than under any detailed plan of military organization which would impose on the Colonies fixed financial obligations?"[62] Surprised at the unanimity of the Canadian rebuff, and more than a little disappointed at Laurier's seeming reversal of attitude from the soothing phrases of 1897 and his imperial rhetoric in defence of his South African policy, Chamberlain dropped the suggestion. But it was not without significance. At once it revealed Laurier's hardening attitude toward imperial affairs and the widening gulf between what Laurier and what Chamberlain understood to be imperial unity.[63]

Chamberlain's proposal for a "real Council of the Empire to which all questions of imperial interest might be referred" reappeared on the agenda of the Imperial Conference of 1902.[64] In the guise of the "weary Titan" struggling "under the too vast orb of his fate," Chamberlain and his colleagues proposed integration of imperial politics, economics, and defence. Lord Selbourne deprecated local defence schemes and plumped for "a single navy under one control." Laurier, backed by Mulock and Borden, Fielding and Paterson, would have none of these schemes for centralization. He and his fellow colonials resolved in favour of periodical imperial conferences, informal and uncommitted, in place of an imperial council. In lieu of an imperial naval force, Laurier countered with the suggestion of the establishment of a Canadian navy. From Laurier's point of view, the Imperial Conference was a great success; from Chamberlain's, a dismal failure.[65]

At bottom, the gap between the conceptions of Empire of the Prime Minister of Canada and the Colonial Secretary was unbridgeable. Laurier believed the greatest glory and the greatest strength of the Empire lay in the liberty and freedom of its ambiguity. Chamberlain, and many of Canada's imperialists, regarded the nebulousness of undefined imperial unity as its greatest weakness. Unlike Chamberlain, when Laurier considered imperial relations, as his biographer wrote, "his formulas were never very formal."[66] Put another way, for Laurier the strength of the imperial connection rested upon the principle of volunteerism. The imperial preference, which helped to slow down the decline of British imports to Canada, had been unsolicited, freely given by Canada. The Canadian contingents had been made up of volunteers. And, as Laurier had reminded the Governor General in April 1900, in time of need Canada could always be counted on to respond, fully and freely. But fixed and precise obligations were another matter again. Not only did they make for potentially embarrassing commitments in an unforeseen future, not only did they place potential barriers before the national development of his country, but also obligations that even hinted of compulsion carried the threat of racial and political disharmony in Canada. And that, as Laurier had said many times, was the greatest calamity which could ever take place in Canada. Sadly, the Colonial Secretary found the Prime Minister's position totally incomprehensible.

IV

From his point of view, Laurier was standing four-square with the Empire in South Africa. In return he expected unwavering British support in the continuing informal negotiations with the United States to settle Canadian-American problems. Alaska remained the key to success or failure. In the late spring and summer of 1899 the Canadians adopted the role of critic of British and American initiatives. Laurier's attitude was that

the first overtures should come from the American side. We have not been able to agree upon a compromise. There is nothing left but an arbitration [on Alaska]. . . . Our position is so strong that it is not for us to depart from it in any way.[67]

The British government did not agree. Chamberlain warned Minto that "whatever arguments may be based on letter of Treaty of 1825, careful examination of United States' case for possession of shore of [Lynn] Canal based on continuous uncontested jurisdiction since date of Treaty, the admissions of Hudson [sic] Bay Company, Imperial and Dominion Governments, [sic] that it is unassailable."[68] In other words, if a reasonable solution could be agreed upon with the United States, the British government was not prepared to support Canadian intransigence.

In spite of the warning, Laurier vetoed three proposals relating to the adjourned Commission between May and September. A renewed suggestion from McKinley that the Commissioners proceed with the other questions was flatly refused. A suggestion for arbitration on the lines of the Venezuela Treaty was made by Lord Pauncefote and Joseph Choate, the American Ambassador in London, with the proviso that Dyea and Skagway at the head of Lynn Canal remain in United States possession. Canada demanded an equal guarantee for Pyramid Harbor to which she had never laid any claim and which had only been considered by the Canadians when it had been offered to them by the Americans a few months before! A Colonial Office official ruefully observed that "we must try to persuade the Canadian Ministers that they would not be wise to press claims which will preclude a settlement . . . which is more important for Canada than for the U.S."[69] Finally, Chamberlain and Tarte proposed a ninety-nine year lease of a suitable place on Lynn Canal where Canada would enjoy full commercial privileges but where American sovereignty could be maintained. When Tarte cabled from London seeking Laurier's approval, the Prime Minister curtly replied, "No, leave matter altogether to us here."[70]

The surrender of the diplomatic initiative to the senior partners in the North Atlantic triangle meant that Canada placed her chances for improved relations with the United States in the hands of the Foreign Office where interest in maintaining Anglo-American understanding was distinctly more powerful than in Canada. As early as February 1900, the first chink in Canada's Alaskan armour was made when London, under great pressure from the United States and severely embarrassed by the humiliation of the British armies in South Africa, finally agreed to abrogate the Clayton-Bulwer Treaty, allowing the United States to build a wholly American-controlled Panama canal. Canada had urged since the previous spring that Great Britain hold out for an Alaskan solution in return for the agreement, but it was not to be. In December 1900, the American Senate ratified the treaty, but with amendments which were unacceptable to the British government. The amended treaty was in turn rejected by Great Britain early in 1901, and Pauncefote and Secretary of State Hay began their efforts to resolve Anglo-American differences. Hay shortly produced not one but three draft treaties, one for the canal question, one on Alaska, and a third dealing with most of the other Canadian questions which had been before the Joint High Commission. In essence, the Secretary of State conceded what Canada demanded, parallel negotiations on the revisions of the Clayton-Bulwer Treaty and on Alaska.

Hay went even further than that. For the first time his proposal for arbitration of the Alaska boundary omitted a clause reserving Dyea and Skagway to the United States. He proposed that the Joint High Commission reconvene for the sole purpose of signing an agreement to arbitrate the boundary upon the basis of the unratified Anglo-American arbitration treaty of 1897, which stipulated a tribunal of six, three from each side. And presumably, if Laurier was to be taken at his word, once that matter had been settled the other Canadian-American problems could be resolved; hence the third draft treaty.

Sir Wilfrid objected to the Alaskan draft, principally because it called for an even-numbered tribunal. Despite British warnings that Canada was being given its last chance, Laurier refused to consider Hay's proposals. Unfortunately, the Prime Minister failed to take sufficient account of the pressures upon both the British and American governments to reach accord. The Hay-Pauncefote Treaty on the canal problem was accepted by the British Government in the fall of 1901. By holding out for a settlement on Alaska that would confirm Canada's position, Laurier had taken a huge gamble. He lost. As one student has observed, Canada "woke up one day to find a new canal treaty concluded and the main basis of her diplomacy with the United States undermined. She lay exposed, far more vulnerable to American pressure than before."[71]

In the summer of 1902, while Sir Wilfrid attended the Imperial Conference, he had a number of conversations with Foreign Secretary Lansdowne, and Henry White and Ambassador Choate of the United States Embassy, about Alaska. Momentarily freed from the watchful gaze of his cabinet colleagues, Laurier seemed prepared to concede everything to the United States. Lansdowne told Choate that the United States must retain Dyea and Skagway and that Canada, provided a properly framed question could be put to arbitration, would withdraw its objection to an even-numbered tribunal. These London conversations led directly to the final agreement to submit the dispute to a "judicial" tribunal in the spring of 1903. This strange reversal of policy was partly inspired by Laurier's realization of the weakness of his position, more especially since strong-willed Theodore Roosevelt had succeeded the assassinated President McKinley in the White House. Equally important was the renewed determination of Newfoundland, with British approval, to open separate reciprocity negotiations with the United States. Should they prove successful, Canada's position on almost all major Canadian-American questions would be hopelessly undermined. Thus, the Prime Minister probably decided to give way on Alaska in the hope that he could short-circuit a Newfoundland-United States agreement when it reached the Foreign Office.[72]

In January 1903, the British government signed the Hay-Herbert Treaty, which provided for a judicial tribunal by "impartial jurists of repute." Only after this signature was Canada notified, though the British had known for some days that Roosevelt had arrogantly appointed Secretary of War Root and Senators Lodge and Turner as his three "impartial jurists." From Ottawa's point of view it was a deliberately crude manoeuvre and they urged reconsideration. Great Britain not only refused Canada's advice but quickly exchanged ratifications with the United States. The British, Sifton bitterly observed, "deliberately decided . . . to sacrifice our interests at any cost, for the sake of pleasing the United States."[73] There was some truth in his assessment. But Sifton might have added that Canada had been repeatedly warned that might happen by numerous British officials and politicians since the summer of 1899. Rejecting a British suggestion that similarly partisan members be appointed to their side of the tribunal, the Canadians insisted upon adherence to the letter of the treaty. The British members were Lord Alverstone from Great Britain, Sir Louis A. Jetté and Justice Armour from Canada. The last died before the tribunal met and was replaced by a prominent Toronto lawyer, A.B. Aylesworth.

Roosevelt's interventions breaching the spirit of the treaty did not cease. The President was convinced that the Canadians had no case.[74] But it was beyond his powers of self-restraint to let the matter rest with his trusted appointees. Lodge, Turner, Root, Choate, and White received a flood of letters urging them to stand firm and apply pressure upon the British government for a final settlement. While the tribunal met the message was conveyed to both Prime Minister Balfour and Foreign Secretary Lansdowne and there is little doubt that Lord Alverstone was made aware of the President's threats.

The main point of the dispute, whether or not the United States had a continuous lisière in the panhandle, was decided in America's favour by 4-2 vote, Jetté and Aylesworth dissenting. And on that point the American case was especially strong.[75] But it was on a seemingly minor point that the true nature of the tribunal appeared. Lord Alverstone, apparently believing a compromise was necessary, tried to give the Canadians as much as possible on the minor questions. On October 12, he announced his belief that four small islands at the southern tip of the panhandle belonged to Canada. Five days later, under intense pressure from the Americans, he reversed himself and announced that the two smaller and westernmost islands would go to the United States. Jetté and Aylesworth, and Sifton who had been responsible for preparation of the British case, were furious at Alverstone's "treachery." The Canadian judges, not totally above partiality themselves, filed a minority decision wholly in line with the British case and injudiciously published a remonstrance against Alverstone. Laurier considered Alverstone's decision "one of those concessions which have made British diplomacy odious to Canadian people."[76]

In Ottawa the tribunal's award was interpreted as intolerable in form and dangerous to Canadian interests in substance. Port Simpson on Observatory Inlet had recently been selected as the western terminal for the Grand Trunk Pacific Railway. It was thought that Sitklan and Kannaghunut, the two islands Alverstone had given to the United States, could be armed by the Americans and thus threaten the shipping lanes to and from Port Simpson. Still more infuriating was the conduct of the tribunal. Laurier concluded that "we should ask the British Parliament for more extensive powers so that if ever we have to deal with matters of a similar nature again, we shall deal with them in our own way, in our own fashion, according to the best light we have."[77] As for the Americans, Roosevelt's truculent diplomacy was inexcusable though probably predictable. But it did not augur well for disposition of the many remaining problems. In the spring of 1904 the Prime Minister announced that "we are always ready to . . . negotiate with them on fair terms, but we shall not take the initiative for new negotiations. If new negotiations are to be made, it must be on their initiative."[78]

The Alaska boundary question was a sorry episode in Canadian-American relations. None of the participating nations could be proud of its performance. Under McKinley the Americans, negotiating from strength, acted moderately; under Roosevelt, their conduct and his were shameful. The British, under great pressure to maintain and enhance Anglo-American accord, tried the impossible, to accommodate Canada's particularist interests to the larger strategic demands of the Empire. From 1899 on they had warned Canada that it might not work and in the end they were as responsible as was the United States for making a mockery of the judicial character of the tribunal. Nor was Canada's position anything like as virtuous as Laurier and his colleagues sought to make it appear in the uproar after the award. The government's public posturing from strength contrasted sharply with the Prime Minister's private confessions of weakness. The result was to call into question what merits there were in Canada's case and to estrange Canada from its major source of support, the Colonial and Foreign Offices in London. Self-righteous recriminations against both Great Britain and the United States in the fall of 1903 gave vent to Canadian sentiment. But they did little to enhance cordial relations with either of Canada's senior partners in the North Atlantic triangle.

CHAPTER 4

Opening Up the Land of Opportunity

I

"The Premier of Canada recently expressed the idea, which is that of all Canadians, that as the 19th century was the century of the United States, the 20th century is the century of Canada," an immigration pamphlet, entitled *Canada: The Land of Opportunity,* announced in 1909. " . . . The United States is the America of achievement, but Canada is the America of opportunity."[1] Optimism was Canada's most striking characteristic during the Laurier years. At least in English Canada, the Boer war had stimulated a strong sense of pride; it had been wounded, but not slain, by the Alaska boundary award. Underlying this new self-confidence, even brashness, were the comforting facts of economic success and the expectation that the future was limitless. At last the country had passed out of the doldrums of world depression. The unfulfilled promises of the first thirty years of Confederation soon seemed but vanishing memories.

The Liberal government, anxious to display its leadership, quickly moved to take advantage of the new opportunities. The goal was to make the national developmental policies, already set out in previous years, a success. The basic transportation system, the Canadian Pacific Railway, had been established; the tariff would only be tinkered with. Now the crying need was to fill up the west with hard-working settlers whose needs and products would make the system work. Agricultural settlement was the last, but in many ways the most important, link in the east-west chain that was to bind the national economy, and even the national identity, together.

By 1896 changing world economic conditions, as well as internal Canadian factors, virtually guaranteed accelerated Canadian development. The discovery of large quantities of gold in South Africa in the mid-nineties, and its absorption into the world monetary system, resulted in a sharp rise in prices that was particularly advantageous to Canada. The price of raw materials, especially food, rose much more rapidly than manufactured products. This was due largely to the rapid pace of industrialization in western Europe and the United States between 1896 and 1914. Competition among the industrial nations for export markets for their manufactured goods, plus the growing need for foodstuffs to feed increasingly urban populations, placed Canada in an especially favourable position. In that period the average increase in the price of all Canadian exports was thirty-two per cent, with grains leading the way by increasing some sixty-six per cent. During the same period imports rose only about twenty-four per cent. Equally important, since Canadian exports were bulky, was the sharp decline in ocean freight-rates. Such favourable conditions contributed greatly to an increase in foreign investment in the Canadian economy. Improved expectations of profit, plus interest rates lower than at any period in recorded history, ensured Canada the volume of foreign investment necessary for the development of newly discovered resources and the expansion of secondary industry.

By almost any measure the country's growth rate was astonishing.[2] The population increased only 24 per cent between 1881 and 1901; in the next twenty years, it leapt forward by 64 per cent. Real growth in population during the first twenty years of the century increased steadily from 5,371,315 in 1901 to 8,788,949 in 1921. Most striking of course was the growth of the prairie west, though every other part of the country increased its population too. Farm acreage expanded 125 per cent and the value of field crops quadrupled as did total external trade in the same period.[3] "Not only businessmen, but politicians, the clergy, the press, and every other vocable instrument is preaching, praising, prophesying," John Hobson wrote of the mood of Canada in 1906. "Now Canada (no longer the United States) is 'God's country, sir!' Now the twentieth century belongs to her. Now her population and her prosperity will swell until she becomes the corner-stone of the temple of the British Empire."[4]

II

The successful settlement of the prairies had long been seen as fundamental to the fulfilment of the grand plan of a viable east-west economy. Its agricultural products would provide the freight needed to ensure the profits of the C.P.R., and its demand for manufactured goods would give eastern industry a long-awaited prosperity. W.S. Fielding, in his budget speech in 1903, explained the Laurier government's developmental policy in terms that Sir John A. Macdonald would have heartily applauded. "The best way you can help the manufacturers of Canada," he maintained, "is to fill up the prairie regions of Manitoba and the Northwest with a prosperous and contented people, who will be consumers of the manufactured goods of the east."[5] In the years between 1896 and 1921, the prairies became the most dynamic element in the country's economic growth. The potential of the plains attracted capital and labour in amounts never before experienced by Canada, and the results filtered through the entire economy.[6]

The west benefited enormously from changed world economic circumstances, as did the whole country. Of particular importance were declining interest rates, which indicated an increasing availability of investment capital, and lowered freight rates, which greatly assisted in keeping the price of Canadian wheat competitive. Farmers constantly complained about the Canadian Pacific Railway, but it was nevertheless a fact that the railway was absolutely indispensable to their well-being: it brought in new settlers and their effects and hauled out their produce. Moreover, settlement growth was determined by the increasing price of wheat and other foodstuffs on the overseas markets. A bushel of wheat that brought eighty-four cents in Liverpool in 1896 was worth one dollar and thirteen cents by 1913. And, of course, there was much more grain for sale as more land was broken and better grains and improved farming techniques were developed.

Of particular importance to the success of the western agricultural economy were certain farming techniques peculiar to the dry climate of the central plains. Dry farming, as it was called, had already been developed in the American west and northwest in the 1880s and 1890s. The Dominion Experimental Station at Indian Head had naturally been especially concerned with the problem of the low rainfall that characterized most of the prairies, and with discovering the best means of utilizing it to the full. The solution was described by Angus Mackay, a leader in the development of the dry farming technique in 1889.

Our seasons point to only one way in which we can in all years expect to reap something. . . . at present I submit that fallowing the land is the best preparation to ensure a crop. Fallowing land in this country is not required for the purpose of renovating it, as is the case with worn-out lands in the east, and it is a question yet unsettled how much or how little the fallow should be worked, but as we have only one wet season during the year, it is found beyond doubt that the land must be ploughed the first time before the wet season is over if we expect to reap a crop the following year. The wet season comes during June and July, at a time when every farmer has little or nothing else to do, and then this work should be done.[7]

It was the refinement and spread of such techniques as these that helped to make the dry prairies bloom.

There were also the advantages of agricultural technology most often developed in the United States.[8] The chilled steel plough cut through the rich prairie sod, straight and deep, opening up thousands of new acres each year: 15.4 million acres were under production in 1901, 57.7 in 1911, and 87.9 in 1921. Improved harrows and seed-drills made spring-time seeding more efficient while threshing equipment helped the farmer, in the short western growing season, to get the crop off the fields before the early snow of the prairie fall. By the years of the Great War a mechanical revolution was beginning in western agriculture: the gas-driven tractor had begun slowly to replace the horse on the more prosperous farms, and the farm equipment firm, with its factory in the east, became an important establishment in every prairie town and village.

Improvements in farm machinery did not come without a price to the farmer. While it made his operation more efficient and less back-breaking, it also increased his debt load. When added to the often heavy mortgages, bank loans, and indebtedness to local merchants, the increasingly heavy investment in machinery made the farmer's financial position highly vulnerable. A single crop failure could put him near bankruptcy. Fluctuating world grain prices, changes in freight-rate structures, high dockage by local grain dealers or failure by the railway to move the grain quickly enough in the fall could mean seriously straitened financial circumstances. It was this sensitive financial position which moved the farmers to organize themselves against the vagaries of the system and which made them a politically volatile community.

No less important than the new farming technology were improvements in grain varieties. The relatively short growing season in the prairies, especially in those potentially fertile areas in the north such as the Peace River district, needed a wheat strain that matured quickly while maintaining the hardness and high protein content that had made Manitoba Number One Northern world famous. Until about 1911 the predominant wheat in the west was the well-established Red Fife. But as early as 1892 William Saunders had experimented with a variety he hoped would mature more rapidly. His son, C.E. Saunders, who became Dominion Cerealist in 1903, continued to develop this cross between Red Fife and Red Calcutta, first in Ottawa and by 1908 in the west.[9] Marquis, as the new strain was registered, proved an immediate success. It was eight days shorter in maturation time than Red Fife and was seven bushels heavier in yield. By 1911 it was being widely distributed, and contributed heavily to the rise of Canada from a position of third largest to that of second largest exporter of wheat by the end of the Great War.[10] In 1928 the Dominion Cerealist, L.H. Newman, reported that the introduction of

Marquis wheat "into Canadian agriculture completely overshadows in importance any other single event, marking as it undoubtedly does a new epoch in the agricultural life of the Dominion."[11] By the end of the Great War the introduction of Marquis had probably added some $100,000,000 annually to farm income.

It would be impossible to underestimate the significance of wheat to the rapid development of the prairie west and to the Canadian economy generally. From Winnipeg west through the fertile plains of Portage la Prairie and Brandon almost to the foothills of the Rockies, wheat was king. In the twenty-five years after 1896 its production and export soared, bringing increasing amounts of foreign capital into Canada, and attracting a growing flood of new settlers to the west. In 1896 wheat production in Canada stood at 7,855,274 bushels. Five years later it had jumped to 26,117,530 bushels and a further threefold increase had taken place by 1911. Though the 1918 and 1919 crop years were extremely poor, total wheat production had risen to nearly 151 million bushels by 1921.[12]

Economic growth of this magnitude underlay the often exuberant confidence of Canadians, and especially western Canadians, in the years before the Great War. There were minor setbacks, of course, as with the slowdown of 1907, but that could only be temporary. Few Canadians, and even fewer westerners, would have agreed with the realistic comments of a writer in the *Queen's Quarterly* in 1902. "At present, and with excellent reason," he wrote,

> everywhere throughout the West the note of confidence prevails and, even in its most extravagant forms, is quite catching. Already the future is mapped out for the next quarter or half century in a geometric ratio of increase from the progress of the present. Yet those who are unpatriotic enough to look both before and after, will be apt to discount the extravagant estimates of the present as liberally as the doleful predictions of the past or those which may follow.[13]

Much more common, and acceptable, were the views of the speaker at the Winnipeg branch of the Canadian Club who in 1906 offered the heady prediction that "in forty or fifty years Canada will have a population of forty or fifty millions, and Saskatchewan and Alberta will be greater than Ontario in population, and Winnipeg will have surpassed Toronto and Montreal."[14]

Such predictions were perhaps not so unreasonable in the years when even the most arid region of the west – the famous Palliser Triangle – was filling up with settlers. If faith in the agricultural potential of that area was possible, there could surely be no bounds to man's confidence. And every year the settlers arrived in rapidly increasing numbers.

III

More fundamental than the scientific advances in grain-growing or the improvements in farm machinery in the successful opening of the west was, obviously, the rush of settlers into the open prairies. In the years prior to 1896, nothing had been more disheartening than the country's failure to attract and keep the large number of people necessary to fill up western Canada's vast and almost empty spaces. For the most part the problem was not want of effort in Canada but lack of motivation on the part of potential immigrants. Apart from the world depression, which had kept grain prices low and therefore left Canada's agricultural lands unattractive, a considerable amount of land in the western United States was still available for settlement. Europeans, and even Canadians, appeared to prefer the United States to Canada. But by the mid-nineties these conditions had begun to change. The world depression was lifting just at a time when demand for agricultural products was also on the rise. And the American frontier was virtually closed, with nearly all good agricultural land, and some that was not so good, filled up. The Canadian west increased rapidly in attraction to immigrants. George Parkin, who travelled across Canada in 1893 preparing a series of articles for *The Times* of London, observed the significant inflow of settlers from the United States.[15] This was just the beginning, a trickle that would soon become a flood.

Undoubtedly the most important member of Laurier's first cabinet, next to the Prime Minister himself, was the Minister of the Interior and the representative of the west, Clifford Sifton. Sifton was a no-nonsense Manitoba businessman with an almost unbounded confidence in the potential of western Canada. His optimism was expressed neither in flights of romantic oratory, nor in the flamboyant braggadocio of many western salesmen. Instead he preferred that his faith should manifest itself in works. His goal was to reorganize the Canadian government's immigration service, and bring to the west the kind of settler he believed most suited to meet the rough challenges of pioneer rural life. Sifton's extensive personal knowledge of prairie conditions was matched by a strong will and a powerful mind. And he was a born organizer, a talent he used to the great benefit of the country and the Liberal party. In the election of 1896 he put his view of the problem of the west in this way:

> Since 1882 the progress of Manitoba has been disappointing; it has not developed as it should have done if a proper policy had been developed at Ottawa. The land policy of the Government alone was enough to kill any new country. Today the great need is to have as Minister of the Interior one who will grapple with this question in an intelligent vigorous way. It was useless to spend thousands of dollars in bringing immigrants here when there was no proper means of locating them. What was needed was a study of the agricul-

tural needs of the country, the problem of education, and the settling of the vast quantity of vacant land.[16]

On becoming Minister of the Interior in 1896 Sifton turned his attention at once to these problems. In the past, large blocks of land had been set aside for the railways as subsidies. Though some 24,000,000 acres had been earned by the railways only a small portion of this acreage had actually been selected by the companies, leaving large areas, often fertile prairie lands, closed to settlement. Sifton took immediate steps to end this land grant system and to pressure the railways into making their choice of lands so that the remainder could be thrown open to general settlement. By the time of his resignation in 1905 this problem had been virtually extinguished.

His next problem was to reorganize his department, which he had once described as a "department of delay, a department of circumlocution."[17] His answer was centralization: all final decisions would be made in Ottawa where he could keep an eye on them. The Land Board in Winnipeg was abolished. Its bureaucratic fumbling had caused endless frustration for prospective settlers awaiting designation of their lands. It took about two years to clear the backlog of applications, and in the meantime Sifton set about simplifying procedures by widening the discretion of the Minister and his officials in settling land grant policies. Though he was roundly criticized by the opposition for his apparent determination to set himself up as sole judge of how policy should be applied, he was convinced that such centralization allowed speed and efficiency, and, above all, succeeded in getting settlers on the land. Sifton's approach, while subject to abuse, nevertheless brought a new flexibility into the operations of the Department. It became simpler to obtain a homestead, prices for additional acreage were lowered, patents were more easily registered and on fairer terms. These changes removed many causes for complaint after settlers had arrived in Canada. But much more important was getting the immigrants to come.[18]

In Sifton's judgment the goal of immigration policy was to settle the prairies with farmers as quickly as possible. Therefore the selection of immigrants had to be made with that goal uppermost and through the application of one discriminatory principle: urban immigrants were not wanted. That policy was frankly defined by Sifton's energetic Deputy Minister and fellow Manitoban, James Smart, in 1900. "If a settler is one who has been engaged in agricultural pursuits in the old land, is possessed of his full faculties, steady, honest, sober, and willing to work whether he be rich or poor, Galician, Austrian, Russian, Swede, Belgian or French, we believe it most desirable to encourage him to occupy our land and to break up our soil and assist in developing the resources of the country, and in this way enrich himself and Canada."[19] And, as Sifton himself often declared publicly, immigration agents were instructed to discourage "labouring men and mechanics,"[20] though this policy was in fact not always effectively enforced when it conflicted with the needs of the Canadian labour market.[21]

What Canada offered the new settler was set out in the Dominion Lands Act first enacted in 1872, and subsequently amended, though not altered in principle. Under this legislation the settler was granted a quarter section of free land, provided he lived on it and cultivated it for a period of three years. Moreover, an additional 160 acres, adjoining the initial holding, could be placed under a three-year pre-emption to purchase. A settler had to become a British subject before obtaining the final patent to his land.[22] To transform this untilled land into a productive farm, a new settler needed a small amount of capital, which he either brought with him, as happened most often with Americans or Englishmen, or earned as a railway or farm labourer, if he was an impecunious peasant.

One estimate of the most elementary needs of the new settler ran to approximately $250, including $180 for a yoke of oxen, $30 for a milch cow, $20 for a wagon, and $14 for a breaking plough. That estimate made no provision for a house or household effects, which some, though certainly not all, settlers brought with them. Professor James Mavor, who made this calculation in a report he prepared for the British government in 1904, added a very telling footnote stating that "such an estimate may be taken as valid for the peasant settler from Continental Europe or to settlers accustomed to a like standard of comfort. For others a larger initial expenditure would be necessary. This expenditure must vary from $500 to $600 for the provision of minimum requirements to $1,500 and upwards for more ample and comfortable settlement." He offered no estimate of the cost of housing, noting only that "the peasant immigrant builds one with sods or with logs cut by himself on or near his own land, and the outside is sometimes daubed with clay."[23]

Mavor's comment was not entirely accurate, for many settlers of different origins and backgrounds, including at least one American doctor who turned to farming in Alberta,[24] began their new lives in sod houses. Nor was this type of shelter totally lacking in comfort. As one pioneer described her first prairie home: "Slabs of sod were placed around the lumber shack and another room was added – all sod. The inside was plastered with mud, with a nice smooth finish. As the years passed the mud plastering was papered over with building paper. The sod walls were three feet thick. There was a good shingle roof and board floors. It was a warm cosy place."[25]

In addition to constructing a house, the pioneer had to clear and break his land and prepare for spring planting. Thus it was important to be near the railway line so that tools, equipment and seed grain could be shipped in, and, later, the crop shipped out to market.[26]

The settler's success in the west depended very much on his background. That was the reason for the government's insistence upon farming experience. Canadian immigration agents set out in three general directions. First there was the British Isles, the traditional source of immigrants to Canada. Second, there was the United States, transformed from a powerful attraction for Canadian emigrants into a prime source of some of the best settlers who established themselves in the west. Finally, there was a large new source, Europe and especially eastern Europe: it was to add an element to the Canadian population which, if not entirely new, now grew to such a size as to alter the whole complexion of the Canadian prairies.

Attacting immigrants from the British Isles was a relatively simple matter. Common membership in the Empire was an obvious advantage, and Canada's contribution to the Boer War served as useful publicity for the country.[27] With many Britishers already settled in Canada, the family connection also played an important part. Until 1903 the immigration services were under the control of the High Commissioner, but Sifton never found this an entirely satisfactory arrangement. In that year he decided to establish an immigration office in Charing Cross Road that was effectively independent of the High Commissioner's office. This arrangement, if increased immigration is taken as evidence, was a marked improvement. In 1900 fewer than 1,200 people from the British Isles settled in Canada. Five years later the total reached more than 65,000, exceeding the numbers arriving from the United States. But the largest year of all came in 1912-13 when 150,000 Britishers arrived in Canada. Apart from the Barr Colony, most settlers from Britain came as individuals in search of a better standard of living and in the hope of escaping the rigidities of the English class structure. For the most part they proved highly satisfactory immigrants.[28]

Some problems were created in 1907 when a downturn in the world economy encouraged a substantial number of unacceptable emigrants to leave for Canada, with a consequent increase in deportations; in 1908 about seventy per cent of all deportations were to Britain. It was suspected, probably on good evidence, that a large number of these people had been shipped to Canada under the auspices of charitable organizations with the intention of shortening British relief rolls. Such people were not warmly welcomed in Canada. "Now we know something of the dreadful conditions existing in the cities in England," a Methodist minister especially concerned with immigration problems wrote in 1907. "We sympathize with the poor people sent to us. We would gladly see them given a better chance. We rejoice that some of them make a success of the new life. But at the same time we are Canadians, and must remember the best interest of Canada."[29] That was a mild comment compared to some. It was probably this type of immigrant who caused signs reading "No English need apply" to appear in the windows of some western employment agencies.[30] Such injunctions were also, of course, the result of the superior attitude adopted by some Englishmen who expected to be granted a special status in the "colony." At any rate, amendments to the Immigration Act in 1910 stipulated that only charitable societies accredited by the Canadian government would be allowed to sponsor landed immigrants. On the whole British immigrants were readily absorbed into the pioneer conditions of western Canada, and moved easily into positions of prominence in local politics, farm and labour organizations. The one British group settlement, the Barr Colony at Lloydminster, nearly proved a spectacular exception.

The Barr, or Britannia Colony as it was later called, was conceived by Rev. Isaac Barr, a Canadian-born Anglican clergyman, who was anxious to do something to save Canada for the British Empire. Apparently caught up in the imperial fervour of the Boer War years, Barr set out to become the Cecil Rhodes of Canada by gathering together a group of British settlers who would be placed on contiguous lands in a northwest which was then filling up with "foreigners."[31] Barr was an enthusiast, even a visionary, who knew something of the Canadian west having worked as a missionary there. He was joined in his work by G.E. Lloyd, a more practical clergyman who also had western experience, having served with Colonel Otter at Cutknife Hill in 1885. Lloyd began as chaplain to the colony, but quickly became its leader. Had it not been for the suffering involved, the Barr colony story would read like an uproarious farce.

Barr and Lloyd recruited nearly two thousand Englishmen, most of whom were city people with no farm experience, to join their adventure. Barr assumed responsibility for nearly everything – obtaining the land, collecting settlers' fees, arranging transport, buying supplies, even establishing a form of medical insurance. But it all proved too much for him. From the day the colonists sailed on the S.S. *Lake Manitoba,* nearly 2,000 of them in a ship equipped to carry about 550 passengers, things went wrong. On arrival, Barr told a Toronto newsman, "We have in this party five earls' nephews, several capitalists, many clergymen, lawyers, doctors and whatnot." The description was somewhat inaccurate, but no more so than the clergyman's description of his forthcoming utopia. "With respect to the mode of laying out the colony the natives of each county will be placed together," he stated. "Thus all the Somersetshire people will be placed alongside one another, the same for the Surrey people and so on. It's the solidarity and purely British character of the colony that attracts the people."[32]

The ocean voyage was bad enough, but many of the English soon discovered that immigrants' trains had their own special pleasures. "I can only say that the 3rd class carriages on the English railways are a king to the filthy cars we were huddled into. No sleeping accommodation, and as to the lavatory arrangements they were simply a disgrace to civilization, and in this misery we were boxed up to spend just one week."[33] Worse was yet to come. In Saskatoon a tent city was erected while the settlers, already beginning to dwindle in number, prepared for the two-hundred-mile trek to Battleford and beyond. Most settlers chose railhead locations for their homestead; Barr, expecting railway construction was imminent, chose an isolated site with tragic consequences. A reporter for the *Manitoba Free Press* described part of the scene in Saskatoon: "Here the men affect horsiness and sportiness of attire, whipcord breeches, leather leggings, sombreros and ties that wake the echoes, and stroll around camp with setters and pointers at heel, exhibiting to admiring friends their 'hammerless or Savage.' A stroll through this section of the camp is like ladies' day at Westpoint [*sic*] or Bisley."[34]

The trouble was now beginning, as doubts crept into some colonists' minds about Barr's ability and even his honesty. Baggage mix-ups, high prices, and lack of effective organization caused growing dissension. Finally, however, oxen, horses, and wagons were purchased and the increasingly dismayed party began to set off for "the Promised Land." Having seen Galicians, Doukhobors, and many other unusual homesteaders, there was little that could surprise a westerner. But the Barr colonists certainly were something new, and pathetic. "Owing to the fact that almost every wagon carried a load which taxed the strength of the horses, women and children had to walk almost the entire distance," the *Saskatchewan Herald* reported. "The weather during the latter part of the week when many of the settlers started from Saskatoon was mild and fine, but Monday when a large number of them were on the trail the cold caused intense suffering."[35] Soon after their arrival, Barr, who was now charged not merely with incompetence, but also with profiteering at the expense of the colonists, was deposed, and the chaplain, G.E. Lloyd, put in his place.[36] During the autumn and winter the colonists, many of whom had not the slightest idea of how to go about establishing themselves as homesteaders, declined in numbers as some went off to find work elsewhere. Those who remained were given assistance by the immigration authorities through the local Mounted Police, and when spring came they were provided with seed grain.[37] Though the beginnings were spectacular, and so nearly tragic that the British government established a parliamentary investigation, the colony gradually found its feet, and with Lloyd's leadership and the aid of the railway was a thriving venture by 1910.[38] Even the bad publicity surrounding the adventure did not prevent the continued growth of British settlement. Isaac Barr died in Australia, while G.E. Lloyd became the Anglican Bishop of Saskatchewan.

The settlers who were most easily absorbed into the agricultural life on the Canadian prairies were the Americans who moved northward into "the last, best West." Rising land prices in the United States pre-disposed many farm labourers, renters, and even farm-owners to move to the Canadian northwest.[39] As one prospective settler wrote to a Canadian immigration agent, "I have four sons old enough to take land. We are farming out here [in South Dakota], but land is too high in price to buy a large enough farm for myself and the boys."[40] The American settlers – often enough returning Canadians – were for the most part English-speaking, though there were Germans and Scandinavians among them.[41] They had a wide familiarity with the conditions of prairie agriculture and the techniques of dry farming, before they arrived. And they frequently brought with them far more capital, in the form of hard cash and equipment, than any other immigrant group.

It was for these reasons that Sifton's agents made a special effort to spread the message of the great potential of the Canadian west in the United States. Advertisements were regularly placed in farm journals and rural newspapers emphasizing the benefits of cheap, fertile land in Canada as compared with the increasing costs of farm ownership south of the border. Newspaper editors were provided with free excursions to the prairies in the justified expectation that they would go home to provide free publicity for Canada.[42] A profusion of pamphlets was issued by the Department of the Interior, describing the possibilities of the prairies. The best known of these was entitled *The Last, Best West* (1906), but there were many others with titles almost as enticing: *The Evolution of the Prairie by the Plow; The Wondrous West; Canada In a Nutshell; Where and How and All About It: Information and Facts for the Prospective Settler; One Thousand Facts about Canada,* issued in 1906, multiplied into *Five Thousand Facts About Canada* five years laters.[43] Despite the titles, most of these pamphlets gave accurate accounts of western conditions, for Sifton was convinced that overselling would only produce large numbers of disappointed settlers. Finally, tours were arranged for thousands of prospective immigrants, with the government and the railways acting as joint hosts.

In addition to government-sponsored immigration, colonization companies, largely American-owned, obtained large tracts of land and sold them to settlers. These companies used vigorous salesmanship, as is evident from a description by a Canadian: "The companies work on different lines altogether from any of the real estate agents here with whom we have hitherto done business. They go after their purchaser, pay railway fares, accompany them to the land, personally conduct them over it and stay with them, eat, sleep and drink with them if necessary until a sale is made or they fail in the attempt."[44] One of the most effective, and controversial, of these groups was the Saskatchewan Valley Land Company. This American-controlled group purchased in 1902 nearly 840,000 acres of land at $1.53 per acre, which had previously been granted to the Qu'Appelle, Long Lake and Saskatchewan Railway and Steamboat Company. The land company agreed to sell this tract, and the government-owned lands interspersed with it, within five years. Eventual sale prices varied from $8 to $12 per acre. These arrangements, arrived at in Sifton's characteristically secret way, led to charges of corruption and collusion between the Liberal party and the land company, but nothing was ever proven, and Sifton could always point to the enormous success of the Company in settling land, much of which had previously been judged useless.[45] Not surprisingly, a number of other companies were organized with the intention of emulating the Saskatchewan Valley Land Company, and some were nearly as successful.

Altogether the campaign for settlers in the United States was a tremendous success – so much so that worries about depopulation were expressed by the American authorities, and some steps taken to halt or slow the northward flow.[46] In 1900, approximately 19,000 settlers moved into Canada from the United States; five years later that number had increased to nearly 58,000, and in 1912-13 some 139,000 Americans flowed in. Because of returning Canadians, and also because it was an easy matter to pass over the border without being counted by immigration officials, there are no completely accurate figures on the total number of Americans who arrived,[47] but something on the order of 500,000 seems a reasonable estimate. Nor is it possible to establish the number of those who remained permanently, though it is clear that the outbreak of war in 1914 brought the flood to an end, and may even have encouraged a number of Americans to return home.[48] But whatever the exact numbers involved, a would-be poet caught the spirit of the American invasion when he wrote in the *Grain Growers' Guide* in 1911:

> The Yankees in the land abound
> For Uncle Sam gets all around,
> And with his push and grit and go
> Is sure to make the country grow.[49]

One group of Americans who did not receive the warm welcome immigration officials usually gave prospective American settlers were the blacks. Generally these people were judged unsuited to Canadian conditions and, though climate was usually given as the reason, the real obstacle was colour. A number of proposals were made to Canadian agents by black spokesmen suggesting group settlement on the prairies, but these were consistently discouraged. The clearest policy statement came in 1911 when a significant number of blacks in Oklahoma indicated a serious interest in moving north. They were given no encouragement and, as one immigration official explained to the black leader, W.E. Du Bois, though there was no law against blacks entering Canada "all restrictions respecting health, money, etc., are strictly enforced."[50] In effect, that was an unusually frank admission that blacks were not admitted, a policy which might have been made more explicit if black votes in Nova Scotia and southern Ontario had not been important to the Liberal Party.[51]

Most of the U.S. immigrants were either Americans by birth or Canadians returning after some years away. But there was also a significant number of men and women who had come from Europe, and settled briefly in the United States, only to move north. Two townships near Claresholm in Alberta were settled by Norwegians with almost two decades of life in North Dakota behind them. So, too, there were large numbers of German-Americans, Icelandic-Americans, and Hungarians who took the opportunity to better themselves. Certain group settlements with a religious basis also originated in the United States. Of these the most prominent were the Mormons who left Utah in thousands to join the small settlement begun by Charles Ora Card in 1887 in southern Alberta. By 1903 a very substantial settlement existed and these stalwart pioneers brought with them a knowledge of irrigation techniques that proved extremely important in developing the dry lands of the Palliser Triangle. The Americans were viewed as a foreign group, and by some as bringing with them the threat of "americanization." But they were obviously not so "foreign" as many other new groups in the west and quickly made themselves at home. Their past experience in agriculture as well as in agrarian politics ensured that many of them would become prominent leaders in the community.[52]

The organization and ingenuity of Sifton's immigration officials was best seen in their activities on the European continent. Here they faced barriers, both cultural and governmental, that were absent in the English-speaking countries. Most European nations were hostile to Canadian immigration agents, and attempted at least to limit their capacity to induce their citizens to emigrate, and in some cases prohibited their activities outright. The government of France actively campaigned against immigration to Canada, while Germany, among other countries, prohibited immigration agents and set heavy licence fees for steamship lines carrying emigrants. In order to surmount these obstacles the Canadian government made a necessarily secret agreement with a group of German steamship agents, which operated under the name of the North Atlantic Trading Company. The company's purpose was to divert agricultural immigrants originating in countries stretching from northern Italy north to Finland, Norway and Belgium and into Roumania, Bulgaria and Serbia on the east, to Canada. For each immigrant landed in Canada the company was paid a bonus. The secrecy of the company, while understandable, was open to various criticisms, all of which were made by Sifton's opponents. It lapsed soon after Sifton left the government, but only after having brought many thousand settlers to Canada.[53]

The Europeans were by far the most interesting and varied of the new settlers. In a real sense they were "foreigners" since, for the most part, they shared neither the cultural, economic nor political experiences of the British and United States immigrants. It is true that they were largely agricultural in background but few had experienced the peculiar conditions of the Canadian west. Probably even fewer had dreamed of the opportunities this new country had to offer them and their children. They were men with strong backs and strong wives, usually uneducated in any formal sense, but full of the ingenuity and courage that made a successful western pioneer. These were the people in whom Clifford Sifton placed unbounded faith and of whom he spoke in a well-known summary of his immigration policy. "I think a stalwart peasant in a sheep-skin coat, born on the soil, whose forefathers have been farmers for ten generations, with a stout wife and a half-dozen children, is good quality."[54] These were Poles, Russians, and Ukrainians. Most came from the Austro-Hungarian Empire. Nearly 6,000 in 1900, over 10,000 five years later, over 21,000 in 1912-13. Taken together with Germans, Italians, Dutch, and Scandinavians, as well as a sprinkling of newcomers from almost every part of Europe, these hardy people opened up some of the most isolated, some of the most fertile, and some of the most arid parts of the Canadian west.

Perhaps the most striking example of Sifton's willingness to open Canada's doors to a variety of immigrant groups was the case of the Doukhobors. With Professor James Mavor, of the University of Toronto and a friend of Tolstoi, acting as an intermediary,[55] this persecuted Russian minority negotiated an agreement with the Department of the Interior in 1898. Under it some 7,400 Doukhobors entered the country and settled on three blocks of land in the northwest, near Yorkton, amounting to some 400,000 acres. Included in their agreement with the federal government was a clause recognizing the Doukhobors' religious objection to military service. Generally a simple and peaceful people, they soon settled quickly into their communal ways and spartan religious practices. But one radical wing caused a sensation in 1902 by setting out from the Swan River colony on a trek to Winnipeg. Whether the purpose was to discover a warmer climate, or to meet their leader, for Peter Veregin was expected at the time, is unknown. Some 1800 men, women and children were among the trekkers, and for days the Manitoba newspapers carried almost nothing but front-page accounts of this long march. In the end, the last of the ill-clad and poorly fed group were placed on trains and returned to their colonies, but the march foreshadowed the appearance of more serious troubles.

In 1902, Veregin arrived in Canada after a Siberian exile which had separated him from his followers for more than fifteen years. He was an exceedingly impressive, yet mysterious man. "His physique, powerful and energetic, and his character, reserved and detached, fitted him for command, and he was accustomed from childhood to be treated with deference and to be obeyed by his people"; this was James Mavor's description of Peter the Lordly.[56] Veregin was anxious to shape the Canadian Doukhobor community to his own philosophy, but at the same time he knew that a state of peaceful co-existence had to be established with the society in which they had settled. Neither task was an easy one, and some members of the sect doubted their compatibility. This became plain within six months of the leader's arrival when a small radical group, the Svobodniki or Sons of Freedom, offered the first exhibition of what was to become their trademark of protest – the nude march. As one Freedomite wrote, "We went in the manner of the first man, Adam and Eve, to show nature to humanity, how man should return to his fatherland and return their ripened fruit of its seed."[57] Veregin treated the radicals firmly, even brutally, for he had no desire to see his community destroyed by the actions of a small fringe element. He found the Canadian government more difficult to deal with, especially now that the west was filling up rapidly and the Doukhobor lands growing more valuable. More and more, Doukhobor non-conformity was looked upon with suspicion. Worst of all the Doukhobors' strongest defender, Clifford Sifton, left office in 1905, and Frank Oliver, his successor, had little sympathy for "Slavs" of any kind.[58] Two points were at issue: first, by holding the lands communally, many Doukhobors had failed to fulfil the letter of the homestead legislation, which required individual entry. Second, the Doukhobors' religious convictions prevented them from taking the oath of allegiance, which was necessary to acquire final title to lands. After several years of discussion and pressure the axe fell in 1905. More than half the Saskatchewan lands were confiscated. To some it appeared that Tsarist persecutions were again beginning. Once more the Sons of Freedom re-emerged, setting off on a great trek to Winnipeg and then on, through the snow, to Fort William.

Veregin again acted decisively. Now it was necessary to buy new lands for part of the community. This time the site chosen was in the Kootenays, near Grand Forks, British Columbia. By 1912 some 14,000 acres had been acquired and the community had again been established on a solid basis. This was by no means the end of the sect's troubled history, for internal divisions and conflict with the outside world continued. But at least as long as Peter the Lordly lived, as he did until 1924, the community proved able to meet both challenges.[59]

The newcomers who seemed no less mysterious, and perhaps even more threatening because of their numbers, were the original "men in sheepskin coats": the Ruthenians, Galicians, and Bukovinians who later became known collectively as the Ukrainians. These people were mainly illiterate peasants attracted to Canada by the promise of *vilni zemli* – free land. In 1895 a Galician professor of agriculture, Dr. Josef Oleskow, began plans to encourage his countrymen to move to Canada to escape "overpopulation, sub-division of land holdings, heavy taxation, and unfavourable political conditions."[60] But it was not until after Sifton took office that Oleskow's proposals began to receive concentrated attention. Then the mass movement of Slavic peoples to Canada began.

The agricultural experience of the Ukrainians seemed to guarantee that they would thrive in the pioneering and climatic conditions of the prairie west. Altogether some 200,000 arrived between 1896 and the outbreak of the Great War.[61] Their desire was to settle in blocks, and the vacant acres of the prairies, as well as western past experience, made this plan eminently practical. Though some new settlers, having sold their small holdings before their departure, arrived with a modest capital, others were nearly destitute. These were the people who clustered together in crowded tenement houses in north-end Winnipeg and began their new lives as navvies on railway gangs or as farm labourers. When they moved on to homesteads, they formed compact settlements near Dauphin, Yorkton, and northeast of Edmonton in the Edna-Star district. They preferred wooded lands, which reminded them of home, rather than the bald, flat prairies. Soon they set about breaking the land, acquiring tools and animals, and constructing homes for their families. As a visitor noted in 1904, one building could often serve several purposes in those early years.

> The main building was a single combination home-barn structure that housed all the farm stock, cattle, hogs, and chickens in one end, with a large room in the other for the family, father, mother and a number of young children, including a baby. . . . At one end of the room there was one of those large home-built continental stoves, that following the usual pattern had quite a small fireplace but an extensive platform surrounding it on which the family slept. At the other end of the room there was a large table, set into a corner, with wooden benches extending along the walls on one side and one end of the table. The building was of logs, plastered inside and out with the usual mixture of clay and straw and the same material furnished the floor. Overall the building was topped with a thatched roof.[62]

The Ukrainians quickly earned a reputation for hard work and determination. An immigration officer in 1898 reported in detail on the Edna-Star settlement. Petro Melnak was fairly typical: he had come in 1894 with only six dollars in his pocket. Four years later he had cleared forty acres, constructed a house, stables, a granary and outbuildings, acquired a wagon, a plough, a mower and rake, three horses, six cattle, and six pigs. "Has the deed to his farm; speaks a little English and is highly pleased with the country," the agent concluded.[63] But not every newcomer experienced such success. There was the cold, sometimes drought, occasional fires, the ubiquitous mosquito, and the heartbreak and loneliness of isolation. Then, too, there was the suspicion and hostility of some of the society around them. Since the Ukrainians spoke a foreign language, often dressed in an unusual and distinctive manner, and practised a religion not easily fitted into normal Canadian categories, they were easily lumped in with those "southern races" which were thought undesirable and unassimilable.[64] Their extended and sometimes boisterous wedding celebrations were frequently pointed to by temperance workers and others as the ultimate example of the evils of alcohol – and of "foreigners."[65] Even a rather tolerant observer was moved to comment in 1904 that the Galician "cannot be said to be a high class farmer; but he is very industrious. He is generally frugal, though sobriety is not a conspicuous characteristic."[66]

The Ukrainians were a deeply religious people, and from their first arrival in Canada were anxious to establish the institutions which would guarantee the continuation of their religious traditions. While some Protestant groups attempted to convert them, the majority remained attached to either the Greek Catholic or Russian Orthodox faith. Soon their tricupola, onion-domed churches sprang up in prairie communities, standing in striking contrast to that other temple of western architecture, the tall, angular grain elevator.[67] But religious life was not always sedate and free of uncharitable strife. A quarrel between the adherents of the Greek Catholic Church and the supporters of the Russian Orthodox tradition over a small $1500 church in the Star community lasted six years before the Judicial Committee of the Privy Council finally settled in favour of the Orthodox believers. The decision was reached at a cost of some $100,000. Surely that was one clear measure of the importance of religion.[68] But far more important to most Ukrainians were the comforts of regular Mass and such joyous celebrations as Christmas with its Holy Supper of twelve dishes, and Easter with brightly painted eggs and blessed *paska*. These religious ceremonies provided both spiritual strength and a reminder of the historic past of a people gradually coming to terms with the demands of a new society.

Forming a close-knit group the Ukrainians sometimes aided each other in financing the transition from railway camp to homestead.[69] By 1910 they had their own newspaper, the *Ukrainian Voice;* two years later Bishop

Budka was appointed as head of the Orthodox Church. Moreover, they rapidly organized their own school districts, often employing teachers drawn from the Ruthenian Normal School in Winnipeg.[70] Their determination to preserve their culture caused serious concern among some groups of native Canadians. The slow pace of assimilation was often attributed to the concentration of settlements, and the activities of church leaders. In fact, there was little contact with English-speaking society and from the outset, according to one group of concerned investigators, the Ukrainians "held tenaciously to their language, religion, national costumes and racial customs."[71]

Few people outside the Ukrainian community doubted that assimilation was necessary. This was the task for the schools and the churches. "We must see to it," Principal Sparling of Wesley College in Winnipeg insisted, "that the civilization and ideals of Southeastern Europe are not transplanted to and perpetuated on our virgin soil."[72] The Methodists were especially active in attempting to work with the Ukrainians. All Peoples' Mission in Winnipeg offered aid to those huddled in the overcrowded and insanitary tenement houses, and a medical mission was established near the northeastern Alberta settlements. "To Canadianize them, they have to be Christianized," one Methodist wrote revealingly in 1909.[73] But even their detractors had to admit that "much of the rough work of nation building in Western Canada is being done by the despised Galicians."[74]

Several of the group settlements in the west, including the Mennonites, Mormons, and Doukhobors, were determined to maintain their cultural and religious distinctiveness.[75] That, after all, was their essential reason for coming to Canada. The federal immigration authorities, especially under Sifton during the first ten years of the Laurier administration, exhibited a remarkable liberality in the reception of these people – a liberality, of course, that was made possible by the pressing need for agricultural colonists. The policy was well stated by James Smart in answer to enquiries from a colony of Hutterians anxious to move from the United States to Canada to escape the martial spirit of the Spanish-American war. The group did move to Canada and settled at Dominion City, Manitoba, where they remained until 1905 when they returned to the United States. Events were to prove that they had not left Canada permanently. But before coming north the Hutterians had requested exemption from military service and oath-taking, and the right to hold their lands communally. All this was granted. Moreover, Smart assured them that "these people will not be molested in any way in the practice of their religious services and principles, as full freedom of religious belief prevails throughout the country. They will also be allowed to establish independent schools for teaching their children if they desire to do so, but they will have to be responsible for their maintenance themselves. Their children will not be compelled to attend other schools if their education is properly provided for."[76] Evidently the immigration authorities had no desire to "Canadianize" every newcomer in the same mould.

IV

Not every Canadian was satisfied that the liberality of the immigration authorities was in the country's best interests. Indeed, Frank Oliver, Sifton's successor, had never favoured the "open door" policy.[77] When he became Minister in 1905 he moved almost immediately to make the Immigration Act more restrictive by broadening ministerial powers to reject and to deport.[78] Even that did not satisfy some of the government's critics, especially those who believed that group settlement presented an insurmountable obstacle to "Canadianization." W.F. Cockshutt, a Conservative M.P., spoke for this viewpoint when he told the House of Commons in 1907 that "we must have one citizenship in the Dominion of Canada, and that the citizenship of broad Canadianism; but this we can never have if we are going to keep together in one settlement the immigrants coming from any section of Europe, whether they will be Doukhobors or any other. They will never get over the evils that they have brought in."[79] Further changes in the Immigration Act in 1910, and the use of administrative procedures to exclude "undesirables," made it possible for Oliver to assert by 1911 with accuracy that his policy was "restrictive, exclusive and selective" in comparison with his predecessor's.[80]

Chinese, Japanese, and East Indian immigrants were looked upon by most Canadians as largely unassimilable and therefore undesirable. The centre of controversy over Oriental immigration was British Columbia and the demand for restrictive legislation began well before the turn of the century. In the early 1900s, however, when Japanese and East Indians began to join the Chinese population, the demand for exclusion reached new heights.[81] Since a significant proportion of Oriental immigrants entered the country illegally, there is no way of establishing absolutely accurate figures. But what is certain is that in 1907-8 there were spectacular increases in the entry of Orientals: the figure grew from 400 in 1904-5 to 12,000 four years later.[82] As 1907 was a year of high unemployment and economic recession, increased immigration from the Far East was resented even more than usual. Here was the most direct evidence of the "yellow peril" that British Columbians had been warned of for years. Soon there would have to be a showdown between the teeming masses of Asia, and the White Nations. Canada's role might be crucial. "We must not allow our shores to be overrun by Asiatics, and become dominated by an alien race," R.B. Bennett told a British Columbia audience in 1907. "British Columbia must remain a white man's country."[83]

The increased immigration figures and the economic downturn of 1907 merely brought to a head a festering sore that had existed in British Columbia for years. The demand for restrictive legislation in that province was intense and came from all levels of society.[84] Working-class people were most directly affected because Oriental labour was cheap, but almost every other class (with the exception of well-to-do families who wanted cheap Oriental domestic help), and certainly every political party, expressed concern about the dangers of "orientalization." The problem, however, was a touchy one since Japan was an ally of Great Britain and India a member of the Empire. Moreover, the Laurier administration was seriously interested in developing an Asian market for Canadian products.[85] For these reasons, despite a commitment to provincial rights, Laurier repeatedly found it necessary to disallow British Columbia legislation designed to restrict Oriental immigration.[86] But that alone was no solution. By 1907 events made it necessary to dispatch Rodolphe Lemieux to Japan to negotiate a mutually acceptable exclusion arrangement, for the issue had reached an explosive stage.

That explosion took place in Vancouver in the autumn of the year. A federal-provincial dispute set off the trouble. Fresh from re-election, Premier Richard McBride, who had been feuding with Ottawa about subsidies,[87] chose the Oriental immigration question as an advantageous ground on which to renew his battle. As he no doubt foresaw, the new Oriental exclusion legislation which he had the legislature pass in 1907 was reserved by the Lieutenant-Governor. That Lieutenant-Governor Dunsmuir himself was an employer of Oriental labour added a spark to the powder. "Western civilization is and will be threatened everyday and as long as a system of immigration exists that invites or admits unrestricted numbers of any Oriental nation," a Victoria trade union official warned Laurier.[88]

By August an Asiatic Exclusion League had been formed, and one month later a mass meeting, followed by a parade through Chinatown and the Japanese section of Vancouver, was organized. The marchers sang "Rule Britannia" and listened to anti-Asiatic speeches from local personalities and also from the Secretary of the Seattle Oriental Exclusion League.[89] Then some stones were thrown at Japanese windows and the rioting began. The whites by no means proved their superiority. "In the later rioting," Laurier informed the Governor General, "the Japs showed fight, turned upon their assailants, and routed them. This is at once a cause for rejoicing and for anxiety; rejoicing because the rowdies got a well deserved licking; anxiety because it may make the Japs very saucy, and render an adjustment of the trouble very difficult."[90]

Laurier appointed his Deputy Minister of Labour, W.L.M. King, to investigate the causes of the disturbances, while Lemieux set off for Tokyo.

Though King apparently went west in a frame of mind sympathetic to the Japanese, his attitude was altered by what he found on arrival. He ordered a raid on the Japanese immigration offices, which produced information suggesting that an organization known as the Nippon Supply Company, working in association with the Canadian Pacific Railway, and perhaps with the tacit support of the Japanese government itself, was engaged in bringing Japanese immigrants into Canada illegally. Whether or not King agreed with the Governor General, who had concluded that "of the two evils, the yellow invasion or the yellow boycott, of course the first is the most serious,"[91] the object of Lemieux's mission was now easily identifiable: the Japanese government had to be convinced that self-restriction was imperative.[92]

Lemieux found the Japanese government in a flexible and accommodating mood. A so-called Gentleman's Agreement was negotiated whereby the Japanese government, in effect, promised to permit no more than four hundred Japanese to leave for Canada annually. By this time the findings of King's commission had convinced the Liberal government that Asiatic immigration was a far more serious problem than it had previously been willing to admit.[93] In addition to the Gentlemen's Agreement, which worked largely because of Japan's new interest in diverting immigration to Manchuria, the Laurier government added new provisions to the Immigration Act in 1908, which, by insisting that immigrants must come by direct passage from their home country, cut off the flow of Japanese and Hindu immigrants from Hawaii. The Canadian Pacific Railway, anxious to maintain its flow of cheap labour, attempted to challenge this continuous voyage principle in 1908 and nearly succeeded, but the government stood firm.

The problem of Chinese immigration was free of the complications of the British alliance system. Nevertheless, the Canadian government attempted to settle it on the Japanese pattern. While attending the meetings of the International Opium Commission in late 1909, W.L.M. King approached the Chinese government with the suggestion that a "Gentleman's Agreement" be worked out. Though an agreement was reached in principle, it was never practised and Canadian controls over entries from China were exercised by a capitation tax set at $500 in 1903. While Japanese and Hindu immigration fell off drastically after 1908, Chinese immigration continued to increase, reaching a record high of nearly 7,500 in 1912-13. This situation, which virtually excluded citizens from Canada's sister nation in the Empire and from Britain's ally, while admitting Chinese immigrants, was an ironic comment on Canada's membership in the British Empire.[94]

The most spectacular anti-Oriental incident on the Pacific coast occurred after the defeat of the Laurier government. In May 1914 a Japanese immigrant ship, the *Komagata Maru*, arrived in Vancouver harbour carrying 376 East Indians. The group's sponsor, a wealthy Punjabi merchant, probably intended to test regulations which were enacted to exclude these British subjects from Canada. Port authorities, supported by Ottawa, refused to allow the ship to dock. Insults, and on occasion missiles, were exchanged between the ship's passengers and immigration officials, during the two months that the vessel lay in harbour. Finally on July 23, with local citizens cheering it on, Canada's newly acquired H.M.C.S. *Rainbow* went into its first, and only, action. It escorted the *Komagata Maru* to sea.[95] Not even British citizenship was sufficient to penetrate the white exclusionist barriers that had been erected upon assumptions that a Vancouver politician, H.H. Stevens, made explicit when he declared: "The real simonpure Canadian life is the highest that I know under the face of the sun; and it is that type that I wish jealously to guard, and which I hold it to be the duty of the people of Canada to guard, and to cherish, and go as far as possible to keep pure and free from the taint of other peoples."[96]

The Asiatic exclusion issue raised in extreme form the general question of the kind of society and culture Canadians wanted to create. Sifton's readiness to welcome virtually anyone, provided he could farm, was certainly not without its critics. Some of that criticism was obviously well deserved. Despite the goal of directing newcomers to the land, substantial numbers of immigrants either remained in the cities, or drifted in after agricultural failure. Often they were forced to live in the most slum-ridden sections of cities like Winnipeg and Toronto, where disease and crime were the predictable products of ignorance and poverty. These conditions increasingly concerned such socially conscious clergymen as J.S. Woodsworth, whose two books, *Strangers Within our Gates* and *My Neighbor*, though tinged with some of the prevalent racial prejudices of the age, were significant attempts to focus public attention upon the problem of the immigrant. In addition to poor living conditions and unemployment, urban social critics often expressed worries about the impact that the "foreign" vote was likely to have on the political system. "These people know absolutely nothing of representative government; Anglo-Saxon institutions are meaningless to them," one generally sympathetic writer maintained, "yet their vote is as good as yours or mine. Elections mean a good time, free beer, yes, and hush! something more – you know."[97] So, too, the "foreign" vote was often suspected of being used to "block prohibition measures."[98] Finally, the young unmarried immigrant was often believed to be the chief source of trade for the houses of prostitution "the social vice," that flourished in most Canadian cities, and certainly on the prairies.[99]

But it was not the social problems created by immigrants that was the major cause of public concern. Far more attention was devoted to the cultural question, the question of how to "Canadianize" this large group of foreigners. Could the country absorb and assimilate such a staggering number of newcomers? "When the United States contained our population they received one settler – and found it difficult to Americanize him. We receive thirty-six. What about our task?" J.S. Woodsworth asked.[100] And, indeed, what did "Canadianize" mean? British immigrants raised no serious problems, since, for the most part, it was assumed that Canadian and British standards of citizenship and culture were identical. British immigrants were thus often seen as the most desirable since they provided the necessary yeast in the foreign lump. "The country will profit," *Industrial Canada* remarked in 1910, "by a large influx of British citizens to form the leaven for the great foreign population who, admirable as they are, are still without knowledge of British institutions and principles of life."[101] There were, of course, critics of the British immigrant, but criticism was directed at specific grievances or matters of conduct. In broad cultural terms to be British was to be acceptable, for Canada was a British country.

The same could almost be said of the American settlers – but not quite. While their cultural and political backgrounds made it relatively easy for them to be accepted, the ever-present fear of American manifest destiny assured some hostility. Did the flag follow massive immigration? Goldwin Smith naturally assumed that it did. "The Northwest will be American," he wrote in 1910, but his unfulfilled predictions were becoming a bore.[102] But there were those, especially in eastern Canada, who while deploring Smith's general views, feared that he might be right in this case. Canadian, American, and British periodicals frequently published articles about "The Effect of the American Invasion" and "The Americanization of the Northwest" at the same time as they were noting the northward flow of American people and capital. In 1907 a doctoral thesis was published by Columbia University, entitled *The Americanization of Canada*. It concluded that whether Canadians knew it or not, the process had already been completed.[103] The fact was, of course, that the American settlers, finding a prosperous living in the west, rapidly settled into full citizenship and certainly contributed to making the west more like the American mid-west than the English midlands.[104]

Much more difficult to accept than the Americans were the sharply contrasting groups of Europeans who had neither cultural nor political affiliations with the English-speaking world. The problem they seemed to raise was articulated by Frank Oliver in 1903. "It is not merely a question of filling that country with people who will produce wheat and buy manufactured goods," he told the House of Commons. "It is a question of the ultimate results of the efforts put forward for the building up of a Canadian nationality. . . . This can never be accomplished if the preponderance of the population should be of such a class and character as will deteriorate rather than elevate the condition of our people and our country at large.[105] Few would go quite as far as the prominent Orangeman and Conservative Member of Parliament, T.S. Sproule, whose view was that "Canada is today the dumping ground for the refuse of every country in the world. . . . "[106] But many were deeply concerned about the future of the new immigrants, and especially those whose tongue was incomprehensible, whose religious practices were unorthodox if not offensive, and whose education in the ways of parliamentary democracy had not even begun – or if it had, had begun in the ways of machine politics that were hardly a sign of a healthy future. Such concerns were commonly expressed by such otherwise different people as the Liberal newspaperman, J.W. Dafoe, the social gospel clergyman, J.S. Woodsworth, and the conservative humourist, Stephen Leacock. The answer to the problem seemed always to come down to assimilation, and the means to be the school system. While the Great War gave great impetus to the assimilationist cause, and to the view that the school system should be its major instrument,[107] the idea had been growing since the beginning of the century. That was the reason the school system was the centre of so much controversy in the west: it was the means of "Canadianization." "If Canada is to become in any real sense a nation, if our people are to become one people, we must have one language," J.S. Woodsworth told his fellow Methodists in 1905. "Hence the necessity of national schools where the teaching of English – our national language – is compulsory. The public school is the most important factor in transforming the foreigners into Canadians."[108]

The ideal of "Canadianization" was put somewhat crudely in a poem by the popular western writer, Robert J.C. Stead, in 1905. He called it "The Mixer," and it began:

> They are fresh from all creation, from the lands beyond the seas,
> Where a man accepts existence by the grace of "if you please,"
> From the homes of rank and title, from the slums of want and woe,
> They are coming as the cattle that have nowhere else to go;
> They are haggard, huddled, homeless, frightened at – they know not what;
> With a few unique exceptions they're a disappointing lot;
> But I take 'em as I get 'em, soldier, sailor, saint and clown
> And I turn 'em out Canadians – all but the yellow and brown. [109]

But what was meant by "Canadianization"? To some it was the melting-pot, to others it was assimilation to an essentially Anglo-Saxon standard. And some, like Ralph Connor in his novel, *The Foreigner*, published in 1909, made no distinction. There he related the story of an immigrant in terms which made it plain that his ideal was assimilation to the Anglo-Saxon standard. Yet in the preface he expressed a melting-pot concept. "In western Canada there is seen today that most fascinating of all human phenomena, the making of a nation," Connor wrote, "out of breeds diverse in traditions, in ideals, in speech, and in manner of life, Saxon and Slav, Teuton, Celt and Gaul, one people is being made. The blood strains of great races will mingle in the blood of a race greater than the greatest of them all."[110] Probably most westerners would have agreed with Connor's description of the ideal of the "new nation"; by 1909 the west was certainly beginning to feel an identity distinct in outlook and interest from central Canada. What was emerging was far from obvious, except that it was not a carbon copy of the "east." That disturbed many easterners.[111]

To many inhabitants of the older sections of Canada the worry of the west was its "unBritish character." If Canada's allegiance to the Empire was to be preserved, it would be necessary, George Foster contended, "to keep British stock dominant."[112] To others, the French Canadians, the problem of the west was the lack of recognition of French Canadians as a group unlike the new immigrants. The French-Canadian attitude to immigration, like that of English Canada, was mixed. Certainly the Liberal party, the proponent of large-scale immigration, maintained the support of Quebec voters after 1896. Yet there were voices in Quebec wondering what the future held for French Canadians in a Canada where their overall relative number was decreasing and in a west where their numbers were falling far behind several other ethnic groups.[113] Henri Bourassa was in many ways the barometer of these fears in Quebec. In his first years in Parliament Bourassa had supported Sifton's immigration policy and had criticized the restrictionist views of a Conservative spokesman from Quebec, F.D. Monk, who had suggested the west be the preserve of the English and French-speaking founders of the country.[114] Within a few years, however, Bourassa had come to realize that immigration was shifting the population balance in previously unimagined directions. In 1904 he told the House of Commons that "it never was in the minds of the founders of this nation, it never was in the minds of the fathers of confederation, the men whose names these present so-called Liberals are so fond of evoking, that in order to be broad – or even in order to make land speculators rich – we ought to change a providential condition of our partly French and partly English country to make it a land of refuge for the scum of all nations."[115] The small French-Canadian population in the west, unassisted by any significant amount of immigration from either Quebec or France, was rapidly being drowned in the flood of newcomers.[116]

V

The debate over provincial status for Saskatchewan and Alberta in 1905 further increased the anxieties of French Canadians uneasy about the cultural development of the prairies. It also provided ammunition for Laurier's critics in both French and English Canada, and provoked a major political crisis. The Prime Minister opened the discussion by once more pledging his faith to the promise of "Canada's century,"[117] but the debate soon descended into yet another wrangle over separate schools and the cultural rights of French-Canadian minorities. Laurier must have quickly realized that even a successful and expanding west could not guarantee the disappearance of old quarrels. Indeed the addition of this ambitious new section to the nation made the coveted prize of national unity even more elusive.

Since at least 1903 the people of the northwest had been demanding an end to their subordinate territorial status.[118] Frederick Haultain, the leader of the local government, was an able politician and administrator who wanted a single province created out of the vast prairie area. Others believed that the boundaries of Manitoba should be extended westward to create two roughly equal provinces. The third view, and the one finally accepted by Ottawa, was that two new provinces in addition to Manitoba should be established. Once that decision had been taken, almost every-thing else was simple enough. Reasonably generous financial terms were calculated, and the Liberals, despite their reputation as the party of provin-cial rights, decided to follow the precedent set in Manitoba by maintaining control over public lands so that they could be used in the promotion of immigration. Sifton had told Laurier that "giving them [public lands] to the Provinces would be ruinous to our settlement policies and would be disastrous to the whole Dominion. The mere reports that the lands had been handed over and that there might be a change [in] the policy of administering them would cost us tens of thousands of settlers in the next two years to say nothing of the more distant future."[119] This left only one question, and that the most difficult, unsettled. That was the issue of education.

Laurier had long realized the school issue in the territories bore within itself the seeds of his government's destruction. There were strong pres-sures from both the west and Ontario to give the new provinces unre-stricted control over their educational systems. But from the Catholic population in the west, from the hierarchy in Canada, and from Quebec Members of Parliament, Laurier was under equally strong pressure to ensure that minority school rights were given adequate protection when provincial status was granted. Basically the issue was how extensive the rights granted the Catholic minority should be. By 1902 those rights had been drastically reduced from the status of complete separation and equality granted in 1875. Indeed the educational ordinances of 1901 had established a system whereby all schools were public schools, subject to virtually the same regulations and curriculum. Religious instruction was permitted at the end of the day and Catholic or Protestant teachers were hired according to the wishes of the majority, leaving the minority the right to establish its own school.[120] This situation was far from satisfactory to the Catholics,[121] and the Papal Delegate to Canada, Mgr Sbarretti, was determined the federal government should rectify this situation before the territories became autonomous. Indeed from the time of his arrival in Canada in 1902, Mgr Sbarretti had devoted a great deal of energy to instructing Laurier on his duty to the Catholic minorities in the west and particularly in Manitoba, where he was convinced that very great improvements could be made upon the settlement of 1897 if only the federal authorities would assert themselves. Laurier had not been easy to convince, though he did his best not to alienate the Papal Delegate who could, after all, turn the Canadian bishops against the Liberals very easily.[122]

In order to avoid public controversy, and doubtless in order to obtain an arrangement more satisfactory to the Catholic minority than the existing one, Laurier adopted the strategy of quiet diplomacy. During the election of 1904, which the Liberals won handily, a promise of provincial status for the northwest was made by the government. But every effort was made to prevent discussion of the school question. When the Toronto *News* raised the issue, Laurier pleaded with his biographer and one-time ally, John Willison, who now edited the paper, to avoid the subject.[123] A similar appeal was made by Senator R.W. Scott, who handled many of Laurier's relations with the Catholic Church. "Our only chance of success," Scott told Mgr Sbarretti, "is in keeping the subject out of politics by avoiding all reference to it."[124]

Once the election was over the Liberal cabinet began drawing up legislation establishing the new provinces. Here the makings of a major crisis developed as two leading Ministers adopted contradictory positions. Clifford Sifton, whose major responsibility was the west, expressed determined opposition to separate schools. He was apparently prepared to accept the situation as it existed in the territories including a statement that the federal government would guarantee those existing rights. Pitted against him was Charles Fitzpatrick, recently appointed Minister of Justice, a position which Sifton had hoped to obtain.[125] Fitzpatrick, a Catholic himself, was concerned to satisfy the Catholic hierarchy by improving the status of the minority in the territories. In the process Fitzpatrick appears to have been attempting some kind of reconciliation between Laurier and the increasingly dangerous Henri Bourassa, who certainly took part in the drafting of the original educational clauses in the Autonomy Bills.[126] Thus there was a struggle of power, principle and personality in the Laurier cabinet's discussion of the proposed legislation. But Sifton made his case forcefully, and probably believed he had carried the argument before his health forced him to take a rest in the south in the early winter of 1905.

The bills Laurier placed before the House on February 21 made it plain that Sifton had suffered a serious misapprehension. The wording of the educational clauses, as drawn up by Fitzpatrick in close consultation with Mgr Sbarretti,[127] was clearly open to the interpretation that the federal government wished to see the arrangements of 1875, providing a full-scale separate school system, restored, and that this system would be brought under the provisions of Section 93 of the British North America Act. In an effort to convince the House of the need to accept these provisions, Laurier appealed to those ultimate arguments: religion and nationalism. "We live by the side of a nation," the Prime Minister proclaimed in a revealing peroration,

> a great nation, a nation for which I have the greatest admiration, but whose example I would not take in everything, in whose schools for fear that Christian dogmas in which all do not believe might be taught, Christian morals are not taught. When I compare these two countries, when I compare Canada with the United States, when I compare the status of the two nations, when I think upon their future, when I observe the social condition of civil society in each of them and when I observe in this country of ours a total absence of lynchings and an almost total absence of divorces and murders, for my part, I thank heaven that we are living in a country where the young children of the land are taught Christian morals and Christian dogmas. Either the American system is wrong or the Canadian system is wrong. For my part I say, and I say it without hesitation. Time will show that we are in the right, and in this instance as in many others, I have an abiding faith in the institutions of my own country.[128]

These were not arguments to move Clifford Sifton. Rushing back from the United States he submitted his resignation, insisting that Laurier had gone far beyond what had been agreed. Laurier denied it was his intention to re-establish the 1875 system and present it to his leading western minister as a *fait accompli*. But he knew he had trouble on his hands: Sifton was determined to quit, and Fielding was threatening to go with him. Now an ominous storm was blowing up in Ontario, and the Tories were certain to make electoral profit from it. Robert Borden, the sober Halifax lawyer who had taken over the leadership of the Conservative party in 1901, had detected a fighting issue in the Autonomy Bills, for much of the press in

English-speaking Canada was hostile to the government. Borden, stealing the old Liberal line, had taken up the provincial rights cause and demanded that the new provinces be given full control over both public lands and educational policy. In Parliament the issue had been kept largely to constitutional niceties, but Laurier knew that behind this lurked a much more explosive issue. His old friend Willison put it bluntly to him early in March. "But while I have all this respect and consideration for the natural race sentiment of the French Canadians," he warned the Prime Minister, "no man could be more strenuously opposed to clerical interference in state affairs. And from Confederation down the plain meaning of the constitution has been deliberately perverted to serve the ends of the Roman Catholic Hierarchy."[129] With religious passions rising and political disaster threatening, Laurier moved quickly to modify his first stand.

While Sifton was not invited to return to the cabinet, he was given the responsibility of re-writing the educational clauses of the Autonomy Bills. In the new version it was made plain that the minority rights to be protected were the modest ones allowed by the Territorial Ordinances of 1901. Separate schools were not to be restored. Laurier now had to face the criticism of the other side. Bourassa and the Quebec Conservative leader, F.W. Monk, denounced the betrayal and further embarrassed Laurier by introducing a motion calling for the acceptance of French as an official language in the new provinces as it had been before 1893. But the motion was quickly defeated, and the bill finally passed. [130]

The storm did not abate at once for its fury was worth some political mileage. It seemed, oddly enough, to cause much more damage in Ontario than in the west where the matter subsided more quickly. The Tories attempted to exploit the issue in two Ontario by-elections, without success, and the same was true in the west where the Liberals carried the majority in the elections held in each of the new provinces. Even the Catholic hierarchy in the west, with the exception of Mgr Langevin of St. Boniface who was intransigent as usual, seemed satisfied.[131]

The Autonomy Bills controversy demonstrated that not even prosperity and confidence could completely erase the religious and cultural tensions that were rarely far beneath the surface of Canadian political life. Laurier could set as his life's work the cementing of national unity[132] but his own tactics in the 1905 crisis had contributed to division. His attempt to muffle the problem of separate schools in the west was understandable, given its explosive nature. No one was more aware than he was of the truth of Willison's comments to Borden about the affair. "I do not think it just," the Toronto editor noted, "but it is nevertheless the fact, that a Protestant leader could do what Sir Wilfrid Laurier is doing much more safely . . . ."[133] But his apparent attempt to circumvent Sifton's well-known views could hardly have been expected to pave the way to a harmonious settlement. In the end he lost Sifton without gaining much for the minority. After the immediate crisis that loss may not have seemed too serious, for Laurier was at the pinnacle of his power in 1905. Yet there can be no doubt that the Prime Minister had lost the battle in 1905, especially since he had further increased Bourassa's mistrust of him, and had also lost the support of the strongest man the west ever sent to Ottawa. If Robert Borden could ever capitalize on the power those two forces represented he would be able to replace Laurier at the head of the cabinet table. And it might be that the west that Sifton built would ultimately contribute to another crisis too unmanageable for Laurier to handle. But in 1905 the danger seemed small. Perhaps the Prime Minister was more disturbed by the comments of his one-time friend, Armand Lavergne, whose fiery *nationaliste* oratory made him Bourassa's first lieutenant. "In constituting the French Canadian, who has lived in the country since its discovery, the equal in rights and privileges to the Dukobor [*sic*] or the Galician who has just disembarked," Lavergne told an assembly at Montmagny in September 1905, "we have opened a gulf between eastern and western Canadians which nothing will fill."[134]

VI

Fears about the way of the west, expressed by French Canadians and other easterners, had little impact on the rapid development of the prairies. The statistics of immigration annually reached higher levels: 49,000 in 1901, 146,000 in 1905, 402,000 in the record year of 1913 just before the Great War brought the level down again. Most, though certainly not all, these new people headed for the prairie west. Why did they come? Motives were varied and mixed, like the new population itself. There were some who came explicitly for religious and political reasons. But for most, the Canadian west offered an opportunity for a new life and, above all, a chance for a better material standard and better opportunities for future generations. A somewhat sanctimonious Protestant minister was disturbed by the worldliness of the new settlers' goals, but he probably came very close to an accurate assessment when he wrote: "People are coming to that country not to get educational advantages, not to get religious privileges, not to secure the comforts and sanctities of home; these things were found much more easily in the communities from which they have come; but they are coming to make money – and the material side of life is uppermost in their thought – wheat and lands, dollars and acres, the thirst to have, the rush to get, these are the things that are absorbing the lives of men to the exclusion of other and higher things."[135]

But the materialistic attractions of the new country were often combined with a sense of adventure and the hope that a man could find greater independence in Canada. One English immigrant recalled the day in 1910 when he made the decision to try farming in the Canadian west: "When I went to school, on my way home every day I stopped to look at a big coloured poster of a wheat field in stook. On it was printed '160 acres land free.' I made up my mind, 'That's what I want,' and I got all the pamphlets on it and read all about it. . . . The result was I left home, worked in a hotel and saved my money and sailed in March on the Allen [sic] liner 'Corsican.' I arrived in Winnipeg with thirty cents which I spent on some pork and beans and coffee. I went to work on a farm south of Boissevain for $10.00 a month. After two years I went to Saskatchewan for a homestead."[136]

What the figures from the prairies indicate is the gradual spread of humanity across the previously unsettled grass and parklands of Canada. For most settlers this was an entirely new environment. In some ways it was an easy environment: on the grasslands little, if any, clearing was necessary so that the breaking of the land could often begin without any of the arduous tree-cutting of, for example, settlement in Ontario. On the other hand, there were the difficulties of extreme temperatures and slight rainfall. So, too, the very lack of trees meant that materials to build shelter for humans and animals alike were scarce. Most important of all was the railway: the new settler tried to establish himself near it; if the railway passed him by at a distance, he might find whole villages moving to re-establish near its lines. In 1912 a land agent in the Peace River country wrote: "Many settlers, a large number with their families came to the country during the year, but the difficulties of the trail are so great that the number of newcomers is not so large as the country merits. The one outstanding need of Grande Prairie is railroad connection with the outside world, and until that comes, growth of population can only be comparatively slow."[137] Railway building also brought with it temporary employment for settlers who needed extra work to tide them over until they produced their first cash crop.

Agricultural settlement thus followed the railways as much as possible. And at convenient, and sometimes inconvenient, points along the line there sprang up the little collection of services that formed the nucleus of a village or town: the loading platform, two or three elevators, a general store, a farm implement dealer, a post-office, and, once things were going well, a branch bank. Churches and schools, each frequently with a single room (one building often served for both), brought teachers and clergymen, out from the east on the "mission field." The names of these new towns gave the west a proper air of cosmopolitanism, even if they were not always accurate reflections of the origins of the inhabitants. There were Hungarians at Kipling, Ukrainians at Innisfree, Germans at Melville, Scandinavians at Quill Lake, Belgians and French Canadians at Ste Rose and Ste Albert. Then there were Monmartre, Veregin, Wolseley, Carlyle, Vonda, Bruderheim, Humboldt, Southey, Esterhazy, and Stockholm scattered among more indigenous names like Moose Jaw, Wetaskiwin, Indian Head, Saskatoon, Red Deer, and Swift Current. Whatever the origin of Rosthern, a little Saskatchewan town, its people apparently came from the four corners of Europe. It was described this way in 1904: "Since 1901 almost all the immigration into this district has been foreign immigration. Between 1896 and 1904, about 3,000 Galician familes of about 15,000 souls; about 500 Bukowinians; about 1,500 Hungarians, including 250 Slovaks (speaking Slovak and Magyar) from North Hungary, via Pennsylvania and Ohio; about 48,000 German Catholics from the State of Minnesota (U.S.A.); about 5,000 French Canadians; and some Orthodox and Reforming Jews from Hungary have gone into or are now in the district. About 1,500 Doukhobors are also settled in 13 villages."[138]

By 1901 the rich soil of the Red, Assiniboine, Souris, and Qu'Appelle valleys had been settled, as had the interlake district in Manitoba. A long thin line of settlement followed the route of the Canadian Pacific Railway, and spread out as the ranching population reached from the United States border to the Edmonton region. Five years later this band of settlement had spread rapidly across the Park Belt, and had pushed north to the Forest Belt. The one area which settlement had consciously avoided was the arid Palliser Triangle. High rainfalls in the 1909-11 seasons made even this land attractive, and by 1911 it was filling up rapidly with ranchers and farmers, while in the north people were beginning to move into the Peace River country. During the next decade these developments continued, especially under the stimulus of high wheat prices during the war, so that by 1921 all the best farm land, and some of the worst, on the prairies had been occupied. Though population density naturally varied greatly, a large part of the west had a density of ten persons per square mile by 1921.[139]

For the thousands of new Canadians who settled on the prairies, the decade before the Great War was a period of experiment, hard work, co-operation, achievement, and disappointment. Cold winters and year-round isolation were gradually replaced, or compensated for, by the growth of community spirit, the spread of churches, farm organizations and prosperity. The world seemed endlessly prepared to buy all the grain that the prairies could yield. Prices were good, and rising; yields regularly increased; and even transportation facilities improved. There were, of course, problems and not all of them caused by nature. The east lacked a sympathetic understanding of the potential and ambitions of the west, while politicians and businessmen sometimes seemed determined to shackle the agriculturalist. None the less, the west looked upon itself as the land of opportunity. Many were the stories of fevered speculation and booming growth. One journalist in 1911 wrote of the founding of Mirror, Alberta, in terms which while perhaps a little unusual, recalled similar incidents in many places. "When the town site of Mirror was first placed on the market," he wrote, "July 11, and 12, 1911 there were 577 lots sold at auction in 660 minutes. The aggregate purchase price of these lots was $250,000. That was the beginning. Many more lots have been sold since. Before Mirror was a month old it had two banks, five stores, three lumber yards, one hotel, three restaurants, two pool rooms, a sash and door factory and a newspaper. When it reaches the mature age of one year it will be a wonder."[140]

There can be no doubt that the west was new, that it developed out of its hardships and successes, and out of its polyglot population, a sense of its own destiny. It was Canadian, but with a special flavour. For most settlers, the west meant a new beginning where everyone had a chance in the competition for success. An English visitor, Canon J.B. Bickersteth, caught the spirit very well in the title of his exceptionally able travel book – one of hundreds written in these years when the Canadian west was one of the wonders of the world. Bickersteth called his book *The Land of Open Doors*, and in it he wrote, "One is now in a country where it is no shame to work with one's hands. Manual work is not necessarily menial work. The possession of wealth may give some kind of social pre-eminence, but the absence of it certainly does not imply social inferiority. It is a case of every man playing for his own hand, and the weakest go to the wall."[141] That was the kind of west that Clifford Sifton had set out to build: individualistic, competitive, prosperous.

CHAPTER 5

The Triumph of Enterprise

I

The optimism of Canadian life in the new century had its roots in the freshly broken sod of the prairie west. The gloom of a previous generation vanished and was quickly forgotten as trainloads of settlers rushed to stake out and break new land. The enthusiasm was general and all encompassing. Where once the hinterland of central Canada had seemed barren and inhospitable, its vast resources of timber, pulp, minerals, and waterpower now held the promise of a prosperity scarcely imaginable. "Fate holds in store for this young Dominion a golden future," two Canadians proudly told a British audience. "In her vast forests, her coast and inland fisheries, her exhaustless coal deposits, her gold and silver mines, iron, copper, nickel, and nearly every other known variety of mineral, and, above all, in the tremendous possibilities of her grain fields, Canada holds the promise of such commercial prosperity as the world has seldom seen."[1]

The key to the golden treasure, they believed, remained Canada's arable land – "Canada will always be primarily an agricultural nation." Prairie grain would find markets in the far-flung corners of the globe. The farmers of central Canada, having switched from grain crops to stock raising, dairying, and vegetable and fruit farming, would have ever-increasing markets in the nation's growing cities and beyond her shores. But Canada was also "destined to take no mean place among the manufacturing nations of the world."

> Even now she produces all the staple articles of modern industry, and as her population increases, and home and foreign capital becomes available for the development of Canadian industries, she will not only supply most of her own wants, but will be in a position to compete, and compete successfully, with her foreign rivals in the markets of the world.[2]

"Modern industry" grew out of the demands of a booming agricultural economy for more extensive transport and communications facilities, for

83

new railways, new and improved roads, bigger lakes grain carriers, refrigerated ocean steamers and the machines and tools needed to produce them, and a host of other sophisticated manufactured products. It grew under the protective umbrella of the federal government's tariff policy. It grew with the expanding cities, which at once provided labour for its factories, and people demanding an increasing array of consumer products. It grew with the stimulus of new technology and the infusion of millions of dollars of investment capital. And finally, it grew with the active encouragement of provincial governments, which adopted their own "national policies." They actively sought out foreign capital investment, gradually reformed their educational systems to conform to the demands for more skilled labour, and, with the cities, offered enormous bonuses, subsidies and guarantees to industrialists to locate new plants within their boundaries.

The exploitation of minerals, timber, and pulpwood was representative of the rapid transition in Canada's economy in the new century. Here, success depended upon equally heavy amounts of government assistance and capital investment, most of the latter from foreign sources. As with wheat, the ultimate destination of the products was foreign markets. As with wheat, their sales abroad brought much-needed capital to Canada to further develop the country. To produce the staples and to get them to eager foreign buyers required huge investments of private and public capital in a broad range of other enterprises. New railways, harbours, canals, roads, telephone and telegraph lines were necessary. Existing industries had to expand their plants and modify and diversify their products. New industries, such as chemical and electrical products, had to be established. In short, the prerequisite to the sale of Canada's new exports abroad was the expansion and diversification of Canada's industrial economy at home. As Professor Mackintosh observed, from 1900 to 1923 the chief characteristic of the economy was "not merely an expansion of exports but expansion *plus* a greatly extended specialization and integration within the Canadian economy."[3] Table I indicates the extent of that growth in the industrial sector.

TABLE I
Net Value of Production[4]

	1900 ($000)	1910 ($000)	1923 ($000)
Rubber Products	606	3,438	30,178
Tobacco	8,078	13,199	41,889

Boots and Shoes	7,623	16,000	22,958
Textiles and Textile Products	32,874	67,282	157,995
including:			
Clothing	*19,960*	*43,657*	*79,470*
Cotton Textiles	*6,537*	*13,032*	*39,342*
Furniture	4,280	8,018	16,582
Iron and its Produce	34,967	106,313	208,821
including:			
Agricultural Implements	*5,469*	*10,667*	*14,434*
Boilers, Tanks and Engines	*2,842*	*7,585*	*2,786*
Machinery	*831*	*2,332*	*19,857*
*Primary Iron and Steel**	*3,111*	*14,919*	*17,500*
Railway Rolling Stock	*5,178*	*25,221*	*28,008*
Wire and Wire Goods	*769*	*2,239*	*11,500*
Automobiles	——	*2,444*	*33,462*
Chemicals and Chemical Products	3,910	12,167	56,800
Electric Light and Power	1,960	12,892	67,500
Total of Above**	94,298	239,309	602,723
Other Manufactures	120,228	325,158	701,834
Grand Total, All Manufactures	214,526	564,467	1,304,557

*Excludes Iron-smelting in 1900 and 1910

**Includes Total of textiles and
  textile products and of iron and
  its products.

The patterns of growth, of course, differed from region to region. British Columbia's lumber was sent south to build the growing American cities and east to construct the homes of the prairie settlers. The province's other exports, non-ferrous metals, coal, and fish, found markets across the continent. On the prairies wheat was king, but Winnipeg was the fourth largest manufacturing centre in pre-war Canada, producing goods for both local and national consumption. Quebec's economy was more complex.

Resting upon a centuries-old agricultural base, and with Montreal domi-
nating Canadian commerce and finance, manufacturing had taken firm
root in the province in the eighties. By 1910 the development of the pulp
and paper industry in the provincial hinterland was well under way. The
Maritime economy was also mixed, producing pulp, paper, and fish products for export, and refined sugar, coal, iron and steel products for
domestic buyers. Productivity increased significantly in the Atlantic provinces in the pre-war years, but it was greatly out-paced by the growth in
central Canada.[5]

It was in Ontario that expansion, specialization, and integration were
most evident. There, and especially from south-central Ontario through
the peninsula, it seemed as if hardly a week passed without the announcement of a new company being formed, a new factory being built, and
hundreds of new men being hired to man the production lines. Some
towns in eastern Ontario – Brockville, Cornwall, and Kingston were representative – which had flourished with small manufactures in the eighties and early nineties, declined as industries consolidated in the provincial
heartland. But the general trend was toward growth, with astonishing
gains in population, capital investment, and total industrial work force.
Berlin was a thriving centre for the production of furniture, footware,
rubber goods, engines and motors, pianos and organs, and a host of small
wares. Brantford and Guelph factories produced engines, bicycles, farm
implements, woollen goods, cigars, glue, carpets, stoves, biscuits, carriages, piping, and stoves. Optical goods were produced in St. Catharines
as well as canned foods, farm implements, and other iron products. The
large Canadian General Electric plant and numerous other factories were
located in Peterborough. Hamilton dominated Ontario's heavy industry
and, with Toronto, formed the base of the province's impressive industrial
complex.

At Queen's Park industrialists and promoters were always welcome, as
they were in every city hall. The province encouraged the aggressive
bonusing policies of its municipalities, which were designed to attract new
firms to its cities. Typical was a Guelph by-law of 1902, noted by the
Labour Gazette, "to grant a bonus of $40,000 extended over a period of
years to a company which will produce 2500 tons of piping, tubing, etc.,
per year, and employ about 125 employees."[6]

Railway policy, resource policy, municipal government and education
policy, all were addressed to the maxim that the business of Ontario was
business. The language of business, the methods of business, the concerns
of business for economy and expertise were reflected in the policies of the
Ontario government. They all found expression in the comfortable environment manufacturers found in southern Ontario. They were all implicit
in the provinces's policies for the development of New Ontario.

II

Tapping the mineral wealth of Ontario's northland was an important part of the province's industrial policies. Mining in the north was especially attractive; the industry was labour-intensive and, once opened, would lay to rest the myth that the vast stretches of northern Ontario were an unproductive wasteland. Perhaps even iron might be found in exploitable quantities. In the great age of steel, this was the fondest of hopes. Iron and steel production was at once the prestige symbol of industrialization and the base of any respectable industrial power. Unlike Nova Scotia, where with considerable federal assistance primary steel was being produced, Ontario's industry was essentially secondary, making finished and semi-finished goods from steel manufactured elsewhere. An observer expressed the anxiety of both the industrialists and the government when he noted that "one cannot point to any nation in the world that amounts to anything which does not manufacture its own iron and steel."[7] But iron was only one of many minerals that might be found. The potential for the mining industry was much more broadly based.

As early as 1890 the Ontario government's Royal Commission on the Mineral Resources of Ontario and Measures for their Development had submitted its influential *Report.* It was a broad examination of all the factors behind the province's failure to develop its mineral resources. The *Report* pointed out the disappointing results of previous attempts at mineral exploitation and noted that the failure to attract the large amounts of capital required by the industry and the lack of a skilled labour force were at the heart of the problem. A vigorous government role in promotion and education was strongly recommended. The Mowat government responded by revising its mining legislation and establishing a Bureau of Mines in 1891. The Bureau's purpose was significant: "to collect and publish information and statistics on the mineral resources and mining industry." Without a regular and reliable flow of data on the industry and its potential, there was no way to attract investment capital. As the Bureau put it in its first report, "Statistics are to industry what pulse and temperature are to the human body; they enable us to observe symptoms and study conditions and in an intelligent way to suggest and apply remedies when remedies are needed."[8] The anticipations of the Bureau were realized in the next decade. The great gold discoveries at both Porcupine and Kirkland Lake began with the geological exploration surveys of its staff in the 1890's[9].

The Bureau's primary role was educational, the promotion of all the province's potential mineral resources from iron, copper, and nickel to mica, corundum, and peat moss. Annual reports were replete with information on "the best economic methods whereby raw material may be utilized and converted into finished articles," analyses of the reasons for failure of abandoned mining projects, cautionary advice against the purchase of new and untried machinery, and admonitions against speculation. "Signs are too evident," it observed in 1906,

> that the Cobalt mining district is to be the scene of another joint-stock company boom. The undoubted richness of the district is attracting to it not only those who wish to engage in legitimate mining, but also that class of speculator that descends upon every rich mining camp in order to turn to personal advantage the hopes of gain roused in the public breast by the sight of the suddenly revealed mineral wealth.[10]

Part of the provincial education campaign was directed at upgrading the skills of Ontario workers to qualify them for employment in the mining industry. At the top level, the Ontario School of Mines was established at Kingston, adjacent to Queen's University in 1892, offering a degree programme in mining engineering. The School of Practical Science in Toronto was given financial assistance to offer courses in mining education. Perhaps of greater importance, and certainly more imaginative, was the founding of short summer school courses in basic mining technique right at mining camps themselves.

One monument to the Ontario government's efforts to open up New Ontario was Francis Hector Clergue's huge industrial empire in Sault Ste Marie. It seemed to incorporate all the government could have wanted. The capital investment was enormous and came from the United States. With it, as the Bureau of Mines continually emphasized and applauded, came "American know-how," experience, and technical skill so lacking in the province.[11] Most important, Clergue's empire was an ideal integration of all the industries capable of exploiting the richness of the northland, including the production of primary steel. On February 18, 1902, the first steel poured from the furnace and the *Sault Star* vividly described the event:

> The vessel shot the sparks up to the top of the building and they fell in beautiful showers, a great sparkling curtain. Gradually the sparks gave way to flame that grew whiter with the minutes. In a little while the loudly soaring fire was too white to look at. Then the blower knew the cook in the vessel was done, – was cleansed enough to pour. . . . Now it was steel.[12]

Consolidated Lake Superior Company included hydro-electric power production, timber and pulp mills, nickel processing, chemical products, iron and steel, steamships, and the Algoma Central Railway. From small beginnings with municipal assistance in 1894, it became a giant, capitalized at $117,000,000 in 1901. Much of the stimulation had come from the Ontario government. Its lucrative enticements to expansion illustrate how far the province was willing to go beyond educational and promotional campaigns to develop New Ontario. Provincial largess included railway land grants, bonuses, timber leases and mineral rights. (Liberal assistance had also been received from the federal government in Ottawa in the form of railway subsidies.) In 1903 the corporation suddenly plunged to disaster when Clergue's incautious financial schemes caught up with him. The province, so generous in the days of building, came to the rescue again with a guarantee of a loan by a New York financial house. "Leaving out of the question for the moment that American capitalists had been getting little for their investment and that it would be desirable to encourage such investments in Canada for the future," the Premier explained, "it is of great importance to the people of Ontario . . . that the industries should be revived and put on a strong financial footing, and carried on on lines originally projected, as it would encourage the investment of American capital for the development of Ontario resources."[13]

The concessions that the provincial government made to the American-controlled Canadian Copper Company were less spectacular but equally as important in the steady development of the nickel industry at Sudbury. Canadian Copper led the mining companies' campaign against a royalty provision in the 1891 Ontario mining legislation. By 1900 the government had abandoned any claim to royalties under steady corporate pressure. The 1900 legislation, however, following the successful practice of placing export duties on raw materials in the lumber industry to encourage processing in Canada, provided for an export duty on nickel matte. Up to that time the ore was simply mixed and concentrated at Sudbury by the Canadian Copper Company. Refining was carried out by the Orford Company, the other half of the concern that would soon become the International Nickel Company, in New Jersey. Again, the strong protests of Canadian Copper, plus threats to withdraw from Sudbury, ended the 1900 export duty. It was not until the middle of the Great War, in the wake of the *Deustchland* allegations, that INCO consented to move the refining stage of the industry to Canada.[14]

Gradually the interests of the provincial government and the resource industries became more closely intertwined. Frank Cochrane, Premier Whitney's appointment as Minister of Lands and Forests in 1905, was deliberately chosen because of his prominence as a former mayor of Sudbury and his close ties with the entrepreneurs of New Ontario. Cochrane quickly called a convention of the province's mining men, who proposed detailed revisions of the Mines Act, many of which were accepted in the legislative session of 1906. Before Cochrane joined Borden's cabinet in late 1911, the mining, timber, and pulp barons of New Ontario were always assured of a sympathetic audience at Queen's Park. And in 1912 the Bureau of Mines initiated the procedure of consulting with the Canadian Institute of Mines, the owners' association, before suggesting further changes in mining legislation to the government. Ontario's policy of developing the mining industry to broaden the province's industrial base, backed by wholehearted encouragement of and generous concessions to the mining entrepreneurs, was a success.

Not so successful were the government's efforts to upgrade the mining skills of Ontario workmen. There is no doubt that the short summer school courses given at the mines themselves, an idea borrowed from New Zealand, were very popular. But their impact is difficult to measure. Especially at "boom towns" like Cobalt, as in the Klondike a few years before, the labour force was constantly shifting and changing. As with gold in the Yukon, so too silver in Cobalt, and soon gold again at Kirkland Lake, attracted all manner of men, young and old, experienced and raw, from around the globe. Provincial policy for the education of miners was predicated upon the assumption of a stable labour force. But the rough, hazardous work, the poor working conditions in the mines, and the unanticipated huge expansion of the industry in New Ontario all encouraged fluidity rather than stability.

Several factors, then, worked at cross purposes to the government's programme of mining education – including the success of the other part of the provincial scheme, attraction of the industry to New Ontario. Mining, ore processing and refinement, iron and steel at the Sault, nickel at Sudbury, silver at Cobalt, and gold at Porcupine all expanded so rapidly that the training of skilled labour and junior management personnel simply could not keep up with the demand. In addition, many skilled miners moved on from mine to mine in northern Ontario as one "boom town" succeeded another. Whether they stayed or moved, when they and their less skilled brothers tried to better their lot by organizing and striking for higher wages, the owners, without hesitation, broke the strikes by importing unskilled immigrant labour. So the mines were opened. And they added an important new element to the industrialization of Ontario. But the miners, rather like the ore they dug, remained an exploited resource in the province's business economy.

III

One sign-post of transition in industry was the gradual change from coal and steam power to electricity as the driving force for factory machinery. Electrically driven machines were much safer than their steam-powered predecessors; they were also more precise and complex. More sophisticated skills were imperative for both operators and maintainance men. Another indication of change was the adoption of the joint-stock company as the basis of corporate finance. In the nineties, much Canadian industry was personally owned in small units; if joint ownership was required, the stock was usually held by a few friendly entrepreneurs. But the expansion and integration of industrial units, and their switch over to new power sources and more sophisticated production techniques, were too expensive for most individual owners or small groups of capitalists. "Public" financing, the issuing of stocks and bonds to the public at large, became the basic source of necessary capital. This method of financing, generally new to Canadian manufacturing, helped integrate and consolidate industry in the first decade of the new century.[15] Table II illustrates the growth of capitalization of Canadian industry.[16]

TABLE II

Year	No. of Companies formed with Dominion Charter.	Total Capitalization. New Companies.	Increased Capitalization. Existing Companies.	Grand Total.
		($000)	($000)	($000)
1900	53	9,558	3,351	12,909
1901	55	7,662	3,420	11,082
1902	126	51,182	5,055	56,237
1903	187	53,405	5,584	58,989
1904	206	80,597	5,366	85,963
1905	293	99,910	9,685	109,595
1906	374	180,173	32,403	212,576
1907	378	132,686	19,091	151,777
1908*	64	13,299	865	14,164
1908-09	366	121,624	72,293	193,917
1909-10	493	301,788	46,589	348,377
1910-11	544	458,415	24,715	483,130
1911-12	658	447,626	42,939	490,565

* First three months of 1908.

A close student of the subject has concluded that the "consolidation movement" in Canadian industry began in 1909. In that year nine consolidations with an authorized capitalization of $134 million were made. Twenty-two mergers, capitalized at $157 million, took place in 1910, among them the formation of the Canadian Cereal & Milling Company, Dominion Canners Limited (a consolidation of thirty-four factories of

Canadian Canners and fourteen independent companies), Dominion Steel Corporation, and the British Columbia Packers Association. In 1911 the Canada Bread Company and Sherwin Williams Company of Canada were but two of fourteen new consolidations capitalized at $96 million. Again, in 1912, thirteen mergers with capitalization of $97 million took place. Then, suddenly, the trend slowed. Further combinations were effected during the war, and after, but the rush towards consolidation slackened with the depressed times of 1913 followed by the financial uncertainty engendered by the war.[17]

The stated purpose of these consolidations, the *Monetary Times* observed, was "to bring about economies of management and to systematize production and distribution." The Canadian Machinery Company, it was said, could expect "increased efficiency and economies by specializing the output at the different factories and by eliminating the unnecessary duplication both in output and patterns, etc."[18] But there was another aspect of the movement that is more apparent in retrospect: "the most potent factor in bringing about these consolidations was the promoter; and ... too often the primary object to be achieved was the realization of 'promoter profits.' "[19]

Indeed, a whole new class of industrial financiers, the professional promoters, Max Aitken, A.E. Ames, Cawthra Mulock, Rodolphe Forget, and others, came into their own during the heyday of consolidation. They were both imaginative initiators of mergers, and, because of their over-capitalization – an important source of their fees, – the origin of future financial problems for many of their creations. One of the most successful, Max Aitken, the future Lord Beaverbrook, unblushingly explained, albeit privately, his part in the organization of Canada Cement to Robert Borden. "I didn't make one dollar in cash," he wrote, "and not one of my associates made any cash, but expended $135,000 in cash! The total profit of all the promoters did not amount to more than two and one-half million dollars of stock, and my own profit, directly and indirectly for promotion and underwriting and every other service, amounted approximately to one million and one-half dollars of Common Stock, worth at the moment about $300,000. .... Either the system of bonus stocks is good or bad. It has been generally practised, and it is countenanced by the Companies Act."[20]

Many combinations failed to meet their capital indebtedness, and consequently had to be reorganized and refinanced on sounder financial principles. So extreme were some cases of excess capitalization that the *London Economist* painted a dim picture of the City's experience with Canadian industrial securities:

> [They were] floated with a large capital of ordinary shares conveying to the unsuspecting investor the idea of stability for the bonds or debentures for

which he is asked to subscribe, whereas in reality all this capital was so much water, being taken by the promoters for the value of their services, while the bondholders had to provide all the money for capital expenditure and sometimes for the promoters' expenses as well. The bonds in such a case have no more security than if they were the ordinary stock of the concern, and the price at which they were issued is out of all proportion with their worth.[21]

The political repercussions of the combination movement were potentially explosive. After years of public propaganda against the evils of "trusts" in the United States, and with rapidly rising prices after 1907, it seemed as if monopolies and their notorious price-fixing practices were about to become firmly established in Canada. The federal government responded with legislation introduced by the Minister of Labour, W.L. Mackenzie King, in 1910. The bill's essential purpose was made apparent in its title – *An Act to Provide for the Investigation of Combines, Monopolies and Mergers.* As King explained:

> The legislation differs in some particulars from legislation . . . in other countries in that it is not aimed against combines or mergers as such, but rather against the exercise on the part of combines, mergers or monopolies, in an unfair manner, of the powers which they may get from that form of organization. This is an age of organization and not merely of local or national competition but of world-wide competition and any industry or any nation which wishes to hold its own in the field of competition must do much in the way of perfecting organization. . . . This measure seeks to afford the means of conserving to the public some of the benefits which arise from large organizations of capital for the purpose of business and commerce. . . . [22]

The benefits of organization without exploitation were to be achieved by a complicated process. A complaint against an apparently offending corporation could be initiated by six persons. It would be reviewed judicially and then passed on to an investigating board. If the board did find the combination acting in restraint of trade, or fixing prices, a fine could be levied against it. But the main emphasis was on publicity. King naively thought that the potential threat of public exposure would be quite sufficient to deter industries from acting contrary to the general public interest. The sceptical leader of the opposition observed that "the measure is capable of becoming useless on the one hand, and of being abused on the other."[23] In fact, he was only half right. No machinery was established to enforce the act, and in its nine years before repeal only one case was pursued under its provisions. Most Canadians would have agreed with King that it was neither desirable nor necessary to nip the growth of industrial integration in the bud. It is less certain that they thought the Combines Investigation Act, a mere sop to public sentiment, was the most effective way to assuage their legitimate fears of some of the economic and social effects of the combination movement. Businessmen had accurately detected little to fear in the anti-combines policy of the Laurier Liberals.

For industry itself, the new mode of financing and the integration of industrial production, either horizontal or vertical, dramatically changed the management level. The small, privately financed company of the 1890s often ran quite well under the overall supervision of the individual entrepreneur. "Public" ownership through joint-stock company financing did away with all that; too many interests – promoters, banks and security houses, heads of many of the amalgamated firms – had a stake in the future of the large reorganized firms, and had to be given places on the boards of directors. At the same time the large firm was much more complex, demanding the supervision of highly skilled men who, unlike many of the directors, had been brought up in the business, knew its intimate details, and worked with it daily. These men, the general managers, men like Frank Jones of Canada Cement and Joseph Flavelle of Davies Packing Company, who had acquired managerial skill, became responsible for both day-to-day operations and much overall policy.

Like the industrial financiers, the managers were a new breed of Canadian businessmen, characteristically able administrators rather than flamboyant salesmen. Efficiency was up to them. They were responsible for the economies of production and distribution, the introduction of precise cost accounting and analysis in the plants, long-term planning of the whole operation. To them gravitated much of the power in the expanding Canadian business community, and more of the responsibility for its welfare.

New sources of power, more elaborate machines, and more sophisticated production techniques demanded more skilled workmen and foremen. Throughout the first two decades of the century most of these men had to be recruited from the United States. Where, *Industrial Canada* asked in 1905,

> is the training ground from which we are to recruit our department foremen, our factory superintendents, and the men who are to guide and direct the practical side of our national industries? . . . The skilled help problem is rapidly becoming the most serious problem which the manufacturer is called upon to contend with. He has been compelled to import, and to import freely.[24]

The problem and the solution were thought to be educational; the schools had not kept pace with the economy, but publicly supported technical education could help to close the gap. Ontario's Minister of Education, Richard Harcourt, had noted the problem as early as 1899. "The advance of applied science, with the resulting sub-division of labour so marked at the present day, has rendered instruction in technical education essential, in view of the changed economic conditions," he argued. "The country must adapt itself to these new requirements."[25]

In that year the Ottawa Board of Trade helped set up a meeting in Toronto where prominent businessmen and civic leaders argued the case for publicly supported, technical education. By 1902 the Canadian Manufacturers' Association and the Trades and Labour Congress had joined the campaign. Both provincial and federal governments were subjected to persistent lobbying. A response was difficult. Education, of course, was a provincial responsibility, but many lobbyists argued that technical education was more directly a federal matter, related to trade and commerce. Equally frustrating was the stout resistance of the academics at both school and university levels against any corruption of their established curricula with the introduction of "practical" courses. Gradually, however, progress was made in several provinces. In 1903 Ontario set up grants for both manual training and its counterpart for women, domestic science. In 1911 the Industrial Education Act was approved by the Whitney government, establishing general industrial schools for instruction in basic trades and special industrial schools for a more theoretical approach to technical education. Instruction could be pursued in both primary and secondary schools, and, for those already "on the line," in evening classes. Four years earlier the Province of Quebec had established secondary technical education schools in Montreal and Quebec City; a third was opened in Shawinigan Falls in 1911. In 1907 Nova Scotia incorporated its evening mining classes into the provincial education system and opened the Nova Scotia Technical College for post-secondary training. Before the war Prince Edward Island, Manitoba, and Saskatchewan had all appointed investigatory commissions on the subject, and Alberta and British Columbia had appointed directors of technical education in their school systems.[26]

The response of the federal government was more cautious. For a number of years Laurier treated the pressure from the C.M.A. with wary indifference. Eventually Mackenzie King took the subject in hand, and, after getting approval from the provincial premiers, established a Royal Commission on Industrial Training and Technical Education in 1910.[27] The *Report* was received by the Borden government in 1913 and 1914. The Commission recommended, first, that Ottawa subsidize elementary-level manual training with a grant of $350,000 per annum for ten years, and, second, that Ottawa establish a Dominion Development Fund to subsidize technical education in secondary schools at a cost of $3,000,000 per annum for ten years. Both grants were to be divided among the provinces upon the basis of population.[28] It was only after the war, in association with its reconstruction programme, that the government acted. The Technical Education Act of 1919 established a fund of $10,000,000 for technical education, to be spent over the next decade. Each province was to receive an annual grant of $10,000 plus quarterly grants in proportion to population, provided that the province expended an equal amount each year on technical schooling. Federal funds were to be used for buildings, equipment, and the training and payment of teachers.[29]

Conservation was another activity which the federal government moved into, responding to the needs of a rapidly changing nation. Indeed the Commission of Conservation, established in 1909, pointedly illustrated how demands of the urban-industrial society forced government to participate in a multiplicity of new activities. Moreover, the *ad hoc* nature of the response, and flexible definition of the Commission's responsibilities, revealed the extent to which Canada's public institutions, particularly the civil service, were unprepared for the ongoing transformation of the country. The Commission's work also displayed the commitment of both business and government to rational, scientific methods in organizing Canadian society. Like Mackenzie King's Department of Labour, the Commission of Conservation was part of the new, efficient, expert bureaucracy that was an emerging counterpart of the industrial society.

Complaints about unplanned, wasteful exploitation of Canada's natural resources had already been expressed in the late nineteenth century. One result was the new profession of forestry.[30] Another was the establishment of a few areas as parks for recreational uses – the National Park at Banff, and Algonquin in Ontario.[31] Then in 1906 the Laurier government convened a Canadian Forestry Convention to assess problems of forest management, sylviculture, and improved forestry education.[32] The guest speaker was Gifford Pinchot, the apostle of conservation and scientific management in the United States. Those same principles, to some extent borrowed from the United States,[33] guided the organization and operation of the Canadian Commission of Conservation.

The Commission's establishment was the direct result of the North American Conservation Conference, which assembled at the call of President Theodore Roosevelt in 1909. On the recommendation of that meeting the Laurier government founded the Commission and appointed Clifford Sifton as its first chairman.[34] That choice, in itself, was immensely significant. Few Canadians better typified the spirit of development and the concern for rational planning than the former Minister of the Interior. Under his guidance, conservation policy could hold no serious threats for businessmen, nor cause exuberance among wilderness preservationists, if any of the latter existed in Canada. The Commission was organized as a non-partisan advisory body, financed by federal funds, but including federal and provincial representation since resource development was largely a provincial responsibility. From the first the experts employed by the Commission were its most important members. Dean B.E. Fernow of the University of Toronto Forestry School, Dr. Charles Hodgetts, a one-time

Medical Officer of Health in Ontario, and Thomas Adams, a leading British town-planning specialist, were well qualified to conduct studies of waterworks and sewage systems, soil fertility, rural life, fur farming, lobster fishing, and many other topics.[35]

The Commission's viewpoint naturally reflected the practical outlook of the businessmen and professionals who composed it. It was recognized, as one conservationist noted, that "Canadians have lived for many years in a fool's paradise as to their natural resources. We are not possessed of the inexhaustible natural wealth which our people believe we have."[36] But the Commission's primary goal was not preservation; it believed that conservation meant planned development. "The principles of conservation," the 1911 *Report* stated, ". . . do not stand in the way of development, but make possible the best and most highly economic development and exploitation in the interest of the people for all time."[37] The key to the Commission's success lay in dispelling the fallacious belief that "any ordinary capable amateur can do work which ought to be done by a trained scientific man."[38]

The Commission set about its work with vigour and imagination, offering studies and advice to whatever authority seemed appropriate or sympathetic. Sifton made sure the Commission even played a role as watchdog over the national interest in power development. In 1910 he waged a successful campaign to prevent the export of power from the St. Lawrence system to the United States. Once this power was exported, Sifton maintained, vested interests would be created across the border that no Canadian government would ever be able to resist if Canadians decided to redirect the power to meet their own needs.[39] Water pollution, forest fire prevention, land drainage, and mining techniques also commanded the Commission's attention.[40] The protection of wild life and birds, which eventually led to the establishment of the Migratory Birds Convention in 1917, was also investigated thoroughly. And the doctrine of usefulness apparently even dominated wild life conservation for, as one expert wrote, "nothing can ever equal our wild life as a means of increasing human efficiency where the tendency of modern life is to work under the high pressure of city conditions."[41]

Nor did the Commission confine its attentions to natural resources and wild life. From the outset human resources in city and country were considered to be within its proper domain. "There are two vital factors in the question of national conservation," Dr. Charles Hodgetts contended in 1912, "the physical and the vital. The former relates to the protecting of our land, our forests, our minerals, our waters, our sunlight, our fresh air; the latter to the prevention of diseases, to health and to the prolongation of life."[42] Agricultural land use and social organization, public health and housing, therefore became central concerns, and brought the centralizing tendencies of the Commission into conflict with local authorities and vested interests. In 1914 the Commission hired the British Garden City Movement leader, Thomas Adams, to supervise work in urban planning. He immediately set about consulting local authorities, forming a Civic Improvement League, and attempting to win approval for the establishment of Departments of Municipal Affairs and Central Town Planning Boards. Many of his schemes ended in frustration and by 1919 he was ready to move to a position in the United States.[43]

It was in its studies of city problems that the Commission of Conservation revealed the complexity of the new urban and industrial Canada. But the ever-widening range of the Commission's activities, jealously regarded by private interests and government bureaucracies alike, led to the institution's downfall. A jurisdictional dispute between the Commission and the federal cabinet in 1918 resulted in Sifton's resignation. Three years later the Commission was abolished on the official grounds that it had served its purpose and its work could now be done within the regular departments of government.[44] An almost unmourned death ended the body, which, for a decade, had done impressive and pioneering work in bringing before governments and the public carefully gathered information, and in advocating a more rational, efficient use of Canadian resources. Nowhere, perhaps, was the need for the Commission's work more obvious, and the limitations of its philosophy of rational expertise more evident, than in the transformation in progress in Canada's cities.

IV

Canadian cities grew at an astounding rate during the first decades of the new century. As industries expanded, workers were drawn in from the countryside or from overseas to fill places in the factories or to operate the burgeoning service facilities. A profound change in the character of Canadian society, and more important, in the lives of individual Canadians, is expressed in the cold statistics of city growth in Table III.

Table III
Population of Canadian Cities, 1891-1931[45]

	1891	1901	1911	1921
Montreal	219,616	328,172	490,504	618,566
Toronto	181,215	209,892	381,833	521,893
Vancouver	13,709	29,432	120,847	163,220
Winnipeg	25,639	42,340	136,035	179,087

Hamilton	48,959	52,634	81,869	114,151
Quebec	63,090	68,840	78,710	95,193
Ottawa	44,154	59,928	87,062	107,843
Calgary	3,876	4,392	43,704	63,305
Edmonton	–	4,176	31,064	58,821
Halifax	38,437	40,832	46,619	58,372
Regina	–	2,249	30,213	34,432
Saskatoon	–	113	12,004	25,739
Saint John	39,179	40,711	42,511	47,166

Montreal and Toronto more than doubled in size, Vancouver and Winnipeg increased fivefold, while Calgary, Edmonton, Regina, and Saskatoon burst from nowhere. Ottawa also doubled, a sign of the expanding civil service.

Rapid, unplanned growth of this magnitude meant skyrocketing land prices, especially in downtown areas. Consequently, cities like Winnipeg, London, Halifax, Ottawa, Montreal, and Toronto built street railways to open the surrounding countryside to the suburban real estate boom. Across the country, banks and insurance companies built monuments to their financial power. Prairie cities reflected their origins and sources of strength in multi-tracked railway strips, flanked by large stations proclaiming the wealth of the giant corporations, which cut through their centres, and often provided a significant social division between rich and poor. Characteristically, the other large buildings were often retail outlets for the Hudson's Bay Company, T. Eaton's, and the branches of eastern banks. The new harbour facilities of Vancouver and Halifax were creatures of the National Policy at last come into its own. These two cities, and Montreal, were the principal beneficiaries of the rising export trade in Canada's new staples. And Montreal probably shared with Hamilton and Toronto the distinction of being Canada's grimiest cities. Industrial smoke, the Commission of Conservation noted, "disfigures buildings, impairs the health of the population, renders the whole city filthy, destroys any beauty with which it may naturally be endowed and tends, therefore, to make it a squalid and undesirable place of residence, and this, at a time when economic influences are forcing into our cities an ever increasing proportion of our population. These conditions press especially on the poor who must reside in the cities and cannot escape from these evils by taking houses in the suburbs."[46]

Every city from Montreal westward was something of a "boom town" during these years, but none more than "the Chicago of Canada," Winnipeg. "The entire structure of such a city changes every few years," an English traveller observed.

The present handsome and commodious railroad station is the third in twenty years, while the big building going up on Main Street is the third post office. The "best hotel" last year is replaced by a "better" one this year, and the omnipotent C.P.R. is erecting a palace of its own, which will absorb the wealthy travellers next year.

All the modern conveniences of street railways, electric light, etc., are furnished in abundance; the brand-new Manitoba Club, where the city magnates meet for lunch, leaves nothing to be desired in comfort and "elegance," while the store set up by Eaton of Toronto occupies a solid block, with a flat roof, on which storey after storey will be added as required. [47]

Winnipeg set the style for the west, as Montreal and Toronto, each in its very different way, claimed to do for the east. It was the centre of prairie commerce, the hub of the region's transport network. But even Edmonton, relatively insignificant by comparison, was a fascinating place for a homesteader's young son to visit for the first time in 1913:

The buildings tower over the street two or three storeys high and even brick and stone buildings of six storeys. Whoever imagined so many buildings, or such variety? And the signs advertising their owners' business, painted in large letters, some illuminated and all overhanging the street in bewildering confusion, why, they make your head swim! . . . it was only after dark that the king of the signs stood out in all its glory over the Selkirk Hotel. This one, done in many lightbulbs, showed by successive combinations a man pouring a glass of beer, lifting it to his lips, and then quaffing the liquor. If I had seen nothing else in all the city, this would have been enough. [48]

It was a striking commentary on the values of city life that the great power of "white coal" was so used in every Canadian city. Street lighting was, at best, selectively installed, first in the broad streets of commerce and then perhaps on the tree-shaded lanes servicing the homes of "the better elements" of society. In Vancouver, one writer reported, "in the residential sections the lighting is poor, one arc lamp generally being placed at each street intersection and the intervening distances of 150 to 200 yards being left in darkness." [49] Downtown behind the great stores and hotels, on the narrow back streets, the ugly masses of hydro and telephone lines and poles passed through without connections to the small, dingy, crowded flats.

There were no sewer lines to service these neighbourhoods; outside "conveniences" could be found in the back alleys. In 1904 the Assistant Relief Officer of Toronto reported that

there is scarcely a vacant house fit to live in that is not inhabited, and in many cases by numerous families; in fact . . . respectable people have had to live in stables, tents, old cars, sheds (others in damp cellars), where we would not place a valued animal, let alone a human being. [50]

"In these homes there is a lack of proper sanitary conditions," read another report in 1909, "one outdoor closet for dozens of men, women, and children. It is simply disgraceful. Then looking out you can see the garbage piled up as high as the window. Nauseating odours and sights on every hand."[51]

In short, the Canadian city at the turn of the century was a place of violent contrasts, a home for the very rich and the very poor, for the rural immigrant from a neighbouring county or a far distant land and the native urbanite, for respectable church-goers and for prostitutes, a place of conspicuous expenditure and forced destitution.[52] "In country districts people are to a large extent on a level," wrote J.S. Woodsworth, the superintendent of All Peoples' Mission in Winnipeg,

> but in the cities we have the rich and the poor, the classes and the masses, with all that these distinctions involve. The tendency is that the well-to-do gather together in more or less exclusive suburbs, while the poor are segregated in slum districts, and between these there is comparatively little direct intercourse. The employer may meet his employee at business, but there is little bond of connection beside what Carlyle called the "cash nexus." A woman may superintend laundry operations in her own house, but she knows little or nothing of the home life of her washerwoman who has come several miles to give her days [sic] service. They live in two worlds. . . . This condition is intensified and more complicated when large numbers of foreigners are brought into our civic life. Differences of language, of race and of religion, often running parallel, deepen and broaden the chasm. The people who most need help are separated from those who best could help them.[53]

In the 1880s and the 1890s attempts to alleviate the misery of the poor and the working class in Toronto were made by the Humane Society and the Children's Aid Society, successively inspired by the leadership of a *World* municipal reporter, Joseph Kelso, and through reform legislation at the municipal and provincial levels of government.[54] In Montreal, Herbert Ames, a businessman deeply influenced by municipal reform movements in the United States, attempted to promote privately financed, low cost housing for the working class, arguing that private philanthropy was both necessary and profitable.[55] Across Canada the churches responded to the declining congregations in and the slums rising around their downtown pastorates with extensive welfare programmes and elaborate social surveys to assess the causes of urban blight. And in Winnipeg Woodsworth devoted his attention to the welfare of the "people who most need help," the foreign immigrants.[56] But the reformers soon learned, as had their counterparts in American cities, that dedicated private service and impressive social legislation were not enough. The problems were too big, too interlocked, and they grew larger and more complex as the

cities expanded. What was needed was equally dedicated public action by
the executive branch of government.[57]

In Toronto another newspaper reporter, who had covered the municipal beat for the *News* in the nineties, gave that kind of leadership when
he was elected mayor from 1912 to 1914. H.C. Hocken, who rose from
newspaper compositor and reporter to become an owner and publisher,
had served on the city's Board of Control from 1907 to 1911. He tried
to bring to the mayor's office a "new spirit in municipal government." It
"has ceased to be a matter of construction and maintenance," he explained; it had become "work that looks to the serving of those human
instincts which, when properly provided for, make a healthy, moral and
intelligent community." His reform programme was broadly based. Parks
were now opened to the use of the people – "the parks are for walking
in, not for athletic sports," C.S. Clark had reported in 1898[58] – and playgrounds with supervised recreation were added to the system: "it takes a
boy who has been playing in the alleyway and puts him into the hands of
a young man or young woman who has a good outlook on life . . . teaches
him . . . how to play, [and] inspires him with the club idea." The variety
of recreation facilities is interesting: 36 baseball diamonds, 29 soccer
fields, 9 rugby fields, 98 tennis courts, 3 lacrosse fields, 10 cricket creases,
8 bowling greens, 2 croquet grounds, 2 quoit grounds, 33 hockey cush-
ions, and 39 skating rinks and toboggan slides. Public health measures
included the establishment of public baths, installation of a sewage treatment plant and a filtration plant, and extension of the sewer system, a
public health nursing programme and the distribution of fresh milk to
infants in the slums. In the first eight months of 1910 Toronto's death rate
from communicable diseases had been 114 per 100,000; in the same time
period in 1914 it was 27 per 100,000. The city, in a measure initiated by
the socialist Controller James Simpson, adopted a minimum wage of $15
per week for municipal workmen. It reformed both its judicial and penal
systems, establishing separate courts for female and child offenders and
correctional farms for minor offenders. A housing company was formed
to build houses for rent at cost. And, to combat the "meat trust," the city
purchased and operated both an abattoir and a cold storage plant "to keep
all the small wholesale butchers in business, and prevent the great meat
trust . . . from driving out the small dealer."[59]

Hocken's extensive reform programme, as he acknowledged, had been
inspired by and accepted guidelines from the experience of municipal
reformers in the United States. In addition, public assistance rested upon
growing Canadian sentiment for a "new spirit in municipal government."
The breadth of the issue was suggested by the Ottawa *Free Press* as early
as 1898.

The question of municipal reform involves the election of competent officials, and the selection of trained subordinates; the enactment of new laws and the enforcement of those already on the statute books; the maintenance of law and order, and the suppression of vice; the determination of whether a city shall own and operate its own franchises, or lease them to a private corporation, or give them away to private parties; municipal functions; of cleanliness, health, and sanitation; municipal standards, taste and finally, of civic patriotism.[60]

Clearly, municipal reform involved a multiplicity of very complex problems. The example of the franchise question was but one of them. "Local control of streets," to use the Mayor of Westmount, W.D. Lighthall's phrase, was a central issue. Municipal governments had no control over where or how or why the lines of Bell Telephone were strung. The company had received a Dominion charter in 1882 with federal acknowledgment that it was "for the general advantage of Canada." Under the powers granted to it, the company could distribute and withhold its services at will (some local telephone companies set up to compete with it were denied access to its long distance trunk lines), free from provincial or municipal control. The effect, from the municipality's point of view, could be disastrous. According to Lighthall:

> it is the enemy of competition, low rates, and municipal control: its inevitable aim is to crush out all competition and attain the sole monopoly in the future. It occupies and tears up valuable streets, occupies the space beneath them, crowds the streets with poles and wires, destroys their appearance, causes great loss at fires, refuses to contribute anything to taxation, and sets a most dangerous precedent to speculators in charters. . . . *The streets are the city* – for public purposes. They are the only lines of communication between citizens, and between the home and the outer world. If private companies can control them, the people are not free.[61]

The Bell franchise, and electric light and street railway franchises, raised conflicts of jurisdiction between the municipal and federal and provincial governments and gave rise to demands for "home rule." It posed serious questions as to whether the utility franchises were, or were not, "natural monopolies." And, if they were, how could they be controlled? If these utilities, and gas and water systems, were privately owned, how could they be taxed? Or was it cheaper, and more efficient, to provide them through municipal ownership?

Questions of this kind led Lighthall, disturbed by the powers of Bell and irritated at similar powers granted by the Quebec government to Montreal Light, Heat and Power, to propose to Mayor Howland of Toronto, "the formation of a League of Canadian Municipalities, for mutual protection against such encroachment" in 1901.[62] In Toronto in August the Union of Canadian Municipalities was formed. Among its more important objects were the elimination of parties from municipal politics and "the future extension of the principle of Municipal ownership and control of public utilities."[63] In succeeding years the U.C.M. grew rapidly, along with associations in Ontario, Manitoba, Alberta, and British Columbia. It campaigned vigorously for "home rule," for city planning and beautification schemes, and against the evils of "bonusing" industries, either by direct municipal payments of land grants or tax exemptions. Run generally by reform-minded businessmen, it spouted the rhetoric and accepted the ideals of business and industry. In essence, the U.C.M. argued, a city's administration was a business proposition to be conducted on business principles. Politics and the ward system interfered with the proper conduct of civic affairs. Thus, if the commission form of municipal government were adopted, it would at once drive out ward heelers at city hall and encourage better men to accept municipal office.[64] "Municipal office would then be accepted by many capable men, who are averse to undergoing the turmoil and excitement of annual elections," observed the *Municipal World*. "Experienced members would always be found at the council board and a business-like management of every department of the municipal service would result."[65]

The municipal reformers achieved many improvements in city government and city life: more parks, better sewage disposal, cleaner streets, better lighting, and more efficient transportation systems. But perhaps the major achievement of the movement, and one which illustrates clearly the coincidence of business and urban reform goals, came with the establishment of Ontario Hydro. By the turn of the century the increasing use of "white coal" for domestic, civic, and industrial purposes naturally stimulated business and civic leaders to search for its sources and for ways of ensuring it could be obtained economically. By 1896 electric power was being successfully transmitted from Niagara Falls to Buffalo, New York. Within a few years Toronto businessmen were expressing interest in obtaining guaranteed power sources for the city's industry, while smaller western Ontario centres, concerned that "Hogtown" should not gain control of the riches of Niagara, were beginning to think of means to ensure a fair distribution of electricity. The 1902 coal strike in the United States further intensified interest in electrical power, since the coal shortage sent fuel prices skyrocketing and also revealed the embarrassing dependence of Ontario industry upon the United States for its major energy source.[66]

Already by 1902 some municipal leaders in western Ontario had begun to examine the idea that public ownership of transmission lines might be the best manner of ensuring a fair and inexpensive distribution of electricity. On the initiative of two proponents of this idea, E.W.B. Snider of

St. Jacobs, and D.B. Detweiler of Berlin, a conference of municipal leaders was held in Berlin in mid-1902. Alderman F.S. Spence of Toronto, who believed in public ownership of hydro and in prohibition of alcoholic drinks with equal fervour, was the leading speaker. He called for the establishment of "a government Commission which would have power to arrange for the transmission of electricity to the various municipalities desiring it . . . preventing in this way the power from falling into the hands of any monopoly, and in this way securing to the industries of this Province advantages of cheap electric energy."[67] The meeting resolved that a detailed study of the proposal should be carried out.

The "monopolies," of course, had other views. The two main competitors for the sale of Niagara power were the American-owned Ontario Power Company, and the Electric Development Company operated by William Mackenzie, railway builder, Henry M. Pellatt, financier and castle builder, and Frederick Nicholls, an electrical equipment manufacturer. Each of these syndicates was anxious to obtain the franchise for power distribution, which would be worth millions, and would give to its owners a major influence over the development of Ontario industry. The power companies and the public ownership advocates each knew that the key to success lay in winning the support of the provincial government.

The public ownership proponents, with the growing support of western Ontario municipal governments, called a second conference to meet at Berlin in 1903. This more widely attended meeting received the study of the feasibility of public ownership, commissioned by the earlier meeting. The conference accepted the report, enthusiastically endorsing the demand that the Ontario government pass legislation making it possible for municipalities to enter the business of transmitting electricity. Moreover, it was at this conference that an effective leader for the public power movement emerged. He was Adam Beck, a successful cigar-box manufacturer who had turned to politics, first as mayor of London, a post he later combined with membership in the Ontario legislature where he sat as a Conservative. After 1903 Beck became the uncompromising, pugnacious, and ambitious evangelist for public power.[68]

The new movement was now in full swing. Its first victory was a decision by Sir George Ross' Liberal government to enact legislation allowing municipalities, after a referendum, to construct and operate transmission lines. But it was only after James Whitney and the Conservative party took power in 1905 that the public ownership advocates were able to gain the initiative. Beck now became a Minister without Portfolio whose first task was to act as chairman of a commission of enquiry appointed to examine the electricity problem.[69] In 1906 the commission reported, recommending public ownership of transmission lines.[70] At first Whitney was cautious, hoping to find a way to satisfy both sides. That seemed especially necessary since he feared that the possible collapse of the Canadian-owned Electric Development Company would leave the U.S.-controlled syndicate with a monopoly of power production at Niagara. But his anger at the underhanded tactics of the power interests, who appeared to be doing their best to destroy the province's financial reputation abroad, and the obvious popularity of Beck's proposal, finally won him over. In August 1908 the Hydro-Electric Commission let contracts for the construction of the transmission lines.

Public ownership was now a fact, though not one the power interests wanted to recognize. They turned first to the courts, but were outflanked by Whitney, who had the legislature legalize all contracts, and remove them from the jurisdiction of the courts. When the aggrieved parties turned to Ottawa for relief, asking Laurier for disallowance, they obviously expected better treatment. "Bankers, bondholders and financial writers all feel that part of the foundation on which they relied for safety in Canadian investments is being swept away," Byron Walker of the Bank of Commerce told Laurier.[71] Though the federal Liberals expressed sympathy, there was no legal justification for disallowance. Only the people of Ontario could punish a confiscatory government, Laurier replied. That view was obviously correct, but it hardly satisfied the spokesmen for the power interests, many of whom were friends of the federal Liberals, and some of whom decided to support Borden's Conservatives in 1911.[72]

But it was far from accurate to suggest that all Ontario businessmen shared the opinion of the "bankers, bond holders" and the private power interests. Indeed the movement for public power, while popularly supported, had been led from beginning to end by businessmen and their allies. Ontario's manufacturers, large and small, local Boards of Trade, and municipal councils fought for public ownership because they believed it was the most efficient method of getting cheap power immediately. And that power was used to turn the wheels of private enterprise throughout the province. They would have agreed with Adam Beck's rejection of *laissez-faire:* "I do not understand that any revelation has ever been made from Heaven to the effect that a democratic government commits an unpardonable sin when it assists in the establishment of a great and necessary public work for the well being of the people of whose interests it is the trustee."[73] But that was because a clear coincidence existed between the interests of business and the interests of the general public. Ontario Hydro was simply another example of that businessmen's "socialism" which was an established part of the Canadian tradition.[74]

Here was the central weakness of the municipal reform movement. Its goals, and those of the industries it sometimes sought to restrain, were frequently identical.[75] The expansion of industry was at the heart of the difficult problems faced by municipal governments, and the spread of slums and the breakdown of social order were the results of urbanization. Yet the cities of Canada were often lavish in their assistance to new industries, hoping to attract them away from competitors. And the confident materialism of the age reigned supreme. One municipal reformer put his finger on the central issue when he wrote of Winnipeg in 1911: "Her mad passion for evidences of expansion, her insistent demand for figures to prove growth, be it by building permits, or by bank clearances, or by customs receipts, or by pavement mileage, or peradventure by the price of vacant land, any process of growth demonstration, have blinded her to the fact that cities cannot live by growth alone."[76] The captains of industry, assumed to be the leaders of the community,[77] were often both the advocates of growth and the leaders of municipal reform. Consequently, the response of the cities to industrial development was most often on industry's terms: expansion, efficiency, economy, and expertise.

It took a Stephen Leacock to portray the irony of municipal reform. He did it brilliantly, and bitterly, in "The Great Fight for Clean Government," in 1914. McGrath, the Champion of Pure Government, and O. Skinyer, the People's Solicitor, had finally driven the rascals out. The Mausoleum Club, on Plutoria Avenue, was the scene of great rejoicing; romantic music wafted through the air while the victorious reformers congratulated each other on their splendid triumph. "And as they talked, the good news spread from group to group that it was already known that the new franchise of Citizen's Light was to be made for two centuries so as to give the company a fair chance to see what it could do. At the word of it, the grave faces of manly bondholders flushed with pride, and the soft eyes of listening share-holders laughed back in joy. For they had no doubt, or fear, now that clean government had come. They knew what the company could do."[78]

CHAPTER 6

Labour and the New Society

"Unionism is undoubtedly a good thing, in some ways," the editorial voice of the Canadian Manufacturers' Association announced in 1909, "but like strychnine, it must be taken in small doses."[1] That comment adequately sums up the businessman's attitude to trade unions during the quarter of a century before the Treaty of Versailles. For working people, unions were becoming indispensable. The impersonal work place, the national and often international organization of business enterprise, and the economic fluctuations which brought slowdowns and unemployment, necessitated unionization to provide protection and security. Moreover, labour was directly affected by immigration, for the newcomers were not merely agricultural pioneers. Perhaps a third of them went in search of work in mines, mills, factories, and on the railways. Naturally, organized labour strenuously opposed cheap contract labour and "open door" immigration policies. Though both the Laurier and Borden governments paid lip-service to labour's immigration principles, in reality the economic imperatives of a capitalist labour market governed immigration policy.

Only strong unions could give the workers an effective voice at the bargaining table and with government. But union organizers had a difficult time in these turbulent years, years which witnessed frequently bitter labour strife and sometimes violence. The source of the greatest trouble was in the coal mining industries in British Columbia and Nova Scotia, in the west coast fishing industry (where class conflict was complicated by Japanese-Indian-white animosity), and in the Quebec textiles industry. But, in fact, few areas were left peacefully untouched. Winnipeg was the scene of a bitter street railwaymen's strike in 1906 that revealed the potential for serious cleavage in that city. Brockville, and other railway towns, experienced rioting and property damage during the 1910 Grand Trunk strike. At Fort William, during a freight handlers' walkout in 1909, eleven special constables and an unknown number of workers were wounded during a pitched battle. In 1911 Canada's newly acquired second-hand cruiser, *The Rainbow*, helped to suppress a violent strike of street labourers in Prince Rupert. While not entirely typical, the events surrounding a saw mill employees' strike at Buckingham, Quebec, during September and October 1906 brutally revealed the division of power in the Canadian industrial world. After the company had refused a mediation offer from the Department of Labour, on the ground that it would not deal with an "international union," violence broke out. Even the unemotional prose of the *Labour Gazette* could not hide the underlying savagery. "On October 8th, the company attempted to bring down some logs with the help of men working under the protection of special police and detectives. A large number of strikers had gathered and, in an effort to prevent the work from proceeding, a serious riot occurred in which two strikers were shot and killed and several others injured. One detective was fatally injured, and three others seriously injured." Then the militia, and later regular troops, arrived to restore order. "No agreement was ever reached, but on October 24th the mill resumed normal operations, the strikers either having capitulated or found work elsewhere."[2] In circumstances such as these union organization was slow and demanding work.

I

Trade unions and working men's associations had begun to develop permanent structures in Canada by the middle of the nineteenth century. For the most part they were limited to skilled trades such as printers, shipwrights, and engineers. Often the Canadian unions were associated with parent unions in Great Britain or the United States, or were begun by immigrants with union experience in their homelands. The Amalgamated Society of Carpenters and Joiners was an example of a British union transplanted to Canada at mid-century, while the Knights of Labour crossed the border from the United States in the 1880s. By 1883 the first serious stirrings of a movement toward labour unity were in evidence. In 1886 the Trades and Labour Congress of Canada was founded, composed almost exclusively of unions in Ontario and Quebec.[3] Unionism fared poorly during the economic slump of the nineties, but gained new momentum with the general improvement of economic conditions toward the end of the century. Indeed these years witnessed the greatest expansion of labour organization in the country's history up to that time.

The organization of Canadian workers continued under the auspices of two major labour associations. The first was the increasingly powerful group of international unions associated with Samuel Gompers' American Federation of Labour. The other was a Canadian body, the Trades and Labour Congress of Canada, whose goal was to become the national labour centre for Canadian unions. Of approximately 20,000 unionists in

Canada in 1900, only about 8,000 were in Canadian unions, the rest being A.F. of L. affiliates.[4] Events were already proving that the Canadian labour centre was too weak and too short of funds and organizational skills to meet the challenge of the American affiliated unions. Increasingly, Canadian workers joined the A.F. of L. unions with the result that the Canadian labour movement, to a large extent, became part of a continental organization. The T.L.C., instead of becoming a Canadian Federation of Labour, fell into the role of something close to a state federation within the A.F. of L.[5]

Accompanying the growing influence of the A.F. of L. unions in Canada were two important developments. Since the Gompers' type unions eschewed independent political action, those Canadian working men who took a cue from their British brethren and wanted to form a labour-socialist political movement were left without a broad, unified base. Secondly, while the A.F. of L. unions brought strength to certain segments of Canadian labour, and doubtless aided in improving wages and working conditions, they also contributed to the fragmentation of the Canadian movement. Jealous of their power, and especially suspicious of "political unionism" or "dual unionism," the A.F. of L. unions forced deviationist groups out of the central T.L.C. organization. Consequently, some Quebec workers, fearful of the American influence in the internationals, and anxious to retain an association with the Roman Catholic Church, remained aloof from the major labour central. So, too, more radical unionists on the west coast, and to some extent on the prairies, found the "business unionism" of the internationals timid and unacceptable. They, too, remained outside, preventing a unified national movement from emerging. The British Labour politician, Ramsay MacDonald, remarked shrewdly on this state of affairs after a visit to Canada in 1906. "Canada," he noted, "could not be treated as a whole. There are three different sections. . . . [In Quebec] the workers were organized on a national basis. They would have nothing to do with the other parts of the Colony. . . . The middle section was a long narrow strip of territory including Ontario and the great western agricultural districts with its centre at Winnipeg. In this division there was a strong trades union feeling but, strange to say, the governing power was situated in Washington, United States. The remaining section was that of the Western side of the Rocky Mountains to the sea."[6] MacDonald might also have observed that even in Quebec and British Columbia the American influence was far from absent: the Knights of Labour, though very much Canadianized, still had a strong following in Quebec, while the more radical U.S. unions, such as the Western Federation of Miners, were making an important impact on the volatile labour scene beyond the Rockies. The most important group in the Maritimes, the Provincial Workmen's Association, was carrying on a losing battle with the internationals.

The reasons for the growth of the U.S. based unions in Canada were manifold. Not least important was Samuel Gompers' vision of the international unity of the working classes–a unity which he hoped to see develop under A.F. of L. leadership. He attempted to build up associations with unions throughout the industrialized world, but the greatest success was in Canada.[7] There were other, more concrete, factors. One was the movement of working people across the international boundary. Canadians who moved into the United States during the depressed nineties often participated in union activity. It was natural enough that upon their return home they should bring their union affiliations with them. Moreover, men engaged in similar trades on either side of the international border felt certain common interests. Equal pay for similar work seemed a reasonable demand that could best be obtained by a united front. From the U.S. workers' viewpoint, parity of wages and conditions of work may have appeared desirable to prevent U.S. industries from moving to Canada to take advantage of cheaper labour.

And, of course, United States capital was moving into Canada partly to exploit Canada's rich resource industries, partly to take advantage of Canada's tariff policy, and, no doubt, partly to take advantage of Canada's less well organized labour force. If capital was becoming "international," it seemed perfectly normal that labour organization should follow suit. The flag might not follow investment, but trade unions did. Gompers himself emphasized this during a strike at a United States owned firm in London, Ontario, in 1900. Speaking in Toronto, he urged the workers to "put forth the greatest efforts to help the men in London to put down the American capitalists who have come into the country to oppress Canadian workingmen. When the Yankee capitalist did this it was but natural that the Yankee agitator should follow him."[8]

Whether the development was as natural as Gompers suggested is questionable. Certainly his Washington office expended a good deal of energy in supporting the growth of the International's hegemony over the Canadian labour movement. Most Canadian labour leaders gave their support, though not uncritically, to the growth of Gomperism in their country. Often they even asked for more: more organizational help and more financial support, though they occasionally complained loudly about union dues flowing into the A.F. of L. coffers in Washington. But their solidarity with the U.S. leadership was strong, the more so no doubt because of the habit of Canadian business leaders, and their political allies, of branding strong unions with the foreign domination iron. "The glaring lies, the naked and unashamed mendacity of the salaried American strike-breeders . . . actuated solely by a desire to do damage, to run amok,"[9] was the way one business journal described A.F. of L. organizers in 1909. If the employing classes, who were not always above importing strike-breakers from the United States (as was done to break the Rossland Miners' strike in 1901[10]) denounced "foreign agitators," it was a sure sign that these same agitators were helping Canadian workers. Certainly during a bitter strike in Glace Bay in 1909, the support given by the employers to the Provincial Workmen's Association against the United Mine Workers of America was based on more than unmitigated patriotism. "It is simply bluff and hypocrisy on the part of the Company when they set up the cry that they are opposing this new union because it is a foreign organization which is seeking to control Canadian industries," a Glace Bay priest wrote realistically. "If the new union were a weak and miserable organization like the Provincial Workman's [sic] Association, which became a tool of the company and a traitor to the poor miners, the Company would soon recognize it, if it were even a Chinese union."[11]

The dominance of the A.F. of L. unions in the Canadian labour movement was not achieved without a struggle, for there was opposition from some businessmen, some politicians, and some trade unionists. As early as 1896 some Canadian labour leaders were expressing a desire to preserve and increase the autonomy of their organizations. Among the most notable were the men associated with the Knights of Labour assemblies which were strong in Quebec. These unions maintained their traditional hostility toward the A.F. of L. unions, though in constrast to the United States, the craft unions and the Knights in Canada worked fairly successfully together in the T.L.C. But the Knights were at a disadvantage once the T.L.C.'s need for money and organizational experience forced it into a growing dependence upon the A.F. of L. By 1898, in return for fees paid by Canadian workers to A.F. of L. unions, the T.L.C. was receiving an annual grant of $100 from Washington to finance pressure for improved labour legislation. Between 1898 and 1902 unions in Canada grew at an unprecedented rate. Unions sponsored by the T.L.C. and the A.F. of L. spread into a variety of new trades, and from almost every part of the Dominion appeals came into the T.L.C. offices for organizational and monetary assistance. In 1899, as part of a general organizational campaign the A.F. of L. vastly enlarged its Canadian operation. The following year, John Flett of Hamilton was appointed as a full-time general organizer for the A.F. of L. in Canada.[12] As vice-president of the T.L.C., Flett was an extremely able and energetic organizer and, since he was a Canadian, he was immune to the charge that he was a foreign trouble maker. Almost alone, he was responsible for the largest share of the more than 140 international union locals chartered in Canada in 1900. By the end of 1902 there were 60-70,000 organized unionists in Canada, and much of this increase was due to the aggressive activities of the A.F. of L. unions. That same aggressiveness allowed the A.F. of L. to undermine the T.L.C. as a national labour centre.[13]

Early conflicts between the A.F. of L. unions and the T.L.C. turned on a variety of questions. One source of friction was the continued activity of the Knights of Labour in Canada. This old enemy of the Gompers' unions provided severe competition for new members, and opened jurisdictional conflicts with the A.F. of L. unions in important centres like Montreal. The goal of the A.F. of L. unions quickly became the expulsion of the Knights from the T.L.C., after which they could be destroyed. Some of the leaders of the Knights favoured the development of a wholly autonomous Canadian labour movement, and in this they had the support of T.L.C. president, and Member of Parliament, Ralph Smith. Without going quite this far, several Congress officials favoured the development of the T.L.C. as the central authority in organizational matters without cutting off A.F. of L. affiliations. By 1901 there appeared to be a movement building up within the T.L.C. for strengthening the Canadian labour centre against the independent activities of the U.S. unions. This was a development which Samuel Gompers viewed with considerable distaste and even alarm. In 1902, at the Berlin Convention of the T.L.C., steps were taken to nip this nationalist labour sentiment in the bud.

The controversy at Berlin centred on two essential questions. First was the question of the status of the delegates representing Knights of Labour Assemblies. Second was the position of those Trades Councils, such as the one in Montreal, which had not been chartered by the A.F. of L. In fact, both disputes boiled down to the question of whether the T.L.C. was to exist as an autonomous labour centre under its own rules, or whether it was to be run according to the wishes of the A.F. of L. unions. "If we are to do anything for the trade union movement in Canada," the British Columbia vice-president of the T.L.C. wrote accurately in 1902, "we must do it at once, or else all our organizations will become American organizations."[14] The outcome of the Berlin meeting was to give the A.F. of L. unions effective control over the T.L.C. The Congress accepted a report excluding the Knights of Labour from membership, denying recognition to the Montreal Trades Council, and ruling against recognition of national unions in trades where internationals already existed. John Flett's election as president of the T.L.C. clearly displayed the triumph of the international unions.

The result of the Berlin congress was a profound division in the ranks of Canadian labour. Twenty-three organizations, mostly from Quebec, were driven out of the Trades and Labour Congress of Canada. These unions subsequently formed the Canadian Labour Federation. This, in itself, seriously limited the right of the T.L.C. to represent itself as an all-Canadian labour centre. Though the internationals retained some support in Quebec, the basis was now laid for the growth of a separate, Catholic labour organization among French-speaking workers. Moreover, the T.L.C., in accepting the demands of the A.F. of L. affiliates in membership standards, had agreed to occupy the position of a state federation of labour. Thus the 1902 decision meant not merely the fracturing of the east-west ties of the labour movement, but also the establishment of an essentially continental association for a large segment of the organized Canadian work force.

Thus, while the ranks of unionized labour grew rapidly in the first decade of the new century, advancing to some 100,000 members by 1914, it lacked unity. The divisions in the labour movement reflected in part, but also contributed to, the country's sectionalism. This meant that labour spoke with a divided voice on public matters affecting the welfare of the workers. In the face of divisions, even among the minority of the workers who were organized, governments could move at their own chosen speed in introducing legislation to improve working conditions and to remove the danger of serious conflict in a society rapidly moving into an industrialized state.

Certain kinds of workers, often those most in need of protection, were left unorganized. This class included, in particular, the navvies, "foreign" and "white," who worked in clearing bush, mucking, and laying the road beds for the railway builders. These workers, or bunkhouse men, often lived like indentured labourers. Their wages were low; their dependence on the contractor or sub-contractor for transportation, food, clothing and accommodation was nearly total; and their ability to obtain redress of grievances was almost non-existent. The work crews were usually a miniature vertical mosaic with the Canadians, French and English, holding the best positions, and the other ethnic groups descending down the scale. The new immigrant, unfamiliar with the country, often unable to speak English, and desperate for work, frequently became the exploited navvy of the northern work camps, the "coolies" of the twentieth-century railway builder. "As the wage system actually worked out on the National Transcontinental," Edwin Bradwin wrote, "apart from losing his personal liberty, a man would have been more comfortable, less molested with flies and mosquitoes, would have had a real bed and much better sanitary surroundings if, instead of going for six months to railway camps, he had gone to Kingston penitentiary."[15]

These conditions often produced dangerous discontent, though less frequently than might have been expected. At a Grand Trunk Pacific camp, where a violent strike took place early in 1912, the cause was obvious enough. "In one of the Tierney camps," a reporter wrote, "the bunks were built three tiers high and the men after waking each morning . . . with raging headaches, tore down the top bunk. . . . In other camps the floors were laid directly upon the ground instead of 18 inches above (as provided by law), insufficient air space was allowed and wash houses and bath houses were of the vilest sort."[16] Though there were some government regulations about fair wages and sanitary working conditions, they seem often to have gone unenforced perhaps because inspectors were neither numerous nor diligent enough.[17] Despite the fact that these men were obviously in need of union support, orthodox labour leaders made little effort to reach into the labour camps, apart from passing occasional resolutions at Congress meetings. What little union activity there was among these workers, particularly in British Columbia, was that of radicals like the International Workers of the World. Even that was only sporadic and largely ineffective.[18]

The presence of the "wobblies," and other radical agitators, was nevertheless unsettling, and indicated there was need for some serious attention to the men in the camps. It was to provide some assistance to these men that Rev. Alfred Fitzpatrick, a socially conscious Presbyterian minister, established the Reading Camp Association, later known as Frontier College, in 1899.[19] Its purpose was to bring the rudiments of education to the men in the camps, thus providing them with some opportunity for better use of leisure time and ultimately for increased social mobility. For the foreigner the Reading Camp Association representative was the means whereby he could become "Canadianized." This, in turn, was supposed to insulate him against radical agitators, "to determine whether there is evolved a Lincoln or a Lenin," as one Frontier College leader put it.[20] Whatever their effect on the political views of the navvies, the Frontier College teachers played an enormously significant part in breaking down the isolation of work camps, and providing avenues for some men to move into more satisfying employment.

A second though very different group which received very little attention from union organizers were women. In 1900 the Canadian labour force contained about 100,000 women, of whom about ten per cent were younger than sixteen.[21] These women workers engaged in a wide variety of employment, especially in the canning and textiles industries. Generally speaking their wages and types of work were on a lower scale than those of their male counterparts. A contemporary comment on the condition of labouring women reveals, both intentionally and unintentionally, some of the causes for this inequality. "It is true in the majority of establishments where both men and women are employed, women are assigned to inferior and less important work, not being, as a rule, so thoroughly trained, or able physically to do men's work. . . . This discrepancy will doubtless always exist between the wages of men and women until the latter go in more generally for scientific training, and also until they take a leaf out of the men's book, and form themselves into strong unions for mutual protection. This species of co-operation, however, seems to be more-or-less foreign to woman's nature."[22] Insofar as this was accurate, trade union leaders did little to resolve the problem, at least until the war years made women a more significant part of the labour force. In the meantime, conditions which women faced in the world of work provided stimulus for the suffragists, who felt that only the vote would guarantee fairer treatment.[23]

II

The failure of the established unions to rise to these challenges was not due, in any large measure, to self-satisfied inertia. Even in the easily accessible industrial centres, union organizers met formidable opposition. While unions had legal recognition, that did not prevent employers from resisting their growth. The Canadian Manufacturers' Association was especially active in opposing legislation to improve the position of unions, and employers banded together to form common fronts to fight union demands, and particularly to defend the open shop.[24] Not all employers would have dared to express themselves as bluntly as James Dunsmuir, one-time premier of British Columbia and near lord of all he surveyed. But many would have sympathized with the answer he gave to a Royal Commission in 1903:

QUESTION :   Do you know of any real cause for the difficulty which the men have now in the mines?

ANSWER :   No I do not. The only trouble is because I won't let them belong to the union. They can belong to the union if they like. I don't care. I have my rights. I can hire them if I like, and they can work if they like.

QUESTION :   Have you not, when you became aware of a man belonging to the union got rid of him?

ANSWER :   You mean fired the heads of the union?

QUESTION :   Yes.

ANSWER :   Every time.[25]

Some employers, combining genuine concern for their workers with a desire to weaken the union organizers' appeal, introduced various plant improvements for their work force: baths and showers, company excursions and picnics, profit-sharing and, in a few cases, pensions.

Employers could often rely on governments to come to their assistance if labour difficulties got out of hand. Describing an especially tumultuous strike in the British Columbia fishing industry in 1900, one reporter wrote, "the militia has been called out to maintain order at the fishing village of Steveson . . . where 1500 fishermen, attached to 47 canneries, are on strike, preventing 4,000 Japanese and Indians from fishing. . . . Colonel Woarsh, Officer Commanding, announced that his men had not come there for amusement, but for business; that each man had four rounds of ball cartridge and at the first sign of interference they would fire and the work would be short but quick."[26] Similarly in the long and violent strike at the Dominion Coal Company in Glace Bay in 1909, where the standard wage was $1.50 per day and earnings averaged $381.45 annually,[27] troops were called in on the pretext of preserving law and order. But the action was also clearly to the benefit of the company.[28] One newspaperman remarked that "the military are used not only to preserve order where so far there has been little disorder, but they are a material assistance to the mining companies in wearing out the patience and the capacity to resist of the men."[29] Nor were businessmen slow to express their appreciation to the federal authorities for the expeditious defence of their interests. "Permit me to congratulate you," the President of the Bank of Montreal wrote to Sir Wilfrid, "on your prompt action in sending troops to Cape Breton. It is undoubtedly saving riot, bloodshed and much destruction of property, and as we have large interests in that section of the country, we have reason to be thankful."[30]

Employers, though often either American financed or affiliated, were particularly concerned about the increasing strength of the A.F. of L. unions in Canada. Obviously these unions added great strength to the Canadian labour movement, and employers were fully aware of the gains the A.F. of L. unions were winning in the United States. Therefore it is not surprising that there were frequent denunciations of the "Americanization" of the Canadian worker. Shortly after the Berlin congress of the T.L.C., a major effort was launched by spokesmen for Canadian business to rid the country of American unions. In April 1903 the Senate debated a proposal, put forward by a western Conservative, James Lougheed, which would have made it a crime punishable by two-year imprisonment for a citizen of the United States to enter Canada to assist striking workers. The effect of the proposal, had it become law, would have been to destroy the A.F. of L. base in Canada and to weaken the Canadian labour movement. Senator Lougheed set the tone of much of the debate when he remarked that " . . . the conditions of labour in the Dominion of Canada and the United States are vastly different. We know very well that certain classes of labour in the United States are becoming very largely tainted through the importation of those anarchistic classes from southern Europe that have [caused] the very many upheavals of industrial life in that country."[31] Some Senators felt that the bill was too limited, failing to name the A.F. of L. specifically. A few opposed it. In July the bill passed the Senate and went to the House of Commons.

The lower house was not untouched by the sentiments of the Senate debate. The years 1902 and 1903 had been marked by widespread labour unrest with major strikes, from the miners and railwaymen of British Columbia to the longshoremen of Montreal. The Laurier government consequently was under increasingly heavy pressure from employers to take some action that would curb labour and display to Canadian workers "the injuries that have come to them because of the interference of the American union."[32] Labour was not unaware of this mounting hostility. Gompers and Flett set out to counter it by organizing Canadian labour leaders to oppose publicly the Lougheed bill.[33] The result was that the bill died before it was considered by the House of Commons.

In 1903 a federal Royal Commission was appointed to examine the troubled labour scene in British Columbia. The Commission's *Report* was highly critical of the activities of United States unions on the west coast, particularly the radical Western Federation of Miners, but its recommendations pointed to investigation, conciliation, and arbitration as the best means of avoiding future labour-management conflicts. It also suggested the need to curb "illegitimate" trade unions controlled by foreigners.[34] The Commission's *Report* produced no immediate results. The Laurier government was apparently unwilling to face the hostility of the T.L.C. that any legislation limiting A.F. of L. activities would produce. Indeed the Liberals appear to have gradually accepted the conclusion that A.F of L. unions were legitimate, even desirable, in contrast to the dangerous "revolutionary socialists" who were thought to be behind much of the strife in British Columbia.[35] A successor to the Lougheed bill, introduced into the Senate in 1907 at the instigation of the Canadian Manufacturers' Association, died a quick death.[36]

If United States unions were a source of worry to businessmen and politicians in Canada, United States businessmen were also sometimes a source of labour unrest. The Grand Trunk Railway president, C.M. Hays, was an American citizen. Though the recipient of government largesse, Hays' railway did little to provide model conditions for Canadian workers. In fact, it was the centre of several long and brutal strikes. During a dispute at the Stratford shops in 1905 Sir William Mulock told the Prime Minister that the time had come to put Hays in his place. "I have had to do with a good many employers of labour in Canada," the Minister wrote in anger, "and with all truthfulness can say that the most heartless, cruel, and tyrannical employers that have ever come under my observation are those of the Grand Trunk."[37] Laurier took no action, and he may later have regretted it. In 1910 another strike took place against the Grand Trunk. Despite the best efforts of the Minister of Labour, W.L.M. King, Hays refused even moderate concessions, instead firing workers, and later, despite an agreement, refusing to reinstate them. King's failure with Hays may well have contributed in a small way to the Laurier government's downfall in the 1911 election, for labour was left disenchanted with the Liberals.[38]

Despite the hostility to unions among many employers the trade union movement, at least among the skilled workers, made large strides during the early years of the century. The growing economy and the consequent demand for labour gave the union organizers leverage to win workers to the movement. As the country became increasingly industrialized and the unions grew in strength, governments found it politically profitable to listen to at least the moderate claims of the working classes. In several important areas legislation was enacted to aid in smoothing the advance of the country toward an industrial society.

III

Until the end of the nineteenth century labour problems were not an area of great responsibility for Canadian governments. Jurisdiction was divided between federal and provincial authorities with the latter holding the preponderant power. Before 1909 there was no separate Minister of Labour in the federal cabinet and it was really only in 1900 that a labour department staff began to develop. The Minister responsible for these beginnings was Sir William Mulock, the Postmaster General. In 1909, speaking in support of the legislation establishing a separate Department of Labour, Sir Wilfrid Laurier summed up the preceding period. "This legislation," he noted,

> in our judgment, is rendered necessary by the ever-growing dignity and importance of labour questions and labour problems. The word "labour" is a rather complex term. It has many significations but so far as this legislation is concerned, we understand by labour the relations between wage-earners and wage-payers. It is not disputed that for generations and generations the wage earners had scarcely any standing in the community. The only right the law acknowledged to the labouring men was that they could sue in a court of law for the miserable pittance paid to them. As to the other rights of labour, as to the dignity of labour as a class, the views of the civilized world, up to perhaps fifty or sixty years ago, were very crude. . . . At last labour has been advanced to the dignity of a class in itself, and quite as important in the economy of society as any other class.[39]

W.L.M. King was the chief architect of the Department of Labour and of the policies of the Laurier government in the labour field.[40] In 1909 he became the first Minister of Labour. At twenty-six, fresh from studies in economics and social science in the United States and abroad, the grandson of the rebel of 1837 had been appointed editor of the newly established *Labour Gazette* in 1900. The establishment of the *Gazette* was one indication of the government's growing sensitivity to the labour question, and of the new bureaucratic demand for detailed information. The labour publication was welcomed by the unions, and opposed by the Canadian Manufacturers' Association, who viewed it an organ for labour propaganda. In attempting to allay this fear, King revealed his own thinking about the government's role in industrial relations. "The subjects dealt with will of course be those which primarily concern the working classes but there is no intention to make the publication other than an entirely impartial one, which should commend itself to the manufacturers as well as to the men. If it fails to do this its chief purpose would be lost for as an official publication it is not sent out in the interest of any special class but for the good of the industrial community as a whole."[41]

King was certainly no radical; he was not even a labour man. Rather he was, among other things, one of a new breed of social scientists who were appearing in many parts of North America, filled with the desire to find the means of resolving the tensions of industrial society. The first steps toward solution lay in serious, empirical investigation, after which reasonable men could come to agreement about necessary action. When agreement could not be reached by conflicting parties in an industrial dispute, government arbitration would then be necessary. In this context government was viewed as a neutral party, representing the general interest. Certainly this was not a radical philosophy, but even the extent to which King recognized the importance of labour and unions, and his willingness to promote government intervention in industrial disputes, placed him in advance of most members of the Laurier government. In 1903, King set out his views in a Royal Commission report. "One of the results of the spread of unionism throughout the various trades," he wrote,

> has been to put the workman in a better position to make terms with his employer; to preserve his independence of character, he is now able to drive a hard bargain and does not have to accept a dole. Formerly employers were too often in the habit of regarding their men as so many machines or units of labour, and those of them who felt humane instincts thought they fulfilled their whole obligation if they gave an occasional extra remuneration or bonus, or conferred some benefit which they regarded as a gratuity. But the workman of modern times demands as his due a fair day's pay for a fair day's work, and that he shall get a reasonable share of the product of his toil; what he seeks is honourable employment, not slavery, he wants fair dealing and justice, and not charity or patronage.[42]

King's ideas, and those of the Laurier government, placed the government in the role of umpire. Even before King entered the Department of Labour this attitude had been displayed, to some extent, in the Alien Labour Law of 1897. This enactment, requested by the unions, was designed to prevent aliens from entering the country as contract labour. In essence it was a response to similar legislation in the United States, and Laurier only accepted it on that basis. He would have preferred a "free" labour market, but was forced to intervene on behalf of Canadian labour because of the action of the U.S. authorities.[43] So, too, the government was willing to pass a Fair Wages resolution to prohibit sweating in industries working under government contract. More characteristic of the Liberal approach was the series of acts designed to prevent labour disputes from ending in strikes and lockouts by using conciliation and arbitration. The first of these acts, under which the Department of Labour itself was established, was the Conciliation Act of 1900. It authorized the federal government to appoint conciliation officers or a conciliation board, on the request of employers or workmen involved in a dispute. Neither party was obliged to accept the conciliation board's conclusions. Rather the report was intended to focus attention on the dispute and, and through public education, force a reasonable settlement. There were some successful settlements under this legislation, notably in the textiles industry at Valleyfield in the autumn of 1900. But where the sides in the dispute were too far apart, or too rigid, as at Rossland, B.C. in the 1901 miners' strike, conciliation proved ineffective.[44]

Nevertheless the government did not lose faith in this voluntary approach. A strike of C.P.R. trackmen in 1901 led to the enactment of the Railway Labour Disputes Act in 1903. It differed from the earlier conciliation legislation in that it permitted the Minister of Labour to take the initiative in appointing a tri-partite conciliation board. The act was invoked only once, and produced a settlement. This experience contributed to the federal government's decision to broaden the legislation's application in 1907 following a nearly calamitous strike in the Alberta coal fields. That strike began in March and stretched on into the fall and early winter of 1906. For many prairie people Alberta coal was crucial to survival in the far-below-zero weather of a western winter, and some farmers were reduced to burning almost anything at hand to save themselves from the cold in November. King was dispatched to the strike scene where he found both sides adamantly opposed to a compromise. But heavy public pressure finally forced them to do so, and also convinced the Laurier government that new, more effective means of strike settlement were required. The result was the Industrial Disputes Investigation Act, prepared by King but guided through the House of Commons by Rodolphe Lemieux in 1907.

The Lemieux Act contained an important new departure for federal labour legislation: a minor element of compulsion. The act prohibited strikes and lockouts in public utilities and mines until the dispute had been investigated by a three-man board. Conciliation was still the essence of the procedure; in the final analysis neither party was to be bound by the investigatory board's finding, and public opinion was expected to force a settlement. The somewhat unrealistic liberal philosophy behind the act was well expressed some years later by the Deputy Minister of Labour, the act's architect. "Investigation is letting in light," King wrote, " . . . willingness to investigate is *prima facie* evidence of consciousness of right. In the absence of good and sufficient reasons, refusal to permit investigation is equally *prima facie* evidence of weakness and wrong."[45]

Labour's response to the Lemieux Act was somewhat ambiguous. Alphonse Verville, a Labour M.P. and one-time president of the T.L.C., endorsed the Act when it was introduced. The T.L.C. Convention of 1907, after a lengthy debate, also gave its approval to the new legislation. Nevertheless, there was some fear among unionists that the period of delay provided by the procedure would allow the employer to engage strikebreakers. There was also concern that the Act might lead eventually to compulsory arbitration.[46] By 1910 the T.L.C. reversed its position, having now had three years of experience under the legislation, and indicated its opposition to the Lemieux Act, an attitude strongly favoured by the Washington headquarters of the A.F. of L.[47]

The Industrial Disputes Investigation Act epitomized the Laurier government's policy on labour matters. In industrial disputes it was prepared at best to act as a neutral, at worst as a partisan of management. Under the act, strikes, lockouts, boycotts, and picketting were prohibited while the investigation was in process. But nothing prevented employers from discharging employees or running their plants with strike-breakers. While the legislation gave partial recognition to unions, in practice there was a strong tendency to settle disputes between employers and "committees of employees" rather than official union representatives; the principles of union recognition and collective bargaining were not fully accepted. Moreover, increasing labour conflict after 1907 suggests that the Industrial Disputes Investigation Act did little to achieve even its major goal: the prevention of strikes and lockouts.[48] Along with the Combines Investigation Act of 1910, the Industrial Disputes Investigation Act clearly revealed how tentative was the Laurier government's willingness to guide the development of the new industrial society. Both these pieces of legislation placed heavy emphasis on investigation, and displayed obvious faith in the rationality of public opinion. The government's basic view was that in a free market economy public authorities could set down guide lines, but in the end public opinion would have to force compliance.

The new Department of Labour, among many other activities, gathered statistics under the capable direction of Robert Coats, later the first Dominion Statistician; attempted to enforce fair wages agreements; and assisted in the work of Royal Commissions, on such matters as Oriental labour.[49]

Since labour legislation was only partly a federal responsibility, many enactments to soften the harshness of a burgeoning industrial system were passed by provincial legislatures. Even the Lord's Day Observance Act, passed in 1906 to prohibit most types of Sunday work, thus guaranteeing labouring people at least one day of rest, was left in the hands of provincial Attorneys General for enforcement, not least of all because of a Quebec suspicion that the act was a Protestant attack on Catholicism.[50] The provinces, especially Ontario and Quebec, moved cautiously into many areas of labour and social legislation. Every province except Prince Edward Island had established Workman's Compensation legislation by 1911. So, too, factory acts setting minimum ages for employment, limiting hours of work for women and young persons, and setting up safety regulations were passed in nearly every province by the outbreak of the Great War. Gradually a team of inspectors was recruited to enforce these laws, although action was not always effective. In 1910, in an effort to find the means for working men to upgrade their skills, the Laurier government appointed the Royal Commission on Industrial Training and Technical Education.[51]

IV

While most working people, when they had time for politics, gave their support to the Liberal and Conservative parties, the late nineteenth century witnessed the birth of small groups advocating labour and socialist politics. Radical political views often came to Canada with the immigrants from the United States and Great Britain. As immigration, urbanization and industrialization picked up momentum after the turn of the century, there was a proliferation of often unconnected and competing groups advocating fundamental reform of Canadian capitalism. Spokesmen for these organizations often made their voices heard at the conventions of the T.L.C. and other labour bodies, but they were never able to win over the official labour bodies either to effective labour political action or to the acceptance of a socialist political programme. No doubt this was partly due to the ascendancy of the A.F. of L. type unions in Canada; these preferred the Gompers' tradition of rewarding friends and punishing enemies irrespective of party stripe.[52] But there were other reasons too. Unionization seemed more important than political action, and the years of relative prosperity, even for the workers, reduced the attraction of radical doctrines.

From its foundation the T.L.C. had worked as a pressure group demanding legislation beneficial to the working classes, and by the mid-nineties it was advocating direct political action. The problem was to choose the most effective means. By the end of the century there already existed a branch of Daniel De Leon's Socialist Labour Party, and a more moderate

Christian socialist group, the Canadian Socialist League, which supported candidates in the Ontario provincial election of 1902. The following year two socialists won election in British Columbia. Many other urban centres, notably Winnipeg where the staunchly labourite paper, the *Voice*, had been established, witnessed the birth of small labour and socialist groups anxious to win the support of workers for their plans to replace capitalism with a more humane, co-operative, and egalitarian society.

Sometimes the differences between various socialist and labour political groups were as deep as the differences between the socialists and their capitalist foes. In endless disputes over doctrine and tactics, some groups demanded the preservation of pure socialist doctrine, and others called for a coalition of socialist and reform groups such as the British Columbia Progressive party. Still others insisted that labour should work for reform independent of the doctrinaire, middle-class socialists who claimed, without credentials, to speak for the workers. British Columbia exhibited all the extremes, and representatives of almost every imaginable socialist sect found some small support in the warm west coast climate. One group in Nanaimo, calling itself the Revolutionary Socialist Party of Canada, denounced its rival Socialist Party of British Columbia and declared righteously: "The Revolutionary Socialist Party of Canada proclaims itself the political exponent of the working class interests. It will deviate neither to the right nor to the left of the line laid down in its platform. It will neither endorse nor accept endorsement. It has no compromises to make."[53]

British Columbia, despite sectarian quarrelling, was the area where labour was most active in politics. The fluidity of the political scene, and the rudimentary working conditions in many of the frontier industries, gave labour an opportunity it lacked elsewhere.[54] The election of Ralph Smith, a long-time advocate of independent labour politics and president of the T.L.C. (1898-1902), was really the result of a Lib-Lab alliance. Some Liberals were quick to recognize the implications. "Should your policy be advanced to cover their reasonable demands," a British Columbia Liberal advised Laurier, "I am of the opinion that forming a new political party will be quite unnecessary. It is as you know not an easy matter to keep a new political party in existence especially where a progressive party is moving to advance its lines."[55] Smith, who was never trusted by the more radical elements in British Columbia, eventually became a straight Liberal. The next Labour M.P. to win election was Arthur Puttee of Winnipeg, who sat as a member of the Independent Labour Party. A third, who also had served as president of the T.L.C., was Alphonse Verville of Montreal. Like Smith he was very close to the Liberals on most issues. After several efforts he won government approval in 1910 for an eight-hour-day regulation in the federal jurisdiction. The bill was lost in the Senate.[56] In federal politics labour was not nearly strong enough or united enough consistently to elect members without the support or co-operation of one of the existing parties, usually the Liberals. For the most part they turned out to be men like Ralph Smith, who readily admitted that "it is the Liberal cause for which I have strong sympathy."[57]

The victories of Smith and Puttee in 1900, and the activities of labour in British Columbia politics, acted as a spur to the T.L.C. But there were profound differences over the best means of taking political action. On the one hand there was serious and growing criticism of the manner in which men like Smith were co-opted by the Liberals. Then there was conflict between the advocates of a strictly labour party, and those who wanted a party with a strongly socialist platform. These divisions went a long way toward neutralizing labour's political effectiveness. So, too, the expulsion of the Knights of Labour in 1902, and the dominance of the A.F. of L. philosophy, meant that the impulse toward politics was weakened. Without unity of purpose there could not be strength.

But interest in political action never died out. Perhaps because of Labour's victories in Great Britain in 1906 – Ramsay MacDonald attended the T.L.C. convention that year – the issue was taken up with fresh vigour at the Victoria convention. Some of the socialist delegates, including T.L.C. Vice-President James Simpson of Toronto, called upon the Congress to organize either an independent labour party or a socialist party. Underlying this demand was the belief that it would be in "the best interests of the wage workers of Canada if they will voluntarily sever their connection with all parties not organized in the interest of the proletarian class."[58] But the Congress was not ready to go that far. Instead, it endorsed a long statement of legislative goals, and called for the election of labour representatives to Parliament.

In subsequent months an effort was made by the Congress to organize a Canadian labour party. But the competition between labourites and socialists, especially in British Columbia, made the effort virtually impossible.[59] This internecine war was to continue for many years leaving the growing labour movement politically divided and weak. Perhaps the T.L.C. leadership was gradually being weaned away from the Liberal party, and there was obviously a developing sense that independent political action was necessary. But there was no consensus, not even an emerging one, on tactics. Ramsay MacDonald observed this problem: "Out here there is the nucleus of a fine Labour party. Our victories in the old country have been a great spur to the Trade Unionists here, and the men who have been hitherto Liberal and Conservative are prepared to throw in their lot with an independent party of labour. But the socialists do not understand the position. They are grinding away at their cold aggressive academic formula about 'class war,' 'economic determinism,' a 'class conscious proletariat,' and everyone who does not agree with them is a faker or a scoundrel of some degree or other."[60]

The stirrings were certainly present. The working classes had experienced most directly the impact of the new industrial society. They were forming unions to protect their interests and better their lives in the new society. A few felt that more was needed, that labour should engage directly in politics in order to change the society in a direction that would give the workers a greater share of the prosperity they saw around them. "Labour produces all wealth, and to labour it should justly belong," one socialist manifesto declaimed; "in order to free the working man from his slavery to the capitalist the wage system must be abolished and to this and other ends labour must take the reins of government away from capital."[61] But this rhetoric was too strong for most workers. They continued to support the existing parties, accepting the modest reforms of the Laurier administration and hoping to win better terms at the bargaining table. The majority of the workers still remained unorganized by 1914. So, too, there were deep divisions even among the organized workers. The T.L.C., with its A.F. of L. affiliations and business union attitude, was dominant. In parts of Quebec, the internationals were held suspect. In other parts of the country, especially on the west coast, the T.L.C. was seen as too staid and conservative, too much dominated by the complacent east. These divisions within the movement were kept in control during the years of growth. But they were nevertheless present, ready to burst forth, along with new debates over political action, during the latter years of the Great War.

CHAPTER 7

French Canada and the New Industrial Order

The rapid development of Canada after 1896 brought with it both dangers and opportunities for French-speaking Canadians. From the centre of the Empire in London, and from many parts of English-speaking Canada, came pressure for closer Canadian involvement in imperial affairs. French Canadians showed very little enthusiasm for this idea; to them integration in an English-speaking Empire had little emotional attraction but rather suggested a further reduction of their influence in shaping the community in which they lived.[1] The Boer War was the first storm signal to show the coolness of French Canadians toward involvement in imperial affairs. It also warned the French Canadians that it would not be easy to stay out.

French Canadians also felt a growing concern about the domestic development of Canada. The very success of the Laurier government's immigration policies meant that the relative power of French Canada was reduced. At Confederation Quebec had been one of four provinces; it was one of nine by 1905. Only the continuing high birth rate of French Canadians ensured that they did not fall drastically below that one-third of the total Canadian population they had represented in 1867. Certainly immigration did little to aid their numerical strength: between 1901 and 1911 only about 30,000 of some 1,500,000 immigrants were French-speaking. The consequence was obvious. "It is impossible to maintain our position," *La Tribune* of Sherbrooke observed, "when the races which surround us receive each year the reinforcement of three or four hundred thousand immigrants."[2]

Moreover, newly opening areas of the country showed little willingness to recognize French and Catholic linguistic and educational privileges. "Our apprehensions become much more lively," one French Canadian warned in 1910, "when we see forming in the vast Canadian northwest a new people, strangers to our beliefs, to our race, to our political ideals, a people which grows by the millions, and which we see will not respect the federal compact any more than is necessary. If for twenty years we

127

have only ceded our rights, what will become of us, of the official rights of our language, of our provincial franchise, of our religious liberty, when instead of a third of the population of Canada, we have become only a thirtieth?"[3]

Yet another, more subtle, more profound change within Quebec gradually became a cause of deep concern. That change was the movement away from the traditional agricultural society toward an urban and industrial one. Of course this transformation was shared with many other parts of the country, but for a variety of reasons it had an especially marked impact upon Quebec. Population movement is one measure of the change: in 1890 about one-third of Quebec's population was urban, while by 1910 the figure had risen to nearly half. By 1911 slightly less than one-third of Quebec's population was engaged in agriculture. As sociology, *Maria Chapdelaine* was already obsolete when it was published in 1913. Despite its reputation as a rural province, Quebec's economic growth and rate of production were almost identical with those of Ontario.[4]

Much of Quebec's new industry was small-scale manufacturing using skills French Canadians had acquired during earlier periods of immigration to New England: textiles, gloves, shoes, saw and flour milling, cigar and cigarette manufacturing, and bakery products. These were, for the most part, industries which employed many hands at relatively low wages, industries which were well suited to the large and generally unorganized labour force in Quebec. But there were also two new industries, which contributed in a major way to Quebec's economic growth: hydro-electricity and pulp and paper. These two industries were closely linked, one providing power for the other. Between 1900 and 1910 power production in Quebec increased by 310 per cent from 82,876 to 334,763 horse power. The pulp and paper industry developed almost as rapidly, gradually becoming the major supplier for the United States market. The aluminum and carbide industries, also associated with electricity, experienced similar rapid expansion.[5] Clearly, as André Raynauld has concluded, "the province of Quebec, like the rest of Canada and thanks to it moreover, experienced a period of 'take-off.' "[6]

Whether this "take-off" represented progress toward a better material standard of life for the majority of Quebeckers is a more complex question. Certainly at the beginning of the period conditions in a city like Montreal were far from ideal. Indeed, all the elements of a potentially serious social crisis were present. In his pioneering essay in urban sociology, Herbert Ames set out many of the problems that beset people who lived in *The City Below the Hill*.[7] Those problems were legion: low wages, long hours, frequent unemployment, child labour, overcrowded housing, inadequate or even non-existent sanitation, and high infant mortality rates because of poor diet and lack of milk pasteurization. Ames drew the contrast between the two Montreals: "The sanitary condition of the 'City Below the Hill' is a disgrace to any nineteenth century city, on this or any other continent. I presume there is hardly a house in all the upper city without modern plumbing, and yet in the lower city not less than *half* the homes have indoor water closet privileges."[8] The general lot of the working people probably did not improve, and may even have grown worse, in the so-called "boom" years before 1914. On the basis of a 1910 cost-of-living investigation, Father Joseph-Papin Archambault concluded that in 1912 the majority of the workers in Montreal lived below a decent subsistence standard. Increases in the cost of living, which exceeded wage increases, as well as lack of health and housing improvements, suggest declining conditions for working-class people even in the years of prosperity. Heavy unemployment in years of recession, such as 1907 or 1913, naturally aggravated the distress.[9]

Nevertheless, industrialization brought some distinct benefits to Quebec society. An increasing variety of occupational opportunities was opened up, and for some the general standard of living increased. Per capita income in Quebec increased at a rate equivalent to that of the national increase, though it remained below Ontario's in absolute terms.[10] But perhaps the most striking benefit of industrialization was that it provided more jobs at home for the expanding labour force of the province. Since the 1850s many hundreds of thousands of young French Canadians had found it necessary to emigrate, most frequently to the United States, in order to make a living. Now this trend was radically altered. One careful estimate clearly illustrates the change: net emigration from Quebec – 1881-91: 132,000; 1891-1901: 121,000; 1901-1911: 29,-000.[11] Industrialization thus provided an answer to what many French Canadians had considered the most serious threat to their community's survival in the later part of the nineteenth century. It was for this very reason that spokesmen for the Church, and the provincial government, worked vigorously to attract industry to Quebec. The editor of *Le Bien Public*, Bishop Cloutier's paper in Trois-Rivières, summed up this attitude very well when he wrote: "We form part of an industrial and commercial centre of the first order; our city is surrounded by five little villages and important parishes which wish only to grow; in working with all our strength for the progress of our region, *Le Bien Public* is determined to destroy the legend that the titles Catholic and French are synonymous with incompetence in business and stagnation in industrial matters."[12] In many areas the campaign to attract industry was successful: extensive resources, a large labour force, and very often low royalties and taxes, ensured capital investment.

But capital investment came only infrequently from French-Canadian sources, and for some French Canadians this was a most disturbing feature

of the new industrialization. Only a few French Canadians became successful financiers and entrepreneurs. There were the two Forgets, Senator
Louis Joseph and his nephew, Sir Rodolphe, who moved with ease in the
English-dominated financial circles of Montreal. Sir Rodolphe, who was
elected president of the Montreal Stock Exchange in 1908 and sat as a
Conservative Member of Parliament, played a major role in many new
enterprises, including Sir Herbert Holt's giant Montreal Light, Heat and
Power Company.[13] Another enterprising industrialist was Alfred Dubuc,
whose Chicoutimi Pulp Company dominated the Saguenay region and
produced a major share of the province's pulp and paper output. Other
extremely successful French-Canadian businessmen included F.L. Béique,
G.N. Ducharme, J.D. Rolland, Senator Raoul Dandurand, and Georges
E. Amyot, a powerful textiles magnate. But these men were exceptions in
a world dominated by English-Canadian, British, and American capitalists.

One reason for the relatively small representation of French Canadians
in the industrial élite of Quebec was a lack of access to capital. A striking
example of this was seen in the development of the Shawinigan Water and
Power Company. As early as 1895 a group of French Canadians from
Trois-Rivières set out to develop the hydro potential of the falls at
Shawinigan. In 1897, after some litigation, the group arranged to purchase the falls for $10,000. But before the transaction could be completed
a provincial election had brought a change of government. The new
Liberal regime of Félix Marchand was much more aware of the true
potential of the falls than its predecessor, and the terms of sale were now
steeply raised: the successful bidder would now have to pay $50,000 for
the site, agree to invest $4 million in the next two and a half years, pay
out $200,000 annually in wages, and agree to bring the plant into opera-
tion in twenty months. The local French-Canadian operators simply could
not meet these terms. The government was apparently fully aware of this,
and also aware there already existed an American group with access to the
necessary capital and technology. Consequently the founders, and chief
beneficiaries, of the giant Shawinigan Water and Power Company were
John Joyce and J.E. Aldred, two American promoters who worked in
co-operation with a group of Montreal financiers, including L.J. Forget,
J.N. Greenshields, and the ubiquitous Herbert Holt. Aldred, though a
financier by training, was the moving force in the operation and proved
himself something of a genius both as a promoter and as a technological
innovator.[14]

French-Canadian businessmen apparently lacked access to pools of capital. The major financial institutions in Quebec, such as the Bank of Montreal, were English-Canadian owned. There were French-Canadian banks,
including the *Banque provinciale* and the *Alliance nationale*, but their hold-

ings were small compared with their English-Canadian competitors. According to one source, English-Canadian banks held assets worth $772 millions in 1915 compared to a mere $77 millions in French-Canadian banks.[15] Indeed, it would appear that even French Canadians preferred to keep their savings in the more affluent, but non-French-Canadian banks, a state of affairs which caused one *nationaliste* to complain: "It is deplorable to notice that certain of our communities, which have millions to place, are piling up fortunes in the coffers of English-Canadian banks."[16] Nor did French capital come into Canada in sums sufficient to counterbalance British and American funds available to English-Canadian investors. When French investors did explore the Canadian market, they seemed most often to favour English-Canadian investment houses and banks.[17]

It is impossible to measure the extent to which French Canadians were actually anxious to gain access to capital for the purpose of developing the resources of Quebec. Since commerce and finance had long been largely English-dominated in that province, many French Canadians seemed often to assume that this was the way things should be. It may only have been a matter of making a virtue of necessity, but many French-Canadian intellectuals argued that business activity was naturally Protestant, materialist, and Anglo-Saxon, and should be avoided by a people Catholic in faith, spiritual in temperament, and ethnically French. Jules Paul Tardivel, the ultramontane nationalist editor of *La Verité*, put the argument in its most extreme form in 1902: "It is not necessary for us to possess industry and money. We would no longer be French Canadians but Americans like the others. Our mission is to possess the earth and to spread ideas. To cling to the soil, to raise large families, to maintain the hearths of spiritual and intellectual life, that must be our role in America."[18] Henri Bourassa, though by no means totally opposed to business and industry, stated the case somewhat more moderately. The French Canadian's ambition, he wrote in 1902, "does not sway him to huge financial operations. Rather given to liberal professions, to agricultural life, or to local mercantile and industrial pursuits, he is more easily satisfied than the English-speaking Canadian with a moderate return for his work and efforts. He has kept out of the frantic display of financial energy, of the feverish concentration of capital, of the international competition of industry, which have drawn his English-speaking fellow citizens to huge combinations of wealth or trade."[19]

There were, of course, those who felt that the French Canadians' apparent inability to achieve first rank in business and commerce was due to the influence of the Church, particularly in education. There was an element of truth in this contention. Certainly the Church controlled the curriculum of the school system jealously, and consistently fought off proposals for educational reform such as compulsory schooling. That type of proposal was usually attributed, rather cavalierly, to the dark and mysterious influence of the Free Masons or to the surreptitious designs of English Canadians bent on undermining French-Canadian values.[20] These attitudes were well expressed in a hostile comment on André Siegfried's well-known book, *Canada: Les Deux Races*, published in 1906. Among other criticisms this French Protestant had made of French Canada was one that the Church exercised too much control over the educational system. "What our so-called educational reformers do not see and what M. Siegfried, blinded by his sectarian prejudices, sees no better than them," his reviewer responded, "is that education will be the corner stone of our nationality only if it remains above and beyond the influences of politics under the supreme direction of the Church. The English, who have political sense, know it and everywhere they can make war upon Catholic education."[21]

In practice the Church, while determined to maintain its predominance in the educational system, was nevertheless far from hostile to the introduction of new scientific and commercial subjects into the school system. But there was always a proviso: these new subjects could not be allowed to take precedence over spiritual matters. It should also be added that the state was not without its responsibility; its budget for education, though it greatly improved by 1914, was far from liberal. But Quebec was not alone in this. Nevertheless, both in its support for education generally, and in its efforts to promote commercial and technical education, the Quebec government's record was probably not as good as most other provincial governments' in the country.[22]

The educational system performed one function which may have inhibited the advancement of French Canadians in the industrial and commercial power structure. The Church and the school, along with the family, were the central institutions in the lives of French Canadians. It was the function of these institutions to instill in the people of Quebec the values by which they lived and which strengthened their will to survive as a distinct community. Above all, the French Canadian was taught that survival depended on the faithful practice of the Roman Catholic religion and on the preservation of the French language. The young French Canadian had set before him the ideals of national service exemplified by priests, writers, and politicians who had struggled for the preservation of French Canada. That ideal provided little place for the successful entrepreneur who was more naturally part of the alien English culture. Education, then, had a moral and patriotic function, to which practical training for economic life was secondary. "Our education," the economist Edouard Montpetit wrote, "has lived for a long time beyond reality, in the realm of the spirit. It has been especially literary and philosophical, a bookish

philosophy without contact with life."[23] It was not merely that the entre-
preneurial impulse developed out of a more pragmatic educational
philosophy than the Quebec educational system's. It was also that the
commanding heights of the Quebec economy were increasingly occupied
by Anglo-Saxons. This meant a language barrier had been raised that the
French Canadian found difficult to cross. He had no desire to abandon the
language which he knew was the key to cultural survival, while the English-Canadian entrepreneurs showed little willingness to accommodate
their economic system to the language of the French-speaking majority in
Quebec.[24] All these factors, then, help to explain the English dominance
of the industrial revolution that was taking off in Quebec at the turn of
the century.[25]

II

French Canada was not without people who were acutely aware of the
difficulties the new industrial society could create. Indeed, many of the
new social and political organizations developed in the first decade of the
century were quite obviously responses to changing social and economic
circumstances. As early as 1901 the distinguished sociologist, Léon Gérin,
warned his compatriots of the need to reform their educational institutions
in order to prepare themselves for a larger role in the economic life of the
new century. Gérin, like his nineteenth-century ancestor Étienne Parent,
had long been a critic of what he considered the lack of individualism and
initiative among French Canadians. To compete successfully with the English he believed that the virtues of individualism would have to be encouraged. Otherwise Quebec would continue to have an unbalanced
social system in which "we lack an essential factor of organization and
progress: a class of great industrial leaders, initiators of large enterprises
in culture, construction, transportation and commerce." He then pointed
perceptively to the logical consequence of this condition: "Due to the gap
in our social organization, the mass of our population depends for its
existence on English employers, on the great English companies in
Canada, and especially (and here is the greatest danger that we run at
present) in the United States."[26]

A more thorough assessment of the economic problems of French
Canadians was made by Gérin's friend, and one of the first French-
Canadian economists, Errol Bouchette. Early in the century Bouchette
began to publish a series of carefully researched articles designed to
convince his compatriots that industrialism was the wave of the future, and
that, unless they participated actively in the process, it and its Anglo-Saxon
initiators would dominate them. In 1906 he gathered his material together

and published it in a massive volume entitled *L'Indépéndance économique du Canada français*. The young *nationaliste* Jules Fournier was not guilty of overstatement when he described the treatise as "probably the most remarkable published so far by a Canadian on the question of political economy."[27] Taking as his slogan, *Emparons-nous l'industrie*, to strike a contrast with the traditional nationalist slogan *Emparons-nous du sol*, Bouchette argued that a full-scale revaluation of institutions and attitudes was required if French Canadians were to participate fully in the newly emerging society. "A true central school, good industrial laws, a system of state support for industry, that in my opinion must be the basis of industrial work in the province of Quebec."[28] What especially concerned this French-Canadian economist was the invasion of Quebec by big business, especially the American "trusts," and, while not opposed to foreign investment, he was convinced that steps had to be taken to prevent foreign corporations from taking over completely.[29] What then was to be done? Bouchette detected two fundamental weaknesses in Quebec: a lack of capital and a deficient educational system. The solution to the second problem lay in the establishment of schools of commerce and technology to provide French Canadians with the specialized practical knowledge required in business careers, and to encourage a new favourable attitude to economic pursuits. "If the French-Canadian group in Canada wishes to conserve its legitimate influence in public life," he wrote realistically, "it must not be content to live in the contemplation of past glories."[30] As to the problem of a shortage of investment capital, Bouchette advocated the development of co-operative enterprises and, more radically, the utilization of the resources of the state. "In a country such as ours," he insisted, "where there is so much to do, and rapidly, if we wish to have an absolute guarantee of our survival as a distinct political entity in America, reform cannot be carried out without an impulse, direct or indirect, by the collective will of the citizens, that is by the state."[31]

Bouchette's modest proposals were by no means entirely acceptable to French Canada's intellectual élite. Though he vigorously denied any sympathy for "socialism," even his limited approval of a more active state was viewed with suspicion. Spokesmen for the Church, always ready to defend that institution's priority in education, responded negatively to his brand of ideas about the school system.[32] Some politicians were more sympathetic. In 1907 the Gouin government, despite the open disapproval of some Church leaders, established the *École des Hautes Études Commerciales* to provide young French Canadians with an opportunity for a business-school education. Moreover, the provincial government began to tighten up the regulations under which the province's natural resources were exploited. But on the whole, the Quebec government followed a laissez-faire policy, perhaps even more faithfully than other governments in

Canada. Once basic public works were attended to, the main areas of economic development were left in private hands. Such a development as hydro-electricity, which elsewhere was frequently looked upon as a public utility to be operated by government, was left in the hands of the private entrepreneur in Quebec.[33] And private hands, for the most part, were non-French-Canadian hands.

One exception to this condition was the highly successful *caisse populaire* movement. This "people's bank" was the brain child of Alphonse Desjardins who had, at various times, been a journalist, publisher of the debates of the Quebec Assembly, and finally stenographer of the Canadian House of Commons. Desjardins had long been concerned about what he considered the lack of thrift among ordinary French Canadians, and the absence of French-Canadian financial institutions. Some time in the late nineties he came across Henry William Wolff's book *The People's Bank*, which described the international credit and co-operative movement. Almost as if he had discovered his life's mission – and he had – Desjardins set about thoroughly investigating the subject by reading and by establishing personal contact with the leaders of the movement in Europe. (Because of the language barrier Desjardins had much closer relations with the European co-operative movements than those in western Canada.) By the end of 1900 Desjardins was ready to establish his first co-operative savings and credit organization at Lévis. He had already taken the trouble to gain the approval of leaders of the Church, but at first he had considerable difficulty in attracting popular support. One difficulty was the lack of legal recognition for the *caisse*, and a series of efforts to gain a federal charter ended only in frustration and failure. It also ended the possibility for an important national institution: a Canada-wide co-operative movement. Finally in 1906 the Gouin government provided the *caisses populaires* with a provincial charter. After that, despite the hostility of the French-Canadian-owned *Banque nationale*, the movement spread rapidly throughout much of Quebec. It quickly won the active approval of both the Church hierarchy and the local clergy, members of which often acted as managers or directors of local branches. To the Church the *caisse* was both a moral and a financial institution. According to Cardinal Bégin, writing in 1910: "The Credit Unions offer several great advantages. Among others to accustom our young people to economy, to restrain them from the dangers of intemperance and luxury, and to supply them, when credit is needed, with the money needed to pay a debt, buy a house, or procure agricultural implements, etc."[34]

While a popular success, the *caisses* were never financially strong enough to offer serious competition to the established banks and credit institutions. In 1907, after an especially successful year the capital of the movement stood at only $48,337.69, a great leap forward from 1900, but hardly a sum to cause tremors on St. James Street. Nevertheless, Alphonse Desjardins had laid the basis for one of French Canada's most successful, permanent economic institutions.[35]

III

The economic transformation of Quebec during the first years of the twentieth century was accompanied by the birth of a number of organizations dedicated to the survival of the French-Canadian culture in Canada. These were *nationaliste* movements. While primarily concerned about the future of French Canada, only rarely did these groups envisage the future in terms of political independence for Quebec. Only an aging Jules Paul Tardivel or a youthful Arthur Saint-Pierre went that far.[36] But many other individuals and groups, worried about the changes they saw and over which they seemed able to exercise very little control, indicated a deep anxiety about the survival of the French culture in Canada. Industrial and urban growth atomized the traditional structures of French-Canadian society with its close organic association of family and Church. While it did not, at least at first, destroy the value system of these institutions, it brought them mildly into question, and sent people in search either of new values or ways to modify the old ones. The very extent to which old values were challenged often seemed to stimulate the defence of those same values. The *nationalisme* that developed in the early years of industrialism was, in part, exactly that kind of reaction. Given the role played by non-French Canadians in the industrial transformation of Quebec, it was almost inevitable that the reaction of French Canadians to change should have a *nationaliste* flavour. It was as natural as the reaction of the English-Canadian farmer who responded to industrial growth by defending the values of the family farm, or the English-Canadian intellectual who sought to fashion a new sense of community through the doctrines of the Protestant social gospel. All these reactions stemmed from the same sense of insecurity in a time of rapid change. Since Quebec has a long-established and well-developed sense of ethnic community, it is not surprising that its reaction was often *nationaliste.*[37]

For the most part, members of the various *nationaliste* organizations were relatively young and came from the classically educated middle-class professional elite. This was the traditional source of French Canada's political and intellectual leadership. Their relationship with the Church was usually close, though an occasional hint of anti-clericalism could be detected among young firebrands like Olivar Asselin. Though the political significance of these groups was relatively slight, they were united in a distrust of politics and politicians, especially Liberal politicians in power.

Yet those same politicians were not unaware of the growing significance of the *nationaliste* groups who seemed able to mobilize opinion and even votes on such critical issues as minority schools, imperial relations, and, to a lesser extent, "foreign" economic domination. These were issues that apparently touched a wide spectrum of French-Canadian opinion, as the naval debate in 1910 and 1911 was to show.

The most important of the new groups was *La Ligue Nationaliste Canadienne,* founded in 1903. Its significance lay neither in its size, for it never had a mass membership, nor in the profundity of its programme, which contained only three rather general planks. Its influence resulted largely from its association with a man who was popularly viewed as its leader, though he was not even an official member. He was Henri Bourassa, the very independent Member of Parliament who had broken with Laurier over the issue of Canadian participation in the Boer War. From that date onward Bourassa began to cast about for a suitable means through which he could express his views and influence public opinion without limiting his independence. He had toyed briefly with the idea of founding an anti-imperialist political movement in co-operation with such unlikely partners as Goldwin Smith and Jules Paul Tardivel. But he quickly realized the futility of that project. Ultimately, in 1910, he established *Le Devoir,* a daily newspaper which was virtually his private platform for more than a decade. But in the interim, this stern, uncompromising Roman Catholic thinker and orator played an important role in active politics, and propagated a brand of *nationalisme* which he believed met the needs of both French and English Canadians. Gradually his views and activities brought him into direct and irreconcilable conflict with the man he had once admired, Wilfrid Laurier. In 1911 Bourassa played a significant role in driving Laurier and the Liberals from office.

The major ideas for which Bourassa stood were set out in the programme of *La Ligue Nationaliste Canadienne,* though they were much embroidered upon in the columns of *Le Nationaliste,* a weekly newspaper established the following year, and in a growing flood of speeches, articles and pamphlets. The three central principles of the *Ligue* were first, the preservation of Canadian autonomy within the British Empire; second, the maintenance of the rights guaranteed to the provinces under the British North America Act and respect for linguistic dualism and separate school rights; and finally, the intellectual and economic development of Canada by and for Canadians.[38] The *Ligue* itself never became more than a paper organization.[39] Nevertheless, its doctrines were widely propagated through the speeches and writings of Bourassa himself and those of a handful of young followers, the chief of whom were Armand Lavergne, Olivar Asselin, Jules Fournier and Omer Héroux. While naturally concerned about every development in imperial relations and every infringe-

ment, real or imagined, on the rights of French-speaking minorities outside Quebec, a great deal of the *Ligue*'s intellectual energy was devoted
to the problems of the new industrial society. Asselin, in fact, described
the organization's social and economic proposals as "possibly the most
important article in the Nationalist programme."[40] While they failed to
develop a realistic, or at least a politically acceptable, alternative to the
predominantly capitalist developmental philosophy of the age, they did
succeed in drawing public attention to a number of glaring abuses and
injustices. Their concern, naturally, was particularly directed toward the
impact of change on French Canadians, though in all their endeavours
they insisted that their perspective was Canadian rather than merely
French Canadian.

While Bourassa was more sceptical than Errol Bouchette about both the
benefits of industrialization and the value of state-directed education, he
and his followers accepted much of the economist's programme.[41] As
French Canadians, they were deeply concerned about the problem of
"foreign" domination of the Quebec economy. "We will be working to
enrich the foreigner in our very own forests, at our very own waterfalls,
in all of our own resources," Fournier complained in 1908. "They will
have the money and consequently the power and we, we will be the
drawers of water and hewers of wood."[42] But what could be done to
prevent this impending tragedy? French Canadians could pool their resources in French-Canadian banks, insurance companies, and especially
the *caisses populaires,* and thus develop some of their own resources. So,
too, the *nationalistes* demanded a thorough policing of the trusts, particularly the giant Montreal Light, Heat and Power and the Montreal Tram-
ways Company. Asselin, and some of the younger members of the
movement, were full of admiration for Adam Beck's Ontario Hydro.[43]
But public ownership did not play a large role in their thinking; they
hoped rather to find a mean between what Bourassa called the "calamities
of communism and corporate domination."[44] They gave their support to
the trade unions, especially Catholic unions, advocated higher wages for
workers and better salaries for teachers, publicized slum housing, and
demanded improved sanitary conditions in urban areas.

Bourassa and his associates were above all moral reformers in the tradition of social Catholicism. Like their counterparts in English Canada in the
Protestant social gospel movement, they were deeply offended by the
materialism and corruption of the age of unrestrained economic progress.
They hoped to encourage an educated elite to place religious and moral
values above personal gain and pecuniary standards. Uncontrolled competition brought out the worst in man and the *nationalites* believed that Leo
XIII's social encyclicals pointed the way toward a more just and moral
society. This did not mean, of course, that material advance was unneces-

sary; it had merely to be set in its proper, secondary place in the scale of society's values. "So that our patriotism is truly practical it is necessary to take into account at the same time both high aspirations and material needs," Bourassa explained. "Without doubt we must take part in all movements, in all progress in economic life. We must also conserve and develop in us all of the elements of moral and intellectual superiority. Let us give our people a healthy spirit in a healthy body."[45]

Increasingly Bourassa and the *nationalistes* became convinced that the root of much of the evil lay in politics. And that meant the Liberals: Gouin at Quebec, Laurier at Ottawa. The trouble was, as Bourassa saw it, that the existing political parties were not divided by principle, but only by a competing desire for the fruits of office. Their leaders were too often merely the spokesmen for the country's powerful economic interests. Olivar Asselin described the parties at Ottawa in terms that could well have been written by a radical western agrarian. "It is a well-known fact," he asserted, "outside of fool's paradise, that the contest in Ottawa is not so much between Liberals and Conservatives, as between this and that combination of railway interests."[46] In 1907 Bourassa withdrew from federal politics to devote his efforts to the defeat of the provincial Liberal government, believing that this would produce some necessary provincial reforms and ultimately destroy the Laurier machine. As he explained to his friend, Goldwin Smith, "I have thought, and still think that it is useless to expect any strong, well-reasoned and fruitful effort on the part of French Canadians – as a national factor – until we have imbued them, through their whole public life, with a strong sense of their rights, and duties as a component part of Canada and the Empire. As our public life stands at present – and the curse of party slavery and patronage and the predominance of selfish interests allied to the natural disposition of the race towards hero worship – and the whole race is at the mercy of a clever and charming opportunist – Laurier – aided by a few office seeking and public money distributors."[47]

While Bourassa's career in provincial politics was not a brilliant success, the Gouin government did begin to pay attention to more flagrant examples of bad public management. But an important by-product was that Bourassa and the *nationalistes* found themselves gradually thrown into an uneasy alliance with the local Conservatives. Here the basis was being laid for their association with F.D. Monk and R.L. Borden in the election of 1911. When the naval debate moved to centre stage in federal politics, Bourassa was once more drawn magnetically to his central interest – imperial affairs. In January 1910 he began publishing *Le Devoir*, devoted to the defeat of Laurier, to the preservation of Canadian autonomy, to continued discussion of the many issues raised by the *nationalistes* in the previous decade, and, it must be added, to the greater glory of Henri

Bourassa. By 1910, Bourassa's influence was reaching its apex and through his newspaper his views were available to a wide audience. Much of that audience was composed of other *nationaliste* groups that had begun to develop in these same years.

IV

While Bourassa and his fellow *Ligue* members distrusted established politicians, they had an almost unbounded faith in the rising generations. The young men in the schools and classical colleges, if given a proper introduction to *nationaliste* doctrine, would eventually provide more adequate moral leadership for French-Canadian society. In these years there was certainly a stirring of discontent among French-Canadian youths. Indeed in the same year the *Ligue Nationaliste* was founded, steps were being taken to establish a new youth organization whose objects were even more traditionalist and nationalist (in a French-Canadian sense) than those of Bourassa and his friends. This organization adopted the title of the *Association Catholique de la Jeunesse Canadienne-Française.* [48] The movement grew out of the desire of some college students, encouraged by a few clerics and journalists, to establish an intercollege organization devoted to the promotion and protection of French-Canadian and Catholic interests.[49] There seems to have been a vague fear among some churchmen that secularism, and even anti-clericalism, were making inroads with Quebec's youth, and the new organization was designed to remove this danger. The first youth conference convened in Montreal in June 1903. Its major decision was to appoint a committee chaired by Joseph Versailles, who later became a highly successful banker, to investigate the potential for a permanent youth organization. In March 1904, on the recommendation of that committee, the A.C.J.C. was founded. Two articles in the constitution reveal the essence of the new group's philosophy, and set it off sharply from *La Ligue Nationaliste:*

1. The members of the Catholic Association of French-Canadian Youth believe that the French-Canadian race has a special mission to fulfil on this continent and that it must for this end, guard its distinct character from that of other races.

2. They believe that the progress of the French-Canadian race is in a special fashion attached to the Catholic faith, which is one of the essential and specific elements.[50]

The *Association's* object was to promote study of religious, national, and social questions. Believing that French Canada was in the midst of a religious and national crisis, the Association's founders concluded that "logically . . . all renovation of a race must begin with youth."[51] Good Catholics would be good French Canadians, and vice versa, and in applying the social doctrines of the Church to the needs of society the special mission of French Canada would be fulfilled. The young Abbé Groulx, one of the *Association*'s chief mentors, described the *Association*, which he called "The Adolescents' Crusade," in these lyrical terms: "On all the surface of the globe, there is perhaps at the present time, few sights as beautiful, as moving as that of this young French-Canadian race encircled by a hundred million foreigners, having against it, against the dream of its survival, all the laws of history, which has nevertheless sworn not to die, not in the goal of money or damnation but to guard a flame on the heights of the new world, the flame of its faith and of its ideal."[52]

The activities of the *Association* were both ceremonial and practical. It circulated petitions demanding greater use of the French language in the economic life of Quebec, opposing the Autonomy Bills in 1905 and the Naval Bill in 1910. It organized demonstrations marking such historical events as the anniversary of Champlain's landing in 1608 and the two hundred and fiftieth anniversary of Dollard des Ormeaux's defence of New France at the Long Sault. And it participated in the struggle against attempts by suspected Free Masons in Godfroy Langlois' *La Ligue d'Enseignement* to obtain some reforms in Quebec's educational system.[53] Its members also advocated legal recognition of trade unions, and legislation limiting hours of work, improving working conditions, and establishing accident compensation.

While conservative in its outlook, the A.C.J.C. was another sign of growing ethnic self-consciousness among French Canadians and of their concern about the new social issues created by industrial and urban growth. There were several other manifestations of that same unease. Among these were the *Société du parler français*, devoted to the promotion of spoken French and to protecting the language from corruption. It sponsored a very large and successful conference on the French language in Canada (though it also included Franco-American representation) at Quebec in 1912.[54] Ultimately more important, was *La Ligue des Droits français*, later named *La Ligue d'Action française*, which attacked the exclusion of French from business and commerce in Quebec. "We are passing through a period of very marked national indifference," one of the organization's founders wrote in 1913, "when the country has taken a gigantic leap towards material prosperity. Our language, because we have willed it, has been excluded little by little from the commercial and industrial sphere."[55] The *Ligue*'s major activity, apart from its publications, was to encourage French Canadians to patronize those business establishments where French was the working language.

These years also witnessed a renewed interest in the history of French

Canada. Abbé Groulx, teaching at Valleyfield, and Thomas Chapais contributed to this development. Henri Bourassa gave it his warmest approval. His campaign for the establishment of university courses in Canadian history met with success in 1915, when Abbé Groulx was given a part-time chair at Montreal, and Chapais began teaching in Quebec City.[56] The teaching of Canadian history, Bourassa and the other *nationalistes* agreed, was essential if French Canadians were to understand fully the reasons for their struggle for cultural survival.[57]

Few French Canadians would have questioned the major moral which Bourassa drew from his people's long, heroic history: faithfulness to the Church and its leadership was the main assurance of survival.[58] Certainly during the first decades of the new century the Church was playing its long-established role as vigorously as it had in the past. That was likely as long as men of such quality as Cardinal Bégin and Archbishop Bruchési provided leadership in spiritual and sometimes temporal matters. Without giving up their traditional pastoral and educational role, the leaders of the Church wanted to ensure that in the new, more pluralistic society that was emerging, the moral and spiritual influence of Catholicism would not diminish. That was plain from the orientation of such Catholic action movements as the A.C.J.C. It was also quite obviously in the mind of Cardinal Bégin when he established the Catholic daily *l'Action Sociale* in 1907 to "promote the true interest of the fatherland, the cause of God, religion and souls."[59] The purpose of Catholic action groups was to bring the social teachings of the Church to bear upon the social and economic life of Quebec, thus providing French-Canadian Catholics with the means of organizing themselves against the abuses of laissez-faire capitalism while at the same time protecting them against the unacceptable materialistic doctrines of socialism.[60]

While the Church recognized the right of workers to organize for collective bargaining purposes, it had serious reservations about two aspects of the Canadian labour union movement. The Church condemned the doctrine of class conflict, which it felt was promoted by strikes; the techniques of arbitration and conciliation, especially when they recognized a role for the Church, were warmly approved.[61] Secondly, the Church deplored the concept of "neutral" unions, especially the "internationals" that dominated the Canadian labour scene. Mgr Labrècque of Chicoutimi expressed this attitude in a pastoral letter of 1912 directed against the introduction into his diocese of "international unions with socialist tendencies or attached to the vice of neutrality."[62] Like all important social institutions, the trade union touched upon the faith and morals of its members, and therefore the Church believed that she had a fully legitimate part to play in labour unions.

The answer to this problem was obviously Catholic trade unions, and at the turn of the century the Church set about extending its influence into the labour movement. In 1901 Mgr Bégin made a personal intervention in a bitterly waged strike at a Quebec City shoe factory. The prelate's arbitration resulted in a contract which included union recognition, adoption of conciliation procedures, and the appointment of a union chaplain. This settlement set the pattern for the gradual development of Catholic syndicalism in Quebec, a development which was slow but which soon attracted the support of *nationalistes* like Henri Bourassa. Since Bourassa was a faithful Catholic he strongly approved of the Church taking an active role in labour affairs. He also hoped that Catholic unions would displace the American-dominated "internationals," which he feared were denationalizing French-Canadian workers. Even some French-Canadian union leaders, like Alfred Charpentier, who had achieved some recognition in international and Canadian union circles, were gradually drawn toward the Catholic unions, though this development was hastened by the war years.[63] These Catholic unions were highly paternalistic and rarely militant. While they doubtless protected the culture and religion of their members, it was sometimes at the price of lower wages and poor working conditions. Consequently, most unionized French Canadians continued to hold memberships in the Canadian and international unions. But most important, the existence of Catholic unions indicated that the Church was making a serious effort to come to terms with the industrial order.

By the end of the Laurier years, Quebec was well along the road to industrialization and urbanization. Many of the problems these changes created had been identified, and in some cases efforts had been made to resolve them. These new conditions gave a strong stimulus to French-Canadian national consciousness, as did the other developments of the period, both within and without Canada. This was not surprising in a society where most of the great economic enterprises of the period were initiated and controlled by *les étrangers*. Many French Canadians were consequently left with a sense of powerlessness, a feeling that their future was in someone else's hands. Frustration and *nationalisme* were the consequences of a condition graphically described by Errol Bouchette, the ablest commentator of the period. "We are thus in the presence of people detached from the soil by the loss of their lands and unprepared for industry by their education: the two careers which create riches are thus closed to them, and even commerce, by which wealth is accumulated," he wrote. "There remains to them yet, it is true, political action and especially the high influence that is given to them by the Church, the magistracy, the professions and intellectual pursuits, but this influence is by its very nature indirect and exclusively moral."[64]

CHAPTER 8

Farmers, Railways, and the Tariff

The Laurier Liberals fully understood that the settlement of the west was fundamental to the economic growth of Canada. Indeed, a prosperous west was the link that would, at last, bind together the east-west economy, integrating it into a prosperous nation. What the Liberals did not anticipate was that a burgeoning agricultural economy and a populous west might not fully appreciate the role that it was assigned in the national economy. And that would create political difficulties undreamt of before 1896. As events were to show by 1910, the success of the Laurier government's western settlement policies bore the seeds of the Liberals' destruction. Instead of fitting themselves obediently into the national economic and political system, the farmers, particularly of the prairies but also of central Canada, began demanding loudly that the system be revised to suit their needs. Sometimes the agrarians were successful in their demands, particularly those demands related directly to problems within the agricultural economy itself. But on what the farmers considered the most important issues, those related to policies regulating the national economy, results were far more meagre and in 1911 the farmers, like the Liberals, suffered a major defeat.[1]

What prairie farmers learned quickly was a lesson already digested by the agriculturalists in central Canada and the United States: organization was the principle of survival in the new national economy. Increasingly, the major economic groups of the country drew together to promote and defend their interests collectively. The Canadian Manufacturers' Association was, of course, not a new organization in the Laurier period but as the process of industrialization intensified, so did the strength and ambition of the C.M.A.[2] Similarly trade unions, trade associations, and professional organizations were developing collective strength on a nation-wide scale. The new industrial society sang the praises of individualism and free competition; businessmen and farmers alike would have agreed that "rugged individualism," characterized by what Clifford Sifton called "hard work, frugality and self-denial," provided the key to success. Yet the reality was often at variance with the rhetoric. Organization, which limited competition, was the more effective road to growth, prosperity, and profits. Anti-combines legislation had existed since the 1890s but it was openly admitted by a retail merchants' newspaper in 1907 that "agreements are now made and entered into in many lines of trade, with a view of preventing ruinous and unfair competition."[3] Moreover, the development of the cooperative movement, which won support among western farmers, Quebec workers, and maritime fishermen, was also, in part, a collectivist response to the insecurities of free competition.[4]

The farmers faced with organized business, especially in the grain trade, realized that they too must present a collective response. "The day has gone by for remaining scattered, unbanded communities, a tempting bait to the ambitious designs of others," W.R. Motherwell, a founder of the Territorial Grain Growers' Association, asserted in 1902. "No one can deny that the farmer extracts the wealth from the soil by his industry and skill in conjunction with the forces of nature, and no one can deny that in the past his rights have been ruthlessly trodden upon by dealers and transportation companies. It is a fact that other branches of agriculture such as dairy, fruit, and stock interests, all have recognized organizations, and it seems strange that grain growers have not before this realized the importance of organizing also."[5] Only through union could the farmer hope to impress railways with the need for better service, governments with the need for better policies, and the Canadian people with the view that what was good for agriculture was good for the country.

Organization, of course, grew largely in response to specific grievances: a shortage of freight cars at harvest time, low prices, growing monopolies, high freight rates, protective tariffs, and rural depopulation. But the ideas and rhetoric of farm leaders arose not only out of specific grievances, but also out of widespread experience. Farm organizations in Ontario and Quebec dated back to the 1870s with the Grange and the Patrons of Industry, which in turn drew much of their inspiration from the United States. But there were British influences also. Young W.C. Good, a future leader of Ontario farmers, had not yet gone off to university in 1896, but he was already fully familiar with the populist platform in the United States and with such English socialist ideas as those expressed in Robert Blatchford's "Merrie England."[6] Many Ontario farmers moved west after 1896 and some, at least, took their ideas about agrarian politics with them. Both E.A. Partridge, the most imaginative of all the agrarian radicals, and T.A. Crerar traced their origins back east. But there were other strains of thought, too. Men like James Douglas and Charles Dunning were immigrants from Great Britain, brought up like thousands of other westerners in the atmosphere of free trade, the new social Liberalism of Lloyd George, and the beginnings of socialist politics. They knew the evils of industrial capitalism even though the prairies provided a radically different context. A businessman, speaking at the annual convention of the Canadian Manufacturers' Association, was not far off the mark when he pointed his finger at the British immigrant as the source of a disease which his associates found threatening. "There is not the slightest doubt that the free trade germ has been started, and it is growing," he warned, "and as we are looking for our immigration from the Old Country to a great extent, the free trader from the Old Country will be coming over here, and the free trade germ will grow more rapidly."[7]

James Douglas, the maverick Liberal from Assiniboia, represented another source of agrarian dissent: social Protestantism.[8] Like many farm leaders, including R.C. Henders of Manitoba and William Irvine of Alberta, Douglas moved from rural pulpit to rural politics, hoping that his efforts would help to build at least a new earth. J.S. Woodsworth, though primarily an urban reformer, contributed regularly to farmers' newspapers, while Rev. Salem Bland urged the farmers, and others, into battle from the pulpit, the Chautauqua, and at grain growers' conventions.[9] "Society is steeped in unrighteousness," Bland thundered from a Methodist pulpit. "We have the elements of moral destruction among us. . . . We must begin the great work of attacking all the ties of our commercial life, all the rascalities of high finance, all the abominations of our political system."[10] Such rhetoric increasingly appealed to agrarian ears.[11]

The Chautauqua, with its origins in the United States, points up yet another significant source of Canadian agrarianism: the embattled farmers of the American west who had been raising both hell and corn for two generations. The thousands of settlers from the United States, often coming to Canada to escape the "trusts," brought their populist gospel with them. Most notable was Henry Wise Wood, who had a long background in agrarian politics, but there were also John W. Leedy, a one-time populist governor of Kansas, and George Bevington, a recognized authority on that perennial panacea for rural ills: "soft money."[12] Out of this mixture of men and influences came a remarkable group of organizations devoted to defending farmers' interests and destroying the "new feudalism." In the end their impact upon the structure of the Canadian economy was limited, though important, for out of these movements came the cooperative enterprises that contributed greatly to easing the farmers' financial burdens, and gaining better grain prices, fairer grain purchasing practices, and more equitable freight rates. But their greatest impact was political, for the farmers not only won control of some of the existing parties in the prairie provinces, but they also established a new one. Nationally, they destroyed the two-party system.

I

1896 was a bad year for farm politicians in North America. In the United States the Populists first succumbed to the blandishments of the Democrats and then went down to defeat with William Jennings Bryan. In Canada the story was not much different. The Patron victories in Ontario in 1894 had raised high hopes for the 1896 federal contest. But the party suffered defeat nearly everywhere, and evidence that some Patron officials had made arrangements with the Liberals left the movement divided and spiritless. Had it not been for the backing of that perennial *laissez-faire* liberal, Goldwin Smith, who took over control of the *Farmers' Sun* in 1896, even that voice of farm discontent would probably have disappeared. Indeed it took another half-dozen years for the Ontario farmers to reorganize effectively again. In 1902, on the *Sun*'s initiative, a substantial group of farmers came together at Exhibition time in Toronto and established a new, non-political group, calling itself the Ontario Farmers Association. Its first president was C.A. Mallory who was also president of the *Sun*. The work of organizing began at once and success was almost immediate. The Association's major criticisms were directed against high transportation costs, the protective tariff, and inequitable tax policies. Within a few years it became clear that the major weakness of farmers in Ontario was division. Despite the Association's success in organizing and pressing its demands, the Grange had never completely died out. The Grange, still a lodge with all the paraphernalia of secrecy, began to make overtures to the younger organization in 1905. Two years later the groups merged. Among the leaders of the new unified organization, soon to adopt the name of the United Farmers of Ontario, were E.C. Drury and J.J. Morrison.[13] This movement towards unity in Ontario was indicative of a gradual coalescence of farmers throughout the country. And as unity increased, so did militancy.

In the west, farmers' organizations had been outspoken and radical from their foundation.[14] Moreover, because of the nature of their major products and the consequent importance of transportation, they set their sights on Ottawa's national policies almost from the outset. The Liberal appeal on the prairies prior to 1896 had been based on the party's low tariff platform and its willingness to criticize the "interests," especially the Canadian Pacific Railway. But the farmers quickly realized, once the Liberals had taken office, that rhetoric was very slow to translate itself into action. The new government did take one immediate step which met with the farmers' approval: the Crow's Nest Pass Agreement. In 1897 an agreement was reached with the C.P.R. whereby a subsidy, not to exceed $3,633,000, was granted to the railway to build from Lethbridge through the Crow's Nest Pass to Nelson, British Columbia. In return the railway

agreed to reduce rates on grain and flour moving east to the Lakehead by
$.03 per hundredweight, and on agricultural machinery and settlers'
effects going west by 10 per cent.[15]

While the relief on freight rate costs was welcome, there were other
monopolies, in addition to the C.P.R., that the farmers wanted controlled.
Most important was the elevator combine. Though there were several
companies – Ogilvie, Lake of the Woods, Northeast, and Manitoba –
there seemed to be very little price competition. Western Members of
Parliament, and especially R.L. Richardson and James Douglas, raised this
issue in 1898 and the following year the Laurier government appointed
a Royal Commission to examine the whole question, a commission heavily
weighted in the farmers' interest. The report concluded, among other
things, that "the evidence . . . shows that in many cases there is little, if
any, competition between elevators as to prices."[16] The outcome of the
Commission's report was the Manitoba Grain Act in 1900, which provided for a more stringent system of grain regulation, particularly in matters concerning loading platforms, flat warehouses, and car allocation.

The problem of car allocation was crucial. If, at harvest time, railway
boxcars were not fairly allocated, or worse, if there was a serious shortage,
crops could not be carried to market. It was exactly this situation that led
to the foundation of the Territorial Grain Growers' Association in 1901,
and the Manitoba Grain Growers' Association in the following year. The
problem was a grain blockade in the autumn of 1901, the year of the
heaviest harvest in western history to that point: some 16 million bushels.
When shipping time arrived, the C.P.R. had far fewer cars available than
were necessary; when navigation closed in December, only about one-
third of the crop had been moved. It was at Indian Head, in eastern
Assiniboia, that the grain blockade was at its worst, and it was there that
the Territorial Grain Growers' Association got its start. Among its first
leaders was a young farmer from Abernethy, W.R. Motherwell, whose
career in western politics stretched over more than three decades.[17] Once
established, the organization spread rapidly, especially after it proved its
earnestness by taking the C.P.R. to court in the Sintaluta case in 1902 and
forcing the railway to abide strictly by the car allotment regulations of the
Manitoba Grain Act.[18]

II

The long-term solution to the farmers' transportation problems was not
the enforcement of the law on the existing railways, but rather the construction of new facilities. It was the potential of the west and the pressing
needs of the farmer that partly explain the railway construction boom of

the Laurier years. Had the farmers' needs alone spurred railway growth, a sensible national policy might have been developed. Unfortunately, there were numerous other ambitions, needs, and pressures at work. Taken together, these helped to produce a railway policy awesome in its scale but shaky in its foundations.

Western farmers needed more boxcars to move expanding grain production. Ever greater numbers of new settlers each year suggested that potential expansion was virtually unlimited. The needs of mining and mineral development, and colonization programmes in northern Ontario and Quebec, also depended on improved railway communications. But added to these real needs were less measurable ones. First there were the empire-building ambitions of railway promoters, their financial backers, and the scores of hangers-on who thrived on the profits of contracts and sub-contracts, land speculation and just plain boodle. Second, there were the politicians, empire-builders in their own way, who recognized that reputations were made and broken, votes won and lost, through the promotion of enterprises of continental magnitude. They, too, had their hangers-on: the local politicians who knew that a branch line could ensure re-election, and the brokers of subsidies, land grants, and influence. Some of these men sat in every legislature in the land. Finally, there was that elusive but potent spirit of the age. If the twentieth century belonged to Canada, as clearly it did since the Prime Minister said so, could there then be any limit on the number of miles of railway the country could sustain? There might be a few errors along the way, such as the collapse of the Quebec bridge in 1907 at the cost of seventy-five lives and countless dollars. Or a contractor might fail to meet his deadline, as happened on the Winnipeg-to-Superior-Junction section of the National Transcontinental, thus losing the profits of several heavy crop years. But, since the future seemed boundless, errors could be rectified, or at least forgotten.

By the early years of the new century, the clamour for railway expansion from almost every crossroad, hamlet, and city on the prairies was becoming irresistible. "We want all the railways we can get," the *Manitoba Free Press* announced in 1899, "for Manitoba's proper policy is free trade in railways and we have got to have more railways if the crop of this country is to be moved out in any reasonable time."[19] Some of these western demands had to be met, and it was certainly more feasible politically to build a railway than to lower the tariff. But a new transcontinental would meet the needs of others besides the westerners. It could, if properly manipulated, satisfy the demands of those financiers, engineers, clerics, and politicians in Quebec who were once more talking about *la colonisation* as a panacea to save French Canadians from the perils of urban life.[20] Moreover, railway construction was linked to the general development of the country. New railways would put men and machinery into northern

Ontario to exploit the mineral riches, and into northern Alberta to reap the harvest of the fertile lands of the Peace River Valley.[21]

These were real needs. They were needs that powerful, and sometimes devious, men were anxious to meet: men like Sir Wilfrid Laurier, the Prime Minister; Charles Rivers Wilson, the British President of the Grand Trunk Railway and his American General Manager, Charles M. Hays; and finally those two Canadian entrepreneurs who proved their ability to compete with the best and the worst in the age of the great barbecue, Donald Mann and William Mackenzie, the creators of the Canadian Northern Railway. These men, and a host of smaller characters, played on a field stretching from the Yukon to London, England, and passed through board rooms and cabinet chambers. They played for high stakes in both money and power, often at the expense of the Canadian people, though the railway tycoons, like the politicians, always insisted that their own interests coincided with those of the nation. They stayed in the game to the bitter end, though not all had the dramatic flourish of Sir William Mackenzie who, at his first meeting with his future partner, is reported to have outdone Mann in a dispute over the ownership of a carload of mules.[22]

Mackenzie and Mann were first into the race to build a second transcontinental. In a few short years these two skilful promoters had built up a railway empire in the west through the acquisition of near-defunct charters, which often included substantial land grants. Through clever financing and political influence, they were ready in 1901 to announce their intention to extend the Canadian Northern Railway across the continent by 1908. This ambitious plan was welcomed in the west where Mackenzie and Mann were popular, since they had made a point of providing service where the Canadian Pacific refused to do so. Indeed, to some degree Mackenzie and Mann had built their reputations on the long-standing unpopularity of the older railway on the prairies, and they had early learned that public relations were at least as important as engineering skill in building a railway. And financing was more important than either.[23]

The western railway promoters knew that the federal Liberals, who had consistently criticized Macdonald's generous railway policies, would not make land grants to railway builders. Yet it was equally clear that public support was needed if their new system was to be commenced, let alone completed. They therefore bought up old charters, which contained subsidies and land grants from the past, and approached provincial governments for direct subsidies and bond guarantees. So successful was this scheme that by 1911 they had built enough of their line to convince the Laurier government that federal aid in constructing the long section from Montreal to Port Arthur was justified.[24] Their financial history was complicated, and their methods produced a ramshackle structure controlled personally by Mackenzie and Mann. They had a bond issue for every occasion: Gold Mortgage Bonds, Land Grant Bonds, Consolidated Debenture Bonds, and Perpetual Debenture bonds, among others. And for all of their vaunted private enterprise independence, Mackenzie and Mann collected some $218,215,409 from the Canadian taxpayer and six hundred acres of land per mile of railway. [25] In addition to the Canadian Northern their interests encompassed telegraph communications, steam shipping services, mining and real estate properties. Their enterprise epitomized the reckless spirit of development that reigned over the Laurier years. [26]

Whatever chance of success and financial viability the sprawling creation of Mackenzie and Mann may have had in 1901, it was greatly reduced the following year when the Laurier government decided to back another transcontinental project. One new railway, perhaps combining the eastern holdings of the Grand Trunk with the Canadian Northern's western lines, would have been an obvious solution. Even the railway entrepreneurs themselves had recognized the need for cooperation. On several occasions the two groups entered into discussions, but these came to nothing. Here was where the government might have stepped in to force agreement. But beyond recognizing the political and economic needs for a new railway, the Laurier administration had no real plans. Late in 1902 the Grand Trunk revealed a scheme to extend its own facilities to the Pacific coast. Laurier, using the stick of proffered subsidies, might well have seen this as an opportunity to bring the competing railways together. Rivers Wilson of the Grand Trunk certainly perceived this possibility. "I think Sir Wilfrid Laurier would be well advised if he undertook the part of intermediary between the Grand Trunk and Messrs. Mann and Mackenzie," he wrote in February 1903; " . . . the moment seems opportune for the handling of the matter by Sir Wilfrid as the 'honest broker.' " [27]

Laurier, whose cabinet was deeply divided over railway policy, recognized that a decision would have to be reached before the forthcoming federal election. He arranged at least two meetings between the principals of the two railways, but to no avail. Mackenzie and Mann were obviously unwilling to accept any proposal that would limit their control over the Canadian Northern, at least in the west; Hays was equally determined that the Grand Trunk should hold the controlling reins in any agreement. The Grand Trunk manager bargained in the most hard-nosed fashion hoping to force his competitors to sell out. [28] But, "we were too young and ambitious to sell at the time," Donald Mann admitted years later. [29]

Since Laurier was unwilling to force a merger between the competing lines, his only option now was to back one or the other of the competitors. He chose the Grand Trunk scheme. The choice was extraordinary in a number of ways. First, it was apparently based on the blithe assumption

that a country of some five million people could support three transcontinental railways. And if that assumption was not questionable in itself, then
it certainly became so when it was realized that 2,500 miles of the new
road was to pass through utterly uneconomic wilderness. The eastern
section was to be a colonization road that would obviously be of assistance
to the Liberal party. As Hays had remarked during the negotiation of the
contract, "Members obviously appeared far more interested in increasing
local rail facilities than in the viability of the entire project."[30] Moreover,
the government agreed to build the eastern section of the National Transcontinental, from Winnipeg to Moncton via Quebec City, thus placing
financial responsibility for some 1800 miles of the railway on the public
treasury. The Grand Trunk Pacific, a subsidiary of the Grand Trunk,
agreed to construct the western section. It would then lease the eastern
route for fifty years at an annual rent of three per cent on the cost of
construction, though the first seven years were to be rent free. Finally, the
federal government became the guarantor for seventy-five per cent of the
bonds issued for the Grand Trunk Pacific.

The proposal, not surprisingly, met strong opposition both in cabinet
and in Parliament. The Minister of Railways and Canals, A.G. Blair, who
favoured a publicly owned line and was doubtless close to Mackenzie and
Mann, had been largely ignored during the negotiations with Hays. He
resigned from the cabinet rather than accept the new scheme. He briefly
took up a position as chairman of the Board of Railway Commissioners
before joining a complicated intrigue designed to defeat Laurier in 1904.
Leading the opposition attack in the House of Commons, Robert Borden
insisted that the country could not afford either this particular arrangement or the resulting duplication of railway services. He insisted that the
competing railways should find a way of pooling their operations. By 1904
he had come to the conclusion that public ownership was the most practical method of providing the country with a second transcontinental.[31] In
defence of his grandiose plan, Laurier appealed to all the arguments his
party had so firmly rejected two decades earlier: the country could not
wait. Another railway would help decrease Canadian dependence upon
the United States. His last refuge was to resort to that expansive, optimistic
patriotism designed to tar his critics with the brush of anti-Canadianism.
"I am aware," he orated, "that this plan may scare the timid and frighten
the irresolute. But I may claim that every man who has in his bosom a stout
Canadian heart will welcome it as worthy of this young nation, for which
a heavy task has no terrors, which has strength to face grave duties and
grave responsibilities."[32]

Patriotic rhetoric came cheaper than ties, rails, and grades. But for the
time being the country seemed fully willing to accept the cost of both.

Despite the efforts of A.G. Blair and a group of fellow conspirators to defeat the Liberals in the 1904 election, Laurier easily carried the day.[33] "Our victory is so complete as to leave no doubt that our railway policy is extremely popular," Laurier wrote proudly, "the opposition made a grave mistake in adopting a policy of government ownership and operation."[34] The country at large apparently shared Laurier's optimistic estimate of the future. The railway suffered the inevitable setbacks in tight financial years like 1907, and experienced problems with construction and even occasional labour troubles. But worse than economic fluctuations and engineering failures was the repeated political interference: a branch line here to aid a local politician in electoral trouble, the appointment of a political friend there to help ease his way out of a tight spot, such as the premiership of Quebec. "Given honest and dynamic administration and a measure of good luck," the railway's historian has written, "it had a bare chance of success; under the dead weight of party politicians, greedy contractors and arrogant managers, it had none."[35]

In the short run the construction of the railway, and the work on the Canadian Northern, created employment, opened up new areas for settlement and exploitation, and contributed to the general economic growth of the country. But it did not remove the western farmers' grievances. After all, slow construction prevented the railways from providing the much needed additional freight volume in a hurry. Moreover, the farmer knew that transportation improvements, while essential, could not alone guarantee his prosperity.

III

Perhaps it was hopeless to expect to satisfy the farmer. It was not only politicians who were rapidly reaching that conclusion. A Methodist minister, who knew the west well, caught the essence of the agrarian spirit when he wrote in 1906 that "farmers are noted as grumblers, and the prairie farmers are no exceptions. They consider the railroads and implement firms as their natural enemies, and are continually growling about frost and drought. At the same time, however, inconsistent as it may appear – there appears the unquenchable spirit of hopefulness. The golden age lies not in the past, but in the future. There is on every side the most rapid advancement. Retrogression is never dreamed of."[36]

But even the successes of the Sintaluta case, and the promise of better railway facilities, did not completely clear the horizon for that prosperous future golden age. There were still those excessive freight rates that the farmers never stopped agitating against. Even more serious were the grain marketing institutions: the line elevators and the Winnipeg Grain Exchange. Once the farmer had defeated the elements and successfully harvested his crop, he faced another factor as unpredictable as the weather: the Northwest Grain Dealers' Association whose tentacles stretched all the way from the Grain Exchange in Winnipeg out to the local elevator agent. These men were the "syndicate of syndicates," who controlled prices, set grades, and funnelled the farmers' golden grain out of the west into the markets of the world. Convinced that they were not receiving a square deal on the market, the Sintaluta Branch of the Territorial Grain Growers Association decided to conduct an investigation in 1905. They appointed as investigator one of the most remarkable, energetic, and erratic men that ever crossed the agrarian political scene in the Canadian west. The "Sage of Sintaluta," as E.A. Partridge was called, was half practical organizer and half visionary – and the latter half usually won out in the end.[37] Partridge was a muscular, deep-voiced former school teacher from Simcoe County in Ontario, who had moved west in the 1880s and become thoroughly assimilated. In January 1905, Partridge arrived in Winnipeg to examine the workings of the Grain Exchange, an experience which convinced him, if he needed further convincing, that the financial interests and the farmers were enemies. He was doubtless the farmer who convinced the Winnipeg grain dealers that the farmers "believe that all wheat's no. 1 Hard, all grain buyers are thieves, and that hell's divided equally between the railways and the milling companies."[38] Partridge discovered very little in his investigation except that the grain buyers ran a secretive, closed corporation. The solution, he rapidly concluded, was for the farmers to own and operate their own grain-buying and selling system. Partridge was nothing if not a missionary. By the following year, firmly backed by his Sintaluta local, Partridge was well on his way to becoming the first president of the Grain Growers' Grain Company and its representative at the "House with Closed Shutters" – the Winnipeg Grain Exchange.

The first few years of the Grain Growers' Grain Company's history were, to say the least, difficult. The Exchange, unhappy at the idea of the farmers doing their own buying and selling, found a pretext to expel Partridge: a cooperative grain company, paying dividends, could hardly be expected to meet the requirements of a bastion of finance capitalism. But the directors of the Exchange acted without calculating the farmers' political power. By pressuring Premier Roblin of Manitoba, the Grain Growers were able not only to get themselves reinstated on the Exchange, but even to get a reconsideration of the rules. Partridge did not resume the seat on the Exchange, however; he had other schemes to float. In July 1907, young T.A. Crerar became president of the Grain Growers' Grain Company, which was now launched upon a healthy career.

Partridge had two more ideas he wanted the farm organization to support. One became known as the "Partridge Plan." No longer satisfied with the Grain Growers' Grain Company, Partridge had moved to the advocacy of public ownership of elevators: the provinces should assume ownership of local elevators while the Dominion government would control the terminal elevators at the Lakehead. In 1906, the Saskatchewan Grain Growers' Association put the "Partridge Plan" before a new federal Royal Commission. The proposal was rejected. At the same time provincial governments were pressed to move into elevator ownership locally. In 1910 the Roblin Conservative government in Manitoba went into the elevator business. Two years later the system collapsed and the line of elevators was leased to the Grain Growers' Grain Company. The blame for failure probably lay as much with bad management on the government's part as with the idea itself, but whatever the cause, the experiment was not repeated elsewhere.[39] In Saskatchewan and Alberta, a cooperative elevator system, with heavy government financial assistance, was the alternative tried and with a great deal more success than the Manitoba debacle.[40]

While the issue of control over local elevators was thus partially resolved, the problem of terminal elevators remained fundamental. "Just as long as these 'terminal' elevators remain in private hands," the *Grain Growers' Guide* declared on December 28, 1909, "there will be temptation to private gain. There is only one possible method by which the system of robbing the farmers' grain at the terminals can be abolished. That method is by Federal Government ownership."[41] But neither Laurier nor his successor was prepared to meet that radical demand.

Partridge's second project was a greater success. That was the establishment of a regular agrarian newspaper, the *Grain Growers' Guide,* as the organ of the western farm organizations. These three organizations, the Manitoba Grain Growers' Association, the Saskatchewan Grain Growers' Association, and the United Farmers of Alberta had come together in 1907 to form an inter-provincial council. The following year that council endorsed a decision of the Grain Growers' Grain Company to finance "a non-political paper." The first issue of the new monthly appeared in June 1908, and since E.A. Partridge was editor, most of its space was devoted to the "Partridge Plan." Characteristically, Partridge soon left the paper, and Roderick MacKenzie and the brilliant publicist, George F. Chipman, assumed control. By 1909, the newspaper had become a lively, very political weekly, complete with editorial cartoons from the superb pen of Arch Dale. Chipman described the *Guide*'s aims well in 1910: "designed to give uncoloured news from the world of thought and action, and honest opinions thereon, with the object of aiding our people to form correct views upon economic, social and moral questions, so that the growth in society may continually be in the direction of more equitable, kinder and wiser relations between its members, resulting in the widest possible increase and diffusion of material prosperity, intellectual growth, right living, health and happiness."[42] In the columns of the *Guide,* western farmers read not merely of grain prices, new agricultural techniques, and fertilizer; they also read the Rev. J.S. Woodsworth's "Sermons for the Unsatisfied," Francis Beynon's appeals for women's rights, Gustavus Meyers' *History of Canadian Wealth,* Edward Porritt's unending revelations about the corrupting influence of the protective tariff, and, of course, they learned about the campaigns of E.A. Partridge for a "cooperative commonwealth."

The cooperation of the three western farm organizations through the inter-provincial council gave impetus to a more inclusive ecumenism. The fact was that Canadian farmers had many common problems, and their strength could be increased by greater unity. In 1909, the westerners decided to approach the Dominion Grange with a proposal to establish a national farmers' organization. The Grange, now headed by E.C. Drury, proved immediately responsive. Out of a meeting in Toronto late in 1909 came the Canadian Council of Agriculture. It was to serve as the central clearing house for information concerning agricultural problems, to aid in organizing farmers throughout the Dominion, and to lead in pressing for improved government agricultural policies. Nothing had been more effective in uniting different farm groups than the growing conviction of farmers almost everywhere in Canada that central to their various ills was a single virus: the protective tariff.

The tariff, as the farmer viewed it, forced him to buy the necessities of life at prices artificially protected, while he had to sell his products on an unprotected and highly competitive international market. The obvious conclusion was that the farmer was paying the profits of inefficient eastern industry. So the farmer was able to convince himself that in calling for tariff reductions, he was asking for the simple justice of equal rights for all.

> The farmers of the prairie lands know well the foe they fight,
> The profiteers of Privilege, full armed with legal right;
> Against that giant bluff we need to solidly unite,
> For Equal Rights to All.[43]

To the contention that the tariff was not a mere method of fattening the manufacturers' profits, but rather a fundamental nation-building device,[44] the farmers responded with healthy scepticism. After all, they were nation-builders too, more important surely than the manufacturers. The farmer's philosophy was based on the assumption that rural life was the good life; urban living a necessary evil – God made the country, man made the town. Policies detrimental to agriculture were therefore ruinous of the good life. "Our future destiny and *national* character," one rural leader insisted, "depend on the quality of life that we can maintain in our rural districts."[45] The manufacturer's plea for protection, then, was pure self-interest. "Always bear in mind," the *Grain Growers' Guide* pointed out in 1910, "that the good old patriotic slogan of the C.M.A., 'Canada for the Canadians' means Canada for 2,500 Canadians."[46]

Central Canadian farmers were able to unite with westerners in an anti-tariff crusade for a reason particularly their own: rural depopulation. By 1910, Ontario and Quebec were fast becoming predominantly urban provinces. For the Ontario farmer who saw his family farm declining or his sons and daughters succumbing to the bright lights of the city, the major source of this evil was obviously the protective system. Gordon Waldron, of the *Weekly Sun*, put the argument quite explicitly in 1910. The causes of rural depopulation, he stated, were "protection and the exclusion of farmers from the markets of the United States."[47] W.C. Good devoted his farewell address as Master of the Dominion Grange to the same theme in 1913:

> Our national policy has deliberately and persistently fostered urban industries at the expense of rural. Our cities have grown with feverish haste, not because their growth provided advantages for the average city resident, but because it gave opportunity to the Big Industries and big landowners to exploit the labour of a large number of workers and to gather into their own pockets the "unearned increment." A class of idle rich has grown up in our cities, to whose love of ostentation commerce and industry are now pandering. These enervated and miserable specimens of humanity rush about the country in great cars, flaunt their wealth in our faces, tear up our roads and cast their dust upon our fields.[48]

Motivated by a potent combination of moral outrage and self-interest, the farmers' criticism of the tariff became much more than a mere dollars-and-cents calculation; it assumed all the dimensions of a crusade.

The farmers' great hopes for relief from the protective tariff when the Liberals came to power in 1896 had been quickly dashed. The farmers recognized that while the British preference was a slight help, Laurier was unwilling to knock any serious holes in the national policy. In 1900, he candidly explained the facts of political life to a farmer in Crystal City, Manitoba. "The truth of the matter is that you are more advanced in the West than we are in the East," he wrote:

> Our tariff may have been somewhat disappointing to our friends in the West, because it was not radical enough, but it has been perfectly satisfactory in the East and, on the whole, I have always been sorry that our friends did not accept it as a very important step in the direction of their views. You know as well as I do that we have to deal with the electorate as we find it, and that numbers must control.[49]

Laurier was saying something the farmers could simply not accept: the east controlled tariff policy. Moreover, Laurier's reference to the "step in the right direction" hardly seemed borne out by the trend of events. The reality was that the manufacturers were constantly pressing for increases. By 1905 Laurier's Minister of Finance, W.S. Fielding, was under strong pressure from all sides for tariff changes. He chose to appoint a commission to examine the problem. Fielding himself was joined by William Paterson, Sir Richard Cartwright, and L.P. Brodeur, and together they crossed the country hearing briefs. Mindful that they had not made their views heard very effectively at commission hearings preceding the 1897 tariff, the farmers turned out in droves for the 1906 sessions. The usefulness of their newly established or revived organizations was never better demonstrated. Fielding and his associates were given a thorough education in the benefits and the evils of the protective tariff. As the commission travelled over 14,000 miles, farmers everywhere argued their case for reductions to the level of tariff for revenue only. Otherwise, the foreseeable long-term result would be the destruction of the agricultural class. "Such a condition," E.C. Drury asserted, "cannot fail to have disastrous effects upon the nation at large, not only on its material prosperity, but on its political, social and moral life, the backbone of which is, and must be, the farm home."[50]

Against this social philosophy, the Canadian Manufacturers' Association argued that Canadian industries simply could not compete, on the same trade terms, with United States competitors. And without a strong industrial base, the country could not survive. "Not only has 'the protective tariff' been conducive to Canada's material prosperity," W.K. McNaught of the C.M.A. wrote, "but it has without doubt engendered a national sentiment previously unknown amongst our people."[51] The establishment of home industry was a major goal, and to do this, foreign investment was necessary. That foreign investment, some of the strongest supporters of the protective tariff noted with pride, came from "Americans who have established industries in Canada."[52]

Argument was long and vigorous. The farmer's closing shot was fired on November 16, 1906, when a delegation from the Manitoba Grain Growers' Association put the farmer's case as succinctly as it could.

> We therefore ask in the coming revision of the tariff, that the protective principle be wholly eliminated; that the principle of tariff for revenue only, and that tariff based on an honest and economic expenditure of public funds, be adopted, and as proof of our sincerity, we will, if the position be adopted by the government, gladly assent to the entire abolition of the whole list of duties on agricultural imports.[53]

The result of the commission's investigations, as embodied in the second

Fielding tariff in 1907, was hardly revolutionary and fell far short of the farmers' demands. Some reductions beneficial to the agricultural community were effected, especially in the farm machinery schedules. A three-tiered structure was set up, with general, intermediate, and preferential levels, thus further complicating the tariff, but meeting some of the manufacturers' complaints against the British preference. On the whole, however, the commission's hearings and the subsequent tariff changes appeared to confirm Edward Porritt's contention that the "protective policy is to be permanent" and "reciprocity with the United States is a dead issue in Canada."[54]

The new tariff satisfied neither the farmers' organizations nor the C.M.A. But anti-tariff agitation briefly died down as the farmers concentrated on a wider variety of issues: the growth of monopolies and combinations, the elevator question, the Hudson Bay Railway, and the ever-threatening signs of rural depopulation. As rumblings in the west grew louder, Sir Wilfrid Laurier, who had not been west since 1894, decided to become the first incumbent prime minister to inspect the progress of the prairies. In June 1910, the Prime Minister set out on a three-month tour, which took him right across the wheat lands to the Pacific coast. In a sense, it was a triumphant tour. Everywhere he went he was welcomed enthusiastically. But everwhere he went he also found that after the ceremonies of welcome came the farmers' petitions. Of course he had expected nothing else. Western supporters had warned him and briefed him. Just before he left, George Chipman of the *Grain Growers' Guide* had sent him a long letter, outlining the five major questions the farmers hoped to raise: the tariff, terminal elevators, the slow progress of the Hudson Bay Railway, a government-assisted chilled meat plant, and legislation supporting cooperative enterprises.[55]

But no issue received more attention from the farmers than the tariff. At every whistle-stop Laurier found farmers who could quote his pre-1896 attacks on the protective tariff. Where now was the tariff reformer of yesteryear? At Saskatoon one farmer pressed hard. "In 1896 you promised to skin the Tory bear of protection. Have you done it? If so, I would ask you what you have done with the hide?"[56] The best that the one-time free trader could do was to admit that his "blood is a little cooler now."[57] He could also hint that there were new opportunities developing for better trading relations in the United States.

The trip was an arduous one, but the aging Prime Minister enjoyed it. He returned to Ottawa in September with the voices of his prairie constituents ringing in his ears. Something short of public ownership could be done to improve the elevator situation,[58] and the developing trade negotiations with the United States would ease some of the western discontent. So, too, the Hudson Bay Railway could be hurried along a little, but there could be no question of accepting the general and increasingly radical agrarian programme. Laurier knew that, for the most part, there was little sympathy for the farmers' complaints, at least among eastern businessmen. After all, the west had been opened up and settled not merely for the benefit of the rest of Canada, but also at its expense. J.W. Flavelle, a prosperous Toronto meat-packer, and a man who rarely refused to offer advice to anyone he felt needed it, put the case forcefully in an "Open Letter Addressed to the Honourable Minister of Agriculture for Ontario," in the summer of 1910. "The farmers of this and the other provinces," the Toronto tycoon pontificated,

> have been diverted from enterprise and have been encouraged to look for returns through agitation, frequently ungenerous and generally wrong, which has had for its keynote that farmers were being deprived by the greed of others, of a legitimate share of the returns of their labour. Farm journals, the press generally, the departments of agriculture . . . have all followed the same course and have lost sight of the fact that the farmer, like everyone else in the community, can, in the last analysis, secure results only by his own effort, supported by intelligence, sound sense and industry.[59]

But the farmer, who prided himself on "sound sense and industry" too, believed that men like Flavelle enjoyed certain artificial advantages that were not frankly admitted. The tariff, for example. By 1910 the farmers had no intention of taking lessons from Toronto businessmen or of letting the Laurier government ignore agrarian aspirations.

In the autumn of 1910, Ontario farmers sent out a call to their western brethren to attend a great gathering in Ottawa. On December 16, some eight hundred farmers congregated for the "siege": five hundred from the west, three hundred from Ontario, and a handful from Quebec and the Maritimes. The following day, they trooped up Parliament Hill into the House of Commons where the oratory supporting the petition began. E.C. Drury spoke for Ontario, Partridge made a plea for a land tax to replace the tariff, and E.W. McCuaig, President of the Canadian Council of Agriculture, presented the main petition. Its philosophy was clearly, if awkwardly stated:

> Believing that the greatest misfortune that can befall any country is to have its people huddled together in great centres of population, and that the bearing of the present customs tariff has a tendency to encourage that condition and realizing also that the constant movement of our people away from the farms, the greatest problem that presents itself to the Canadian people today is the problem of retaining our people on the soil, we come doubly assured of the justice of our petition.

Laurier's response was dignified, complimentary, and evasive. Then they moved off to Rideau Hall where the Governor General, Earl Grey, held a reception, which undoubtedly exceeded the style to which most of the farmers were accustomed. Nevertheless, George Chipman, conscious no doubt of a few sneering eastern journalists, felt confident in remarking that "although their clothing was not of the latest cut, nor their whiskers trimmed in the most approved style, they realized the part they were playing in the upbuilding of the nation, their feeling of dignity did not desert them."[60]

Laurier's response to the farmers' delegation had been diplomatic. In fact, he saw little reason to believe that their programme would win acceptance outside the agricultural community. "The requests of our farming friends are too radical to stand the test of discussion and have no chance to be adopted in the east," he told an Ontario supporter.[61] If this was so, what was left for the farmer who believed his platform represented the minimum necessary for his prosperity? Yet neither political party seemed willing to take up his cause. Indeed, on matters that touched the farmers' interests, there seemed very little to choose between Liberals and Conservatives. Some farmers already believed that a farmers' party was the only solution. But the official view remained more cautious. It was expressed by the editor of the *Grain Growers' Guide* in 1911:

> The formation of a third party is a hazardous undertaking and one which is very liable to the purposes for which it is undertaken. The logical method to be pursued then is for the people to adhere to the respective names of which one designates parties and take charge of the party caucuses and see that the men nominated for Parliament are men who will support the demands of the people.[62]

Perhaps there was still reason for confidence in at least one of the established parties. On January 26, 1911, W.S. Fielding reported to the House of Commons on the trade negotiations with the United States. He had arrived at a reciprocity agreement covering natural products, which, though not all the farmers had hoped for, sounded like a good beginning. As the *Weekly Sun* remarked optimistically of the business community's hostility to reciprocity: "They see that the promised success of the agitation by the farmers for the opening of the American market to farm products may be a prelude to an assault on the whole citadel of Special Privilege."[63]

But before that assault took place, farmers, and other Canadians, were made to realize once again that more than trade was involved in a discussion of reciprocity with the United States. In fact, by 1911 reciprocity had become so confused with imperial relations and the future of Canada as a nation that the economics of farming was almost completely drowned in the uproar.

CHAPTER 9

Imperialism, Nationalism, and Reciprocity

The Boer War and the Alaska Boundary dispute troubled that relatively small number of Canadians who concerned themselves about Canada's place in the world. Both events had stimulated national feelings. But the difficulty was that those feelings took many different forms. To some the Alaska Boundary award proved that Canada could not rely on Britain's support in disputes with the United States. Yet the idea of going it alone, of breaking the imperial tie, was unthinkable. After all, there was no reason to believe that direct and independent dealings with the United States would produce any more satisfactory results.[1] That consideration probably dampened Laurier's enthusiasm, expressed shortly after the Alaska affair, for greater Canadian autonomy in external relations.[2] The Prime Minister, privately at least, admitted the truth in Lord Minto's realistic reminder that "if Canada wishes to possess complete treaty-making powers, she must be prepared to back her claims with her own forces."[3]

But the Alaska award had also heightened suspicion of the United States and concern that the "big stick" might again be raised toward Canada. This suspicion was only gradually removed, partly through the efforts of two British officials, Lord Grey, the new Governor General, and James Bryce, the British Ambassador to Washington. Both men subscribed to a general and vague belief in the moral unity of the English-speaking world. A step toward this ideal lay in "cleaning the slate" of the remaining differences between Canada and the United States.[4] By 1910 this was largely achieved, though the eruption of anti-American sentiment in 1911 suggested that Laurier's government had recovered from the bruised feelings of 1903 more quickly than large segments of the population.

The Boer War, too, had aroused national feelings and opened a long debate about Canada's place in the imperial family. Perhaps, above all, the war indicated the existing relationship was unsatisfactory. The fact was, as perceptive critics of Laurier's policy in both French and English Canada noted, that Canada had played the role of a colony responding to the appeal of the mother country in 1899. For many English Canadians that position was humiliating: Canada should have assumed a fuller role and in this fashion asserted her equality as a nation within a united British Empire. Principal Grant of Queen's University, now nearing the end of a long career as an advocate of a united empire of equal nations,[5] predicted nearly all the disputes that would grow out of the war in 1900:

> The larger patriotism which has now taken possession of Canadians, cannot possibly vanish. . . . We are henceforth a nation, and as every great statesman of the American Republic, from Washington to Cleveland, always urged upon their fellow countrymen "the nation that cannot resist aggression is constantly exposed to it," so, we must make our militia force a reality; must organize a naval reserve; must defend our coasts; must attract Newfoundland into Confederation; and must do these things at once. The party that does not understand the necessity of action is not loyal to Canada, or it is blind to the signs of the times.[6]

But not all Canadians agreed that greater involvement in imperial and world affairs was the most desirable way of asserting Canada's national status. Few French Canadians felt the sentimental attachment to Britain evident in large segments of English Canada. Even less did they feel responsible for the defence of a far-flung, multi-racial empire. "We are Canadians before all, and above all," one Quebec newspaper announced in 1901; "all our patriotism, all our love, all our aspirations, all our memories, all our soul attaches us to the Canadian land, to this ancestral soil where our fathers sleep: it is our only fatherland."[7] Henri Bourassa acted on exactly that assumption when he so strongly, and unsuccessfully, insisted that Laurier played a colonial role in 1899 in making a contribution to an overseas war in which Canada had no interest and over which she could exercise no control. "The French Canadian," Bourassa wrote in a British periodical in 1902,

> is decidedly exclusively Canadian by nationality and American by his ethnical temperament. People with world-wide ambitions may charge him with provincialism. But after all, this sentiment of exclusive attachment to one's land and one's nationality is to be found as one of the essential characteristics of all strong and growing peoples. On the other hand the lust for abnormal expansion and imperial pride have ever been the marked features of all nations on the verge of decadence.[8]

The French-Canadian position on the empire and defence matters was really very simple. Perhaps that is why it was so often misunderstood. The French Canadian insisted that he was loyal to the British Empire, loyal to the Crown, but in his own way. For him that meant a responsibility to defend only that portion of the British Empire which was his homeland: Canada. As Armand Lavergne told the Military Institute in 1910, French

Canadians had defended the Empire in 1775 and in1812, and they would do so, in the same fashion, again. "The Nationalists of Quebec today are willing and ready to give their last drop of blood for the defence of the British flag and British institutions *in this country.*"9

One obvious reason for misunderstanding between French and English in Canada was the almost total lack of social and intellectual intercourse between the two communities except, of course, in politics. Even in Montreal, where French and English lived side by side, each group followed its own instincts with little concern for the other. Staunch proponents of closer imperial ties like Andrew Macphail and Stephen Leacock contributed their articles to the *University Magazine* at McGill, almost oblivious to the opinions propagated by Henri Bourassa and Olivar Asselin in the pages of *Le Nationaliste* and *Le Devoir*. The *Montreal Star*, Sir Hugh Graham's yellow journal of jingoism, might just as well have been published in London.10 Lord Minto, a shrewd and sympathetic observer of Canadian society, was appalled at what he found in Montreal in 1902. "Society there is most peculiar and difficult," he told his brother, "full of cliques and petty jealousies, and the racial division in society absolutely distinct. I am really ashamed of the narrowness of the Britisher – he taboos the French entirely – he chooses to say that they are disloyal – and practically has nothing to do with them, and we found the leaders of society of both races unacquainted with each other."11

Added to the conflicting views of English and French Canadians was the worrisome question of the impact that the new immigrants would have on Canada's relations with the outside world. Could Ruthenians, Galicians, Germans, and Russians and for that matter, even Americans, be expected to glow with warmth at the sound of appeals for imperial solidarity? As early as 1902, before the largest numbers had yet arrived, a Canadian journalist raised and answered that question:

> The newcomers from America and Europe may make good enough Canadians, but will they become loyal subjects of the British Empire? The two terms are not synonymous. . . . Will not the present feeble separatist movement gather strength when the time is ripe, when the Dominion has increased in prosperity, and the population has been further swollen by foreign peoples, and particularly Americans, who are never weary of pointing to the progress of the United States as an independent power?12

That concern explains why some Canadian "imperialists" became immigration restrictionists, while others advocated rapid "Canadianization" through the "national" school system.13

It was through the shoals of these conflicting conceptions of Canada's interests that the Laurier government attempted to guide the country in its relations with the outside world. The storm signals had been raised in

1899, and for the next decade much of Laurier's energy was devoted to finding ways of avoiding a repetition of that crisis. The result was a policy of extreme caution, which oscillated between the narrow limits of either defending the status quo or, when forced to move, taking short, ambiguous steps in the direction of increased autonomy for Canada. It was an unheroic policy which satisfied neither French-Canadian *nationalistes* nor British-Canadian nationalists. But behind it lay a sharp political sensitivity to the potential division in the country, and the threat to his own power that would result if those divisions were allowed to grow. "Our existence as a nation is the most anomalous as has yet existed," he told a critic in 1909; "we are British subjects, but we are an autonomous nation; we are divided into provinces, we are divided into races, and out of these confused elements the man at the head of affairs has to sail the ship onwards, and to do this safely it is not always the ideal policy from the point of view of pure idealism which ought to prevail, but the policy which can appeal on the whole to all sections of the community."[14] In formulating his imperial policy, then, Laurier always kept a sharp eye on the domestic scene, especially on Quebec, for he was utterly convinced that domestic tranquillity could be seriously endangered by external events.

I

Laurier's cautious moves in the direction of greater Canadian autonomy were most obvious in the field of increasing Canadian control over local military forces. Yet even here, the initiative often came as much from Britain's desire to terminate expensive military commitments as from any wish by the Canadian government to enter into new military expenditures. This was clearly so in the 1904 decision to withdraw the British garrisons from Halifax and the later transfer of authority over the naval establishment at Esquimalt from Britain to Canada.[15] Rather more rancorous was the lengthy dispute surrounding the role of the General Officer commanding the Canadian Militia, a British-appointed officer. The GOC's position, under the Militia Act, was a difficult one. Though subordinate to the Minister of the Militia, he bore a responsibility to nurture an imperial military connection and to develop an efficient militia force. Ever since Confederation there had been friction between successive ministers and generals, as the imperial and military goals of the GOC were often at variance with the financial and patronage needs of local politicians.

The first serious clash in the Laurier years came during the Boer War, when the strong-willed and imperially minded Colonel Edward Hutton crossed swords with his Minister, Sir Frederick Borden. Hutton had practically ensured this conflict by taking what the Liberal government considered unauthorized initiatives in preparing the militia for South African service. To the government, the GOC appeared to be attempting to force its hand.[16] After the first contingent was finally dispatched, Hutton and Borden continued their dispute: the new issue was that of political appointments in the militia and patronage in the purchase of supplies for the expeditionary force. The relationship had so deteriorated by 1900 that Lord Minto, who had sympathized with Hutton in earlier disputes, found it politic to sign the order for the GOC's recall, though the blow was softened when Hutton was called for service in South Africa.

That Hutton had pointed to serious deficiencies in the Canadian militia is beyond question. Yet his apparent unwillingness to work in cooperation with his minister, and his obvious willingness to dabble in Canadian politics himself, made him the cause of his own downfall. His successor found Borden willing to move toward militia reform at a reasonable speed, but a speed determined by the minister, not the GOC. For the Earl of Dundonald, who became GOC in July 1902, this was not an entirely satisfactory arrangement. Ambitious and imperious, he almost at once became convinced that his immediate job was to sweep the militia clean of patronage, inefficiency, and apathy. Nor was he prepared to brook any opposition from a government which he strongly believed did not take the militia seriously. Sir Frederick Borden was equally determined to protect his ministerial authority, a point he made evident by carefully editing Dundonald's first, damning report on the state of the militia. Almost at once Dundonald took to the public platform to proclaim his imperialistic and militaristic opinions. Equally soon he became the centre of political controversy. Laurier, however, was not to be intimidated. "If the General commanding the militia has advice to tender," he informed the House of Commons, "it is not his right – I say it deliberately – to offer advice to the public, but it is his duty to offer it to the minister, and for that policy the minister shall be responsible."[17]

Throughout the conflict Borden proceeded slowly with reforms and alterations in militia procedures and practices. Most important, and to Lord Minto's dismay, the minister prepared an amendment to the Militia Act that would open up the GOC's post to Canadian officers. In 1903 the Governor General succeeded in having the amendment postponed on the ground that Borden should first consult with the British authorities. Shortly thereafter, on his return from meetings of the Committee of Imperial Defence, Borden announced that his proposals had received British approval. But there was still opposition to the change within Canada itself. This was led by the redoubtable Colonel Sam Hughes, M.P., who allied himself with Minto, and Dundonald, who still hoped to forestall the change. But Dundonald ruined any chance of defeating or even further delaying the measure by quarrelling with Sidney Fisher, the acting

Minister of the Militia, over the old question of patronage in militia promotions. The GOC decided to take his case before the court of public opinion and in so doing he sealed his own fate. This was conduct which the government could not accept, nor the Governor General condone. Dundonald was dismissed. There was a brief flurry of rumours that he might stand for Parliament as a Conservative candidate, but he finally left the country in July 1904. To the large crowd of well-wishers who waved him farewell, he cried dramatically, "Men of Canada, keep both hands on the Union Jack!"[18] The new Militia Act was passed, and the new Militia Council formed, in 1904. The new legislation represented an important step toward making the military force a Canadian institution, and certainly the new arrangements improved the militia's efficiency. But it was still a long way from the kind of force that could adequately provide for the country's defence needs. It would take more than an altered Militia Act to remove the feeling Dundonald had accurately described in 1903. "The mainspring of the difficulty," he wrote, "is the confessed belief of some of the members of the government that military expenditures and preparations are in themselves mistaken and unnecessary. In their eyes, the militia is merely a make-believe to keep the Jingoes and ultra-loyalists quiet; and this belief as to military preparations is not confined to politicians. It is widespread among the people and is commonly expressed both in conversation and in the press."[19] He might have added that one of the greatest weaknesses of the militia was its failure to attract any very significant number of recruits from among French Canadians. The result was that the militia was for all practical purposes an English-Canadian institution.[20]

Laurier showed similar studied caution both to the regular Colonial and Imperial Conferences held after 1897, and to plans to regularize and formalize imperial structures. His considered view was that the vague, undefined relationship that existed among the members of the Empire was an entirely satisfactory state of affairs. While always full of expressions of warmth and gratitude toward Britain and the Empire, Laurier never failed to insist that Canada's responsibilities within that association would be decided in Canada, by Canadians.[21] His fondest hope was that no crisis would arise that would necessitate any very substantial increase in Canadian responsibilities. His basic argument was that Canada fulfilled its imperial duties, and exhausted its financial capacities, in building up an economically strong and politically united nation. Thus, he was uninterested in, even hostile to, proposals for imperial reform, repudiated even the most vague commitments such as those accepted by his Minister of Militia when he attended the Committee on Imperial Defence in 1903,[22] and rejected every scheme designed to formalize imperial discussions.[23] While this attitude was often portrayed as the battle of an heroic colonial nationalist combatting the wily moves of the centralizers in the Colonial

Office, it was hardly that.[24] Both Joseph Chamberlain and his successor at the Colonial Office, Alfred Lyttelton, certainly had hopes for a more functionally integrated Empire. But these were never pressed very hard. Subsequent British governments, Liberal governments, were less and less interested in imperial integration, though they were concerned about such practical matters as imperial defence, especially after 1909.

Indeed, to some extent after 1905, the British were often embarrassed by the imperial ardour of some colonies, notably Australia and New Zealand, and were probably glad to find Canada applying the damper. Certainly in both 1907 and 1911 that was true: Australia and New Zealand put forward proposals to give the colonies both a greater equality of status in the Empire and increased responsibility for imperial policy. In opposing these schemes Canada and South Africa found no need to quarrel with Great Britain, for the mother country had little interest in sharing her power with the colonies.[25] Imperial enthusiasts like Dr. L.S. Jameson, Premier of the Cape Colony, found Laurier infuriating; after the 1907 conference Jameson told his friend Rudyard Kipling: "that damned dancing-master bitched the whole show."[26] Lord Milner, a self-appointed missionary for closer imperial unity, was cooler and shrewder. "I am sure you will be struck by noticing how small a part Sir Wilfrid Laurier played throughout," he remarked to R.L. Borden, "and how purely negative his attitude was when he did intervene in any discussion. His whole attitude seemed to be one of preferring the present dependent Colonial position with the prospect of future separation to a position of national equality with the United Kingdom which would involve closer union between the different parts of the Empire."[27] But what that assessment lacked was any understanding of the domestic divisions which lay at the root of Laurier's caution. Since Laurier personally did not favour closer imperial unity ("I suspect he dreams of Canadian independence in a future age,"[28] Minto observed accurately), he did nothing to remove the domestic obstacles to any policy but his own. Not long after the 1907 Imperial Conference, escalating Anglo-German naval rivalry resulted in exactly the problem Laurier's cautious diplomacy had sought to avoid.

Late in 1908 British public opinion was enflamed by rumours that the German naval programme had been secretly accelerated to overtake Britain's superiority in capital ships. More Dreadnoughts at once, became the cry: "We want eight and we won't wait." Campbell-Bannerman's Liberal government was forced, much against its will, to double its naval construction programme.[29] This atmosphere of mounting crisis was soon telegraphed across the Atlantic to the English-speaking population of Canada. The Toronto *Globe* was far more restrained than many other newspapers in demanding that Canada should "fling the smug axioms of commercial prudence to the winds and do more than her share."[30]

Though Laurier had committed his government to the formulation of a naval defence policy as early as the 1902 Colonial Conference, nothing had been done to fulfil the pledge aside from assuming responsibility for Halifax and Esquimalt. Now the naval scare forced Laurier's hand, though the leaders of both political parties knew the issue was highly divisive. On March 29, 1909, Sir George Foster, on behalf of the Conservative opposition, moved a resolution declaring that Canada "should no longer delay in assuming her proper share of the responsibility and financial burden incident to the suitable protection of her exposed coast line and seaports."[31] The resolution was general and avoided commitment to either of two responses being discussed outside the House: the establishment of a Canadian navy, or a direct financial contribution to the British Admiralty. On the Conservative side, particularly outside of Parliament, there was a growing feeling that the best way to display Canada's concern in the emergency was a direct contribution. That would result in more rapid construction of additional Dreadnoughts. Many members of the parliamentary Conservative party, including Robert Borden, were prepared to support that view as a temporary emergency measure, but not necessarily as an alternative for a Canadian navy. The resolution which Laurier placed before the House, as a substitute for Foster's motion, established the principle of a Canadian navy that would cooperate with the British Navy, and rejected the idea of regular financial contributions to the Admiralty. By implication, at least, it left open the possibility of a temporary "emergency" contribution.[32] The generality of the resolution allowed it to pass unanimously. The deep divisions, especially within the Conservative party but also in the country, were thus at first disguised under a superficial unity. It did not last long.

Following the passage of the 1909 resolution, L.P. Brodeur, Minister of the Marine, and Sir Frederick Borden, Minister of the Militia, were dispatched to Britain to attend an Imperial Defence Conference. The occasion was to be used to sound out British officials about naval policy. There is no doubt that Brodeur and Borden set out with their conclusions already in mind; their goal was to obtain the imperial imprimatur. Laurier had already decided to establish a small naval force, and he wanted imperial sanction for this policy in order to undercut opposition charges that the Liberals were set on destroying imperial unity. Brodeur found that the British, and especially the Admiralty officials, favoured a united imperial fleet. But the Canadian ministers rejected this suggestion and made it plain to the Admiralty that what the Canadian government had in mind was a relatively small expenditure. After much discussion the British cabinet recognized that the only practical solution was to allow Canada to set her own best policy, and to hope that it could be fitted into an overall imperial scheme.[33]

On January 12, 1910, Laurier introduced the Naval Service Bill, which provided for the establishment of a Canadian navy composed of five cruisers and six destroyers. There was also to be a permanent naval force, including both reserves and regulars. While the navy was to be under Canadian command, the bill provided that in time of war, and with the consent of Parliament, it could be placed under imperial control. Thus the Naval Bill was an almost perfect expression of Laurier's ambiguous view of Canada's status: a nation neither independent of the Empire nor fully integrated into it. "When Britain is at war," Laurier declared, "Canada is at war; there is no distinction."[34] That was a principle of international law. But the Naval Bill, and Laurier's speech supporting it, made it clear that the extent of Canadian participation in any imperial war would be decided by Canada alone.

By this moderate and somewhat ambiguous policy, Laurier hoped he could keep his own party united, while at the same time driving a wedge into the opposition forces. It was an old strategy, and one that he had perfected to such a degree that, at first, it looked as though it would succeed. Laurier apparently never suspected that there might be a means whereby the two ends could unite against the middle. But that is exactly what happened. At first, the naval policy announcement produced obvious discomfiture for Borden's Conservatives. By January 1910, Borden's English-Canadian supporters had moved quickly to the position that a direct contribution to the Admiralty was the only respectable response to the imperial naval crisis.[35] His few French-speaking followers, led by the troublesome and ineffective F.D. Monk, opposed both the idea of a contribution and Laurier's policy. Already, the Quebec Tories had been working towards an alliance, provincially and federally, with Henri Bourassa's nationalistes.[36] While the naval debate divided the Conservatives as a whole, it also had the effect of bringing nearly to fruition the Conservative-nationaliste alliance in Quebec. Borden attempted to bridge the gap between his French and English followers by insisting that a policy of direct financial contribution was purely temporary and that no permanent policy would be established before Canada was given a voice in the shaping of imperial affairs.[37] For the moment, at least, he was unsuccessful. Even the heavy-handed efforts of the Governor General, Lord Grey, could not bring Monk and his followers into a proper imperial frame of mind.[38] The Quebec Conservatives decided to go their own way, opposing both Laurier and their own party's official policy. Their proposal was to hold a referendum before any policy was adopted.[39]

After a lengthy and emotional debate, Laurier's bill, establishing what some Tories now derisively called a "tin pot navy," was passed. Soon the first two ships, the aging British cruisers *Rainbow* and *Niobe*, which were to serve as training vessels, were transferred to the Canadian command.

Because of the debate now spreading through the country, those two ships became the sum and substance of the Canadian navy for some years to come. The naval debate had opened up a controversy which led to profound divisions in the nation, undermined Laurier's power base in Quebec, and contributed greatly to the Conservative victory in 1911.

The hottest place in the continuing naval controversy was the Province of Quebec, and the leader in that debate was Laurier's one-time protégé, Bourassa. The Boer War had made a rift in their association; the Autonomy Bills in 1905 had broken it. From then on, Bourassa had grown completely convinced that Laurier was interested in nothing but remaining in power. Frustrated by his role in Ottawa, Bourassa had withdrawn to enter provincial politics in 1907, partly in the hope that he could thus help to destroy Laurier's provincial allies. Laurier never underestimated Bourassa's capacities. In 1907 when Bourassa left Ottawa, the Prime Minister reportedly remarked: "I regret your departure. We need men like you at Ottawa . . . though I would not want two."[40] He kept a close eye on his disappointed disciple, probably anticipating that if the imperial question were raised again he would have to do battle with Bourassa. What concerned Laurier especially was Bourassa's apparent influence with the leaders of the Church in Quebec. The "religious wars" of his early years were never far from Laurier's mind, and he feared that Bourassa, the *Castor-Rouge*, was the man who could relight sectarian flames. His nervous anticipation proved accurate.

Bourassa's associations with the provincial Conservatives, in a common fight against the Gouin government, had been quickly recognized by men like F.D. Monk and T.C. Casgrain as an opportunity to rebuild their party in Quebec. Laurier had stolen the "national cause" from them in 1896; Bourassa would help them win it back. The naval question offered the occasion to cement that alliance. By 1909 Bourassa's interests were again turning toward the federal scene, for he saw in the revival of the imperial question a threat to his conception of Canada. He may also have seen an opportunity to destroy Laurier. The debate on the Foster Resolution galvanized him into action. The time had now arrived for him to fulfil a long-standing ambition: the establishment of an independent, *nationaliste* daily newspaper. In January 1910, when Laurier brought down the Naval Service Bill, Henri Bourassa's new journal, characteristically called *Le Devoir*, was waiting with its editorial guns levelled. The paper was an almost immediate success, not as a mass circulation daily, but as a journal for that elite which liked some intellectual fare. Bourassa's influence was once more on the upswing.

An early sign of that growing influence was Bourassa's triumph at the Twelfth Eucharistic Congress of the Roman Catholic Church, which assembled in Montreal in 1910. The Congress itself worried Laurier, for he did not want to associate himself too closely with it for fear of awakening Protestant animosities. Yet he had his own people to think about. Under pressure from some of his supporters, he hurried back from his tour of the west to appear at the Congress.[41] Perhaps it was something of a relief to escape from those free-trade farmers. But the relief was short-lived. Bourassa was the star. He succeeded in upstaging every other Canadian, politician or prelate, when he challenged Mgr Bourne of Westminster, who had pleaded for the recognition of English as the language of Catholicism in North America. Nothing could have been better calculated to stimulate Bourassa to an oratorial triumph. "I do not wish," he proclaimed, "through a narrow nationalism, to say – that would be contrary to my thought, and I do not say it to my compatriots – that the Catholic Church ought to be French in Canada. No, but say with me that among the three million Catholics, descendants of the first apostles of Christianity in America, the best safeguard of the faith is the conservation of the idiom in which for three hundred years they have adored Christ. Yes, when Christ was attacked by the Iroquois, when Christ was denied by the English, when Christ was fought by all the world, we confessed him, and confessed him in our language."[42] That *tour de force* received a tumultuous response. The following day, when the Congress paraded through the streets of Montreal, no mitred head won the hero's applause that was given Bourassa by the throng along the route.[43]

Laurier had anticipated the developing alliance between Bourassa and the Church. In August 1910, he instructed Rodolphe Lemieux, then setting off for a European and African tour, to visit Rome and inform his old friend Mgr Merry del Val of this new threat of clerical interference in Canadian politics. He was especially anxious that such Church-controlled newspapers as *l'Action sociale* should be prevented from campaigning against the Naval Service Act.[44] Whatever effect Lemieux' delicate mission had, a new threat to Laurier's power came in November when the ballots in the Drummond-Arthabaska by-election were counted. That seat had been opened through the appointment of Laurier's old friend Louis Lavergne to the Senate. Lavergne had assured his leader that the Liberals would easily retain the riding. Laurier should have been more cautious; after all, he had once suffered personal defeat in the same riding in the 1870's. In fact, in 1910 the local riding association was in poor shape, and when an Arthabaskaville lawyer was chosen to contest the election, serious disaffection appeared in the Drummond section of the riding. The Conservatives left the field open to Bourassa and his friends, who put up a local farmer, Arthur Gilbert. Everything was now ready for an emotional re-run of the naval debate. Led by Bourassa, the *nationalistes* flocked down from Montreal to warn of the dangers of the navy – it was merely a prelude to conscription. The Liberals found it necessary to throw in their heaviest artillery. As candidates and supporters moved through endless *assemblées contradictoires*, the debating honours were repeatedly carried off by the enthusiastic *nationalistes*. But even Bourassa was not sanguine enough to expect victory. On election eve he prepared an editorial for the next morning's *Le Devoir* explaining that Liberal corruption had won again.[45] It was never printed. The *nationaliste* candidate carried the day by two hundred votes.[46]

Laurier was crushed; he insisted bitterly that "there are defeats more honourable than victory. This victory was won not by loyal opposition, but by His Majesty's disloyal opposition."[47] Nor could Borden take much immediate satisfaction out of the defeat, for, though Monk and the Quebec Conservatives had joined the *nationaliste* ranks, there seemed little hope of finding common ground between Bourassa and the official Conservatives. Confusion was the most immediate result of the returns from Drummond-Arthabaska, but one perceptive Conservative journalist saw the real meaning of the result: "It is a nationalist victory and as you will see the Quebec wing of the Conservative party is now completely swallowed up by the nationalists and owns Bourassa as its real leader. . . . Unless something occurs to mitigate the effect, the incident will make it far easier for Conservatives to campaign in English-speaking Canada. Hitherto they had to contend with the view that Laurier had a solid Quebec behind him and was unbeatable. . . . Unless something very spectacular occurs the Liberals will be unable to use this argument and instead will be confronted by the feeling that Laurier has lost his hold on Quebec and that his day as a dispenser of gifts is done."[48]

The naval question had forced Laurier to move out of his normal safe berth of non-commitment in imperial relations. The result was what he had always feared: disunity in the country, which threatened the ascendancy of the Liberal party. Drummond-Arthabaska was the first significant chink in the armour of the white-plumed knight. No longer did he seem invincible. And he seemed less and less so, as external policy assumed a larger role in the political debate in the country.

II

As the threat to British security from the direction of the North Sea grew ever more ominous, maintaining friendly relations with the United States became a primary imperative in British strategic planning. War with the United States was, of course, unthinkable. The Committee on Imperial Defence concluded in 1908 that it would be "not merely the supreme limit of human folly, but also . . . as unlikely as to be a contingency against which it is unnecessary to make provision."[49] But that was only the negative side of the problem. Equally important was the desire to enhance the friendly relationship. And in that area of policy Canada was all-important. Smarting from wounds inflicted by the Alaska affair, Canada's distrust of both Great Britain and the United States and their behind-the-scenes diplomatic schemes explained her reluctance to open up new discussions on the many remaining problems in Canadian-American relations. Those very problems provided the greatest outstanding obstacle to enlarging Anglo-American friendship. Until 1906 all three parties stood firm; neither Canada nor the United States was anxious to make any generous move toward the other; Great Britain, fearing another embarrassing blow-up in Ottawa, was reluctant to intervene.

Not entirely by coincidence, the replacement of Lord Minto by Lord Grey at Rideau Hall in 1904, of John Hay by Elihu Root at the State Department in 1905, and, finally, of Sir Mortimer Durand by James Bryce at the British Embassy in 1907, provided the occasion for a total reversal of positions. Reluctance, indecision, and evasion gave way to a feverish "cleaning of the slate" of Canadian-American problems. By 1913 Bryce could proudly tell the Ottawa Canadian Club that "we have, so far as human provision can go . . . dealt with all the questions that are likely to arise between the United States and Canada."[50] Signalling the new attitude in Ottawa, Laurier told the House of Commons in 1907 that "we can never conceive of war between us, or of war between Great Britain and the United States. We mean to settle all our difficulties with that nation by peaceful means, by diplomatic action, by negotiation, but never by war."[51]

He was as good as his word. In the next five years the host of issues hanging over from the Joint High Commission was quietly and effectively resolved in a series of treaties and agreements. The fisheries question was referred to the Hague Tribunal, which generally upheld the case of Canada and Newfoundland in 1910. The following year Great Britain, on behalf of Canada, joined the United States, Russia, and Japan in an agreement for the international regulation of the exploitation of fur seals in the North Pacific. Less spectacular, but no less important, were the agreements on regulation of inland fisheries, conveyance of prisoners, wreckage and salvage, boundary commissions and the like. All in all, Bryce, Grey, Root, and Laurier all had reason to be proud of their work.[52]

More significant than the resolution of the many nineteenth-century conflicts was the signing of the Boundary Waters Treaty of 1909, which established the International Joint Commission. Both in its origins and in its ultimate provisions, the treaty reflected the new century's growing concern with resource management and regulation. The vastly increased and more diversified use of water resources common to both Canada and the United States at the turn of the century provided the stimulus for early diplomatic resolution of a potentially divisive issue between the two countries.

In the west in the late 1890s, the source of conflict was rivalry over the use of the waters of the St. Mary and Milk Rivers for irrigation of the semi-arid land in the Palliser Triangle. In Alberta, Elliott Galt and Charles Magrath of the Alberta Irrigation Company, encouraged by Clifford Sifton, made an agreement with Mormon leaders in Utah for the construction of an irrigation canal and settlement on the company's lands south of Lethbridge. The plan called for diversion of water from the St. Mary River and was well under way by 1900. Similar schemes were being promoted in Montana, proposing to use the same waters. As early as 1895 John S. Dennis of the Department of the Interior had foreseen a conflict of interest and recommended "a commission to consider the question . . . of the division of the waters which might then be made the subject of a treaty between the two countries."[53] In the same year Dennis collaborated with Mexican delegates at the International Irrigation Congress in Albuquerque, New Mexico, in introducing a resolution requesting an international commission to adjudicate "the conflicting rights . . . on streams of an international character."[54] In 1896, Ottawa indicated its desire to cooperate with the United States in the regulation of international streams for purposes of irrigation[55] but received only an evasive response from Washington. The Alberta Irrigation Company's scheme then went ahead, with the use of the St. Mary and Milk Rivers for irrigation purposes by the two countries unresolved.

To the east, at Sault Ste Marie, the waters of the St. Mary River had been used for canals between Lakes Superior and Huron for some decades, and by the 1880s were also being used for hydro-electric development on the American side of the river. Canadian development for the same purpose became significant with the building of Clergue's industrial empire at Sault Ste Marie. In 1898 one of Clergue's companies, the Michigan Lake Superior Power Company, applied to the United States government for approval of the construction of a power canal and diversion works in the river. The following year the United States Corps of Engineers recommended against approval of the project and urged "the formation of an international commission" to consider the many legal, technical, and international questions involved in use of boundary waters for water power purposes.[56]

In 1889 the Illinois State Legislature set up the Sanitary District of Chicago, a "quasi-municipal corporation," and empowered it to remedy that city's growing water pollution and sewage disposal problems by building a canal from the Chicago River to the Des Plaines River. The purpose of the plan was to divert water from Lake Michigan through the canal into the Des Plaines and down the Mississippi River system rather than continue the practice of dumping raw sewage into the city's water supply, Lake Michigan. By 1900 the canal was open, and the Sanitary District was withdrawing large quantities of water from the lake. It had thus created one of the perennial technical disputes in Canadian-American relations in the twentieth century, because the amount and rate of diversion of water into its canal directly affected lake water levels (and hence navigation) in all the lower lakes of the Great Lakes system.

The other area of major boundary water difficulties was the Niagara River. The rapid industrialization of the lower Great Lakes states and the Province of Ontario depended on the growth of shipping on the lakes, and the use of larger and larger lake carriers. These, in turn, increased maintenance and improvements costs for harbours in the lake ports, especially for the cities on Lake Erie. One potential solution of the problem was to raise the level of Lake Erie by constructing a dam at the head of the Niagara River. In 1900 the United States Board of Engineers on Deep Waterways reported on the plan, calling attention to the necessity of Canadian cooperation in any such project. At the same time, growing concern was expressed on both sides of the border over the chartering of hydro-electric companies at Niagara Falls, which could divert water from the river without restriction thus impairing the scenic value of the Falls.

In February of 1902, on behalf of the President of the New York State Reservation at Niagara Falls, Senator Platt introduced a resolution in the United States Senate asking President Roosevelt to "invite the government of Canada to join in the formation of an international commission" to investigate the diversion of boundary waters. A month later, the Member of Parliament for North Victoria, Sam Hughes, introduced a similar motion in the House of Commons. Hughes' motion was withdrawn when he was assured that the government was giving the matter adequate consideration.[57] Platt's resolution had a more fruitful end. It emerged from Congress as a clause in the Rivers and Harbors Bill of the House of Representatives. In response to it, the President asked the British government to appoint three Canadians to join an equal number of Americans on the International Waterways Commission. The Canadian government agreed to accept the invitation in April of 1903 but it was not until January of 1905 that its three members were appointed.[58]

Meetings of the I.W.C. over the next two years made clear the number and variety of problems concerning boundary waters that resulted from increasing demands of industry and agriculture, as well as the need for rules and regulations governing the use of boundary waters and for some permanent agency to deal with these problems as they arose. By the spring of 1907 the Canadian and American governments had charged George Gibbons of Canada and George Clinton of the United States, leading members of the I.W.C., with drafting a comprehensive boundary agreement. After more than a year of diplomatic manoeuvering and particularly skilful negotiating by Gibbons, both with Laurier and the Americans, the Boundary Waters Treaty was signed in 1909.[59] After last-minute hesitations on the part of the Laurier government, ratifications were exchanged in 1910.

Arguing against the treaty in December of 1910, Robert Borden attempted to picture it as another surrender of Canadian interests: "Whatever the attitude of the United States may be with regard to matters of great international import, we are obligated to accept it, because we can do nothing but expostulate."[60] The Governor General, on the other hand, believed that "we have got, in my opinion, the best of the bargain – an uncommonly good treaty."[61] Both opinions were coloured, but Lord Grey's was closer to the mark. The point was that both of Canada's central demands, the establishment of fixed principles governing the use of boundary waters and a permanent commission – the International Joint Commission – to oversee them, were embodied in the treaty. They were of major significance. Henceforth the use of shared water resources would increase beyond all expectations, but under regulations and procedures agreed to by both nations. Even more important, the treaty recognized the highly technical complexities of international water use management. Of course, establishing the I.J.C. did not, in itself, solve the problems of using international waters by the citizens of either or both countries. After 1912, when the Borden government appointed the first Canadian members,[62] there was running disagreement among Commission members about the relative importance of its regulatory or judicial functions. But what the I.J.C. did do was to provide an appropriate body for the recommendation of solutions to boundary water problems – navigation, pollution, conservation of water resources, and so on – that were at once technically practical and equitable to the resource users of both nations. And it was at least one step removed from parochial political pressures and interest groups.

A constant source of irritation throughout this period of intense diplomatic activity was the apparently dilatory attitude of the Canadian government. In part the reluctance of the Canadians to come to decisions did stem from the government and especially the Prime Minister. Laurier was unquestionably overworked, and he did pay much closer attention to domestic than to external developments. But that was only one part of the problem; as Lord Grey explained to the Foreign Secretary, the very process of diplomatic procedures was too cumbersome, too complicated, too time-consuming.

The road between Ottawa and Washington should be shortened. The present route is as follows – Laurier approaches me, I pass on his communication to the Colonial Office, the C.O. passes it on to the F.O., the F.O. to Durand who then calls on the S. of State – and his answer comes back via this long circuitous route to Laurier. The result of all this is that Ottawa and Washington don't know each other.[63]

Grey's solution to the problem, that Canada "be allowed to attach to the British Embassy at Washington a man nominated by them and approved by me," was at least a decade in advance of official opinion in both London and Ottawa and anticipated similar considerations at the end of World War I.[64] In part that aspect of the problem was circumvented with the appointment of Bryce, who made it his special concern to give adequate representation to Canadian interests at Washington, and who short-circuited the official route to Ottawa via London with direct communications from Washington.

But even that was solely a mechanical solution, though its implications for the ever-sacred diplomatic unity of the Empire raised several eyebrows in the Foreign Office. Much more serious was the sudden realization that, however good their intentions, the Canadians simply were not able to negotiate *any* problem properly. Position papers on any subject, as they had discovered in 1898-99, were at best inadequately prepared; often, records of previous negotiations were so scattered that no position, aside from the impulse of the moment (and that might contradict records as recent as a year before), could be taken at all. There was no systematic collection of records, there were no advisers, there was no policy. This deplorable situation was outlined by the Under-Secretary of State, Joseph Pope, in a memorandum to the Civil Service Commission in 1907. Pope explained that in the earlier years of Confederation,

the Prime Minister of the day kept [external affairs] pretty much in his own hands; but with the growth and development of the Dominion this is no longer possible.

The practical result . . . is that there does not exist to-day in any department a complete record of the correspondence. . . . It has been so scattered, and passed through so many hands that there is no approach to continuity in any of the departmental files. Such knowledge concerning them as is available, is, for the most part, lodged in the memories of a few officials. . . . If some reform is not soon effected it will be too late.[65]

Pope recommended the creation of a Department of External Affairs – "a small staff of young men, well educated and carefully selected . . . and . . . specially trained in the knowledge and treatment of these subjects" – and henceforward carried on a quiet campaign with Laurier's ministers for support. Lord Grey heartily supported Pope's recommendation: "Sir W. Laurier's work would be ever so much facilitated, and Canada would be prompt and satisfactory to deal with, instead of the swollen impossible cork, the extraction of which almost bursts a blood vessel."[66] By 1908 Laurier was convinced, and, with the election of 1908 safely over, the Department of External Affairs was created in 1909 and attached to the office of the Secretary of State. Pope found himself appointed Under-Secretary, inadequately housed and staffed in a room above a barber shop on Bank Street. A serious anomaly remained. The Secretary of State was the responsible minister for the department but the Prime Minister in fact determined the guidelines of foreign affairs. In 1912, the new Borden administration, in a more concerted and systematic approach to foreign policy problems, transferred responsibility for the department to the office of the Prime Minister.[67]

<h2 style="text-align:center">III</h2>

One remaining problem in Canadian-American relations, as old as Canada itself and ever changing in its dimensions, was the difficulty of arriving at trading arrangements satisfactory to both nations and their consumers. By the time the Canadian Council of Agriculture presented its brief to Parliament in December 1910, praying for tariff relief, negotiations with the United States for a new trade agreement were well under way. Political pressure from the farmers coincided with diplomatic pressure from the republic to break the bonds of reciprocity in protective tariffs that had characterized Canadian-American trade for more than three decades. The American initiative was at once coercive and friendly, growing out of the Payne-Aldrich tariff of 1909. That "reform" of the United States tariff adopted the European model of protectionism, setting the previous general level of protection as its minimum level and establishing a twenty-five-per-cent higher maximum level. This schedule was to be applied to trading partners judged to be discriminatory in their trade practices against the United States.

In 1907, after an extensive cross-country inquiry, the Laurier government had also modified its tariff structure by inserting an "intermediate" tariff level between the general tariff and the British preference. The object was to reach more satisfactory trade agreements with non-British nations on the basis of reciprocal agreements below the general rates. In the same year such an agreement, limited in scope, was made with France, soon followed by less important treaties with Japan and Italy. After the passage of the Payne-Aldrich tariff, the United States was forced to regard these minor treaties as discriminatory and threatened to apply its new maximum penalty rates to Canadian imports.

At the same time, President Taft was reluctant to impose the trade penalties upon Canada and, even more, was under heavy pressure from

Democrats and insurgents in his own party to lower the tariff. A face-saving arrangement with Ottawa was worked out in the spring of 1910; in the fall, the Americans proposed full-scale discussions on reciprocity. From the first it was clear the Americans were anxious to go much further than their neighbours. By mid-January 1911, a comprehensive agreement had been reached. At Canada's insistence it was to be implemented by concurrent legislation rather than to take the form of an Anglo-American treaty. The agreement itself was in four parts: first, most natural products of either country and a very few manufactured items were to be accorded free entry into the other; second, identical lower rates were to apply to secondary food products, agricultural implements, and some commodities; finally the Canadians were to reduce duties on some other American goods, but not to the level of similar items in the American tariff, and the same was to be done to some articles in the American tariff. President Taft called Congress back into special session in the spring to consider the agreement and approval was finally given in July.[68]

Fresh from Washington, Fielding enthusiastically presented the agreement to Parliament on January 26. Most Liberals were surprised and jubilant; after decades of degrading begging for reciprocity, each plea being met with insolent refusal from Washington, not only had Washington now come to Ottawa on bended knee but a broad agreement for freer trade had actually been accomplished. For their part, the Conservatives were thunderstruck. "There was the deepest dejection in our party, and many of our members were confident that the government's proposals would appeal to the country and would give it another term of office," Borden observed.[69]

On the face of it, reciprocity was difficult to oppose. In Saskatchewan, Haultain, leader of the Conservative opposition, joined in a unanimous vote in the legislature in favour of the agreement. Among the Conservative provincial premiers, only Roblin of Manitoba stood against an obvious favourable reaction – "until it was announced the drift was undoubtedly against the government but now it is just the other way about," J.W. Dafoe reported to Laurier.[70] McBride of British Columbia, Hazen of New Brunswick, and Whitney of Ontario all hesitated before denouncing reciprocity. Eventually all of them managed to get anti-reciprocity resolutions through their legislatures on straight party votes.[71]

It soon became clear, however, that if attacking reciprocity itself was dangerous, a frontal attack on its "inner meaning" was not. What reciprocity seemed to imply was yet another assault by the Laurier government against the imperial connection, a long step on the road toward commercial and eventually political union with the United States. So interpreted, the agreement provided a golden opportunity for Whitney, McBride, Hazen, and Roblin to wreak revenge on the Laurier government for its

degrading stand on the naval issue. "The Liberals have failed in their duty
. . . by the half hearted measures they have adopted," McBride told
Borden.[72] This also seems the most reasonable explanation for Roblin's
action, in light of his ardent advocacy of reciprocity in natural products
as the leading plank in a Conservative platform as late as 1907.[73] So
interpreted, a campaign against reciprocity could arouse the latent anti-
Americanism in Canadian national sentiment against the apparent anti-
imperialism in Laurier's naval policy. And this was the main ground of the
fight that ensued. In Ontario, pictures of the American flag were censored
out from moving pictures. Across the country reciprocity became the
symbol of the destruction of Canadian home life "because divorces would
immediately become prevalent . . . and . . . every conceivable kind of ill
would be let loose." "The 'Ultra Imperialists,' " the American Consul
General in Ottawa reported, "really represent their loyalty to the British
connection to be a much poorer thing than I believe it is, for they seem
to think it can only exist by keeping up an isolation of the Canadian people
from outside influences."[74]

The clue for a successful attack on reciprocity, picked up by the Tory
premiers, came from the shrewdest group of Canadian lobbyists, the businessmen. Nurtured by and supporters of Laurier for fifteen years, they
suddenly broke with the Ottawa government when they perceived their
vested interests in national transport, commercial and industrial policy to
be threatened. On February 20, eighteen Liberal Toronto businessmen
and financiers (Sir Edmund Walker, J.L. Blaikie, W.D. Mathews, W.K.
George, Z.A. Lash, W.T. White, G.T. Somers, R.S. Gourlay, Sir Wm. M.
Clark, R.J. Christie, H. Blain, Henry S. Strathy, L. Goldman, G.A. Somer-
ville, W. Francis, J.D. Allen, E.R. Wood, and J.C. Eaton) issued a manifesto against reciprocity because, they said, it would "weaken the ties
which bind Canada to the Empire . . . and make it more difficult to avert
political union with the United States."[75] "Although a Liberal, I am an
Imperialist," Walker explained, "and the national reasons against the
proposals are perhaps more frequently in my mind."[76] As the anti-reciprocity campaign developed, the Canadian Manufacturers' Association quietly set up the Canadian Home Manufacturers' Association in Toronto,
with links in Winnipeg and Montreal where the similarly rooted Anti-
Reciprocity League was founded. The C.H.M.A. was the collection centre
for business contributions against reciprocity, and the origin of anti-reciprocity propaganda distributed by Lash's Canadian National League to
some three hundred daily and weekly papers, which regularly printed
their prepared copy.

For Robert Borden the defection of prominent Liberals from Laurier's
camp was a particularly welcome omen. For many years there had been
rumours of impending alliances with dissident Liberals as a result of one

or another of Laurier's policies, and it was no secret that Borden's door was open. As early as 1907, B.A. Macnab of the *Montreal Star* was playing the role of intermediary between Bourassa and Borden, and a year later Roblin reported that "the alliance with Bourassa is pretty close now."[77] At the same time Willison served as an effective link with Sifton and by 1910 his Ottawa correspondent was advising Tory friends "to leave Sifton alone."[78] And in 1910, as well, Sam Hughes reported that some Toronto businessmen who objected to Laurier's naval policy were ready to bolt.[79] Of the six Hughes named, Walker, Flavelle, George, Wood, White and Clark, only Flavelle, who was not a Liberal, did not sign the February manifesto. All that seemed to be needed was a convenient issue upon which to make a public break. Reciprocity, perhaps less a cause than an excuse, gave the signal for desertion.

Now the pieces of Borden's strategy of wooing suddenly fell into place. Sometime in February Lloyd Harris, a Liberal M.P. and Ontario manufacturer who had crossed the floor because of reciprocity, sounded out Borden. He found him "afraid of the division in his own following and disinclined to fight." The chat was heartening to both men and Harris went away to rally "recalcitrant Liberals" in Ontario. On March 1 he returned to Borden's office with Lash, Willison, and Sifton, who had denounced reciprocity in the House of Commons a week earlier. All were now ready to join Borden in the fight against reciprocity and the four agreed upon a general set of guidelines for a new administration if they were successful.[80]

Given these developments, Borden's mood shifted from doubt to confidence, his policy from hesitant confusion – should he or should he not force an election?[81] – to a determination to filibuster the reciprocity bill in the House while anti-reciprocity sentiment was whipped up in the country. The debate was adjourned for Laurier to attend the Imperial Conference, only to be resumed when he returned in July. At the end of the month the Prime Minister had had enough. He challenged the Conservatives to a September election.

Apparently the Grits, despite the defections, were impressively strong; the Tories were woefully weak. Reciprocity, after all, was an attractive issue and it would be a fitting climax to fifteen years of unprecedented prosperity under a popular Liberal administration. In contrast, Borden seemed the epitome of respectability and integrity in politics, but he did not "take" with the people and was no leader of his party.[82] His first election, 1904, had been a personal disaster, when Fielding had engineered a sweep of Nova Scotia, and the opposition leader's humiliating defeat. Serious attempts at national organization had begun in 1906 and 1907. In 1907 Borden had announced his progressive – as he called it – Halifax Platform, but he did so without consulting his caucus, and its emphasis on public ownership deeply offended Montreal businessmen. Then in 1908 Laurier had stolen and half-heartedly implemented two of his other planks, rural free mail delivery and civil service reform. Borden's "purity in politics" sessions in the House from 1906 to 1908 had fanned the smoke of Liberal scandals, but revealed no telling sources of fire. With organization incomplete and financing inadequate, internal dissension over his platform, and a prosperous public uninterested in hints of malfeasance in the Liberal administration, the Conservatives held their own in the 1908 election, but did no better than before. A planned convention of the party was postponed in 1910 because of differences between French and English members over the naval issue,[83] and an open revolt against Borden's leadership occurred after he had replaced "regular" party men by Perley as chief whip, and H.B. Ames as national organizer.[84]

The 1910 revolt was quashed when Borden threatened to resign and Whitney and Roblin came to his aid, the latter advising him to "have the courage of a lion, and a face of flint and exercise your rights as leader in as autocratic a manner as does the Czar of Russia."[85] Then in 1911 the "regulars," led by Reid, Northrup, and William Price, struck once more at Borden's leadership just as the reciprocity campaign got under way. Again the ostensible cause seemed to be dissatisfaction with problems of organization; the movement, Hughes reported, was against the lieutenants, Perley and Ames, rather than Borden himself.[86] But it coincided with Borden's first flirtatious meetings with the Liberal bolters, and it seems clear that the staunch party men were really challenging their leader because of their desire to have no more truck and trade with the Grits or Bourassa's *nationalistes* than with the Yankees.

It was all very embarrassing and did not augur well for the forthcoming election. But appearances could be, and were, deceiving. Trouble at the top, within the Parliamentary party, did not filter down to the constituencies. There, and especially in Ontario where the crucial battle would be fought, local organization which had begun so feebly in 1907 had nicely coalesced by 1911.[87] In Manitoba and British Columbia as well, and to a lesser extent in New Brunswick, local organization had taken on strength because of close cooperation between federal Conservatives and the ruling provincial parties. That cooperation, with the added strength of party financing by anti-reciprocity businessmen, gave the lie to the apparent weakness of the Conservative contingent and its Liberal and *nationaliste* allies.

Correspondingly, the strength of the Liberals was deceptive. They had all the weapons of a ruling party at their disposal, all the power of federal patronage, and a revered leader in Laurier. Laurier himself was very confident of the outcome. A month before the vote he confided to Lord Grey that "unless appearances are deficient, we will do much better than

I had expected. The main issue is strong, but there are in several constituencies local troubles which are likely to jeopardize a few seats."[88] There was no one who could or who would challenge his leadership; the decision of the defectors to bolt rather than fight from within was clear enough evidence of Sir Wilfrid's grasp of the reins of power. But also unlike the Conservatives, Liberal strength at the top rested upon crumbling foundations. Fielding could probably hold Nova Scotia and its maritime neighbours in check with the lure of reciprocity; so might Premiers Scott and A.L. Sifton in Saskatchewan and Alberta. But doubts about Laurier's grip on his own province were confirmed late in June when the threatened alliance between Bourassa and Borden's Quebec spokesman, Monk, was consummated. Granted, party regulars like William Price, the Conservative organizer, had mixed feelings about the event. "All the news I get is most encouraging," he wrote,

> the one black spot is the position in this blessed province. Monk has again put us into a most horrible mess. He has made a definite alliance with Bourassa and the Nationalists, and this new combination is calling itself an Independent Conservative Party, under the leadership of Monk. They will not be able to obtain much funds for organization, but they will, at any rate, take several seats from the Liberals.[89]

Needless to say, whatever doubts some Tories had were small consolation to the Prime Minister. His vulnerability on the naval question, the key issue in Quebec, had been revealed the previous November in Drummond-Arthabaska.

In Ontario the situation was even worse. There Laurier seemed to be fighting on the wrong side of both the navy and reciprocity questions. If increased trade with the United States meant at best the stopping of American industrial investment capital flowing into Canada, and at worst the closing of Ontario's factories, reciprocity would hardly appeal to the people in the province's growing cities and industrial towns.[90] And even specialist producers in the agricultural community were either dubious about or hostile to the agreement. Moreover, the Liberal leadership and organizational structure in Ontario was virtually non-existent. Aylesworth, Laurier's Ontario lieutenant, recognized by 1911 that he had long since lost control of his province, but stayed powerless at the helm out of a deep devotion to his leader. Beneath him the party tore itself to pieces with internal rivalry, and there was no younger man in the fold with sufficient power, or attractiveness, to put it back together. "Whatever Conservatives may do, Liberals will not follow that leadership," Newton Rowell warned in 1910.[91] Many did not.

On September 21, after months of argument through pamphlets, leaflets, articles and editorials, and of cajoling by party leaders, the electors cast their ballots, perhaps for reciprocity, perhaps against the "tin-pot" navy, perhaps for a candidate they knew, perhaps for a promised bridge, road, wharf or post office. Any and all these considerations, cool self-interest and heated emotion, oratory and whiskey influenced the decision. The over-all popular vote was extremely close; 666,074 for the Conservatives, 623,554 for the Liberals. But that did not count. What did was the number of seats each party held, and on that basis the Conservative victory was amazing; 134 seats to 87 for the Liberals. In Quebec the Bourassa-Monk alliance had paid off; a gain of 18 seats for a total of 27. In Ontario, perhaps as expected, the Liberals were smashed. Borden, Whitney, and Sifton had returned 73 Conservatives to Laurier and Aylesworth's 13 Liberals.[92] Bitterly, an Ontario Liberal poured out his feelings to the defeated Minister of Labour, Mackenzie King. "In a manufacturing town," Stratton observed,

> with the well known and usual activity of manufacturers when they get their Irish up, with an unintelligent rural body, and with the working men being controlled by the manufacturers, what use is there attempting to legislate for the working man or farmer? I fought a good fight on a cause I did not believe in and which I will never do again. Fighting for the "full dinner pail" and the "farmer" is poor policy – neither appreciate your efforts on their behalf, and are controlled by their employer when it comes down to the finally final. . . . I am neither laughing nor weeping – I am just thinking what damn fools we were.[93]

Robert Borden received the joyous results at party headquarters in his old riding in Halifax. After a few days' rest with his family in Grand Pré, he boarded the train for Ottawa, prepared to accept the seals of office. By that time Conservatives from across the land were descending on the capital, anxious to assume both the responsibilities of power and a long-awaited division of the spoils of victory.

IV

A mood of surprise and expectation spread across the country. There was excitement and speculation about what the new administration might do for Canada. Fifteen years had passed since the last change of government, and during that time the country had expanded and changed in many striking ways. Two new provinces and two million people had been added to the nation; in 1911 nearly seven and a quarter million people lived in Canada. The western plains had been filled with agricultural pioneers who made wheat the country's new staple product. Yet the greatest population increases had taken place in the urban areas, though rural people still outnumbered their urban cousins by about one million.[94] In central Canada the rise of modern manufacturing drew men and women to the cities from the farm and from overseas; in 1911 the majority of Ontarians lived in urban areas.[95] Among that growing population was a new element, "the foreigners" whose impact upon the nature and outlook of the country was still an unknown and, to some, a disturbing factor. New cities and towns had sprung up, new railways and industries had been built, and new highways to carry the increasingly popular automobile were under construction. And in February, 1909, J.A.D. McCurdy had flown his biplane *Silver Dart* at Baddeck, Nova Scotia, the first flight in Canada.

The Laurier years had been a time of boom and prosperity. A new Canada had emerged. But the inequalities and materialism of the age had produced vocal social critics: farm and labour leaders who believed that their followers had received less than a fair share of the new affluence, French-Canadian *nationalistes* fearful for the future of their society's distinctiveness, feminists demanding political equality, urban reformers concerned about slums and sanitation, prohibitionists zealous to "Banish the Bar," and advocates of "Canadianization" uneasy about the foreign immigrant. These critics, sometimes vaguely, sometimes precisely, demanded new public policies to ease the transition from an agricultural to an industrial age. By 1911 Laurier had begun to sense this need, yet the only new policy he could offer was an old one: reciprocity with the United States. But the new Canada was not to be satisfied with a panacea from the past. The Liberal leader clung to his essential political convictions despite an awareness that they were being challenged. "I must tell you frankly," he wrote to a man who asked his opinion about public ownership of terminal elevators, "that for my part and with my strong convictions, borrowed from the English Liberal school of politics, I am not much in favour of the growing view of substituting collectivism to individualism in the relations of the government with the people."[96] But the individualistic Gladstonian liberalism to which Laurier owed allegiance had already passed into the collectivist liberalism of Lloyd George. John Willison went straight to the mark when he observed in 1911 that though Laurier "was classed in Canada as a Liberal, his tendencies would in England have been considered as strongly Conservative; an individualist rather than a collectivist, he opposed the extension of the state into the sphere of private enterprise."[97]

The increasing irrelevance of Laurier's kind of liberalism was, ironically, one major consequence of the country's rapid growth from 1896 to 1911. What the reform movements represented, in part, was the search for a new public philosophy. One reformer, increasingly attracted by collectivism, summed up the essential problem of the new Canada. "The fact is that in Canada," J.S. Woodsworth wrote, "industrialism has been suddenly thrust into what was essentially an agricultural society. Many of our laws are not modern. . . . Improvement comes slowly and is resisted, because the Canadians who largely dominate the situation do not understand the new social order. Country-bred men, essentially individualistic in thought and ethics, have attained positions of responsibility in highly organized industrial concerns."[98] He was thinking of the plutocrats of the Mausoleum Club: "Practically every one of them came from Mariposa once upon a time."[99]

Stephen Leacock's *Sunshine Sketches of a Little Town* not only immortalized the election of 1911, but also symbolized some of the changes in Canada during its transition to the industrial age.[100] But despite his great hopes for the new Conservative regime, even Leacock found it difficult to believe that the long Liberal ascendancy was ended. It had almost become a permanent part of the Canadian romance:

> The leader with his white plumes typified, as it were, purity and chivalry: his bilingual eloquence recalled the union of the two races on which the Canadian Commonwealth was built. Beside him was Sir Richard Cartwright, the Nestor of the Senate, whose views on Free Trade were known to be so profound that they figured, without further utterance, as a solid asset of a Protectionist government. Here, too, was Mr. Fielding the magician of the legend who could spin you a yearly surplus out of the palm of an empty hand as easily as a juggler twirls a billiard ball out of nothingness. Near him, lest the reproach of senility might be brought against a government growing grey in office, was Mr. Mackenzie King, a sometime economist now "gone bad" in politics, whose boyish countenance was useful as typifying the fire of youth and in its gentle moments was supposed to beam with all the roguishness of political childhood. The debonair Mr. Fisher presided over agriculture and the weather, becoming, in the Liberal mythology, the god of the Harvest, just as Mr. Pugsley had become the god of Wharves and Bridges and Sir Frederick Borden, from his repulse of the Fenians in 1866, the god of Scientific Warfare.[101]

That Liberal mythology had been shattered. Now the country, so changed during the fifteen years of Laurier's rule, waited to see how the newly elected government would deal with the problems those changes had created.

CHAPTER 10

An Attempt at Reform

I

The transfer of power began respectably enough. After Borden arrived from Nova Scotia, there was a triumphant Conservative victory parade through the streets of the capital. And, in contrast to the deplorable squabble in 1896 between Tupper and the Governor General over the former's numerous "midnight" appointments,[1] the defeated Laurier government wound up its affairs with quiet dignity. Parliament Hill was still, but the same could not be said of the crowded hotel suites where hungry Tory office-seekers gathered to plot and gossip, or of the railway station where special trains bearing "important personages" puffed in and out at all hours of day and night, or of the impressive residence of the Prime Minister designate on Wurtemberg Street where all sorts of men came seeking favours, offering advice, threatening reprisal if a rival faction got the plum. To one waiting – too long, he thought – to be called by his chief, it was intensely frustrating: "More people – more wire pulling, deputations galore and general suspense. [Borden] seems helpless on the surf," wrote Sir George Foster.[2] Another Conservative, one of the few who apparently wanted nothing for himself, disgustedly reported: "There was hardly a member of the party who did not rush to him [Borden] and say he had to make him a cabinet minister. It was a most humiliating spectacle, this rush for the spoils of office, this playing pussy in the corner."[3]

Even Borden was surprised and probably appalled at the performance of his followers, though he should not have been after fifteen years in federal politics, and ten as leader of the opposition. But he was not helpless before the tide of seekers. Coolly and very correctly he received the Governor General's best wishes, an offer of assistance, and the characteristically meddlesome warning that "the presence of Mr. Monk as one of your colleagues on the Treasury Bench" might "mean a weak or retrogressive Naval Policy."[4] There were, of course, many contending factions to be conciliated and placating them all, balancing the forces

Borden needed in his cabinet with those which he wanted, took both time and skill. The Parliamentary party and the party regulars both needed strong representation. So too did the Quebec members from the Monk-Bourassa alliance. But beyond that both the Liberal defectors and the Tory provincial chieftains who had played so prominent a part in the victory deserved representation. Borden skilfully weighed the advice of Sifton, Whitney, Monk, Forget, and dozens more, and finally satisfied most of the claimants by the evening of 9-10 October. He was President of the Privy Council and would also assume the important External Affairs portfolio early in 1912.[5]

The new Prime Minister was not a colourful man. He was shy and diffident on the public platform, aloof from his followers in his party. He was not given to grandiose visions of his own capabilities, still less to those of most of his colleagues. One quick appraisal summed him up as "pre-eminently the businessman of Canadian politics"[6] and, in measure, it was true. He spoke the language of the business community often enough, his style was dry and practical, and he did admire the achievements of business leaders in developing the country. But even more was Robert Borden a lawyer; he was devoted to his chosen profession, he thought the law to be the fundamental civilizing influence in society, and he never abandoned the habits and attitudes he had acquired in his eminent legal career. "Every fibre of his being – even on the golf links – acts obedient to law. His very smile is forensic,"[7] another observer noted. For him, unlike most of his fellow politicians, legal training was not a doorstep to a political career; political service was a duty to one who had become a leader in the legal profession.

Borden never totally gave himself to politics. Its seamy but necessary side he found distasteful and left to more willing men. He was wholly committed to duty to the state but, unlike some of the regulars among his followers, drew a personal distinction between it and extreme partyism. Others might believe that Conservatism and the good state were one; for Borden the meanness of partisanship was the root cause of inefficiency in the administration of the state. Similarly, he was committed to the catchwords of North American progressivism, morality (individual and collective), earnestness, responsibility, duty, efficiency, rather than to theoretical political principles, be they Conservative, Liberal or Socialist. His approach to politics and statecraft was functional rather than philosophical; that had been evident in his Halifax Platform and again in his 1911 platform. Both included tariff planks that managed to avoid using the cherished Tory term, protectionism, and emphasized a "scientific tariff" and a "permanent tariff commission." Both advocated state ownership and control – in 1907 generally, in 1911 more circumspectly – where public interests could be better served by state than private enterprise. Both emphasized extensive national development and, as a necessary corollary, a reformed and more efficient civil service. The essential message of both seemed to be that Canada was a progressive twentieth-century state being governed by the shoddy and partisan methods and men of the nineteenth century. It was time for a change.[8]

Of those he chose to be his cabinet colleagues, the Minister of Finance, W.T. White, most closely approximated Borden's own outlook. White had a strong champion in Premier Whitney – "he is the keystone of the arch"[9] – and the approval of both Sifton and Willison. Moreover, he represented the defecting Liberal faction of the Ontario business community. Equally important, he was young (forty-five) and, like Borden in 1896, without political experience. As Vice-President of the National Trust Company, White was a leader in the Canadian financial community. A proven administrator without strong party attachments, he quickly established himself as a trusted adviser and close friend of the Prime Minister. Sir George Foster, who had had years of experience as Finance Minister before 1896, was, justly or not, "somewhat smirched in the public mind,"[10] because of his involvement in the Foresters affair of 1906-7. He was deliberately passed over and first offered the chairmanship of the anticipated tariff commission. Eventually, like Cartwright before him, Foster accepted Trade and Commerce.

Borden later wrote that "one should never select a colleague by the standard of one's personal likes or dislikes."[11] Some of his colleagues found entrance to the cabinet because of political necessity rather than personal respect. Among them was the Minister of Customs, J.D. Reid, who had been prominent in the intrigues against Borden's leadership in 1910-11, though he became a loyal and dependable administrator. Reid, however, was pre-eminently an organizer and with the Minister of the Interior, Robert Rogers, and the Minister of Railways, Francis Cochrane, formed the government's triumvirate of party managers. They were, William Price enthusiastically advised, "men who can do things."[12] The latter two also acknowledged the assistance Premiers Roblin and Whitney had given to the 1911 victory. Cochrane, moreover, brought to the cabinet extensive experience with northern development and resource entrepreneurs from his years as Whitney's Minister of Lands and Forests. J.D. Hazen, Minister of Marine Fisheries and Naval Service, was the only Tory provincial premier to join the cabinet. McBride, like the others, was offered a post but when he hesitated, Borden almost too quickly assigned Agriculture to their mutual friend from British Columbia, Martin Burrell. T.W. Crothers, who probably had conspired against Borden in 1910,[13] but was supported by Whitney and approved by Sifton, became Minister of Labour. The long-time Conservative member for Marquette, W.J. Roche, as Secretary of State, joined Rogers as a Manitoba representative.

And, after a severe warning about "his past vagaries, his lack of tact and his foolish actions and words on many occasions,"[14] Colonel Sam Hughes became Minister of Militia and Defence. The impulsive Colonel begged forgiveness for past indiscretions and set out on a spectacular career of compounding them.

In selecting the English-speaking representatives from the Province of Quebec, Borden did not follow the maxim he had adopted from Macdonald about personal friendship. Both Judge C.J. Doherty, an Irish Catholic, who assumed the prestigious office of Minister of Justice, and George Perley, Minister without Portfolio, were friends of the Prime Minister and distinctly personal choices. Doherty had had a distinguished career in law, had been a puisne judge of the provincial Supreme Court, and was professor of civil and international law at McGill. He was also close to the Montreal financial community, a director of La Banque Provinciale, Montreal City and District Savings Bank, Prudential Trust, and Capital Life Assurance Company, and president of the Canadian Securities Corporation. He had entered Parliament in 1908 after retiring from his judgeship. Perley, who had represented Argenteuil since 1904, was a millionaire lumber baron from the Ottawa Valley. Long a loyal supporter of Borden, he had been made Chief Whip in 1910. Both men would remain influential advisers of the Prime Minister. The other two Ministers without Portfolio were also personal choices. A.E. Kemp, millionaire Toronto manufacturer, had been the party's organizational patron and pocketbook in Ontario since 1907.[15] J.H. Lougheed, Calgary lawyer, became government leader in the Senate.

The French-Canadian representation was a more difficult matter. Monk, of course, was assured a portfolio, though Public Works was hardly suited to his legal training or his sensitive conscience.[16] But what of the other half of the electoral alliance? Monk, aware of the weakness of his own position without strong *nationaliste* support, urged Bourassa to come in. As one of Monk's correspondents made clear, without Bourassa in the cabinet the future of the alliance in Quebec was in jeopardy: "The French Canadians want to incarnate their principles in a man; or rather they make an abstraction of their principles in order to give themselves completely to a man. There must be a man in the new ministry who can be the idol of the province. . . . At the present time Bourassa alone can fill this role. . . . it is the existence of the national movement which is at stake. Bourassa in the ministry is a flag, a power. . . . If you do not make Bourassa enter the ministry you will be preparing the restoration of Laurier in the province as the Bourbons prepared the return from the Island of Elba."[17] But Bourassa refused and so too, apparently, did Lavergne, though both advised Monk on the selection of his Quebec colleagues.[18]

Some traditional French-Canadian *bleus*, T.C. Casgrain, Mathias Tellier and L.T. Maréchal, as well as financier Rodolphe Forget, were considered for inclusion. As Bourassa later explained, the "orthodox" Quebec Conservatives "rested in a long sleep, . . . talked in stentorian tones; starved by a long fast, they had an immense appetite. Forced to accept Mr. Monk, whom they had been cursing for a long time, they demanded that his colleagues be real Tories, free from any Nationalist alloy."[19] But Monk and Lavergne would have none of them, and two men acceptable to the *nationalistes,* W.B. Nantel (Inland Revenue and Mines), and L.P. Pelletier (Postmaster General), whom Bourassa described as having a "propensity for complicated affairs," became Monk's cabinet colleagues. All in all, the French-Canadian representation was weak, too much of a compromise between the demands of the *bleus* and the *nationalistes* to satisfy either.

Borden's cabinet accurately reflected the forces which had joined to forge his electoral victory. It was a coalition of interests, many potentially in conflict. The Prime Minister had performed a delicate and skilful task in putting them together; even more skill would be demanded to keep them all in harness. Still, there was agreement among them all on some things. Certainly none disputed that Laurier's government had had to go, and most agreed with their leader's platitudinous pledge that clean, efficient government must be brought to Ottawa. More than that, all accepted Borden's ten electoral pledges to the Canadian people, though, significantly, direct reference to the naval question was carefully excluded from the list. There was great political potential in the cabinet if only the coalition could become a working unit willing to compromise its differences in future policy formation. Correspondingly, the cabinet's greatest weakness was its collective inexperience in the government and administration of the state. True, some members soon revealed real administrative talent, especially White and, in lesser degree, Reid and Perley. But except for Foster on the federal scene, and Hazen, Cochrane, and Rogers at the provincial level, all the members were new to the exercise of great power and responsibility. And even one former provincial administrator seems to have had trouble adjusting to the more complicated ways of Ottawa. It was rumoured, the gossipy *News* correspondent, C.F. Hamilton, reported,

> that Rogers is trying to open all his own letters – 300 to 400 per day – & is stodged up. Burrell also is said to be a bit overwhelmed. They are all oppressed by the bigness of the work & the number of interruptions.[20]

II

Borden and his followers assumed office convinced that their predecessor's administration had harboured a well-protected nest of boodlers. Though the 1906-8 "scandal sessions" and subsequent opposition probes had turned up little concrete evidence of extensive corruption, the Conservatives believed this was mainly due to the skilful guile by which Sir Wilfrid's colleagues had covered their crooked paths. The new administration, in turn, was pledged to clean up Ottawa, even to extend the provisions of the Civil Service Act of 1908 to the outside service. To their dismay, they found that election planks were easier to formulate than fulfil.

In fact, it soon became apparent that the inside service, the very heart of everyday government and administration, was a massive tangle of inefficiency and incompetence. As soon as the government took office, an inquiry was launched by Kemp into the purchasing practices of the various departments. By January 1912, he had established that in fact there was no common system of purchasing in the government, and that expenditures were being made in generally uncontrolled and sometimes unexplained ways.[21] Meanwhile, in December, Borden appointed a Public Service Commission to inquire more generally into the state of the civil service in the interest of "securing increased efficiency and more thorough organization and co-ordination of the various departments."[22] In an interim report in the spring of 1912, the commissioners noted that since Confederation the government had grown like Topsy:

> Owing to the great development of the country exigencies have arisen from time to time, and services have been created to meet these exigencies, but no organized effort had been made to co-ordinate these services with the various Departments of the Public Service as a whole, and assign to each the proper status and duties in the general machinery of the administration.[23]

Indeed, though the Laurier government had passed the Civil Service Act with flourishes of reform just before the 1908 election, with a few exceptions Sir Wilfrid's ministers had found it unnecessary or inconvenient to implement its organizational provisions in their departments. So they remained in the spring of 1912, perpetuating inequality of treatment in the public service and lending colour to suspicions of wrongdoing.

Equally important was another of the commission's findings. Very few cases of personal malfeasance in office had, in fact, been found. Rather, the wastage of public moneys, the inaccuracy of estimates of expenditures for public works, was more often than not simply the result of inadequate planning and incompetent execution of projects undertaken.[24] Even if a minister's conduct and intent were entirely scrupulous, the very lack of system and control in administrative procedures could make him an unwilling victim of less discreet contractors doing business for the government. Then, too, the time of ministers was so taken up with administrative trivia, both in their departments and in cabinet, that important questions of public policy and careful consideration of the larger implications of public expenditure were necessarily given inadequate attention.[25]

The situation was so serious that in September 1912, Sir George Murray, who had been Permanent Secretary to the British Treasury from 1903 to 1911, was appointed to do a complete investigation of the public service. His report, issued two months later, was an indictment of the system from the ministerial level to the lowliest civil servant, and it recommended a complete overhaul of Ottawa's governmental machinery. The proper role of ministers, he observed, was to serve as the political heads of their departments; administrative and executive details should be left to subordinate officers in the permanent service. Open competitive examinations for positions should apply to both the inside and outside service. Generally tighter administrative procedures and control of appointments and promotions should apply throughout the service.[26]

Though the report was received with enthusiasm by some ministers,[27] immediate and full implementation was well-nigh impossible. Some of the more important recommendations were too closely modelled on British practice and inappropriate in the Canadian governmental context. For some others, the irony of it all was that the existing service was so inadequate that it was incapable of effecting quickly its own reform. Clearly, as Borden later noted, time was needed to execute a thorough change. The war intervened and complicated the problem before a solution could be implemented.[28]

Still, some progress was made. Two minor amendments to the Civil Service Act were passed in 1912, one providing for a higher grade of private secretaries for ministers, the other for a third Civil Service Commissioner. And consideration was given to the critical problem of reforming and expediting cabinet procedures.[29] More encouraging was the success of Borden's search for qualified people to assume positions on some of the government's regulatory bodies. In the Laurier years these appointments had often been flagrantly political. Two of Borden's appointments in vital positions reversed that practice. The appointment of Henry L. Drayton, a lawyer with extensive experience as city solicitor and corporation counsel for Toronto, and R. W. Leonard, a distinguished civil engineer, to the Board of Railway Commissioners and the National Transcontinental Railway Board, contrasted sharply with such Liberal appointments as S. N. Parent, deposed Premier of Quebec, as Chairman of the National Transcontinental Railway. All in all, then, a beginning had been made. The essential problem of government administration had been carefully identified: the ship of state was powered in the twentieth century by dilapidated machinery manufactured in the mid-nineteenth century and merely greased, patched, and tinkered with ever since. A new engine could not be built overnight. Patching and tinkering would continue for a while.

Some electoral pledges could, however, be carried out more quickly. They depended not upon a cumbersome bureaucracy but upon the government's impressive power in the House of Commons – or so it seemed. Especially important were the pledges made to Canadian farmers who had voted for reciprocity. Politically it was vital that Borden's own promises be fulfilled to show the government's good faith with the agriculturalists. The reason was simple. Outside of Ontario the new government was not strong, and some advisers believed that the Quebec alliance was both fragile and ephemeral. "Surely it is in the West that the Conservative party must chiefly build for the future," one wrote.[30] Accordingly, the contract to J. D. McArthur to build a portion of the long-promised Hudson Bay Railway, which the Laurier government had issued on the eve of the election, was reviewed by the Borden government and revised to allow the contractor to build a complete line to Port Nelson, where terminal facilities were begun in 1913.[31]

Of greater importance at the time was the passage of the Canada Grain Act of 1912. Here again, the Liberals had long promised new legislation controlling the ownership and operation of grain elevators. As with the Hudson Bay Railway, on the eve of the election Cartwright had introduced a bill in the Senate consolidating and amending previous federal grain legislation. The following year the new government revived the measure and with some further amendment it became the new Grain Act. It had two outstanding features, both carried over from the earlier Liberal bill. The first established a powerful Board of Grain Commissioners to supervise grain inspection and regulate the grain trade. The second was a clause enabling the government of Canada to build or acquire terminal elevators and operate them. The nationalization of the terminal elevators, Cartwright admitted, was "a strong step and a new step" and though vigorously urged to do so by the western farmers Cartwright assured his fearful fellow-Senators that as far as the Liberals were concerned, "it will not be resorted to if we can help it."[32] The Conservatives, while unwilling to fulfil completely their unqualified pledge of nationalization, did read the clause more positively than their predecessors. The government, Foster promised, would "put into operation the principle of government ownership either by construction or leasing, but to what extent the government will go is not yet determined."[33] Clearly they would not go as far as the farmers wished. But in 1913 a government terminal elevator was erected at Port Arthur and, in 1914-15, interior government elevators were opened at Moose Jaw, Calgary, and Saskatoon. A small transfer elevator was opened in Vancouver in 1916 coincident with the opening of the Panama Canal in an effort to demonstrate the feasibility of the Pacific route for grain shipment.[34]

The government's agricultural legislative programme was designed to do more than simply woo western voters. Deep concern had been expressed throughout the country at the growing disparity between the attractiveness of urban and rural life and at the increasing depopulation of rural areas. The Conservatives, in a typically North American progressive fashion, seized upon that universal cure-all, education, as a solution to this social dilemma and promised federal assistance to the provinces for upgrading agricultural instruction programmes. When the legislation was introduced in the spring of 1913, the government's objective was clearly stated by Martin Burrell. Canadians could be and should be proud of their cities, he said, but not too proud. "The swelling of urban population with a diminution in the ranks of the producers has its sequence in the added cost of living, in the increase in squalor, hunger and crime." The "solitary figure in the distant furrow, that stooped form tending the hearth of the isolated home – symbols and types of our national necessities, our national virtues and our national strength" were being forgotten in the rush to the cities. But "there can be no health in the cities without corresponding health in the country." Therefore, the government, "following the best methods of the most progressive countries," was giving aid, over a ten-year period, to agricultural education administered by the provinces. "It is not alone a betterment of economic conditions that we should aim at," Burrell noted, "but something finer – the creation of a rural civilization which will at once ensure a fuller and happier life to those in its midst, and prove a source and fount of strength to the State itself."[35]

Some of the same reasoning was behind two other government measures: the extension of rural free mail delivery and government bills in 1912 and 1913 to provide funds to the provinces for use in provincial highway construction. The first had been a plank in Borden's Halifax Platform and was hastily and partly adopted by the Liberals just before the 1908 election. Both measures, the Minister of Railways now argued, would better the condition of rural living and lessen the isolation of the farmer from urban Canada. The second would also substantially improve the farmer's marketing potential by affording him better access to his markets. A striking feature of the Highways Bill – and of federal assistance to agricultural education – was that it proposed a new pattern in dominion-provincial fiscal relations. Up to 1911 all federal subsidies to provincial governments had been given unconditionally. The Highways Bill was the first proposal by the federal government to establish conditional grants to the provinces.[36]

The Prime Minister explained that the dominion's power to build interprovincial highways, or even to declare a highway within a province to be for "the general advantage of Canada," remained unimpaired. But this bill was for a different purpose; it was designed to provide an incentive to the provinces to develop their own highway programmes. The Liberals, who could not see why it was necessary to do other than increase the general subsidies to the provinces, argued that the act was unconstitutional. As Senator Ross put it, "It is a subversion of the fundamental principle of the constitution, namely, when certain duties are assigned to a province that the Dominion Government has *no* right to step in and interfere in the discharge of these duties nor to supplement these duties by any legislation of its own."[37] The Prime Minister, who regarded himself as no mean champion of provincial autonomy, patiently pointed out that the rights of the provinces were inviolate; not a dollar could be spent by the federal government without the prior sanction of the provincial legislature and executive. But provincial autonomy in dominion-provincial fiscal relations was not to be equated with either dominion licence or impotence. It was no longer good enough to hand out all funds to the provinces without any controls attached. General subsidies would, of course, remain. But at least some portion of the federal government's money should be spent for purposes which it thought necessary. Laying down the cardinal principle of all future fixed grants in dominion-provincial fiscal relations, Borden said: "It is not only the right but it is also the absolute duty of the government of Canada who are responsible to this parliament, . . . to provide that the money shall be applied to that particular purpose and no other, and that it shall be expended in such a way as to result in permanent benefit and advantage."[38]

The Highways Bill was also part of the government's programme of continued national economic development. It was included in the grand scheme with the completion of the Hudson Bay Railway. Both were linked with proposals for the creation of national harbour facilities, with enabling legislation for the acquisition of branch lines by the Intercolonial Railway and with federal assistance to Ontario's provincially owned Temiskaming and Northern Ontario Railway. It was a general plan of expansion and consolidation of transport facilities, especially those under public ownership and control. A corollary was the encouragement of development of the shield country surrounding Hudson and James Bays. Here the federal government's role was largely jurisdictional. In 1912 the long-promised settlement of the Manitoba-Ontario boundary was finally achieved. Concurrently the federal districts of Keewatin and Ungava became parts of the vastly enlarged provinces of Manitoba, Ontario, and Quebec.[39]

Unfortunately many parts of the Borden government's generally impressive pre-war legislative programme never found their way into the statute books. The Senate, dominated by Liberals bitter with recent defeat, amended piece after piece of legislation in a manner unacceptable to the government. The Highways Bill was rejected in both 1912 and 1913. Also turned down were the proposed aid to the Temiskaming and Northern Ontario Railway and the Intercolonial Branch Lines Bill. Equally shattering was the rejection of the Tariff Commission Bill in 1912. The object in this case was not, as some Liberals supposed, to set up some

super-tariff agency which would deprive Parliament of its fiscal responsibilities. Rather, the Finance Minister explained, what was desired was to
find a way to decide tariff questions in a more sophisticated fashion in
keeping with the growing complexity of the twentieth-century Canadian
economy. At the moment, he observed,

> We have not tabulated any accurate information on which we can rely, we
> do not know the facts as we should know them, in regard to the industries,
> the business, the callings and the occupation of the people. We have not the
> facts with regard to the cast and conditions of production that we should have
> before we can intelligently approach the question of tariff consideration [and
> tariff modification].[40]

It was that information which the tariff commission was intended to provide. But the Senate added it to a long list of Borden government proposals that ended up as unfulfilled good intentions.[41]

III

The Borden government had come to power at the peak of expansion of
the Canadian economy. One of the primary arguments of the anti-reciprocity men had been: why trade our present prosperity (which, it was
assumed, would continue unabated) for an uncertain economic future? In
1912 the Minister of Finance could proudly note in his budget speech the
largest surplus on record. In January of 1913 a representative report from
one of the Finance Department's regional officers stated that "the year just
closed has been phenomenal as to increase, the amount being almost
double that of last. The bank clearings show an increase of app[roximately]
35% while the total value of building permits issued practically 100%
. . . the outlook for 1913 is even better."[42]

Unfortunately, the forecast was both premature and wrong. Even
though the 1913 and 1914 federal budgets were cast in generally rosy
hues, the fact was that in 1913 Canada began to slip into a severe depression, which continued until long after the outbreak of war. As early as
1912 it was clear the consumer was caught in a tight squeeze with housing
and food prices rising far more rapidly than wages. "Both house rents and
living expenses have advanced during the past two years fully 50% – and
of course the working man and those on fixed salaries are feeling the
pressure most,"[43] a government official wrote early in 1912. By spring
1913 the economic downturn was clearly evident across Canada. The
Deputy Receiver General in Winnipeg reported that "the present financial stringency is being felt very acutely throughout this whole Western
Country and businessmen are inclined to take a gloomy view of the

outlook."[44] The expansion of the economy, the growth and consolidation of industry, was dependent upon a continual supply of liquid capital. But the prime source of much of that capital, the London money market, had dried up. The Vice-President of the Grand Trunk, William Wainwright, described the situation to the Prime Minister as "the almost impossibility of floating securities, except at a great sacrifice."[45] By October, White was warning Borden of "a possible falling-off of revenues" and urging that it was "most desirable that no further tenders should be called in cases where the work can stand until next year."[46]

The tide of industrial expansion had reversed. It had risen higher and higher, on ever more foamy waves of optimism, since 1909. In part the turn around of 1913-14 was due to the realization that expansion had gone too far, that the productive capability of industry had greatly surpassed the absorptive capacity of the Canadian market.[47] But an equally potent factor was the growing distrust by foreign financiers of Canadian securities. Investment in Canada seemed like a bottomless pit: the supply of securities was infinite, the prospect of return was minimal. Even public securities were of doubtful value. British investors, the *Market Mail* savagely remarked in 1914, "have applied for municipal and city bonds, thinking that Canada would benefit by the money, whereas the bulk has been swallowed by issuing houses, financial parasites, and underwriters. . . . People begin to realize that Canada is playing the risky game of keeping solvent by borrowing more with which to pay back, and that only while money is advanced can the country keep straight." In March 1914, the Assistant Superintendent of Emigration in London reported that "nearly 80% of the most recent Dominion Government loan remained in the underwriters' hands."[48]

Cutbacks in industrial production and expansion resulted in serious unemployment in urban areas. And the tightening of credit was even more severe for rural Canadians. Across Canada farmers had invested more and more of their earnings, actual and potential, in machinery. In the west, where the machinery was at once so necessary and so expensive, the pinch was especially severe. Bankers refused to extend further credit, mortgage companies threatened to foreclose, and a flight from the land, smaller certainly than that in the 1930's, but nonetheless real, began. Farmers, their sons, their tenants and hired men, along with a continuing flood of immigrants – over 400,000 in 1913 – poured into the cities to join the growing ranks of urban unemployed in the fruitless search for work if possible, for relief if necessary.[49]

The federal government responded in December 1913, by appointing an investigatory commission on the high cost of living. And Borden urged the railways to maintain as full employment as possible during the winter of 1913-14. A year later Ontario appointed a commission on unemployment. Beyond that, at both levels of government policy was dictated by the traditional economic verities, and expenditures were cut to the bone in an attempt to preserve or restore credit ratings in the financial markets. Municipal employment bureaus were set up in Montreal, Toronto, Ottawa, Winnipeg, Edmonton, Calgary, Vancouver, New Westminster, and Victoria. But most of the work was done by commercial employment agencies, which exacted high fees for the positions they found for the unemployed.[50]

Few people were more aware of the magnitude of the problem of unemployment or of the degradation of the unemployed than Mayor Hocken of Toronto.[51] "After we spend all the money we have to spend, after we find all the work that it is possible to find, we feel absolutely helpless in dealing with the problem as we find it today," he observed. "It is too large for the city. . . . It has to be taken hold of in a more comprehensive way than any municipality can do." As the Mayor put it, each level of government bore a portion of the blame for "the very climate in which we live" and it was up to every level of government to assume a portion of responsibility for solving the problem. "No serious or effective steps have been taken to solve the question. . . . we have never tried to find the solution, as we should have done."[52] Support for Hocken's position came in the report of Ontario's unemployment commission, which observed that "no amount of caution. . . can absolve our governments and people from the duty of making preparation during good times, for periods of depression."[53] But it was too late; the commissioners reported late in 1915.

Here, as inevitably as a change in the weather, entered the country's two greatest supplicants for government largess: the uncompleted transcontinental railways. The Grand Trunk Pacific and the Canadian Northern had been caught in the now common vise of rising prices and declining sources of capital. Traffic revenues on their completed sections had been good in 1912 but insufficient to meet the skyrocketing costs of construction. And neither the swashbuckling financiers of the Canadian Northern, Mackenzie and Mann, nor the sober managers of the Grand Trunk Pacific and its parent, the Grand Trunk, could find a ready market for a further issue of their securities. Naturally, and without hesitation, they turned to their ultimate benefactor, the government of Canada. For its part, the government vividly remembered, in its partisan moments, not only the cosy relationships of the railways with its predecessor, but also that the problem was not of its making. "What a legacy Laurier left to Canada in his foolish and criminal railway blundering," George Foster ruefully observed after a particularly heated caucus on railway policy.[54] But whatever the legacy, the responsibility was now theirs. With the country's finances in deep trouble, upon the fate of the Canadian Northern rested the fortune of one of Canada's largest banks, the Bank of Commerce, and its associated trust company, the National, in Toronto. More important still, upon the fate of both railways rested the fortunes of all four western provinces, which had recklessly participated in financing the new transcontinentals and their myriad networks of branch lines. The Laurier government, Borden later recalled, "initiated not only a second but a third transcontinental railway for which the credit of Canada was pledged. Then we had to face . . . the actual or potential insolvence of the four western provinces if aid was withheld."[55] Such a prospect, whatever the price of avoiding it, was unthinkable.[56]

The first encounter was with the National Transcontinental system, made up of the Grand Trunk Pacific in the west (being built by the Grand Trunk) and the National Transcontinental (being built by the government of Canada from Winnipeg to Moncton). Over the years the National Transcontinental Railway had been flagrantly partisan, and in January 1912, Borden, in part motivated by revenge, appointed a royal commission to investigate the construction of the eastern section. The commission's report, issued two years later, was a scathing indictment of government involvement in waste and corruption on the eastern section[57] Additional pressure was applied by the government in July 1912, when it asked the Grand Trunk Pacific to fulfil the terms of its 1904 lease and take over operation of the completed parts of the eastern section. The company countered by reminding Borden and his colleagues that the terms called for takeover only after the government section was completed, still a year in the future, and added that the government should continue to operate the section indefinitely. Borden then pointed out that such a step would inevitably mean "taking over Western Division by gov't assuming all liabilities."[58]

The Prime Minister's position was that if the Grand Trunk was to be relieved of its contractual obligations for the eastern section, then the government should take over the western section also. The "more statesmanlike proceeding" would be to admit now that the deal with the Liberals had been a bad one and turn the whole line over to the government. After considering the matter for a few weeks, the company, in a long and argumentative reply, concluded that "to ask the company to give up all it has worked for, and all it has risked during the last eight years, solely on the condition of being relieved from a hypothetical liability ten or twelve years hence, is a course they could not recommend to their shareholders."[59] There the matter rested for more than a year and a half. In June 1914, the government, anticipating further contractual difficulties with the Grand Trunk, obtained authority for the eastern section to be temporarily operated as part of the Canadian Government Railways.

Meanwhile the Grand Trunk was at the government's door seeking a $15 million loan for the western section, and claiming that it had a commitment to the loan from the previous administration. Partly because of the company's refusal to take over the eastern section, the loan application was refused. Still, however bitter the sparring between the partners in this venture in disaster, the government could not, and would not, let the company go under. Discussions on the loan were renewed in 1913 and in June a loan of $15 million was granted to the Grand Trunk Pacific. A year later the government guaranteed the principal and interest on $16 million of Grand Trunk Pacific four per cent bonds. For its generosity to the company the government extracted a price; it assumed a first mortgage on the western section.

The complicated affairs of the National Transcontinental, in comparison with the dealings with its rival, the Canadian Northern, seemed almost simple and direct. The Canadian Northern had the advantage of friends at court, foremost among them the Minister of Finance. But even the friends of Mackenzie and Mann were astounded by the magnitude of the demands made upon the government. In January 1913, Sir William Mackenzie coolly proposed to the Prime Minister that the government lend his company $30 million and, in addition, give it a subsidy on another 2200 miles of railway. Debate in Council continued for months. In May, White came out strongly against the subsidy and Mackenzie scaled down his request a few days later. "Mackenzie wants us to grant him subsidies to C.N.R. of 22 millions," Borden recorded. "Told him it was too large an order."[60] A month later, subsidies for more than $15 million were granted by the government, in return for the assumption by the government of $7 million of Canadian Northern common stock. Even so, the government was severely criticized for assisting the almost universally distrusted proprietors of the Canadian Northern. The President of the Canadian Pacific, Sir Thomas Shaughnessy, "grumbled" and told Borden that "he has many grievances which he wants to ventilate at an early visit to Ottawa."[61] And a government member told White that "the pill that the western Conservatives had to swallow in that outrage of giving $15,-000,000 to Mckenzie [sic] & Mann was not sugar coated, and it was legislation that we find it very difficult to defend, and let me assure you that with one exception there was not one western Conservative that was not very much opposed to the legislation." "I wonder," he asked, "if the government today know how much of the $15,000,000 of the people's money goes into railway extension or goes to make these gentlemen richer by aiding their investments in all parts of the world?"[62]

It was a good question. Just how good the government discovered early in 1914 when Mackenzie and Mann returned, their over-large cup in hand. Now they wanted a "loan or guarantee to prevent their securities from being defaulted." Borden "could hold out no hope" and they "seemed depressed and resentful."[63] But they would not go away. And Sifton called in February "to urge that Canadian Northern Railway should not be allowed to smash."[64] Certainly, the Canadian Northern's position was precarious, and within days F. Williams Taylor of the Bank of Montreal appeared, "very nervous and apprehensive as to effect of default on London market and on banking situation."[65] But just how precarious no one, not even the principals of the railway, knew. When Mackenzie was asked for a detailed accounting of the railways' affairs, he produced a statement that was "very unsatisfactory. Told him it would not go either in council or in caucus."[66] A committee of government officials, including the newly appointed Solicitor General, Arthur Meighen, descended upon the company's Toronto offices and began their own tedious examination of the C.N.'s finances. They found three things: that the company's affairs were an incredibly chaotic maze of interrelated and complex dealings; that, so far as one could tell, Mackenzie and Mann were entirely honest and had not been milking the public through the Canadian Northern; and that the railway did indeed need assistance – lots of it.[67]

That was all very well, but it would take a lot of convincing to win over the company's enemies, inside and outside the government party. At a mid-March caucus Borden gave "a plain and business like statement of the C.N.R. situation" and was greeted by "fierce invective against M. & M."[68] By the end of April the government had worked out its policy. It would guarantee $45 million of Canadian Northern bonds. In return the company's affairs were to be completely reorganized, and Mackenzie and Mann would turn over to the government a further $33 million of Canadian Northern common stock. The government also assumed a mortgage on the consolidated company with power to take over the railway in case of default. R. B. "Bonfire" Bennett, the C.P.R.'s Calgary solicitor, and W. F. Nickle, bolted over the assistance to the C.N.R. But the premiers, Liberal and Conservative alike, of Nova Scotia, New Brunswick, and the four western provinces, all supported the measure with audible sighs of relief.[69] Some leading financial men and others, observing the trend of government policy toward both railways, encouraged it to go all the way and assume full ownership of both the C.N.R. and the N.T.R.[70] Clearly, a step in that direction had been taken by the summer of 1914, but the time was not yet come.

IV

Just after taking office, the Borden government took pains to assure the United States that the result of the election did not mean the beginning of an era of hostility in Canadian-American relations. Reciprocity had been rejected, but good relations with the United States remained important to Canada. Soon, the Canadian representatives on the International Joint Commission were appointed and began their work. The encouragement of American investment in Canadian industrial development continued. Wisely, the contentious tariff issue was left at rest during 1912, an election year in the neighbouring republic. Then, in 1913, the victorious Wilsonian Democrats passed the Underwood Tariff, indirectly granting to Canada many of the concessions gained in the abortive 1911 agreement. All in all, a mood of sweet amiability prevailed in Ottawa. As the United States Consul General reported, "Mr. Borden, Mr. White and other members of the Cabinet are taking considerable pains to express friendliness to the United States. I have no doubts of the genuineness of their feeling."[71]

Just as quickly, the Prime Minister hinted at a new approach to the Canadian-American relationship. For Canada the bilateral relationship was important, but even more crucial was her place in the Ottawa-Washington-London diplomatic triangle. Anglo-American accord was the key to Canada's well-being. In the past Canada's passivity had seemed to result in Anglo-American understanding at the sacrifice of Canadian interests. But it did not need to be that way. A more active Canadian policy, based upon the assumptions that Canada knew Washington better than London and London better than Washington and could successfully mediate between them, would at once provide insurance against the future sacrifice of Canadian interests and serve a useful function in the Anglo-American relationship. As early as November 1911, Borden put the case in a Halifax speech.

> Canada is an autonomous nation within the British Empire and is closely and inseparably united to that Empire by ties of kinship, of sentiment, and of fealty, by historic association and tradition, by the character of its institutions, and by the free will of its people. By ties of kinship, by constant social and commercial intercourse, by proximity and mutual respect, and good-will, this country is closely associated with the United States. Canada's voice and influence should always be for harmony and not for discord between our Empire and the great Republic and I believe that she will always be a bond of abiding friendship between them.[72]

There was platitude in this; it was good after-dinner talk. But there was more. Playing the self-assumed lynch-pin role in Anglo-American relations portended a more vigorous approach to external relations, both Canadian-American and Anglo-Canadian. The more active role the Prime Minister intended to take himself was signalled in the transfer of the external affairs portfolio to his office in the spring of 1912. The more active role of the Department was suggested in the very gradual increase in its staff, which began with the hiring of the Harvard-trained, Nova-

Scotia-born lawyer, Loring Christie. His credentials reflected the new interest in triangular diplomacy. Christie came from Washington, where he had held a senior position in the United States Justice Department, and had intimate connections with, and was warmly recommended by, members of the staff of the British Embassy.

The central aim of the new policy in external affairs was to alter relations with the mother country. Though the aging Lord Strathcona was kept on as High Commissioner, Perley, as Borden's chief administrative trouble-shooter, was sent to London to reorganize the chaotic affairs of the Canadian office.[73] An over-enthusiastic reading of the election results, meanwhile, had led the British Tories to plead with Borden to join their crusade for imperial preference against the Asquith government. But the Canadian Prime Minister would have none of it. After all, he had to deal with Asquith, not the opposition, at Westminster. Besides, this was a domestic British political quarrel.[74] Nor was he inspired by the visionary centralist schemes of the Round Tablers. After an evening in London with Milner, Curtis, Jameson, and some others, he noted that he found much of what they said to be "impracticable and any advantage too remote and indirect."[75]

What was practical and, he thought, obtainable, was a greater voice for Canada in imperial foreign policy. Borden had long believed this was both necessary and appropriate to Canada's maturing stature in foreign affairs, and it was essential to any practical working out of "a bond of abiding friendship" between the republic and the mother country. It would not, he knew, be freely given. At the 1911 Imperial Conference, Asquith had categorically denied the possibility of a Dominion voice in imperial foreign policy. But the Prime Minister believed he had a strong bargaining hand. His trump was a Canadian contribution to naval defence.

Almost certainly, Borden had decided upon an emergency contribution to the Imperial Navy before he left for Great Britain, in June 1912, to discuss the naval situation with the British government. In March, he had announced that Laurier's naval programme would be halted, adding that when a new permanent policy was decided upon, the country would be consulted, and that "if the various Dominions . . . do enter into a system of Naval Defence which shall concern and belong to the whole Empire, those Dominions . . . cannot be very well excluded from having a greater voice in the councils of the Empire."[76] But an emergency contribution was one thing, a permanent policy another; properly used, the former could be a preliminary wedge into "the councils of the Empire."

On June 1, Borden had sought the advice of a number of trusted friends outside the cabinet "as to the necessity or expediency of an effective contribution for the temporary purpose of meeting conditions which undoubtedly confront the Mother Country at the present time." Borden clearly did not question the existence of a naval crisis – "conditions which undoubtedly confront the Mother Country" can have no other meaning. What was at issue was whether it was "necessary" or "expedient" for Canada to make a contribution. Not surprisingly, the advice received was generally to the effect that an emergency contribution was both "necessary" and "expedient," as Premier Whitney put it, to "our self-respect as a nation."[77]

The Prime Minister was very much aware that he was risking the alienation of his Quebec colleagues with a policy of emergency contribution, and Monk's refusal to accompany him to England emphasized the point. (Pelletier, Hazen, and Doherty went with him.) But how great was the risk? There was some evidence that the proviso of a plebiscite before contribution, made by Monk and his friends, did not apply to an emergency contribution – or, at least, so Borden might have thought. In November 1909, Monk had told Borden that "under the circumstances which existed last winter, it was essential that our resolution of the 29th of March should be unanimous," adding, "if the same thing happened again, I should think we should pursue the same course," and that "course" did not exclude an emergency contribution.[78] In March 1910, Martin Burrell reported that the French and English Conservatives were "agreed on the desirability of giving a contribution in case of emergency, but not agreed on the fact of emergency."[79] And if Lavergne's account of the conditions Monk made on entering the government is to be believed, including "no Canadian participation in Imperial Wars before the people have pronounced on this question through a plebiscite,"[80] nothing in those conditions excluded the possibility of an emergency contribution in a crisis without a plebiscite. Borden believed that a crisis did exist in the late spring of 1912. In light of the furore in the British government caused by the publication of the German *Novelle* on March 22,[81] he may have judged it to be not just "the same thing happened again" but even more serious.

Even if the Prime Minister was convinced of both the "necessity" and the "expediency" of an emergency contribution, it is clear that his sceptical French colleagues were not. And here was the the heart of the problem. The government had no better information about the "fact of emergency" than did any other Canadians who read the daily press. It had not been, indeed could not be, privy to the continual re-evaluations of supremacy going on in the Admiralty, of the abortive results of the Haldane mission. Borden went to England to get that information, perhaps to reassure himself of the rightness of the decision he had already made, certainly to get concrete evidence with which to convince his colleagues. Moreover, he wanted to make clear to the British government that no contribution, emergency or permanent, could be expected unless and until his government had been taken into the confidence of and assumed a share of British foreign policy planning. On July 16, he candidly explained his position to Churchill at the Admiralty. Afterwards he noted that the interview was "quite satisfactory. He is quite willing to play the game. Will give assurance in writing as to necessity [of an emergency contribution]."[82]

Over and over, in private and in public, Borden stressed that the price of any Canadian contribution to imperial defence was a Canadian voice in imperial foreign policy. At closed meetings of the Committee of Imperial Defence he learned that while a dominion voice in foreign policy had been denied at the Imperial Conference of 1911, a resolution had been passed recommending dominion representation at C.I.D. meetings when dominion problems were discussed. The resolution had not been published nor, at Laurier's request, officially communicated to Ottawa. Borden thought that as a "temporary measure" the recommendation was a step in the right direction. He told a public audience that his country had no intention of becoming "merely silent partners in such a great empire. If there is to be imperial cooperation, the people of Canada propose to have a reasonable and fair voice in that cooperation."[83]

Prime Minister Asquith replied: "There rests with us undoubtedly the duty of making such response as we can to their obviously reasonable appeal that [the dominion] should be entitled to be heard in the determination of the policy and the direction of imperial affairs." And Borden, taking Asquith at far more than his word, jubilantly told the Canadian House of Commons a few months later that "no important step in foreign policy would be undertaken without consultation with . . . a representative of Canada."[84] This, of course, was nonsense. A worried Colonial Secretary hastily wired the Governor General that he had carefully explained to Borden that the C.I.D. "is a purely advisory body and is not and cannot under any circumstances become a body deciding on policy."[85]

Borden returned home armed with two memoranda from the Admiralty, drafted by Churchill and himself, to convince Parliament and his cabinet of the necessity of an emergency contribution.[86] As discussions proceeded in cabinet, it became clear that Monk, at least, would remain uncooperative. He agreed that the situation was "grave and emergent" but "there should be an appeal to the people by plebiscite. Ontario men and Hazen as well as Rogers, Burrell and Roche strongly opposed to this as indicating weakness and indecision."[87] On October 18 the Minister of Public Works resigned. For a while it seemed that Nantel would go with him – "Nantel is merely his echo"[88] – but he eventually fell into line. In late November Borden took his proposals to the French-Canadian members of his caucus. "Boulay, Barette, Bellemare, Achim and Guilbault said they agreed that proposals are wise but they are bound by promises. Lavallée and Gauthier said notwithstanding promises they would vote for us. Also Paquet, Rainville, Blondin and Sévigny."[89] A few days later, on December 5, the Prime Minister introduced his Naval Aid Bill, proposing a grant of $35 million, the cost of three Dreadnoughts for the Royal Navy. "We cannot and we shall not wait and deliberate until any impending storm shall have burst upon us in fury and with disaster," Borden said, amidst the constant cheering of his followers.[90]

Strenuous opposition came from the Liberals as the debate proceeded. In part, their ire had been aroused by government's precipitate discontinuance of the Liberal's naval programme. An emergency contribution and placating generalities from the Prime Minister about a future permanent policy seemed hardly an adequate substitute. Beyond that, they were convinced that the "emergency" was a sham, that "Borden has been trying to induce the British government to say something to afford an excuse for some policy that will help him out of the hole."[91] Fielding did report from London in January that Churchill had told him that if the Naval Aid Bill was defeated, "he must ask the British Parliament to make good the difference." But the former Finance Minister was more interested in the doings of a group of Liberal M.P.'s who had petitioned Asquith in December to resist what they considered the "extravagant and dangerous tendencies of the Admiralty. The negotiations between Mr. Churchill and Mr. Borden are they think a part of this objectionable policy."[92] Fielding worked closely with this group, encouraging any activity on their part that would cast a shadow of doubt from England upon the "fact of emergency."[93]

In Ottawa Liberal obstruction became more and more intolerable as the weeks of debate wore on. Second reading finally was passed, 114-84, Feburary 27, with seven French-Canadian members of the government party voting with the Liberals. Then, in early March, in committee, the House sat continuously, excepting Sundays, from the 3rd to the 15th. On April 9, after two abortive attempts at cooperation with Laurier, the frustrated government introduced a motion for closure, precipitating a new debate, which lasted until April 23. On May 15, Borden's motion for third reading was finally passed. "Laurier and Guilbault contended for the honour of moving six months hoist and Laurier won by a neck or rather by a mouth. Five Nationalists against us and we had a majority of 33."[94]

Meanwhile the Prime Minister had given private consideration to a permanent naval policy, which, he believed, should be quite separate from any discussion of the emergency contribution. Some early thoughts had been intimated to the cabinet and to French-Canadian members during the last weeks of 1912. The following March he had taken up the subject in earnest with the Governor General. By late March he had prepared a memorandum on permanent policy, which the Duke of Connaught took to Great Britain.[95] On the surface it was true that Borden's permanent policy, as he told an emissary from Asquith some months later, "approximated very closely" Laurier's programme.[96] It contemplated the building of dry docks for naval and commercial use, the establishment of naval bases and fortification of harbours, the development of extensive shipbuilding facilities in Canada capable of building small cruisers, the subsidization of modern merchant carriers and extension of the Fishery Protective Service and the training of officers and men for the naval service. But on three points the emphasis was quite different. First, Borden's plan placed greater emphasis on the commercial development of a total naval service than did the Laurier programme. Second, the idea of separate navies in war-time was totally rejected – "defence of the Empire upon the high seas cannot be successfully accomplished by a series of scattered navies." Indeed, the three Dreadnoughts contemplated in the emergency contribution, which were "subject to recall by Canada upon reasonable notice," might become the basis of a Canadian fleet "unit or units of an Imperial Navy." Finally, as always, Borden stressed "the cooperation of Canada in the establishment of an Imperial Navy, carrying with it responsibility and a voice on foreign policy."

> It has been said in Great Britain that any such proposal would abnegate the control by the people through their representatives of foreign policy relations. This argument seems to proceed upon the assumption that the people who can properly be entrusted with such control reside wholly within the United Kingdom. The people are undoubtedly entitled to control foreign policy but there are at least fifteen millions of them outside the United Kingdom. . . .

"Cooperation" meant just that; "responsibility and voice in foreign policy," not token monetary contributions to some seemingly superior authority.[97]

Two weeks after the Naval Aid Bill passed in the House, it was returned by the Senate with the cryptic message, "This House is not justified in giving its assent to the Bill until it is submitted to the judgement of the country." Since late April the government leader, Senator Lougheed, had been negotiating with Sir George Ross, Liberal leader in the Upper House, seeking to find some compromise acceptable to both parties. Ross was as anxious to see the emergency contribution go through as anyone, but, not unreasonably, thought some small appropriation for a permanent naval policy might be made. And Borden, as anxious as he was to keep a clear division between emergency and permanent policy, was probably ready to accept such an amendment from the Senate. What he had not counted on was the furious anger of the Liberals in the House of Commons after the introduction of closure. If the Tories could gag debate, the

Liberals, as they were getting in the habit of doing, could block policy. Fielding undoubtedly spoke for many Liberals in the Commons when he told Laurier that "I am not much in favour of the Senate obstructing the Commons, but in this case if the Naval Bill is carried through the Commons by use of closure, I believe the Senate will be fully justified in rejecting it."[98]

The great naval debate, which had begun on so high a plane and with such admirable motives four years before, had degenerated into a petty, vindictive, partisan shambles, an embarrassment to the nation, if not its leaders. Both parties and both leaders had to share the blame. Despite professions to the contrary, neither leader had played the part he so often assumed in public, as "statesmen"; both had been partisan. Borden had unwisely cancelled Laurier's naval programme before he had any acceptable substitute to put before the nation. Laurier had replied by obstructing passage of the Naval Aid Bill. Borden had introduced closure; Laurier had forced an outright rejection of the bill in the Senate.

The whole sorry spectacle once again highlighted the central fact of Borden's pre-war administration: the obstructionist role of the Senate in his government's legislative programme. With reason Borden was convinced that in both domestic and foreign policy that august body had become less a chamber of sober second thought, more a house of partisan second chance. As early as his 1912 visit to London, the Prime Minister had suggested the connivance of the British government in "packing" the Senate by implementing the clause of the B.N.A. Act permitting the appointment of six additional senators. But the Colonial Secretary had wisely shied away from the proposal, refusing to involve himself and his government in a Canadian political quarrel. The vote on the rejection of the Naval Bill had been 51 to 27, revealing the huge Liberal preponderance in the Senate. In the spring of 1914 the Prime Minister, in conjunction with the decennial redistribution of House of Commons representation worked out by a bipartisan committee,[99] made an agreement with Sir Wilfrid for an increase in the number of western senators. In the House of Commons the measures were unanimously approved on June 11. Two days before, Laurier had told Borden that he "agrees that our resolution with respect to increased Senate representation shall go through. Asked him about the Senate and he said there would be no difficulty there so far as he knew."[100] But the following day Borden angrily wrote: "The Grit Senators, doubtless in collusion with their friends in the Commons, deliberately violated the agreement to pass the resolutions for increase in Senate representation. Laurier looking uneasy and ashamed but our men believe that he permitted it and connived at it."[101]

There was one alternative to continued obstruction: to appeal to the people. A year earlier an election, making the tactics of the Senate the issue, had been considered.[102] But that was hardly good enough; even if the party was returned with a large majority in the House, Liberal domination of the Senate would remain. The government would have to propose a substantial reform of the Senate itself. Borden, who had privately favoured Senate reform on the elective principle for many years,[103] had a resolution prepared for presentation to the House of Commons in the aftermath of the Senate's rejection of the representation measures. It noted that the Senate "has not fulfilled the expectations" of the framers of the B.N.A. Act and that "federal systems both within the British Empire and in foreign countries [have] strongly tended in the direction of election of members of the Upper House instead of appointment thereto by the Executive." It proposed a plebiscite "upon the following question: 'Are you in favour of abolishing the Senate of Canada as at present constituted and of substituting therefor a Senate elected by the people?'"[104] The resolution was not presented as the government rushed to the conclusion of the long and frustrating 1914 session. But it did indicate Borden's thoughts on the matter, and the way in which he might present Senate reform to the people.

Late in July the Prime Minister went off to Muskoka for a brief holiday and a chance to ponder his three years in office. They had been good years in part. A start had been made at administrative reform and some of his legislative programme was well under way. There had been less division in his ranks over the naval policy than might have been anticipated. But there was much undone. The economic depression was worrisome. And the obstructive Senate seemed prepared to block his every move. An election would be risky at best with high unemployment, and an unsophisticated electorate more concerned with the government's unfulfilled promises than with reasons for their lack of accomplishment. But an election it probably would have to be.

Then, suddenly and ominously, his private secretary called him back to Ottawa as the festering sores of European diplomacy broke. Passing through Toronto on July 31, he found "everyone anticipates war." The next morning he breakfasted in his railway car and went directly to his office. Thoughts of an election and Senate reform were of concern no more. The easy days of party battles were over.

> Blount under my telegraphic instructions had instructed ministers to return immediately. Sladen showed me tlgm. from Stamfordham to Duke that situation most serious but a faint hope of peace. Council at 11, again in afternoon and at office all evening. Sent several despatches to Harcourt as to alien army reservists, assisting by Expeditionary Force, etc. Also tlgm. for publication stating that Canadian people will be united to support if war shd. ensue.[105]

CHAPTER 11

Organizing for War

I

Canadians went to war little suspecting the ultimate consequences of their Prime Minister's pledge "to put forth every effort and to make every sacrifice necessary to ensure the integrity and maintain the honour of our Empire."[1] An outburst of enthusiastic patriotism, rooted in the complacent assumption that imperial forces would quickly prevail, greeted the news of the declaration of war. No one, public official or private citizen, even at his most pessimistic, could foretell the destruction that would be wrought on a whole generation of young Canadians in the slimy trenches of the western front. No one imagined the enormous boost war manufacturing would give to Canadian industry, the incentive it would create for establishing new industries, and the stimulus it would provide to the growth of trade unionism.

In the initial excitement, no cabinet member could predict that voluntary effort would soon wane or that coercive measures would be needed to organize and control nearly every aspect of Canadian private and public life. In December, in Halifax, Sir Robert Borden confidently pledged that "there has not been, there will not be, compulsion or conscription. Freely and voluntarily the manhood of Canada stands ready to fight beyond the seas."[2] Few, indeed, were the politicians and party organizers who did not assume that the war would unite the electorate in common purpose. The spirit of unity in the face of common danger was so great that Sir Wilfrid Laurier solemnly promised the 1914 war session of Parliament that "if in what has been done or in what remains to be done there may be anything which in our judgment should not be done or should be differently done, we raise no question, we take no exception, we offer no criticism, and we shall offer no criticism so long as there is danger at the front."[3] Both leaders would break their promises, not because of dishonesty, but because the corrosion of the Great War forced the breaking of promises and the shattering of many, early, confident expectations.

212

Even as Laurier spoke, much, in fact, had been done in defence of the nation. Certainly Canada was ill-prepared, for the most part unprepared for war. It was true that in the months preceding the conflict the government had prepared a War Book, which, when implemented in August, put its fledgling bureaucracy upon what was thought to be a war footing. In the hectic days of mid-August, scores of Orders-in-Council were passed activating the Militia, providing for home defence, taking control of communications networks, establishing censorship of trans-Atlantic cables, and shoring up the credit of the banks against an anticipated run on their funds.[4]

The government also took upon itself unprecedented authority, in essence the surrender by Parliament of its powers to the government for war purposes, with the introduction and quick passage of the War Measures Act. W.F. O'Connor, who drafted the act and believed that "no one could foresee what it would need to contain to be effective and that the only effective Act would be one of a 'blanket' character," later recalled that the Liberal party wholly supported his proposal. E.M. Macdonald, speaking for the opposition, told him to "make absolutely sure that you omit no power that the government may need."[5] The "blanket" character of the act is revealed by some of the provisions of clause 6:

> The Governor in Council shall have power to do and authorize such acts and things, and to make from time to time such orders and regulations, as he may by reason of the existence of real or apprehended war, invasion or insurrection deem necessary for the security, defence, peace, order and welfare of Canada; and for greater certainty, but not so as to restrict the foregoing terms, it is hereby declared that the powers of the Governor in Council shall extend to all members coming within the classes of subject hereinafter enumerated, that is to say:

> (a) censorship and the control and suppression of publications, writings, maps, plans, photographs, communications and means of communication;
> (b) arrest, detention, exclusion and deportation;
> (c) control of the harbours, ports and territorial waters of Canada and the movements of vessels;
> (d) transportation by land, air, or water and the control of the transport of persons and things;
> (e) trading, exportation, importation, production and manufacture;
> (f) appropriation, control, forfeiture and disposition of property and of the use thereof.[6]

Canada's first line of defence, however, was beyond the seas. On August 6 the cabinet authorized mobilization of the militia units "to be composed of officers and men who are willing to volunteer for overseas service."[7] Two days later Lord Kitchener told Sir George Perley in London that "he can use all you think best to send" and that he anticipated at least a division of 25,000 men.[8] Meanwhile the Minister of Militia and Defence, ignoring his department's mobilization scheme, had broadcast an appeal for volunteers by nightletter to 226 unit commanders. Chaos reigned in militia headquarters in Ottawa as a result of Colonel Hughes' precipitate decision to supervise personally the recruitment of the expeditionary force. Sir George Foster, no friend of Hughes, observed that "the Militia Department is lawless and Kaiserism runs mad."[9]

The department decided to assemble the eager volunteers at Valcartier, a few miles northwest of Quebec City. The site had been planned as a central training area for the Quebec militia since 1912, but it was not until June 20, 1914 that the cabinet authorized the purchase of land for the camp.[10] When war broke out, no work had been done. But by late August a huge training camp had been built. Amid construction and confusion the recruits began to pour in. Somehow Colonel Sam, ably assisted by Honorary Lieutenant-Colonel William Price, timber baron and Quebec Conservative Party organizer in charge of building the camp, wrought a miracle in the wilderness, characteristically capped by the minister's own castle from which he surveyed his domain and his army. Even the detractors of Colonel Hughes were impressed – to a degree. After a tour of the camp, Sir George Foster wrote:

It is a fine site but very dusty . . . the lay of the ground for shooting excellent. 32000 men & 8000 horses are living here – in tents. Water supply & sanitary arrangements appear to be good, as also the food. Sam has small castle built for his convenience over which floats the flag. Saw and conversed with several men & officers & find universal dissatisfaction [with Hughes], swearing – interfering – taking matters out of officers hands etc., etc.[11]

A Montreal reporter provided the most convincing explanation of the choice of Valcartier as the site for mobilization:

There has been some criticism of the plan of mobilization at Valcartier. Many have wondered why Petawawa or Farnham were not used. One reason was the economy which will be made in transportation when mobilization is completed and the troops are trained. They will be marched from the camp to Quebec where they will embark. The expense of horses, the transport wagons, supplies, the equipment and the artillery from one of the other camps would have been great. The delay would have been long. The present plan saves all this.[12]

During a visit to Valcartier on September 21, the Prime Minister made the decision that all 31,200 men should be sent to England instead of just the 25,000 making up the divisional force. Hughes, who had agonized over the choice of who should and who should not go, "broke down and sobbed" in relief.[13] At the end of the month, again amid great confusion, the men, horses, and equipment were loaded on transports at Quebec.

The convoy assembled in Gaspé harbour to await its Royal Navy escort and eventually sailed for Europe and battle on October 3. The day before the Minister of Militia passed among the ships in a launch, with his personal valedictory. Unable to slight his own accomplishment, he told them:

> Soldiers! the world regards you as a marvel. Within six weeks you were at your homes, peaceful Canadian citizens. Since then your training camp has been secured; three and a half miles of rifle ranges – twice as long as any other in the world – were constructed; fences were removed; water of the purest quality was laid in miles of pipes; drainage was perfected; electric light was installed; crops were harvested; roads and bridges were built; ordinance and army service corps buildings were erected; railway sidings were laid down; woods were cleared; sanitation was perfected so that illness was practically unknown, and 33,000 men were assembled from points, some of them upwards of 4,000 miles apart. You have been perfected in rifle shooting and to-day are as fine a body – officers and men – as ever faced a foe. The same spirit as accomplished that great work is what you will display on the War fields of Europe.[14]

They were, indeed, a fine body of officers and men, but they were hardly as prepared to face a foe as Colonel Sam enthusiastically proclaimed. They had but a few weeks of elementary training in the art of modern war. They were poorly equipped and inexpertly led by officers and staff, most of whom lacked any war experience. They were undisciplined. Though the Canadians never would wholly and unquestionably submit to superior authority, and were perhaps better soldiers because of their stubborn independence, fundamental discipline, co-ordination, and cooperation between men and units had yet to be instilled. That was the responsibility of General Alderson, who assumed command of the First Division and oversaw their further training in England during the winter of 1914-15. There, in dreadful weather and with inadequate shelter and clothing, useless or inadequate equipment was scrapped in favour of standard British army issue. Men were drilled, drilled, and drilled again in the ways of war. By spring, when the division entered the line in France, it was a tough and effective unit. Later in April it was "blooded" in the Ypres salient in the first, horrifying gas attack of the war. On the Canadians' left, the French colonials broke in terror. But the Canadians held, and a German breakthrough was averted. Now the Canadians were all the Minister said they were, and more.

At home the high level of volunteer enlistments over the winter of 1914-15 was matched by the low level of organization for adequate training of recruits. The dispatch of a second division to England was held back because of the appalling conditions of the training camp on Salisbury Plain; in Canada the men could at least be sheltered from the elements. But in some places that was about the most that could be said for Canadian training facilities. In Winnipeg, one veteran recalled, the recruits were housed in the Horse Show Building, sleeping on straw palliasses in the spectator seats, and drilling, in a cloud of dust, on a floor covered with sawdust and powdered manure. Mess was served, three times a day, after a brisk march, a mile away in a warehouse in Portage Avenue. The militia, of course, had always trained in months of warm weather. In consequence, almost no winter clothing was available and what there was had gone to the First Division.

> For weeks in the increasingly cold weather men had nothing to wear but their blue jeans, light footwear and even straw hats in which they had come directly from the harvest fields. Even after uniforms came there was still a great shortage of boots and many pairs were bought by officers out of their own pockets for the most needy. Mittens, shirts and caps came in dribbles. The quartermaster sergeant kept his stores in the hockey penalty box and men had to go to him and beg for some needed articles.[15]

After advanced training in England, the Second Division went to France to join the First, in the newly formed Canadian Corps, commanded by Alderson, in September, 1915. At Christmas the Canadians' strength was augmented with the formation of the Third Division. But trouble was developing for the Corps commander. For some time disturbing reports had circulated about the inefficiency of the Ross rifle with which the Canadians were equipped, reports supported by Alderson. The soldiers, it was said, frustrated at the performance of their "Ross" in the muddy warfare of the trenches, downed their rifles to a man and picked up dependable British Lee-Enfields from their fallen imperial comrades.

The Minister of Militia and Defence was a stout defender of the Ross, Canada's own weapon. It was a superb target rifle, vastly superior to the British weapon, he claimed, and that was true. But Hughes refused to acknowledge that the weapon he championed, so fine under the orderly conditions of the target range, was of little more use than a club on a grimy battlefield. The issue came to a head in the spring of 1916 when the Corps did badly and suffered heavy casualties in the battle of the St. Eloi Craters. Part of the blame rested with the friction between Alderson and the commander of the Second Division, General Turner. But part was also attributed to the Ross, large numbers of which jammed in the heat of battle. Severely attacked by Hughes, Alderson was supported by neither his British army superiors nor the Canadian government, and was replaced as Corps commander by Sir Julian Byng. But Hughes did not win all. Following a War Office recommendation, and investigation and testing of the Ross, Canada's rifle was gradually withdrawn from service in the Corps and replaced by the Lee-Enfield.

The Ross rifle affair was but one of a growing number of episodes in which the Minister of Militia and Defence, now both a general and a knight, was a source of embarrassment to the government. A year before, charges of gross corruption in Sir Sam's Shell Committee[16] had been laid in Parliament and the Prime Minister had had to assume control of Hughes' department. In England confusion and contradiction reigned supreme in the Canadian training command structure. "Canadian methods of administration are rather being laughed at over here," was the gloomy report from Sir George Perley, the High Commissioner, as early as May 1915.[17] Sir Sam was seldom in his office, leaving the complicated task of administering his department unattended, either flitting off to England to interfere in the affairs of his subordinates or rushing from city to city at home in vain attempts to win new recruits to his forces. Gradually the work that was rightly his was assumed by others. At the end of 1915, the Shell Committee was reorganized as the Imperial Munitions Board. Canadian government war contracts were turned over to the War Purchasing Commission, chaired by A.E. Kemp. F.B. McCurdy was appointed Parliamentary Secretary to the department and assumed responsibility for much of the department's routine work. In the fall of 1916 R.B. Bennett was made chairman of the National Service Board, and Perley assumed the Ministry of Overseas Military Forces, charged especially to clear up the organizational mess in the United Kingdom. Hughes especially objected to the last appointment and accused Sir Robert Borden of a breach of faith. Borden countered by demanding Sir Sam's resignation. Kemp was named as his successor on November 23. "I saw no tears, heard no regrets," wrote Sir George Foster. "The nightmare is removed."[18]

"A mad distorted dream," one historian's phrase summing up a soldier's life at the front,[19] would disappear neither so easily nor so quickly. By 1916 it was clear that victory was nowhere in sight. After St. Eloi Craters, the Canadians fought again in June at Mount Sorrel in the salient, then moved from Flanders to the Somme. In September the Corps took Courcelette and won their feared reputation as "storm troops." The price for that reputation was high; 24,029 casualties in the battles of the Somme, 1,373 at the St. Eloi Craters, and 8,000 at Mount Sorrel.[20] It was a horrible war, with even the best of soldiers discouraged at times. "Cold, windy, wet. How I hate this country," a Canadian captain wrote home. "I am absolutely fed up with the war this week. The amount of work to be done on the line is immense. Sometimes hundreds of men work on the line all night in the rain to do a piece of trench, and the next day the Germans throw a thousand shells or so at it and flatten it out." And then there was the mud. The same young officer reported from the Ypres salient: "It is so deep that it is not possible to walk in it. Men lie on their llies and wallow and wiggle through it! Then rifles and ammunition become useless, and they are exhausted before the real attack starts."[21] The worst was yet to come. The cost of static warfare was again seen, in April 1917, when the Corps, even after the most careful preparations and behind a devastating moving artillery barrage, lost 10,602 men - 3,598 killed – at Vimy Ridge.

Preliminary bombardment of the German defences began on March 20 and steadily increased through the last day before the attack. At 5:30 a.m. on Easter Monday, the Canadians, who had crept into forward positions during the night, jumped off. "Our barrage," a soldier recalled,

> involved a gun to every 25 yards of the Boche front, and was regular as a clock and as sweet as a sewing machine. Nothing human could stand against it, and, combined with the gale, it sent the Hun helter-skelter for cover, smashing his forward positions and converting his support lines into a morass. It is no exaggeration to say that the ground at the crest of the Ridge and for rods behind it looked . . . like nothing so much as a rich plum-pudding before it goes to the boiling.[22]

That afternoon, an officer who had remained behind the lines at a communications post, walked across no man's land. There he saw "in that awkward humpbacked posture" of death his dinner companion of the night before. Then he came upon the results of the Canadians' wrath.

> The first dead German I saw was spread-eagled against the parados, or back-wall, of his trench, arms flung out as though crucified. Where his head had been was a red pulp like a crushed strawberry. Many of the dead lay as though sleeping without a mark of disfigurement and I am certain felt no pain, but others were disembowelled or with limbs shattered and clothing torn from their bodies by the blast of high explosives. The water in the shell holes was stained blood red.[23]

Vimy was a great victory for the Canadians. The Corps, now four divisions strong, attacked all together for the first time in a carefully co-ordinated operation. The casualties were high, very high, but much less than they might have been had not the operation been skilfully planned, and the whole Corps fought together as one terrible, efficient machine of death. The tributes to the victors were many and well deserved. Not least was the esteem with which the High Command held the Corps. When their commander, Byng, was shortly after promoted to command of the Third Army, Field-Marshall Haig recommended that a citizen soldier from Canada, Brigadier-General Arthur Currie of the First Division, be promoted and take Byng's place.

As the hope of easy and quick victory faded, then vanished, and as the casualties mounted, and mounted again, the government's early commitments of one division, and then an additional 16,000 men, became ludicrously unreal. Reality took the form of the enormous wastage of men in the trench warfare of the western front. The authorized total force levels rose to 150,000 in July, 1915, 250,000 in October, and finally 500,000 men, including those already sent overseas and those in garrison and guard duty in Canada, on January 12, 1916.[24] More training camps were built, others were enlarged, and recruiting drives were launched, culminating in the disappointing National Registration scheme of 1916. As a last effort at volunteerism, it was designed to provide a basis for the most efficient allotment of manpower to both the domestic and overseas war effort. Able-bodied young men, often employed in essential war production industries at home, suffered under the abusive label of "slacker." Well-meaning but increasingly intolerant private citizens and voluntary groups continually pressured the government to increase its commitment to the expeditionary force. Numerous organizations were founded – Win-the-War and Recruiting Leagues – to assist the government's own recruiting efforts.

Especially prominent in the recruiting drives were Canada's women, ably assisted by such prominent British ladies as Lady Aberdeen and Mrs. Pankhurst. The latter, on a cross-Canada tour, asked a Vancouver audience in 1916, "How will you like to think that the man you love has allowed other men to do his duty for him while he sheltered himself behind the sacrifice of other men? How will you like to feel as the mother of sons when other mothers have sacrificed their sons for you and your sons? It is the duty of women to remind men that they are not fully awake to the war and their need of service."[25] At Toronto on June 12 a mass meeting of women war workers was told by Constance Boulton that

> The voluntary system is testing our democracy through the individual response of our men to their national obligations. If they do their duty the voluntary system is the finest system in the world, but if they are going to let others fight their battles, it is the most degraded, the most cruel, the most selfish system that ever existed in the world.

The militant ladies then proceeded to pass a resolution asking the Canadian goverment to "register all men of military age, and to give badges to all those who are required at home for the essential industries of the nation, including women, and those who are medically unfit, and further, to classify all sources of national wealth, including the services of women."[26] Eventually, all efforts were not enough. Attempting to shame men from behind their wives' skirts did little to force them to volunteer for the carnage in France, and, in part at least, ignored the ever-increasing labour demands of war industries in Canada. But speeches and propaganda did help create an atmosphere of crisis, the necessary first step in leading Canadians from volunteerism to compulsion.

Sir Robert Borden's New Year's message for 1916, raising the man-power commitment to 500,000 men was greeted with brief enthusiasm. In January nearly 30,000 men enlisted and in March almost 35,000. But increased labour demands for war production at home and ever-gloomy news from the front both ate away at the enthusiasm for volunteer service. By July enlistments were down to around 8,000 men; in December a mere 5279 responded to the calls to the colours, and about the same number were recruited in February and March of 1917.[27] The Secretary of the National Service Board estimated that some twenty per cent of Canadian males between eighteen and sixty-five failed to return their registration cards. Of the more than $1\frac{1}{2}$ million who did, only 286,976 were not engaged in essential occupations.

To these the recruiters turned their attention. In military district 10 (Winnipeg) a canvassing of almost 2000 men produced not a single recruit. In district 5 (Quebec) four recruits were produced from a list of 4500.[28] In the spring of 1917 a scheme to establish a home defence force, to release men already enlisted for service overseas, was a dismal failure. In May, with the knowledge of Vimy's 10,000 plus casualties to balance against less than 5,000 April enlistments, and with no prospect for change from battles of attrition at the front, Borden announced his intention to introduce conscription.

The Borden government was committed to maintaining the strength of the Canadian Corps in France and, in those terms, the Military Service Act of 1917 was a military necessity. "The only solution of the problem of Canadian recruiting is conscription," said the newly appointed commander of the corps. "My experiences in France have shown me, as a soldier," Currie added, "the necessity of conscription if we desire to maintain at full strength our fighting divisions to the end of the war."[29] The Military Service Act was also a political necessity in urban English Canada, in large part because of the frenzied crisis atmosphere created by the volunteer recruiting societies. But it was a political disaster for French Canada and in agricultural communities from coast to coast. The political contradictions were reflected in the broad exemptions policy of the act, especially in the agricultural workers' exemptions. In mid-October, 1917, all Class I men – bachelors and childless widowers between twenty and thirty-four years old – were called to register for service. A month later about 20,000 had reported for service and more than 300,000 had applied for exemptions.[30]

In the meantime the Canadian Corps had won its grimmest and most futile victory at Passchendaele, suffering 15,654 battle casualties in the last phase of Field Marshall Haig's misguided Flanders offensive. In the spring of 1918 the Allies suffered crushing reverses in the great German counter-offensive. The Canadians, weary and wounded, stayed out of the initial stages of the defensive action. But they would soon be engaged again in attack; indeed, though no one could know it at the time, playing a vital role in the crushing of the Germans in the last hundred days, climaxed by Currie's triumphal entry into Mons on Armistice Day.

As the Allied armies suffered serious reverses and heavy casualties in April 1918, Borden called a secret session of Parliament to reveal the nature of the crisis and to announce the cancellation of exemptions. By summer there were nearly 28,000 defaulters from registration under Class I. Some 5,400 of these had reported under an amnesty in August.[31] Ultimately about half of the men registered under the act, some 220,000, were granted exemptions. When further deductions were made for the defaulters, for men serving in the British forces, and for medical discharge, 99,999 drafted men had been secured for the Canadian Expeditionary Force. The objective set by the act had been 100,000 men. As the official historian concludes, "While the administration of the Military Service Act was often inefficient and attended by many gross malpractices, the Act itself was neither a failure nor ineffective . . . it did produce the military results it was designed to produce."[32]

II

War imposed a new sense of social as well as military responsibilities upon Canadians. Of particular importance was their obligation to sustain the families and dependants of the nation's soldiers. Here, too, the voluntary response to the call of duty was immediate and enthusiastic. And like the military effort, the social service cause began in confusion. As one observer put it, "so far as organization was concerned, Canada was as unprepared for war as a South Sea Islander for a snow storm."[33]

The I.O.D.E., which regarded the war as an opportunity for "prompt and united action . . . by the women and children of the Empire," was prominent in relief work across the country, forsaking an image of social pretension for one of social utility.[34] The chief function of the Canadian Red Cross, with some 1,200 local branches, was to "furnish aid to sick and wounded soldiers as an auxiliary to the Army Medical Corps." But Red Cross clubs in many cities and towns provided a place for lonely soldiers' wives to meet and work with new friends.[35] The work of the Lucan (Senior) Women's Institute was probably typical of the 30,000-member Women's Institutes of Ontario:

> During World War I, the Institute did marathon Red Cross work in knitting, sewing, packing parcels, serving meals, holding dances, collecting paper and all manner of such work. A drive was sponsored which netted thirty-two tons of food for relief and a gramaphone was purchased for an English hospital.
>
> At home, a room was furnished in the Byron Sanitorium, a flagpole purchased for the Public School, suppers served to returned men and chickens canned and sent overseas.[36]

The Great War Veterans' Association, the Next-of-Kin Association, the Y.M.C.A., Consumers Leagues, Women's Patriotic Leagues, Vacant Lot Garden Clubs, and the Women's Volunteer Reserve all gave time and money in innumerable projects.

Probably most important was the work of the Canadian Patriotic Fund, incorporated by Parliament in the short war session of August 1914, and the separately organized Manitoba Patriotic Fund. Like the other organizations, they helped relieve the natural anxieties of soldiers overseas. "We are willing to put up with the hardship," a private in the 10th Canadian Field Ambulance told the Prime Minister,

> but sir, it adds to a married man's worry etc. when he receives a letter from his wife to say that they are practically starving. . . . Before I went to the war, I had a comfortable home one which I built myself . . . I was on the G.T. Rly. and made good wages, my wife and children had all the comforts that could be given them and we both worked hard to get our home together. I am no beggar sir and all I ask for, is that my wife and children are looked after while I am away and my house and bit of land protected.[37]

With the aim of "preserving the families' economic status in comfort and decency, as a partial recognition of the services of the soldiers overseas," the fund worked through volunteer local committees under the general direction of an Ottawa headquarters.[38]

At the beginning of the war a soldier's family could receive up to $30 per month in eastern Canada and $40 per month in the west from the Patriotic Fund. With the rise in the cost of living during the war, the maximum allowance was raised to $50 per month across the country by 1918. (Wealthy detractors complained that the fund was responsible for the lamentable shortage of domestics in Canada!)[39] Fund workers helped set up budgets for recipient families and acted as the families' business agents in dealing with the government concerning separation allowances and pension claims. Frequently local fund offices acted as mediators between creditors and debtor families, and set up small cooperatives to buy food and fuel and sell it at cost to the soldiers' dependants.

The activities of the Montreal branch illustrate the wide scope of the fund's activity. Helen R.Y. Reid, Convenor of the Ladies Auxiliary, described their efforts, carried out in both languages, as

> a social service work of wide scope, embracing all the family interests that are affected by the war. In order that a man may fight well he must be assured that his family is not suffering personal privation and making further sacrifices at home. . . . The homes, so sadly broken as a consequence of war, have to be doubly safe-guarded if the nation is to maintain its civilized standards at the level reached before the war.
> With the startling increase in juvenile delinquency (41% in the third year

of the war) and with the heavy rate of infantile mortality (182 per thousand), Montreal may well emphasize the need for patriotic home service on the part of every man and woman of the city.[40]

Montreal relief committee workers were provided with lists of doctors, nurses, hospitals, and milk stations. They relayed reports of health, sanitation, and housing inadequacies to City Hall. Aid was given to illegitimate children. Trust accounts were opened, first for a blinded returned soldier in November 1914, and later for those who suffered from intemperance, insanity, consumption of drugs, illness, the neglect of a guardian, and the death or imprisonment of a mother. In 1915 an employment bureau was set up to settle returned soldiers back into the community. All this work, of course, required careful planning and a large commitment to volunteer social work. In Montreal nearly two hundred volunteers gave a minimum of three half-day's weekly service to the sixteen different departments of the local fund organization.[41]

One general consequence of the wide range of voluntary war work by Canadians was a decided shift in social attitudes. This was particularly true of Canadian women, who were crucial to most voluntary organizations. Canadian attitudes toward the proper role of women in society, including the attitudes of women themselves, were liberalized by the conspicuous contribution women made to the success of voluntary groups.

Equally important, the voluntary organizations were the direct predecessors, sometimes the initiators, of public social welfare programmes. No matter how hard they tried, the private organizations could never completely dispel their image as paternalistic charities. Support from the Patriotic Fund often seemed to the recipient demeaning rather than an unquestioned national obligation. Partly as a result of this unfortunate attitude and partly because the work surpassed the capabilities of volunteers, some functions of the voluntary groups were taken over by governments. Saskatchewan mainly and New Brunswick wholly eventually relied upon provincial taxation to support soldiers' dependants. Early in 1917, Alberta implemented a Patriotic Tax Act to assist in the same cause. After 1916 widows and dependants' pensions were assumed by the Canadian government rather than the Patriotic Fund. By war's end the dominion government, through agencies like the Department of Soldiers' Civil Re-establishment, the Women's Bureau and the Food Board, was performing social services initiated in voluntary organizations. As an accepted public responsibility, these social services were scarcely thought of before the war. The voluntary organizations played the intermediary role between private social accountability and public welfare. They accustomed the public, both recipient and donor, to think in terms of government responsibility for social services.

III

Canada was a nation of immigrants. About 100,000 of them were native-born Germans or Austro-Hungarians, and another 400,000 were of alien enemy extraction. What was to be done about these people who had freely come to live in Canada and who had been and were contributing so much to her economic and social development? That they posed a potential problem to the government – "a menace" was the way Sam Hughes put it to the cabinet in August 1914 – was obvious. And not the least unreasonable of early suggested solutions was his: that "they be encouraged to go to the United States."[42] That their potential plight was unsympathetically regarded by much of the Canadian public was equally obvious. The tiresome and often irresponsible debate of the previous five years over the naval issue had conditioned Canadians to regard the "foreigners," especially German immigrants, with disfavour and distrust at best. On August 7, after recommending a rigid system of registration and curfews for alien immigrants, a Toronto newspaper hysterically concluded: "Anyone disobeying these orders to be court martialled and shot as a spy."[43]

Dispassionate consideration of the problem was further hindered by rumours of imminent invasion of Canada by large forces of German-Americans. "The Germans all over the United States are holding meetings," read one report to J.D. Hazen,

> their intentions are to invade Canada on the lines of the Fenian Raid. . . . Their headquarters is Milwaukee. They are getting all the automobiles they can possibly get without causing suspicion; they intend to muster 150,000 men along the border and invade in three or four places, destroy the canals, the railroads and grain elevators; their plans are for inland invasion; they have plenty of money behind this.[44]

Crank letters like this, and a warning from the British Ambassador at Washington that Germans were drilling in Milwaukee in preparation for a raid on Canada,[45] all had to be checked carefully by the Dominion Police, the Mounted Police, and private detective agencies hired for the purpose. There were a very few isolated cases of sabotage by German agents in later years,[46] but happily both the Commissioner of the Dominion Police and the Comptroller of the Royal North West Mounted Police were able to assure the Prime Minister that fears of an invasion from the United States were groundless.[47] The results of the rumours were two: substantial numbers of militia were placed on guard duty at bridges, railways, canals, public buildings, and factories; more important, the irresponsible, sensational publicity given to these rumours further heightened Canadian anxiety about the "enemy" within their gates.[48]

Government policy attempted to put the problem on a higher plane. Reservists in enemy forces who attempted to return to their native countries were detained. But for the most part a proclamation, in August 1914, assured enemy aliens of the rights and privileges they held before the war. As Sir Robert Borden explained a few months later, "So long as they do not attempt to aid the enemy they are entitled to the protection of the law." "Having invited them to become citizens of this country, we owe to them in the trying circumstances in which they are placed the duty of fairness and consideration."[49] Still, some concessions were made to public demands for restriction. Enemy aliens were barred from possession of firearms and explosives by an Order in Council passed in September and a month later were subjected to a system of registration with police authorities. Failure to report monthly, to register, or suspicion of complicity with the enemy resulted in internment in one of the camps established for the purpose by the Department of Militia and Defence.[50]

Despite government policy, harassment of aliens, collectively and individually, increased during the war. The Anti-German League was founded in Toronto in 1916. The Dean of Trinity College, Toronto, urged that the head tax on Chinese immigrants ($500) be doubled for future German immigrants, that their families be barred entry, and that they be kept under police surveillance.[51] In 1918 the Great War Veterans Association called for a 10 per cent supertax on enemy aliens, the dismissal from work and internment of all not engaged in critical jobs, and restriction on the travel of others to five miles from their homes without passports.[52]

"I have moved to Canada where I think the country very nice," one Saskatchewan farmer wrote to the Prime Minister:

> but as I am a German I am called the horiblest names and I dont want to harm no one and if they leave me a lone I wont say nothing they was a man just today called me a dam low down German trash. . . . I wont take anymore of his abuse and I think you will agree with me on this as I know you are a onst man.[53]

In Northern Ontario, acting on the current suspicion that aliens were not contributing their share to drives like the Patriotic Fund, seventeen of the "foreign element" were arrested, searched, and had their funds recorded.[54]

Clearly the public did not respond to the government's plea for a policy of tolerance and restraint. Indeed, lower level public officials bowed to demands for harassment. In Montreal a plaintiff of alien origin who sought to sue under the Industrial Accidents Act for damages from an accident he suffered in January 1914, had his case thrown out of Superior Court because, as an enemy, he was not entitled to sue. "An alien enemy cannot maintain any action in our courts," declared Mr. Justice Bruneau, "even in a case where the right originated before the commencement of hostilities, but . . . this right is not destroyed; it is only suspended during the war."[55] On appeal, the Court of King's Bench overthrew this decision and upheld the protection of the law guaranteed to aliens in the government's proclamation of August 1914.

To safeguard the rights of aliens was not easy, and became less so as the war dragged on. Censorship of the foreign language press was vigorous, and much more restrictive than regulations for English and French language newspapers. Even so, administrative officials regarded the measures as half-hearted, and urged a total ban on foreign language publications. When the increasingly powerful Great War Veterans' Association joined the chorus of complaint, and when a government investigator of radical activities in Canada reported a presumed dangerous growth of Bolshevist sentiment, the government relented.[56] On September 25, 1918, an Order in Council made it an offence to print, publish or possess any publication in an enemy language without a licence from the Secretary of State.[57] Three days later, a number of "foreign" organizations – including the International Workers of the World – were banned as were meetings of other groups at which enemy languages were used.[58] More flagrant still was the passage of the Wartime Elections Act of the previous year, which disfranchised naturalized citizens who had been born in enemy countries and naturalized after 1902.[59]

That restrictions upon aliens intensified during the war is undeniable, as is the evidence of the government's decreasing resolve to uphold its 1914 pledge to protect their rights. But it is also likely that the government's actions held in check the unrestrained enthusiasm of native Canadians to persecute their fellow citizens. That was only accomplished by compromise and hard work upon the part of senior political and judicial officials and the national police forces. For their efforts, these officials received no thanks from their fellow Canadians.

The organization of manpower for war, then, began in confusion and chaos. Neither governors nor governed knew what to do nor how to do it. Both began with enthusiasm and with the haphazard volunteerism of a free, peaceful society. Both assumed the war would quickly and victoriously go away. It did not. A military effort that began with the combined attributes of a Scout Jamboree and a citizens' crusade ended with a tough and terrifyingly efficient Canadian Corps, led by Canadian citizen soldiers and backed by compulsory military service. Supplemental services to the soldiers and their dependants, started by well-meaning, charitable, middle-class civilians, gradually became the responsibility of the state.

Throughout the war, people's impulse was to persecute their fellows who, by chance, suddenly became enemy aliens. The state interposed itself between the native-born and the unfortunate "foreigners" to protect the latter from possible harsher abuses. By 1918 the governors had become regulators and controllers, the governed regulated and controlled. The comfortable and complacent late summer of 1914 seemed very far away indeed.

CHAPTER 12

The War Economy

I

In 1919 Sir Thomas White observed that "in war time, the treasury loses control to a large extent over expenditures. . . . Finance becomes secondary in war time; the money must be found."[1] It was certainly true, in some measure, that the Minister of Finance lost "control . . . over expenditures" during the war years. The government's decision to maintain the country's great capital projects, especially the transcontinental railways, during the war, combined with enormous war expenditures, notably in the Department of Militia and Defence, led White to complain, early in 1915: "I have come to wonder whether the Minister more immediately concerned in all these matters being myself has anything whatever to say in the administration of this country's affairs."[2] It was equally true that the money had to be found. But financing Canada's war effort was hardly "secondary"; in fact, it was an essential part of the nation's war machinery. To supply the funds, accepted modes of government finance had to be abandoned, though gradually, and new methods of raising money adopted.

To meet the immediate fiscal crisis in August 1914, the government passed Orders in Council,[3] later given legal sanction by the Finance Act, 1914, and the Dominion Notes Act,[4] to protect the credit of the Canadian banks and to increase the money supply. Under the first act the Minister of Finance was permitted to advance dominion notes to the chartered banks upon the pledge of satisfactory securities; the banks could make payments in their own notes rather than dominion notes or gold; the excess circulation privilege of the banks, formerly seasonal to finance wheat exports, was extended to the whole year; the redemption of dominion notes in gold was suspended; and the government could declare a general moratorium.[5] To meet the government's monetary requirements, the Dominion Notes Act authorized an increase of dominion notes which could be issued against a 25 per cent reserve from $30 to $50 millions.

Sixteen millions were advanced to the Canadian Northern and Grand Trunk Pacific Railways, and $10 millions of dominion notes issued for general purposes later in the fall of 1914 received legislative sanction in the Confirmatory Act of 1915.[6] In addition a War Appropriation Act for $50 million was passed,[7] tariff duties on coffee, sugar, spirits, and tobacco products and excise taxes on spirits, beer, and tobacco were increased, and $60 million was borrowed on the London market. In 1917 a further issue of $50 million in dominion notes was made to finance British war purchases in Canada.[8]

The extremely close cooperation between the chartered banks, through the Canadian Bankers' Association, and the Minister of Finance in the war years provided a near equivalent to a centralized banking system. White later recalled: "I discovered when I was Minister of Finance that the Canadian banking system is the most perfect instrument that a Minister of Finance could have at his hand in floating a loan. . . . What had I to do? Just call up on the telephone the president of the Canadian Bankers' Association: 'I want all the branch banks of Canada notified to do a certain thing.' It was done."[9]

Throughout the war the tariff remained the foundation stone of the government's financial structure and, in the early years, the most important source of revenue. In 1915 the only major change in the tariff during the war was made, with an *ad valorem* increase of $7\frac{1}{2}$ per cent in the general and intermediate schedules and a 5 per cent increase in the British preferential rates. "The chief source and mainstay of our revenue is the tariff and it is to this we must look principally for relief of our present financial condition," White said in his budget speech. "Taxation imposed by increased customs duties," he argued with decades of traditional financial sentiment to support him, "bears upon all classes because all are consumers and in paying additional taxation each member of the community will feel that he is to that extent contributing to the cost of the war and the defence of his country."[10]

Despite later criticism, the government's adherence to orthodox fiscal policy was entirely understandable. However dour the predictions of the Minister of Finance, during none of the war years did war expenditure exceed ten per cent of the national income.[11] More important, new methods of raising revenue seemed unnecessary in the general expectation, in Britain as well as in Canada, that the war would be of short duration. This sense of optimism prevailed throughout 1915. Accordingly, the government firmly intended to maintain an image of stability by continuing traditional policies and procedures. Indeed, as late as 1917 White argued that "it should . . . always be kept in mind that Canada has been in the past and will likely be for many years in the future a country inviting immigration and capital to develop its resources and contribute to its prosperity.

Especially should we in considering taxation measures for the period following the war keep in view the desirability of the flow of settlers and capital to Canada not being retarded through fear on their part of heavy Federal taxation."[12]

Direct taxation, especially the imposition of an income tax, was both politically unacceptable and fraught with constitutional and administrative problems. "Such a tax is not expedient," Sir Thomas observed in 1915, "at all events for the present."

> In order to bring into force an income tax the Government would be obliged to create machinery for assessment, revision and collection. This would involve a heavy expense as compared with the amount which would be realized. ... My chief objection, however, to an income tax is the fact that the several Provinces are also likely to be obliged to resort to [such] measures for raising additional revenue and I am of the view that the Dominion should not enter upon the domain to which they are confined to a greater degree than is necessary in the national interest.[13]

The other major source of revenue was the bond market, and it eventually became the greatest source of government funds. Like the tariff, it was a traditional method of government financing. The Borden government added another sentimentally appealing if economically questionable rationalization for the large increase in bonded debt during the war. "We are justified in placing upon posterity the greater portion of the financial burden of this war, waged as it is in the interests of human freedom, and their benefit in equal if not in greater degree than for our own," said White in 1916. "Canada in future years of peace, with the prosperity which will be her heritage from the development of unbounded resources, will be able to meet the interest and sinking fund charges upon such debt as we shall be obliged to incur in defence of our country and its liberties."[14]

Even in this well-established area of government finance, war conditions forced important changes in practice. After early 1915 the traditional market for Canadian securities, London, was effectively closed to further borrowing, and in August the government floated its first loan in New York for $45 millions. The step was taken with misgivings. As the General Manager of the Bank of Montreal put it, "It becomes more of a national question as to whether or not you should go to the New York market. ... It is true that several of the provinces of Canada and our two principal cities have recently borrowed in New York, but for the government of the Dominion of Canada itself to go there might be, well, just a little *infra dig.*"[15] Beyond that, the Canadians did not like the high commissions charged on the New York loan. Nonetheless, further issues were floated in New York of $75 millions in March 1916 and $100 millions in July 1917.

Much more important was the opening of the domestic market to dominion securities. Early in the war the Minister of Finance was extremely sceptical of the many suggestions he seek funds from the Canadian public. "It is not a matter of raising five, ten, fifteen or twenty or even fifty million dollars," he pessimistically replied to one correspondent, seriously underestimating the strength of the well-developed pre-war domestic capital market. "No doubt your company and others would do their best but the gross amount would be relatively quite small."[16] In 1915 the Minister did float a loan of $50 millions, which was doubly subscribed. But White remained unconvinced – and worried by the high costs of the New York market. "My New York money has certainly cost me dearly," he wrote, "and I only wish that we were in a position in Canada to finance our own requirements but this does not appear to be possible."[17]

In fact, it was possible. The expansionary policies of the first war years now paid their dividends. Issues in 1916 and 1917 were, like the first, oversubscribed. Then, in the crisis summer of 1917, a second loan was floated, the first "Victory Loan," for $150 millions. It yielded over $400 millions. In 1918 the second "Victory Loan" of $300 millions yielded $660 millions. Another "Victory Loan" in 1919 was equally successful.[18] The last three issues were made in low denominations to enable small investors to subscribe. Previous issues had largely been taken up by financial institutions but over 800,000 buyers participated in the first "Victory Loan" and more than a million subscribed to the "Victory Loan" of 1918. Additional funds from the "popular" savings market were secured with the issuance of War Savings Certificates in 1917 and of War Savings Stamps in 1918.[19]

As optimistic predictions of early victory dwindled, Canadians demanded fulfilment of their pledge of "every sacrifice" in financial as well as military affairs. Federal fiscal innovations that would have been politically unthinkable in 1914 and 1915 were being urged upon the government with increasing force. The first break with tradition came in 1916 with the introduction of a Business Profits Tax. By then it was clear that the war had become a tremendous stimulant to the Canadian economy. The munitions manufacturers were only the most obvious benefactors; producers of all the sundry necessities of war – food, clothing, boots, blankets, and wagons, to name but a few – were making huge profits. "Their position being advantageous as compared with less fortunate fellow citizens," observed the Minister of Finance, "it is just that a portion of their advantage should be appropriated to the benefit of the state."[20]

Even more than the Business Profits Tax, the introduction of the federal income tax was inspired by political rather than fiscal pressure. In his April 1917 budget, Sir Thomas White still defended his reluctance to impose an income tax. But as a late concession to growing demands for conscription of wealth to accompany conscription of manpower, he reversed his position and introduced the Income War Tax Act on July 25, 1917. "There has arisen, in connection with the Military Service Bill," he acknowledged, "a very natural and, in my view a very just, sentiment that those who are in the enjoyment of substantial incomes should substantially and directly contribute to the growing war expenditure of the Dominion." He justified the moderate rates imposed, 4 per cent on corporate profits, 4 per cent on personal income and a graduated supertax on incomes over $6,000 of from 2 to 25 per cent, and the generous exemptions on personal incomes, by pointing out that

> the cost of living has materially, and indeed greatly increased in this country . . . and that has a bearing upon the question of exemption which should be allowed in an income tax measure.[As well], in most of the provinces of the Dominion there is a municipal tax upon income, more or less heavy, running as high as two or three percent. In addition to that, there is in some provinces a direct income tax levied by the province itself . . . when this measure becomes law the people of this country whose incomes make them subject to the several income taxation laws in force in Canada will be liable to three different sets of income taxation.[21]

As Table I shows, the rates on personal income were raised in both 1918 and 1919. In 1918 the exemptions were lowered.

Table I
Dominion Income Tax Payable in 1917, 1918, and 1919

Income	Single			Married		
	1917	1918	1919	1917	1918	1919
$	$	$	$	$	$	$
1,500	–	10	20	–	–	–
2,000	20	30	40	–	–	–
2,500	40	50	60	–	10	20
3,000	60	70	80	–	20	40
5,000	140	150	160	80	100	120
10,000	420	452	662	360	399	620
20,000	1,320	1,463	2,132	1,260	1,408	2,090
30,000	2,520	2,783	4,127	2,460	2,728	4,085
50,000	5,320	5,863	9,692	5,260	5,808	9,650
100,000	14,820	17,688	32,792	14,760	17,633	32,750
200,000	43,820	51,842	97,892	43,760	51,785	97,850[23]

In spite of the 1918 and 1919 changes, most Canadians were exempt from federal income taxation during the war years. Average annual earnings for supervisory and office employees in manufacturing industries rose from $1,317 in 1917 to $1,810 in 1920, and for production workers from

$760 in 1917 to $1,090 in 1920. On average, then, all married employees were exempt and if single employees paid any federal income tax it was clearly minimal. [22] The imposition of the income tax on agricultural labour was also minimal, as Sir Herbert Ames explained to the House of Commons in June 1919. Wages for seasonal summer labour by males had increased from $36 per month, including board, in 1914 to $78 per month in 1919, and for females from $19 per month in 1914 to $43 per month in 1919. Annual wages for agricultural labour by males increased from $323 to $764 over the same period and for females from $189 to $465. The average value of board included in these figures rose from $14 per month to $24 per month for males and from $11 per month to $19 per month for females. Ames revealed that 31,130 Canadians had paid an income tax in 1918. Of these, 3,623 were farmers, 14 per cent of the total. And the farmers had paid $3\frac{1}{2}$ per cent of the total income tax receipts in that year. [24] In short, the income tax fell most heavily, if not exclusively, upon the professional and managerial classes, those whom White had described as citizens "in the enjoyment of substantial incomes," those whose incomes had probably been most enhanced by war prosperity.

Fiscal and monetary policy were decidedly inflationary and along with extraordinary demand for Canadian goods and services contributed directly to the rise in the cost of living. Those who suffered most were Canadians who could least afford it, people with fixed or low incomes who lost considerably in terms of real purchasing power. In 1933 the Royal Commission on Banking and Currency noted that the Finance Act of 1914 had been "the efficient agency which made effective the policy of inflation which Canada, in common with all belligerent countries followed." Sir Thomas White, in a heated rejoinder, admitted the existence of credit inflation – though attributing it to circumstances of the war rather than to government policy in the Finance Act; [25] but he denied any "policy of inflation." The minister's defence that government issues of dominion notes were all "secured" by suitable securities betrayed his definition of inflation as simply the issuance of unsecured paper money, and revealed more about the lack of economic sophistication in the war-time Finance Department than about the existence of inflation. [26] It is true that taxing power was not used to check inflation during the early war years because of optimistic forecasts of victory and public reluctance to accept new tax burdens. It was also true that very few Canadians – economist O.D. Skelton was one – regarded the power to tax as a valid instrument of social policy.

In fiscal matters, as in other wartime policies, the traditional reliance on the tariff and on bond issues for revenue was slowly augmented by direct taxation in the Business Profits and Income War Tax Acts of 1916 and 1917. Even then, attention was focussed more on immediate political and

fiscal needs than on long term economic and social planning. As J.H. Perry
has written, "The official attitude in World War I was simply a desire to
surmount the immediate *financial* problem presented by the war without
giving much consideration to the underlying economic effects of various
alternative paths of action."[27]

II

Business and industry benefited most from the government's inflationary
policies. Plagued with great unused productive capacity at the start of the
war – "We are only operating at 40% of our capacity" was a typical
complaint from the president of the Lake Superior Corporation in December 1914[28] – Canadian industrial plants were vastly expanded and even
then stretched to their limits before the Armistice. Export markets for
staple products and manufactured goods grew far beyond the fondest
expectation of Canadian businessmen. Before 1913 about 7 per cent of
Canada's manufactured goods were sold overseas; between 1916 and
1918 the proportion was over 40 per cent. Acreage in field crops rose
from 35 million in 1913 to 53 million in 1919; in the prairies wheat
acreage increased 80 per cent. These exports paid a considerable part of
the cost of the war. Export sales, in turn, were possible because of the
expansion of credit, which financed the purchasers of the goods Canada
produced.[29]

But inflation was only one force responsible for eventual business prosperity. The government made large demands upon the economy for war
supplies and the continuance of capital projects. The Prime Minister spent
much time – some thought inordinate amounts – seeking markets for
Canadian goods. It was a frustrating and, until 1916, not a very successful
effort. The Allied governments, reasonably enough, concentrated their
North American purchasing of war material in the United States. In one
of a series of complaints about early British and French purchasing practices, Borden wrote: "A very painful and even bitter feeling is being
aroused throughout the Dominion. Men are going without bread in
Canada while those across the line are receiving good wages for work that
could be done as efficiently and as cheaply in this country."[30]

Borden's problems did not stop there. There were hundreds of rumours
of unsavoury and corrupt dealings associated with the orders, domestic
and foreign, which Canadian industry did receive. Neither business nor
government, of course, was prepared for the demands of a war economy.
And much that seemed corrupt was the result of administrative chaos and
productive inefficiency rather than dishonesty. (This seems to have been
true of the boots and field-glasses "scandals.") Still, each rumour had to

be checked, and evidence of corruption, though slight, was found. Two members of Borden's party, Messrs Garland and DeWitt Foster, were found to have engaged in corrupt practices in the acquisition of drugs and horses for the military and were declared *persona non grata* by the Prime Minister in a speech in April 1915, in which he announced the establishment of a War Purchasing Commission to oversee Canadian war contracts.[31]

More serious, at least politically, were the charges against the Shell Committee. It had been set up in the early weeks of the war in a typically haphazard fashion by Colonel Hughes, and included some members of the Militia Council and a few manufacturers representing industries potentially capable of producing munitions. Its function was to act as a contractor – more particularly a purchasing agent – for the British government for the procurement of munitions in Canada. Initial orders had to be placed in the United States. But by 1915 a substantial munitions production industry had been created, almost solely through the efforts of the Shell Committee, in Canada. As with other Hughes enterprises, the creation was a magnificent testament to his energy and imagination, but some of its methods were compelling evidence of his lack of judgement and casual disregard of basic administrative responsibilities.

In March 1916, the Liberals charged that members of the committee had personally benefited from the contracts they issued, that contracts were not put out to tender, that large orders had been placed in the United States rather than Canada, and that Hon. Colonel J. Wesley Allison, a crony of Hughes who was a free-lance agent for the committee, had pocketed considerable gain at the expense of the British public. A Royal Commission found that the committee members, including Hughes, had not used their position for personal gain. It was true that the contracts were not put out to tender, but such was the practice of the British government in all its munitions purchases in North America. It was also true that large orders had been placed in the United States; Canadian industry, initially, had been very reluctant to plunge into the business at great retooling expense and had neither the skilled men nor the machinery necessary for shell production. As for Allison, whom Hughes stubbornly defended to the end, he had taken a considerable rake-off on a questionable contract to an American firm. His punishment was farcical, as were most things in a Hughes' endeavour. He was censured by the Royal Commission and deprived of his honorary militia rank.[32]

Meanwhile, the services of Allison and the Shell Committee had ended. The shell crisis of 1915 had led to the establishment of a Ministry of Munitions in the British government. Following talks between Borden and the minister, Lloyd George, during Borden's summer visit to London, representatives of the ministry were sent to Ottawa to reorganize the

Canadian end of the supply line. By the end of the year the Shell Committee had been replaced by the Imperial Munitions Board directly responsible to the British Ministry of Munitions, and chaired by the energetic and
opinionated president of the Wm. Davies Packing Company, Joseph Flavelle. Under Flavelle's dictatorial direction the I.M.B. was a stupendous
success – as he was always the first to point out. By 1918 it was producing
not only shells but also airplanes, boats, and other material. It had established its own "national factories." And it was even serving as a substantial
supplier to the United States Ordnance Department when its productive
capacity had outstripped British requirements.[33]

From the beginning munitions production was an exceptional enterprise in Canada. Even under the Shell Committee, it remained a state-
induced and state-regulated business. Generally, in the early war years,
Canadian businessmen were assured they could carry on with little fear of
interference from a meddling government. "The policy," Borden told the
House of Commons in March 1915, "is not to interfere with the business
activities of the country." That was understandable enough. Business was
still suffering from the depression of the previous two years. The coming
of war had been a further shock rather than a stimulant to business confidence. And, given the accepted attitude of business toward government
interference, the tariff always excepted, reassurance seemed appropriate.
But the Prime Minister did add a proviso, the potential significance of
which he himself hardly realized: "except in so far as this is absolutely
necessary and imperatively demanded of it by reason of the war or by
reason of conditions arising out of the war."[34]

Both the war and the conditions it created led to a revocation of the
apparent pledge of "business as usual." The Business Profits Tax of 1916,
and the 1917 corporate income tax indicated the changing trend. But
there was more to it than fiscal policy. The experience of the grain trade
exemplified the lengths to which the government would go when forced
by circumstance. In the early years, the trade functioned through its normal channels. The only exception, albeit a major one, was the sudden
commandeering under the War Measures Act of a substantial portion of
the 1915 crop for sale to Italy.[35]

The first step away from traditional trading was the establishment of
centralized Allied (Britain, France, and Italy) purchasing, in November
1916, under the Wheat Executive Agreement. This led to the formation
of the Wheat Export Company in the United States and the Wheat Export
Company of Canada, central buying and export agencies replacing the
regular North American exporters. Then, in the spring of 1917, indica-
tions of inadequate wheat supplies for Allied needs led to a run on futures
trading at Winnipeg. May wheat jumped from $1.90 to $3.00 per bushel
during April. The Canadian government assumed control of the grain
trade for the duration. A Board of Grain Supervisors, given monopoly

control over Canadian wheat sales, was established in June, to determine domestic and foreign requirements, and to regulate domestic distribution "in such a manner and under such conditions as will prevent to the utmost possible extent any undue inflation or depreciation of values by speculation, by the hoarding of grain supplies, or by any other means."[36] Futures trading reopened on the Winnipeg Exchange for a few days in July 1919, then again was cut off by the government. The responsibility for the remainder of the 1918 crop and for the 1919 crop was given to the successor to the Board of Grain Supervisors, the Canadian Wheat Board.[37]

Faced with the possibility of a serious fuel shortage in the winter of 1917-18 – especially of anthracite coal from the United States – and consequently a shutdown of war industries and widespread domestic hardship, the government of Canada appointed Charles A. Magrath as Fuel Controller in June 1917. He was given authority "to make regulations, subject to the approval of the Governor in Council, governing the price of coal, wood and gas, and the production, distribution, sale, delivery, consumption and use thereof."[38] Magrath and his officials worked closely with their opposite numbers in the United States Fuel Administration, set up shortly after Magrath's appointment, to establish a continental zoning system for the distribution of U.S. anthracite.[39] Price controls on coal in Canada were adopted on the principle of restriction of the net profits of coal dealers. Pit-head prices and transportation rates were fixed from time to time, and local coal dealers were compelled to render monthly statements of their transactions to the Fuel Controller. "Heatless Days" became a regular feature of life in central Canada, from Rivière du Loup to Fort William, during the following winter. The number of passenger trains on Canadian railways was reduced to save coal. The threat of strikes, in the Maritime and Alberta mines in 1917, led the Controller to appoint a director of Coal Mining Operations in Alberta and a Royal Commission in Nova Scotia. The director mediated the Alberta strike and the Royal Commission prevented a strike in Nova Scotia. Thereafter both the price of coal and miners' wages were regulated by the government.[40]

In the summer of 1917 the provinces appointed representatives to assist the Fuel Controller by allotting the distribution of fuel within the provinces and encouraging the use of bituminous coal or alternate fuels. In turn, the municipalities appointed fuel commissioners whose work Magrath described as "to develop team work among the various dealers in their municipality, and, in periods of coal stringency to prevent panic among consumers. To this end they were empowered, when necessity demanded, to pool the stocks of all dealers, and ration consumers."[41]

W.J. Hanna was appointed Food Controller at the same time Magrath took up his position as Fuel Controller. "The people were demanding cheaper food and they thought that the office was created solely for the purpose of reducing prices," Hanna reported in 1918 when his functions were taken over by the new Canada Food Board headed by the Minister of Agriculture, T.A. Crerar. The problem was not reduction of prices, he added, but to conserve food and increase production so that greater quantities could be released to overseas consumption. Reducing prices "would have been disastrous to both objects."[42] Special volunteer committees reported to Hanna on particular problems; provincial committees studied local food requirements. And the Food Board enrolled 8,000 commercial travellers to report on local conditions and to urge Canadians to follow its orders.[43]

Food control followed the paths of encouragement, restriction, and persuasion. More than 1,000 tractors were purchased from Henry Ford & Son and distributed to farmers across the country at cost. Fish display cases were distributed to butchers and fish retailers, the government assuming half the cost of the cases. Beef and pork use was restricted in restaurants on certain days, and eating places were allowed twenty-one pounds of sugar for every ninety meals. Food dealers were licensed and subject to fines of up to $1,000 and three months imprisonment for violations of food regulations. Potentially among the most coercive of all war measures for individual citizens, the "Anti-Loafing Law" of 1918 demanding useful employment for all males between sixteen and sixty, resulted directly from a Food Board suggestion to the government.

But most food control effort took the form of persuasion towards voluntary restraint from waste and encouragement of change in eating habits. Films condemning waste or emphasizing the merits of nourishing but little-used products were shown in theatres and churches. Each province had a "Keep a Hog" campaign and a "Soldiers of the Soil" movement, which enrolled boys for farm labour. Slogans such as "Eat fish as a patriotic duty" or "Eat fish and reduce the cost of living" were broadcast across the country – backed up by a "Sea Food Special" on the Canadian Government Railways to rush fish from the Maritimes to interior markets. Every restaurant-goer was admonished by the menu:

> All persons in ordering their food ought to consider the needs of Great Britain and her Allies, and their armies, for wheat, beef, bacon, and fats, and the Canada Food Board desires the public to do everything in their power to make these commodities available for export by eating as little as possible of them, and by making use of substitutes, and avoiding waste.[44]

The mode of government interference with traditional business practice during the war, then, varied with the nature of the business itself.[45] Centralized control of the wheat market in Europe forced government monopoly control of the wheat crop under the Board of Grain Supervisors and the Wheat Board. Fuel control, because of international markets and because of the limited number of sources of supply, was a half-way house between government regulation and exhortation to consumers. Food control, as the Report of the Food Board observed, also took a middle road between the British method of compulsion and the American effort at volunteerism.[46] But because both production of food and its consumption were so diverse and individually oriented, the main emphasis was upon persuasion. All the same, by 1918 the war had carried the governments of Canada, national, provincial and municipal, to an overseers' role in Canadian business.

III

The enthusiasm with which men volunteered for service in the Canadian Expeditionary Force was directly related to employment prospects in Canada. Thousands of men, the young and not-so-young, signed up in 1914 and 1915 not so much from patriotism as because the army offered steady, though hazardous, employment. "Recruits were more numerous in districts where employment was scarce," observed the Patriotic Fund.[47] Nor was it mere accident that volunteer recruitment fell off badly in 1916 when, as the Minister of Labour put it, "unemployment has been transformed into a labour shortage continually becoming more acute" and that organized labour supported conscription only with the deepest misgivings.[48]

In the winter of 1914-15, with the exception of those in the Maritimes where employment increased with the beginning of war, Canadian workmen faced a dismal future. The Prime Minister was urging the Militia Department and his ministers responsible for allotting war contracts that it was "most desirable that there should be such an allotment of the work as will give a reasonable share to every part of the country and particularly to those communities where unemployment largely obtains." The *Labour Gazette* reported that of twenty-seven industrial wage changes in the last quarter of 1914, twenty-two were reductions.[49]

Financial restrictions forced many cities to abandon their public works projects and to get relief work under way. In Ontario, the Commission on Unemployment reported,

> Rents are unpaid, families living on not half rations, and in many homes not knowing where the next meal is coming from. Many heads of families are feeling the pressure mentally; two men, one with a wife and seven small children, the other with a wife and two small children, have been unable to stand up against the depression. One became mentally unbalanced and died of starvation in the hospital, and the other took his own life, both leaving their families destitute.[50]

Even where work projects continued, there were too few jobs for too
many workers. Montreal, the *Labour Gazette* noted,

> has been obliged to call in the help of the police to maintain order among
> those who fight for tools each morning in order to get a day's work in laying
> water pipe. . . . There have been 350 men trying each morning to get 150
> men's work.[51]

Parties of workmen were encouraged to leave Canada for war work
overseas. A group went to northern Russia to assist in railway construction, and another, of western Canadian miners, volunteered to work in
British mines. Trade unions in Canada cooperated with their counterparts
in the United Kingdom in sending some of their unemployed members
to British jobs. And a mission from the British government took back
about 2,000 skilled mechanics to work in munitions plants.[52]

Recruitment into the armed forces or for overseas labour, and a growing flood of war contracts, resulted in much higher employment by
the end of 1915, a return, said the *Labour Gazette*, "to almost normal activity."[53] In succeeding months, the employment picture continued to
brighten and by the third quarter of 1916 thirty-one changes in wages and
hours, involving nearly 19,500 employees, resulted in one reduction in
hours for 325 men, higher wages and shorter hours for 500 men, and
higher wages for all the rest. Coincident with higher wages was the continual rise in the cost of living. A list of thirty staple foods, averaged in
sixty Canadian cities, which cost $8.02 in November 1915, had risen to
$10.05 a year later.[54] Orders in Council,[55] in November 1916, charged
municipalities with responsibility for enforcing regulations against combinations in or hoarding of the necessities of life, in an effort to curtail price
increases. But with the government pursuing an inflationary fiscal policy,
they had little effect. In November of 1918 an average weekly budget was
$13.49 as compared with $12.10 in November 1917, and $7.96 in
November 1914.[56]

One indicator of the scarcity of labour was the growing number of
female employees in business and industry. First noticed as a trend by the
Labour Gazette in July 1916, it was re-emphasized in November with the
announcement of "a pronounced shortage of female labour in nearly all
lines of factory work . . . due partly to the increasing number of women
being utilized in metal factories."[57] Trade unions a year later, with some
evidence to support their case, condemned the "unnecessary dilution of
labour by the introduction of female labour before proper steps had been
taken to utilize available skilled mechanics."[58] Women worked on farms
assisting with the harvest, in offices, on streetcars and trains, and on
assembly lines, amazing their employers and male co-workers, if not themselves, with their endurance and rapidly acquired skills. In 1918, when

Massey-Harris first employed one hundred women to do men's work, the company reported that "women are engaged in drilling plates, bending metal sheets, sharpening mower blades and collecting goods for shipment. They are not employed in blacksmith shops, where the heat is extreme and the physical strain severe; but it is expected that they can be employed in piling lumber in the yards, as this open-air work should not prove too arduous."[59]

Eventually more than 30,000 women were employed in munitions factories and tens of thousands of others in hundreds of jobs closed to their sex before the war. Their place in the labour market became significant enough that the Trades and Labour Congress executive was empowered to investigate the possibility of organizing them (only 4,000 were then organized) in September 1918.[60]

By 1918 rising wage scales in urban industries had attracted so many young men to the cities from rural areas, that rural depopulation, already a serious problem before the war, appeared to reach crisis proportions. To meet the agricultural labour problem, one farmer told the Prime Minister that men should not be conscripted for service overseas, but from city factories to work on the farms at military rates of pay.

> Young or old men will not work on a farm as long as such exorbitant wages are paid in the Shell factories, and Young farmer boys that never earned a dollar off the farms in their lives are getting as high as five and six dollars a day. A young ladd [sic] on the next farm about sixteen years is making six dollars per day, at the Shell Factory. How do you expect The Farms to be carried on at that rate? It will be impossible to make Sugar or even put in the Crops. There are men, doing nothing that will not work for less than Three Dollars, as they see that the Factories are paying so much.[61]

A sign of the growing strength of labour during the war was the recovery and expansion of membership in trade unions, which had lost many members during the pre-war recession.[62] Confident of their increased bargaining power because of the labour shortage, and angered by the failure of wage increases to keep pace with the rising cost of living, workmen resorted to more and more strikes during the later years of the war.[63] The director of coal mining operations in western Canada – District 18 of the United Mineworkers of America – had been empowered by the government to adjust miners' wages quarterly according to changes in the cost of living. But that was a very exceptional case. Most employers faced with a strike energetically looked for, and found, scapegoats to explain the halt in production. Typical was the managing director of the Union Steamship Company of British Columbia, who told the Prime Minister that the totally "unnecessary" strike of B.C. longshoremen was due to the men being influenced by a lot of windy demagogues who were demanding recognition on a Trade Union basis with the attendant evils of a closed shop. We may say that we do not believe that this strike would ever have taken place if the government had shown any strength of mind in dealing with the situation at the start.[64]

The Canadian government's response to the problems of the working man was hesitant. Certainly, the effort put into securing foreign war contracts and the government's own war orders were the main factors in relieving unemployment. In 1916 the munitions industry was brought under the terms of the Industrial Disputes Investigation Act. The Canadian government had fair wage clauses in all its contracts and tried to have them inserted in the contracts of the Imperial Munitions Board. But Joseph Flavelle curtly refused, even after pressure from Borden and Crothers and Lloyd George in England. Flavelle's attitude was that his workers were lucky to have jobs anyway and ought to be satisfied with their lot. "The work people associated with many of these factories would be out of employment were it not for the labour conditions which have been created through these War Orders being executed here."[65] The cost-of-living investigations and Orders in Council prohibiting hoarding of the necessities of life were ineffective weapons against constantly rising prices.

In mid-1918 the government finally began to move on the labour front. The Employment Office Co-ordination Act charged the Department of Labour with responsiblity for formulating a national labour policy and "standardizing the work of the provincial employment systems in line with that policy through subsidies provided in the Act."[66] In June a compulsory registration of every male and female between sixteen and sixty was undertaken, including a series of questions relative to his or her usefulness for national purposes. Approximately five million Canadians were so registered.[67]

Then, in mid-July, Canada's "War Labour Policy" was proclaimed through Order in Council.[68] Strikes and lockouts were thereafter prohibited for the duration. All employees were assured of their right to organize into such associations as they chose. Employers were prohibited from firing or refusing to hire employees who were union members, and union shops were to continue where they existed. "All workers, including common labourers, shall be entitled to a wage ample to enable them with thrift to maintain themselves and (their) families in decency and comfort, and to make reasonable provision for old age." Regarding female workers, the policy required equal pay for equal work. The eight-hour day was to continue where it was established, and elsewhere hours of work were to be settled with regard for the "necessities" of the government and the health and welfare of the workers. Agreements between workers and employers were to be established for the remainder of the war subject only to changes in the cost of living.

On paper it was a rather enlightened labour policy. But it came much too late. Like the whole of the government's policy toward the working man during the war, it responded to rather than anticipated the conditions the Great War imposed on labour. Like their employers, workmen were in serious trouble before the war. Like their employers, they did well during the war. But their employers did better.

IV

Maintaining the railways was a vital part of the national war effort. The government relied on them for the assembly and transport of military men. War industries depended on them for coal and raw materials, and for the delivery of shells, guns, clothing, food, and equipment to seaside for shipment to the front. Needless to say, the problems of maintenance were complex. Shortages of cars, many not returned by American lines, halted traffic on numerous occasions. Shortages of coal also threatened halts, and forced consolidation of schedules and cancellation of some passenger service. Traffic on the great main lines grew during the war years, bringing increased revenues. But costs rose even more. A locomotive which cost $20,000 in 1914 was priced at $50,000 in 1917. The price of freight cars tripled in the same years. There were similar cost hikes for ties and rails, complicated by lack of supplies of these vital replacement materials for long periods during the war. And despite numerous appeals from the companies, the government refused to raise freight rates.[69]

The greatest shortage, as ever, was money; not so much for the well-established C.P.R. or even the Grand Trunk, but for the latter's unwanted child, the Grand Trunk Pacific, and for the Canadian Northern. Neither had been completed when war broke out, their private sources of capital had dried up in the depression, their fixed charges increased, and public money was being spent for destruction rather than construction. Government grants in 1914 and 1915 had been sparing, given only after hard bargains had been driven and a measure of control exerted through mortgages taken on the lines. Still, two points were abundantly evident to the Borden government in the winter of 1915-1916. Both the C.N.R. and the G.T.P. would be back soon on bended knee, and to allow either to go under was unthinkable.

But what was to be done? The government also knew that neither the people nor Parliament would stand for continual bleeding of the public treasury into the ever-thirsty sponges of the new transcontinentals. The public did not, could not, understand how millionaires like Mackenzie and Mann, with enterprises flung half-way around the world, or the Grand Trunk with 100,000 sturdy British shareholders, could be going broke.

In Parliament, a fragile party truce would be broken and the Liberals and obstinate Tory back-benchers like Bennett and Nickle would revolt if further aid, especially to the despised Canadian Northern, was proposed. Then too, the wrath of the hard-hearted but powerful Canadian Pacific could be expected. In December, Sir Thomas Shaughnessy told Borden that "the idea that parliament would give the credit of the country to aid this [the C.N.R.], or any other railway enterprise, to any extent whatever at a time when the indebtedness of the country is being increased by leaps and bounds to meet war expenditures, is so obnoxious, that I am confident that it would not receive, at your hands, one moment's consideration."[70] That was easy enough to write, expressing the view of the Canadian Pacific and its ally, the Bank of Montreal. It was less easy for the Prime Minister to accept. He knew that the fate of the Montreal companies' rivals, the Toronto-based Canadian Northern and the Bank of Commerce, hung in the balance.

In fact, the idea received not "one moment's" but many months' consideration. The solution, which Meighen thought "diabolically clever,"[71] was to avoid railway legislation and prolonged debate by slipping aid for the railways into the supply estimates. A commission would be established to inquire into and recommend a solution of the whole tangled mess of railways and politics. Finally, very confidentially, with only White apparently in on the deal, Borden gave repeated promises to the Bank of Commerce to reimburse it, if it continued to bail out the Canadian Northern until the railway problem had been settled by the government.[72]

Sir Thomas White presented the estimates, not to exceed eight millions for the Grand Trunk Pacific and fifteen millions for the Canadian Northern, in May 1916. "The collapse of the two railway systems in question, with the involvement of the Grand Trunk, would have a most disastrous effect upon our entire credit, federal, provincial, municipal and industrial," he explained.[73] A final effort at finding capital for the C.N.R. was made with New York financiers in June, but they demanded a government guarantee of the principal and interest on the bonds. "This," Borden noted in his diary, was "out of [the] question."[74] Shortly thereafter the membership of the inquiry commission was announced. A.H. Smith of the New York Central was chairman, and Sir Henry Drayton, chairman of the Board of Railway Commissioners, and the British economist, Sir George Paish, were the other members. Because of illness Paish was unable to serve and was replaced by W.M. Acworth, another British railway authority.

When the commissioners reported in 1917, they did not agree to a solution. The chairman, Smith, while recognizing the Canadian railway system was overbuilt and needed consolidation, was optimistic that some tinkering, and a continuance of substantial government aid, would see the

G.T.P. and the C.N.R. through "to the not distant day when the country
will have survived the war and resumed its prosperous growth."

> Let the Grand Trunk operate the eastern lines now held by that company and
> by the Canadian Northern; let the Canadian Northern operate the western
> lines, now held by that company and the Grand Trunk Pacific system; let the
> government operate the connections [exclusive of the C.P.R. lines] or procure
> their operation by private companies.[75]

Drayton and Acworth, after proclaiming that "it is not in the interests of
Canada that the operation of its railways should be in the hands of the
government," proceeded to a series of recommendations that made nationalization inevitable. "Not only the Grand Trunk Pacific Company but
also . . . the Grand Trunk Railway Company of Canada should be surren-
dered into the hands of the people of Canada," they wrote. As for the
Mackenzie and Mann enterprise, "it seems logical . . . that the people of
Canada should assume control of the property."

In a tortuous effort to avoid nationalization, they recommended that the
C.N.R., G.T.R., G.T.P., the National Transcontinental (which the Grand
Trunk had refused to take over from the government), and the Intercolonial all be transferred to an independent Board of Trustees incorporated as the Dominion Railway Company. The government would
assume responsibility for the interest on all existing securities, but ownership of the lines would be vested absolutely in the new company and its
board would not be subject to government control.[76]

Neither plan was satisfactory. Smith essentially left things as they were.
His was a recommendation of prayers for peace and prosperity, and an
open till for the railways until the millenium arrived. Drayton and Acworth came closer to an acceptable solution but also assumed too much
generosity on the part of the people and their elected representatives.
Canadians could never agree to pay for the acquisition of the lines, continue to assume all their fixed charges, and then casually turn them over
to a board of managers, no matter how talented, beyond their control. No.
If the railways were going to be taken over by the people of Canada, then
they must be run, indirectly, by the people of Canada.

A recommendation for nationalization of the railways, which Smith had
ardently rejected in his minority report, and which Drayton and Acworth
tried to circumvent, was hardly new. The Prime Minister had played with
the idea in 1904 during the debate on the Grand Trunk Pacific. Many
people had mooted it during the long and sorry financial history of the
new transcontinentals. Sir Joseph Flavelle had suggested it in June
1915.[77] Even Sir Thomas Shaughnessy had advocated nationalization
of all Canadian roads – on condition they be run by his company's managers.[78] In May 1917, after the Smith and Drayton-Acworth reports

were published, Shaughnessy urged that the C.P.R. take over the Canadian Northern and the government the Grand Trunk Pacific.[79] Indeed, the Prime Minister had considered the idea of public ownership sufficiently attractive politically that in 1915, when plotting election strategy, he decided on "a bold policy of government ownership of [the] two [new] transcontinental lines."[80]

In the cabinet, opinion was divided. Cochrane, White, Rogers, and Reid had been in on the 1915 policy discussions and supported government ownership. Meighen stated that he preferred Smith's plan, though Borden had curtly rejected it as "wholly impracticable."[81] Others were undecided: "many objections to White's proposal but no alternative plan," Sir Robert recorded after a June cabinet meeting.[82]

On June 14, Borden broke the news to Sir William Mackenzie at an early morning conference: "I told him we must take over road. No other action possible politically. He broke down, a very distressing scene. Told me he was ruined financially. I consoled him as best I could."[83] Later in the morning, the government's decision was sanctioned by caucus and the first step toward the creation of the Canadian National Railways system had been taken. In August, Sir Thomas White presented legislation to authorize the take-over of the Canadian Northern. The government, which already held forty per cent of the stock, would now acquire the remainder. A board of arbitrators would determine the amount to be paid in compensation, up to a limit of $10 million, to Mackenzie and Mann. For the moment the government would give another $7.5 million in aid of the Grand Trunk Pacific to keep it afloat. But its fate, and the Grand Trunk's, were sealed. The two railways were the necessary eastern complement to the Canadian Northern to provide an integrated national system. Their acquisition, comments the official historian, "was implicit in any plan to take over the Canadian Northern."[84]

There was little opposition to the take-over itself. Mackenzie and Mann, who would end with one hundred shares apiece in their enterprise and slight regard for more than a decade of daring effort, were almost friendless. There was much opposition to paying any compensation at all. The Liberals charged that it was merely a pay-off to the traitors of 1911 in the Canadian Northern and the Bank of Commerce. But with Whips on, there was little danger the bill would be defeated. And the real reason for compensation, as the Prime Minister explained, was that simple confiscation would be disastrous to a country so dependent upon borrowed capital from sensitive foreign creditors.

> It would be exceedingly unfortunate that it should go abroad to the United States of America, to Great Britain, or to any of the other great lending countries of the world, that the people of Canada are represented in parliament by men who are disposed . . . to deny to those whose property is taken

against their will, the right and opportunity to make good their claim as to its value before an impartial and properly constituted tribunal.[85]

The bill was passed in September. In December an Order in Council established the Board of Management of the Canadian National Railways, independent in its management of the line but answerable to Parliament for its decisions. Borden told the House of Commons on March 15, 1918, that "we shall leave the administration and operation of the road to be carried on absolutely under that Board of Directors and we shall use every means available to the government . . . in order that anything like political influence, political patronage or political interference . . . shall be absolutely eliminated from the administration of that road."[86]

The take-over of the Grand Trunk and Grand Trunk Pacific was a messy business that took another two years. A government offer to the parent company was brusquely rejected as were a series of counter-proposals by an increasingly hostile government.[87] White, never a friend of the Grand Trunk, urged confiscation under the War Measures Act. And Meighen, once nationalization was a reality, took a hard line in negotiations with the British company. In March 1919, the railway threatened to shut down operations on the Grand Trunk Pacific, and White, as acting Prime Minister, immediately placed the western line in receivership and ordered the Minister of Railways to compel the Grand Trunk to honour its G.T.P. obligations. A further default by the Grand Trunk on its G.T.P. securities in September was followed within a month by the introduction of arbitration legislation. In May 1920, a Board of Management took over operations of the Grand Trunk system, and in September the arbitrators decided the company's unprotected stock issues were worthless. The government of Canada would pay an annuity on the preferred issues only.[88]

The nationalization of the railways was bitterly opposed by a large segment of the business community. Most politicians regretfully accepted it as an inevitable outcome of war conditions. Those who opposed, opposed not the deed so much as the way it was done. Few indeed – the Prime Minister was one – saw much merit in the principle itself. But once finished, it symbolized the great change in the Canadian economy during the war.

V

By 1918 the free-wheeling economic activity and business practices of pre-war years had been replaced by government regulation, government control, and, in a vital sector of the economy, a healthy dose of government ownership. The government of Canada taxed both profits, and private and corporate incomes. It encouraged the consumption of some products and discouraged, rationed or regulated the use of others. It controlled the wheat economy from the farmer's field to distant international markets. It cooperated with the United States in regulating the use of anthracite coal across the whole of the continent north of the Rio Grande. Provincial and municipal governments worked with it, in fixing prices and consumption of fuel for businesses and home owners alike across Canada. The government eventually assumed control of the working lives of Canadians, regulating the wages and hours of some, preventing strikes by all.

Canadians had been given an ample taste – and many thought it bitter – of state intervention in their private and public lives. It had come about gradually though not, save perhaps for Hughes' Shell Committee, in a fit of absence of mind. It had created, at all levels of government, a new group of bureaucrats, the unseen and impersonal regulators of Canadian economic life. For some of the regulators, the war provided an impetus and a motivation for what they did; for others, a rationalization. For a few men in both business and government, the war provided an opportunity to put the power of the state behind the goals of efficiency and organization, in both society and the economy, which they had championed in less hectic but less auspicious times. On occasion, the government of Canada took the initiative, providing exemplary leadership to the governed. At other times it merely responded, hesitantly or forcefully, to the demands of individuals and groups with motives both high and low.

The discernible break with the pre-war way of things came in 1916. In that year, the business of war triumphed over "business as usual," as the second over-subscribed domestic war loan finally convinced the Minister of Finance of the feasibility of large-scale war financing independent of foreign money markets. That same year Sir Thomas White also led the first federal government attempt at direct taxation with the introduction of the Business War Profits Tax. In 1916, the Imperial Munitions Board replaced its predecessor's record of chaos with an efficient, tightly organized system of munitions production. The establishment of the Wheat Export Company of Canada was the first step to control of the grain trade, and concern over waste of vital materials and luxurious consumption foreshadowed regulation of trading in food and fuel. In 1916, an abundance of manpower for Canadian industry gave way to labour shortages and a significant movement of women into the work force. The first Orders in Council to check the rising cost of living were passed, and union membership approached its pre-depression level and strength. Thenceforth, there would be no turning back to volunteerism.

A later generation might judge this to be innocent, simple, and decidedly amateurish. The actors themselves found their commitment real enough, their work often exciting, and sometimes frightening in its implications Some could even see a certain irony in what had taken place. It had, after all, been done in the name of preserving "civilization" – a civilization that was rooted in the assumed continuance of a *laissez-faire* style of economic life in pre-war Canada. In the attempt to preserve that way of life, the government of Canada had changed it almost beyond recognition.

CHAPTER 13

The Clash of Nationalisms

I

"There are no longer French Canadians and English Canadians," the Montreal newspaper *La Patrie* announced on August 5, 1914. "Only one race now exists, united by the closest bonds in a common cause."[1] So it may have seemed in the first flush of emotion as Canadians heard the news that their country would be part of the grand coalition fighting to halt the Kaiser's aggression. Some people really believed the war would unite Canadians as never before, turning their eyes away from those preoccupations with tariffs, freight rates, separate schools, and language controversies, which seemed more and more to divide them. Here was a chance, perhaps, to acquire that "lean eager patriotism and sacrifice of a people bred for war" about which Professor Stephen Leacock had written in 1907. At last the "turkey cocks of Ottawa" would have to stop feathering their own nests and "the little man of the province" with his "Gospel of Provincial Rights" would have to subordinate his petty interests to the greater cause.[2] Here was a war for Christian civilization that should arouse a vibrant Canadianism. Charles W. Gordon provided the rhetoric under the title of "Canada's Duty:"

> No sudden rage, no fluke of diplomacy, not Austria's greedy ambition leaping at the chance of war afforded by the wicked act of a mad Servian student – not these things nor things like these have caused Germany to plunge into this war. Never did a nation more deliberately take a purposed and long planned step. For forty years Germany has cherished ambitions, has fed upon philosophies, has extended her commerce, has built her industries, has established her fortresses, has perfected her siege guns, has built her navy, has drilled her eight million soldiers, has fired her young men with lust for the Satanic glory of war with one purpose only – that she might war in a supreme effort after world power.[3]

The rhetoric of this, and hundreds of other speeches and articles from pulpit and press, was not surprising. But to expect the war to unite the country was simply to ignore the depths of the divisions in the nation and to misunderstand the extent to which Canada had changed in the twentieth century. First, there was the unresolved issue of the status of the French language outside Quebec. Then there was the precarious position of the Borden government, especially in Quebec. And finally there was the obvious fact that for the previous fifteen years Canadians had fought intermittently, but passionately, over the very problem the war brought to a head: the nature of Canada's relationship to, and responsibility in, the British Empire. The sensitivity of this issue, and the country's apparent inability to resolve it, were symbolized in those two aging ships, the *Rainbow* and the *Niobe*. Those not very fearsome vessels represented the sum total of five years of acrimonious debate, years which had seen two different policies produce the same result: deadlock and division. Though few people realized it in August 1914, the war would finally make it brutally necessary to force a conclusion on what had been a hung jury for a decade and a half.

Still, it was quite true that the country was united at the outbreak of war. Francis Beynon, women's editor of the *Grain Growers Guide*, called upon women to refuse to send their sons "to be shot down in order to settle a dispute between nations or to gratify the greed of gun-making corporations,"[4] but she, and pacifists like J.S. Woodsworth, were few and far between. In neither French nor English Canada was there any effective opposition to Canadian participation in the war. It was almost universally believed that Britain's cause was just, and that Canada had a clear responsibility to aid in the triumph of that cause. The Prime Minister doubtless spoke for most Canadians when he told the House of Commons that "as to our duty, we are all agreed, we stand shoulder to shoulder with Great Britain and the other British Dominions in this quarrel. And that duty we shall not fail to fulfil as the honour of Canada demands."[5] Sir Wilfrid Laurier was even more eloquent and fervent in his support for the cause. "It will be seen by the world," he exclaimed, "that Canada, a daughter of old England, intends to stand by her in this great conflict. When the call goes out, our answer goes at once, and it goes in the classical language of the British answer to the call to duty: 'Ready, Aye Ready.'"[6]

If there were French Canadians who were wondering what the war had to do with them, they received an answer not only from politicians but also from their spiritual leaders. "England has protected our liberties and our faith," Archbishop Bruchési informed a group of volunteers setting out for Valcartier. "Under her flag we have found peace, and now in appreciation of what England has done you go as French Canadians to do your utmost to keep the Union Jack flying in honour to the breeze."[7] Even Henri Bourassa, the man who had protested dramatically against Canadian participation in the South African campaign in 1899 and who had constantly attacked the imperial policies of Laurier and Borden, offered no resistance to Canadian involvement in 1914. Yet his assessment of the situation was more realistic and calm than most. In a long editorial on September 14, entitled "The National Duty" (similar in title but worlds apart from the Rev. Charles Gordon), he forewarned of things to come. Bourassa took the view that it was proper for Canada to participate in the war, though certainly not because her interests were directly threatened; they were no more in jeopardy than those of the United States, which remained neutral. Canadian intervention was justified only because of the "thousand ethnic, intellectual and economic ties" with Britain and France, from which flowed a powerful natural desire to see those two mother countries victorious. But while contributing, Canada should not forget her own vital interests: "Canada must begin by resolutely envisaging its real situation, to take exact account of what it can do, and to ensure our own internal security before starting or pursuing an effort that it will perhaps not be in a state to sustain until the end."[8] It was a sensible warning, but not likely to receive much attention during the first heady patriotic months of the war. Even later when it became brutally plain that there was more to war than glory – mud, gas, and death, for example – Bourassa was rarely heeded, for he, it was widely believed, had always been less than one hundred per cent loyal.

In August 1914, on a wave of unifying nationalism, in a conflict between good and evil, democracy and tyranny, there was hardly room for any calmer analysis of the deeper causes of European conflagration. Professor W.L. Grant of Queen's University was one of the few Canadians who suspected the war raised questions about the values of the civilization to which Canada belonged. "The contribution of the nineteenth century to political organization, had been the self-conscious nation," he wrote; "more and more we allowed the nation to assert its self-consciousness against its neighbours, not in patriotic rivalry for good, but in mere satanic pride and bellicose highness of heart."[9] It remained to be seen whether Canada's new-found national self-consciousness could avoid those excesses during the hypertensions of war.

II

Borden's government had already completed nearly three years of a normal mandate when war broke out. At most, it had two years of life before an election would be unavoidable. Even before the war there had been signs that Conservative fortunes were declining. In the west, many farmers, still smarting from the defeat of reciprocity, were beginning to talk seriously about independent political action.[10]Moreover, the economic recession had brought trouble. "Increased cost of living, low wages, unemployment, industrial disputes – such are the ugly facts that confront social workers in nearly all Canadian cities," one social worker remarked in the spring of 1914.[11] But the most dangerous condition was in Quebec where the Conservative-Nationalist alliance had become unstuck. There the problem was both political and personal. By 1914 several prominent Conservative-Nationalists had found safer berths on the bench or in the civil service, leaving Borden with minor men whose reputations were based chiefly on having denounced Laurier's naval policy in particular and the British Empire in general in 1911. The tragedy was that, as the credibility gap between Borden's erstwhile *nationaliste* supporters and the Quebec electorate widened, the country was moving into a period when a strong French-Canadian presence in the federal cabinet was critical for the country's unity. Since the most influential French Canadian in Ottawa was Leader of the Opposition, the deep divisions which began to appear in the country almost immediately took on a political colouration. That made it virtually inevitable that the rupture would widen, with each side claiming the other was motivated by politics.

The issue over which serious cultural disunity first began had its roots in pre-war years. It was another of those minority education questions that had periodically ruptured the surface of French-English amity in Canada since before Confederation. This time the scene of the trouble was Ontario, though there was still a festering dispute in Manitoba, and a developing one in Saskatchewan. Though the controversy over bilingual and separate schools had never been entirely dormant in Ontario at any time since Confederation, it had been nearly so during the early years of the new century. Nevertheless, the growing French-language population of Ontario – about ten per cent of the province's population by 1910 – caused unease in some quarters of the province. What did this growing Franco-Ontarian population mean? That the revenge of the cradle was becoming a reality? Some French Canadians apparently thought so. "From Cape Breton to Lake Superior," one wrote in 1910, "the whole country will become an almost exclusively French land. There will be nothing more than the south of Ontario and certain parts of Nova Scotia where French will not be spoken."[12]

A mere idle dream perhaps, but for others it had the quality of a nightmare. Two of these groups, the Orange Lodges and the English-speaking Catholics of Ontario and the west, rarely shared dreams or nightmares, but the politics of bilingual schools made strange bedfellows. The Orangemen had no doubt about the stand necessary to win the newest Battle of the Boyne. "It is part of the great ambition of the French that French be equal with English," the *Sentinel* thundered in 1910; "should that demand ever be conceded . . . the battle waged for a century will have been lost, and the barrier that Ontario has so long opposed to the oncoming tide of French settlement will have been swept away. All that would mean to the destiny of Canada cannot be readily imagined. It would almost inevitably mean French domination and papal supremacy."[13]

Papal supremacy was entirely acceptable to the Irish Catholics of Ontario, but French domination was something else. Mgr Francis Michael Fallon, who in 1910 was appointed Bishop of London, had intimate knowledge of that problem, and strong views about it. His recent ministry in the United States had been preceded by a period as Vice-Rector of the University of Ottawa. There he had seen the growing French-Canadian population and had even interpreted his removal from academic life as the result of that expansion. This bilingual cleric strongly suspected the French-Canadian bishops were behind the growth of *nationalisme* in Quebec, and were using it for their own personal advancement. "Are not the wider interests of the future Canadian Catholic Church at stake?" he asked a fellow bishop somewhat rhetorically in 1911; "does not the nationalism of Quebec threaten to ruin the Catholicity of Canada? We are playing our part in the making of a great English-speaking nation and so far as I am concerned I intend . . . to take my stand on the side of the manifest destiny of Canada."[14] Here was a strong-minded leader for the wearers of the green, who, improbable as it might seem, joined forces with the defenders of the Orange to rekindle the fires of cultural conflict in Ontario.

For some years there had been growing friction between French and Irish Catholics. By 1910 it was intensified by changing population figures in the Church; as French-speaking Catholics increased, those of Irish origin declined. The growth of the Franco-Ontarian population brought that group both new confidence and increased financial needs for education. Thus the Franco-Ontarians became the centre of a growing solidarity among French-speaking minorities outside Quebec. Gradually these minority groups established organizations dedicated to the protection and extension of their language and religious privileges in education.[15] All seemed inspired, to greater or lesser extent, by Bourassa's conception of Canada as a society of two equal cultures. The most important group was the *Association Canadienne-Française d'Éducation d'Ontario.* In January 1910, about one thousand delegates met in Ottawa to discuss French-language education in Ontario, and to make recommendations for improvements.[16] Many delegates were highly critical both of the quality and extent of French-language education.[17] But the major recommendation of the congress to the Whitney government called for the extension of French education and for alterations in the provincial school grants system in order to encourage bilingual education. Underlying the resolutions of the congress was the conviction that Ontario, like Quebec, should be a bilingual province providing educational equality for French and English citizens.[18]

This conception of a bilingual Ontario found little sympathy among English-speaking Ontarians. There were even many who viewed with alarm the growing pretensions of the French-Canadian population. Such fears were encouraged by the widely serialized and distributed work of the editor of the *Huntington Gleaner*, Robert Sellar. *The Tragedy of Quebec*, which went through four editions between 1907 and 1916, was a warning about French-Canadian expansionism. It described how the growing French-speaking population of Quebec, led by the priests, had gradually spread into the Eastern Townships, transforming these former English-language preserves into a French and Catholic domain. This expansion Sellar attributed to a clerical plot designed to extend, ultimately, the writ of the Pope throughout Canada, to transform Canada into Quebec. "The watchword of present day Nationalism is French-Catholic supremacy in the Dominion. This is what Nationalism stands for and nothing else," Sellar wrote; " . . . the term Nationalist implies a man striving for another government than that he lives under. In Quebec it indicates one who is satisfied with the government of the province but who desires to change the federal government by bringing it into harmony with that of Quebec."[19]

Sellar's views were close to those of the Grand Orange Lodge in Ontario. And, oddly enough, despite Sellar's denunciations of "clericalism," his views were also quite similar to those of Bishop Fallon and an important segment of the English-speaking Catholic community. These people were greatly upset by the aggressiveness of the Franco-Ontarians and were especially annoyed that, contrary to past practice, the French-speaking Catholics had approached the government separately in 1910 with their demands for changes in the educational system. This division in the Catholic common front, English-speaking members believed, jeopardized any hope of Whitney government support for more extensive aid to separate schools. Therefore a campaign began, whose intention can only have been to undermine the Franco-Ontarian position. In May 1910, Bishop Fallon had an extensive interview with W. J. Hanna, the Ontario provincial secretary, which was later reported to the Minister of Education. Fallon expressed almost total opposition to bilingual schools, which he insisted failed to give Franco-Ontarian children an adequate training for their future in an English-speaking province.[20] That same autumn, the English-language bishops, meeting in Kingston, delegated Fallon to express their "alarm for the future of our Catholic educational system in Ontario because of the agitation that culminated in the French language Congress in Ottawa in January 1910."[21]

By this date Premier Whitney had already informed the Franco-Ontarian leader, Senator Belcourt, that his government had rejected all proposals for extension of bilingual education. He pointed out that constitutional guarantees for minorities in Ontario covered only religious and not linguistic rights, and that he had no intention of further dividing the school system by adding schools "organized on a racial basis."[22]

The sides in the debate were now clearly drawn. Bishop Fallon's view, as expressed to Hanna, became public in the fall of 1910 when Hanna's account of the meeting was leaked to the press. Replies were soon forthcoming from Quebec, particularly from Le Devoir. The Whitney government now moved to regain the initiative by appointing a commission to investigate French-English bilingual schools. In February 1912, Dr. F.W. Merchant's report was presented to the Ontario legislature. It was a judicious document, which concluded that the central problem was the inadequate training of many teachers in the bilingual schools. It noted that "the French-English schools are, on the whole, lacking in efficiency. The tests combined to show that a large proportion of the children in the communities concerned leave school to meet the demands of life with an inadequate equipment in education."[23] The report made no specific recommendations about reforms.

In April 1912, the Whitney government announced its policy, which was known as Department of Education Instruction 17, or more popularly, "Regulation 17." Its intent was clear: public funds would go only to schools which employed teachers fully capable of teaching in English, and additional supervisors would be appointed to ensure the fulfilment of this condition. English instruction was to begin on school entrance, with French as a language of communication only where existing conditions demanded it and in no case beyond the first form (normally, the first two elementary years).[24] The Whitney government justified this policy, and its later modifications, on two grounds. First, it was a policy in the interest of Franco-Ontarians themselves, who needed an adequate knowledge of English in order to thrive in Ontario. Second, it was repeatedly claimed that the policy was not new at all, but merely a formalization of existing practices, and that it in no way contravened the Canadian constitution.

Most Franco-Ontarian leaders, their nationaliste allies in Quebec, and a large number of other French Canadians, disagreed vehemently with the Ontario government's policy and its assumptions. While few French Canadians would have denied that a knowledge of English was of crucial importance to most Franco-Ontarians, they nevertheless interpreted Regulation 17 as an attempt to proscribe the French language totally as a language of instruction. Here was the crux of the matter. The Ontario government would accept French as a subject of study; the Franco-Ontarians wanted French recognized as a language of instruction. Second, the Franco-Ontarian leaders and their Quebec allies were convinced that Regulation 17 was not a codification of existing practice, but an assault upon their already limited rights at a time when they were asking for an extension of those rights. And this view was based on a proposition which directly contradicted the position of the Ontario government and of most English-speaking Canadians: that the constitution guaranteed equal rights for French and English throughout Canada. "The constitution, natural law and justice, every rule of a pedagogy, rights acquired by the minority, British fair play and last, but not least, common sense all stand out in unison against [Regulation 17]," Senator Belcourt insisted; "the constitution has decreed the equality of the English and French languages in the treatment of all matters of Dominion-wide concern."[25] Until the court decision in favour of the Ontario government was handed down by the Judicial Committee of the Privy Council in 1916, neither side wavered from its stand. The result was an increasingly bitter atmosphere, based upon a fundamental misunderstanding, not only in Ontario, but between French and English-speaking Canadians throughout the country. And an issue which raised such bitterness could hardly but affect the course of federal politics just when the demands of war were becoming more pressing and divisive.

The bitterness in Ontario might not have reached such proportions if the Franco-Ontarians had been able to express their grievances through one of the provincial political parties. But the Liberals led by Newton Wesley Rowell, a straitlaced Methodist lawyer, were unwilling to buck the rising tide of anti-French sentiment in Ontario. Indeed there were those who thought that Rowell was more dependable on the school question than Whitney. W.R. Plewman, one-time editor of the *Orange Sentinel*, threw his support behind the Liberals in the provincial general election of 1914, predicting that "we are on the verge of the greatest political upheaval in the history of Canada. The bar will be banished and the English language will be preserved."[26] But that dry Anglo-Saxon utopia still lay in the future, for Whitney was easily re-elected. The Franco-Ontarians now had nowhere to turn for aid but to Quebec, which meant that the quarrel would almost certainly erupt into federal politics.

That the centre of Franco-Ontarian discontent was Ottawa further ensured that federal M.P.'s would be drawn into the struggle. In the capital city, under the leadership of separate school trustee Samuel Genest, the French-speaking population decided to resist Regulation 17. At some schools, pupils marched from the classrooms when the supervising inspectors arrived.[27] By 1915, in the face of these and similar tactics, the Ontario government, now headed by William Hearst, placed the Ottawa School Board under trusteeship. This step added injury to insult. In January 1916, two teachers appointed by the commission to teach in the Guigues' school were denied entry to the building by an angry group of mothers. Two other teachers, the Desloges sisters, took up the positions instead. For several days, near riot existed while parents, often armed with such domestic weapons as hat pins, protected the school. After a few days, three to

four thousand teachers and students paraded through the streets of Ottawa
carrying lighted candles and singing:

> Little children, guard our language
> Never obey the oppressor!
> It is a sacred heritage from our ancestors
> Our young hearts must remain French
> O God of Jeanne d'Arc, protector of France,
> Save Canada, conserve forever
> In all our children's hearts the faith and courage
> In spite of everything to remain French-Canadian.[28]

This growing resistance among Franco-Ontarians was accompanied by,
and encouraged by, increasingly shrill criticisms of Ontario from Quebec.
From *nationalistes* came frequent comparisons between Regulation 17 and
the German treatment of minorities in Europe. In Ottawa, *Le Droit* addressed an open letter to French Canadians overseas, warning them that
"you will soon find your wives and children and sisters in the trenches in
Canada for the defence of their language and schools against the might
of a persecuting government. You can therefore say with reason: 'Of what
use is it for us to fight against Prussianism and barbarity here when the
same conditions exist at home.'"[29] Bourassa, Lavergne, and other *nationalistes* urged French Canadians to boycott goods produced in English
Canada. The president of the Montreal Saint-Jean-Baptiste Society went
further, reportedly asking in February 1916, "Has not the time arrived
for us to revolt against persecution? If it keeps up perhaps we shall be
compelled to take guns in our hands just as our confreres are doing in
France."[30] Increasingly the battle in Ontario was linked with the war in
Europe, and the Ottawa River with the western front. "This morning's
dispatches," *Le Devoir* remarked early in 1916, "announce the death on
the field of honour of four soldiers of the French-Canadian 22nd and the
wounding of seven others. . . . But does anyone believe that as a result of
their sacrifice, that the Boches of Ontario and Manitoba will suspend the
war that they make against our language?"[31]

By 1916 Manitoba had been added to Ontario as a battlefield, and there
were ominous signs that the language war would soon spread to
Saskatchewan.[32] The agitation in Manitoba culminated in the abolition of
all bilingual schools by the recently elected Liberal government of T.C.
Norris. A long campaign against these schools had been carried on by the
Manitoba Free Press whose editor, J.W. Dafoe, was, with some justification,
described by a former French-Canadian friend as the "father of the new
school legislation."[33] As in Ontario, the English-speaking Catholics had
little sympathy for bilingual schools. Indeed, in 1915 during the controversy over the division of the diocese of St. Boniface, an action which itself
reflected the linguistic division among Manitoba Catholics, a group of

English-speaking Catholics complained to the Pope that the French-speaking clergy were more interested in nationalism than in Catholicism. The only solution to the problem was "one Church, one pastor, one school, one teacher, one college, one language and one set of books."[34]

As in most of these school reforms, the need for greater efficiency was given by the Norris government and its supporters as the reason for its policy. In fact the underlying assumption was that efficiency and the English language were co-partners, and, while the primary aim of the Manitoba legislation may have been to anglicize "foreigners," the French Canadian found himself swept into the melting pot too. The Manitoba Minister of Education put the case quite explicitly: "in an English-speaking country, as this is, a knowledge of English is more necessary than a knowledge of arithmetic. . . . A grave injustice is done to the children who do not receive a satisfactory education in English. . . . We wish to give them the same consideration as is accorded to our own children to fit them to earn their way through life, and take their places as citizens in our Canadian nationality."[35] The Franco-Manitoban Canadian reply was: "We will not be assimilated whether you like it or not."[36]

In the light of developments in Ontario, Manitoba, and elsewhere, it is not surprising that a growing number of French Canadians began to suspect English Canadians were using the heightened sense of nationalism the war had stimulated as an occasion to destroy the French culture in Canada. And there were certainly English Canadians who viewed the struggle as one for the soul of the country. In the 1916 edition of *The Tragedy of Quebec,* now selling better than ever, Sellar exhorted Ontarians to stand up for Regulation 17. "The issue . . . is fundamental and admits of no compromise," he wrote, "it is one that is not local but affects the future of the entire Dominion. It is simply whether this Canada of ours is to be British, and nothing else than British, or whether it is to be a mongrel land, with two official languages and rules by a divided authority. Should Ontario knuckle under to the demand now being made upon her, farewell to the hope of Canada being British."[37]

Soon the controversy erupted into provincial and federal politics. The Quebec premier, Sir Lomer Gouin, was first to respond to the issue. In January 1915, two English-speaking Liberal members of the legislative assembly presented a motion expressing regret that the dispute should have arisen, and recalling that "one of the fundamental principles of British liberty in all of the Empire is respect for the rights and privileges of minorities."[38] The motion passed unanimously. Shortly after, Gouin wrote to Hearst defending the action of his province's legislature. Hearst, not unexpectedly, rejected both the motion and the defence.[39] In March 1915, Laurier's close friend, Senator L.O. David, presented a motion in the Senate very similar to the one passed in Quebec. It was debated, but never voted upon.[40]

Throughout 1915 the dispute raged on. In May the A.C.J.C. organized a mass conference at the Monument National in Montreal. It was presided over by Senator Phillippe Landry, a Quebec Conservative recently elected president of the Franco-Ontarian Association. Landry told the crowd: "Our race has survived more sombre days on this continent than those we now pass through. . . . Our race will survive even in Ontario, and the little children of our persecuted compatriots will speak French in the family and at school. We want it, you want it, God wants it."[41] A few months later when a bill was before the Quebec Assembly authorizing Montreal to contribute to the Patriotic Fund, Armand Lavergne moved an amendment allowing the city to provide financial support to Franco-Ontarian schools. Gouin chided him for mixing the two questions, but the following day a Liberal introduced a bill permitting all Quebec municipalities to subscribe to the Ontario school battle fund. The bill passed quickly and easily and stirred new resentment in Ontario.[42]

By early 1916 pressure was rapidly building up within the federal Liberal caucus to take some official, public action on the French-language question. Three aspects of the problem disturbed Laurier. First, was the damage of the continuing agitation to the war effort. Second was the danger that, if his party failed to take a stand on the issue, the field would be vacated to Bourassa. And third, he knew that if he could not unite his party on the language question, he would lose all hope of ever returning to power. Knowing that he would soon have to make his views on the issue public, he set to work to win the support of the provincial party in Ontario. But its leader, N.W. Rowell, and the editor of the party's major newspaper, the *Globe,* both knew that the Ontario government had the full support of the electorate in this controversy. Indeed Rowell himself found nothing to disagree with in Regulation 17.[43] His assessment of public opinion in his province was probably accurate. "The propaganda which has been carried on by the Nationalists in Quebec against recruiting," he wrote to his federal leader, "based in some measure at least upon the bilingual situation in this province and assertions by the Nationalists of the constitutional right of the French language in the schools of this province, have greatly aroused and incensed public opinion here, and any action which would look like interference with Ontario would, in my opinion, be deeply resented by an overwhelming majority of the people of this province."[44] Laurier and his English-speaking supporters were approaching a breach.

Similarly Borden was losing what little confidence remained among his French-Canadian supporters. Ever since Regulation 17, Quebec Conservatives had been warning that it would have serious detrimental effects on the party in their province. Premier Whitney rejected every appeal, insisting that no injustice had been done and therefore no rectification was in order.[45] He evidently convinced Borden that he was correct.[46] Borden, of course, was fully aware of the growing agitation, and its damage to his party in Quebec and, more generally, to the war effort. Yet he was convinced there was nothing that either he or his government could do. When, in April 1916, his three French-Canadian ministers, T.C. Casgrain, P.E. Blondin, and E.N. Patenaude, suggested the matter be investigated by the Committee of the Privy Council in Great Britain, and indicated their intention to absent themselves from cabinet until a decision was reached, Borden rejected the proposal.[47] Nor did he offer any alternative. Nothing could have more clearly indicated the weakness of Borden's French-Canadian supporters, nor highlighted the dangerous gap opening between the Conservative government and French-Canadian opinion.

The way was thus left open for Laurier to take advantage of the Conservative weakness – and to display his own. By the spring of 1916, Laurier's hand was being forced, not by his own caucus, but by young Paul-Émile Lamarche who had been elected as *nationaliste* in 1911. Lamarche was one of the few *nationalistes* who had consistently stood by his principles, and he now intended to raise the Ontario language question in the House of Commons. After a variety of meetings among French-Canadian M.P.'s of all parties,[48] Laurier grasped the initiative. Ernest Lapointe was delegated to move

> that this House, especially at this time of universal sacrifice and anxiety, when all energies should be concentrated on winning the war, while fully recognizing the principle of provincial rights and the necessity of every child being given a thorough English education, respectfully suggest to the Legislative Assembly of Ontario the wisdom of making it clear that the privilege of the children of French parentage being taught in their mother tongue be not interfered with.[49]

The resolution was carefully worded and moderate in tone. The subsequent debate was far less so, though there was little of the harsh, even violent, language now frequently heard outside the House. When the vote was finally taken, the motion failed, as was expected. But the significance of the vote lay in the division: five Conservatives from Quebec crossed party lines to support the Lapointe resolution, while all eleven western Liberals deserted their leader. The members from Ontario and the Maritimes stuck to their party allegiances, thus preventing a clear division along French-English lines, but the vote indicated that the country was moving toward just such a crisis.

The debate served some purpose beyond consolidating the Liberal hold on Quebec and weakening it elsewhere, by providing a public forum for strongly felt views. It also showed, as nothing had since Louis Riel's hanging, the powerlessness of French Canadians at Ottawa when English-Canadian nationalism was aroused. In the end, however, it was not the

Canadian Parliament, but two external authorities who contributed most to cooling the language issue. In September 1916, Pope Benedict XV addressed a letter to the Canadian hierarchy, which managed to straddle the fence, favouring both the rights of the Franco-Ontarians and the position of the Ontario government. But, above all, it counselled moderation.[50] Two months later, the Judicial Committee of the Privy Council ruled that Regulation 17 was within the jurisdiction of the Ontario government. It also ruled, however, that the suspension of the Ottawa Separate School Board was beyond the power of the provincial authority.[51]

The papal letter and the judicial decision failed to bring the matter to an end. Franco-Ontarians had no intention of giving up the struggle. Nor were good relations within the Church quickly restored. Mgr Fallon remained as intransigent as ever, and despite outward appearances there were still profound internal rumblings. Early in 1917 Cardinal Bégin informed the Pope that the controversy had revealed conclusively "that the immediate and principal cause of our school troubles is less the English-Protestant government of Ontario than a group of ecclesiastics hostile to French influence and desirous of establishing on the ruins of this influence their own domination."[52] But now the law was clear, as was the official Church view. Still, neither court judgement nor Church ruling could repair the harm done. All passion was by no means spent. Now it merely took a new direction, and focused upon the recruitment question, which, if anything, was more volatile than the language dispute.

III

There was something depressingly symbolic in the fire that gutted the Houses of Parliament on February 3, 1916. It was like a forewarning that, close to the fiftieth anniversary of Confederation, the country was entering a period of profound trouble. Though French Canadians had accepted participation, their apparent early enthusiasm largely dissipated with the heavy demands of modern warfare. At no time during the war did the French Canadians volunteer in numbers proportionate to those enlisted in English Canada. That, however, was to be expected. From the outset, the most eager volunteers had been the British-born. By the end of 1915, they composed over sixty per cent of the enlistments.[53] So, too, there had been a greater response from urban than rural areas, as the army provided work that the pre-war depression had denied. English Canada, especially Ontario, was more highly urbanized than Quebec. Then there were special problems with the recruiting programme in Quebec. The first was Sam Hughes, the Minister of the Militia, who had a long and deserved reputation as a vociferous critic of Roman Catholicism. There was nothing especially Machiavellian in the appointment of a Methodist Minister as Director of Recruiting in Montreal since an attempt had been made to find a Catholic counterpart. But it did nothing to assure French-Canadian Roman Catholics that they would be at home in the Canadian forces.[54] Then there was the evident reluctance of the military authorities to organize designated French-Canadian regiments. During the first year of the war, French Canadians were dispersed among other troops, thus exacerbating language difficulties, encouraging desertion, and discouraging recruiting. It was almost despite Hughes that the Royal Twenty-Second was established in October 1914, the first – and last – French-Canadian battalion in the Canadian Corps. This difficulty merely revealed a problem rooted deep in the history of the militia. Despite some efforts to rectify the situation, the militia had never been organized to appeal to French Canadians. Few if any French-Canadian military traditions had been incorporated into the Canadian forces, and almost no effort had been expended in making French a language of training and command. The result was a militia which for all practical purposes was English.[55] Hughes did nothing to change this situation. His insensitivity to French-Canadian needs was especially unfortunate when French Canadians had less powerful emotional commitments to the war than their English-Canadian compatriots.

Unlike English Canadians, many of whom felt the call of the blood in 1914, the French Canadian was almost totally North American in outlook. For him the British Empire was a perfectly acceptable institution, at least in the short run, as long as Canada was growing toward greater autonomy. But his attachment to that Empire was founded largely upon a calculation of self-interest, and very little on any feeling for imperial grandeur. Some, including Laurier, hoped that French Canadians might compensate for lack of emotional attachment to Britain by affection for France. As early as 1915, eminent Frenchmen had been brought to Canada to promote the war effort. In the spring of 1917, General Joffre received an enthusiastic welcome in Quebec, but the visit had none of the anticipated impact on recruiting. France was not a mother country for French Canadians in the way that Britain was for many English Canadians. Indeed, some French Canadians were strongly convinced that the gulf between the atheistic republic and Catholic Quebec could not be bridged. This view was especially strong among certain elements of the clergy who had observed, with distaste, the anti-clerical laws of modern France, and had even on occasion personally experienced the hostility toward priests of some segments of French society. "In the Paris of 1907," the historian Lionel Groulx recalled many years later, "I had every occasion necessary to taste French anti-clericalism fully unleashed."[56] Some French-Canadian priests even refused to support appeals for relief for French families dispossessed by the war, claiming that such aid would only assist the anti-clerical authorities As one priest wrote: "I do not wish to be the object of the gratitude of the France which will thank us and send us the agents of the Lodges to educate us in the ways of the world, as they say so candidly."[57]

Thus, lacking strong sentimental attachment to either France or Britain, the French-Canadian attitude toward the war depended heavily upon the approach of the authorities at Ottawa. Borden and Hughes appear to have cared little, and to have understood even less, about the complexity of French-Canadian sentiments. Consequently their recruitment plans were poorly conceived and ineffectively implemented. The very real enthusiasm French Canadians had expressed at the beginning of the war was quickly dissipated and even transformed into icy hostility.[58]

The sharp decline in recruitment was recognizable by 1916. That was the reason for the establishment of the National Service Board. Its main achievement in Quebec was to raise the bogey of conscription. To calm these misgivings, Borden approached the leaders of the Church who had consistently supported the war effort. With two of his ministers, he called on Archbishop Bruchési early in December, and succeeded in satisfying him that registration was not a prelude to compulsory enlistment. Bruchési, after some hesitation caused no doubt by anticipated hostility from the *nationaliste* press, gave his public support to registration and called upon his clergy to follow his example.[59] At just about the same time, however, Sir Robert was refusing a request from a group of labour leaders that he should pronounce his unalterable opposition to conscription in all circumstances. He did reiterate his often-expressed hope that conscription would not be necessary, but added that "if it should prove the only effective method to preserve the existence of the state and the institutions and liberties which we enjoy I should consider it necessary and I should not hesitate to act accordingly."[60] Put in those extreme terms, the position was unexceptionable. But the statement showed that Borden had by no means excluded conscription from the range of recruiting possibilities. In fact Sir Robert had been thinking about conscription and its relation to the poor enlistment figures in Quebec since at least the beginning of 1916. At that time he had written to Sir Charles Hibbert Tupper, "I do not know that I can say more as to the question of enforced military service than was expressed in our personal interview in Ottawa. We have more than two and a half million French Canadians in Canada and I realize that the feeling between them and the English-speaking people is intensely bitter at present. The vision of the French Canadian is very limited. He is not well informed and he is in a condition of extreme exasperation by reason of fancied wrongs supposed to be inflicted upon his compatriots in other provinces, especially Ontario. It may be necessary to resort to compulsion. I hope not, but if the necessity arises I shall not hesitate to act accordingly."[61]

Borden's observations were probably very close to the thinking of many English Canadians. Certainly, similar views were held by the men who organized the *Bonne Entente* movement in 1916. The movement was begun by two Toronto Liberals, J.M. Godfrey, a lawyer, and Arthur Hawkes, a journalist. They soon acquired the active assistance of Colonel Lorne Molloy, a blind veteran of the South African War. On the face of it, the movement was intended to promote understanding between French and English Canadians. It organized trips by prominent English Canadians to Quebec, and return visits by Quebeckers. But under a desire to heal the nation's wounds, a desire that was genuine enough, were other, more mixed motives. One was the hope of some English-Canadian businessmen that *Bonne Entente* would help them win back business in Quebec lost as a result of boycotts organized to protest Regulation 17. Secondly, several leading *Bonne Ententistes,* including Godfrey himself, hoped that the movement would win French Canadians over to compulsory military service and a coalition government.[62] The movement experienced some initial success, attracting to it such prominent figures as Sir Lomer Gouin, the provincial premier, and Sir Georges Garneau of the National Battlefields Commission. It was in the spirit of the movement that Lt.-Colonel L.G. Desjardin wrote *L'Angleterre, Le Canada et la Grand Guerre,* a detailed and effective defence of Canada's war effort directed against critics like Henri Bourassa.[63] But a movement whose objectives were never really fully shared, or perhaps even understood, by both French and English-Canadian members could hardly be a permanent success. French Canadians appear to have hoped that *Bonne Entente* would aid in a satisfactory resolution of the language issue in Ontario; English-Canadian members expected it would convert their French-speaking compatriots to a greater enthusiasm for the war. By 1917 *Bonne Entente* had failed, and its English-Canadian sponsors had moved openly to the advocacy of conscription and coalition under the new name of the Win-the-War Movement.[64] A correspondent of *Le Devoir* had early underlined the source of *Bonne Entente*'s fatal weakness: "When an English Canadian pronounces the word patriotism, he wishes to say love of Empire, while the French-speaking Canadian, with the same word, thinks only of Canada."[65] It would take more than a *Bonne Entente* movement to bridge that gulf.

The evolution of *Bonne Entente* did, however, indicate the growing impatience in English-speaking Canada. The war dragged on, enlistments declined, and politics continued as usual. Was there no way out of this vicious circle? Perhaps a coalition government, free of politics, would put new vigour into the war effort. More and more frequently, too, the ideas of conscription and coalition were linked, as a means of ensuring Canada would live up to her commitments. In October 1916, the editor of *Industrial Canada* expressed a growing public sentiment. "Possibly Canada made a mistake at the early stages of the war in not forming a coalition government. . . . It seems clear beyond question that there were no insuperable obstacles to coalition in Canada had its advantages in relation to the prosecution of the war been properly appreciated. Even yet it should not be too late to correct a mistake, if a mistake has been made."[66]

This sentiment was widely echoed in the press of English-speaking Canada.[67] Most striking, it was a non-partisan sentiment. Even Liberal newspapers such as the *Manitoba Free Press,* which had lost what little confidence it once had in the Borden administration, no longer favoured the return of the Liberals to power.[68] Two assumptions lay behind this non-partisan attitude. One was that a great national responsibility like winning the war should be above politics. This seemed especially important in view of the somewhat besmirched reputation of the Conservative regime. Second was the sometimes implicit, and occasionally explicit, concern that if the Liberals replaced the Conservatives, Quebec would once more be in the driver's seat. That would hardly result in a re-invigorated war effort. By the end of 1916, the problem of declining enlistments and the growing clamour for some shuffling of political forces intensified with the realization that Parliament was nearing the end of its legal existence. A one-year extension beyond the normal limit had been unanimously agreed to in 1915, but a second extension seemed very unlikely. The Laurier Liberals had experienced a series of provincial successes; between August 1915 and June 1917, the Conservatives lost general elections in seven provinces. Moreover, deep partisan divisions, stimulated by the Lapointe Resolution debate and a series of charges of corruption against the government, made a continuation of the uneasy political truce almost impossible.

Crucial to the political temper of the country, as it moved well into the third year of war, was the recruiting problem. At its heart was the growing controversy over the low level of enlistments in Quebec. Not even the most staunch defenders of the French-Canadian record, such as *La Presse,* could do much more than suggest that the record was better than it looked on the surface.[69] Nor was it easy to disguise the fact that every effort to step up enlistment in Quebec proved a more dismal failure than the last. Almost every recruiting meeting in Quebec met with some hostility, for the anti-war propaganda of the *nationalistes* appeared to be capturing an ever-growing audience. Indeed Bourassa's influence was spreading so rapidly that the Church, through Abbé d'Amours, editor of *l'Action Catholique,* attempted a counter-attack in a widely distributed pamphlet entitled *Où Allons-Nous? Le Nationalisme canadien.* In it d'Amours reiterated the official position of the Church in support of the war, a position which Bourassa had attacked privately,[70] and Asselin publicly.[71] D'Amours warned French Canadians of the dangers of the growing divisions in the country, and attacked the idea of a Catholic or French-Canadian political party, which would completely alienate English-speaking Canadians.[72]

It was a powerful statement, but certainly less in tune with the mood of Quebec than Bourassa's brilliant polemic, *Hier, Aujourd'hui et Demain*, in which he repeated his long-standing critique of imperialism, asserted his conviction that Canada had done enough in the war, and demanded that the domestic grievances of French Canadians be redressed.[73] Nothing could have emphasized the mood of French Canada better than the recruiting trip made by P.E. Blondin, one of Borden's *nationaliste* ministers, and General F.L. Lessard (a French-Canadian officer who, having made a reputation in the Boer War, had settled in Ontario), in May 1917. Their campaign lasted a month as they criss-crossed the province, making public appeals to the people and private appeals to the curés. The result of their effort was ninety-two volunteers.[74]

By this time, of course, enlistment was falling off everywhere in Canada. In April and May 1917, 3,000 men volunteered for infantry service while more than 20,000 Canadian casualties were recorded at the front. Obviously the Canadian forces could not be maintained at strength unless recruiting methods drastically changed. More and more, the finger was pointed at Quebec. Nor was everyone thinking of the overseas front when recruitment was discussed. "Is it fair to leave the province of Quebec to retain its strength in numbers," Dr. Dwight Chown, General Superintendent of the Methodist Church wrote late in 1916, "ready for any political or military aggression in the future, while our Protestants go forth to slaughter and decimation?"[75] Whether the problem was on the home front or in France, whether it was the political difficulties of the Borden government or the military problems of the Canadian Expeditionary Force, the same solution offered itself with increasing frequency. Conscription. In May 1917, Sir George Foster, the acting Prime Minister during Borden's absence at the Imperial War Conference, drew the obvious conclusion. "Enlistment is at a very low ebb," he wrote in his diary. "Only compulsory service can meet the situation; and although it is full of grave difficulties, come it must."[76] A week later Foster's leader arrived home, having reached the same conclusion.

Borden returned to Canada in the spring of 1917 in a mood of justifiable triumph. He had won acceptance for a new view of imperial relations which appeared to recognize all members as equals. But his mood had moments of despair. During his overseas visit, the Prime Minister had been made aware of the continuing seriousness of the war and of the heavy Canadian losses at the front. Nor had domestic political problems been banished from his mind: the government had either to win acceptance, unanimous or nearly so, for a further extension of the parliamentary term, or an election would be inevitable. Central to all these worries was recruiting policy. The men at the front had to be reinforced; to let them down would be a disgraceful betrayal. So, too, if Canada failed to continue to pull her weight in the war, who would take seriously her claims to equal status in the Empire? And finally, would not a radical change in enlistment policy have a catalytic effect on domestic politics by forcing a coalition of those groups who genuinely placed winning the war above every other consideration? On May 17, Borden wrote in his diary: "Sat in Council from 10:30 to six and debated at great length conscription and extension of parl't'y term. All agreed that conscription necessary. Patenaude and Blondin said they are prepared to stand by us but that it will kill them politically and the party for 25 years. Question of coalition government came up in this connection and there was considerable divergence of opinion majority favouring it. . . . Great division of opinion as to putting through extension by majority vote. . . . Very weary with all this discussion and would gladly relinquish post."[77]

On May 18, Sir Robert addressed the House of Commons, reporting on his work at the Imperial War Conference. Then he turned to enlistment policy. The voluntary system had failed, he said, and Canada would now have to adopt compulsion. There was no choice if faith was to be kept with the men at the front. There could be no drawing back now, for Canadian men, Canadian interests, and Canadian liberty were all at stake. Then came the crux of Borden's view of the war, a view with which some Canadians, especially French Canadians, disagreed. "All citizens are liable to military service for the defence of their country, and I conceive that the battle for Canadian liberty and autonomy is being fought today on the plains of France and Belgium. There are other places besides the soil of a country where the battle for its liberties and its institutions can be fought; and if this war should end in defeat, Canada, in all the years to come, would be under the shadow of German military domination."[78]

In making this surprise announcement, Borden ushered in one of the most critical periods in Canadian history. He, of course, was fully aware of the strength of the opposition to compulsory military service in Quebec. Some of his ministers even feared that the anti-conscription riots that broke out in Montreal on May 24 foreshadowed French-Canadian determination to disobey the conscription law when it came into force. It was this threatening situation which convinced Borden and his cabinet of a second radical conclusion: Sir Wilfrid Laurier should be invited to join in the formation of a coalition.[79] On the following day, when Borden met with Laurier to discuss the union, he revealed a further concern. "Our ministers," he recorded, "are afraid of a gen. election. Think we wd. be beaten."[80]

Borden's offer to Laurier was a generous one: a coalition of equal numbers from each party, excepting the Prime Ministership. But from the outset the aging Liberal leader indicated one insuperable problem. As Borden recalled the conversation, Laurier said "he could not accept conscription and expressed great regret and concern that it had been introduced. Fears consequences in Quebec if it is enforced by present parl't without a referendum."[81] He did not reject the offer of coalition totally, however, and agreed to speak with some of his supporters. He was fully aware of the recruitment problem and anxious to see it resolved. Equally, however, he knew that conscription was utterly unpalatable in Quebec, that Bourassa's influence had reached a new high, and that not even he, Laurier, could change the minds of his compatriots.

Then there were the immediate political considerations. Until conscription had been thrown into the discussion, the Liberal party's fortunes had been waxing, and a return to office was not beyond realistic hope. Laurier believed that if he could hold his followers together (and that was a very large if), he might still resume his seat on the right-hand side of Mr. Speaker. As for coalition, the sticking point was conscription. On May 29, Borden offered a new concession: a coalition should be formed, conscription enacted but not enforced until after an election had confirmed the new government in office.[82] Laurier again agreed to examine the proposal with his supporters, this time in Montreal. On June 6, Laurier gave Borden his final answer. It was negative. He could not join a coalition in which conscription was a precondition. To do so would mean freely handing Quebec to Bourassa. He had already explained his position to an old Ontario Liberal friend. "In the province of Quebec I have been accused by the Nationalists of being a conscious or unconscious Jingoist and of leading the country to Conscription. This was on account of the truth which I often proclaimed that our position in the British Empire might make it imperative for us to participate in wars in which Britain might be engaged. At the same time I asserted that this did not lead to conscription, and that I was opposed to conscription. The statement was never objected to by either friend or foe, the Nationalists excepted. If I were now to take a different attitude, I would simply hand over the province to the Nationalists, and the consequences may be very serious."[83]

The die was finally cast. The coalition movement was not halted, but Laurier's refusal to join ensured that there could not be a new government representing all parts of the Canadian population. Why had the effort failed? Some believed that Borden's offer had never been sincere, and that conscription had been introduced to smash the Liberal party, as it was bound to do. Sir Clifford Sifton, later an influential supporter of the Union government, was of this opinion. "If Borden had put his cards on the table and called Laurier in when he came back from England," Sifton wrote in

June, "I am confident that the whole question could have been adjusted, a national government formed and recruiting put on a satisfactory basis."[84] Why had Borden not taken this approach? He appears to have been convinced by the spring of 1917 that conscription was absolutely necessary with the shortest possible delay. It was a military necessity. Moreover, though aware of the seriousness of the Quebec situation, he seems to have been convinced that Laurier could nullify Bourassa's influence and bring the province into line with the rest of the country. So, too, he was conscious of the growing demand for conscription in English Canada, and realized his government would be seriously weakened if decisive action was not taken. And, of course, there would be some political pay-off.

The tragedy was that the forces now splitting the political parties along cultural lines accurately reflected a country no longer at peace within itself. On May 27, 1917, Mgr Bruchési, whose loyalty to the war effort was unquestioned, sent off two agonizing letters to the Prime Minister. In the first he recalled the repeated pledges of the government to maintain the voluntary system, and pleaded with Borden to stick to these promises. The second, highly emotional, warned the Prime Minister of the threat of serious disorders in Quebec. "I have recommended to my diocesans to exercise their rights as free citizens with calm and moderation. But you know that an excited crowd does not easily govern itself. Excess will be repressed by force, I agree. But after force has been employed, after blood has flowed, what has one gained for the good of the nation? Hatred is born in the hearts of men that is not extinguished; history is there to prove it."[85]

The Prime Minister replied with care and firmness. His concern about the turbulent situation in Quebec was profound, he insisted. Yet he had to balance that situation against the powerful emotions evident in the rest of Canada. "If the measure were abandoned or if no such measure had been introduced and the present government should persist in attempting to carry on the affairs of the country, in the face of so intense and vehement a feeling, disorders as grave, perhaps even graver than those which Your Grace apprehends would be extremely probable if not inevitable."[86] No doubt both the prelate and the Prime Minister exaggerated somewhat. But feelings were reaching a fever pitch, and the Borden government, which had never adequately understood French Canada, was now responding almost exclusively to pressures from English Canada. And Laurier, whose stand on the Lapointe resolution in May 1916 had shown where the centre of gravity in his party lay, was just as obviously responding to the views of Quebec. An irresistible force had met an immovable object, and the country was splitting into unequal parts.

Once Laurier had finally rejected the coalition offer, Borden turned to winning the support of Liberals willing to break with their leader. At first

this seemed easy enough, since many of Laurier's English-Canadian supporters had crossed party lines in the vote on the Military Service Act in
July. Laurier had attempted to delay the passage and to unite his party, by
proposing a referendum. But he had failed, and his party's wounds were
now open for all to see. Still, he had not lost everything. In Toronto on
July 20, and three weeks later in Winnipeg, Liberal conventions expected
to reject the federal leader had remained loyal.[87] But these victories were
only temporary.

During nearly three months, following the passage of the conscription
legislation, fitful negotiations for a coalition continued among Borden,
some of his cabinet colleagues, the energetic and mysterious Clifford
Sifton, a variety of Liberals in Ontario and the west, and a few farm
leaders. One thing had now become crystal clear: no further extension of
the existing parliamentary term was possible. But almost equally clear to
the government was the evidence that not even the popularity of conscription would be enough to ensure election victory. "Laurier hopes to win
with a solid French and foreign vote," J.D. Hazen, Minister of the Marine,
wrote, "and the Liberals are banking on the fact that only a small portion
of the votes of the soldiers overseas can be polled."[88]

Here was a problem that had already troubled some members of the
cabinet. As early as October 1916, Arthur Meighen, the Solicitor-Gen-
eral, had remarked that removing the vote from the "doubtful British and
anti-British of the male sex" and giving it to "our patriotic women" would
be "a splendid stroke."[89] Conservative defeats in the Saskatchewan and
Alberta provincial contests further emphasized the need to alter the franchise.[90] On August 15, 1917, Charles Doherty, the Minister of Justice,
introduced the first of two pieces of legislation designed to eliminate these
problems. The Military Voters Act enfranchised all members of the armed
forces, male and female, regardless of length of residence in Canada. The
act further provided that military voters would be asked to cast their
ballots for or against the government, rather than for named candidates.
If a voter could not specify his home riding, his vote would be assigned
by the electoral officer. A month later Arthur Meighen brought forward
a more far-reaching "reform" of the franchise, bearing the name of the
Wartime Elections Act. By this legislation all female relatives (mothers,
wives, sisters, and daughters) of servicemen were given the vote. All
immigrants from enemy countries who had arrived since 1902, and all
conscientious objectors, were disfranchised. The injustice of this measure
and its political motivation were readily obvious. While some supporters
of votes for women pronounced the measure a forward step,[91] Dr. Margaret Gordon, President of the Canadian Suffrage Association, denounced
it. "It would have been more direct and at the same time more honest,"
she remarked, "if the bill simply stated that all who did not pledge themselves to vote Conservative would be disfranchised."[92] The Liberals

agreed and fought the measure with all the energy of a party struggling for its life. The government was forced to resort to closure. The bill passed and Parliament prorogued on September 20.[93]

The new electoral legislation played a large part in re-activating the stalled negotiations for coalition. Western Liberals quickly recognized that the bottom was now totally out of their plans to fight an election before entering a coalition. Arthur Sifton, premier of Alberta, J.A. Calder of Saskatchewan, and T.A. Crerar, the prominent Manitoba agricultural leader, were now prepared to talk seriously. On October 3, the log jam broke: C.C. Ballantyne and Hugh Guthrie, two eastern Liberals, were sworn into a new Borden cabinet. Everything was moving now: the sound of Liberals rushing to Ottawa could almost be heard across the land. "Caesar is no longer disposed to wait," Calder warned N.W. Rowell, the Ontario Liberal leader.[94] On October 12, the new cabinet was announced.

A wartime election followed automatically upon the formation of the Union government. In that election the major issue was brutally simple: for or against conscription and Union government. In Quebec the case for the government was virtually impossible to make. In 1911 Borden had had the *nationalistes* with him; in 1917 they were his sworn enemies. Bourassa had long since declared himself. "Every Canadian who wishes to combat conscription with an effective logic must have the courage to say and to repeat everywhere: No Conscription! No Enrolment! Canada has done enough!" he exclaimed in a widely circulated pamphlet.[95] In his view conscription resulted from a combination of British imperialism reaching into Canada, and the Conservative need for a good election issue.[96] His policy was not the same as Laurier's, for the Liberals called for the continuation of the voluntary system. But the *nationalistes* had little choice other than to vote for Laurier; the lesson of 1911 had been learned. There was no room for a third party.[97]

With the *nationalistes* neutralized, the Liberals' sailing in Quebec was smooth. Indeed, it hardly seemed necessary for Laurier to bother campaigning.[98] That did not prevent some party stalwarts from stirring up their supporters and roundly denouncing the coalition. The most prominent argument was that the Union government was part of an imperialist scheme to subordinate Canada to Downing Street. "Why have the Tories imposed conscription upon Canada?" Rodolphe Lemieux asked rhetorically. "To create a precedent, in order that Canada may become for England a reservoir of men for the wars of the future. That is the basis of Imperialism."[99] Bourassa had used that argument as long ago as 1899 against the Liberals!

Outside Quebec, the Liberals faced a wall of hostility, though their anti-conscriptionist stand won some support among the working classes, even though the Unionists had received an imprimatur from the President of the American Federation of Labor, Samuel Gompers.[100] There was also some support for the Liberals among the rural population, which objected strenuously to the conscription of farmers' sons. Two weeks before voting day, the cabinet passed an Order in Council giving them an exemption, thus neutralizing their opposition. Government forces had a monopoly on patriotic fervour, and anti-Quebec sentiment. Enthusiastic Unionist newspapers identified Laurier with the hated Bourassa and placed them both in the Kaiser's camp. Sir George Foster set the tone for a Toronto audience in September: "Every alien enemy sympathizer, every man of alien blood born in an alien country with few exceptions, is with Sir Wilfrid Laurier, and every Hun sympathizer from Berlin to the trenches, from Berlin to the Cameroons, wishes success to Laurier, with his anti-conscriptionist campaign."[101] From election platform and Protestant pulpit the Unionist cause was sanctified and the Liberals damned.[102] On December 11, the *Manitoba Free Press*, once Liberal but now Unionist, ran a banner headline on its editorial pages reading "Shall Quebec, which will neither fight nor pay, rule?"[103] A week later, when the returns were counted, a front-page photograph of Laurier had the caption, "Swept Aside by Patriotic Canada."[104]

The results were decisive, at least in seats. The government carried 153 constituencies, of which three were English-speaking Quebec seats. The Liberals held the other sixty-two Quebec seats, carried ten of twenty-eight in the Maritimes, eight of eighty-two in Ontario, and two of fifty-seven in the west. The civilian vote gave the government a popular majority of one hundred thousand, but the soldiers added another two hundred thousand to the majority.[105] Borden interpreted his victory as a triumph for nonpartisanship and for his policy of compulsory enlistment for overseas service. For him, it was obviously a great personal achievement. For Laurier, it was a serious defeat, though not an unexpected one. At seventy-eight, he was able to take it stoically. "I did not expect to win and therefore I feel no disappointment," he told his old friend, Lady Aberdeen. "I am conscious that I was in the right; that is quite sufficient for the present."[106] A younger Laurier would never have been satisfied merely with being right. Ambition was obviously spent.

Neither leader referred to the most striking aspect of the Canada that emerged from the winter election of 1917: it was politically divided along cultural lines to a degree not witnessed since Lord Durham's day. The French Canadians had rallied around their old leader, Sir Wilfrid. The rest of the country, or most of it, had closed ranks around Sir Robert. What had brought the country to this critical state? Henri Bourassa, with surprisingly little bitterness, offered a thoughtful explanation early in the New Year. He wrote:

It is not the first time in the history of Canada that English and French Canadians have found themselves deeply divided over some great national issue. So long as English Canadians remain more British than Canadian, these differences are bound to happen every time there is a conflict between the demands of British Imperialism and the resistance of Canadian Nationalism. The present war was bound to produce antagonism along these lines. The only way to have alleviated the danger would have been to have maintained the participation of Canada within reasonable bounds, and especially to make it exclusively national. Unfortunately, under the spell of the intense propaganda of Imperialism, carried on for the last twenty years, our rulers have chosen to turn Canada's intervention in the war into an Imperial contribution. They have also lost all sense of national requirements, and, from the start decided to bankrupt Canada to help the Mother Country. On both grounds this was bound to raise the instinctive opposition of French Canadians, who, looking upon Canada as their only Motherland, are not prepared to make heavier sacrifices for other countries, British or foreign, than the people of those countries would be disposed to make for us; nor were they willing to accept the Gospel of Imperial solidarity as sufficient justification to govern Canada and sap her vitality in a war for which she had no responsibility whatever.[107]

Bourassa here adopted a dichotomy which many French Canadians found compelling: imperialism versus nationalism. The French Canadians were the nationalists, their only loyalty being to Canada. The English Canadians were left to be cast in the evil role of imperialists. But Borden and many, perhaps most, of those who supported him in 1917 also considered themselves to be nationalists. To them Canada's interest, her status, and her future were closely bound up in the outcome of the war. Never once did Borden conceive of Canada as a subordinate or colonial participant in the war: Canada was fighting in her own right, though Britain had often to be reminded of it. This theme ran through the whole of Borden's wartime policy, and it was a policy that attracted many former critics to his support in 1917. Many of these men could sniff an imperialist as quickly as Bourassa. Clifford Sifton, Newton W. Rowell, and John W. Dafoe were prominent examples.[108] What Bourassa failed to perceive was that the sentiment which he called imperialism was another expression of Canadianism, different from his own, but still nationalism.[109]

But Borden and his allies were no less myopic. They failed to realize that Bourassa, too, was a Canadian nationalist. His vision of Canada's future was one of increasing independence from imperial commitments and responsiblities. Indeed he favoured the dissolution of the Empire unless it could accommodate itself to "the just nationalist aspirations of each of the British countries."[110] These two versions of Canadian nationalism clashed in 1917, and victory went to the British-Canadian nationalists. It was their most resounding triumph. But it was also their last.

CHAPTER 14

The Continent and the Empire-Commonwealth

I

When Britain was at war, Canada was at war. But Canada was not at war simply as a matter of legal status. Canada joined the Great War because Canadians, anxious for a place in the imperial crusade, would not have it otherwise. But neither reason in itself explained the totality of Canadian commitment to the war effort. As far as an inexperienced and administratively weak government was capable, every man and every dollar were to be expended for victory. For Canada also went to war with a deep sense of duty to the Empire and even more to "civilization" in peril. Germany's "military aristocracy" threatened to unhinge the world, to dissolve the bonds of law and order that held civilized society together. This, the Prime Minister explained repeatedly, was why Canada must commit herself to "every sacrifice." "The people of Canada entered this war from a profound conviction of duty to the Empire and to the civilized world," Borden wrote in 1918, proudly adding, "Probably no part of the Britannic Commonwealth was more disinterested in reaching a decision as to that duty."[1]

But not totally disinterested. It was true that Canada had no great territorial ambitions, and that most Canadians–at least in the beginning–shared Borden's lofty war aims. But no nation would have been expected to shed so much blood and expend so much treasure for an abstract principle alone. What Canada demanded in return was the right to belong to the family of nations, no longer as an adolescent, but as an adult member. The country was committed to a mature role in the world's greatest war; henceforth she sought full partnership in the councils that waged war and made peace.

Where better to look for proof of Canada's maturity than at her relations with her closest neighbour? Because of their responsible attitude, Canadians believed their relations with the United States to be in good order. Indeed they had been and were being conducted, as the International Joint Commission illustrated, on the highest, most civilized plane, "in a thoroughly judicial spirit," said the Prime Minister.[2] More than that, because Canada's continental affairs were in such good standing, and because her continental relations were so intimate and so comprehensive, Canada, if given a chance, could make a unique contribution to the imperial war effort by providing the link of understanding between Britain and the United States.

It was no secret that Anglo-American relations were badly strained by 1915. In Washington, Britain's apparent war objectives were viewed with scepticism, her methods with growing anger. In London, Geoffrey Dawson observed that "nothing would be so popular here as a real anti-American outburst and the sacking, let us say, of poor old Page's house [Walter Hines Page, U.S. Ambassador to the Court of St. James]."[3] For the United States the sorest point of contention was Britain's economic war effort against Germany, more particularly the blockade of Germany. American complaints against violation of the freedom of the seas in respect of her ships were answered with cold contempt. Here, Borden believed, was a place for Canadian initiative. It was certain that the blockade would not be lifted, but if the Americans were able to understand the high purpose for which the blockade had been mounted, then a grave crisis in Anglo-American relations could be averted. Borden suggested that a word from Britain, expounding the moral principles behind the British war effort, would serve the purpose. But the British refused to issue a proclamation of morality.[4]

In fact, the British silence served Canada's purpose; if the British Foreign Minister would not speak, then the Canadian Prime Minister would, making even more apparent Canada's usefulness as interpreter and intermediary. In the fall of 1916 Borden went to New York to give what he considered to be one of the most important speeches of his career; he spoke to the Lawyers' Club. The points he made were succinctly stated in a memorandum by his assistant, Loring Christie:

1. That an inconclusive peace would be disastrous to the liberty of the world.
2. That England was doing her share in the contest.
3. That the question of the control of the seas is a vital one to civilization; that Britain has maintained it for the cause of liberty; and that the subject should be considered in the light of that fact.[5]

Borden assured the leaders of the New York legal community that what was at stake was a world in which the rule of law would replace the rule of force among nations. "It is as certain as my own existence that modern civilization will ultimately disintegrate and perish if it fails to achieve this ideal."[6]

But by late 1916 carrying a propaganda torch for the imperial war effort was only a small part of Canada's concerns with the United States. Already New York had replaced London as the source of government's external borrowing.[7] For some time American industry had contracted to supply munitions to the Shell Committee and the Imperial Munitions Board, in many instances through branch plants established for the purpose in Canada. United States citizens, illegally but with a cautious welcome from some members of the government, made up most of the 97th Battalion of the C.E.F.[8] After the United States entered the war in the spring of 1917, Canadian-American cooperation grew more intimate. Food control, and, more particularly, fuel control and wheat marketing were decidedly cooperative ventures. For Canada, the great difficulties were her part in the Anglo-American exchange crisis of 1917-1918, her growing trade deficit with the United States, and an apparent unwillingness on the part of the Americans "to use facilities of Canada" to correct the trade imbalance.[9] Early in 1918 Borden went to Washington to seek a solution to these problems, which, if unresolved, might bring the Canadian war effort to a halt.

The trip was a smashing success. The Americans were "exceedingly cordial," and willing to do all he asked. With obvious delight, the Prime Minister reported that "they expressed the view that the resources of the two countries should be pooled in the most effective cooperation and that the boundary line had little or no significance in considering or dealing with these vital questions." And, again, Secretary of the Treasury McAdoo "means to redress our adverse balance of trade" by "warmly approv[ing] of utilizing the facilities of Canada in the production of munitions to as great an extent as possible."[10]

Simultaneously, unprecedented military cooperation was being developed. The Admiralty, fearing submarine attacks in the northwest Atlantic upon North American shipping, and unable to provide adequate defence against such attacks, urged Canada and the United States to work out a joint submarine defence plan based on cooperative sea and air patrols. The Commander-in-Chief, North American and West Indies Station, signalled on April 15 that "patrols and air service now under joint consideration with Canada and United States to obtain immediate best results with means at disposal."[11] On the sea, patrol responsibilities were divided at the 65th meridian, the United States covering the area west and Canada covering the area east of the line. For the air patrols, Canada supplied bases in Nova Scotia, and the United States provided the planes and the flyers.[12]

This was a far cry from the atmosphere of the 1911 election campaign. And it was a very different kind of continental relationship from that of the pre-war years. In the private sector, of course, there had been extensive sharing of development capital and resources for a long time. But now the boundary line "had little or no significance" in the pooling of money, material, and, to a limited extent, manpower, by the deliberate policies of the governments in Washington and Ottawa. Clearly, the prewar machinery for cooperation was inadequate to the demands of the new and more intricate relationship. It was true that before the war, the British Embassy in Washington had been largely concerned with Canadian affairs. But the war had changed that. Now the more intimate Anglo-American relationship occupied nearly all the time of the Embassy personnel. Now, as well, because Canadian-American affairs had become so complex, Canadians could no longer even hope that British Foreign Service officers would have the slightest acquaintance with any Canadian interests they were charged to protect. And, finally, the old way of doing business was just not suited to war time. Leisurely passage of crucial notes, information, and decisions through the innumerable channels of the Foreign Office was utterly inappropriate.

The Canadians became acutely aware of the functional limitations of pre-war channels of communication between Ottawa and Washington, and of the inadequate representation of the status Canada had attained through her war effort. The government suggested a dramatic change. Just after the United States declaration of war, Borden, attending the Imperial War Cabinet meetings, received a cable advocating a "permanent representative at Washington . . . at least while war continues."[13] By October he had concluded that:

> The multiplicity of departments and commissions at Washington leads to disastrous delay if negotiations are conducted through the Embassy. . . . I propose therefore to appoint Hazen and to give him the designation of High Commissioner or some suitable title. In matters that may concern the whole Empire he will of course consult with the Embassy but in matters solely touching our own affairs he would communicate direct with the United States government and its various commissions.[14]

Though sympathetic to Canada's problem, the British government had great doubts about the proposal, which would "raise a grave constitutional issue" in war-time. Especially worrisome was the Canadian insistence that their representative "in respect of matters directly and solely concerning Canadian interests should have recognized diplomatic status."[15] Then, at the end of October, it was learned that the financial arrangements for Hazen's appointment were quite inadequate for the demands of a mission in Washington. Hazen, excluded from the Unionist government and unable to afford the uncertain diplomatic post, accepted the Chief Justiceship of New Brunswick. Borden again pressed the case for a Canadian mission but then, lacking an appointee, backed down on the matter of diplomatic status.[16]

Clearly, functional problems were more important at the moment. To resolve them, the government appointed a Canadian War Mission in Washington under the chairmanship of Lloyd Harris, formerly the Imperial Munitions Board representative there. Significantly, Harris, who was "directly responsible to the Cabinet," was empowered to negotiate for Canada in "purely Canadian affairs" with the Americans and "with the other British or Allied Missions operating in the United States in connection with the war."[17] Harris, then, was what Hazen would have been, except in name. And there the matter rested, functionally adequate and constitutionally beclouded, until the end of the war. A variation on the theme of representation in Washington was played out in the spring of 1919 when Lloyd George offered the British Ambassadorship at Washington to Sir Robert Borden. Borden was tempted but refused because of his "political obligations" to his party in Ottawa.[18] Besides, a Canadian representing imperial and especially British interests, and subject to Foreign Office control, was hardly the same thing as a Canadian Minister in Washington taking his instructions from Ottawa.

That the latter was desirable was all the more clear by war's end. The Chairman of the Canadian Trade Commission, after two years' experience in Washington, firmly recommended that Canadian business "be carried on direct by [a] Canadian High Commissioner, and not in conjunction with, or through, subordinates of the British Ambassador."[19] In October the government decided to appoint a Canadian representative in Washington of ministerial rank, "directly responsible to the government of Canada." He would be part of the British diplomatic establishment and, to ensure cooperation, he would arrange with the ambassador "for continuous consultation in all important matters of common concern and for such necessary concerted action, founded on consultation, as they may determine."[20] Finally, after a good deal of haggling with the British government over the appointment, and some real concern on the part of the United States about the implications of accepting a Canadian minister – would the United States have to reciprocate in Ottawa? would that lead to domestic pressure for diplomatic recognition of Ireland? how could a united Empire speak with one voice on one occasion and two or more voices on other occasions? – Sir George Foster announced on May 10, 1920 that the Canadian government was going to appoint a Minister Plenipotentiary in Washington, receiving instructions from and reporting to Ottawa. In the absence of the British Ambassador, he would be the chief imperial representative in Washington.[21]

The change in the Canadian-American relationship was the result of "war conditions." Unexpectedly, the war had driven two distrustful neighbours into each other's arms. During the war years, their differences were submerged in the interest of a cooperative war effort; the resources, the money, the manufacturing and transport facilities, and, to some extent, the manpower of the continent were as one for war purposes. As important for Canadians were their awareness of the distinctiveness of their war contribution, and their demand that it be accorded appropriate recognition formally as well as functionally, in London as well as Washington. That Canada was in neither status nor stature a British colony any longer, but an equal partner on the North American continent was the message conveyed by the announcement of the ministerial appointment in Washington. The constitutional implications of the announcement within the imperial family remained to be resolved. But the forceful manner in which the Borden government pushed for the establishment of a Canadian mission did demonstrate that where Ottawa perceived Canadian interests to be at stake, those interests would take precedence over the formalities of imperial diplomatic unity.[22]

II

The steady growth of contact between Canada and the United States dispelled many of the fears of the United States harboured by Canadians before the war. The war years produced less happy conclusions about relations with the mother country. The easy sense of security from membership in the invincible imperial family was shattered by the repeated successes of the German army and the cruel enemy U-boat campaigns. Anglo-Canadian cooperation, on a scale unparalleled in Canadian history, seemed to bring to reality the great vision of imperial theorists in both Canada and Britain. But for the actors, the politicians in Ottawa who had to make decisions, it was a tarnished vision indeed. In fact, until 1918, there was no cooperation on any recognizable basis of equality. At least until 1917, the British government more often acted on the assumption that Canada was a crown colony than a self-governing dominion, an outpost of Empire whose resources of men and material could be appropriated and disposed of at will by junior bureaucrats at the War Office, the Admiralty, and in other departments of the Imperial government. For Canadians the experience was galling, nothing less than a rude shock.

Naturally, there were grievances on both sides. The War Office readily admitted that Canada's civilian soldiers were tough, reliable troops who performed brilliantly in the field under the command of talented and resourceful civilian officers. But the Canadians did so in spite of, rather than because of, the direction of their higher command structure in England and in Canada. The British war administrators found the confused and often contradictory training command hierarchy in England a source of continual bewilderment and frustration. For that matter, the Canadians themselves, until Hughes resigned and a Ministry of Overseas Forces was created, seldom knew who was in charge of what at any given time. The upper echelons of the C.E.F. in England seemed to the War Office like a band of squabbling, jealous children, dependent upon a politically conscious and administratively inept minister in Ottawa. In addition, Hughes complicated matters in England by constantly commissioning all and sundry from Ottawa. A staff officer suggested the minister be reminded "of the number of surplus officers we have on this side, and that if every Tom, Dick and Harry is granted a commission we will soon have a Brigade of officers run by a handful of privates."[23] It was an accurate impression.

Then, too, initial Canadian complaints about war orders going to the United States could be seen from London as more a cry for a slice of imperial patronage than a realistic assessment. Where were the factories in Canada? Where was the precision machinery or the trained labour force to produce munitions? With money in short supply, why should it be spent on retooling inadequate Canadian plants when effective facilities existed in the United States? With skilled labour in short supply, why should it be drained from British factories to man machines in Canada? Canada wanted a piece of the action, but where was her ante?

In Ottawa, doubts about the capabilities of the professional British officer corps grew with each passing month and year of the interminable war. Complaints from Hughes and McBride were backed up by a letter from a Canadian officer at the front who cited the "lack of foresight and incompetence of British. 'They send us on every forlorn hope.' "[24] The Canadians fought bravely, but were the thousands of casualties worth the few yards of trenches gained in futile assaults? As for the supply problem, apparent Canadian manufacturing inadequacies were dwarfed by the British bungling that produced the shell crisis of 1915. During his London visit of 1915, Sir Robert Borden heard a "damning indictment of department negligence" from the newly appointed Minister of Munitions. He recalled a few months later that Lloyd George "in speaking of the officers of another department said that he did not call them traitors but he asserted that they could not have acted differently if they had been traitors. They are still doing duty and five months have elapsed."[25]

There were legitimate grievances on both sides of the Atlantic. And there were petty problems which, in calmer days, would have been recognized as such. But so pressing was the war crisis, so deep the commitment to victory, so depressing the stalemate on the western front, that every problem was soon elevated to a harsh exchange of contending principles.

At the heart of the matter was a blatant disregard by the British of Canadian sensitivities. The British treated Canada not as a partner but as a junior clerk in the imperial firm conducting the business of war. From Ottawa's viewpoint, the rub was not so much in the requisition of

Canadian ships by the Admiralty as in the Admiralty's failure to consult Ottawa before the ships were taken. Canadians expected their government to be responsible for the military actions and war policy to which they were committed. But how could they be responsible if they were not consulted? An embarrassed government learned about military activity and policy decisions from the same source as the governed – the censored daily press. An effort was made to convince the British of the necessity of consultation. The Colonial Secretary had decades of imperial presumption behind his cool reply. "I fully recognize the right of the Canadian government to have some share of the control in a war in which Canada is playing so big a part," he wrote. "I am, however, not able to see any way in which this could be practically done."[26] That was that!

Bonar Law's reply reflected the complacency and self-confidence that still possessed Britain's first coalition government at the end of 1915. A year later, when Lloyd George's coalition took power, there was a dramatic change. Confidence of victory had been replaced by the threat of defeat. The new Prime Minister quickly realized the dominions could no longer be treated indifferently. "We must have even more substantial support from them before we can hope to pull through," he observed. "It is important that they should feel that they have a share in our councils as well as in our burdens."[27]

The Imperial War Conference of 1917, summoned by the new British government, and the parallel meetings of the Imperial War Cabinet – the War Cabinet with dominion representation added – opened the door for the first time to consultation between the imperial government and the dominions on war policy. The Imperial War Cabinet was an opportune stroke by Lloyd George. Dominion criticism of imperial war policy would be defused there. And he could turn the frustrations of the dominion prime ministers at the conduct of the war to his own account in his battle for the control of strategy with the British High Command.[28]

Lloyd George opened the meetings of the Imperial War Cabinet with the grim warning that for the members to hope for victory in 1917 "might be a miscalculation which would be fatal to the whole of our purpose."[29] What was necessary was a decision on imperial war aims. Future policy could be adopted accordingly. Consequently, committees were struck to determine the territorial and non-territorial goals of the imperial war effort. Canada was represented by Hazen on the first and by Borden on the second committee, which discussed economic problems, freedom of the seas, and proposals for a league of nations.[30] Hazen, obviously with Borden's agreement, presented a novel variant of dominion territorial aspirations: the others wanted captured enemy colonies but Canada desired territory from an ally! He "urged the British government to consider whether it would not, by the surrender of territories elsewhere, e.g., British Honduras or some other West Indian possession, persuade the United States to surrender to Canada part or the whole of the Alaska 'pan-handle.' "[31]

The report of the territorial committee revealed the division of opinion within the British government over war aims. The British Prime Minister, like Borden, was a firm advocate of victory in Europe; Lord Milner, ably assisted by L.S. Amery of Lloyd George's staff, and seconded by Smuts of South Africa, argued, in Smuts' words, for a "reasonable peace" in Europe and the security of the Empire first and foremost. Smuts told the War Cabinet that imperial interests were "not so much with the particular settlement of European frontiers as with the maintenance of intercommunication between the different parts of the Empire itself."[32] From this point of view it followed, as Smuts reported in April, that an offensive should be launched in Flanders to clear the channel ports, not, as Lloyd George wanted, as a step toward the defeat of Germany, but rather as a basis for a negotiated peace with Germany.[33] This critical difference of opinion between the victory and negotiation factions of the Imperial War Cabinet was not resolved in 1917, and policy was thus left the creature of circumstance rather than of decided goals.

Meanwhile the Imperial War Conference met side by side with the War Cabinet. There, resolutions on a host of subjects were passed, including one concerning imperial preference. The outstanding accomplishment of the Conference was the passage of Resolution IX, which, with some ambiguity, asserted the equality of status of the dominions and put off to a more peaceful time the constitutional adjustments necessary upon a recognition of such status. Canadians initiated and carried through Resolution IX, and its terms reflected special Canadian concerns. "I insisted on a clause declaring our right to an adequate voice in foreign policy," Borden wrote of his negotiations with his dominion colleagues, Smuts and Massey of New Zealand. "Smuts fears this may involve responsibility for financial aid in defence, etc."[34] Borden won out: the resolution included the assertion of the dominions' right "to an adequate voice in foreign policy and in foreign relations."[35]

Despite the continuing ambiguity of future war policy, the Canadians were delighted by the results of the 1917 meetings. They had been consulted, they had taken part in policy discussions at the highest level. More than that, their status, and the right to "an adequate voice in foreign policy" which they had pressed for since 1912 had at last been recognized, in word and in deed. But their enthusiasm was naive. After they returned home, the War Cabinet sanctioned the disastrous Flanders offensive. In the spring of 1918 the German spring offensive was singularly successful against the British armies, dangerously weakened in their futile fall campaign of 1917. Throughout it all, the Canadian government was not consulted. The incompetence of the High Command seemed to have reached a peak at Passchendaele; though thousands of Canadians had been needlessly killed and wounded, there remained an utter "lack of detailed information."[36] Clearly the matter would have to be settled at the 1918 meetings of the Imperial War Cabinet.

At the second meeting of the 1918 session, Borden bluntly asked the War Cabinet the "cause for our failure." Clearly it was not the fighting men themselves. Rather, blame rested at the top where "the unfortunate results which have obtained during the past year, and especially during the past three months, are due to lack of foresight, lack of preparation, and to defects of system and organization."[37] General Currie, whom Borden had summoned to London, had given him "an awful picture of the war situation among the British. Says incompetent officers not removed, officers too casual, too cocksure."[38] Jealousy among the professional British officers had held up the promotion of young officers proven in the field; it "amounts to scrapping the brains of the nation in the greatest struggle of history."[39] Angrily Sir Robert concluded:

> Canada will fight it out to the end. But earnestness must be expressed in organization, foresight, preparation. Let the past bury its dead, but for God's sake let us get down to earnest endeavour and hold this line until the Americans can come in and help us to sustain it till the end.[40]

There was no direct answer to Borden's quest for the causes of failure. But he knew it well enough, and had singled it out in his statement. He also knew of the great battles between the western front strategists in the Imperial General Staff and the Prime Minister, who urged a holding action in the west and attacks in the east to open a second front. The indirect reply came from Lloyd George, who quickly established a Committee of Prime Ministers within the Imperial War Cabinet to review war strategy and recommend future policy. This committee apparently resembled the 1917 one, but in fact it had a qualitative difference. Then the dominion representatives had wandered in generalities, and speculation about the future. Now the prime ministers were presented with a detailed review of past mistakes, and sought equally detailed projections of the future from the High Command.

The Committee of Prime Ministers, not unexpectedly with Lloyd George in the chair, asserted the primacy of the politicians over the military in war policy. "The government," read the report, "is in the position of a Board of Directors who have to insist that before committing the resources of the Company in some great enterprise, they shall be fully appraised of its prospects, cost and consequences."[41] On particular points, the Committee agreed that the manpower situation was critical and no victory could be anticipated in 1918 or probably in 1919. Certainly the western front was decisive. "So far," however, it had "proved the doom of every attempt to reach a decision." Therefore, the best hope rested in a defensive strategy in the west and offensive activity in the east with a possible attack from Italy in 1919. But the "most promising" prospect was "in the creation of such embarrassment to the enemy in Russia as to bring about the withdrawal of a substantial number of German divisions to deal with the situation there." The Russian front had collapsed during the previous year and the revolutionary government had withdrawn from the war. Borden, under strong pressure from Lloyd George, Milner, and Smuts, had already agreed to commit a brigade to the Russian intervention. Now he wholly agreed with the Committee's view that "future operations on the western front must turn to a considerable extent upon events in the east."[42]

The report of the Committee of Prime Ministers was concrete evidence of the change in Anglo-Canadian relations brought about by the war. It was a long time in coming. In the process Sir Robert Borden, stubbornly insistent upon gaining an adequate Canadian voice in imperial foreign policy, had made very large commitments of Canadian resources and manpower to the war effort. It was, he believed, his only tangible asset with which to bargain with the British government. Even then it took the prospect of an imperial defeat and the clever opportunism of Lloyd George to bring about the necessary recognition of Canada's right to a voice in decisions so gravely affecting her. The form of equality and formal recognition came in 1917. Further disasters and an angry challenge by Borden in 1918 brought an actual imperial foreign policy for war from the Committee of Prime Ministers. But fate precluded its implementation. Even as the Committee's report was being drafted and Borden was returning to Canada, Germany's western front, which appeared so impregnable but days before, was collapsing. Though Borden did not know it, within weeks he would be rushing back to Britain to discuss not war but peace.[43]

III

On Sunday, October 27, Lloyd George urgently requested Borden to return to England to assist in the preparations for a peace conference.[44] Two days later Sir Robert's cabinet discussed the request and an accompanying message regarding the forthcoming armistice. The war would be over in a matter of days. Looking back on it, the cabinet was overwhelmed by the terrible price their countrymen had paid to crush Germany's threat to civilization. Nearly 620,000 Canadian men and women had served in the C.E.F., another 10,000 in the Canadian Navy, and about 24,000 more in the British air forces. In the army alone there had been a dreadful toll of life and limb. There were just short of 60,000 Canadian dead. Another 173,000 non-fatal casualties included many who would be permanently maimed and handicapped.[45] Though less important, the huge increase in the public debt was still significant. By the end of November 1918, Canada's war expenditure totalled one billion two hundred ninety million dollars – and still the cost of demobilization and resettlement remained. The public debt in March 1914, had been $336 million; in March, 1919 it was estimated that it would be one and a half billion dollars.[46]

And for what? Was the defeat of Germany enough? Was the easy cooperation with the United States in defence production and the lately won voice in imperial war policy enough? Was the great boost given to Canadian industry and agriculture by war orders enough? Certainly these were all gratifying. But the cabinet recognized that these products of war conditions could vanish if not consolidated as part of Canada's peace settlement. The government had an enormous task of "reconstruction" ahead to ensure continued domestic development. But of immediate importance was the assertion of Canada's right to a say in the making of peace equal to and, if possible, greater than her voice in the waging of war. With cabinet approval, Borden cabled back to Lloyd George that "the press and the people of this country take it for granted that Canada will be represented at the Peace Conference." Borden clearly recognized the demand would create problems within imperial circles and among the allies. But Canadians, he added, "feel that new conditions must be met by new precedents."[47]

Lloyd George was not so sure. As much as he seemed to want Borden in London, he was not anxious to have the Canadian government suddenly clamouring for recognition in world councils. Borden had been and could still be useful to him, partly to calm down Australia's W.M. Hughes, who was making the same noises about representation in a most embarrassingly public way. But the Canadian Prime Minister was not as crucial a supporter as he had been in the war-time duels with the military. Lloyd George was studiously vague in reply. "Come," he said; "I should value your presence greatly." As to representation, "it is impossible to solve by correspondence the many difficult problems which it raises and which you fully appreciate."[48]

As soon as Sir Robert reached London, Lloyd George and Bonar Law put forward a proposal to appease Borden and, it was hoped, take the wind out of Hughes' sails. There were to be five British representatives at the peace table. "They propose L.G., Balfour, Barnes, B. Law, and myself to specially represent Dominions. [Lloyd George] thought I shd be selected by Dominions." Very flattering. And personally gratifying, Borden must have thought. But it was not the same thing as Canadian representation – far from it. Nor did he have any assurance of dominion support. Nor was there reason to think he should have. "I said I did not think I shd have any special status to represent Dom's but same as others."[49]

It was a tiresome, constantly uphill fight for separate dominion recognition, first within the Imperial War Cabinet and British Empire Delegation (as the Imperial War Cabinet was styled in Paris), and then with the Allies. The longer he stayed in London, the less satisfactory the existing state of affairs seemed to Borden. "I am beginning to feel more and more that in the end, and perhaps sooner than later, Canada must assume full sovereignty. She can give better service to G.B. and U.S. and to the world in that way."[50] Certainly the I.W.C. - B.E.D. was proving less and less desirable as a vehicle for policy formation. Too much was being decided above it, in the Inter Allied Conference and the Council of Five; too little was being communicated back until unalterable decisions had been made. "I had a long confc. with Milner," Borden wrote in January 1919; "told him very frankly my apprehension that the present system of Imp. War Cabinet wd. not be adequate or satisfactory [for the future]."[51]

Then there were American objections to Canada's aspirations. President Wilson was sympathetic to the dominion case but worried that representation for the British Empire, plus seats for the dominions, would make just too much of a British Empire voice in the peace deliberations. Secretary of State Lansing even had the effrontery to ask "why Canada should be concerned in the settlement of European affairs?" Lloyd George bluntly reminded him that both Canada and Australia "had lost more men than the United States in this war."[52] Newton Rowell wrote from Ottawa that "if after all the sacrifices Canada has made it is decided that she cannot be represented at the Peace Conference, it does not require much vision to see the political possibilities and implications that might grow out of such a position." "The people of Canada," he added, "will not be content to have their Prime Minister occupy a subordinate position in relation to the Conference."[53] Borden succinctly expressed the rationale of the Canadian position: "It was largely a question of sentiment. Canada got nothing out of the war except recognition."[54]

Still, the British proposal in November contained the root of a solution to the problem of dominion representation at the peace talks. That Borden should be among the five British delegates as a representative of all dominion interests was an unacceptable form of tokenism. Separate representation was essential. "Canadian people would not appreciate five American delegates throughout whole Conference and no Canadian entitled to sit throughout Conference nor would they appreciate several representatives from Great Britain and Canada none," White cabled early in January.[55] And Hughes was even more insistent than Borden on that point.[56] But it quickly became apparent that the real work of the Peace Conference would be done by the five Great Powers. Separate representation would be useful only when the special interests of the dominions were at stake. For the influence of the dominions to be felt on the more general questions, it would be necessary to have a voice in the British delegation at the Great Power talks. The British Empire Delegation agreed to a form of panel representation for the five British Empire seats at the end of December. In mid-January, after much persuasion, President Wilson proposed separate representation of two delegates for each of Canada, Australia, South Africa, and India, and one delegate for New Zealand at the plenary conference. Newfoundland, denied separate representation, was represented through its prime minister on the panel for the five seats at the Great Power talks.[57]

It then remained only for Borden, on behalf of the dominions, to urge separate dominion signatures and ratification of the eventual peace treaties. With that, recognition of the dominions' contribution to the war effort was acknowledged.[58] For the future, confirmation of the dominions' newly won status depended upon separate membership in the League of Nations, the right to separate election to the League of Nations Council and to separate membership in the International Labour Organization. As with representation at Versailles, each step required endless frustrating work: careful scrutiny of draft clauses of conventions, composition of scores of memoranda, listening to and offering hour after hour of arguments in the British Empire Delegation. That each was achieved was a testament to the persistence and patience of the dominion representatives and especially the Canadian delegation.[59]

Various members of the Canadian party, Borden, Doherty, Christie, and Colonel O.M. Biggar, had spent many hours discussing the structure and functions of the proposed League of Nations. But none of them made any particularly significant contribution. It was Smuts' draft proposal which so deeply impressed Wilson and the members of the League of Nations Commission.[60] Aside from their main concern over membership, the Canadians were most worried by the draft Article X, which stated:

> The High Contracting Parties undertake to respect and preserve as against external aggression the territorial integrity and existing political independence of all states members of the League. In case of any such aggression or in case of any threat or danger of such aggression the Executive Council shall advise upon the means by which their obligation shall be fulfilled.

"This Article should be struck out or materially amended," Borden wrote in a memorandum on the draft Covenant. It assumed that League members agreed that all existing territorial boundaries were "just and expedient," that they would continue to be so and that the League would assume responsibility for them. But it was clearly "impossible to forecast the future." "There may be national aspirations to which the provision of the peace treaty will not do justice and which cannot be permanently repressed." Other articles of the Covenant admitted the possibility of war between two member states without the active participation of other signatories. If the nation attacked, eventually occupied, and proposed to annex, with the consent of the majority of the population, some of the territory of the aggressor, "what is to be the operation of this Article?" In short, Article X seemed to impose unreasonable obligations upon members of the League and was inconsistent with subsequent articles.[61] But the protest was for naught. Lord Cecil, the British member of the Commission, informed Borden: "I was unable to persuade my colleagues . . . to agree to its alteration."[62]

Throughout his memorandum Borden exhibited a measure of scepticism about the League of Nations. He noted "the reluctance of each nation to relax control of matters within the scope of its sovereignty."[63] Adoption of the Covenant would certainly be a welcome step toward the acceptance of the rule of law among nations. But "clearly it is not within the competence of any human power absolutely to prevent war."

> The means selected are discussion, publicity and mediation. As President Wilson has truly said, there is force in the background, but only in the background. It is a Covenant of peace and not of war.[64]

The Covenant was an insurance policy for peace. But force remained the ultimate resort of diplomacy and, sadly, the ultimate deterrent to war. How might it best be mobilized to guarantee peace in the future? Long before Borden gave much thought to the League of Nations, he had concluded that it rested in "the two great English-speaking commonwealths which are of themselves sufficiently powerful to dictate the peace of the world if they can subordinate to a common aim the jealousies and divergences which naturally arise from time to time, and through such an understanding or alliance between Britain and America to have a less active and intimate relation to the minor complexities and rivalries of European politics. . . . In this ideal I see the greatest hope for the future."[65]

The United States had to be induced, "however reluctant, to undertake with us any responsibilities for securing the welfare, the advancement, and the safety of backward races."[66] The Americans, Borden urged at the Imperial War Cabinet, ought to take the responsibility of governing captured German territory in the Near East.[67] The British position on the captured colonies must absolutely convince the Americans (and the Canadians) that they had not gone to war "to add to the territory of the

British Empire."[68] This placed the Canadian at odds with his fellow dominion representatives. Their territorial aspirations were to annex the colonies they had captured; he thought they should forego annexation in favour of their claims to be appointed mandatory powers under the League, as Wilson wished.[69] Eventually Borden yielded to his colleagues in so far as their arguments could be based upon the security of their own territory. But Australia's claims were extravagant: "Hughes wants to reach from one island to another across the Pacific. He has very little vision beyond his own personal interests."[70] When a crisis developed in the Council of Ten between the contending views of Hughes and Wilson, Borden's intervention and mediation averted a possible breakup of the peace talks.[71]

Sir Robert Borden left Paris in mid-May with the success of the Peace Conference still in doubt. The Treaty of Versailles – "the terms are too severe"[72] – had been submitted to the Germans but there were rumours they would refuse to sign it. Still, there was cause for satisfaction. Canada's sacrifice in the Great War had been vindicated. Out of the war years had come a new basis for her relations with the Empire-Commonwealth, one befitting the stature of Canada evident in the war. At Paris, Canada had received recognition of her nationhood from the world community. In return, Borden had served that community as an influential member of the committee delimiting the boundaries of Greece and would gladly have headed the Prinkipo Conference among the Russian factions – a conference he had originally suggested – had it taken place.[73]

Status by itself, Borden recognized, the right to consult here, the right to a seat there, was meaningless. It was the concurrent responsibility to act that counted, the willingness of Canada to take on duties beyond her boundaries commensurate with the status she proclaimed. That was why Borden had stayed on in Paris, "listening to disputes, sometimes to stupidities and sometimes to inanities,"[74] despite pleas from his Ottawa colleagues to return home. And that was why it was necessary to call a session of Parliament in September to ratify the Versailles Treaty. For Canadians themselves were as querulous and sceptical of the status and responsibilities their government was touting as were some foreign powers.

The Prime Minister's speech opened the September debate with a rehearsal of Canada's war-time accomplishments, of the development of Canadian representation at Paris, and a description of the "peculiarly effective" performance of her representatives there. All of this climaxed in the Treaty Parliament was now asked to ratify, the Treaty ensuring "the future peace of the world." Questioning came in two directions from the opposition. D.D. Mackenzie, the temporary Liberal leader, and the traditionalist W.S. Fielding were especially worried about all this talk of an autonomous Canadian status. "We are not a nation in the true sense of the term," Mackenzie argued. "We are a part of a great Empire of which we are proud, and we are nothing else. I maintain that it is not a strength but a weakness for us to put ourselves to one side, to separate ourselves from the rest of the Empire, and attempt to become a separate nation, or a separate part of the Empire as far as these Treaty obligations are concerned." Ernest Lapointe was also concerned about this but raised another "fundamental question." If the League had to invoke sanctions against Great Britain, would Canada live up to her League membership obligations and make war on the Mother Country? He and Fielding then moved an amendment which presaged the future: that the nature of any Canadian action under the Covenant be reserved to the decision of the Canadian Parliament. There was, of course, no doubt about the outcome of the debate; the Unionist majority saw to that. But it did reveal the immaturity and confusion of the country's response to the government's activist assumptions in foreign relations.[75]

The debate also raised questions about the continuing ambiguity of the imperial relationship. Resolution IX had asserted Canadian autonomy but put aside the constitutional implications for a future Imperial Conference to consider. The work of the British Empire Delegation and the Treaty ratifications pointed toward a common imperial foreign policy. Could it continue in the post-war world? If so, how would it work, what machinery would be required to establish and to execute it? Could the autonomous dominions pursue "independent" foreign policies when it was in their interest to do so? Could they remain within the Empire if they did so? And what was the implication of independent representation at the League of Nations?

The first post-war Imperial Conference focused directly on these questions. The original intention of a meeting to settle the constitutional aspects of dominion autonomy was set aside at the desire of both the British and Canadian governments.[76] Instead, a meeting styled on the Imperial War Cabinet precedent was held in London, in June 1921, to discuss current foreign policy problems. Foremost among them was the pending amendment and possible renewal of the Anglo-Japanese alliance. In November 1920, Loring Christie had learned of American concern about renewal of the alliance at the League Assembly meetings in Geneva. The United States, as one of the three predominant Pacific powers, viewed renewal as a detriment to its interests. This same position was strongly put to Rowell by prominent Americans during his visit to the United States in early February 1921.[77]

Deeply disturbed by the developing rift in Anglo-American relations, Meighen advised Lloyd George on February 15 that "there is a danger that a special confidential relationship concerning that region between ourselves and Japan to which [the United States] was not a party would come to be regarded as an unfriendly exclusion and as a barrier to an English speaking concord." Instead, Meighen suggested, a conference of the Pacific powers should be convened to resolve their differences; it would "end the Alliance with good grace and would reconcile our position in respect of China and the United States." He added that Borden would be willing to go to Washington to sound out the Americans and "the proposal seems best calculated to succeed in Washington if put forward by Canada."[78]

Lloyd George rejected the idea, preferring to leave his options open until the meeting of the forthcoming Imperial Conference. On April 1, Meighen took the daring step of telling him that if the Alliance was renewed, Canada would ask to be excluded from its terms.[79] Unknown to the Canadians, a Foreign Office committee had come to a conclusion on the Alliance similar to their own.[80] But arrayed against them were the Prime Minister and the Foreign Secretary, both of whom favoured renewal, and the Premiers of Australia and New Zealand, who regarded renewal as a necessary check to Japanese ambitions in the Pacific.

The Canadian case was briefly put by Meighen at the Imperial Conference. Beginning with the assumption that foreign policy differences within the Empire had to be resolved by continuous consultation, he went on to detail the "distinctively Canadian relations with the United States" and to assert that their control "has become and must remain a matter incident to our autonomy." It had become "an indefeasible constitutional recognition" that "in the determination of questions affecting, not the Empire as such and the United States, but affecting Canada and the United States, the Dominion should have full and final authority." As far as the Alliance was concerned, because its renewal would be so detrimental to Anglo-American friendship, "the pivot of our world policy," and to Canadian-American relations, he would be "compelled to oppose the renewal." And playing the theme of Canada as the lynchpin in Anglo-American accord to the full, Meighen grandly proclaimed that "we have a special right to be heard . . . because we know, or ought to know, the United States best."[81]

Advocating the primacy of a dominion viewpoint in foreign relations when its special interests were at stake was a two-edged sword. Canada might, as Meighen hyperbolically claimed, be the "Belgium" of an Anglo-American war, but that was hardly conceivable whether or not the Alliance was renewed. It was much more likely that the interests of the Pacific dominions would be threatened if non-renewal left Japan unchecked in the Pacific. The position really confronting the Conference was this: Canada demanded rejection of the Alliance and a Pacific powers conference in its place. The British government also favoured a Pacific powers conference, but gave primacy of place to renewal of the Alliance and was vigorously supported by Australia and New Zealand. The British suddenly broke the deadlock by reversing their priorities. The threat of the impending end to the Alliance, and consequently, the urgency of renewal, disappeared. Lloyd George's law officers now seemed to say that the Alliance could go on indefinitely until specifically renounced by one of the parties – an unlikely event. Thus, a Pacific conference now became the first order of the day. Negotiations were quickly opened with the United States, and a conference was arranged to begin at the end of November in Washington. For the British, representation would follow the Versailles formula. Sir Robert Borden from Canada and representatives from Australia and New Zealand would join the British in a reconstituted British Empire Delegation.[82]

In the immediate aftermath, the Canadians judged the results of the Imperial Conference as a victory for their position and proof of the feasibility of a common Imperial foreign policy.[83] In fact, the Conference results were inconclusive. The idea of a Pacific powers conference was hardly original to Canada; it had been put up as an alternative to renewal of the Alliance by a Foreign Office committee and was very much "in the air" in London and Washington as well as Ottawa. Undoubtedly, Meighen's strong stand at the Imperial Conference was a powerful influence leading to a reversal of British government priorities, but only one influence among many. And the Canadian position included a demand that the Alliance be renounced. That demand was not met. The Alliance remained in force and would continue to do so until the Washington Conference supplied an acceptable alternative.

In the end, of course, the Treaties emanating from the Washington Conference obviated the necessity for renewal of the Anglo-Japanese Alliance. Luck, circumstance, and the demands of the great powers made visions of a Canadian contribution to big power diplomacy and to a common Imperial foreign policy appear larger than they really were. But what the Alliance episode did demonstrate, just as the simultaneous drive for separate Canadian representation in Washington had revealed, was that Canada's relations with the United States had a high priority in her external policies. The ties of Empire and the appeal of an Imperial foreign policy had to be accommodated to that basic consideration. With that understanding in mind Sir Robert Borden, a decade after the anti-reciprocity campaign, went to Washington to speak for Canada.

CHAPTER 15

———

O Brave New World . . .

I

The bitterly fought election of December 1917 had one very obvious meaning: in endorsing the coalition and conscription, most Canadians had affirmed that Canada should continue to make a maximum contribution to the war effort, regardless of cost. Those who felt reservations about this policy, whether French Canadians, labour leaders or members of "alien" immigrant groups, were swept aside by a swelling tide of British-Canadian nationalism. Winning the war was the first, to many the sacred, objective of Union government. "Canada was saved yesterday," the *Manitoba Free Press* announced jubilantly in its election post-mortem, "–from shame, from national futility, from treachery to her Allies, from treason to the holiest cause for which men have ever fought and died."[1]

But the Union government represented a broader, and vaguer, sentiment than the simple desire to win the war. It was in many ways the culmination of ideas and impulses at work in Canadian society for more than a decade. A widely publicized congress in Ottawa, in March 1914, exemplified those impulses. It was sponsored by the Social Service Council of Canada, a body of representatives of the Protestant churches, some farm and labour organizations, and the Woman's Christian Temperance Union. The meeting, in Rev. Charles Gordon's words, focused upon "the impressive fact that in this civilized and Christian country both civilization and Christianity are challenged by the economic, industrial and social conditions upon which the fabric of the state is erected." The solution was to begin building the Kingdom of God on Earth. "For there is in our nation," he asserted, "so deep-seated a sense of righteousness and brotherhood that it needs only that the light fall clear and white upon the evil to have it finally removed."[2] This sense of "righteousness," which was often associated with "Canadianism," was not smothered by the militant patriotism of the war years, but rather stimulated and siphoned into the Unionist movement. The war became the great patriotic challenge which would purge Canada of petty politics, materialism, and corruption; Unionism was the embodiment of what the Rev. Salem Bland called the "New Canada Movement." The triumph of the Borden coalition therefore awakened expectations that no government could fulfil. "For the first time in Canadian history," one reformer wrote, "Canada possesses a government so constituted as to personnel, and dowered with a mandate so weighty and insistent, that policies quite Utopian in normal times may not be merely practical, but obligatory. . . . Canada has spoken out of a full heart, and has placed behind her new government a volume of moral power that will justify undertakings that no ordinary administration dare hazard."[3]

That same hope for national regeneration inspired a collection of essays by prominent Canadians in 1917. *The New Era in Canada,* edited by the Principal of Ridley College, J.O. Miller, had a title as significant as its contents, and took as its theme a set of ideas that were on many lips, all over the Anglo-Saxon world, in the later war years. "The final triumph of Democracy can only be assured by the willing subordination of the individual to the state, for the common good," Miller explained. "That is the lesson Canadians have to learn in the New Era, a lesson made easier for them by the heroic example of Canadian youth in war and the devotion of those who willingly gave them to a noble cause."[4] Only a better Canada, a regenerated Canada, could fully repay those who had sacrificed so much in war.

To a considerable extent these reformist views had their roots in pervasive religious sentiments of Canadians, especially in the new, socially oriented Christianity. The spread of liberal theology on the wings of nineteenth-century historical criticism and natural science had brought with it both secularism and a renewed interest in the social application of Christianity. Maurice Hutton, a professor at the University of Toronto, remarked on this phenomenon early in the war in one of those interminable essays which purported to explain the moral virtue of Britain and her allies, and the moral vice of the Central Powers. Germany had experienced a collapse of traditional morality whose place had been taken by militarism. "How has the decay of creeds affected us – affected Canadians, and the United States and Britain?" Hutton asked. "Obviously you can all see it – by substituting the practice of Christianity for the theory – for dogmas and creeds and confessions. Everyone talks of social betterment and social uplift and the amelioration of the condition of the submerged tenth."[5]

While the war might have raised doubts about man's potential for perfection, it seems rarely to have done so. W.L. Grant was unusual in concluding that "the war gives the lie to the believer in the upward march of humanity. We asked for righteousness and behold oppression, for judgement, and behold – the cry from butchered Louvain."[6] More common was the view of the President of the University of Toronto, Sir Robert Falconer, who though rejecting perfectionism believed that "even through our great gloom we get glimpses of sunshine which promise a brighter day for those who will succeed us."[7] Even long-time supporters of the international peace and conciliation movement such as the Rev. James Macdonald, editor of the Toronto *Globe*, could view the war as a step toward a better, more democratic world.[8] Many of the writers in Andrew Macphail's *University Magazine*, a philosophically conservative journal, welcomed the war as a means of purifying the world "sunk in sensuality and sloth."[9]

The Protestant churches, increasingly influenced by social gospel doctrines, expounded the idea that the war provided the seedbed for social reform. In 1916, the Board of Home Missions and Social Services of the Presbyterian Church concluded that "we are experiencing and witnessing a social revolution."[10] Two years later, the Rev. Samuel Dwight Chown, General Superintendent of the Methodist Church, rose to his most fulsome rhetoric in describing the war as "a contest between an insane desire for personal power and the aspirations of a society towards perfection. . . . The war is a divine challenge to build the Tabernacle of God amongst men, that he may dwell with them and be their god." He then called upon his fellow Methodists, attending their Church's General Conference, to rise and join him in singing "The Battle Hymn of the Republic." Subsequently the gathering endorsed a report entitled "The Church, The War and Patriotism," which mixed militant nationalism with a call for the thorough reconstruction of Canadian society on Christian socialist principles: "Nothing less than the transference of the whole economic life from a basis of competition and profits to one of cooperation and service."[11]

The war had brought two, long sought reforms – though not everyone viewed them as true signs of progress; in each case, it had turned the tide in favour of the reformers. Prohibition and voting rights for women, both achieved in the latter years of the war, were surely harbingers of the new era. The prohibition and woman suffrage movements had long been closely linked, not least of all because those most anxious to end the evils of alcohol quickly realized that women's votes would probably weigh heavily on their side of the cause.

In several respects both movements were epitomized in the life and works of the irrepressible Nellie McClung. She fully displayed the reforming spirit of the Anglo-Saxon middle class, with its broad human sympathy centring on the woman's lot in the home and in the world of work. A naive, almost utopian, belief in the perfectibility of society and the purifying effect of women on politics characterized her thought. She was also sure that moral reform could be forced by majority vote upon Canadian society, wets as well as drys. An ardent member of the Woman's Christian Temperance Union and a leader in the suffragist movement, she tirelessly turned out essays, short stories, and novels to promote the causes in which she believed so passionately. Her dramatic imitation of Manitoba Premier Roblin rejecting a plea for female suffrage was famous throughout the west – and it softened many a male heart.[12] "Humanity," she wrote in her widely read book of essays entitled *In Times Like These.* "can do anything it wants to do. There is no limit to human achievement."[13] But there were obstacles that had to be cleared away – especially the demon drink and political discrimination against women. Her hopes for the future happiness of society were based on her assessment of the profound impact women voters would have on the political system. "We wonder at the disparity between our individual ideals and the national ideal, but when you remember that the national ideals have been formed by one half of the world – and not the more spiritual half – it is not surprising," she wrote enthusiastically. "Our national policy is the result of male statecraft."[14] Mrs. McClung had no doubt that the first change women would make in the national policy would be an immediate attack upon the trade in alcoholic beverages. "Any nation which sets out to give a fair deal to everyone must divorce itself from the liquor traffic, which deals its hardest blows to the non-combatants," she asserted. "We despise the army of the Kaiser for dropping bombs on defenceless people, and shooting down women and children – we say it violates the laws of civilized warfare. The liquor traffic has waged war on women and children all down the centuries."[15]

Nellie McClung's enthusiasm and energy gave the twin movements of prohibition and suffragism a powerful momentum. But there were, of course, thousands of others who joined the causes. Nor would all the women's leaders have shared Mrs. McClung's approach or expectations. Cora Hind at the *Manitoba Free Press.* an early suffragist, quietly and competently proved that a woman could become one of the best agricultural journalists in the country.[16] Emily Murphy, the creator of "Janey Canuck" and the first woman police magistrate in the British Empire, attended to the problems of her sex's inferior legal status and fought a long battle against the narcotics trade and for prison and mental hospital reform.[17] Both the National Council of Women, the central women's organization established in 1893, and the Catholic Women's League of Canada, officially founded in 1920, concerned themselves with a wide range of reforms from women's education and public health to consumers' leagues and children's playgrounds.[18] It was only in 1910 that the National Council endorsed the demand for woman suffrage. Many women would certainly have agreed with one feminist's sober and conservative conviction that, while the vote was important, "training and skills in women's employments' was even more so if real equality was ever to be achieved.[19]

The arguments for and against woman suffrage had been heard for years. Conservatives such as Stephen Leacock and Andrew Macphail continued to insist that woman's greatest contribution was to be made in the home, despite the fact that growing numbers of them were joining the labour force.[20] (One almost suspects that Leacock, at least, feared that votes for women would indeed bring prohibition as well!) They would have agreed with Mgr L.A. Paquet, whose views carried the day in Quebec for several more generations. "Under the name of feminism," the learned prelate wrote ominously in 1918, "a perverse movement, a fallacious ambition, draws in its way the most elegant half of the species, and menaces the very basis of the family and society."[21] Occasionally the women, unwittingly, gave the opponents of female suffrage cause to shake their heads. Certainly neither a Leacock nor a Paquet could accept the claim of Dr. Augusta Stowe Gullen, daughter of a founder of the women's rights movements in Canada, who claimed in 1915 that "when women have a voice in national and international affairs, war will cease forever."[22]

It was, nevertheless, the war which finally forced the male leaders of Canadian society to give women voting equality. On the side of feminism was now the fact that women were playing a quite remarkable part in the war effort: they not only sent their sons into the front lines of the fighting, but they had also taken up places on the assembly lines and in the patriotic organizations.[23] Mrs. F.H. Torrington, President of the National Council of Women, was only repeating what the politicians themselves were saying when she told the annual meeting in 1917 that "the courage, self-forgetfulness, and persistence shown by the women of Canada in all forms of war work, and indeed in all forms of work, since the outbreak of the war has in the greater part of the country swept aside the last barriers of prejudice and misunderstanding which in the minds of our men stood between us and the franchise."[24]

The province where Nellie McClung had fought her greatest battles was the first to fall. In January 1916, the Manitoba Legislature, "amid scenes of unparalleled enthusiasm" as the *Free Press* reported,[25] passed legislation giving women political equality. Its two western neighbours, Saskatchewan and Alberta, followed. That was as it should have been, for on the prairies, in the recent pioneer years, women had always shouldered at least half of the burdens of opening up the new country.[26] British Columbia and Ontario were next. Then, in the autumn of 1917, political expediency caused the Borden government to enfranchise the women relatives of soldiers; once the breach was made, the further step of total female enfranchisement had to come, as it did in the spring of 1918. The three maritime provinces then fell into line, so that by 1922 only Quebec women were left partly disfranchised – they could still not vote in provincial elections. [27]

The struggle for woman suffrage had been prolonged and vigorous, but it lacked both the drama and the bitterness that often characterized the suffragist movement elsewhere. Though feminist leaders had contact with their counterparts in Great Britain and the United States, the Canadian movement always remained essentially moderate, even conservative, and failed to produce any very strong philosophical statement of the kind evident in feminist groups elsewhere. [28] The Canadian movement was well described by one of its British Columbia supporters, who wrote in 1918 that "certainly a few women put up a determined fight, but the masses of women at no time, and in no place, were with them, so that it would be wrong to conclude that women's political emancipation came about solely through her own efforts and desire for freedom." [29]

That it had been a struggle rather than a fight is perhaps explained by the essentially traditionalist outlook of most Canadian feminists. Beyond prohibition and better working conditions and educational opportunities, no really radical demands were made by Canadian women. Certainly no attack was launched on either marriage or the family. [30] Indeed, most Canadian suffragists viewed their movement as one to defend those traditional institutions against such evils as alcohol and its attendant vices. For example, Mrs. A.V. Thomas, of the Manitoba Political Equality League, told the "Women's Congress" in Saskatoon in 1913: "Women's place is in the home, I hear, but do you think it is part of a mother's mission to sit quietly by and see her sons and daughters growing up under conditions which she knows are bad but, through lack of power, is unable to remedy?" [31] So, too, women found many men willing to aid them in their struggle. This was especially so in the west where the farmers' organizations quickly allied themselves with the demand for women's votes. Perhaps it was the relative ease with which women won the vote in Canada that also gave them a sense of realism about the future, once the vote had been won. "Let no one be so simple or sentimental," wrote a member of the suffragist movement in Manitoba in 1920, "as to imagine that the vote has opened the door for women, into the promised land. The key is in their hands. But they have not learned how to make use of it. Nor are they likely to do so for some time." [32]

Just as the war made votes for women respectable and possible, it also provided a new impulse for the enemies of alcohol. Ever since Laurier's failure to act on the 1898 plebiscite, prohibitionist forces had continued their struggle, chiefly at the provincial level. Though the movement was not without some supporters in Quebec and among the new immigrant population, its leadership was essentially Protestant and Anglo-Saxon. [33] It was therefore no coincidence that the dry forces of righteousness won their greatest victory against an abuse which often filled homes with "hatred begotten of violence, poverty, privation and actual hunger,"[34] during the war. Now to the fight against those real social evils could be added patriotism. During the 1916 plebiscite on the liquor question in British Columbia, the dry forces ran an advertisement which read:

Are We To Do Our Duty by the Empire
Or Are We To Neglect It?

Are we to "Be British" indeed, and remove a
"greater enemy than the Hun" from our midst?
Is the Sacrifice made by our soldiers for us
On the battlefield to be the only sacrifice?
The Bar or the War? That is the Question of the Hour.[35]

Repeatedly the prohibitionist groups appealed to the spirit of patriotism and sacrifice: liquor production did nothing for the war effort; it consumed products better used for food; drink reduced industrial and military efficiency. Women worried about the prospect of their sons being corrupted by the free flow of alcohol in the military canteens in Great Britain. In 1914 the National Council of Women resolved that while they were willing to send their sons abroad for the defence of a just cause, it was "with acute pain that they have learned that in so doing they have not only imperilled the lives of their loved ones, but in addition have subjected them to influences, the result of which may be more deadly than even shrapnel or shell."[36]

By 1915 these arguments were having a wider public impact than any prohibitionist plea before. Moderates, who favoured temperance in the past rather than abstinence, now moved over to the side of the "drys." Prohibition rallies were nearly as frequent as "win-the-war" meetings, and often the two were the same. More and more people in English Canada decided that the time had come to fulfil Billy Sunday's dream; that American divine, a favourite orator at "dry" gatherings all over the continent, told Torontonians in 1919: "I hope you will be able to make Ontario and the whole American continent so dry that you will have to prime a man before he can spit."[37] Again it was the western provinces that led the way. Saskatchewan was first, followed in rapid succession by every province except Quebec in 1915 and 1916. And even Quebec was about to fall – briefly. In April 1917, the Dominion Prohibition Committee issued a ringing manifesto demanding that the federal government act to make prohibition total. Prohibition was now presented almost exclusively as an act of pure patriotism.[38] One of the first actions of the newly-formed Union government, free as it was from "foreign" influences, was to prohibit the use of grain and other substances of food value in alcoholic production. No doubt the "drys" were pleased, and showed their gratitude in supporting the Unionists in December 1917. Within a week of the election, Sir Robert Borden announced the total prohibition of the manufacture, importation, and transportation of any beverage containing more than $2\frac{1}{2}$ per cent alcohol.[39]

The great crusade had succeeded – at least for the duration of the war. It is, however, a difficult matter to judge its effectiveness, especially since the federal prohibition lapsed with the War Measures Act at the end of 1919. Officially at least, prohibition was total and figures are therefore lacking on consumption.[40] Yet illicit supplies were still available, and consumption for "medicinal" purposes was never abolished. It may not have been typical, but one British Columbian observer noted a drastic increase in illness at times of normal celebrations. He wrote in 1919: "Toward Christmas especially it looked as if an epidemic of colds and colics had struck the country like a plague. In Vancouver queues a mile long could be seen waiting their turn to enter the liquor stores to get prescriptions filled. Hindus, Japanese and Chinese varied the lines of the afflicted of many races. It was a kaleidoscopic procession waiting in the rain for a replenishment that would drive the chills away; and it was alleged that several doctors needed a little alcoholic liniment to soothe the writer's cramp caused by inditing their signatures at two dollars per line."[41]

Nor had the prohibitionists been wrong in fearing that Canadian boys might be corrupted overseas. Once these men returned, the forces of moderation once again took courage, and in almost every province movements for repeal and government sale began to develop. It may also have been noticed elsewhere, as it was in British Columbia, that Quebec, where beer and wine had reappeared early in 1919, was experiencing a boom in the tourist trade.[42] And finally, of course, militant patriotism disappeared with the war. The movement that had won its greatest victory with the aid of that spirit could not help but suffer. "Was prohibition a mood – all blue – or was it a conviction? Did we give up drink because giving up things was the fashion? Did we give it up because it was the easiest, safest, long distance way of martyrizing ourselves – of suffering something for the war which implied personal discomfort,"[43] one journalist asked in 1919. The answer was probably yes. The problem of enforcement had never been satisfactorily solved. In British Columbia, even the Prohibition Commissioner, a former leader of the People's Prohibition Association, turned bootlegger and was sentenced to two years in jail.[44] Finally prohibition had always had class, and even ethnic, overtones. Middle-class Anglo-Saxon Protestants viewed John Barleycorn as a moral enemy, whose victims were most often among the workers and the immigrants.[45] As the Winnipeg labour paper, the *Voice,* suspected, prohibition was "intended not to save them [the workers] but to get more work out of them."[46] By the end of the war neither workers nor "foreigners," nor a growing number of other Canadians, were willing to accept the wartime reform as permanent. Controlled sale, which provided revenue for the public coffers, was accepted by a growing number of provinces as a better solution to the liquor question than prohibition.

Nevertheless it was the enfranchisement of women and the prohibition of liquor sales that gave reformers cause for hope. As if to symbolize the great victory of the combined cause, the Alberta Provincial President of the W.C.T.U., Mrs. L.C. McKinney, became one of the first two women elected to a provincial legislature in Canada in 1917.[47] Here were signs of a whole new beginning. "Province after province has sought to abolish the liquor evil, that fruitful mother of moral and physical degeneration," wrote Sir Clifford Sifton, a somewhat unexpected utopian. "While our sons have been fighting in Europe the moral leaven has been working at home. . . . Men who scoffed a few years ago are the foremost now to demand reform."[48]

That was in 1917. Within the next few years, a flood of books appeared with a broad selection of nostrums and panaceas that would, once adopted, usher in the kingdom of justice. There was W.C. Good's rather belated appeal for the implementation of the single tax.[49] William Irvine's *The Farmers in Politics* was a secular sermon, which took as its text the observation that "everywhere there is evidence of a spirit entirely different from that which was the expression of the individualistic past."[50] Most urban reformers took up the same theme. In 1918 Mackenzie King's turgid but important *Industry and Humanity* pointed out, as few others did at the time, that Canada's future was urban-industrial, and that reformers would have to turn their eyes to new types of problems. The volume was filled with platitudes and generalities, but that hardly distinguished it from other books of the day. Salem Bland's *New Christianity*, a social gospel manifesto, was designed "to give a vision of the Promised Land" where Christian socialism would prevail.[51] The book was seen as subversive in some official quarters, notably by the R.N.W.M.P.,[52] though Bland left his conception of socialism in such wispy generalities as the identification of the Holy Spirit and the labour movement. One author, at least, had a solution for every problem based upon education reforms that would ensure "teaching of the higher citizenship."[53] In 1920 Stephen Leacock published his blueprint for the new era entitled *The Unsolved Riddle of Social Justice*. Like *Industry and Humanity*, Leacock's book stopped a good deal short of exhorting the masses to the barricades, but it did assert that a new age was unfolding in which society, through its elected government, would have to assume much broader responsibilities for the welfare of its citizens. Catching the spirit of the age very accurately, Leacock wrote: "Put in the plainest terms we are saying that the government of every country ought to supply work and pay for the unemployed, maintenance for the infirm and aged, and education and opportunity for the children. These are vast tasks. And they involve, of course, a financial burden not dreamed of before the war. But here again the war has taught us many things. It would have been inconceivable before, that a man of great wealth should give one-half of his income to the state. The financial burden of the war, as the full measure of it dawned upon our minds, seemed to betoken a universal bankruptcy. But the sequel is going to show that the finance of the war will prove to be a lesson in the finance of peace. The new burden has come to stay."[54]

The patriotism and idealism let loose by the war centred on the idea of building a better Canadian nation. Only in this fashion could the great sacrifices of the war be repaid. But what kind of new nation was it to be? Many reformers were convinced that the new Canada was to be, above all, Anglo-Saxon. One mistake, or at least shortcoming, of pre-war years had been the failure to assimilate fully the newcomers. The future had to be different. "Most of us would like to see this Dominion mainly British in spirit and race," one reformer wrote in 1916.[55] A few, like J.S. Woodsworth, recognized the valuable contributions that immigrant groups had made,[56] but a young Saskatchewan educator seemed more in keeping with the temper of the times. J.T.M. Anderson summed up the argument of his study, *The Education of New Canadians*, by saying: "When the vastness of this immigrant tide that has almost unceasingly set toward our Dominion during the past ten years is considered we may ask whether this in-sweeping immigration can ever be assimilated . . . the success of the process of unification will eventually be achieved only when we as Canadian citizens come to the full realization of its absolute necessity. Unless this fact is realized there can be little likelihood of our developing in these peoples a true Canadian spirit and attachment to British ideals and institutions."[57]

This desire to keep Canada British was not without unpleasant consequences. The war had deepened suspicions of "foreigners," and, even after a victory won for freedom and democracy, the "alien" question preoccupied some parts of the country. Often the spokesmen for the Great War Veterans expressed strongly nativist sentiments, demanding that "aliens" be dispossessed of their property and deported to their homelands. In 1919 Arthur Meighen received a memo from a journalist in the west, which noted the increasing number of anti-foreign speeches and resolutions being heard on the prairies. "The result is that today in western Canada," he observed, "there are literally thousands of homes of which the members are sitting up at night discussing their future in anxiety, if not in terror."[58] It was this same sentiment which fundamentally altered immigration policy early in 1919. The group immediately affected were the Hutterians. Late in 1918 representatives of this pacificist and communitarian group, then suffering persecution in the United States, had approached the Minister of Immigration about moving to Canada. James Calder approved their request, indicating they would have the protection of the 1898 Order in Council, which recognized their religious practices. Immediately the Hutterians began to sell their American properties and a forward party, mainly of men, entered Canada. Their arrival set off a storm of protest in the west, with the result that, in April 1919, the Borden government repealed the 1898 Order in Council, which had protected conscientious objection. A month later, a second Order in Council was passed prohibiting the entry of immigrants "deemed undesirable owing to their particular customs, habits, modes of living and methods of holding property and because of their probable inability to become readily assimilated or to assume duties and responsibilities of Canadian citizenship within a reasonable time."[59] The effect of this ruling was to prevent the entry of the remaining members of the Hutterian community, though eventually the next-of-kin of those who had already arrived were allowed to join their relatives. The rest remained in the United States, though they had sold their homes and property, until the Order in Council was repealed in 1922.[60]

Nor was it only the federal government's policies that began to minimize ethnic diversity. The prairie provinces, beginning with Manitoba in 1916, reformed their educational systems. Their major goal was to ensure that English would be the sole language of instruction in the schools; in this the French language was usually lumped together with foreign tongues. The war had provided a new argument for that attitude. "French must go, Quebec failed us during the war," a Saskatchewan Presbyterian chaplain asserted during the language debate in his province. "Let all enlightened citizens speak, write and wire until French goes with German."[61]

Sometimes even those with impeccable British credentials suffered. In 1920 the British Columbia government withdrew from that province's schools a history of Canada widely criticized for insufficient loyalty to British and Protestant values and excessive sympathy to French Canada. Its author was W.L. Grant, son of the imperial federationist, the Rev. G.M. Grant. In 1917, W.L. Grant had been appointed Head Master of Upper Canada College, shortly after recovering from heavy wounds sustained while serving as a major in the Canadian Expeditionary Force at the Battle of the Somme.[62] The standards of loyalty in some parts of Canada were obviously demanding and well understood. Apparently there was no room for a man who believed his school was educating the leaders of the nation, and who argued that "we must be Canadian; but in the cause of Canada we must search the world for new ideas."[63]

These, of course, were the excesses of the new self-confidence and sense of nationalism that the war had helped to create among some Canadians. There was a new nation to be built. "We are no longer humble colonials," a young war artist wrote confidently in 1919; "we've made armies, we can also make artists, historians and poets."[64] But A.Y. Jackson and his fellow painters found it much easier to fulfil their aspirations than did the politicians, who quickly discovered, if they did not already know, that it took much more than idealistic rhetoric to build a new Canada. Or, for that matter, even to keep the old one together.

II

While most English-speaking Canadians greeted the triumph of Union government with enthusiasm, it evoked no similar response among French-speaking Canadians. The Unionist victory gave impetus to a spirit of reform and national self-confidence among its supporters; in Quebec, it induced a sense of defeat and introspection. The young Abbé Groulx, writing on the fiftieth anniversary of Confederation in the newly founded *l'Action française,* expressed a profound pessimism: "Alas! What would the Fathers of Confederation say, if, for a moment, they reappeared in our political arena? Fewer than fifty years have sufficed for their heirs to sabotage their great work. The work of destruction is almost completed, and we are going to leave to history one of the most striking examples of the lamentable bankruptcies that can attend federal unions."[65]

After the election returns in December 1917 that mood deepened, and for a short time there was a serious threat of trouble, even of violence, in Quebec. The first reaction came as a motion presented to the Quebec Legislative Assembly by the Liberal, J.N. Francoeur, on January 17, exactly one month after the election. It stated: "That this House is of the opinion that the province of Quebec would be disposed to accept the breaking of the Confederation Pact of 1867 if, in the other provinces, it is believed that she is an obstacle to the union, progress and development of Canada."[66] A vigorous debate ensued with many members participating. Here was an opportunity to give vent to a long list of pent-up grievances: the treatment of French-speaking minorities outside Quebec, the centralization of power in Ottawa, the flood of foreign immigrants that threatened to drown French Canadians, and the "imperialism" of English Canadians. Yet not a single speaker called for separation, and many, on both sides of the House, defended Confederation. None was more eloquent than the Premier, Sir Lomer Gouin, who closed the debate. "It is to preserve my country's greatness, to cherish in the hearts of our children all of their hopes, to hand down to them, in a word, the heritage which we received from our fathers, that we should struggle fearlessly against the passing storm, that we should labour ceaselessly and untiringly to develop and maintain the Canadian Confederation."[67] The resolution was withdrawn without a vote being taken.

But the storm did not pass so quickly. On Easter weekend, serious rioting broke out in Quebec City. It began when police arrested a young man in a Lower Town pool hall. He could not produce his draft exemption papers. The arrest touched an obvious sore spot with many Quebeckers, who felt they were under constant surveillance, sometimes by secret agents of dubious character. Large crowds gathered in the Lower Town on each evening on the weekend, taunting police, disturbing the peace, and sometimes damaging private and public property. On March 30, the situation appeared beyond the control of local authorities, and a battalion of troops was ordered into the city. They were English-speaking. On Easter Sunday the scene became tumultuous: great crowds gathered, the troops occupied the Lower Town, and tension rose to the breaking point. An intervention by Armand Lavergne, who offered to act as a mediator, only further excited the crowds. On Easter Monday, tragedy struck. As night fell, troops faced the jeering crowd, some of whom were armed, over a barricade of snow. The first shots probably came from the civilian side; in the ensuing fray, four civilians were killed, and more than fifty wounded. Five soldiers were hospitalized. The crowd now dispersed, and the rioting ended. Three days later *habeas corpus* was suspended.[68]

The rioters in Quebec City were working off a sense of frustration that many French Canadians must have felt. Their specific grievance was what they considered the severe and rigid administration of the Military Service Act. But their frustration was also the result of their powerlessness after the 1917 election. There was no real desire to revolt, and only the insensitivity of the authorities provoked the brief, but tragic rioting. *Le Devoir* expressed both the mood of resignation and the respect for established authority that pervaded most of the province. "Whatever one thinks of conscription and generally of the war policy followed by the two parties," the paper declared, "it is neither legitimate nor practical to combat one or the other by violence. On the contrary, nothing is so likely to increase the burden of the iron yoke that weighs on the country."[69]

Though pessimism reigned in Quebec during the latter years of the war, it did not prevent French Canadians from concerning themselves with some of the social and economic questions also agitating English-Canadian reformers. Although the social gospel is often viewed as an exclusively Protestant development, the fact is that it also made a notable impact on Roman Catholic thinking. At least as far back as the social encyclicals of the 1890s, the Church in Quebec had been attempting to find methods of applying the social teachings of the Church. Throughout the war years, the *École Social Populaire* continued to sponsor discussion of Christian social doctrine. In 1917, one of that group's most significant leaders, Father

Joseph Papin Archambault published his tract, *La Question Sociale et Nos Devoirs de Catholiques*. Like his Protestant counterparts, Father Archambault was disturbed by signs of the declining influence of the Church among the working classes. In order to halt that trend, he urged the Church to pay more attention to the material needs of the workers. Failure to do so would lead to a serious social crisis, for, he perceived, "our society – we believe that it can be proven – itself suffers two ills that Leo XIII warned of and deplored in his encyclical *Rerum Novarum:* the unfortunate condition and the unmerited misery of a good number of workers; a deaf hostility, the generator of conflicts, between employer and employed classes."[70] If the Church failed to show that application of its teachings could ameliorate the condition of the working classes, then that class would certainly fall prey to false, secular doctrines that would destroy the faith and culture of French Canadians. To elaborate and propagate the Church's social teachings, Father Archambault, and a number of clerics and laymen, founded the *Semaine Sociale* in 1920.[71]

The concern of Father Archambault and his friends was based on solid and disturbing evidence. Whatever prosperity and growth the war years brought, they also brought accompanying pressures of rising costs and increasing shortages of housing. Low educational levels, child labour made necessary by low wages, poor housing, and high mortality rates remained the lot of the working class in many Quebec centres. Labour unions protected only a small part of the work force, and even unions could not guarantee that employers would sit down and bargain collectively. In 1919 a Quebec government official reported that "neither revolution nor socialism is rousing the working classes today. No doubt there are ardent theorists and partisans of these dangerous doctrines in our province but the masses are ignorant of them. What the working class wants is improvement in their lot, fair remuneration for work and, above all, that living may not be unjustly too dear for them."[72]

The establishment of the *Semaine Sociale,* where clerics and laymen could gather to discuss social questions every year, was only one example of the Church's growing concern about social conditions. During the war years, labour unrest in Quebec provided the Church with opportunities to extend its influence in the trade union movement. In 1915 a strike was called by an international union affiliated with the radical Western Federation of Miners in the asbestos industry at Thetford Mines. The clergy intervened and, in cooperation with management, formed a Catholic union that successfully squeezed out the radicals.[73] Here, of course, the Church was interested in more than the material conditions of the workers; it wanted to protect its flock against the materialistic doctrines of socialism.[74]

Concern with the impact of international unions on the religion and culture of French Canadian workers was also growing among some union men. Alfred Charpentier, a leader of the International Brotherhood of

Bricklayers, was at first concerned merely with the internationals' possible threat to French-Canadian national identity. But increasingly he fell under the influence of Bourassa for whom Catholicism and French-Canadianism went hand in hand.[75] While at first reluctant to accept the idea of confessional unions, Charpentier's growing involvement in the activities of the *Semaine Sociale,* where he felt the influence of Father Archambault, drew him gradually toward what he called his "conversion." His growing French-Canadian nationalism was given a strong push forward in 1917 when he discovered that there was no class solidarity between French and English-speaking workers on such questions as Regulation 17 and conscription.[76] So, too, the radicalism which he detected in some sections of the Canadian labour movement, especially in western Canada, convinced him that the time had come for a Catholic trade union movement in Quebec. That was a conclusion he shared with Henri Bourassa, who, in the spring of 1919, published a lengthy series of articles under the title of *Syndicats Nationaux ou Internationaux?* In those articles Bourassa, now at the height of his influence in Quebec, argued forcefully for Catholic unions as the best means for Quebec to "maintain social order and national unity."[77]

Already in the early months of 1918 a group of labour leaders and priests had met in Montreal to establish a Catholic union. That same autumn, plans were made in Quebec City for a province-wide organization. After two preliminary conferences, the founding convention of the Canadian Confederation of Catholic Workers was held in Hull in 1921. Charpentier, in a pamphlet revealingly entitled *Dans les Serres de l'Aigle,* put the case for the new movement: "What should our attitude be, faced with two schools of trade unionism ardently competing for the conquest of the Canadian worker? What is there to choose between American trade unionism and English trade unionism? One is denationalizing, the other imperialist; one is centralizing and autocratic, the other half unionist and half political, both are socialist and materialist. . . . Catholic workers of this province! it is a providential mission, a sacred mission that has been conferred on us. These hideous plagues have made their appearance in our Canada, and they threaten to cover our own province: anti-patriotism, socialism, and materialism. The fatherland, society, and our faith are in danger."[78]

The choice was obvious. The Hull Convention adopted a constitution written by Charpentier and Abbé Maxime Fortin, chaplain of the Quebec City unions. It stated that the new association was based firmly on two principles: national and Catholic. While national, in theory, meant Canadian, in practice it meant French Canadian.[79] The new federation attracted only about a third of Quebec's 90,000 organized workers to its banner in the beginning years.[80] But it was a highly significant fragment, which underlined a new division in an already weak Canadian labour movement. Moreover, the foundation of this new, essentially French-Canadian union marked the cultural and ethnic tensions that were major consequences of the war years and were also increasingly apparent in other sections of the country.

III

Outside Quebec, currents of discontent churned through the labour movement in the last years of the war, and reached a dramatic climax in the turbulent year 1919. These years were marked by a rapid increase in union membership, which jumped from 143,000 in 1915 to 378,000 in 1919.[81] This growth, and the wage increases which renewed prosperity brought, did little to dampen labour militancy. Indeed, aggressiveness increased as strength grew. Not the least important stimulus was the spiralling cost of living, which rose 8 per cent in 1916, 18 per cent the following year and $13\frac{1}{2}$ per cent in 1918. Wage increases rarely kept pace with rising living costs. There was also a widespread belief that business was enjoying unprecedented, and not always justified, profits, and that politicians with slight sympathy for labour demands were not always above reproach in the use of public funds. Moreover, federal regulations governing labour activities appeared unduly restrictive of unions, while business was left largely unfettered. Consequently, labour dissatisfaction with the organization of the war economy brought strikes in various sectors of industry – coal miners in Nova Scotia and Alberta; clothing workers in Quebec; street, railway, and electrical workers in several centres.[82]

Nor was the source of discontent exclusively economic. From the outset of the war, labour bodies, notably the T.L.C., had opposed the conscription of men unless accompanied by the conscription of wealth. The latter was a rather vague formula, expressed sometimes by farmers, sometimes by labour, and sometimes even by Liberal politicians. To more radical groups, it meant something more than the income tax implemented by the Borden administration. Nevertheless, when the Military Service Act was adopted in 1917, the T.L.C. dropped its official opposition to conscription, though not without loud voices of dissent calling for a general strike. To deflect criticism, the labour leadership proposed the establishment of a labour party to fight the wartime election. The results were far from spectacular – twenty-seven candidates were nominated and all were defeated, some disastrously. Sam Gompers, President of the A.F. of L., was imported to speak on behalf of the Union government, which obviously had the support of most workers in English Canada.[83]

The dispute in the Congress over conscription, and the demand for more sustained political activity, revealed another cause of discontent within the ranks of labour. By 1917 western labour leaders had developed a radicalism well beyond the attitudes of most of their eastern brethren, and were consequently extremely restive inside the T.L.C. Like some Quebec unionists, westerners resented the American influence in the central labour body; but unlike their Quebec counterparts, they viewed that influence as too conservative. "The labour movement of the east is reactionary and servile to its core," the *B.C. Federationist* proclaimed. "Its vision has never reached beyond the matter of work and wages, the gospel and philosophy of slavery. If there has been any advance and progressive thought it has, as a rule, come forth from the west. . . . It is time that the western labour movement repudiated this servile and suicidal policy and refused to longer be party to it."[84] The outcome of the meeting of the T.L.C. at Quebec City in 1918 further alienated the radicals: on virtually every issue, from policy to the election of officers, the western delegates were routed. In reaction they formed a western caucus, which in turn decided to convene a western labour convention to meet at Calgary in the spring of 1919.

As the date approached, several incidents further increased the strength of the radicals in the western labour movement. One was the continuing increase in the cost of living. A second was the death of a B.C. labour leader, who had taken to the woods to evade the draft. He was killed by an R.N.W.M.P. bullet. And third, there were the increasingly restrictive policies of a somewhat jittery Borden government. In the spring of 1918, Orders in Council were passed covering censorship, sedition, and criticism of the war effort, which seemed aimed directly at labour radicals. Police raids were conducted against labour and socialist offices in Vancouver. Then, in mid-1918, a new war labour policy was promulgated, recognizing collective bargaining rights, but abolishing strikes for the duration. This was a gain for labour, but only at the cost of losing its ultimate weapon. Finally, in September 1918, fourteen radical organizations, including the I.W.W. and the Social Democratic party, were outlawed. The appointment of C.H. Cahan as Director of Public Safety indicated clearly that the Union government was deeply upset by the evidence of radicalism in Canada in the months following the Bolshevik revolution.[85]

It was in this atmosphere of suspicion of the federal government's repressive intent, and dissatisfaction with their economic conditions, that the delegates gathered in Calgary in March. All but 2 of the 239 came from the west. As soon as the conference opened, speakers began to fill the air with radical rhetoric and resolutions: they condemned allied intervention in Russia, called for an end to censorship and the freeing of all "political" prisoners, demanded a six-hour day, and threatened to enforce their demands with a general strike. Above all, they "resolved that this convention recommend to its affiliated membership the severance of their affiliation with their international organizations, and that steps be taken to form an industrial organization of all the workers."[86] One Big Union was the cry, the General Strike the tactic.

How far the delegates intended, or even understood, the full meaning of their demands and declarations is far from clear. What is evident is that some of those outside the circles of radical labour were prepared to take them seriously, and react accordingly. Was Canada ripe for Bolshevism? In April 1919, the acting Prime Minister, Sir Thomas White, cabled Borden in Paris: "Bolshevism has made great progress among workers and soldiers there [B.C.]. We cannot get troops absolutely dependable in emergency and it will take a long time to establish old militia organization. Plans are being laid for revolutionary movement which if temporarily successful would immediately bring about serious disturbance in Calgary and Winnipeg where socialism rampant. We think most desirable British government bring over cruiser from China station to Victoria or Vancouver. The presence of such ship and crew would have steadying influence. Situation is undoubtedly serious and getting out of hand by reason of propagandaism [sic] from Seattle and workers and soldiers."[87] Borden, who had struggled long and hard to convince the British that Canada should be recognized as an equal, pointed out in reply that "as far back as 1885 we attended to our own rebellions." But he recognized the growing cause for alarm, and did not immediately set aside the idea of calling on one of His Majesty's warships.[88]

But cruisers would have been of little use where the next trouble struck: Winnipeg. That city was, perhaps, a perfect Canadian setting for a social and political confrontation in the spring of 1919. Winnipeg was the capital of the west – though no longer unchallenged. It was the home of the Grain Exchange, the railway shops, and a number of industries that had prospered during the war. It had a well-established union movement, a conservative middle class, and three powerful newspapers. Winnipeg had grown rapidly in the Laurier years to a city of some 200,000 people. But that growth had brought with it profound tensions – between the rich of Wellington Crescent and the poor of North Main; between the powerful business establishment and their political allies, and the growing radicalism of labour leaders and some intellectuals; between the orthodox churches and the new labour churches; between the dominant Anglo-Saxons and the polyglot population of recent immigrants.[89] In May 1918, a confrontation between labour and management took place in Winnipeg when a civic workers' strike spread to near general-strike proportions. In the end the unions won most of their demands, including recognition of the right of most civic workers to strike. The victory doubtless increased labour's self-confidence and perhaps even aggressiveness.[90] Another form of strife was revealed, in January 1919, when serious property damage resulted from an assault by returned soldiers on "foreign" owned business.[91] The city's tensions were obviously boiling to the surface.

Winnipeg was also a centre of various ideological currents. For years, many reform ideas had found adherents there – feminism, prohibition, the single tax, initiative, referendum and recall, and socialism. The Norris administration, elected in 1915, had implemented a wide variety of progressive measures, including important labour legislation – though this had not proved sufficient to satisfy organized labour.[92] Some of the most dynamic leaders of the social gospel lived in Winnipeg, and most participated in the public social and political debates. William Ivens, Salem Bland, and J.S. Woodsworth, among others, carried their message to the working classes through such institutions as the Peoples' Forums and the Labour Churches. In Winnipeg, perhaps more than anywhere else in the country, there was a growing conviction, among some segments of the community, that something closer to heaven than the status quo could be built on earth, but not by the established practitioners of "churchianity" who preached "the gospel of those with financial power."[93] In June 1918, two hundred people attending the opening of William Ivens' Labour Church pledged their determination "to support an independent and creedless Church based on the Fatherhood of God and the Brotherhood of Man. Its aim shall be the establishment of justice and righteousness among men of all nations."[94] Expectations of this sort had been encouraged by the optimistic rhetoric of politicians and clergymen, businessmen and labour leaders throughout most of the war to make the world safe for democracy. Some, at least, of those who took part in the troubles in Winnipeg in May 1919, believed that the time had come to transform rhetoric into reality.

Yet what became the Winnipeg General Strike began as a straightforward dispute over wage claims by men in the building trades, and, more important, over collective bargaining rights in the metal trades. Faced with the adamant opposition of the employers, these two groups took their case to the Winnipeg Trades and Labour Council, which, in turn, called for a vote on a general strike. No doubt the previous year's victory was in their minds, and there had been repeated talk of such action at various levels of the labour movement throughout the war years, most recently at the Calgary convention. Though there was no direct connection between the One Big Union meeting at Calgary, and the Winnipeg situation, they were all part of a pattern of unrest. Winnipeg was ripe for action – an overwhelming majority of workers voted to strike. On May 15, some 35,000 workers left their jobs. From that date, until the strike collapsed on June 26, Winnipeg was convulsed with hope, fear, rumour, bitterness, and, finally, violence. While the Strike Committee insisted that its only aim was to achieve recognition of union rights, the very fact that the Committee acted as a quasi-government, which held the city in its grip for more than a month, lent credence to claims of the opposition that a "soviet" was in the making. The Citizens' Committee of One Thousand, composed of Winnipeg's business and professional elite, constantly propagated the view that revolution was afoot. "No thoughtful citizen," the Citizens' Committee newspaper insisted on May 27, "can any longer doubt that the so-called General Strike is in reality revolution – or a daring attempt to overthrow the present industrial and governmental system." The *Manitoba Free Press* referred to "The Great Dream of the Winnipeg Soviet."[95] That was not an atmosphere in which to arrive at a reasoned settlement.

The lines were brutally drawn between the Citizens' Committee and the Strike Committee, each side hurling abuse at the other and jockeying for the advantage. Again and again charges of "bolshevik" and "bohunk" were screamed at the strikers, but no real evidence was offered then or later to support the charge that the strike was either "foreign"- led or inspired by committed revolutionaries. Indeed, much to the consternation of the Citizens' Committee, the strike leaders were virtually all good Anglo-Saxons who increasingly won the support of returned veterans. Over and over again the strikers' newspaper, the *Western Labour News.* cautioned against violence and insisted that restraint and patience were the most potent weapons. The Citizens' Committee had other weapons – ones which eventually led to violence – the support of civic, provincial, and, most important, federal authorities. They also had the sympathy of the international unions, who feared that success in Winnipeg would mean victory for the One Big Union idea.[96]

No doubt, one fear of the Union government was that the strike in Winnipeg might spread to other centres. In fact it did, as sympathetic walkouts of varying success were called in many places, from Prince Rupert to Sydney. By May 25, federal authorities had decided to intervene. On June 6, the House of Commons passed "with unanimity in about twenty minutes" an amendment to the Immigration Act providing for deportation without trial of advocates of the use of force in changing society. That same day, though there had been no violence, the Mayor of Winnipeg banned parades and demonstrations. Soon regular police were replaced by "specials," and the scene was set for a clash. In Ottawa, the Borden government remained convinced that revolution was under way, a view confirmed by reports from the Minister of Labour, Senator Gideon Robertson. After a long discussion in cabinet on June 14, the Prime Minister wrote: "A dispatch from Mr. Robertson which informs us of the intention to arrest several strike leaders. These leaders have plotted to overthrow the government of the country and to establish a Soviet government."[97] Three days later, ten strike leaders were arrested, and union offices rifled. On the twenty-first, the worst happened: returned soldiers called for a parade to protest against the federal government's refusal to hear the strikers' case. But parades were illegal. Mayor Gray read the Riot Act. This was followed by an armed charge by mounted members of the R.N.W.M.P. At Portage and Main, police and strikers met in an unequal melee. The result was one death and an unknown number of injuries. "Bloody Saturday," as the events of June 21 inevitably became known, effectively broke the strike, though it was five more days before an official halt was called.

The failure of the strike and the subsequent conviction of seven of its leaders for "seditious conspiracy" was a tragic defeat for the western labour movement. A strike which had begun with concrete goals had in fact become the testing-ground for the utopian visions of some Canadians at the end of the war. Even when the strike had ended, some of that spirit still prevailed. Writing to his friend Vernon Thomas on June 30, 1919, J.S Woodsworth, who had recently been charged with seditious libel for printing a verse from Isaiah in the *Western Labour News* during the strike, remarked: "Last night we had Labour Church services in all directions just outside the city limits. At my first meeting the chairman was a small manufacturer. An elder in the Presbyterian church led in prayer. . . . The atmosphere was a great religious revival. The movement is a religious revival."[98] The Winnipeg Strike was one product of this millennial mood; the O.B.U. was another. Both failed. Reaction had won. The symbolic result of these months of "red scare" was Section 98 of the Criminal Code. Passed on July 7, this amendment outlawed any organization whose professed purpose was to bring about "governmental, industrial or economic change" by force. Penalties for membership in such an organization included a maximum twenty-year jail sentence. Anyone who attended a meeting, advocated the principles, or distributed the literature of an "unlawful association" was "presumed in the absence of proof to the contrary" to be guilty.[99] Guilt by association thus appeared on the Canadian statute books, while the normal presumption of innocence until otherwise proven was wiped out.

After the strike was broken, labouring men returned to their jobs, and to the difficult task of rebuilding their unions. Some turned from direct action to politics in a city where the scars of the strike were indelibly marked on civic affairs.[100] A handful of labour leaders were immediately elected to city council, the provincial legislature, and, in the case of J.S. Woodsworth, to the federal Parliament in 1921. The Winnipeg Strike and the One Big Union, like the founding of the Canadian Catholic Confederation of Labour in Quebec, illustrated dramatically the depths of class, ethnic, and sectional discontent at the conclusion of the Great War. And there was more evidence yet to come.[101]

IV

If 1919 witnessed the worst year of labour strife in its history,[102] Canadian society was just as upset on another front. As the Winnipeg General Strike sputtered out and relative calm began to return to the industrial scene, class and sectional unrest had already begun to increase among agricultural people. Ever since the defeat of reciprocity in 1911, large numbers of farmers had remained restless and dissatisfied. "We as farmers are downtrodden by every other class," Henry Wise Wood told the United Farmers of Alberta at their Annual Convention in 1917; "we have grovelled and been ground into the dirt; we are determined that this shall not be. We will organize for our protection; we will nourish ourselves and gain strength, and then we shall strike out in our might and overthrow our enemies."[103]

In the west, in particular, independent political action had become a leading topic in farm journals. Eleven farmer candidates received nominations in 1917. Five who supported Union government were elected; the rest suffered the same fate as did labour candidates.[104] But Union government did little or nothing to quiet the growing farm discontent; indeed, it adopted several policies which further enflamed it. In fact, the major impact of the Union government on the farm community was to destroy traditional political ties, and catapult the farmers along the road to their own agrarian movement.

There were three areas, in particular, where Union government action annoyed the farmers. The first was the government's most important policy, the one that justified its existence: conscription. Though some farm organizations, such as the United Farmers of Ontario officially opposed conscription of men unless accompanied by conscription of wealth,[105] there was nevertheless a very strong war spirit among farmers. When Borden first introduced the Military Service Act, farmers had been quick to call for broad exemptions for their sons, whose work was of fundamental importance to the war effort. At first the government resisted the demand. But in early December 1917, with polling day rapidly approaching, exemptions for farmers' sons were promised. At the time the action appeared to some as nothing more than a blatant attempt to buy the farmer's vote. That interpretation gained support when, in April 1918, just as farmers were preparing to begin a new crop season, the government announced the cancellation of all special exemptions.[106] As one farm woman, mixing moral indignation and metaphors, put it: "Farmers have been toyed with, advised, implored, and hoodwinked so often that the worm will turn sometime and this new law is the last straw on the camel's back."[107] Some 5,000 farmers arrived in Ottawa on May 15, 1918, to stage a vigorous protest. Most of the demonstrators came from Ontario and Quebec, led by J.J. Morrison and Manning Doherty of the United Farmers of Ontario, and J.E. Caron, the Quebec Minister of Agriculture. A sprinkling of delegates represented the prairies and the maritimes. Sir Robert Borden met with the delegation but refused to promise any alteration in his government's policy. This, in itself, raised the farmers' temperature, but perhaps no more than the hostile reaction to their demands in some sections of the urban press. Peter McArthur was nearer the truth than his sneering city cousins when he wrote of the Ottawa march that "instead of being the end of a futile protest on the part of the farmers it may be the beginning of a movement that will shape the destiny of Canada."[108]

Much of the opposition to the conscription of farmers' sons stemmed from a long-standing worry about rural depopulation. This was especially deep in Quebec and Ontario where the movement from country to city, already evident before 1914, had been accelerated by the demands of wartime industry. W.C. Good, the most thoughtful of the U.F.O. leaders, expressed this concern eloquently. His philosophy, and that of farm organizations across the country, was pure agrarianism: God Made the Country, Man Made the Town. Therefore rural depopulation was a threat to the very moral fibre of society, to its democratic system, to the nation itself. "Our future destiny, and *national* character," he told the Empire Club in Toronto in 1916, "depend on the quality of life that we can maintain in our rural districts."[109] This agrarian assumption was the basic contention underlying Good's single-tax tract, *Production and Taxation in Canada*. which appeared in 1919. The essence of the argument was that governments had followed public policies favouring urban and industrial growth for too long, and to the obvious detriment of Canadian society. Even the educational system and the churches were "innoculated with the virus of false ideals" and had "taken on an urban bias."[110] Catching the utopianism of current reform movements of the period, Good concluded that "surely, now, when the flower of our manhood has been sacrificed for the purpose of preserving Liberty and Democracy . . . at last we can make an honest effort to establish in this, our native land, a Kingdom of Righteousness, without which we cannot possibly obtain abiding prosperity."[111] As with many other farmers' leaders, Good's writing was crammed with religious phrases and symbols, and infused with the spirit of the revival meeting. Christianity had become secularized in the minds of the reformers. "The line between the sacred and the secular is being rubbed out," was the view of one clergyman who had moved his pulpit from the church to the farmers' movement.[112]

This zealous new spirit was directed against the causes of rural decay, notably the protective tariff and the "old-line" political parties. It was the tariff, above all, that caused the country's problems: combines and trusts, the high cost of living, excessive profits, overpriced farm machinery, rural depopulation, and the corruption of public life. Why was it so, and how could it be overcome? In 1916, the Canadian Council of Agriculture issued *The Farmers' Platform*, which denounced the evils and proposed necessary reforms. These latter included an immediate fifty per cent reduction of the tariff against Great Britain, followed by gradual, total elimination; reciprocity in natural products with the United States; free trade in agricultural machinery and the necessities of life. To replace the revenue lost through tariff reductions, the farmers advocated graduated income, inheritance and corporation taxes, and a direct tax on unimproved land values. Railways, telegraph and express companies were to be nationalized and the alienation of crown lands and natural resources strictly controlled. Then came a series of venerable agrarian political panaceas: initiative, referendum and recall, abolition of patronage, publicity for political party campaign funds, votes for women and prohibition.[113] In introducing the platform, the Council's Secretary wrote, "It is becoming more apparent each year that our parliament is coming more and more under the direct influence of industrial, financial and transportation interests, represented by men of wealth in financial and industrial centres, and if the rural population and the common people, including the wage earners, are to have their viewpoint represented in parliament a democratic system of nomination and electing representatives must be adopted."[114] Direct political action was not far from his mind.

The farmer's discontents and his platform were plain enough by 1918. So was his growing hostility to the Union government. But that did not mean any rush of enthusiasm for the Laurier Liberals. The election of 1917 left that party dominated by Quebec, aided by a scattering of anti-conscription, anti-prohibition elements that held little appeal for the righteous farmer. But was a third party a realistic alternative? There was certainly no consensus among the various farm organizations on that subject. For some farmers it would be enough if more of their representatives could win nominations at the old party conventions. That would ensure that the voice of agriculture would be heard, especially if the initiative, referendum, and recall were enacted. To others, the old parties were unredeemable, and any farmer foolish enough to join them would soon be similarly afflicted. A new farmer-controlled party appeared to be the answer. Yet others were even convinced that parties themselves were the cause of the trouble, and that to start a new one would merely multiply the problem. For men like Henry Wise Wood of Alberta, and J.J. Morrison of Ontario, the political system itself had to be changed. The iron chains of party discipline had to be broken, and, with parties abolished, elected representatives would represent interests, or groups, in a vaguely defined corporate legislature. There competition would be replaced by cooperation, and group government replace the corrupt cabinet and party system. "Pure democracy" was Wood's goal, and once the interests were unmasked, when "humanism" trumphed over "mammonism,"[115] the people would rule. "The Kingdom of Heaven and perfect Democracy," Wood wrote in 1918, "are synonymous terms."[116]

The movement was divided on other matters at least as important as the party system. Some farm leaders, after the experience of the Wheat Board and other government controls during the war, had begun to favour government intervention and economic planning as a solution to farm problems. The state could guarantee prices and subsidize farm products, and thus reduce the insecurities of farm life. The time had come, as R.C. Henders of the Manitoba Grain Growers' Association observed, "to combat the individualistic traditions of the last century."[117] But not every farm leader was willing to give up faith in the doctrines of *laissez-faire* that had once been the purest wisdom of farm movements. For T.A. Crerar, the best-known farm leader, government intervention, even to fix farm prices, was utterly unacceptable. "What we need above everything else," he told a Manitoba correspondent in 1918, "is the freest possible play of the natural laws of trade and a sound healthy application of the principle of cooperation."[118]

These currents and counter-currents were running strongly throughout the Canadian agricultural community, though especially in Ontario and the prairie west, when the war ended in November 1918. For the most part the conflicts and contradictions in the movement were ignored. Just as the war ended, *The Farmers' Platform* was revised, and it was soon christened with a resounding title: *The New National Policy.* The platform was re-issued partly as a response to the activities of the Canadian Manufacturers' Association and Sir John Willison's Canadian Reconstruction Association, both of which had begun to present loud defences of the old national policies. But there were also additions in the new version of the farmers' platform. These included strong demands for a clear definition of Canada's autonomous status in the Empire, and support for a world peace organization. These clauses, and some others, had been prepared for the Canadian Council of Agriculture by Professor O.D. Skelton of Queen's University.[119] The revised document was referred to the provincial sections for approval, accompanied by the suggestion that steps would be taken to ensure "in whatever means they deem advisable" the election of supporters of the "New National Policy" to the next Parliament.[120]

Events were gradually overtaking the farmers and a decision about political action was being forced upon them. Already, with the war over, western Members of Parliament were under pressure from their constituents to stand up for western interests. "Western Canada is watching this government very closely," J.A. Maharg told the House of Commons early in 1919.[121] That spring a caucus of western Unionists met to devise ways of meeting the growing agrarian unrest. But the prairie west was not the only place where the issue was being joined. In October 1918, the farmers of Manitoulin Island had elected a representative to the Ontario Legislature, and five months later, in another by-election, a second agrarian member was returned.[122] By spring, 1919, E.C. Drury stated bluntly that "the United Farmers of Ontario form the nucleus of a new party which is going to sweep the two old parties into a single organization, which they really are, a new party that will stand for wisdom, justice and honesty in public affairs; a party untainted by campaign funds contributed by selfish interests, that will cleanse the whole public life of Canada. . . . We intend to hoe our own row."[123] In October 1919, that same Drury found himself the leader of the largest party in the Ontario legislature, and soon discovered that his row was a tough one. The Ontario electorate had returned forty-three U.F.O. supporters, twenty-eight Liberals, twenty-six Conservatives, twelve Labour, and two Independents. Premier Hearst's Conservative government had collapsed: it had mishandled many issues, including prohibition, and it was also made to pay for the sins of the federal government.[124] The farmers of Ontario, carried forward on postwar discontent and tremendous organizational enthusiasm, had pointed the way to their brethren in the rest of the country.

The movement was spreading rapidly. On June 6, 1919, T.A. Crerar announced his resignation from the Borden cabinet. He was now in total disagreement with the government's tariff policy. Within weeks the western Unionists were bolting party ranks on the same issue.[125] "The break with the government has, I think, been definite," Crerar told a friend; "the plain fact is that the administration is entirely dominated by the Tory element in it and I see no prospect of any change in this regard."[126] Soon, by-election returns confirmed the west's insurgency. In October 1919, in Assiniboia, a farmer candidate swamped W.R. Motherwell, a popular Saskatchewan Liberal and a founder of the farmers' movement. Here was proof that the Liberals had little cause to rejoice at the government's discomfiture. One informed observer even believed that within the varied opinion of the farmers some elements "were more friendly to the Unionists than to the Liberals. I think from what I hear that any attempt to tie up the farmers' movement with the official Liberals will blow both ends out of the barrel."[127] Unless one of the old parties – the Unionists by a radical shift in policies, the Liberals through new leadership and a new programme – could win the farmers' affections back, independent political action now seemed inevitable. The demand was rising from the grass roots and pushing the leadership in that direction. The conflict over the type of political action remained unresolved, and the Canadian Council of

Agriculture sought to face the question in a meeting in Winnipeg in November 1919. There a compromise was reached. While central direction was established to fight for candidates supporting the "New National Policy," there was no suggestion of founding a party or electing a leader. But there was an element of shadow-boxing in this ambiguous action. A party already existed. T.A. Crerar and ten Members of Parliament had formed a caucus and adopted a name: the National Progressive Party. A new class and sectional political movement had been born by New Year's Day, 1920.

V

For several groups in Canadian society, the final years of the Great War inspired great expectations. There were widespread hopes that a new, more humane world was being born out of the ashes of the cruelty and sacrifice that had just passed. But underneath these hopes lay a series of hard, competing regional, class, and ethnic interests. These had been present before the war, but in muted form. The war years, after the initial optimism about the country's unity of purpose had worn thin, exacerbated the old tensions between French and English, between new and old Canadian, between classes, and between city and country. Less than two months after the Armistice, Professor O.D. Skelton wrote a keenly perceptive letter to his old friend, W.C. Good. "Is it not remarkable how class and sectional animosity is growing in Canada?" he remarked;

> I have been astounded by the violence of anti-farmer sentiment among even educated city people, resenting the alleged profiteering, and selfish slackering of the farmers on the military issue. At the same time the gap between workmen and employers is growing rapidly, in spite of well-meaning endeavours to conciliate them. The stupid and short-sighted policy of the government and courts in fining and imprisoning men for having in their possession some harmless socialist rhetoric is manufacturing Bolshevism at a rate I could never have believed possible in Canada. When the returned soldiers get back and post-discharge gratuities give out there'll be another element of discord added. Apparently Canada is not going to escape any longer the ills that older civilizations are suffering.[128]

Skelton's predictions, though perhaps a shade too gloomy, were far closer to reality than the optimistic rhetoric of those years of hope. And the situation he described made the lives of governments and politicians more difficult than at any time since Confederation.

CHAPTER 16

. . . That Has Such People In't

I

"We need a new conception of citizenship," a political commentator wrote in an article entitled "Nation Building" in 1917, "possibly a new conception of religion. More than all, we need men of vision who can point us the way and men of devotion whom we can follow."[1] Though the writer of the article, J.S. Woodsworth, was a pacifist who could not support the Union government,[2] he here expressed a yearning felt by many who followed Borden and the Unionists. But the members of the wartime coalition turned out to be mortal men like all the rest. Devoted to winning the war, they did their best to find the most efficient, and sometimes the most equitable, means of achieving that goal. Certainly no Canadian government had ever used the powers of the state in such a variety of ways: to conscript men for military service, to prohibit the production of alcoholic beverages, to regulate prices, to control the sale of wheat, and to outlaw strikes. Almost everywhere the presence of the federal government was evident. While many Canadians welcomed this intervention, others accepted it only grudgingly as a wartime necessity. For some it went too far, but others thought it was merely a beginning; what for some was unjust and oppressive, others judged progressive and humane. But wartime emotion kept many of these conflicting views muted.

By the time the war ended, patriotic emotion had fallen nearly to the vanishing point. The superficial wartime unity of the country cracked under the pressure of a host of ethnic, regional, and class discontents. The government's successes were quickly forgotten, and its failings constantly held before the public. Governing had become a thankless, perhaps even a hopeless, task. With his customary realism, J.W. Dafoe summed up the problems of the government he had helped to create. "It will bear the sins

321

and blunders of the past four years," he explained to another Unionist who was becoming disillusioned, "and as well an unpopularity which all governments in reconstruction have to bear, that of not being able to accomplish miracles. I think any person who holds office now or at any time during the next five years is entitled to a measure of sympathy. It is going to be demanded of him that he do things that cannot be done; things that are mutually contradictory and destructive; and whatever he does will have more critics than friends. A government not strong enough to do unpopular things will be a menace."[3] The Winnipeg editor was rarely more perspicacious.

The temper of the country, and the demand for public policies to ease the transition from war to peace, were very much on the minds of the members of Borden's cabinet. Some of them were growing increasingly restless, and anxious to begin planning. N.W. Rowell, the leading Liberal in the coalition, had for some time been pressing on his leader the need to devise a clear, reform programme for reconstruction. Without such a set of policies, Canadian society was in danger of flying apart. "After the strain of war during the past four years," he wrote in October 1918, "people are not in a normal condition. There is less respect for law and authority than we probably have ever had in this country. . . . I am persuaded that after the war problems are going to be more difficult to deal with than even the war problems themselves."[4] Borden, preoccupied with winning the war and making the peace, was slow to respond to his minister's importunities.

Nevertheless, the war's end did not catch the Union government totally without reconstruction plans. In October 1917, shortly after the coalition had been formed, a cabinet committee on reconstruction had been organized.[5] In February 1918, the new Department of Soldiers Civil Re-Establishment was created to oversee the numerous problems of demobilization. Its minister, Senator James Lougheed, was charged with responsibility for hospital treatment and vocational training for returned men, the administration of pensions, the re-employment of munitions workers, and the operations of the Soldiers' Land Settlement Scheme.[6] Moreover, the government continued its efforts to build a more effective, non-partisan civil service, by placing some 40,000 outside workers under the jurisdiction of the Civil Service Commission. This frontal attack on a once rich area of party patronage was not without its problems. First, it overburdened the Civil Service Commission at the beginning, creating havoc and resentment.[7] Second, though this reduction of patronage removed a burdensome task from ministers, it also destroyed an important cement that the Unionists might have used to hold their disintegrating forces together.

One item that stirred great interest during the 1918 session of Parliament was the debate over hereditary titles. The discussion itself was another example of the reform sentiment stimulated by the war; the conviction had spread that titles and honours had much more to do with party loyalty than with genuine merit. Knighthoods and political colonelcies had flowered rampantly during the war. The leading opponent of hereditary titles was W. F. Nickle, the Unionist member for Kingston, but he was strongly supported on both sides of the House of Commons. Nickle's motion came up for debate early in April, and during the discussion Sir Robert Borden announced that his government had already requested that the British authorities confer no further hereditary titles upon Canadians. Sam Hughes, a knighted devotee of pomp and circumstance, and a handful of others, unsuccessfully fought to stem the egalitarian tide.[8]

During 1919, a year of labour strife and rising agrarian protest, the government realized it must respond to post-war problems with greater dispatch. That year's budget made it obvious that the income tax was not merely a temporary wartime expedient, but a permanent part of the tax structure. It was even increased, and all business war taxes were continued. Another measure made the Immigration Act more restrictive than ever. In particular, the minister's discretionary power to prohibit entry and order the deportation of foreigners was increased, and a literacy test was added to the qualifications required of newcomers. Moreover, the government announced a new effort to attract British immigrants by offering British ex-servicemen almost identical terms with Canadians under the Land Settlement Act.[9] These changes reflected the anti-foreign feelings stimulated by the war. The *Manitoba Free Press*, whose publisher, Sir Clifford Sifton, had been responsible for the large-scale "foreign" invasion of the pre-war years, now expressed the new spirit of the country. "The open door policy must give place to the policy of the melting pot," the newspaper argued. "The people who come to us in the future must go through the crucible and emerge from it as Canadians."[10]

The government's most persistent and difficult problem, and one at the root of much public discontent, was the rising cost of living. The source of the difficulty was defined by Dr. R.J. McFall, who was appointed Cost of Living Commissioner in May 1919. McFall insisted that the problem resulted from a world-wide food shortage and vigorous competition for war contracts, which had combined to create an inflationary spiral.[11] At the end of May, a select committee of the House of Commons was established to investigate the cost of living. Two pieces of legislation followed its report: a Combines and Fair Prices Act, and a Board of Commerce Act, the latter establishing the machinery to implement combines and price control regulations. The Board was empowered to investigate, judge, and rule on the fairness of price changes, but its decisions were subject to appeal to the cabinet. Here, at least potentially, was an important new form of government intervention in the country's economy. It had a political, as well as an economic goal: as one Member of Parliament frankly put it, the Board "was to have a settling effect upon the people."[12]

The Board of Commerce's history was relatively short and not particularly glorious. This was partly due to inexperience, even after the war years, in the complicated task of economic regulation. There was also some internal conflict within the Board between the chairman, Judge H.A. Robson, who was anxious to avoid taking the initiative, and W.F. O'Connor, who favoured vigorous action in controlling prices. Finally, it was almost impossible for the Board to keep prices down when another government agency, the Wheat Board, was committed to maintaining high grain prices. In 1920, after a Board decision to support a request to maintain the price of sugar at an artificially high level was reversed by the cabinet, all the Board members resigned and no new appointments were made. The Board had been largely ineffective in fulfilling its task, and won the government very little sympathy in any part of the community.[13]

The attempts to control prices were genuine, if rather unsuccessful, efforts to resolve serious economic problems and to quiet public dissatisfaction. So, too, was the Royal Commission on Industrial Relations, and its brainchild, the National Industrial Conference. The Royal Commission, appointed in April 1919, was chaired by Justice T.G. Mathers of Manitoba and included representatives of both business and labour. Its report offered a wide-ranging assessment of the causes of post-war labour unrest: unemployment and job insecurity, long working hours, the rising cost of living, lack of collective bargaining rights, the housing shortage, and unequal educational opportunities. Its recommendations, accepted by five of the seven commissioners, were extensive. It called for minimum wage laws, the eight-hour day, unemployment and accident insurance, legalized collective bargaining, better educational opportunities, and the establishment of industrial councils.[14]

The Royal Commission submitted its report to the government just as the Winnipeg General Strike was sputtering out. The mood which the Winnipeg crisis had created helps to explain the almost total failure of the National Industrial Conference called in September to discuss the recommendations of the Mathers' *Report*. The conference was equally divided between representatives of labour and capital, while a smaller delegation spoke for the "public." For two days the delegates met in the Senate Chamber with capital on the government benches, labour on the opposition side. The symbolism could hardly have been missed. The debates were wordy and sometimes bitter.[15] While some goodwill may have been generated, the exercise was largely futile since the gathering reached a deadlock over the two most important questions: collective bargaining and the eight-hour day.[16] "Legislation," *Industrial Canada* noted in its comment on the conference, "has its function, but legislation which attempts to limit or pervert great natural laws will defeat its own ends and injure those whom it was designed to benefit."[17] Obviously much of the business community had grown tired of government interference. What was wanted was a return to normal conditions, provided, of course, that the tariff was not tampered with. That was certainly the view of a man like Sir Joseph Flavelle, who had himself spent the war years in the government service directing the Imperial Munitions Board.[18] And that was the central goal of the Canadian Reconstruction Association, whose chief propagandist was Sir John Willison.[19]

Nevertheless, the Union government was drawn into an increasing range of activities. Most striking, of course, was railway nationalization. In other areas, the federal authorities repeatedly found themselves involved in policies that raised questions of constitutional jurisdiction. In 1919, a Department of Health had been established, partly in response to the drastic influenza epidemic, which ravaged the country in the winter of 1917-18. The new department was given authority over a wide area of public health problems, though most of this area had traditionally been considered a provincial responsibility.[20] Also in 1919, after long years of delay and controversy, the government brought down legislation providing federal financial assistance for the support of technical education. Here was one measure which at least had the merit of satisfying business and labour, both of whom had long urged the federal government to ignore constitutional scruples in the cause of industrial training.[21] Conditional grants to aid highway construction, the establishment of employment offices, and grants to aid in combatting venereal disease were also authorized in the immediate post-war years.[22] These measures, part of the continuing momentum of the powerful central government of the war years, did not meet with any serious resistance from the provinces, though the years of unquestioned federal ascendancy were now rapidly drawing to a close.

Even within the Unionist cabinet there were growing doubts about shouldering new responsiblities, and a tendency to use constitutional arguments to defend inaction. Nowhere was this more obvious than in the field of unemployment. The economic recession of the immediate post-war years brought demands from labour leaders that the federal government provide assistance to the unemployed. Gideon Robertson, the Minister of Labour, summarized the government's view: "Municipal and provincial authorities must not be permitted to continue – as in wartime – to pass every local question to the federal government to find a solution. In previous periods of depression appeals for aid were always made to the local authority first. We should, I think, guide all concerned in that direction, if municipal and provincial authorities are to properly function."[23] Prime Minister Meighen was in full agreement.[24] The time had arrived for a return to normality.

Nevertheless, the Union government's reconstruction programme had been somewhat imaginative, though seriously lacking in co-ordination. And it had experienced both successes and failures. Among the former was undoubtedly the Soldiers Settlement Scheme, which by 1921 had financed over 25,000 soldiers at a cost of more than $80 million.[25] But its general effort to regulate the economy was, perhaps not surprisingly, less impressive. Fluctuating prices, rapid demobilization, and bad crop conditions, especially in 1921, meant that economic instability exacerbated social tensions. Then there were the political problems of a coalition formed to fight a war and unsure about its own future now that peace had returned. The *Manitoba Free Press*, which, in an increasingly detached way, sympathized with the Union government, summarized the record with reasonable fairness: "The Dominion government is unlucky. No matter what it does it gets into trouble. Few thanks and plentiful kicks are its daily portion. In this it is in part the victim of circumstances; but it is also in great measure the architect of its own misfortunes."[26]

By 1920 the Union government, so securely in office in 1917, was on the verge of collapse. "The government is steadily being dismembered," Sir Joseph Flavelle observed. "We manage to lose a cabinet minister about once a month, without putting anyone in place of the retiring member. The cabinet is headless, so is the government, Sir Robert Borden being away."[27] But complete collapse did not come before some strenuous efforts were made to inject new life into the prematurely aged Unionist organization.

II

By Armistice Day, the Union government had lost favour with some significant segments of Canadian society. Those disfranchised by the War-time Elections Act were awaiting a new election to savour their revenge. The French Canadians had found no reason to change their minds about the government they had opposed *en masse* in 1917. For the farmers, Unionist policies had only confirmed their growing conviction that the old parties were the playthings of the "interests," while organized labour was already making rather ineffective preparations for independent political action. Nor was the business community, which had prospered during the war, uniformly enthusiastic about Unionist policies. Certainly some of the most powerful members of the Montreal business establishment had fought hard against the government's railway nationalization policy. They had lost, but they hoped that a change in government might eventually reverse the score.[28] Perhaps the Toronto business community, whose representatives had been at the centre of power since 1911, were happier, for some of its members had been saved serious financial embarrassment by the government's railway policy.[29] Finally, some Conservatives, who had been left out of the Union government, were now supporting Robert Rogers' demand for a return to party politics.

Some of these problems might have been at least partly overcome if the Union government and its supporters had been able to agree on a definite plan about the future of the coalition. But this decision was made especially difficult by the party leader's long absences from the country, first at the Imperial Conferences and later at the Peace Conference. Borden doubly enjoyed his role on the world's stage: it was interesting work, and it relieved him of the troublesome problems of the domestic political scene. In May 1919, as he boarded the *Aquitania* to sail home, he revealed his growing *ennui* in his diary. "I should be happy to return to Canada," he confided, "were it not for politics."[30] It was well that he kept that sentiment to himself, for it was hardly calculated to evoke the confidence of his colleagues in Ottawa. After all, while he was becoming a minor world figure, they were fighting to defend the government's record, struggling to devise a programme for the future, and, too often, arguing about the best method of ensuring the coalition's permanency. Arthur Meighen, his eyes never far removed from the domestic scene, had long been uneasy about the lengthy periods which his leader seemed willing to spend abroad. "We cannot indefinitely remain a government at large, a sport of every sniper, and every liar and every disappointed partisan," he wrote Borden in Paris. "I think the Unionist party should be formally and definitely launched, that in the course of the session, its enemies will be put in the open, and under your leadership, we can have all the advantages of the offensive."[31] Meighen was particularly conscious of the dangers of drift; if a programme was not hammered out and agreed upon, he feared, the deepening differences among Unionist members over the tariff would split the movement apart.[32] Borden, from his Paris vantage point, lacked the sense of urgency; the problems of the Sea of Marmara seemed more pressing and certainly more to his taste. If Parliament thought the Union government had fulfilled its objectives, that was fine with him, for he "would greatly welcome any respite from the burdens which I have sustained during the past four and a half years."[33] Yet without Borden, with his reputation for solid honesty, the Unionist cause would be hopeless. But could it survive even with Borden?

Even before the Prime Minister returned in the spring of 1919, Unionist hopes had begun to revive slightly despite the threatening social discontents. The death of Sir Wilfrid Laurier on February 17, 1919, obviously gave the government a needed respite. The passing of the old man who had led his party for thirty years had a profound emotional effect upon the country. But in politics neither death nor mourning is without political implications. Now the Liberals, whose confidence had been growing almost daily, were leaderless. Whatever hopes they had of returning to office in an early post-war election were shattered. A new leader would now have to be selected, with all of the dangers of division that the competition for succession held. "The death of Laurier has profoundly affected the political situation here," an informant told Borden four days after Laurier's funeral. "No one now talks of an early election. . . . The opposition is in a state of disorganization from which it will take some time to recover. . . . The French-Canadian members are standing like Cromwell's Ironsides, sullen and disconsolate on the moors, their leader fallen. It will take time, but the solid Quebec is bound to disintegrate."[34]

The analogy may have been confused, but the comment pointed to the Unionists' most immediate task: breaking into Quebec. That problem deeply concerned the Prime Minister. Ever since October 1917, he had been conscious of the problems created by the absence of French-Canadian ministers from his cabinet. He even seems to have hoped that once the election was over, some French-Canadian Liberals would join the coalition.[35] He was anxious that newspapers restrain their comments on Quebec.[36] His relations with most of the French-Canadian leaders, and especially Premier Gouin, remained friendly.[37] But the fact is that neither Borden, nor his advisers, appear to have comprehended how deep and bitter the division over conscription and Union government had been. Borden ignored the emotional barrier, and reasoned that economic issues could be used to lure French-Canadian support. To some extent that was a fair gamble. Borden was correct in believing that Gouin, and some other prominent Liberals, supported the Unionist tariff policy and were distressed by Liberal flirtations with the farmers. But, as Borden discovered during a highly political vacation trip down the St. Lawrence in July 1919, the people of Quebec were far from willing to place economic interests first. As he cruised down the great river, Borden consulted several major Quebec figures, including Gouin, Sir Rodolphe Lemieux, and Ernest Lapointe. They were all very friendly, expressed appreciation for the Prime Minister's efforts to heal the nation's wounds, and Gouin, at least, confirmed Borden's view that there was some dissatisfaction with the federal Liberal party. But even the Quebec premier pointed out that there were grave difficulties about any *rapprochement*, given the deep hostility to Union government among the Quebec people. There was one special sticking point, as Borden noted: "Finally in discussing the complexities and difficulties of the situation he [Gouin] emphasized the strong influence of the Ontario school controversy upon the population of Quebec and especially upon the clergy. He said that the difficulties in Manitoba had much less influence by reason of the comparatively small French population of that province, while in Ontario two hundred and fifty thousand people of French origin were continually in touch with their compatriots in Quebec. He expressed the very earnest hope that I could do something to relieve the situation and he believed that even a small concession would do more than anything else to bring Quebec into line with the rest of the country."[38] The trip was a failure. Borden was unable, and probably unwilling, to take any effective steps to encourage Ontario to alter its bilingual schools policy.[39] Without that there was no hope of attracting Gouin. Moreover, it was increasingly obvious that the Quebeckers would not make any final move before their party chose a successor to Sir Wilfrid.[40]

That event took place in Ottawa in August 1919. In choosing a new leader and devising a new platform, the Liberals faced a problem not unlike their Unionist opponents: a means of uniting various competing elements had to be discovered. They had to regain the support of those thousands of Liberals who had run off to support coalition in 1917. In addition, they had to attract enough agricultural support to convince the farmers that an independent political party would be an exercise in futility. Third, it was obvious that, in a country rapidly moving toward an urban majority, the future lay with the party that could sink deep roots in the cities and among the working classes. And finally, there was the need to hold that precious legacy which Sir Wilfrid had left to the party: a solid Quebec. Of course these aims were at odds with each other, and a platform attempting to satisfy them all would either be a mass of contradictions or commit the party to very little of significance. On the whole, the new platform avoided both these dangers. On most matters it was quite specific – too specific for the new leader, as events were to show. Tariff reductions were promised, though not sufficiently drastic to satisfy the western farmers; old age pensions were proposed, along with a series of other social measures designed for the new urban age. On Canada's place in the Empire, the party moved hesitantly in the direction of greater autonomy. It was a reformist platform, respectable but not radical.[41]

Adopting a platform, or a "chart" as the new leader was later to call it, was demanding enough. The choice of a leader was even more difficult, and more important. From the start there were really only two serious contenders. W.S. Fielding, though seventy, had a large following; as the author of the lamented reciprocity agreement of 1911, he had the farmers' support, and his business activities since Laurier's defeat had won him the confidence of many business elements in the party. He was probably

Laurier's chosen successor. On the negative side was his age and, more important, his break with the party over conscription. He had supported the Military Service Act, but he had not joined the Union government. But that vote for conscription cost him the sympathy of the majority of the Quebec delegation, who were loyal to Laurier above everything. The other major prospect was W.L.M. King, who was forty-five. He had served briefly as Minister of Labour in Laurier's last government, suffered personal defeat in 1911, and had divided the subsequent years among work for the party, work for the Rockefellers in the United States, and planning to become leader of his party. His views on labour, without being radical enough to frighten businessmen, suggested that he was a man of the urban age. But that association left him without much appeal in the farm community.[42] His greatest asset, apart from an ingratiating personality and the conviction that God was on his side, was his loyal support of Sir Wilfrid in the troubled times of 1917. That loyalty ensured that Ernest Lapointe, who rather than Gouin controlled the Quebec delegation, would swing his weight behind King.

From the first vote, King led the race. On the third ballot, he narrowly defeated Fielding – 476 to 438. Afterwards he wrote in his sanctimonious way, "It is right, it is the call of duty. I have sought nothing, it has come. It has come from God."[43] But he knew full well that God was on the side of the big battalions. As one of King's supporters, Sir Allen Aylesworth, explained, "The Frenchmen did a grand thing . . . they voted practically solid – to stand by Fisher and me *because* we were English and had stood by Laurier and the French Canadians."[44] Support from the French Canadians, with their solid voting block, was King's first electoral advantage, though it was not without some disadvantages in the rest of Canada.

For all that the new leader was convinced the hand of destiny was upon him, he had done very little to explain where he thought that destiny would lead. Certainly he believed in the fundamental importance of preserving national unity, and for this he knew he had to maintain the indispensable support of Quebec. But national unity for what, and by what means? King had never offered any clear answers to these questions, and certainly *Industry and Humanity,* though it provided many insights into his general ideas, presented few specific proposals. In fact his mind seemed to delight in ambiguities, and his tongue in high-minded generalities. In January 1920, at Newmarket, he defined his philosophy, if such it could be called. "Liberalism," he maintained, "is to me the expression of a wide human freedom, whether it be for those who work in the country on the farms, or in the cities and towns in the shops and factories; whether it be the well-being of women and children that is at stake in the home or elsewhere or the lot of men in their struggle with their several environments."[45] There were obviously many mansions in King's Liberal house.

But while to some it may have appeared that he was "floundering about like a man on a sandbar who is not sure how far the tide is going to rise,"[46] there was, underneath the woolly rhetoric and the boyish grin, a sharp political intelligence, an intense personal ambition, and a powerful commitment to his conception of Canada. His very vagueness and apparent lack of clear direction provided perhaps his greatest asset in a period when so many strongly held, clashing doctrines were being let loose on the country.

King's selection as leader of the Liberal party virtually ended the Unionists' hopes of cracking Quebec. One further approach was made to Sir Lomer, who had clearly been outmanoeuvered at the convention by Lapointe. But Gouin was a realist, and he closed the door to any further discussions. "He is of opinion," Borden recorded, "that no minister could be elected from the province of Quebec at present."[47] One week later, Borden decided that his health would no longer permit him to carry on. Everything appeared nearly as futile as the Quebec negotiations, and, since his interest in political management and intrigue had never been very great, he was doubtless relieved to be able to discover an honourable way to exit.

But he was not allowed to go finally, as yet. The party would not let him. Even after a year of peacetime administration, the party was incapable of deciding its future. Obviously it needed a new leader, a new policy statement, and a great deal of new organization. Borden could not be allowed to resign until these matters were attended to, at least partly. So he agreed to postpone his departure, and instead to take a long leave of absence in order to recuperate. No doubt this arrangement appeared to be in the best interests of the party, for Borden was the only man who could hold the coalition together. But a clean break might have forced the Unionists to make a decision. Instead the temporizing began all over again. The party needed a platform; Borden preferred to let it wait until his return in the spring. The party needed an organization to fight an approaching election. But nothing much was done. Indeed, the party even needed a name. But who was to do the christening?[48]

While King and the opposition were making yards, and the Progressives gaining strength in the rural areas, the Unionists marked time, their leader resting. "Political conditions in the country have not, I fear, improved," Meighen wrote in his acerbic way in April. "The farmer is elated and defiant, the business world is not bothering, and the labour crowd are increasing the number of extremists – those I came in contact with in Temiscaming [sic] seemed to be on the borderland between rebellion and lunacy. We should get past this epidemic but there may have to be an intervening period of disintegration and hard times."[49] The time had come to organize, he urged his leader, to take a firm grip on the situation, and to prove that the Unionists offered the best alternative to mounting chaos.

Meighen knew that, above all, the government needed leadership; Borden's conviction that he should step down permanently remained unchanged. On his return to Ottawa, with the party in much the same muddled state as when he left, he gave his final decision. He would retire as soon as a successor could be chosen. There was to be no convention of the sort called by the Liberals. Instead, Borden assumed the task of choosing a successor after close consultation with the parliamentary party. He discovered that Meighen had the support of the caucus, but White had the confidence of the cabinet. Borden recommended White to the Governor General, but the now retired former Minister of Finance refused, preferring to remain in private life. That left Arthur Meighen, the choice of the rank-and-file M.P.'s. He accepted with alacrity.[50]

The new Unionist leader had experience, a keen legal mind, a sharp tongue, and an almost unlimited ability for work. These were all qualities he would need. He was also an intense partisan with a strong, even arrogant, sense of the rightness of any course which he chose to follow. Even before he became leader, one of his journalistic admirers had taken his measure in a disinterested fashion: "He is a fine parliamentarian now and a first class political advocate," John Stevenson wrote, "but still regards all Liberals as children of the devil and has too hard and unyielding a mind for the times in which we live."[51] Meighen's most serious disabilities as party leader were some of the very things he considered his greatest successes: his brilliant performance in directing the passage of the Military Service Act, and his defence of the complicated railway nationalization legislation, had won him the warm hostility of both French-speaking Quebeckers and the Montreal tycoons. His determined defence of the tariff was highly satisfying intellectually and appealing to the Canadian Manufacturers' Association, but had little hope of winning favour in the farm community. So complete was his belief in the tariff that he almost certainly failed to discern the political danger, or the irony, in a letter he received from a man who was president of a foreign-controlled oil company, and an ex-president of the C.M.A. "If you had been a manufacturer yourself," S. R. Parsons of the British American Oil Company wrote, "you could not have presented our case more to our liking. In this there is nothing of a sectional or a selfish view, but you have taken high national ground which cannot be refuted."[52] That was certainly not the way his speeches on the tariff struck the Canadian farmer. Early in 1920 Arthur Meighen summed up his approach to politics with clarity, but also with that self-assurance which made it difficult for him to see other viewpoints. "This continual bending of the knee to local notions and prejudices is nothing but weak and foolish humbug and gets no person anywhere," he wrote, with the leader of the opposition firmly in focus. "The only unpardonable sin in politics is lack of courage. Indecision or doubt about a course once entered upon is inevitably fatal."⁵³ In July 1920, after months of uncertainty and rudderlessness, the Unionist forces had a leader who had every intention of putting an end to "indecision and doubt." But time was running very short.

III

Meighen, King, and Crerar. Three new, relatively young political leaders, each with his own views of what was best for Canada, stood before the people in 1920. An election could not be put off much longer. In fact, the campaign began soon after Meighen succeeded Borden, though the new Prime Minister had to attend to regular office routine and participate in the Imperial Conference in London early in 1921. Meighen's position was certainly the most difficult of all of the leaders, for he had to defend the record of his government at the time when the electorate was restless and demanding. But if the cause was difficult, it could not have had a more resourceful and aggressive defender. He knew that the best defence was often offense.

Place a clear, unmistakable set of policies and arguments before the electorate, stick to the facts, and the voters would be won over. That was Meighen's strategy. The ground which he chose was the tariff. He knew that the issue was a source of serious embarrassment to King, who hoped to unite Montreal manufacturers and Saskatchewan farmers behind an undefined policy. Meighen believed that he could expose the fraudulence of the Progressives, with their free trade "evangel which was to emancipate mankind and bring the light and glory of Heaven to the earth."⁵⁴ His own position, he believed, was consistent, understandable, and patriotic. In short, it was right. "We stand for a tariff based on the principle of protection," he told a meeting in Vancouver late in 1920. "Not the kind of protection that will fleece the many for the benefit of the few, but for protection just sufficient to enable Canadian industries to operate in this country, to make Canadian goods for Canadians, to employ Canadian labour, and to build a Canadian market."⁵⁵ As the preliminary campaign moved into the main bout, Meighen spoke on many subjects, but he always came back to the national policy, for that was what was threatened.

Thomas Crerar was at the other end of the political spectrum. His position was, in many ways, the easiest of the three leaders. It is true that his followers were much less united than they appeared to those eastern protectionists who believed that the success of the agricultural hordes would produce "unemployment, exodus of Canadians to American industrial centres, summary stoppage of the establishment of American factories in Canada and a great check to industrial and national development."⁵⁶

But at least for electoral purposes, the differences between Crerar's "Liberals in a hurry" and Henry Wise Wood's "group government" exponents were submerged. The National Progressive party was riding the crest of a wave: in 1919 Ontario had fallen to the farmers, and the next year in Manitoba farmers and labour made large political gains. Alberta fell next, and even in Nova Scotia Progressive politicians made an important breakthrough.[57] But despite these promising signs, Crerar was not entirely happy with Meighen's choice of the tariff question as the central focus of debate. The tariff was his strongest policy in most rural areas (in British Columbia, fruit farmers were protectionists), but it also was the issue that made the charge that the Progressives were a "class" movement ring true. Crerar wanted to evade that charge, and to "broaden out" his following. "I stand opposed to the principle of protection, and I trust I ever shall," he declared. But he was certainly no revolutionary. "We recognize that changes must be brought about in a manner that will give a fair opportunity to Canadian industries, now enjoying protection, to adjust themselves to them."[58] Moreover, Crerar and his supporters insisted that the tariff was not the essential question, but rather what the tariff represented: the ascendancy of the industrial east and the corruption of the political system. The farmers' movement stood for democracy and peoples' power; the old parties, both of them, were merely gramophones for the big interests.[59] This was the message they preached everywhere in an effort not to win power, but a balance of power. That achieved, Crerar believed that a realignment of the party system could be forced, which would result in a tariff party and a free trade party.

Mackenzie King stood midway between the two schools. His platitudinous rhetoric, which infuriated Meighen, often sounded similar to that of the agrarian reformers. "They," he told a western audience in the autumn of 1920, "constitute the real government of this country today, the invisible government of the big interests, of which Mr. Meighen and his cabinet are but the visible embodiment."[60] As to the tariff, he refused to join the issue beyond saying that he disagreed emphatically with Meighen, and less emphatically with Crerar. His own stand was the middle, the undefined way: "The Liberal position is a policy of downward revision of the tariff in the interest of producers and consumers. It does not aim at free trade, but it does aim at freer trade."[61] Tariff reduction if necessary, but not necessarily protection became his most successful theme. Or as Meighen described the Liberal policy: "Protection on apples in British Columbia, Free Trade in the Prairie Provinces and rural parts of Ontario, Protection in Industrial centres of Ontario, Conscription in Quebec, and Humbug in the Maritimes."[62]

After his return from the 1921 Imperial Conference, Meighen gave his undivided attention to cabinet reconstruction in preparation for the hustings. He was especially anxious to bring in some representatives from

Quebec, but he knew that his government was electorally weak in many other parts of the country. In 1917 the Unionist majority was seventy-one; by 1921 it had fallen to twenty-one, with eight seats vacant. In the most recent by-election, called to fill the seat held by Arthur Sifton, the Unionist candidate had been swamped by Robert Gardiner of the Progressives. To delay the election any longer would be courting suicide.[63]

On September 1, 1921, the campaign was officially launched. It was dominated by themes that each party leader had been developing for nearly a year. "If I can get the people of this country to see that the issue is Protection or no Protection," Meighen argued in his home constituency of Portage la Prairie, "the battle will be won."[64] But King had no intention of fighting that battle. He preferred to speak in generalities, and to attack Meighen. "In the mind of the Prime Minister," King asserted, "[the tariff] may be the issue; in the mind of the people, however, the issue is the Prime Minister himself and what he and his colleagues represent of autocracy and extravagance in the management of public affairs."[65] King may have been right, for Meighen soon found it necessary to defend his record. He faced the conscription issue squarely in Quebec, where he was subjected to an extraordinary smear campaign, and in the west he stood firmly by his unpopular tariff policy. He attacked the Progressives as a "class" organization, almost Bolshevist in outlook. King was more conciliatory toward the farmers' party, though toward the end of the campaign, he repudiated the suggestion that he was looking for a Liberal-Progressive coalition.

Crerar struggled manfully to present his party as a national, rather than a class or sectional movement. "Let me say I detest class domination and class legislation," he told a rally at Brandon. "This movement is in all essentials a movement of liberalism."[66] But the fact remained that the Progressives' only real appeal was west of Ottawa. A United Farmers' movement had been started in Quebec, and had even won a measure of sympathy from Henri Bourassa, but the twenty or so candidates who stood for the farmers' cause in Quebec had little chance of withstanding the Liberal tidal wave.[67] In some parts of the Maritimes, the insurgent cause had a little more hope. But the party's tariff policy was easily used against it. "The Agrarian-Socialist ticket," the Sydney Post argued heatedly, "[is] a conspiracy of treason to the basic industry of Cape Breton. . . . Mr. Crerar's western friends want farm machinery and coal placed on the free list . . . asking the coal miners of Cape Breton to vote themselves out of employment . . . the agrarian campaign is sectional, disruptionist and antinational."[68]

From the outset Quebec was virtually conceded to the Liberals and the prairies to the Progressives. "That leaves Ontario as the big battle ground and the deciding factor in the situation," King remarked realistically.[69] There the battle raged, with King and Meighen each spending more than half the campaign time there, and Crerar over a third.[70] In the campaign, the newly enfranchised women were given special attention since 1¼ million of them could now vote. Meighen's manifesto appealed directly to them, recalling that Union government had extended the franchise to women,[71] and both parties used women speakers. Neither of the old parties nominated a woman, though there was some speculation that Lady Laurier might run in Ottawa for the Liberals. Several Progressive and left wing candidates were women, and, when the count was made on December 6, a thirty-one-year-old school teacher, Agnes MacPhail, became the first woman elected to the House of Commons. "The lady wears skirts," the *Flesherton Advance* quipped awkwardly, "but they do not appear to be much of an impediment when the lady takes a notion to run."[72] She sat as a Progressive.

The complete returns revealed what many had expected: a country so deeply divided that no party had been able to win a majority. Meighen had lost, his once mighty party reduced to third place with fifty seats. He had been totally shut out of Quebec where the Liberals carried every seat, and his party had also lost everything in Prince Edward Island, Nova Scotia, and in the three prairie provinces. Even in Ontario, the heartland of the national policy, Meighen's followers had managed to hold only thirty-seven seats, followed by the Progressives with twenty-four and the Liberals with twenty-one. The Prime Minister and nine members of his cabinet suffered personal defeats. Crerar, who had probably been aiming at seventy-five seats and the balance of power, captured sixty-five, a remarkable showing for the party's first election. Thirty-eight on the prairies, two in British Columbia, and a lone seat in New Brunswick, plus Agnes MacPhail and her twenty-three Ontario colleagues make up Crerar's following. As a reminder of the discontents of labour, J.S. Woodsworth and William Irvine each won a seat. King and the Liberals carried 116 seats with a member in every province except Alberta. But Quebec was the sheet anchor; it had given King the party leadership, it now gave him a tenuous grip on the prime ministership.[73] His task now was to cling to office and work at continuing the reconstruction of his party outside Quebec. For Meighen and the Conservatives, ten years of office had come to an end and the party was in its weakest state since Confederation. T.A. Crerar's Progressives had won an astonishing number of seats. But the movement's internal differences remained unresolved, ensuring that its future was less secure than its numbers suggested.

IV

The election of 1921 marked the end of a distinct period of Canadian history. The new men, and one woman, had arrived: King, Crerar,

Meighen, Woodsworth, and MacPhail. Outside Parliament, in Quebec, the leadership of the *nationaliste* movement was passing, slowly, from Henri Bourassa with his broadly Canadian views, to the more Quebec-centred doctrine of Abbé Lionel Groulx. Each of these figures represented a vision of Canada that had been born during the prosperous Laurier era, and had matured during the tensions of the war and immediate post-war years. In 1921 the electorate rejected the status quo and with it the talented and sharp-witted Arthur Meighen. In his place the people elected William Lyon Mackenzie King, who had a reputation as a mild, ambiguous reformer. Crerar was more sure where he stood – but not all his followers stood on that same agrarian-liberal ground. Woodsworth was moving gradually from the social gospel, that had been such a powerful element in pre-war reform movements, to socialism. Agnes MacPhail bore the heavy burden of proving the long feminist struggle had been worth the effort. Groulx, like Crerar's agrarian foe Henry Wise Wood, was more interested in doctrine and propaganda than politics. The energetic priest-historian hoped to prepare his people, the French Canadians, for that day when they would be free from English-Canadian domination.[74] But he feared for the future of French Canadians, faced with danger from "the too rapid industrialization of our province almost completely at the hands of foreign capital."[75]

These were new doctrines and sentiments; they found their roots in the radical changes that had transformed the country in a quarter of a century. The 1921 census revealed those changes: for the first time in the country's history, the 8,787,949 Canadians, an increase of more than three million since 1896, were divided almost equally between urban and rural dwellers.[76] That demographic shift had been a response to industrial growth and western settlement, the two dominant developments of the new century. The result was a much more complex nation where classes, sections, and ethnic divisions were potentially deep enough to make the country nearly ungovernable. The war had accentuated these divisions, but they had been present for many years. And the war years encouraged an uneasy sense that one historical age had ended, and that another with new ambitions and values, as yet undefined, was opening.

Laurier was dead; Borden had retired to his books, his garden, and his private affairs. In those two men, in their personalities and their policies, most of the public aspirations and fears of Canadians for nearly a quarter of a century were summed up. The period had begun with an affirmation of unity and a certainty of progress. "My object," Laurier told a friend, "is to consolidate Confederation, and to bring our people long estranged from one another, gradually to become a nation. This is the supreme issue. Everything else is subordinate to that idea."[77] With that ambition achieved, nothing could prevent Canada from claiming for itself the twentieth century.

Over sixty thousand Canadians died defending that unity, progress, and the new national pride. In time great monuments would be erected to mark the place of those who had fallen. But as the quarter century ended, the searing experience of war and death, the reality of unity shattered and progress brought into question, and the frightening prospect of national responsibilities in a chaotic world, occupied many Canadians' thoughts. On the day the shooting stopped and Sir Arthur Currie led Canada's civilian soldiers into Mons, Sir Robert Borden privately confessed his fears for the future: "The world has drifted from its old anchorage," he recorded in his diary, "and no man can with certainty prophesy what the outcome will be. I have said that another such war would destroy our civilization. It is a grave question whether this war may not have destroyed much that we regard as necessarily incidental thereto."[78]

SELECT BIBLIOGRAPHY
OF UNPUBLISHED SOURCE MATERIAL

Because of the space limitations of the volumes in this series, the authors have been unable to provide a complete bibliography of the material consulted in the preparation of this volume. Most of the published source material we have used is indicated in the footnotes.

I Manuscript Collections

Public Archives of Canada

Aberdeen, Seventh Earl of

Aberdeen, Lady

Bennett, Rt. Hon. Richard Bedford

Borden, Sir Robert Laird

Bourassa, Henri

Christie, Loring C.

Coffee, Fanny Penfold

Dafoe, John Wesley

Dandurand, Raoul

Denison, George T.

Devonshire, Duke of

Fitzpatrick, Sir Charles

Foster, Sir George E.

Gibbons, Sir George C.

Good, William Charles

Gouin, Sir Lomer

Grant, W.L.

Grey of Howick, Albert Henry, Fourth Earl

Kemp, Sir Edward

King, William Lyon Mackenzie

Landry, Philippe

Lapointe, Ernest

Laurier, Sir Wilfrid

Lemieux, Rodolphe

Mabee, J.P.

Magrath, Charles A.

Meighen, Arthur

Minto, Fourth Earl of

Mulock, Sir William

National Council of Women

O'Connor, W.F.

Pacaud, Ernest

Parkin, G.R.

Perley, Sir George Halsey

Pope, Sir Joseph

Rowell, Newton Wesley

Scott, Richard W.

Sifton, Arthur Lewis

Sifton, Sir Clifford

Tupper, Sir Charles

Tupper, Sir Charles Hibbert

White, Sir Thomas W.

Willison, Sir John S.

Woodsworth, James Shaver

Public Archives of Nova Scotia

Borden, Sir Frederick

University of New Brunswick

Crockett, O.S.

Hazen, Sir J.D.

Public Archives of Ontario

Whitney, Sir James Pliny

University of Toronto

Charlton, J.C.

Walker, Sir B.E.

Wrong, George M.

Queen's University

Crerar, Thomas A.

Flavelle, Sir Joseph W.

Foster, John G.

Gregory, William D.

Lambert, Norman

Public Archives of Manitoba

Political Equality League of Manitoba

Dixon, F.J.

Rigg, J.A.

Thomas, Lillian B.

Thomas, Vernon

Public Archives of British Columbia

McBride, Sir Richard

Cornell University

Smith, Goldwin

II Government Records

Public Archives of Canada

Colonial Office Series

Department of Finance

Governor General's Series

Imperial Munitions Board

Department of Interior

Department of National Defence

Department of the Secretary of State

III Unpublished Theses

Acheson, Thomas William, "The Social Origins of Canadian Industrialism: A Study in the Structure of Entrepreneurship," Ph.D., Toronto, 1971.

Allan, John, "Reciprocity and the Canadian General Election of 1911: A Re-Examination of Economic Self-Interest in Voting," M.A., Queen's, 1971.

Allan, Richard, "Salem Bland and the Social Gospel in Canada," M.A., Saskatchewan, 1961.

Armstrong, Christopher, "The Politics of Federalism; Ontario's Relations with the Federal Government, 1896-1941," Ph.D., Toronto, 1972.

Atherton, James J., "The Department of Labour and Industrial Relations, 1900-1911," M.A., Carleton, 1972.

Atkinson, David, "Organized Labour and the Laurier Administration: The Fortunes of a Pressure Group," M.A., Carleton, 1957.

Avery, Donald Howard, "Canadian Immigration Policy and the Enemy Alien, 1896-1919: The Anglo-Canadian Perspective" Ph.D., Western Ontario, 1973.

Babcock, Robert Harper, "The A. F. of L. in Canada, 1896-1908: A Study in Labour Imperialism," Ph.D., Duke, 1969.

Bacchi-Ferraro, Carol Lee, "The Ideas of Canadian Suffragists, 1890-1920," M.A., McGill, 1970.

Barber, Marilyn J., "The Ontario Bilingual Schools Issue, 1910-1916," M.A., Queen's, 1964.

Bercuson, David Jay, "Labour in Winnipeg: The Great War and the General Strike," Ph.D., Toronto, 1971.

Bliss, J.W.M., "A Living Profit: Studies in the Social History of Canadian Business, 1883-1911," Ph.D., Toronto, 1972.

Bothwell, Robert, "Loring Christie: The Failure of Bureaucratic Imperialism," Ph.D., Harvard, 1972.

Boudreau, Joseph, "The Enemy Alien Problem in Canada, 1914-1921," Ph.D., U.C.L.A., 1964.

Brown, A. Gordon, "Nova Scotia and the Reciprocity Election of 1911," M.A., Dalhousie, 1971.

Christie, E.A., "The Official Attitudes and Opinions of the Presbyterian Church in Canada with Respect to Public Affairs and Social Problems, 1875-1925," M.A., Toronto, 1955.

Clippingdale, Richard T., "J.S. Willison, Political Journalist: From Liberalism to Independence," Ph.D., Toronto, 1970.

Coutts, Robert M., "The Railway Policy of Sir Wilfrid Laurier: The Grand Trunk Pacific-National Transcontinental," M.A., Toronto, 1968.

Crunican, Rev. Paul E., "The Manitoba School Question and Canadian Federal Politics, 1890-1896: A Study in Church-State Relations," Ph.D., Toronto, 1968.

Eagle, John Andrew, "Sir Robert Borden and the Railway Problem in Canadian Politics, 1911-1920," Ph.D., Toronto, 1972.

Emery, George Neill, "Methodism and the Canadian Prairies, 1896-1914," Ph.D., British Columbia, 1970.

Hallett, Mary E., "The Fourth Earl of Grey as Governor-General of Canada," Ph.D., London, 1969.

Hallowell, Gerald S., "Prohibition in Ontario, 1919-23," M.A., Carleton, 1966.

Heibert, Albert John, "Prohibition in British Columbia," M.A., Simon Fraser, 1969.

Huel, H.J.A., "L'Association Catholique Franco-Canadienne de la Saskatchewan: A Response to Cultural Assimilation," M.A., Saskatchewan (Regina), 1969.

Humphries, Charles W., "The Political Career of Sir James P. Whitney," Ph.D., Toronto, 1966.

LaPierre, Laurier L., "Politics, Race and Religion: Joseph Israel Tarte," Ph.D., Toronto, 1962.

Lawr, Douglas A., "Development of Agricultural Education in Ontario, 1870-1910," Ph.D., Toronto, 1972.

Levitt, Joseph, "The Social Program of the Nationalists of Quebec, 1900-1914," Ph.D., Toronto, 1967.

Lupal, Manoly S., "Relations in Education between the State and the Roman Catholic Church in the Canadian North West with Special Reference to the Provisional District of Alberta from 1880 to 1905," Ph.D., Harvard, 1963.

MacIntosh, Alan W., "The Career of Sir Charles Tupper in Canada, 1864-1900," Ph.D., Toronto, 1959.

Mackenzie, Anthony, "The Rise and Fall of the Farmer Labour Party of Nova Scotia," M.A., Dalhousie, 1969.

Mackinnon, C.S., "The Imperial Fortresses in Canada: Halifax and Esquimalt, 1871-1906," Ph.D., Toronto, 1965.

McLean, Robert Irwin, "A Most Effectual Remedy: Temperance and Prohibition in Alberta, 1875-1915," M.A., Calgary, 1969.

McLeod, K.A., "A History of the Status of the French Language in the Schools of the North West Territories, 1870-1905, and in Saskatchewan, 1905-1934," M.Ed., Saskatchewan, 1966.

Miller, Carman, "The Public Life of Sir Frederick Borden," M.A., Dalhousie, 1964.

Morrison, Terrence R., "The Child and Urban Social Reform in Late Nineteenth Century Ontario, 1875-1900," Ph.D., Toronto, 1970.

Mott, Morris, "The Foreign Peril: Nativism in Winnipeg," M.A., Manitoba, 1970.

Neatby, H.B., "Laurier and the Liberal Party in Quebec: A Study in Political Management," Ph.D., Toronto, 1956.

Nelles, Henry Vivian, "The Politics of Development: Forests, Mines and Hydro-Electric Power in Ontario, 1890-1939," Ph.D., Toronto, 1970.

O'Connell, Martin F., "The Political Ideas of Henri Bourassa," Ph.D., Toronto, 1954.

Oliver, Peter Nesbitt, "The Making of a Provincial Premier, Howard Ferguson and Ontario Politics: 1870-1923," Ph.D., Toronto, 1969.

Orlikow, Lionel, "A Survey of the Reform Movement in Manitoba, 1910-1920," M.A., Manitoba, 1969.

Orr, Allen D., "The Western Federation of Miners and the Royal Commission on Industrial Disputes in 1903," M.A., British Columbia, 1967.

Palmer, Howard, "Responses to Foreign Immigration: Nativism and Ethnic Tolerance in Alberta, 1880-1930," M.A., Alberta, 1970.

Patrick, Michael Joseph, "The Role of Bishop Francis Michael Fallon in the Conflict Between the French Catholics and the Irish Catholics in the Ontario Bilingual Schools Question, 1910-1920," M.A., University of Western Ontario, 1969.

Pinno, Erhard, "Temperance and Prohibition in Saskatchewan," M.A., Saskatchewan (Regina), 1969.

Prang, Margaret, "The Political Career of Newton Wesley Rowell," Ph.D., Toronto, 1959.

Ralston, H.K., "The 1900 Strike of Fraser River Sockeye Salmon Fishermen," M.A., British Columbia, 1965.

Regehr, Theodore David, "The Canadian Northern Railway: Agent of National Growth, 1896-1911," Ph.D., Alberta, 1967.

Reid, John M., "The Erection of the Roman Catholic Archdiocese of Winnipeg," M.A., Manitoba, 1961.

Robertson, Susan Mann, "L'Action Française: L'Appel de la Race," Ph.D., Laval, 1970.

Roy, P.E., "Railways, Politicians and the Development of the City of Vancouver as a Metropolitan Centre, 1886-1929," M.A., Toronto, 1963.

Royce, M.V., "The Contribution of the Methodist Church to Social Welfare in Canada," M.A., Toronto, 1940.

Stamp, Robert M., "The Campaign for Technical Education in Ontario, 1876-1914," Ph.D., Western Ontario, 1970.

Stapells, H.G., "The Recent Consolidation Movement in Canadian Industry," M.A., Toronto, 1922.

Stevens, Paul Douglas, "Laurier and the Liberal Party In Ontario, 1887-1911," Ph.D., Toronto, 1966.

Tennyson, B.D., "The Political Career of Sir William Hearst," M.A., Toronto, 1963.

Tetu, Michel, "Les Premiers Syndicats Catholiques Canadiens, 1900-1921," Ph.D., Laval, 1969.

Thompson, John H., "The Prohibition Question in Manitoba, 1892-1928," M.A., Manitoba, 1969.

Troper, Harold Martin, "Official Canadian Government Encouragement of American Immigration, 1896-1911," Ph.D., Toronto, 1971.

Warner, Catherine L., "Sir James P. Whitney and Sir Robert L. Borden: Relations Between a Conservative Provincial Premier and his Federal Party Leader, 1905-1914," M. Phil., Toronto, 1967.

Willms, A.M., "Sir Robert Borden

at the Paris Peace Conference," M.A., Toronto, 1950.

Wolff, Claudette Bégin, "L'Opinion Publique Québécoise face à l'Immigration," M.A., Montreal, 1970.

ABBREVIATIONS

A.H.R.: American Historical Review
C.A.R.: Canadian Annual Review
C.H.A.: Canadian Historical Association
C.H.A.A.R.: Canadian Historical Association *Annual Report*
C.H.R.: Canadian Historical Review
C.J.E.P.S.: Canadian Journal of Economics and Political Science
C.O.: Colonial Office
D.C.E.R.: Documents on Canadian External Relations
I.W.C.: Imperial War Cabinet
P.A.B.C.: Public Archives of British Columbia
P.A.C.: Public Archives of Canada
P.A.M.: Public Archives of Manitoba
P.A.N.S.: Public Archives of Nova Scotia
P.A.O.: Public Archives of Ontario
R.H.A.F.: Revue d'Histoire de l'Amérique française
U.N.B.: University of New Brunswick

NOTES TO CHAPTER ONE

1. M.C. Urquhart and K.A.H. Buckley, eds., *Historical Statistics of Canada* (Toronto, 1965), 14.

2. H.G.J. Aitken, *American Capital and Canadian Resources* (Cambridge, Mass., 1961), 31-57.

NOTES TO CHAPTER TWO

1. Howard A. Scarrow, *Canada Votes* (New Orleans, 1962), 23.

2. Paul Stevens, "Wilfrid Laurier: Politician," in Marcel Hamelin, ed., *The Political Ideas of the Prime Ministers of Canada* (Ottawa, 1968), 68-86; John W. Dafoe, *Laurier: A Study in Canadian Politics* (Toronto, 1922).

3. P.A.C., Laurier Papers, Laurier to Gregory, 11 November 1904.

4. P.A.C., Willison Papers, Sifton to Willison, 27 August 1907.

5. P.A.C., Laurier Papers, George H. Bertram to Laurier, 2 July 1896; Laurier to J.S. Ewart, 20 April 1896.

6. *Ibid.*, George H. Bertram to Laurier, 27 June 1896.

7. D.C. Harvey, "Fielding's Call to Ottawa," *Dalhousie Review*, XXVIII, 4, 1949, 374-6.

8. P.A.C., Laurier Papers, Willison to Laurier, 25 June 1896. Paul D. Stevens, "Laurier and the Liberal Party in Ontario, 1887-1911," (unpublished Ph.D. thesis, University of Toronto, 1966), 154-7.

9. Laurier L. LaPierre, "Politics, Race and Religion in French Canada: Joseph Israel Tarte," (unpublished

Ph.D. thesis, University of Toronto, 1962).

10. Robert Rumilly, *Henri Bourassa: La Vie Publique d'un Grand Canadien* (Montreal, 1953), 37-8.

11. John W. Dafoe, *Clifford Sifton in Relation to His Times* (Toronto, 1931), 115-16.

12. See John T. Saywell, "The Cabinet of 1896," in F.W. Gibson, ed., *Cabinet Formation and Bicultural Relations: Seven Case Studies* (Royal Commission on Bilingualism and Biculturalism, Ottawa, 1966), I, 87-107.

13. Mgr Langevin à Chanoine Bruchési, 29 juin 1896. Cited in Jean Bruchési, "Sir Wilfrid Laurier et Mgr Bruchési," *Transactions of the Royal Society of Canada*, 1946, I, 6.

14. Paul E. Crunican, "The Manitoba School Question and Canadian Federal Politics, 1890-96: A Study in Church-State Relations" (unpublished Ph.D. thesis, University of Toronto, 1968), 545-613.

15. J.T. Saywell, ed., *Lady Aberdeen's Canadian Journal* (Toronto, 1960), xxv-xxvi.

16. P.A.C., Laurier Papers, J.S. Ewart

to Laurier, 27 June 1896; also R.W. Scott to Laurier, 25 June 1896.

17. *Ibid.*, Fitzpatrick to Laurier, 27 June 1896 and 17 July 1896.

18. *Ibid.*, A.B. Routhier to Laurier, 1 September 1896.

19. O.D. Skelton, *Life and Letters of Sir Wilfrid Laurier* (London, 1922), II, 17.

20. P.A.C., Laurier Papers, Willison to Sifton, 17 August 1896.

21. *Ibid.*, Peter Ryan to Laurier, 21 November 1896, and Wm. McGregor to Laurier, 24 November 1896. See Stevens, "Laurier and the Liberal Party" *op. cit.*, 161-5.

22. *Ibid.*, Dandurand à Laurier, 20 novembre 1896.

23. *Ibid.*, Laurier à Charles Angers, 9 décembre 1896.

24. *Ibid.*, Laurier à Proulx, 23 novembre 1896.

25. *Ibid.*, Proulx à Laurier, 5 octobre 1896.

26. Montréal, 1896.

27. Robert Rumilly, *Histoire de la Province de Québec* (Montréal, n.d.), VIII, 141.

28. P.A.C., Laurier Papers, Tarte à Laurier, 14 janvier 1897.

29. *Ibid.*, Fitzpatrick to Laurier, 21 January 1897.

30. *Ibid.*, Russell to Lord Russell, 30 January 1897.

31. *Ibid.*, Laurier to Russell, 24 February 1897.

32. Bernetta Quinn, *Give Me Souls: A Life of Raphael Cardinal Merry del Val* (Westminster, Md., 1953).

33. P.A.C., Laurier Papers, Mgr Merry del Val to Laurier, 16 June 1897.

34. *Ibid.*, unsigned memo in del Val's hand.

35. *Ibid.*, R.W. Scott to Laurier, 12 July 1897.

36. *Ibid.*, Charles Russell to Laurier, 27 November 1897.

37. *Canada, House of Commons Debate*, 11 May 1898, 5335ff.

38. P.A.C., Fitzpatrick Papers, Laurier to Fitzpatrick, 27 December 1897.

39. Langevin à Bégin, 22 janvier 1898, cited in Rumilly, *op. cit.*, IX, 46.

40. H.B. Neatby, *Laurier and the Liberal Party in Quebec* (Toronto, 1973), 99.

41. P.A.C., Laurier Papers, Laurier to Greenway, 11 February 1898.

42. *Ibid.*, T. Rochon to W.R. Scott, undated.

43. *Ibid.*, T. Rochon à Laurier, 16 février 1899.

44. *Ibid.*, Laurier to A.S. Hardy, January 1897.

45. *Ibid.*, Bruchési à Marchand, 22 novembre 1897.

46. *Ibid.*, Tarte à Laurier, 3 décembre 1898.

47. Louis-Philippe Audet, *Histoire de l'Enseignement au Québec, 1840-1971* (Montreal, 1971), II, 228-38.

48. P.A.C., Laurier Papers, Bruchési à Laurier, 9 juin 1898.

49. Eugène Normand, *Le Libéralisme dans la Province de Québec* (n.p., 1897), 18. See also "Mémoire sur la Question des Écoles du Manitoba: l'Origine de cette Question," *R.H.A.F.*, VI, 3 décembre 1952, 440-42.

50. P.A.C., Laurier Papers, Cardinal Rompolla à Laurier, 5 juin 1899.

51. *Ibid.*, Bruchési à Laurier, 7 juin 1899.

52. *Ibid.*, Merry del Val à Laurier, 1 avril 1904.

53. P.A.C., Denison Papers, Denison to Lord Salisbury, 2 May 1896.

54. *Morning Chronicle*, 6 August 1896.

55. P.A.C., Willison Papers, Laurier to Willison, 29 June 1896.

56. P.A.C., Laurier Papers, Geo. W. Ross to Laurier, 30 March 1896.

57. *Ibid.*, W.S. Kennedy to Laurier, January 1897.

58. *Ibid.*, Laurier to Charlton, 18 January 1897.

59. *Ibid.*, Laurier to Wiman, 21 January 1897.

60. *Ibid.*, Charlton to Laurier, 30 April 1897.

61. P.A.N.S., Sir Frederick Borden Papers, Sydney Fisher to F.W. Borden, Easter Sunday, 1897.

62. *Canada, House of Commons Debate,* 1897, 1891 *et seq.*

63. O.J. McDiarmid, *Commercial Policy in the Canadian Economy* (Cambridge, Mass., 1946), 206-7.

64. *Canada, House of Commons Debates,* 1897, 1132.

65. P.A.C., Denison Papers, Denison to Salisbury, 1 May 1897.

66. J.L. Garvin, *The Life of Joseph Chamberlain* (London, 1934), III, 194.

67. P.A.C., Laurier Papers, Sifton to Laurier, 29 April 1897; R.C. Brown, *Canada's National Policy, 1883-1900* (Princeton, 1964), 262-80.

68. *Report of the Royal Commission on the Liquor Traffic,* Ottawa, 1894-95.

69. R.E. Spence, *Prohibition in Canada* (Toronto, 1919), 231-36.

70. Richard A. Olmsted, *Canadian Constitutional Decisions of the Judicial Committee of the Privy Council* (Ottawa, 1954), I, 343.

71. Spence, *op. cit.,* 245.

72. *Canada, Sessional Papers,* XXXIII, 14, 1899, no. 20, 1-312.

73. *Ibid.,* x.

74. P.A.C., Laurier Papers, Laurier to Spence, 4 March 1899, cited in Spence, *op. cit.,* 350-52.

75. *Winnipeg Tribune,* 4 April 1902, cited in John H. Thompson, "The Prohibition Question in Manitoba, 1892-1928" (unpublished M.A. thesis, University of Manitoba, 1969), 45.

76. J.S. Woodsworth, "Foreign Immigrants and Temperance," *Christian Guardian,* 13 April 1910.

77. Nellie L. McClung, *The Stream Runs Fast* (Toronto, 1945), 67-68.

78. See Edith Luke, "Woman Suffrage in Canada," *Canadian Magazine,* V, 1895, 335; S.G.E. McKee, *Jubilee History of the Ontario Woman's Christian Temperance Union, 1877-1927* (Whitby, n.d.), 43.

79. For the relationship between prohibition, the social gospel, and general reform in Manitoba, see Lionel Orlikow, "The Reform Movement in Manitoba, 1910-1915," *Transactions of the Manitoba Historical and Scientific Society,* series III, 16, 1961, 50-61; A.S. Sutherland, *The Kingdom of God and the Problems of To-Day* (Toronto, 1898).

80. William Magney, "The Methodist Church and the National Gospel, 1884-1914," *Bulletin of the Archives of the United Church,* 1968, 3-95.

81. *Presbyterian Witness,* 9 October 1907, cited in E.R. Forbes, "Prohibition and the Social Gospel in Nova Scotia," *Acadiensis,* I, 1, 1971, 16-17; see also Salem Bland, *James Henderson, D.D.* (Toronto, 1926).

NOTES TO CHAPTER THREE

1. John Hobson, *Imperialism: A Study* (London, 1902).

2. For a brilliant critique of Hobson and his Marxist imitators, see Elie Kedourie, *Nationalism in Africa and Asia* (New York, 1970), 4-21.

3. John Edward Kendle, *The Colonial and Imperial Conferences 1887-1911* (London, 1967), cited 20.

4. W.L. Langer, *The Diplomacy of Im-*

perialism, 1890-1902 (New York, 1935), 78.

5. Bernard Semmel, Imperialism and Social Reform (London, 1960), cited 25.

6. W.E. Leuchtenberg, "Progressivism and Imperialism: The Progressive Movement and Foreign Policy, 1898-1916," Mississippi Valley Historical Review, XXXIX, December 1952; Walter LeFeber, The New Empire: An Interpretation of American Expansion 1860-98 (Ithaca, 1963).

7. Heinz Gollwitzer, Europe in the Age of Imperialism, 1880-1914 (London, 1969), provides the best short account of the new imperialism.

8. Thomas F. Gossett, Race: The History of an Idea in America (New York, 1965), 310-38.

9. Carl Berger, The Sense of Power (Toronto, 1970), 260-61.

10. Charles Carrington, Rudyard Kipling: His Life and Work (London, 1955), 398.

11. Goldwin Smith, Canada and the Canadian Question (Toronto, 1891); George Parkin, Imperial Federation (London, 1892); J.P. Tardivel, Pour La Patrie (Montreal, 1895); Edmond de Nevers, L'Avenir du Peuple canadien-français (Montreal, 1894).

12. "G," "Current Events," Queen's Quarterly, V, summer 1898, 328.

13. P.A.C., Minto Papers, Minto to Elliott, 26 February 1899.

14. See R.C. Brown, "The Nationalism of the National Policy," in Peter Russell, ed., Nationalism in Canada (Toronto, 1966), 155-63.

15. See S.F. Wise and R.C. Brown, Canada Views the United States (Toronto, 1967), ch. 3; Carl Berger, The Sense of Power (Toronto, 1970), ch. 6; and Norman Penlington, Canada and Imperialism, 1896-99 (Toronto, 1965), passim.

16. Canada, House of Commons Debates, 18 March 1902, 1338-39.

17. D.R. Annett, The British Preference in Commercial Policy (Toronto, 1948), cited 38.

18. P.A.C., Minto Papers, Willison to Minto, 18 July 1903.

19. Annett, op. cit., 34-45; Fred W. Field, Capital Investments in Canada (Toronto, 1911), 22.

20. Garvin, Chamberlain, op. cit., III, 192.

21. Berger, op. cit., 121; see also C.C. Berger, ed., Imperial Relations in the Age of Laurier (Toronto, 1969), ix.

22. W. Sandford Evans, "Empire Day: A Detailed History of its Origin and Inception," Canadian Magazine, XIII, July 1899, cited 277.

23. Kendle, op. cit., cited 23.

24. Penlington, op. cit., cited 56.

25. Skelton, op. cit., cited II, 73.

26. Daily Mail, 7 July 1897.

27. Maurice Ollivier, The Colonial and Imperial Conferences from 1887 to 1937, (Ottawa, 1954), I, 1-39.

28. Ibid., 140.

29. John Buchan, Lord Minto (London, 1924), 127.

30. Skelton, op. cit., cited II, 82.

31. P.A.C., Pope Papers, Copy, Foreign Office Confidential Print 7135, Pauncefote to Salisbury, 10 March 1898. (Hereafter Confidential Print 7135)

32. Laurier proposed the reciprocal abolition of Canadian and American restrictive alien labour legislation. The proposal doubtless reflected Canada's recognition of the developing links between labour organizations in Canada and the United States and, more important, the increasing dependence of Canadian industry upon skilled labour imported from the United States.

33. Confidential Print 7135, Pauncefote to Salisbury, 10 March 1898.

34. Canada, House of Commons Debates, 7 March 1898, 1277.

35. C042/854, Foreign Office to Colonial Office, 10 December 1897.

36. P.A.C., Laurier Papers, Dobell to Laurier, 24 July 1898.

37. P.A.C., Pope Papers, Diary, 25 August 1898.

38. University of Toronto Library, Charlton Papers, Diary, 7 October 1898.

39. Confidential Print 7135, Herschell to Salisbury, 7 February 1899.

40. P.A.C., Willison Papers, Laurier to Willison, 15 February 1899. A detailed description of the negotiations and failure of the Commission may be found in R.C. Brown, *Canada's National Policy, op. cit.*, chs. 10-11.

41. Penlington, *op. cit.*, 218-20.

42. Rumilly, *Henri Bourassa, op. cit.*, 47.

43. *Globe,* 4 October 1899.

44. P.A.C. Laurier Papers, Carling to Laurier, 12 October 1899.

45. Penlington, *op. cit.*, 235-36, 271-72.

46. Robert J.D. Page, "Canada and the Imperial Idea in the Boer War Years," *Journal of Canadian Studies,* V, 1, 1970, 33-49.

47. Marie Dronsart, "Cecil Rhodes," *La Revue Canadienne,* XXXVII, janvier 1900, 25-55; Marie Dronsart, "Le Président Kruger," *ibid.,* XXXVII, février 1900, 87-108; these two articles were reprinted from the Paris journal *Correspondant.* But they were highly recommended by the *Revue's* editor whose own sympathies were expressed in Alphonse Leclaire, "La Guerre de Transvaal et l'Opinion Anglaise," *ibid.,* XXXVII, juin 1900, 405-20. See also Jean-Guy Pelletier, "La presse canadienne-française et la guerre des Boers," *Recherches Sociographiques,* IV, 3, 1963, 337-50.

48. *La Presse,* 5 October 1899, cited in Pelletier, *op. cit.*, 341.

49. Penlington, *op cit.,* 258, 272.

50. P.A.C., Dandurand Papers, Laurier à Dandurand, 4 novembre 1899.

51. P.A.C., Willison Papers, Laurier to Willison, 14 October 1899.

52. *Globe,* 9 January 1900.

53. P.A.C., Laurier Papers, Bourassa to Laurier, 29 October 1899.

54. W. Sandford Evans, *The Canadian Contingents and Canadian Imperialism* (Toronto, 1901); T.G. Marquis, *Canada's Sons on Kopje and Veldt* (Toronto, 1900); Desmond Morton, "Colonel Otter and the First Canadian Contingent in South Africa, 1899-1900," in Michael Cross and Robert Bothwell, eds., *Policy by Other Means* (Toronto, 1972), 97-120.

55. H.B. Neatby, "Laurier and Imperialism," in Berger, ed., *Imperial Relations, op. cit.*, 6.

56. Skelton, *op. cit.*, II, 107.

57. Cornell University, Smith Papers, Bourassa to Smith, 20 January 1900.

58. R.C. Brown, "Goldwin Smith and Anti-Imperialism" in Berger, ed., *Imperial Relations, op. cit.*, 10-22.

59. Cornell University, Smith Papers, Bourassa to Smith, 12 July 1900; Smith to Mount Stephen, 31 August 1900. See also Skelton, *op. cit.*, II, 102-18, and Mason Wade, *The French Canadians, 1760-1967* (Toronto, 1967), I, 479-87.

60. I.O.D.E., *Golden Jubilee, 1900-1950* (Toronto, 1950), 10.

61. P.A.C., Minto Papers, Chamberlain to Minto, 2 March 1900.

62. *Ibid.,* Minto to Chamberlain, 14 April, 1900; Laurier memo, 9 April 1900.

63. For a full discussion of the incident see Richard H. Wilde, "Joseph Chamberlain's Proposal of an Imperial Council in March, 1900," *C.H.R.,* XXXVII, 3, 1956, 225-46.

64. Ollivier, ed., *op. cit.,* vol. I.

65. Kendle, *op. cit.*, 39-54.

66. Skelton, *op. cit.*, II, 289.

67. P.A.C., Laurier Papers, Laurier to Van Horne, 24 March 1899.

68. C042/869, Chamberlain to Minto, in Minto to Chamberlain, 19 July 1899.

69. C042/868, Wingfield minutes on Minto to Chamberlain, 19 July 1899.

70. P.A.C., Laurier Papers, Laurier to Tarte, 12 July 1899.

71. C.S. Campbell, Jr., *Anglo-American Understanding, 1898-1903* (Baltimore, 1957), 240.

72. This point is ably argued in Campbell, *op. cit.*, ch. 12.

73. Dafoe, *Sifton, op. cit.*, 221.

74. This opinion was clearly shared by all the Americans involved. Some of its strength doubtless came from damaging British admissions of weakness. "I have heard from Laurier, and Pauncefote, directly," Secretary Hay wrote, "that they know they have no case" (cited in Campbell, *op. cit.*, 333). See also C.C. Tansill, *Canadian-American Relations, 1875-1911* (New Haven, 1943), 239.

75. "There was ample evidence to sustain the majority in favour of an unbroken coast strip belonging to the United States" (F.W. Gibson, "The Alaskan Boundary Dispute," *C.H.A.A.R.*, 1945, 36).

76. Cited in Dafoe, *Sifton, op. cit.*, 233.

77. *Canada, House of Commons Debates*, 23 October 1903, 14817.

78. A.C. Gluek, Jr., "Pilgrimages to Ottawa," Canadian Historical Association, *Historical Papers*, 1968, cited 68.

NOTES TO CHAPTER FOUR

1. *Canada: The Land of Opportunity*, issued by the authority of the Minister of the Interior (Ottawa, 1909), 20.

2. David C. Corbett, *Canada's Immigration Policy* (Toronto, 1957), 128.

3. W.A Mackintosh, *The Economic Background of Dominion-Provincial Relations* (Toronto, 1964), 40-45.

4. J.A. Hobson, *Canada To-Day* (London, 1906), 6.

5. *Canada, House of Commons Debates*, 16 April 1903, 1411.

6. V.C. Fowke, *The National Policy and the Wheat Economy* (Toronto, 1957), 70-71.

7. A.S. Morton, *History of Prairie Settlement* (Toronto, 1938), cited 106.

8. Harold Innis, "Industrialism and Settlement in Western Canada," in his *Problems of Staple Production in Canada* (Toronto, 1933), 94.

9. E.M. Pomeroy, *William Saunders and his Five Sons* (Toronto, 1956), 141-44.

10. V.C. Fowke, *Canadian Agricultural Policy: Its Historical Pattern* (Toronto, 1947), 233-37.

11. L.H. Newman, *The History and Present Status of Wheat Production in Canada* (Ottawa, 1928), 77.

12. D.A. MacGibbon, *The Canadian Grain Trade* (Toronto, 1932), 81-82.

13. "S," "The North West Boom," *Queen's Quarterly*, X, October 1902, 240.

14. J.W. Longley, *Second Annual Report of the Canadian Club of Winnipeg, 1906* (Winnipeg, 1907), 49.

15. George Parkin, *The Great Dominion* (London, 1894), 39-41.

16. Dafoe, *Sifton, op. cit.*, cited 104.

17. *Ibid.*, 105.

18. James B. Hedges, *Building the*

Canadian West (New York, 1939), 126ff.

19. *Canada. House of Commons. Journals* 1900, 308.

20. *Canada. House of Commons Debates.* 1897, 4071.

21. Donald Avery, "Canadian Immigration Policy and the Foreign Navvy, 1896-1914" (unpublished paper presented to the C.H.A. June 1972).

22. *Revised Statutes of Canada.* ch. 54 (Ottawa, 1903).

23. James Mavor, *Report to the Board of Trade on the North West of Canada. with Special Reference to Wheat Production for Export* (London, 1904), 26.

24. Sarah Ellen Roberts, *Alberta Homestead: Chronicle of a Pioneer Family* (Austin, 1971), 149-53.

25. Elizabeth Ruthig, "Homestead Days in the McCord District," *Saskatchewan History.* VII, 1, 1954, 24. See also C.A. Dawson, *Pioneering in the Prairie Provinces: The Social Side of the Settlement Process* (Toronto, 1940); Wallace Stegner, *Wolf Willow* (New York, 1962); John Warkentin, "Time and Place in the Western Interior," *Artscanada.* 169/170, early autumn, 1972, 20-37.

26. Allan R. Turner, "Pioneering Farm Experiences," *Saskatchewan History.* VIII, 2, 1955, 41-55; W.L. Morton, "The Significance of Site in the Settlement of the Canadian and American Wests," *Agricultural History.* XXV, July 1951, 101.

27. Robert England, *The Colonization of Western Canada* (London, 1936), 69.

28. L.G. Reynolds, *The British Immigrant* (Toronto, 1935).

29. J.S. Woodsworth, "Pump Them In—But Whom?" *Christian Guardian.* 27 November 1907, 10.

30. Basil Stewart, *"No English Need Apply" or Canada as a Field for Immigration* (London, 1909).

31. The literature on the Barr Colony is extensive and controversial. For a good short objective account, see Edmund H. Oliver, "The Coming of the Barr Colonists," *C.H.A.A.R.*, 1926, 65-87; critical accounts of Barr's activities are numerous but G.E. Lloyd's autobiography, *The Trail of 1903* (Lloydminster, 1940), provides the basis for most of them including C. Wetton, *The Promised Land* (Lloydminster, n.d.). Barr is defended in an informative though naive book by Helen Evans Reid, *All Silent. All Damned* (Toronto, 1969).

32. *Toronto News.* 14 April 1903, cited in Reid, *op. cit..* 70-71.

33. Oliver, *op. cit..* 76.

34. *Manitoba Free Press.* 23 April 1903, cited in Reid, *op. cit..* 73.

35. Wetton, *op. cit..* cited 24.

36. For an objective account of these events see Clive Tallant, "The Break with Barr," *Saskatchewan History.* VI, 2, 1953, 41-46.

37. Clive Tallant, "The North West Mounted Police and the Barr Colony," *Saskatchewan History.* VII, 2, 1954, 41-46.

38. Arthur E. Copping, *The Golden Land: The True Story of British Settlers in Canada* (Toronto, n.d.), 71-85.

39. Karel Denis Bicha, "The Plains Farmer and the Prairie Frontier, 1897-1914," *Proceedings of the American Philosophical Society.* 109, 6, 1965, 398-406.

40. P.A.C., Immigration Files, 76/140, 138202, J. Baril to J.M. McLaughlin, 26 April 1908. Cited in Harold Martin Troper, "Official Canadian Encouragement of American Immigration, 1896-1911" (unpublished Ph.D. thesis, University of Toronto, 1971), 67.

41. For an example of the ease with which some settlers passed back and forth across the border, see Laura

Salverson, *The Confessions of an Immigrant's Daughter* (Montreal, 1949).

42. Hedges, *op. cit.*, 135.

43. See Hedges, *op. cit.*, 135-37 and Bicha, *op. cit.*, 119-20, for a discussion of this literature.

44. Hedges, *op. cit.*, cited 142.

45. *Ibid.*, 145-49.

46. Bicha, *op. cit.*, 432.

47. See Duncan M. McDougall, "Immigration into Canada, 1851-1920," *C.J.E.P.S.*, XXVII, 2, 1961, 167-70, for a discussion of this problem.

48. Bicha, *op. cit.*, 438-39, and Troper, *op. cit.*, 270-95. Troper argues that Bicha exaggerates the size of the U.S. exodus from Canada. His argument is well made, though the unsatisfactory character of available statistics necessarily makes it inconclusive.

49. Paul Sharp, *Agrarian Revolt in Western Canada* (Minneapolis, 1948), cited 10.

50. P.A.C., Immigration Files, 76/115, 72552, L.M. Fortier to W.E. Du Bois, March 4, 1911. Cited in Harold Martin Troper, "The Creek-Negroes of Oklahoma and Canadian Immigration, 1909-11," *C.H.R.*, LXIII, 3, 1972, 286.

51. *Ibid.*, 282-83.

52. Paul F. Sharp, "When Our West Moved North," *A.H.R.*, LV, 2, 1950, 290.

53. Mabel F. Timlin, "Canada's Immigration Policy, 1896-1910," *C.J.E.P.S.*, XXVI, 4, 1960, 520-21.

54. Dafoe, *op. cit.*, 142.

55. James Mavor, *My Windows on the Street of the World* (London and Toronto, 1923), II, 2.

56. *Ibid.*, 20.

57. George Woodcock and Ivan Avakumovic, *The Doukhobors* (Toronto, 1968), cited 194.

58. *Canada, House of Commons Debates*, 1901, 2439.

59. This account follows Woodcock and Avakumovic's excellent study. See also J.F.C. Wright, *Slava Bohu* (New York, 1940) for a more popular and highly sympathetic treatment. Harry B. Hawthorn, ed., *The Doukhobors of British Columbia* (Vancouver and Toronto, 1955) is also excellent.

60. Vladimir J. Kaye, *Early Ukrainian Settlements in Canada, 1895-1900* (Toronto, 1964), cited p. 3. See pp. 3-131 on Oleskow's role.

61. Paul Yuzyk, *The Ukrainians in Manitoba* (Toronto, 1953), 31.

62. J.G. MacGregor, *Vilni Zemli–Free Lands* (Toronto, 1969), cited 186.

63. Kaye, *op. cit.*, 351.

64. Marilyn Barber, "Introduction," in J.S. Woodsworth, *Strangers Within Our Gates* (Toronto, 1972), xiv-xv. See also William Kurelek, "Another Person with Me," *Exile*, I, 2, 53-72.

65. Ralph Connor, *The Foreigner* (Toronto, 1909), 87; Rev. (Captain) Wellington Bridgman, *Breaking Prairie Sod* (Toronto, 1920), 163.

66. Mavor, *Report, op. cit.*, 15.

67. Ol'ha Woycenko, *The Ukrainians in Canada* (Ottawa and Winnipeg, 1967), 164.

68. MacGregor, *op. cit.*, 178-82 and 198-203.

69. Mavor, *My Windows, op. cit.*, I, 365-68; Woycenko, *op. cit.*, 66-67.

70. *Ibid.*, 88.

71. J.S. Woodsworth, ed., *Ukrainian Rural Communities*, Report of Investigation by Bureau of Social Research, Governments of Manitoba, Saskatchewan, and Alberta (Winnipeg, 1917), 139.

72. J.W. Sparling, "Introduction," in J.S. Woodsworth, *Strangers Within Our Gates* (Toronto, 1909), 4.

73. Arthur R. Ford, "The Foreign Question Again," *Christian Guardian*, 6 January 1909. See also George

Neil Emery, "Methodism and the Canadian Prairies, 1896-1914" (unpublished Ph.D. thesis, University of British Columbia, 1970), ch. 2; and R.G. MacBeth, *Our Task in Canada* (Toronto, 1912), 21.

74. Woodsworth, *Strangers, op. cit.,* 135.

75. C.A. Dawson, *Group Settlement: Ethnic Communities in Western Canada* (Toronto, 1936).

76. Victor Peters, *All Things Common: The Hutterian Way of Life* (New York, 1971), cited p. 47.

77. W.S. Waddell, "Frank Oliver and *The Bulletin,*" *Alberta Historical Review,* V, 1957, 1-12; *Canada, House of Commons Debates,* 1901, 2939.

78. Timlin *op. cit.,* 523.

79. *Canada, House of Commons Debates,* 1907-8, 7004-5.

80. *Ibid.,* 1911, 5915.

81. *Canadian Annual Review, 1907* (Toronto, 1908), 383-84.

82. Timlin, *op. cit.,* 524.

83. Howard Palmer, "Responses to Foreign Immigration: Nativism and Ethnic Tolerance in Alberta, 1880-1930" (unpublished M.A. thesis, University of Alberta, 1970), cited 210.

84. "Report of the Royal Commission on Chinese and Japanese Immigration," *Canada, Sessional Papers,* 1902, no. 54.

85. Robert Joseph Gowan, "Canada and the Myth of the Japan Market, 1896-1911," *Pacific Historical Review,* XXXIX, 1, 1970, 63-83.

86. G.V. La Forest, *Disallowance and Reservation of Provincial Legislation* (Ottawa, 1955), 66.

87. J.A. Maxwell, *Federal Subsidies to Provincial Governments in Canada* (Cambridge, Mass., 1937), 109-11.

88. P.A.C., Laurier Papers, Silvertz to Laurier, 29 July 1907.

89. Robert E. Wynne, "American La-

bor Leaders and the Vancouver Anti-Oriental Riots," *Pacific Northwest Quarterly,* LVII, 4, 1966, 176-78.

90. P.A.C., Grey Papers, Laurier to Grey, 10 September 1907.

91. *Ibid.,* Grey to Laurier, 27 December 1907.

92. R. McGregor Dawson, *William Lyon Mackenzie King* (Toronto, 1958), 146; Margaret Ormsby, *British Columbia: A History* (Toronto, 1958), 350-53; Mary E. Hallett, "A Governor-General's Views on Oriental Immigration to British Columbia, 1904-11," *B.C. Studies,* 14, Summer 1972, 51-72.

93. *Report of W.L. Mackenzie King, C.M.G., Commissioner Appointed to Enquire into the Methods by which Oriental Labourers have been Induced to Come to Canada* (Ottawa, 1908).

94. See Charles Woodsworth, *Canada and the Orient* (Toronto, 1941); John Norris, *Strangers Entertained* (Vancouver, 1971), 209-29.

95. Eric W. Morse, "Some Aspects of the Komagata Maru Affair, 1914," *C.H.A.A.R.,* 1936, 100-8; Ormsby, *op. cit.,* 369-70.

96. *Social Service Congress, Ottawa, 1914,* The Social Service Council of Canada (Toronto, 1914), 257.

97. Arthur R. Ford, "The Foreign Question Again," *Christian Guardian,* 6 June 1909.

98. J.S. Woodsworth, "Foreign Immigrants and Temperance," *Christian Guardian,* 13 April 1910.

99. James Gray, *Red Lights on the Prairies* (Toronto, 1971); C.S. Clark, *Of Toronto the Good* (Montreal, 1898), 86ff.

100. J.S. Woodsworth, *Strangers, op. cit.,* 165-66.

101. *Industrial Canada,* March 1910.

102. Goldwin Smith, *Reminiscences* (New York, 1910), 414.

103. Samuel E. Moffitt, *The Americani-*

zation of Canada (New York, 1907).

104. Robert Sloan, "The Canadian West: Americanization or Canadianization?" *Alberta Historical Review.* Winter 1968, 1-7.

105. *Canada. House of Commons Debates.* 1903, 6562.

106. *Ibid..* 6591.

107. See, J.T.M. Anderson, *The Education of New Canadians* (Toronto, 1918).

108. J.S. Woodsworth, "The Stranger Within Our Gates," *Methodist Magazine.* July 1905, 36.

109. Robert J.C. Stead, *The Empire Builders and Other Poems* (Toronto, 1908), 15.

110. Connor, *The Foreigner. op. cit.,* n.p.

111. There is a good discussion of some attitudes to immigration in Berger, *The Sense of Power, op. cit.:* we have also been helped by an unpublished paper by Howard Palmer, "Elite Responses to Foreign Immigration in English Canada 1896-1931," York University, 1970.

112. George Foster, "Some Problems of Empire," *United Empire.* December 1912, 957.

113. William Maxwell, *Canada Today* (London, 1911), 14-15.

114. *Canada. House of Commons Debates.* 1899, 8527-41.

115. *Canada. House of Commons Debates.* 1904, 6182.

116. George Pelletier, *L'Immigration canadienne* (Montreal, 1913). See also Claudette Bégin-Wolff, "L'Opinion Publique Québécoise Face à l'Immigration, 1906-13" (unpublished M.A. thesis, Université de Montréal, 1970); Olivar Asselin, *L'Emigration Belge et Française au Canada* (Ottawa, 1913).

117. *Canada. House of Commons Debates.* 1905, I, 1421-22.

118. L.G. Thomas, *The Liberal Party in Alberta* (Toronto, 1959), 3-20.

119. P.A.C., Laurier Papers, Sifton to Laurier, 22 January 1905.

120. M.S. Lupal, "Relations in Education between the State and the Roman Catholic Church in the Canadian North West with Special Reference to the Provisional District of Alberta from 1880-1905" (unpublished Ph.D. thesis, Harvard University, 1963).

121. P.A.C., Fitzpatrick Papers, Evêque de St-Albert à Mgr Sbarretti, 4 octobre 1903.

122. G.R. Cook, "Church, Schools and Politics in Manitoba, 1902-12," *C.H.R..* XXXIX, 1, March 1958, 1-23.

123. P.A.C., Willison Papers, Laurier to Willison, 7 June 1904.

124. P.A.C., R.W. Scott Papers, Scott to Mgr Sbarretti, 11 October 1904.

125. Dafoe, *op. cit..* 280.

126. P.A.C., Fitzpatrick Papers, Apostolic Delegate to Fitzpatrick, 5 March 1904.

127. *Ibid.,* Apostolic Delegate to Fitzpatrick, 9 January 1905.

128. *Canada. House of Commons Debates.* 1905, I, 1458-59.

129. P.A.C., Laurier Papers, Willison to Laurier, 9 March 1905.

130. *Canada. House of Commons Debates.* 1905, II, 3252-84; V, 8751-91.

131. P.A.C., Fitzpatrick Papers, N.D. Beck to Fitzpatrick, 7 August 1905; *Le Canada.* 13 juin 1905.

132. P.A.C., Laurier Papers, Laurier to Gregory, 11 November 1904.

133. P.A.C., Willison Papers, Willison to Borden, 22 April 1905.

134. Armand Lavergne, *Les Écoles du Nord Ouest* (Montreal, 1907), 18.

135. Emery, *op. cit..* cited 20.

136. Evelyn Eager, "Our Pioneers Say," *Saskatchewan History.* VI, 1, 1953, cited 2.

137. A.S. Morton, *History of Prairie Set-*

tlement. op. cit.. cited 141.

138. Mavor, *Report. op. cit..* 26.

139. W.A. Mackintosh, *Prairie Settlement: The Geographic Setting* (Toronto, 1934), 39-74.

140. N. Jeffs, *Homes and Careers in Canada* (London, 1914), 132.

141. J.B. Bickersteth, *The Land of Open Doors* (Toronto, 1914), 11.

NOTES TO CHAPTER FIVE

1. Henry J. Morgan and Lawrence J. Burpee, *Canadian Life in Town and Country* (London, 1905), 238.

2. *Ibid..* 241. See also F.W. Watt, "The Theme of Canada's Century, 1896-1912," *Dalhousie Review.* XXXVIII, 1958-59, 154-66.

3. Mackintosh, *The Economic Background of Dominion-Provincial Relations. op. cit.,* 48.

4. *Ibid.,* 51.

5. *Ibid..* 52-53. A fairly complete picture of the extent of industrialization in Nova Scotia and of the stiff competition from manufacturers in central Canada may be found in *Nova Scotia. Report of the Commission on Hours of Labour. 1910.* 64-121. See also T.W. Acheson, "The National Policy and the Industrialization of the Maritimes, 1880-1910," *Acadiensis.* I Spring, 1972, 3-28.

6. *Labour Gazette.* September, 1902, 138.

7. W.H. Merritt, *Notes on the Possibilities of Iron and Steel Production in Ontario* (Toronto, 1892), 12. The Bureau of Mines *Report* for 1892 added that "Ontario is singular in being almost alone among the great commonwealths of our continent without a blast furnace for the production of metallic iron" (13).

8. *Ontario. Department of Lands and Forests. Annual Report of the Bureau of Mines.* 1891, 4.

9. See *Report of the Bureau of Mines.* 1910, 10, and S.A. Pain, *Three Miles of Gold* (Toronto, 1960), 17-18.

10. *Report of the Bureau of Mines.* 1906, 10.

11. See, for example, *Report of the Bureau of Mines.* 1906, 17.

12. M. van Every, "Francis Hector Clerque and the Rise of Sault Ste. Marie as an Industrial Centre," *Ontario History.* LVI, 1964, cited 197.

13. H.V. Nelles, "The Politics of Development: Forests, Mines and Hydro Electric Development in Ontario, 1890-1939" (unpublished Ph.D. thesis, University of Toronto, 1970), cited 244. See also H.V. Nelles, "Empire Ontario," in Donald Swainson, ed., *Oliver Mowat's Ontario* (Toronto, 1972), 174-88.

14. See O.W. Main, *The Canadian Nickel Industry* (Toronto, 1955), chs. 1-5.

15. William Kilbourn, *The Elements Combined* (Toronto, 1960), 64-66.

16. H.G. Stapells, "The Recent Consolidation Movement in Canadian Industry" (unpublished M.A. thesis, University of Toronto, 1922), cited 11.

17. Stapells, *op. cit.,* 12-13, 18-34. For an excellent description of the formation of STELCO, see Kilbourn, *op. cit..* ch. 5. The interlocking directorates that emerged from the early stages of the movement are outlined in Nathaniel S. Fineberg, "The Canadian Financial Triangle," *Moody's Magazine.*

VIII, November, 1909, 374-81.

18. Stapells, *op. cit.*, cited 59-60.

19. *Ibid.*, 63. The role of the promoter is traced in detail in chapters 4-7 of this thesis. Kilbourn's sketch of Max Aitken's promotion of STELCO is equally instructive (ch. 5, *The Elements Combined*). See also A.J.P. Taylor, *Beaverbrook* (London, 1972), chs. 1-3.

20. Beaverbrook Library, Beaverbrook Papers, Aitken to Borden, 4 July 1911. We are grateful to Professor J.L. Granatstein for bringing this letter to our attention.

21. Stapells, *op. cit., 206.*

22. *Canada, House of Commons Debates,* 18 January 1910, 2058-59.

23. *Ibid.*, 26 April 1910, 7795-98.

24. *Industrial Canada,* November, 1905, 261.

25. *Ontario. Annual Report of the Minister of Education,* 1899, xxii.

26. Robert M. Stamp, "The Campaign for Technical Education in Ontario, 1876-1914" (unpublished Ph.D. thesis, University of Western Ontario, 1970), *passim.* See also, J.D. Wilson, R.M. Stamp, L.P. Audet, *Canadian Education: A History* (Toronto, 1970), 314-25.

27. Dawson, *King, op. cit.,* 200-1.

28. Stamp, *op. cit.,* 275-76.

29. J.C. Hopkins, *The Canadian Annual Review, 1919* (Toronto, 1920), 530-31. Hereafter *C.A.R.*

30. R.S. Lambert and Paul Pross, *Renewing Nature's Wealth* (Toronto, 1967), 150-201.

31. Robert Craig Brown, "The Doctrine of Usefulness: Natural Resource and National Parks Policy in Canada, 1887-1914," in J.G. Nelson, ed., *Canadian Parks in Perspective* (Montreal, 1970), 46-62.

32. F.J. Thorpe, "Historical Perspective on 'Resources for Tomorrow' Conference," in *Resources for Tomorrow*

(Ottawa, 1961), I, 2-3.

33. Samuel P. Hays, *Conservation and the Gospel of Efficiency: The Progressive Conservation Movement, 1890-1920* (2nd ed., New York, 1972), 261-76.

34. Dafoe, *op. cit.,* 347-48.

35. See C. Ray Smith and David R. Witty, "Conservation, Resources and Environment: An Exposition and Critical Evaluation of the Commission of Conservation, Canada," *PLAN,* XI, 1, 1970, 55-70, and XI, 3, 1972, 199-216, for an excellent summary of the Commission's work.

36. Commission of Conservation, *Annual Report,* 1910 (Ottawa, 1910), 16.

37. Commission of Conservation, *Lands, Fisheries and Game, Minerals* (Ottawa, 1911), 406. Cited in Smith and Witty, *op. cit.,* 199.

38. *Conservation,* VI, 12, 47. Mr. Lloyd Evans supplied this quotation.

39. P.A.C., Laurier Papers, Sifton to Templeman, 5 February 1910; Dafoe, *op. cit.,* 446-47.

40. Morris Zaslow, *The Opening of the Canadian North, 1870-1914* (Toronto, 1971), 197-98.

41. C. Gordon Hewitt, *The Conservation of the Wild Life of Canada* (New York, 1921), 15.

42. Commission of Conservation, *Annual Report, 1912* (Ottawa, 1912), 148.

43. Alan H. Armstrong, "Thomas Adams and the Commission of Conservation," in L.O. Gertler, ed., *Planning the Canadian Environment* (Montreal, 1968), 19-35.

44. *Canada, House of Commons Debates,* 1921, IV, 3959-60. Dafoe, *op. cit.,* 452-55.

45. *Canada Year Book, 1932* (Ottawa, 1933), 103.

46. Commission of Conservation, *Annual Report.* 1915 (Ottawa, 1915), 63.

47. J.A. Hobson, *Canada To-Day* (Lon-

don, 1906), 14-15; See also Alan F.J. Artibise, "An Urban Environment: The Process of Growth in Winnipeg, 1874-1914" (unpublished paper presented to the C.H.A., June 1972).

48. J.G. MacGregor, *Northwest of Sixteen* (Edmonton, 1968 edition), 155-56; See also J.M.S. Careless, "Aspects of Urban Life in the West, 1870-1914," in A.W. Rasporich and H.C. Klassen, *Prairie Perspectives* 2 (Toronto, 1973), 25-40

49. C.F. Galloway, *The Call of the West* (London, 1916), 44.

50. S.D. Clark, *The Social Development of Canada* (Toronto, 1941), cited 400.

51. *Ibid.*, 420. Appalling social conditions in city slums were not confined to Toronto or to the older eastern cities generally. See, for example, J.S. Woodsworth's letter to the *Manitoba Free Press*, 12 March 1909, grimly detailing the daily life of "one little foreign girl," cited in K.W. McNaught, *A Prophet in Politics* (Toronto, 1959), 56-57, and Woodsworth, *Strangers Within Our Gates* (Toronto, 1909), *passim.*

52. C.S. Clark, *Of Toronto The Good: A Social Study* (Montreal, 1898).

53. P.A.C., Woodsworth Papers, 28, "Some Aspects of the Immigration Problem" in *The Young Women Of Canada* (December, 1909).

54. I. Bain, "The Role of J.J. Kelso in Launching the Child Welfare Movement of Ontario," (M.S.W. thesis, University of Toronto, 1935).

55. See Herbert Brown Ames, *The City Below the Hill* (Toronto, 1972) with an introduction by P.F.W. Rutherford.

56. See J.S. Woodsworth, *Strangers Within Our Gates, op. cit.*, with an introduction by Marilyn Barber. On the work of All Peoples' Mission, see George Neill Emery, "Methodism and the Canadian Prairies, 1896-

1914: The Dynamics of an Institution in a New Environment," (unpublished Ph.D. thesis, University of British Columbia, 1970), ch. 8; see also "City Mission Work," *Christian Guardian*, December 20, 1899, 248.

57. T.R. Morrison, "The Child and Urban Social Reform in Late Nineteenth Century Ontario, 1875-1900" (unpublished Ph.D. thesis, University of Toronto, 1970).

58. C.S. Clark, *op. cit.*, 5; On the rise of "new" Toronto, see Peter G. Goheen, *Victorian Toronto, 1850 to 1900* (Chicago, 1970), especially ch. 7.

59. H.C. Hocken, "The New Spirit in Municipal Government," *Ottawa Canadian Club Speeches*, 1914-15, 85-97.

60. *Municipal World*, November, 1898, cited 175.

61. P.A.C., Borden Papers, W.D. Lighthall to Borden, 30 March 1906.

62. *Union of Canadian Municipalities: Official Report of the Third Annual Convention*, 3-4.

63. *C.A.R.*, 1901, 438.

64. Much the same argument was used by a young University of Toronto undergraduate, F.H. Underhill. See his paper, "Commission Government in Cities" in *The Arbor*, 1910-11, 284-94.

65. *Municipal World*, November, 1902, 174. Mr. Kenneth Dewar called to our attention some of these sources.

66. Merrill Denison, *The People's Power: The History of Ontario Hydro* (Toronto, 1960), 27-28.

67. *Ibid.*, cited 34.

68. W.R. Plewman, *Adam Beck and the Ontario Hydro* (Toronto, 1947).

69. Charles Humphries, "The Political Career of James P. Whitney" (unpublished Ph.D. thesis, University of Toronto, 1966), 344ff.

70. Nelles, "Politics of Development," *op. cit.*, 422.

71. P.A.C., Laurier Papers, Walker to Laurier, 4 June 1909.

72. Robert Cuff, "The Toronto Eighteen and the Election of 1911," *Ontario History*, December 1965, 169-80. On the disallowance question, see Christopher Armstrong, "The Politics of Federalism, Ontario's Relations with the Federal Government, 1896-1941" (unpublished Ph.D. thesis, University of Toronto, 1972), 146-78.

73. Nelles, *op. cit.*, cited 480.

74. H.G.J. Aitken, "Defensive Expansionism: The State and Economic Growth in Canada," in W.T. Easterbrook and M.H. Watkins, eds., *Approaches to Canadian Economic History* (Toronto, 1967), 183-221.

75. Paul Rutherford, "Tomorrow's Metropolis: The Urban Reform Movement in Canada, 1880-1920," *C.H.A., Historical Papers*, 1971, 203-24, and the same writer's introduction to H.B. Ames, *The City Below the Hill*, *op. cit.*, vii-xviii.

76. A. Vernon Thomas, "The Weight of a New Broom" *Canada Monthly* (London), XVI, 2, June 1914, 91. For an expression of the booster spirit see C.F. Roland, "The City of Winnipeg," in *A Handbook to Winnipeg and the Province of Manitoba Prepared for the 79th Meeting of the British Association for the Advancement of Science, 1909* (Winnipeg, 1909), 26-56.

77. Michael Bliss, Introduction to Alan Sullivan, *The Rapids* (Toronto, 1972), vii-xx.

78. Stephen Leacock, *The Arcadian Adventures of the Idle Rich* (New York, London, Toronto, 1914), 309.

NOTES TO CHAPTER SIX

1. *Industrial Canada*, April 1909, cited in J.W.M. Bliss, "A Living Profit: Studies In The Social History Of Canadian Business, 1883-1911" (unpublished Ph.D. thesis, University of Toronto, 1972), 166.

2. *Labour Gazette*, VIII, 1906-07, 556.

3. H.A. Logan, *Trade Unions in Canada* (Toronto, 1948), 57; Eugene Forsey, "History of the Labour Movement in Canada," *Canada Year-Book, 1957-58* (Ottawa, 1958), 795-802.

4. R. McGregor Dawson, *William Lyon Mackenzie King* (Toronto, 1958), 97.

5. Robert Harper Babcock, "The A.F. of L. in Canada, 1896-1908: A Study in Labour Imperialism" (unpublished Ph.D. thesis, Duke University, 1969).

6. *C.A.R.*, 1906, 303-4.

7. Lewis L. Lorwin, *Labour and Internationalism* (New York, 1929), 117-21.

8. *Globe*, 4 May 1900. Cited in Babcock, *op. cit.*, 105.

9. *Canadian Mining Journal*, 15 September 1909.

10. Paul Phillips, *No Power Greater* (Vancouver, 1967), 33.

11. P.A.C., Laurier Papers, Father John Fraser to Laurier, 23 September 1909.

12. Babcock, *op. cit.*, 97-100.

13. *Ibid.*, 124.

14. Logan, *op. cit.*, cited 72; see also Robert Babcock, "Samuel Gompers and the Berlin Decisions of 1902," in Richard Preston, ed., *The Influence of the United States Upon Canadian Development* (Durham, N.C., 1972), 185-204.

15. Edmund Bradwin, *The Bunkhouse Man* (Toronto, 1972), 212. See also Donald Avery, "Canadian Immigration Policy and the Foreign Navvy, 1896-1914," (unpublished paper presented to the C.H.A., 1972).

16. Phillips, *op. cit.*, cited 53.

17. Bradwin, *op. cit.*, 205-14.

18. Phillips, *op. cit.*, 52-55.

19. Alfred Fitzpatrick, *The University in Overalls* (Toronto, 1920).

20. Bradwin, *op. cit.*, 235.

21. National Council of Women of Canada, *Women of Canada: Their Life and Work* (Ottawa, 1900), 102; see also "Canada's Working Women," *Christian Guardian*, 14 May 1913.

22. Henry J. Morgan and Lawrence J. Burpee, "The Canadian Woman," in *Canadian Life in Town and Country* (London, 1905), 143.

23. Nellie McClung, *The Stream Runs Fast* (Toronto, 1945), 109; P.A.M., *Political Equality League* (Minute Books, 15 May 1913).

24. S.D. Clark, *The Canadian Manufacturers' Association: A Study in Collective Bargaining and Political Pressure* (Toronto, 1939), 9, 39-40. Bliss, *op. cit.*, 158ff.

25. *Royal Commission on Industrial Disputes in British Columbia* (Ottawa, 1903), 240.

26. *Ottawa Free Press*, 25 July 1900; cited in Dawson, *op. cit.*, 96. See also Desmond Morton, "Aid to the Civil Power: The Canadian Militia in Support of Social Order, 1867-1914," *C.H.R.*, LI, 4, 1970, 407-25 and H.K. Ralston, "The 1900 Strike of Fraser River Sockeye Salmon Fishermen" (unpublished M.A. thesis, University of British Columbia, 1965).

27. Stuart Jamieson, *Times of Trouble: Labour Unrest and Industrial Conflict in Canada, 1900-66* (Ottawa, 1968), 102.

28. P.A.C., Laurier Papers, F.L. Wanklyn to Laurier, 14 July 1909.

29. *St. John Globe*, 19 August 1909; cited in Jamieson, *op. cit.*, 153.

30. P.A.C., Laurier Papers, E.S. Clouston to Laurier, 15 July 1909.

31. *Canada, Senate Debates*, 29 April 1903, 143-44.

32. P.A.C., Laurier Papers, Mulock to Laurier, 4 April 1903.

33. Babcock, *op. cit.*, 246.

34. Dawson *op. cit.*, 138; Jamieson, *op. cit.*, 116-21: see also Allen D. Orr, "The Western Federation of Miners and the Royal Commission on Industrial Disputes in 1903" (unpublished M.A. thesis, University of British Columbia, 1967).

35. Babcock, *op. cit.*, 252.

36. *C.A.R.*, 1907, 266-67.

37. P.A.C., Laurier Papers, Mulock to Laurier, 14 September 1905.

38. Dawson, *op. cit.*, 209-11. See also H.S. Ferns and Bernard Ostry, *William Lyon Mackenzie King: The Rise of a Leader* (London, 1955), 105-45.

39. *Canada, House of Commons Debates*, 15 May 1909, 6712.

40. James J. Atherton, "The Department of Labour and Industrial Relations, 1900-1911" (unpublished M.A. thesis, Carleton University, 1972).

41. P.A.C., King Papers, King to S.M. Wickett, 22 October 1900, cited in Atherton, *op. cit.*, 102-3.

42. Dawson, *op. cit.*, cited 141.

43. P.A.C., Laurier Papers, Laurier to Hays, 20 June 1904. See also William David Atkinson, "Organized Labour and the Laurier Administration: The Fortunes of a Pressure Group" (unpublished M.A. thesis, Carleton University, 1957), ch. 1.

44. Dawson, *op. cit.*, 113-15.

45. W.L.M. King, *Industry and Humanity* (Toronto, 1918), 210-11.

46. Atkinson, *op. cit.*, ch. 5.

STOP

47. Babcock, *op. cit.*, 397.

48. Jamieson, *op. cit.*, 128-29; H.D. Woods and Sylvia Ostry, *Labour Policy and Labour Economics in Canada* (Toronto, 1962), 258-60.

49. Atkinson, *op. cit.*, ch. 4. See above, ch. 4.

50. A.C.M. Waterman, "The Lord's Day in a Secular Society: A Historical Comment on the Canadian Lord's Day Act of 1906," *Canadian Journal of Theology*, XI, 2, 1965, 108-23; *Report on Sunday Observance Legislation*, Ontario Law Reform Commission, Department of Justice (Toronto, 1970), 36-62.

51. For an excellent survey, see Edith Lorentsen and Evelyn Woolner, "Fifty Years of Labour Legislation in Canada," *Labour Gazette*, L, September 1950, 1412ff.

52. Babcock, *op. cit.*, 128-67 and 339-96.

53. *Independent*, 24 May 1902, cited in Martin Robin, *Radical Politics and Canadian Labour, 1880-1930* (Kingston, 1968), 41.

54. J.T. Saywell, "Labour and Socialism in British Columbia: A Survey of Historical Developments before 1903," *British Columbia Historical Quarterly*, XV, 3-4, 1951, 129-50; Dorothy G. Steeves, *The Compassionate Rebel: Ernest E. Winch and His Times* (Vancouver, 1960), 10-44.

55. P.A.C., Laurier Papers, Horace Evans to Laurier, 10 December 1900.

56. Atkinson, *op. cit.*, 137-38.

57. P.A.C., Laurier Papers, Smith to Laurier, 30 June 1900. See also A.R. McCormack, "Arthur Puttee and the Liberal Party, 1899-1904," *C.H.R.*, LI, 3, 1970, 141-63.

58. *Proceedings of the Twenty-Second Annual Convention of the Trades and Labour Congress of Canada (1906)* (Ottawa, 1906), 82. See also Martin Robin, "The Trades and Labour Congress of Canada and Political Action, 1898-1908," *Relations Industrielles/Industrial Relations*, XXII, 1967, 187-214.

59. Robin, *Radical Politics*, *op. cit.*, 83-90.

60. *Voice*, 19 October 1906, cited in Robin, *op. cit.*, 97.

61. *C.A.R.*, *1903*, 219; see also Paul W. Fox, "Early Socialism in Canada," in J.H. Aitchison, ed., *The Political Process in Canada* (Toronto, 1963), 79-98.

NOTES TO CHAPTER SEVEN

1. Henri Bourassa, "The French Canadian in the British Empire," *Monthly Review*, VII, September 1902, 68.

2. *La Tribune*, 12 April 1901, cited in Claudette Bégin Wolff, "*L'Opinion Publique Québécoise Face à l'Immigration, 1906-1913*" (unpublished M.A. thesis, Université de Montréal, 1970), 75.

3. Abbé Lionel Groulx, "L'âme de la Jeunesse Canadienne-Française," *Le Semeur*, VI, 8, 1910, 212.

4. André Raynauld *et al.*, *Croissance et structure économiques de la Province de Québec* (Quebec City, 1961) 28-29; for background, see Jean Hamelin and Yves Roby, *Histoire Economique de Québec, 1851-1896*, (Montreal, 1971).

5. W.F. Ryan, *The Clergy and Economic Growth in Quebec, 1896-1914* (Quebec City, 1966), 41-42.

6. Raynauld, *op. cit.*, 28.

7. Herbert Brown Ames, *The City Below the Hill* (second edition, ed. P.W. Rutherford, Toronto, 1972).

8. *Ibid.*, 105.

9. Joseph-Papin Archambault, *La Question sociale* (Montreal, 1917), 40-41; T.J. Copp, "The Condition of the Working Class in Montreal, 1897-1920" (unpublished paper presented to the C.H.A., June 1972).

10. Ryan, *op. cit.*, 46-47.

11. Nathan Keyfitz, "Growth of Canadian Population," *Population Studies*, IV, June 1950, 54.

12. Ryan, *op. cit.*, cited 97.

13. Thérèse-F. Casgrain, *Une Femme chez les Hommes* (Montreal, 1972), 23-72; J. I. Cooper, *Montreal: A Brief History* (Montreal, 1969), 113-14.

14. Gérard Filteau, *L'Epopée de Shawinigan* (Shawinigan, 1944), 87-90; John Dales, *Hydroelectricity and Industrial Development: Quebec 1898-1940* (Cambridge, Mass., 1957), 50-55.

15. J.J. Harpell, *Canadian Industry, Commerce and Finance* (Montreal, 1916), 418.

16. Olivar Asselin in *Le Devoir*, 26 June 1911, cited in Joseph Levitt, *Henri Bourassa and the Golden Calf* (Ottawa, 1969), 40.

17. F.W. Field, *Capital Investment in Canada* (Montreal, 1914), 76-80; Albert Faucher, "Le caractère continental de l'industrialisation au Québec," in his *Histoire économique et unité canadienne* (Montreal, 1970), 161-78.

18. Robert Rumilly, *Histoire de la Province de Québec*, X (Montreal, 1943), cited 83.

19. Bourassa, *op. cit.*, 59.

20. L.-P. Audet, "La querelle de l'instruction obligatoire," *Les Cahiers de Dix*, XVII, 1959, 132-50.

21. Raphael Gervais, "Erreurs et Préjugés," *La Nouvelle France*, V, 10, 1906, 487.

22. Ryan, *op. cit.*, 209-45; Urquart and Buckley, *op. cit.*, 599.

23. Edouard Montpetit, *Les Forces Essentielles* (Montreal, 1940), 22-23. See also Jean Charles Falardeau, "Thèmes sociaux et idéologies dans les romans canadiens du XIXe siècle," in *Notre société et son roman* (Montreal, 1967), 11-38.

24. Ryan, *op. cit.*, 291.

25. The whole question of the role of French Canadians in economic development still awaits definitive answer. For a useful discussion presenting a variety of viewpoints, see René Durocher et Paul-André Linteau, eds., *Le "retard" du Québec et l'infériorité économique des Canadiens-français* (Trois Rivières, 1971).

26. Léon Gérin in *Le Monde Illustré* 17e année, 881, Montreal, 23 mars 1901, 780. See also Jean-Charles Falardeau, "Léon Gérin: His Life and Work," in Laurier L. LaPierre, ed., *French Canadian Thinkers of the Nineteenth and Twentieth Centuries* (Montreal, 1966), 59-76.

27. *Le Nationaliste*, 8 December 1908.

28. Errol Bouchette, *Emparons-nous l'industrie* (Ottawa, 1901), 28.

29. Errol Bouchette, "L'Evolution économique dans la Province de Québec," *Transactions of the Royal Society of Canada*, VII, 2nd series, 1901, Section I, 97-116.

30. Errol Bouchette, *L'Indépendance économique du Canada français* (2nd ed., Montreal, 1913), 94.

31. *Ibid.*, 30.

32. Abbé J.-A.-M. Brosseau, "Etude critique du Livre d'Edmond Demolins: *A quoi tient la supériorité des Anglo-Saxons?*", *La Revue canadienne*, XLVI, March 1904.

33. Kenneth Buckley, *Capital Formation in Canada, 1896-1913* (Toronto, 1955), 55.

34. Yves Roby, *Alphonse Desjardins et les Caisses Populaires, 1854-1920* (Montreal, 1964), cited 123.

35. *Ibid., passim,* and see Albert Faucher and Cyrille Vaillancourt, *Alphonse Desjardins Pionnier de la Coöpération d'Epargne et Crédit en Amérique* (Lévis, 1950).

36. *La Verité,* 15 May 1904; Arthur Saint-Pierre, *L'Avenir du Canada Français* (Montreal, 1909).

37. Martin P. O'Connell, "The Political Ideas of Henri Bourassa" (unpublished Ph.D. thesis, University of Toronto, 1954), 16.

38. *Ligue nationaliste canadienne: Programme* (Montreal, 1903).

39. P.A.C., Bourassa Papers, Bourassa to John Boyd, 3 November 1911.

40. Olivar Asselin, *A Quebec View of Canadian Nationalism* (Montreal, 1909), 44.

41. Armand Lavergne, "Un beau et bon livre," *La Revue Franco-Américaine,* 1ère année, 2, mai 1908.

42. *Le Nationaliste,* 6 September 1908 cited in Levitt, *op. cit.,* 35.

43. Asselin, *op. cit.,* 52.

44. Henri Bourassa, "The Nationalist Movement in Quebec," *Addresses Delivered Before the Canadian Club of Toronto, 1906-07* (Toronto, 1908), 57.

45. *Le Devoir,* 26 June 1911, cited in Levitt, *op. cit.,* 74.

46. Asselin, *op. cit.,* 47.

47. P.A.C., Bourassa to Goldwin Smith, 18 November 1909.

48. The best study of the *A.C.J.C.* is an unpublished research paper by Michael Beheils entitled "L'Association Catholique de la Jeunesse Canadienne-Française: Its Origins, Its Philosophy and Its Activities, 1903-1914" (York University, 1969). We have relied heavily upon it.

49. The atmosphere of the Colleges is effectively evoked in Lionel Groulx, *Mes Mémoires, 1878-1920* (Montreal, 1970), 41-57 and 95-109.

50. *A.C.J.C.,* "Compte Rendu du Congrès de 1904," *Le Semeur,* I, 1-2, septembre-octobre 1904, 38-39.

51. Lionel Cartier, "La Jeunesse et l'avenir," *La Croix,* 27 septembre 1903.

52. Lionel Groulx, "L'Ame et La Jeunesse Canadienne-française," *Le Semeur,* VI, 8, 1910, 215; see Lionel Groulx, *La Croissade d'Adolescence* (Montreal, 1906).

53. Henri Bernard, *La Ligue de l'Enseignement: Histoire d'une Conspiration maçonnique à Montréal* (Montreal, 1904).

54. *Premier Congrès de la Langue française au Canada* (Quebec City, 1914).

55. Pierre Homier, *La Langue française au Canada: Faits et Réflèxions* (Montreal, 1913).

56. Henri Bourassa, "Lord Haldane," *Le Devoir,* 3 septembre 1913; Abbé Lionel Groulx, "L'Enseignement de l'Histoire dans nos Collèges," *Le Devoir,* 27 octobre 1913.

57. Henri Bourassa, "L'Enseignement de l'Histoire," *Le Devoir,* 19 novembre 1913.

58. Henri Bourassa, "En Marge de l'Histoire du Canada," *Le Devoir,* 27 novembre 1913.

59. Mgr L.-N. Bégin, "Lettre Pastorale sur l'Action sociale catholique," *Les Mandements, Lettres Pastorales, Circulaires* (Quebec City, 31 March 1907).

60. *L'Action sociale catholique et l'oeuvre de la presse catholique: motifs-programme-organisation-ressources* (Quebec City, 1907).

61. Jean Hulliger, *L'Enseignement Social des Evêques Canadiens de 1891 à 1950* (Montreal, 1958), 117.

62. *Mandements des Evêques de Chi-*

coutimi, 19 March 1912 (Chicoutimi, 1912), 308.

63. Alfred Charpentier, *Ma Conversion au Syndicalisme Catholique* (Montreal, 1946); Michel Têtu, "Les premiers syndicats catholiques canadiens, 1900-21" (unpublished Ph.D. thesis, Université Laval, 1961); Joseph Levitt,

"Henri Bourassa on Catholic Unionism," *Social History*, VI, November 1970, 107-15.

64. Errol Bouchette, "Les débuts d'une industrie et notre bourgeoisie," *Proceedings and Transactions of the Royal Society of Canada*, VI, third series, 1912, Section I, 156.

NOTES TO CHAPTER EIGHT

1. Fowke, *The National Policy and the Wheat Economy*, *op. cit.*, 93.

2. Clark, *The Canadian Manufacturers' Association*. *op. cit.*, 7-10.

3. *Retail Merchants Journal of Canada*. August 1907, 257. We owe this reference to Professor J.M. Bliss, whose "A Living Profit: Studies in the Social History of Canadian Business, 1883-1911" (unpublished Ph.D. thesis, University of Toronto, 1972), offers many important insights into the businessman's "flight from competition."

4. Ian Macpherson, "The Origins of Canadian Cooperation, 1900-1914" (unpublished paper presented to the C.H.A., June 1972).

5. Alan R. Turner, "W.R. Motherwell: The Emergence of a Farm Leader," *Saskatchewan History*, XI, 1958, 101.

6. P.A.C., W.C. Good Papers, W.C. Good to Uncle John, 2 September 1896.

7. Edward Porritt, *The Revolt Against the New Feudalism* (London, 1911), cited 205.

8. See the speech by Douglas in "The Agrarian Movement in the 1890's," *Saskatchewan History*, VII, 2, 1954, 51-55.

9. Richard Allen, "Salem Bland and the Social Gospel in Canada" (unpublished M.A. thesis, University of Saskatchewan, 1961).

10. *Winnipeg Tribune*, 4 August 1913.

11. Richard Allen, *The Social Passion* (Toronto, 1971), 3-18.

12. Paul F. Sharp, *The Agrarian Revolt in Western Canada* (Minneapolis, 1948), 81.

13. L.A. Wood, *The History of the Farmers' Movement in Canada* (Toronto, 1924), 147-55; See also S.E.D. Shortt, "Social Change and Political Crisis in Rural Ontario: The Patrons of Industry, 1889-1896," in Donald Swainson, ed., *Oliver Mowat's Ontario* (Toronto, 1972), 211-35.

14. Brian R. McCutcheon, "The Patrons of Industry in Manitoba, 1890-1898," *Transactions of the Historical and Scientific Society of Manitoba*, series III, 22, 1965-6, 7-26.

15. *Statutes of Canada*, LX-LXI, Vic., C.5, 1897.

16. *Canada, Sessional Papers*, 1900, no. 81-81a, *Report and Evidence of the Royal Commission on the Shipment and Transportation of Grain*, 1900, 9.

17. Allan R. Turner, "W.R. Motherwell and Agricultural Education, 1908-18," *Saskatchewan History*, XII, 1959, 81-96.

18. Wood, *op. cit.*, 173-80.

19. *Manitoba Free Press*, 4 August 1899.

20. *C.A.R.*, 1902, 56; G.R. Stevens, *Canadian National Railways* (Toronto, 1962), II, 122-23.

21. Morris Zaslow, *The Opening of the*

Canadian North, 1870-1914 (Toronto, 1972), 187-91 and 199-209.

22. D.B. Hanna, *Trains of Recollection* (Toronto, 1924), 118-20.

23. Theodore David Regehr, "The Canadian Northern Railway: Agent of National Growth" (unpublished Ph.D. thesis, University of Alberta, 1967).

24. J.B. Hedges, *The Federal Railway Land Subsidy Policy of Canada* (Cambridge, Mass., 1934), 107-14.

25. Stevens, *op. cit.,* 116.

26. D.B. Hanna's *Trains of Recollection* exudes this spirit in telling part of the Canadian Northern story.

27. Stevens, *op. cit.,* cited 133.

28. P.A.C., Hays Papers, Hays to Wilson, 22 October 1902, cited in Regehr, *op. cit.,* 101.

29. Stevens, *op. cit.,* cited 133.

30. P.A.C. Hays Papers, Memo, 7 May 1903, cited in Regehr, *op. cit.,* 112.

31. Borden, *Memoirs,* I, 14-22.

32. *Canada, House of Commons Debates,* 1903, 7659-61.

33. Regehr, *op. cit.,* 136-42, tells the story of the *La Presse* affair more convincingly than any other commentator.

34. Stevens, *op. cit.,* cited 154.

35. *Ibid.,* 227.

36. J.S. Woodsworth, "Sketches of Western Life, III, The Pioneer Home," *Christian Guardian,* 4 July 1906.

37. Ralph Hedlin, "Edmund A. Partridge," *Transactions of the Historical and Scientific Society of Manitoba,* series III, no. 15, 1960, 58-59; E.A. Partridge, *The War on Poverty* (Winnipeg, 1925); Carl Berger, "A Canadian Utopia: The Co-Operative Commonwealth of E.A. Partridge," in Stephen Clarkson, ed., *Visions 2020* (Edmonton, 1970), 257-62.

38. Hopkins Moorhouse, *Deep Furrows* (Winnipeg and Toronto, 1918), 72.

39. Fowke, *op. cit.,* 139-42.

40. D. Spafford, "The Elevator Issue, the Organized Farmers and the Government, 1908-1911," *Saskatchewan History,* XV, 1962, 81-92, and W.A. Mackintosh, *Agricultural Co-operation in Western Canada* (Kingston, 1924), 76.

41. H.S. Patton, *Grain Growers Cooperation in Western Canada* (Cambridge, Mass., 1928), cited 135.

42. George Fisher Chipman, "The Voice from the Soil," *Canadian Magazine,* XXXVI, 3, 1911, 359.

43. Sharp, *op. cit.,* 63.

44. Watson Griffin, *Protection and Prices and the Farmer's Home Market* (Toronto, 1904).

45. W.C. Good, "Canada's Rural Problem," *Empire Club Speeches, 1915-16* (Toronto, 1917), 309.

46. *Grain Growers' Guide,* 2:5, 23 February 1910.

47. Gordon Waldron, "The Depopulation and Impoverishment of Rural Ontario," *Addresses Before the Canadian Club of Toronto, 1910-11* (Toronto, 1911), 68.

48. W.C. Good, *Farmer Citizen* (Toronto, 1958), 97.

49. P.A.C., Laurier Papers, Laurier to Riley, 8 February 1900.

50. E.C. Drury, "The Farmers and the Tariff," *Canadian Magazine,* XXVI, no. 6, 1906, 560.

51. W.K. McNaught, "Protectionism and Canadian Prosperity," *Canadian Magazine,* XXVI, no. 5, 1906, 432.

52. *Ibid.,* 504.

53. Wood, *op. cit.,* 248.

54. Edward Porritt, "Canada's Tariff Mood Toward the United States," *North American Review,* 182, 4, 1906, 577.

55. P.A.C., Laurier Papers, George F. Chipman to Laurier, 10 June 1910.

56. Wood, *op. cit.,* cited 258.

57. *Ibid.,* 257.

58. P.A.C., Laurier Papers, Laurier to Cartwright, 23 July 1910.

59. Queen's University, Flavelle Papers, "Open Letter Addressed to the Honourable Minister of Agriculture for Ontario," 18 June 1910.

60. G.F. Chipman, *The Siege of Ottawa* (Winnipeg, 1910); See also *Canada.*

Sessional Papers. 1911, 24, no. 113, "The Farmers' Delegation," 1-57.

61. P.A.C., Laurier Papers, Laurier to Nesbitt, 23 December 1910.

62. George F. Chipman, "The Voice from the Soil," *Canadian Magazine.* XXXVI, 4, February, 1911, 359.

63. *Weekly Sun.* 15 March 1911.

NOTES TO CHAPTER NINE

1. J. S. Willison, *Anglo-Saxon Amity* (Toronto, 1906), 12-13.

2. *Canada. House of Commons Debates.* 1903, 14814-18.

3. P.A.C., Minto Papers, Minto to Lyttleton, 25 October 1903.

4. James Bryce, "The Essential Unity of Britain and America," *Atlantic Monthly.* LXXXII, July 1898, 22-24; on Grey see Mary Hallett, "The Fourth Earl Grey as Governor-General of Canada" (unpublished Ph.D. thesis, University of London, 1969).

5. Carl Berger, *The Sense of Power* (Toronto, 1970), 23-33.

6. G.M. Grant, "The Imperial Significance of the Canadian Contingents," in T.G. Marquis, *Canada's Sons on Kopje and Veldt* (Toronto, 1900), 6-7.

7. *La Patrie.* 9 décembre 1901.

8. Henri Bourassa, "The French Canadian in the British Empire," *Monthly Review.* VII, October 1902, 68. Lord Minto, referring to this article, told his brother, "Bourassa's article is really important as I believe expressing the feeling of a large part of French Canada." P.A.C., Minto Papers, Minto-Elliot Correspondence, Minto to Elliot, 2 November 1902.

9. Armand Lavergne, "National Defence as Viewed by French Canadi-

ans," *Canadian Military Institute: Selected Papers from the Transactions of the Canadian Military Institute. 1910* (Welland, 1910), 98, italics added. See also Mgr Bégin à Mgr Bruchési, 15 janvier 1900, "La Loyauté des Canadiens-français," *Revue Canadienne.* I, 1900, 124-27.

10. J.I. Cooper, *Montreal: A Brief History* (Montreal, 1969), 118-19.

11. P.A.C., Minto Papers, Minto-Elliot Correspondence, Minto to Elliot, 14 December 1902.

12. Archibald Hurd, "Foreign Invasion of Canada," *Fortnightly Review.* LXXVIII, December 1902, 1065.

13. Stephen Leacock, "The Political Achievement of Robert Baldwin," *Addresses Delivered Before the Canadian Club of Ottawa. 1903-09* (Ottawa, 1910), 164; Berger, *op. cit..* 147-51; Charles Magrath, *Canada's Growth and Some Problems Affecting It* (Ottawa, 1910).

14. P.A.C., Laurier Papers, Laurier to Gregory, 19 November 1909.

15. Donald C. Gordon, *The Dominion Partnership in Imperial Defence. 1870-1914* (Baltimore, 1965), 182-86.

16. Norman Penlington, *Canada and Imperialism. 1896-99* (Toronto, 1965), 226ff.

17. *Canada, House of Commons Debates,* 1903, 2403.

18. Desmond Morton, *Ministers and Generals: Politics and the Canadian Militia* (Toronto, 1970), cited 181.

19. *Ibid.,* 181.

20. Desmond Morton, "French Canada and the Canadian Militia, 1868-1914," *Social History,* III, April 1969, 32-50.

21. H. Blair Neatby, "Laurier and Imperialism," *C.H.A. A.R.,* 1955, 24-32.

22. P.A.N.S., Sir Frederick Borden Papers, Borden to Alfred Lyttleton, 1 March 1904. Carmen Miller drew this letter to our attention. See his "The Public Life of Sir Frederick Borden" (unpublished M.A. thesis, Dalhousie University, 1964).

23. J.E. Kendle, *The Colonial and Imperial Conferences, 1887-1911* (London, 1967), chs. 4, 5, 10.

24. Laurier's biographers, Skelton, Dafoe and Schull, have all depicted the story in this manner.

25. Keith Sinclair, *Imperial Federation,* Commonwealth Paper no. 11 (London, 1955), 26-45.

26. Charles Carrington, *Rudyard Kipling, His Life and Work* (London, 1955), 396.

27. P.A.C., Borden Papers, Memoir Notes, 352, Milner to Borden, 15 July 1907.

28. P.A.C., Minto Papers, Minto to Chamberlain, 14 April 1900.

29. A.J. Marder, *From Dreadnought to Scapa Flow* (London, 1961), I, 176-79.

30. *Globe,* 23 March 1909.

31. *Canada, House of Commons Debates,* 1909, II, 3484.

32. *Ibid.,* 3564.

33. P.A.C., Laurier Papers, Brodeur to Laurier, 10 August 1909, 26 August 1909.

34. *Canada, House of Commons Debates,* 12 January 1910, 1735.

35. P.A.B.C., Sir Richard McBride Papers, Martin Burrell to McBride, 28 November 1909.

36. P.A.C., Borden Papers, Memoir Notes, 352, Casgrain to Borden, 29 January 1909.

37. Henry Borden, ed., *Robert Laird Borden: His Memoirs* (Toronto, 1938), I, 269-74.

38. Mary Hallett, *op. cit.,* 272-93.

39. P.A.C., Borden Papers, Memoir Notes, 352, Monk to Borden, 28 January 1909.

40. R. Rumilly, *Histoire de la Province de Québec,* XIII, (Montreal, n.d.), 105.

41. P.A.C., Laurier Papers, Charles Murphy to Laurier, 20 August 1910, 25 August 1910.

42. Henri Bourassa, *Religion, Langue, Nationalité* (Montreal, 1910), 14.

43. Rumilly, *op. cit.,* XV, 116.

44. P.A.C., Laurier Papers, Lemieux à Laurier, 11 août 1910.

45. Rumilly, *op. cit.,* XV, 159.

46. Douglas J. Wurtele, "The Drummond-Arthabaska By-Election of 1910," *Dalhousie Review,* XL, 1960-61, 14-33.

47. O.D. Skelton, *The Life and Letters of Sir Wilfrid Laurier* (London, 1922), II, 239.

48. P.A.C., W.L. Grant Papers, C.F. Hamilton to W.L. Grant, 4 November 1910.

49. Marder, *op. cit.,* cited 183.

50. Gluek, "Pilgrimages to Ottawa," *op. cit.,* cited 65.

51. *C.A.R.,* 1907, 401.

52. See Gluek, *op. cit.,* and Peter Neary, "Grey, Bryce, and the Settlement of Canadian-American Differences, 1905-1911," *C.H.R.,* XLIX, 4, 1968, 357-80.

53. P.A.C., R.G. 15, H 1, v 14, Dennis to Pearce, 24 June 1895. See also C. Dawson, *Group Settlement, op. cit.,* and Lawrence B. Lee, "The Canadian-

American Irrigation Frontier, 1884-1914," *Agricultural History,* XL, 4, 1966, 271-83.

54. L.M. Bloomfield and G.F. Fitzgerald, *Boundary Waters Problems. Canada and the United States* (Toronto, 1958), 9, and C.J. Chacko, *The International Joint Commission* (New York, 1932), 71ff.

55. P.C. 3 645/1895, 8 January 1896.

56. P.A.C., Mabee Papers, Colonel S.J. Lydecker to General J.M. Wilson, 23 February 1899.

57. *Canada, House of Commons Debates,* 10 March 1902, 886-88.

58. Mr. N.A.F. Dreisziger of the Royal Military College has kindly brought to our attention some of the material used in the foregoing paragraphs.

59. For a brief account of the negotiations, see Neary, *op. cit.* Some of the Canadian documentation may be found in Department of External Affairs, *Documents on Canadian External Relations,* I, 1909-1918, ch. 4 (hereafter *D.C.E.R.*).

60. *Canada, House of Commons Debates,* 6 December 1910, 911.

61. P.A.C., Grey Papers, Grey to Laurier, 12 February 1910.

62. Borden passed over the Liberal, Gibbons, who was more responsible than anyone else for the existence of the I.J.C., when he appointed Thomas Chase-Casgrain (Chairman), Henry Powell, and Charles Magrath to the Commission. P.A.C., Magrath Papers, Memoir Notes, file 34.

63. P.A.C., Grey Papers, Grey to Sir Edward Grey, 1 March 1906.

64. See below, 278 ff.

65. James Eayrs, "The Origin of Canada's Department of External Affairs" in H.L. Keenleyside, *et al.,* eds., *The Growth of Canadian Policies in External Affairs* (Durham, 1960), cited 16.

66. P.A.C., Grey Papers, Grey to Elgin, 28 March 1908.

67. The origins of the Department of External Affairs are traced in detail in Eayrs, *op. cit.* For the role of Bryce in the creation of the department, see F.A. Coghlan, "James Bryce and the Establishment of the Department of External Affairs" in Canadian Historical Association, *Historical Papers,* 1968, 84-93. An inadequate collection of documents on the subject may be found in *D.C.E.R.,* ch. 1.

68. The negotiations are discussed in detail in L. Ethan Ellis, *Reciprocity, 1911: A Study in Canadian-American Relations, 1875-1911,* (New Haven, 1945), ch. 14; McDiarmid, *Commercial Policy, op. cit.,* ch. 9; and Skelton, *Laurier, op. cit.,* II, ch. 16. See also the memorandum by Wm. S. Culbertson of the United States Tariff Commission in Culbertson to Foster, 10 September 1917, Douglas Library, J.G. Foster Papers.

69. Borden, *Memoirs,* I, 303.

70. P.A.C., Laurier Papers, Dafoe to Laurier, 28 April 1911.

71. *C.A.R.,* 1911, 96-110.

72. P.A.B.C., McBride Papers, McBride to Borden, 3 March 1910.

73. P.A.C., Borden Papers, Roblin to Borden, 3 January 1906, 29 March 1907.

74. Queen's University, Douglas Library, Foster Papers, Foster to Patchin, 31 October 1911; to Pepper, 15 March 1911; to Weikel, 21 February 1911.

75. *C.A.R.,* 1911, 48-49.

76. University of Toronto Library, B.E. Walker Papers, Walker to Ashley, 16 March 1911. See also Walker to Fulton, 16 March 1911.

77. P.A.C., Borden Papers, MacNab to Graham, 9 July 1907; to Borden, 11 July 1907; P.A.C., Willison Pa-

pers, Hamilton to Willison, 19 May 1908 and 3 July 1908.

78. P.A.C., Willison Papers, Hamilton to Willison, 2 June 1906; Willison to Hamilton, 4, 7, and 26 June 1906; Hamilton to Willison, 8 March 1910.

79. P.A.C., Borden Papers, Hughes to Borden, 23 March 1910.

80. Douglas Library, Norman Lambert Papers, Diary, 9 February 1919; P.A.C., Willison Papers, memo of the March 1 meeting, n.d., vol. 105.

81. P.A.C., Borden Papers, Borden to Whitney, 22 March 1911 and Whitney to Borden, 23 March 1911.

82. R.C. Brown, "The Political Ideas of Sir Robert Borden," in Marcel Hamelin, ed., *The Political Ideas of the Prime Ministers of Canada* (Ottawa, 1968), 87-106.

83. P.A.B.C., McBride Papers, Burrell to McBride, 10, 20, 24, and 31 March 1910; McBride to Burrell, 17 and 31 March, 1 April 1910; P.A.C., Willison Papers, Kemp to Willison, 11 April 1910.

84. P.A.C., Borden Papers, Burrell to Borden, 17 October 1932.

85. *Ibid.,* Roblin to Borden, 6 April 1910.

86. *Ibid.,* Hughes to MacArthur, 23 March 1911.

87. P.A.C., Kemp Papers, Carstairs to Borden, 23 May 1912; Charles Humphries, "The Political Career of Sir James P. Whitney," *op. cit.,* 462-70.

88. P.A.C., Grey Papers, Laurier to Grey, 23 August 1911.

89. U.N.B., O.S. Crockett Papers, Price to Crockett, 23 June 1911.

90. *The Tariff and National Prosperity.* Memorial Presented to the Dominion Government by the Canadian Manufacturers' Association, on 13 January 1911; see also John Allan, "Reciprocity and the Canadian General Elec-tion of 1911: A Re-Examination of Economic Self-Interest in Voting" (unpublished M.A. thesis, Queen's University, 1971).

91. P.D. Stevens, "Laurier, Aylesworth, and the Decline of the Liberal Party in Ontario," in C.H.A., *Historical Papers,* 1968, cited 101.

92. J. Murray Beck, *Pendulum of Power* (Scarborough, 1968), 135.

93. P.A.C., King Papers, Stratton to King, 7 October 1911. On the reciprocity campaign and election, see Stevens, *op. cit.;* Robert Cuff, "The Conservative Party Machine and the Election of 1911 in Ontario," *Ontario History,* September, 1965, 149-56, and "The Toronto Eighteen and the Election of 1911," *ibid.,* December, 1965, 169-80; Heath MacQuarrie, "Robert Borden and the Election of 1911," *C.J.E.P.S.,* XXV, 3, August, 1959, 271-86; L.E. Ellis, "Canada's Rejection of Reciprocity in 1911," *C.H.A.A.R.,* 1939, 99-111; Skelton, *Laurier,* II, ch. 16; Borden, *Memoirs,* ch. 16; and A. Gordon Brown, "Nova Scotia and the Reciprocity Election of 1911" (unpublished M.A. thesis, Dalhousie University, 1971).

94. M.C. Urquhart and K.A. Buckley, *op. cit.,* 14.

95. J. Spelt, *The Urban Development of South Central Ontario* (Assen, 1955), 165.

96. P.A.C., Laurier Papers, Laurier to D.R. Wood, 24 December 1910.

97. John Willison, "Sir Wilfrid Laurier," *Encyclopedia Britannica,* eleventh edition (Cambridge, 1910), XVI, 287.

98. J.S. Woodsworth, "Some Aspects of Immigration," *University Magazine,* XIII, 2, April 1914, 190.

99. Stephen Leacock, *Sunshine Sketches of a Little Town* (1912, reprinted, New Canadian Library, 1960), 149.

100. Ramsay Cook, "Stephen Leacock

and the Age of Plutocracy, 1903-1921," in J.S. Moir, ed., *Character and Circumstance* (Toronto, 1970), 163-81.

101. Stephen Leacock, "The Great Victory in Canada," reprinted from *The National Review,* 58, November 1911, 3.

NOTES TO CHAPTER TEN

1. J.T. Saywell, ed., *The Canadian Journal of Lady Aberdeen, 1893-98* (Toronto, 1960), xxviii-xxxi.

2. P.A.C., Foster Papers, Diary, 5 October 1911.

3. H.N. MacQuarrie, "The Formation of Borden's First Cabinet," *C.J.E.P.S.,* XXIII, 1, February, 1957, cited 92.

4. P.A.C., Borden Papers, Grey to Borden, 2 October and 29 September 1911.

5. *D.C.E.R.,* I, 12. Descriptive accounts of Borden's selection of his cabinet colleagues are MacQuarrie, "Borden's First Cabinet," *op. cit.,* 90-104; Borden, *Memoirs,* I, 329-33, and Roger Graham's closely argued essay, "The Cabinet of 1911," in F.W. Gibson, ed., *Cabinet Formation and Bicultural Relations: Seven Case Studies* (Royal Commission on Bilingualism and Biculturalism, Ottawa, 1970), ch. 4.

6. P.A.C., Borden Papers, v. 339, 72.

7. *Ibid.,* 3.

8. On the party platform, see Borden, *Memoirs,* I, 192-95, 322-25. See also Brown, "Political Ideas," *op. cit.*

9. P.A.C., Borden Papers, Whitney to Borden, Sunday p.m., n.d.

10. *Ibid.,* Van Horne to Borden, 24 September 1911.

11. Borden, *Memoirs,* I, 231.

12. *Ibid.,* Price to Borden, 2 October 1911.

13. He did sign the round-robin of that year. See *Memoirs,* I, 310. But see also "Borden's Want of Tact Started the Discontent," *Toronto Daily Star,* 7 April 1910, and P.A.C., Borden Papers, Hughes to Borden, 24 November 1910.

14. Borden, *Memoirs,* I, 330.

15. See P.A.C., Borden Papers, Carstairs to Borden, 23 May 1912. "It was only through the generous assistance of Mr. A.E. Kemp that we were rescued from the debts that had accumulated."

16. Armand Lavergne, *Trente Ans de la Vie Nationale* (Montreal, 1934), 205.

17. Garceau to Monk, n.d., cited, Rumilly, *Bourassa,* 433-34.

18. See Graham, "The Cabinet of 1911," 53-58.

19. Cited *ibid.,* 57.

20. P.A.C., Willison Papers, Hamilton to Willison, 22 November 1911.

21. P.A.C., Borden Papers, Kemp to Borden, 11 January 1912.

22. P. C. 2928, 21 December 1911.

23. P.A.C., Borden Papers, enclosure in A.B. Morine to Borden, 15 March 1912.

24. *Ibid.,* Morine to Borden, 27 May 1912, and P.A.C., Grey Papers, Adam Shortt to Grey, 22 January 1912.

25. P.A.C., Borden Papers, White to Borden, 11 May 1912. The standard account of the public service is R.M. Dawson's *The Civil Service of Canada,* (Toronto, 1929). Professor Dawson was especially harsh in his judgment

of the service during the first Borden administration. See especially ch. 5. In 1931, as President of the Canadian Historical Association, Borden took the occasion of his presidential address to issue a sharp and rather convincing rejoinder. See *C.H.A.A.R.*, 1931, 5-34; see also J.E. Hodgetts *et al.*, *The Biography of an Institution: The Civil Service Commission of Canada. 1908-1967* (Montreal and London, 1972), 28-35.

26. *Canada. Sessional Papers,* 1913, no. 57A, 7-27. Dawson, *Civil Service. op. cit.*, 83-85.

27. See P.A.C., Foster Papers, Diary, 21 December 1912.

28. See Borden, "The Problem of an Efficient Civil Service," *C.H.A.A.R.*, 1931, 15.

29. P.A.C., Borden Papers, Perley to Borden, 26 February 1914, and enclosures.

30. *Ibid.*, Willison to Borden, 5 October 1911.

31. Zaslow, *The Opening of the Canadian North. op. cit.*, ch. 10. Borden had promised "the construction of the Hudson Bay Railway and its operation by independent commission."

32. *Canada. Senate Debates,* 1910-11, 306.

33. *Canada. House of Commons Debates,* 12 February 1912, 3784.

34. Wood, *Farmers' Movements in Canada,* ch. 18, and Fowke, *The National Policy and the Wheat Economy,* 162-63.

35. *Canada. House of Commons Debates,* 24 January 1913, 2147ff.

36. The aid to agricultural education was less clear-cut constitutionally because of shared jurisdiction under section 95 of the B.N.A. Act.

37. *C.A.R.*, 1913, cited 258.

38. P.A.C., Borden Papers, Memoir Notes, 334. On the subject of the con-

ditional grants inaugurated by the Borden governments, see J.A. Maxwell, *Federal Subsidies to Provincial Governments in Canada* (Cambridge, Mass., 1937), chs. 15-16.

39. See Zaslow, *op. cit.*, ch. 10.

40. *C.A.R.*, 1912, cited 229.

41. On Senate amendments of government legislation, 1911-1920, see R.A. MacKay, *The Unreformed Senate of Canada* (Carleton Library no. 6, Toronto, 1963), 98-101.

42. Department of Finance, Deputy Minister's Correspondence, v. 281, D.B. McConnan, Deputy Receiver General, Victoria, to Boville, 11 January 1913.

43. *Ibid.*, 298, H.M. Drummond, Deputy Receiver General, Winnipeg, to Boville, 10 April 1912. See also *C.A.R.*, 1913, 314, and J.S. Woodsworth, "A Workman's Budget," *Christian Guardian,* 11 June, 2, 9 and 16 July 1913.

44. *Ibid.*, Drummond to Boville, 12 June 1913. See also v. 281, McConnan to Boville, 6 May and 21 October 1913. McConnan's second letter mentions "a terrible falling off. . . . Real Estate business has gone flat, there is practically nothing doing."

45. P.A.C., Borden Papers, Wainwright to Borden, 7 May 1913.

46. *Ibid.*, White to Borden, 11 October 1913.

47. *Ontario. Report of the Ontario Commission on Unemployment* (Toronto, 1916), 19.

48. P.A.C., White Papers, clipping, *Market Mail,* 17 June 1914; J.O. Smith to W.J. Roche, 9 March 1914.

49. In Ontario, between January and December 1914, employment dropped significantly in the following industrial categories: iron and steel, timber and lumber, paper and printing, chemicals and allied products, metals

and products other than steel, vehicles for land transportation, and ships. See *Report of the Ontario Commission on Unemployment.* Appendix H.

50. B.M. Stewart, "The Employment Service of Canada," *Bulletin of the Departments of History and Political and Economic Science in Queen's University.* no. 32, July 1919, and *Report of the Ontario Commission on Unemployment.*

51. " . . . there is no sadder sight in any civilized country than to see a man tramping up and down the streets, day in and day out, looking for work that he needs to keep his little family, and unable to find it; coming home every night in a deeper discouragement than he was when he started out in the morning; able to work, willing to work, and can't get work." Hocken, "The New Spirit in Municipal Government," *op. cit..* 96.

52. *Ibid..* 94-96.

53. *Report of the Ontario Commission on Unemployment.* 90.

54. P.A.C., Foster Papers, Diary, 18 March 1914.

55. P.A.C., Borden Papers, Borden to Drayton, 3 November 1934.

56. The history of both railways, of their construction, of the colourful men who built them, and of their connivance with politicians of both parties, is very well told in G.R. Stevens, *Canadian National Railways.* II. The role of the railways in western development is traced in Zaslow, *op. cit..* ch. 10.

57. *Ibid..* 218-21.

58. P.A.C., Borden Papers, Private, Diary, 14 September 1912.

59. P.A.C., Borden Papers, A.W. Smithers to Borden, 18 October 1912. See also Borden to E.J. Chamberlain, 15 January 1915.

60. P.A.C., Borden Papers, Private, Diary, 7 January, 1 May and 16 May 1913.

61. *Ibid..* 13 June and 2 July 1913.

62. P.A.C., Borden Papers, Schaffner to White, 5 September 1913.

63. P.A.C., Borden Papers, Private, Diary, 22 January 1914.

64. *Ibid..* 19 February 1914.

65. *Ibid..* 2 March 1914.

66. *Ibid..* 5 March 1914.

67. Stevens, *op. cit..* 111, and Graham, *Meighen.* I, 78-79.

68. P.A.C., Borden Papers, Private, Diary, 18 March 1914.

69. Stevens, *op.cit..* 110-12; Graham, *Meighen.* I, 79-82. "Saskatchewan, Alberta and British Columbia were ruined undoubtedly if it were not for the present policy of your Government," Sir C.H. Tupper observed. "But where will this lead us? What is to stop these provinces renewing their mad folly in finance?" P.A.C., Borden Papers, Tupper to Borden, 6 May 1914.

70. See for example, P.A.C., Borden Papers, C.A. Bogert, General Manager, Dominion Bank, to White, 23 March 1914; E.B. Biggar to Borden, 11 April 1914; and C.H. Cahan to Borden, 4 May 1914.

71. Queen's University, J.G. Foster Papers, Foster to Patchin, 6 November 1911; Foster to Pepper, 26 September 1911. See also P.A.C., Borden Papers, Borden to Bryce, 14 October 1911.

72. *C.A.R..* 1911, cited 295.

73. P.A.C., Borden Papers, Griffith to Borden, 3 October 1911, and Perley to Borden, 7 February 1912.

74. See *inter alia.* Borden to Amery, 15 March 1913.

75. P.A.C., Borden Papers, Private, Diary, 20 July 1912.

76. *C.A.R..* 1912, cited 49.

77. P.A.C., Borden Papers, Borden to Whitney, 1 June 1912; Whitney to Borden, 15 June 1912.

78. *Ibid.*, Monk to Borden, 2 November 1909.

79. P.A.B.C., McBride Papers, Burrell to McBride, 10 March 1910.

80. See footnote 16.

81. See Marder, *From the Dreadnought to Scapa Flow*, I, ch. 11, and Harold Nicholson, *King George V* (London, 1952), 259-63.

82. P.A.C., Borden Papers, Private, Diary, 16 July 1912. On July 5, "Churchill . . . discussed Naval situation for an hour. Very serious. Feels confident that Germany will strike." *Ibid.*

83. *D.C.E.R.*, I., 268; Borden, *Memoirs*, I, 364. Even though Borden noted that the United Kingdom Parliament "elected upon issues chiefly, if not altogether, local and domestic . . . can hardly be regarded as an Imperial Parliament in the highest or truest sense," he never regarded an "Imperial Parliament" as the proper way to Canadian representation. After a lunch with Bonar Law, he recorded that "he believes in Imperial Parliament; I dissented." *Memoirs*, I, 359-60; Diary, 7 July 1912.

84. *Canada, House of Commons Debates,* 5 December 1912, 692-93.

85. *D.C.E.R.*, I, 277.

86. See G.N. Tucker, *Canadian Naval Service*, I, Appendix VIII, for the text of the secret memorandum which was shown to the cabinet, Sir Richard McBride and Laurier.

87. P.A.C., Borden Papers, Private, Diary, 18 September 1912.

88. *Ibid.*, 30 September 1912.

89. *Ibid.*, 27 November 1912.

90. Borden, *Memoirs*, I, 409.

91. P.A.C., Laurier Papers, Fielding to Laurier, 8 November 1912.

92. *Ibid.*, Fielding to Laurier, 19 January and 5 February 1913. The petition stressed the additional cost to the British taxpayer of maintaining the three ships. Moreover, the M.P.'s were deeply distressed by Borden's pronouncement of December 5 about consultation in foreign policy. "If this proposal entails the admission of anyone outside the cabinet to a position giving any control over foreign policy, we view it with great alarm." From both points of view they stressed the superiority of Laurier's naval programme. It "would show a sense of Imperial responsibility equal to the proposals of Mr. Borden and appear to us much less likely to promote dangerous developments. Nor is any demand made to interfere with foreign policy." P.A.C., Laurier Papers, Liberal M.P.'s to Asquith, 18 December 1912.

93. *Ibid.*, Fielding to Laurier, 18 and 19 March 1913.

94. P.A.C., Borden Papers, Private, Diary, 15 May 1913. The five were Achim, Barrette, Bellemare, Boulay and Guilbault. Lamarche and Mondou, who had joined them on second reading, were absent.

95. *Ibid.*, 6, 20 and 22 March 1913.

96. R.A. Preston, *Canada and "Imperial Defence"* (Durham, 1967), 451.

97. Most of the text of the memorandum on permanent policy is printed in *D.C.E.R.*, I, 279-81.

98. P.A.C., Laurier Papers, Fielding to Laurier, 18 March 1913.

99. *C.A.R.*, 1914, 752.

100. P.A.C., Borden Papers, Private, Diary, 9 June 1911.

101. *Ibid.*, 12 June 1914. The Senate's rejection was in the form of a provision delaying implementation "until the termination of the now-existing Canadian Parliament."

102. U.N.B., J.D. Hazen Papers, Borden to Hazen, 8 May 1913, and Hazen to Bassett, 9 May 1913.

103. P.A.C., Borden Papers, Borden to Ferguson, 23 March 1906.

104. *Ibid.*, 33, no. 13883.

105. P.A.C., Borden Papers, Private, Diary, 31 July, 1 August 1914.

NOTES TO CHAPTER ELEVEN

1. *D.C.E.R.*, I, 37.

2. P.A.C., Borden Papers, 40, no. 17702.

3. Skelton, *Laurier*, II, cited 433.

4. P.A.C., Borden Papers, v. 37, OC187.

5. *Ibid.*, 336, Memoir Notes, 892.

6. For assessments of the exercise of emergency powers by the Canadian government during World War I, see D.E. Smith, "Emergency Government in Canada," *C.H.R.*, L, 4, 1969, 429-48, and R.C. Brown, " 'Whither are we being shoved?' Sir Robert Borden and War Leadership in Canada," in J.L. Granatstein and R. Cuff, eds., *War and Society in North America* (Toronto, 1971), 104-19.

7. P. C. 2067.

8. *D.C.E.R.*, I, 43.

9. P.A.C., Foster Papers, Diary, 12 September 1914.

10. P.A.C., R.G. 24, Records of Department of National Defence, vol. 6328, HQ 67-79-1 has details on the assembly of land for the camp.

11. P.A.C., Foster Papers, Diary, 19 September 1914.

12. *Montreal Daily Star,* 17 August 1914, 2. G.F.G. Stanley, *Canada's Soldiers* (Toronto, 1960), judged Valcartier "wasteful and unnecessary," 311.

13. P.A.C., Borden Papers, Borden to Chisholm, 21 November 1932.

14. *C.A.R.*, 1914, 205. For detailed accounts of mobilization of the first contingent, see Colonel G.W.L. Nichol-

son, *Canadian Expeditionary Force 1914-1919* (Ottawa, 1962), 18-32; John Swettenham, *To Seize the Victory* (Toronto, 1965), ch. 2; and S.F. Wise, "The Borden Government and the Formation of a Canadian Flying Corps, 1911-1916," in Cross and Bothwell, eds. *op. cit.*, 122-44.

15. D.E. MacIntyre, *Canada at Vimy* (Toronto, 1967), 7.

16. See below, 235-36.

17. Nicholson, *op. cit.*, cited, 205.

18. P.A.C., Foster Papers, Diary, 14 November 1916.

19. Swettenham, *op. cit.*, 247.

20. Nicholson, *op. cit.*, 144, 154, 198.

21. A Canadian Captain, "The Trench Raiders," *Atlantic Monthly,* December 1916, 832. The Canadian captain was D.E. MacIntyre of Kirk's Ferry, Quebec, who generously made this material available.

22. I. and R. F. L. Sheldon-Williams, *The Canadian Front in France and Flanders,* cited, R.C. Brown and M. Prang, *Confederation to 1949* (Scarborough, 1966), 152.

23. MacIntyre, *op. cit.*, 112. Yet another account, by a soldier in the Canadian Field Artillery, may be found in W.B. Kerr, *Shrieks and Crashes* (Toronto, 1929), ch. 2.

24. *D.C.E.R.*, I, 58, 81-82, 94, and 107-8.

25. *C.A.R.*, 1916, 422.

26. *Ibid.*, 1916, 424.

27. Nicholson, *op. cit.*, 218, 546.

28. *Ibid.*, 220.
29. *C.A.R.*, 1917, 520. For an account of Currie's despair at the way the politicians handled the issue, see A.M.J. Hyatt, "Sir Arthur Currie and Conscription: A Soldier's View," *C.H.R.*, L, 3, 1969, 285-96.
30. Nicholson, *op. cit.*, 344, 347.
31. When a general amnesty was proclaimed in December 1919, about 15,000 were still at large and an equivalent number were in prison. Nicholson, *op. cit.*, 352.
32. Nicholson, *op. cit.*, 353.
33. P.H. Morris, ed., *The Canadian Patriotic Fund: A Record of its Activities from 1914-1919* (n.p., n.d.), 7.
34. *Imperial Order of the Daughters of the Empire, Golden Jubilee, 1900-1950* (Toronto, 1950), 25-27.
35. *Canada's Part in the Great War*, Department of Public Information, 1919, 43. The work of the Red Cross illustrated the growth of professionalism among community organizations that characterized the war years. The Society stated:
We are not going to be led astray by any wild appeals or sensational reports, but we are adopting a system of making careful enquiries before we take action, and the people may rest assured that whatever we do will be done after due thought and consideration and careful investigation. Canadian Red Cross Society, *Annual Report, 1915*, 16.
36. Mrs. G. Wilson, *et al.*, "The History of . . . North Middlesex District Women's Institutes . . . " (1953), 18. See also, Annie Walker, *et al.*, *Fifty Years of Achievement* (Federated Women's Institutes of Ontario, 1948), *passim.*
37. P.A.C., Borden Papers, M.C. Lewis, to Borden, 18 June 1916, no. 30391-93.
38. Relief Committee, Montreal

Branch, *Report of the Work of the Canadian Patriotic Fund from August, 1914 to August, 1917*, 9.
39. Morris, *op. cit.*, 36, 39.
40. Relief Committee, Montreal Branch, *Report, op. cit.*, 11.
41. *Ibid., passim.*
42. P.A.C., Borden Papers, 334 Memoir Notes, no. 181.
43. *Globe*, 7 August 1914.
44. P.A.C., Borden Papers, R.D. Nixon to Hazen, no day, August, 1914, no. 105969-70.
45. *Ibid.*, Spring-Rice to Governor General, 3 September 1914, no. 105990.
46. See *C.A.R.*, 1915-1917, *passim.*
47. P.A.C., Borden Papers, Sherwood to Borden, 8 September 1914, and Fortescue to Borden, 11 September 1914.
48. Eventually the Chief Press Censor, E.J. Chambers, was able to curtail some of the more flagrant rumour-mongering about invasion threats and the dangers of the aliens within Canada. See P.A.C., Records of the Secretary of State, Chief Press Censor files.
49. P.A.C., Borden Papers, Speech, Montreal, 7 December 1914.
50. Secretary of State's Records, W.D. Otter, "Internment Operations, 1914-1920." A total of 8,579 male prisoners were eventually interned. Of these some 3,000 were in the reservist category and classed as "prisoners of war." Otter also observed that "the tendency of municipalities to 'unload' their indigent was the cause of the confinement of not a few" and that about 6,000 were "parolled" for labour work outside the camps.
51. H.T.F. Duckworth, *No Trading with Germans*, British Empire Union of Canada (Toronto, 1916), 10-11.
52. P.A.C., Foster Papers, Stewart to

Doherty, 22 August 1918.

53. P.A.C., Borden Papers, A.W. Windish to Borden, July 18, 1916, no. 98877-78. On Borden's orders the officers of the R.N.W.M.P. subdistrict investigated and reported that the "man" had been warned not to bother Windish again. Crime Report, Moosomin Subdistrict, 16 August 1916.

54. P.A.C., White Papers, M.J. Galvin to White, 3 July 1918, no. 2948. For an interesting description of the life of an enemy alien businessman, a partner of Mackenzie and Mann, during the war, see T. Regehr, ed., The Possibilities Are Truly Great (Toronto, 1971).

55. Labour Gazette, XV, June 1915, 1453.

56. P.A.C., Borden Papers, Cahan to Doherty, 20 July and 14 September 1918.

57. P. C. 2381.

58. P. C. 2384.

59. See below, 271-72.

NOTES TO CHAPTER TWELVE

1. P.A.C., Department of Finance, Miscellaneous, Correspondence of the ministers, "Report of a Conference in connection with the 1919 War Loan held at the Chateau Laurier, August 1, 1919," 10.

2. P.A.C., Borden Papers, White to Borden, 5 February 1915, no. 2485-88.

3. P.C. 2032 and 2033.

4. Statutes of Canada, 5 George V., chs. 3 and 4.

5. C.A. Curtis, "The Canadian Banks and War Finance," in E.P. Neufeld, ed., Money and Banking in Canada (Carleton Library no. 17, Toronto, 1964), 207-8.

6. C.A.R., 1915, 203.

7. Statutes of Canada, 5 George V, ch. 1.

8. Curtis, op. cit., 209.

9. Cited, ibid., n. 1, 206.

10. Canada, House of Commons Debates, 11 February 1915, 85.

11. J.J. Deutsch, "War Finance and the Canadian Economy, 1914-1920," C.J.E.P.S., VI, 1940, 537. By comparison, during the most intense period of World War II, war spending absorbed nearly fifty per cent of national income.

12. Canada, House of Commons Debates, 24 April 1917, 720.

13. Ibid., 11 February 1915, 86.

14. Ibid., 15 February 1916. O.D. Skelton in his Queen's University Bulletin, "Canadian Federal Finance," II, 1918, properly noted, so far as domestic borrowing was concerned, that this was simply "financial hocus-pocus":

these goods and services must come out of the present, not out of stores inherited from the past, nor out of the activities of generations yet to come. . . If we borrowed every cent of the cost of the war, that would simply mean giving future individual creditors the right to recoup themselves from future individual taxpayers. Conceivably loans and taxes might be so distributed that in the future each man would get back in interest what he had paid in taxes. In any case, the next generation will not be repaying this generation; some individuals in 1935 will be repaying other individuals in 1935.

Cited, J. Harvey Perry, *Taxes, Tariffs and Subsidies,* I (Toronto, 1955), 148.

15. P.A.C., White Papers, F. Williams-Taylor to White, 6 May 1915, no. 1474.

16. *Ibid.,* White to Macaulay, 9 July 1915, no. 1549-50.

17. *Ibid.,* White to Williams-Taylor, 24 August 1916, no. 2087.

18. The enormous resources of the domestic bond market and White's gradual realization of their potential as a source of financing independent of foreign markets were the subjects of his *The Story of Canada's War Finance* (Montreal, 1921).

19. O.D. Skelton, "Canadian Federal Finance–II," *Bulletin,* Department of History and Political and Economic Science, Queen's University, 1918, *passim.*

20. *Canada, House of Commons Debates,* 15 February 1916. Detailed discussion of the Business Profits Tax may be found in Perry, *op. cit.,* 152ff. Suffice it to say here that the rates were increased in both 1917 and 1918 and that it produced 80 per cent of the revenue from direct taxation during the war period.

21. *Ibid.,* 25 July 1917. An excellent description of war-time provincial and municipal fiscal policy may be found in Perry, *op. cit.,* chs. 11-12.

22. From Perry, *op. cit.,* 162.

23. Urquhart and Buckley, eds., *Historical Statistics of Canada, op. cit.,* Table D280-287, 99.

24. *C.A.R.,* 1919, 323, 326.

25. On this point and the inadequacy of White's view, see Curtis, *op. cit.;* see also P.A.C., White Papers, White to Hardman Lever, 18 December 1918, no. 12827-28. "The Banks have already used over fifteen million dollars which we advanced to them in purchase of their loans upon wheat. This,

coupled with their own heavy advances, has brought about a serious condition of currency inflation."

26. See *Canada, Report of the Royal Commission on Banking and Currency in Canada,* 1933, 58-59, 85-86.

27. Perry, *op. cit.,* 149.

28. P.A.C., White Papers, T.F. Taylor to White, 14 December 1914, no. 7389-91.

29. See Deutsch, "War Finance," *op. cit.,* 525-37.

30. *D.C.E.R.,* I, 59. See also 61-64, 66, 68-69, 76-77, 84-89, 99-100 for other dispatches on this subject, and Gaddis Smith, *Britain's Clandestine Submarines, 1914-1915* (New Haven, 1964). Much of Borden's trip to London in the summer of 1915 was taken up with the continuing problem of securing war orders from the Allies.

31. *Canada, House of Commons Debates,* 15 April 1915, 2613-17; Borden, *Memoirs,* I, 476-82, 541-42; *D.C.E.R.,* I, 69-72 gives the text of the Order-in-Council authorizing the War Purchasing Commission.

32. *Report, Royal Commission on Shell Contracts, 1916.*

33. A detailed and biased survey of the work of the Shell Committee and the I.M.B. can be found in David Carnegie, *The History of Munition Supply in Canada, 1914-1918* (London, 1925). See also J.C. Hopkins, *Canada at War* (Toronto 1919), ch. 11, and Michael Bliss, "A Canadian Businessman and War: The Case of Joseph Flavelle," in Granatstein and Cuff, eds., *War and Society in North America, op. cit.,* 20-36.

34. *Canada, House of Commons Debates,* 1 March 1915, 552.

35. *D.C.E.R.,* I, 99-100.

36. Fowke, *The National Policy and the Wheat Economy, op. cit.,* cited 169.

37. For a more detailed discussion see Fowke, *op. cit.,* ch. 9, and Mitchell W.

Sharp, "Allied Wheat Buying in Relationship to Canadian Marketing Policy, 1914-18," *C.J.E.P.S.*, VI, 3, 1940, 372-89.

38. P.A.C., White Papers, "Final Report of the Fuel Controller," March 1919, no. 4791.

39. P.A.C., Borden Papers, Magrath to Borden, 24 January 1918, no. 130887-88.

40. *Ibid.*, "Facts About Fuel Control Work in Canada" by Charles Peterson, Deputy Fuel Controller, October 1918, no. 133507, and Jamieson, *Times of Trouble*, 160-64.

41. "Final Report," no. 4804.

42. P.A.C., White Papers, "Report of the Food Controller," 1918, no. 4501.

43. T.A. Crerar, "Report of the Canada Food Board," 22.

44. "Report of the Food Controller"; "Report of the Canada Food Board"; *Food Laws: Manual . . . of the Canada Food Board*, 1918; and Food Controller for Canada, "War Meals," 1917; *passim.*

45. Other examples of government intervention were the 1918 establishment of the War Trade Board to regulate imports and exports, and the prohibition of the manufacture, distribution, and sale of liquor through provincial and federal legislation in 1917 and 1918. The latter, of course, was considered by many as essentially a long awaited social reform. See P.A.C., Foster Papers, Diary, 31 January and 7 February 1918.

46. "Report of the Canada Food Board," 4.

47. Morris, ed., *The Canadian Patriotic Fund, op. cit.*, 8.

48. P.A.C., Borden Papers, Memorandum, Crothers to Borden, 16 May 1918, no. 75319-32 and Martin Robin, *Canadian Labour and Radical Politics* (Kingston, 1968), ch. 9.

49. P.A.C., Borden Papers, Borden to Foster, 15 December 1914, no. 15386-87; *Labour Gazette*, February, 1915, 965.

50. *Ontario Commission on Unemployment, Report* (Toronto, 1916), 119.

51. *Labour Gazette*, February, 1915, 869.

52. *Ibid.*, November, 1915, 530; P.A.C., Borden Papers, Memorandum, Crothers to Borden, 16 May 1918, no. 75319-32.

53. January, 1917, 33.

54. *Labour Gazette*, December, 1916, 1852.

55. P. C. 2777 and 2957.

56. *Labour Gazette*, December, 1918, 1131. As computed by the Department of Labour, the price index of the family budget for 1911-20 is:

	Total	Food	Fuel	Rent
1920	184.7	217.9	192.1	128.4
1919	158.1	189.2	160.6	107.7
1918	147.2	177.3	149.6	97.7
1917	129.4	155.6	124.1	89.4
1916	105.4	119.8	100.9	83.5
1915	98.7	107.2	95.7	85.3
1914	102.0	105.4	99.5	98.3
1913	100.0	100.0	100.0	100.0
1912	98.3	100.0	95.4	98.3
1911	92.7	97.3	93.6	95.2

From Urquhart and Buckley, eds., *Historical Statistics*, Table J, 128-31, 303.

57. *Labour Gazette,* July, 1916, 1337; November, 1916, 1717.
58. P.A.C., Borden Papers, *Pronouncement of Organized Labour in Canada on*

War Problems (Ottawa, June 1917), no. 123341.
59. *Labour Gazette,* September, 1918, 690.

60. Department of Public Information, *Canada's Part in the Great War* (Ottawa, January, 1919), 45; *Labour Gazette,* October, 1918, 835. 8,000 women were employed in banks and 5,000 to 6,000 in Civil Service. Their increasing importance in the work force is suggested in the following table. The reader should note that the 1921 figures are probably considerably below the war-time figures for 1917 and 1918 due to the release of women from employment that generally is assumed to have taken place after the war.

Females gainfully employed by occupation, 1901-1921

	Agriculture	Manufacturing and Mechanical	Transport and Communication
1921	17,879	89,658	14,836
1911	15,887	96,795	5,340
1901	8,936	70,508	1,322

	Trade and Finance	Professional	Personal	Clerical
1921	47,670	92,754	132,424	90,612
1911	28,651	45,402	137,221	33,756
1901	7,757	34,679	100,306	12,569

From Urquhart and Buckley, eds., *Historical Statistics,* Table C8-35, 59.

61. P.A.C., Borden Papers, J.H.M. Parker to Borden, 17 January 1918, no. 125140.

62. Union memberships, 1911-1920.
(thousands)

	Total Membership	Members of International Unions
1920	373.8	267.2
1919	378.0	260.2
1918	248.9	201.4
1917	204.6	164.9
1916	160.4	129.1
1915	143.3	114.7
1914	166.2	140.5
1913	175.8	149.6
1912	160.1	136.4
1911	133.1	119.4

From Urquhart and Buckley, eds., *Historical Statistics*, Table D412-13, 105.

63. Strikes and lockouts, employers and workers, 1911-1920

	Strikes and Lockouts Beginning During Year	Total Strikes and Lockouts	Employers	Workers
1920	310	322	1,374	60,327
1919	332	336	1,967	148,915
1918	228	230	782	79,743
1917	158	160	758	50,255
1916	118	120	332	26,538
1915	62	63	120	11,395
1914	58	63	261	9,717
1913	143	152	1,077	40,519
1912	179	181	1,321	42,860
1911	99	100	533	29,285

From Urquhart and Buckley, eds., *Historical Statistics*, Table D426-33, 107.

Index numbers of wage rates in selected main industries, 1911-1920. (1949 = 100)

	General Index	Logging	Coal Mining	All Metal Mining	Manufac- turing	Construc- tion	Railways
1920	52.3	65.9	57.8	56.9	47.0	57.5	63.6
1919	44.0	58.9	49.9	48.9	39.0	47.1	52.9
1918	37.4	51.0	46.1	48.7	31.8	40.1	45.4
1917	31.9	44.3	38.2	44.9	27.7	35.0	35.8
1916	27.8	33.8	32.6	40.5	24.9	32.6	30.4
1915	26.0	28.3	29.9	36.6	23.0	32.2	29.3
1914	25.8	29.7	29.8	36.2	22.3	32.1	29.0
1913	25.5	-	-	-	21.7	31.8	28.8
1912	24.8	-	-	-	21.0	30.5	28.1
1911	24.0	30.3	28.5	34.9	20.7	28.7	27.6

Ibid., Table D 1-11, 84.

64. P.A.C., Borden Papers, E.H. Beazley, to Borden, 28 August 1918, no. 136194.

65. *Ibid.,* Flavelle to Borden, 11 December 1915, no. 123293-94. See also Flavelle to Borden, 7 June 1917, no. 123315-17 and Crothers to Borden, 9 June 1917, no. 123319-23; and David Bercuson, "Labour in Winnipeg: The Great War and the General Strike" (unpublished Ph.D. thesis, University of Toronto, 1971), ch. 3.

66. *Labour Gazette,* May, 1918, 354.

67. Department of Public Information, *Canada's Part in the Great War, op.cit.,* 46.

68. P.C., 1743, 11 July 1918.

69. Stevens, *Canadian National Railways,* II, 473, 470. Stevens, however, overstates the case when he remarks that "railways were the only major enterprises which were being denied a share of war prosperity" (470). Nor is it clear that an increase in freight rates would have solved the railways' financial problems.

70. Shaughnessy to Borden, 4 December 1915, cited, Graham, *Meighen,* I, 94.

71. P.A.C., Borden Papers, Private, Diary, 26 November 1915.

72. P.A.C., Borden Papers, File O.C. 167, *passim.*

73. Borden, *Memoirs,* II, cited 644. Three directors, named by the government, were placed on the board of each company. *C.A.R.,* 1916, 790-93.

74. P.A.C., Borden Papers, Private, Diary, 26 June 1916.

75. *C.A.R.,* 1917, cited 399.

76. Stevens, *op. cit.,* II, 474-79; Borden, *Memoirs,* II, 649.

77. P.A.C., Borden Papers, Flavelle to Borden, 28 June 1915, no. 32891-93.

78. Government management would "be ruinous," "management by commission is little better," but if his suggestion was accepted, he boasted, it "would ensure to the combined system the organization of the Canadian Pacific Railway, the name, which is an item of considerable value, particularly in connection with passenger traffic, and the esprit de corps for which the Canadian Pacific staff is famous." *Ibid.,* Shaughnessy to Borden, 16 May 1916, no. 32941-46.

79. P.A.C., Borden Papers, Private, Diary, 16 May 1917.

80. *Ibid.*, 5 May 1915.

81. P.A.C., Borden Papers, Cable, Borden to Blount, for White, 29 April 1917, no. 47409.

82. P.A.C., Borden Papers, Private, Diary, 13 June 1917.

83. *Ibid.*, 14 June 1917.

84. Stevens, *op. cit.*, 483.

85. Borden, *Memoirs*, II, cited 651-52.

86. Stevens, *op. cit.*, cited 510.

87. Stevens ably traces the story of nationalization against a background of biased treatment of the Grand Trunk by the Borden governments. See *Canadian National Railways*, II, ch. 17.

88. Stevens, *op. cit.*, 488-508.

NOTES TO CHAPTER THIRTEEN

1. *La Patrie*, 5 August 1914.

2. Stephen Leacock, "Greater Canada: An Appeal," *University Magazine*, V, April 1907, 133, 136.

3. Charles W. Gordon, "Canada's Duty," *Presbyterian*, XXV, 18, 12 November 1914, 438; see also Rev. (Captain) Wellington Bridgman, *Breaking Prairie Sod* (Toronto, 1920), 156.

4. Carol Lee Bacchi-Ferraro, "The Ideas of Canadian Suffragists, 1890-1920" (unpublished M.A. thesis, McGill University, 1970), cited 117.

5. Borden, *Memoirs*, I, 461.

6. A.B. Keith, *Documents and Speeches on British Colonial Policy, 1763-1917* (Toronto, 1953), 263.

7. *Gazette*, 8 August 1914.

8. *Le Devoir*, 8 September 1914.

9. W.L. Grant, "Current Events," *Queen's Quarterly*, XXII, 2, 1914, 220.

10. W.L. Morton, *The Progressive Party in Canada* (Toronto, 1950), 30-31.

11. J.S. Woodsworth, "Some Aspects of Immigration," *University Magazine*, XIII, 2, 1914, 188.

12. Henri Lemay, "L'Avenir de la Race canadienne-française," *La Revue Canadienne*, LVIII, 1910, 300.

13. *Orange Sentinel*, 3 February 1910.

14. Fallon to McEvoy, 21 January

1921. Cited in Michael Joseph Patrick, "The Role of Bishop Francis Michael Fallon in the Conflict Between the French Catholics and the Irish Catholics in the Ontario Bilingual Schools Question, 1910-1920" (unpublished M.A. thesis, University of Western Ontario, 1969), 137. On the controversy, see also the valuable study by Marilyn J. Barber, "The Ontario Bilingual Schools Issue, 1910-1916" (unpublished M.A. thesis, Queen's University, 1964).

15. R.J.A. Huel, "L'Association Catholique Franco-Canadienne de la Saskatchewan: A Response to Cultural Assimilation" (unpublished M.A. thesis, University of Saskatchewan, Regina, 1969), 22.

16. *Congrès d'Education des Canadiens-Français d'Ontario, 1910* (Ottawa, 1910).

17. *Système scolaire de la Province d'Ontario* (Hawkesbury, 1909).

18. P.A.O., Whitney Papers, N.A. Belcourt to Whitney, 12 November 1910.

19. Robert Sellar, *The Tragedy of Quebec* (Toronto, 1916), 282-84.

20. P.A.O., Whitney Papers, Hanna to Pyne, 23 May 1910.

21. P.A.C., Landry Collection, Memo-

randum of Bishop Fallon to the Bishops of Ontario, 24 January 1917. Cited in Barber, *op. cit.*, 38.

22. P.A.O., Whitney Papers, Whitney to Belcourt, 12 August 1910.

23. F.W. Merchant, *Report on the Condition of English-French Schools in the Province of Ontario* (Toronto, 1912), 69.

24. *Report of the Minister of Education for the Province of Ontario for the year 1912* (Toronto, 1913), 211. See also Franklin Walker, *Catholic Education and Politics in Ontario* (Toronto, 1964), 266.

25. N.A. Belcourt, *French in Ontario* (reprinted from the *University Magazine*, December 1912), 4. See also Association Canadienne-Française d'Education d'Ontario, *Bilingualism in Ontario: A Common Sense View* (Ottawa, 1912).

26. *Globe*, 27 June 1914. On Rowell, see Margaret Prang, "The Political Career of Newton Wesley Rowell" (unpublished Ph.D. thesis, University of Toronto, 1959). See also James Gray, *Booze* (Toronto, 1972), 79.

27. Alphonse T. Charron, *La Langue française et les Petits Canadiens français d'Ontario* (Quebec City, 1914).

28. Robert Rumilly, *Histoire de la Province de Quebec*, XXI (Montreal, n.d.), 137-38.

29. *C.A.R.*, 1916, 526.

30. *Ibid.*, 567.

31. Rumilly, XXI, *op. cit.*, 54.

32. K.A. McLeod, "A History of the Status of the French Language in the Schools of the North-West Territories 1870-1905 and in Saskatchewan 1905-1934" (unpublished M.Ed. thesis, University of Saskatchewan, 1966), and Keith McLeod, "Politics, Schools and the French Language," in Norman Ward and Duff Spafford, eds., *Politics in Saskatchewan* (Toronto, 1968), 124-50.

33. P.A.C., Dafoe Papers, Thomas Côté to Dafoe, 27 March 1917.

34. John M. Reid, "The Erection of the Roman Catholic Archdiocese of Winnipeg" (unpublished M.A. thesis, University of Manitoba, 1961), cited 55-56.

35. C.B. Sissons, *Bilingual Schools in Canada* (Toronto, 1917), cited 150.

36. W.L. Morton, *Manitoba: A History* (Toronto, 1957), cited 352.

37. Sellar, *op. cit.*, 327-28.

38. Rumilly, XIX, *op. cit.*, 137.

39. P.A.C., Gouin Papers, Gouin to Hearst, 3 February 1915, and Hearst to Gouin, 19 February 1915.

40. *Canada, Senate Debates*, 1915, 627.

41. Rumilly, XX, *op. cit.*, 57.

42. *Ibid.*, XXI, 51-52.

43. P.A.C., Laurier Papers, Rowell to Laurier, 29 February 1916.

44. *Ibid.*, Rowell to Laurier, 26 April 1916.

45. P.A.O., Whitney Papers, Pelletier to Whitney, 1 October 1912, and Whitney to Chapais, 16 October 1912.

46. *Ibid.*, Borden to Whitney, 16 October 1912, and Whitney to Borden, 17 October 1912.

47. P.A.C., Borden Papers, Casgrain, Blondin, Patenaude to Borden, 20 April 1916, and Borden to Casgrain, Blondin, Patenaude, 24 April 1916.

48. Rumilly, XXI, *op. cit.*, 55.

49. *Canada, House of Commons Debates*, 1916, IV, 3618.

50. C.B. Sissons, *Church and State in Canadian Education* (Toronto, 1958), cited 91.

51. Walker, *op. cit.*, 298-99.

52. P.A.C., Gouin Papers, Mgr Bégin à Sa Sainteté Le Pape Benedict XV, 7 janvier 1917. See also Fitzpatrick, *op. cit.*, 144-50.

53. Sir Charles Lucas, *The Empire at War* (London, 1923), II, 17.

54. Nicholson, *The Canadian Expedi-*

tionary Force, 1914-19. op. cit., 221.

55. Desmond Morton, "French Canada and the Canadian Militia, 1868-1914," Social History, III, April, 1969, 32-50.

56. Lionel Groulx, Mes Mémoires, I (Montreal, 1970), 127.

57. Louvigny de Montigny, La Langue française au Canada (Ottawa, 1916), cited 168.

58. Desmond Morton, "French Canada and War: The Military Background to the Conscription Crisis of 1917," in Granatstein and Cuff, eds., War and Society in North America, op. cit., 84-103.

59. Jean Bruchési, "Service national et conscription," in Témoignages d'hier (Montreal, 1961), 262-64.

60. P.A.C., Borden Papers, Borden to Waters, Simpson and Rigg, 27 December 1916.

61. Ibid., Borden to Tupper, 2 January 1916.

62. P.A.C., Laurier Papers, Godfrey to Laurier, 12 June 1916.

63. L.-G. Desjardin, L'Angleterre, Le Canada et la Grande Guerre (Quebec City, 1917).

64. J.M. Godfrey, The History of Bonne Entente (n.p., 1917); W.H. Atherton, A Report of the National Unity and Win-the-War Convention (Montreal, 1917); The Bonne Entente: How It Began, What It Has Done and Its Immediate Programme (n.p., 1917). An unpublished research paper by Mr. John Witham at York University provided some of the details about the "Bonne Entente" movement.

65. Rumilly, XXII, op. cit., 16.

66. Industrial Canada, October 1916.

67. R. Matthew Bray, "The National Government Phenomenon: An Analysis of a Popular Movement in Canada" (unpublished research paper, York University, 1972).

68. Manitoba Free Press, 29 November 1916.

69. Our Volunteer Army: Facts and Figures (Montreal, 1916).

70. René Durocher, "Henri Bourassa, les évêques et la guerre, 1914-1918," C.H.A., Historical Papers, 1971, 248-75.

71. Olivar Asselin, L'Action catholique, les évêques et la guerre (Montreal, 1915).

72. Lettres d'un "Patriote," Où Allons-Nous? Le Nationalisme canadien (Montreal, 1916).

73. Henri Bourassa, Hier, Aujourd'hui et Demain (Montreal, 1916).

74. Rumilly, XXII, op. cit., 64; Elizabeth Armstrong, The Crisis of Quebec, 1914-18, (New York, 1937), 161-98.

75. J.M. Bliss, "The Methodist Church and World War I," C.H.R., XLIX, 3, 1968, cited 222.

76. W. Stewart Wallace, The Memoirs of the Rt. Hon. Sir George Foster (Toronto, 1933), cited 187.

77. P.A.C., Borden Papers, Private, Diary, 17 May 1917.

78. Borden, Memoirs, II, 698.

79. P.A.C., Borden Papers, Private, Diary, 24 May 1917.

80. Ibid., 25 May 1917.

81. Ibid., 25 May 1917.

82. Borden Memoirs, II, 722.

83. P.A.C., Laurier Papers, Laurier to Hardy, 29 May 1917.

84. P.A.C., Sifton Papers, Sifton to Wrong, 5 June 1917.

85. Bruchési, op. cit., 269-70.

86. P.A.C., Borden Papers, Borden to Bruchési, 31 May 1917.

87. Ramsay Cook, "Dafoe, Laurier and the Formation of Union Government," C.H.R., XLII, 3, 1961, 200-3.

88. P.A.C., Perley Papers, Hazen to Perley, 9 August 1917.

89. P.A.C., Borden Papers, Meighen to Borden, 17 October 1916.

90. *Ibid.*, Edward Michener to Borden, 11 June 1917; Thomas McNaughton to Borden, 7 July 1917; Meighen to Borden, 7 July 1917; H.C. Simpson to Robert Rogers, 9 August 1917; Joseph Boudreau, "Western Canada's Enemy Aliens, in World War I," *Alberta Historical Review*, XII, 1, 1964, 1-9.
91. P.A.C., Borden Papers, Constance Hamilton to Borden, n.d.
92. *Globe*, 21 September 1917. Cited in Bacchi-Ferraro, *op. cit.*, 125.
93. Borden, *Memoirs*, II, 706-13; Graham, *Meighen*, I, 164-70.
94. P.A.C., Sifton Papers, Calder to Rowell, 4 October 1917. For details of the negotiations with Rowell, see Margaret Prang, *op. cit.*, 397-443.
95. Henri Bourassa, *La Conscription* (Montreal, 1917), 11.
96. P.A.C., Bourassa Papers, Bourassa à Fitzpatrick, 28 juin 1917: Henri Bourassa, *The Case Against Conscription* (Montreal, 1917).
97. P.A.C., Bourassa Papers, Lavergne à Bourassa, 26 octobre 1917.
98. P.A.C., Laurier Papers, Bureau à Laurier, 26 septembre, 1917.
99. *C.A.R.*, 1917, 622.
100. Martin Robin, "Registration, Conscription, and Independent Labour Politics," *C.H.R.*, XLVII, 2, 1966, 101-18; see also Leo Heaps, *The Rebel in the House: The Life and Times of A.A. Heaps, M.P.* (London, 1970), 14-16.
101. *Toronto Mail and Empire*, 25 September 1917.
102. *C.A.R.*, 1917, 602-33, and Bliss, *op. cit.*, 221; and Charles W. Gordon, *Postscript to Adventure: The Autobiography of Ralph Connor* (New York, 1938), 338-39.
103. *Manitoba Free Press*, 11 December 1917.
104. *Ibid.*, 18 December 1917.
105. *C.A.R.*, 1917, 643.
106. P.A.C., Aberdeen Papers, Laurier to Lady Aberdeen, 24 December 1917.
107. *Le Devoir*, 3 janvier 1918.
108. Ramsay Cook, *The Politics of John W. Dafoe and the Free Press* (Toronto, 1963), 66-85.
109. Berger, *The Sense of Power*, *op. cit.*, 264.
110. Henri Bourassa, *Le Problème de l'Empire: Indépendance ou Association Impériale?* (Montreal, 1916), 43.

NOTES TO CHAPTER FOURTEEN

1. P.A.C., Borden Papers, Peace Conference, file 18, Borden to L.S. Amery, 22 August 1918.
2. *Ibid.*, Speech to Pilgrims' Society, New York City, 23 December 1915, no. 175545-48.
3. Cited in D.C. Watt, "America and the British Foreign-Policy-Making Elite, from Joseph Chamberlain to Anthony Eden, 1895-1956," in his *Personalities and Policies* (London, 1965), 19-52.
4. P.A.C., Christie Papers, "Memorandum for the Prime Minister," 27 and 31 January 1916; Perley to Borden, 24 February 1916, no. 1726-29, no. 1730-31.
5. P.A.C., Christie Papers, Memo and draft of speech. V. 2, no. 1385-92.
6. P.A.C., Borden Papers, "Canada at War," Speech to the Lawyers' Club, New York, 18 November 1916, no. 175549-57. It should be noted that this and previous Borden speeches in

the United States were largely sermons to the converted. The New England Society and the Pilgrims' Society (22 and 23 December 1915) were both ardently Anglophile in sentiment. And the President of the Lawyers' Club, after reading an advance draft of his speech, told Borden that "we fully realize that Canada in her Loyalty to the Mother Country is fighting a battle for us as well as herself." *Ibid.*, W.A. Butler to Borden, 10 November 1916, no. 28441-42.

7. See above, 230.

8. This became the cause for an unseemly argument between the Prime Minister and the Governor General. See P.A.C., Borden Papers, file OC322.

9. Borden, *Memoirs*, II, 769-70.

10. *Ibid.*, II, 771-73, Borden to Devonshire, 3 March 1918; P.A.C., Borden Papers, Borden to White, 9 March 1918, no. 51030-31.

11. P.A.C., M.G., 12, A, (Copy) Admiralty Papers, Adm. 116/1400, fo 507, C. in C., N.A. and W.I. to Admiralty, 15 April 1918, Reel B 3444.

12. See P.A.C., R.G. 24, Records of the Department of National Defence, vols. 3831-33 and 4031 and Tucker, *The Naval Service of Canada, op. cit.*, 255.

13. P.A.C., Borden Papers, Meighen to Borden, 14 April 1917, no. 45807.

14. *D.C.E.R.*, I, 24, Borden to Perley, 13 October 1917.

15. *Ibid.*, 25, Governor General to Colonial Secretary, 18 October 1917.

16. *Ibid.*, 27, Governor General to Colonial Secretary, 31 October 1917; Governor General to Colonial Secretary, 5 November 1917. U.N.B., Hazen Papers, Hazen to W.N. Thorne, 16 October 1917 and Hazen to M. MacLaren, 7 November 1917.

17. *Ibid.*, 32-34, P.C. 272, 2 February 1918.

18. P.A.C., Borden Papers, Private, Diary, 26 March 1919; *Memoirs*, II, 911-12, 926.

19. *D.C.E.R.*, III, 4-6. Chairman, Canadian Trade Commission to President of the Privy Council, 17 September 1919.

20. *Ibid.*, 7-9. The latter quotation, significantly, is a direct paraphrase of the last lines of Resolution IX of the Imperial War Conference, 1917, amended for this occasion.

21. *Canada, House of Commons Debates*, 10 May 1920. The history of the origins of the Canadian mission in Washington is reviewed in Robert Bothwell, "Canadian Representation at Washington: A Study in Colonial Responsibility," *C.H.R.*, LIII, June 1972, 125-48. The appointment, of course, was not made for another six years. See John A. Galbraith, *The Establishment of Canadian Diplomatic Status at Washington* (Berkeley, 1951); *D.C.E.R.*, III, 6-21, 23-33, 40-43, and 50.

22. Sketches of Canadian-American relations during World War I may be found in Gaddis Smith, "Canadian External Affairs during World War I" in H. Keenleyside, ed., *The Growth of Canadian Policies in External Affairs*, (Durham, N.C., 1971), 33-58; and Robert Craig Brown, "Canada in North America" in John Braeman, *et al.*, eds., *Twentieth Century American Foreign Policy* (Columbus, 1971), 343-77.

23. Swettenham, *To Seize the Victory, op. cit.*, cited 130. Chapter 8 of Swettenham's book ably discusses the general problem.

24. P.A.C., Borden Papers, Private, Diary, 16 June 1915.

25. *Ibid.*, Diary, 24 August 1915; *D.C.E.R.*, I, 104, Borden to Perley, 4 January 1916.

26. *D.C.E.R.*, I, 96, Colonial Secretary to Acting High Commissioner, 3 November 1915.

27. Lloyd George, *War Memoirs*, IV (London, 1934), 1733. See also Thomas Jones, *Whitehall Diary, 1916-1925*, I (London 1969), 12, and S.W. Roskill, *Hankey, Man of Secrets, 1877-1918*, I (London, 1970), 348.

28. See Borden, *Memoirs*, II, 827.

29. George L. Cook, "Sir Robert Borden, Lloyd George and British Military Policy, 1917-1918," *Historical Journal*, XIV, 2, 1971, cited 375.

30. See Jones, *op. cit.*, 29-34.

31. P.A.C., Borden Papers, Peace Conference, file 18(a), Amery to Borden, 25 September 1918. See also P.A.C., Borden Papers, Amery to Borden 19 August 1918, no. 35977-79.

32. G.L. Cook, "Sir Robert Borden," cited 376, I.W.C., 4, 27 March 1917.

33. W.K. Hancock, *Smuts: The Sanguine Years, 1870-1919*, I (Cambridge, 1962), 446-52.

34. P.A.C., Borden Papers, Private, Diary, 22 March 1917.

35. For the full text of Resolution IX, see Maurice Ollivier, *The Colonial and Imperial Conferences from 1887 to 1937* (Ottawa, 1954), II, 194. On the initiative and drafting of Resolution IX, see R.C. Brown and Robert Bothwell, "The Canadian Resolution," in Robert Bothwell and Michael S. Cross, eds., *Policy By Other Means* (Toronto, 1972).

36. P.A.C., Borden Papers, Borden to Kemp, 31 January 1918, no. 51137.

37. I.W.C., Shorthand Notes, 13 June 1918, P.A.C., Borden Papers, no. 2484-96.

38. P.A.C., Borden Papers, Private, Diary, 12 June 1918.

39. I.W.C., Shorthand Notes, 13 June 1918.

40. *Ibid.*

41. P.A.C., Borden Papers, 340, Memoir Notes, "Report of the Committee of Prime Ministers," II, 2428-67.

42. *Ibid.* An able summary of the Imperial War Cabinet discussions of military policy is presented in G.L. Cook, "Sir Robert Borden," *op. cit.* The Canadian part in the Russian intervention is discussed in Gaddis G. Smith, "Canada and the Siberian Intervention, 1918-1919," *A.H.R.*, LXIV, July, 1959, 866-77, and in J. Swettenham, *Allied Intervention in Russia, 1918-1919, and the Part Played by Canada* (Toronto, 1969).

43. For a summary of Anglo-Canadian relations during the war see Robert Craig Brown, "Sir Robert Borden, the Great War and Anglo-Canadian Relations" in John S. Moir, ed., *Character and Circumstance: Essays in Honour of Donald Grant Creighton* (Toronto, 1970), 201-24.

44. *D.C.E.R.*, I, 218.

45. Nicholson, *C.E.F.*, 535, 548.

46. *D.C.E.R.*, II, 8.

47. *Ibid.*, I, 218.

48. *Ibid.*, I, 219.

49. P.A.C, Borden Papers, Private, Diary, 17 November 1918.

50. *Ibid.*, 1 December 1918.

51. *Ibid.*, 10 January 1919.

52. *D.C.E.R.*, II, 189.

53. P.A.C., Borden Papers, 342, Memoir Notes, Rowell to Borden, 24 December 1918, no. 3134-36.

54. P.A.C., Borden Papers, Private, Diary, 13 January 1919.

55. *D.C.E.R.*, II, 23.

56. L.F. Fitzhardinge, "Hughes, Borden and Dominion Representation at the Paris Peace Conference," *C.H.R.*, XLIX, June, 1968, 160-69.

57. *D.C.E.R.*, II, 190.

58. *Ibid.*, II, 72-73, 109-11, 118.

59. Volume II of the *Documents on*

Canadian External Relations is a most useful documentary account of the Canadian role in recognition of dominion status. See also G.P. de T. Glazebrook, *Canada at the Paris Peace Conference* (Toronto, 1942).

60. See Hancock, *Smuts, op. cit.,* ch, 21; D.H. Miller, *The Drafting of the Covenant* (London, 1928); and George Curry, "Woodrow Wilson, Jan Smuts, and the Versailles Settlement," *A.H.R.,* LXVI, July 1961, 963-86.

61. *D.C.E.R.,* II, 78-79.

62. *Ibid.,* 93. Concern over Article X remained a key point in Canada's League stance. At the first General Assembly in 1920, Doherty moved that it be deleted from the Covenant. See *D.C.E.R.,* III, 446-49.

63. *Ibid.,* 74.

64. *Ibid.,* 82.

65. P.A.C., Borden Papers, Peace Conference, file 18, Borden to Amery, 18 August 1918.

66. *Ibid.*

67. See P.A.C., Borden Papers, 341, Memoir Notes, I.W.C., 43, 18 December 1918, no. 2782-88; I.W.C., 44, 20 December 1918, no. 2789-96.

68. *Ibid.,* I.W.C., 44, 20 December 1918.

69. Borden to Rowell, 25 January 1919, *D.C.E.R.,* II, 41.

70. P.A.C., Borden Papers, Private, Diary, 29 January 1919.

71. See Borden, *Memoirs,* II, 905-7; *D.C.E.R.,* II, 193-98. Borden later acted as an intermediary between the Japanese representatives and the Australians in a dispute over Japanese conditions for entrance into the League of Nations. See *Memoirs,* II, 926-28 and *D.C.E.R.,* II, 104-5, 216.

72. P.A.C., Borden Papers, Private, Diary, 15 May 1919.

73. On the Greek Committee, see

P.A.C., Borden Papers, Peace Conference, file 36a, "Minutes" of the Greek Boundary Committee; Harold Nicolson, *Peace Making, 1919* (London, 1964); Borden, *Memoirs,* II, ch. 36. On Prinkipo, see P.A.C., Borden Papers, Memoir Notes, I.W.C., 47, 30 December 1918; Richard Ullman, *Britain and the Russian Civil War* (Princeton, 1968); and Arno Mayer, *The Politics and Diplomacy of Peacemaking* (Princeton, 1969).

74. P.A.C., Borden Papers, Private, Diary, 10 May 1919.

75. For a useful summary of the debate, see *C.A.R.,* 1919, 104-9.

76. See *D.C.E.R.,* III, 154-55, 157-62.

77. P.A.C., Meighen Papers, Rowell to Meighen, 9 February and 3 March 1921.

78. *D.C.E.R.,* III, 162-63.

79. *Ibid.,* 163-67.

80. See L. Woodward and R. Butler, *Documents on British Foreign Relations,* 14 (London, 1966), 221.

81. *Ibid.,* 170-88. Meighen had had little experience with foreign relations before he assumed the prime ministership. The strong position he took was the product of Loring Christie's efforts, with occasional consultation with Borden and Rowell, in a series of memoranda dating from February 1921. See A.R.M. Lower, "Loring Christie and the genesis of the Washington Conference of 1921-22," *C.H.R.,* XLVII, 1, 1966, 39ff.; Loring Christie, "The Anglo-Japanese Alliance: Recapitulation of Points, 1 June, 1921," *External Affairs,* September, 1966, 402ff.; and especially Robert Bothwell, "Loring Christie: The Failure of Bureaucratic Imperialism" (unpublished Ph.D. thesis, Harvard, 1972), ch. 7.

82. Of the many accounts of events leading up to the Washington Confer-

ence, brief summaries by Robert Bothwell, *op. cit.*, and M.G. Fry, "The North Atlantic Triangle and the Abrogation of the Anglo-Japanese Alliance," *Journal of Modern History,* XXXIX, March, 1967, 46-64, are most useful. Fuller discussion, including treatment of the Conference itself, may be found in M.G. Fry, *Illusions of*

Security: North Atlantic Diplomacy, 1918-1922 (Toronto, 1972). See also Graham, *Meighen,* II, and *D.C.E.R.,* III, chs. 3 and 5.

83. This opinion was re-affirmed by J.B. Brebner, "Canada, the Anglo-Japanese Alliance and the Washington Conference," *Political Science Quarterly,* L, 1935, 45-57.

NOTES TO CHAPTER FIFTEEN

1. *Manitoba Free Press,* 18 December 1917.
2. Rev. C.M. Gordon, "Forward," in the Social Service Council of Canada, *Social Service Congress, Ottawa, 1914* (Toronto, 1914), n.p.
3. James S. Brierley, "The Union Government's Opportunities," *University Magazine,* XVII, February 1918, 14-15.
4. J.O. Miller, ed., *The New Era in Canada* (London, Paris, Toronto, 1917), 6.
5. Maurice Hutton, "The British and German Mind," *University Magazine,* XV, October 1915, 337.
6. W.L. Grant, "Current Events," *Queen's Quarterly,* XXII, 2, 1914, 219.
7. Sir Robert Falconer, "What About Progress?", in *Idealism in National Character* (London, New York, Toronto, 1920), 115-16.
8. James A. Macdonald, *The North American Idea* (Toronto, 1917).
9. Andrew Macphail, "The Day of Wrath," *University Magazine,* XIII, October 1914, 356; G.G. Melvin, "The Cement of Blood," *University Magazine,* XIV, February 1915, 31. See also Paul Rutherford, "Canadian Intellectuals and the Great War, 1914-18" (unpublished research paper, University of Toronto, 1968).
10. *The Acts and Proceedings of the Forty-*

Second General Assembly of the Presbyterian Church in Canada, Winnipeg, June 7-16, 1916 (Toronto, 1916), 13.
11. *Journal of Proceedings of the Tenth Annual Conference of the Methodist Church in Canada, 1918* (Toronto, 1918), 139, 140, 340 *et seq.*. See Richard Allen, *The Social Passion* (Toronto, 1971), ch. 4.
12. Nellie L. McClung, *The Stream Runs Fast* (Toronto, 1948), 118-22.
13. Nellie L. McClung, *In Times Like These* (Toronto, 1915), 176.
14. *Ibid.,* 21-22.
15. *Ibid.,* 163.
16. Kennethe Haig, *Brave Harvest* (Toronto, 1945).
17. B.H. Saunders, *Emily Murphy: Crusader* (Toronto, 1945); Emily F. Murphy, *The Black Candle* (Toronto, 1922).
18. Rosa L. Shaw, *Proud Heritage* (Toronto, 1957); P.A.C., Fanny Penfold Coffee Papers, "History of the Catholic Women's League of Canada, 1910-35."
19. Marjorie MacMurchy, *The Woman–Bless Her* (Toronto, 1916), 151.
20. Stephen Leacock, "The Woman Question," in *Essays and Literary Studies* (Toronto, 1916), 137-60; Andrew Macphail, *Essays in Fallacy* (London, 1910), 1-100.
21. Mgr L.-A. Paquet, "Féminisme,"

Le Canada Français, I, décembre 1918, 233. See also Lionel Groulx, "Méditation Patriotique," in *Dix Ans d'Action française* (Montreal, 1926), 75; Henri Bourassa, "Le suffrage des femmes," *Le Devoir,* 28, 30 mars and 1 avril 1918.

22. Shaw, *op. cit.,* cited 119.

23. Victoria Hayward, "The Women Workers of Canada," *Canadian Magazine,* 50, March 1918, 286-96; Imperial Munitions Board, Canada, *Women in the Production of Munitions in Canada* (n.p., 1916).

24. Shaw, *op. cit.,* cited 116.

25. *Manitoba Free Press,* 28 January 1916.

26. Norman Lambert, "A Joan of the West," *Canadian Magazine,* 46, January 1916, 267.

27. Thérèse Casgrain, *Une Femme Chez les Hommes* (Montreal, 1971), 73ff.

28. Carol Lee Bacchi-Ferraro, "The Ideas of Canadian Suffragists, 1890-1920" (unpublished M.A. thesis, McGill University, 1970).

29. Mrs. Rose Henderson in the *British Columbia Federationist,* 27 September 1918. Cited in Catherine L. Cleverdon, *The Woman Suffrage Movement in Canada* (Toronto, 1950), 7.

30. A very advanced book on the feminist question, which demanded sexual emancipation as well as political equality, was published in Canada in 1911. Written by the South African writer Olive Schreiner, *Woman and Labour* (Toronto, 1911) viewed marriage as the essential obstacle to true equality. It is difficult to establish whether the book had much influence among Canadian women. The copy in the National Library was originally owned, read, and marked by W.L.M. King, who, of course, never contributed to woman's oppression through marriage.

31. June Menzies, "Votes for Saskatchewan's Women," in Norman Ward and Duff Spafford, eds., *Politics in Saskatchewan* (Toronto, 1968), cited 83. See also Nellie L. McClung, *In Times Like These, op. cit.,* 50.

32. Anne Anderson Perry, "Winning the Franchise," *Grain Growers' Guide,* 7 July 1920. See also Wendy Mitchinson, "Canadian Women 1900-21: A Study in the Feminist Role and Ideal" (unpublished research paper, York University, 1971).

33. John H. Thompson, "The Prohibition Question in Manitoba, 1892-1928" (unpublished M.A. thesis, University of Manitoba, 1969), 62-64; Albert John Heibert, "Prohibition in British Columbia" (unpublished M.A. thesis, Simon Fraser University, 1969); E.R. Forbes, "Prohibition and the Social Gospel in Nova Scotia," *Acadiensis,* I, (Autumn 1971), 11-36; Gerald A. Hallowell, "Prohibition in Ontario, 1919-23," (unpublished M.A. thesis, Carleton University, 1966); Erhard Pinno, "Temperance and Prohibition in Saskatchewan" (unpublished M.A. thesis, University of Saskatchewan, Regina, 1969); Robert Irwin McLean, "A Most Effectual Remedy: Temperence and Prohibition in Alberta, 1875-1915," (unpublished M.A. thesis, University of Calgary, 1969); James Gray, *Booze* (Toronto, 1972).

34. James Gray, *The Boy From Winnipeg* (Toronto, 1970), 26.

35. *World,* 19 August 1916. Cited in Heibert, *op. cit.,* 86.

36. P.A.C., National Council of Women Papers, Resolutions, 68, 1914. Wendy Mitchinson drew our attention to this document.

37. Cited in Hallowell, *op. cit.,* 57-58.

38. Ruth Spence, *Prohibition in Canada* (Toronto, 1919), 605.

39. *Ibid.,* 487-88.

40. Robert E. Popham and Wolfgang Schmidt, *Statistics of Alcohol Use and Alcoholism in Canada, 1871-1956* (Toronto, 1958), 15-21.

41. James Morton, *Honest John Oliver* (London, 1933), 199. Cited in Heibert, *op. cit.,* 111-12.

42. Heibert, *op. cit.,* 126. See also R.L. Werry, *The Liquor Traffic in the Province of Quebec* (Board of Home Missions and Social Service, Presbyterian Church in Canada, 1923), 13-14.

43. H.F. Gadsby, "Is the Prohibition Pendulum Swinging Back?", *Maclean's Magazine,* XXXII, April 1919, cited in Hallowell, *op. cit.,* 27.

44. Heibert, *op. cit.,* 131.

45. Pinno, *op cit.,* 303; Thompson, *op. cit.,* 108.

46. *Voice,* 9 April 1915; See also the *British Columbia Federationist,* 14 January 1916, and McLean, *op. cit.,* 121-24.

47. Cleverdon, *op. cit.,* 74; See also Eleanor Harman, "Five Persons from Alberta," in Mary Quale Innis, ed., *The Clear Spirit* (Toronto, 1967), 171.

48. Sir Clifford Sifton, "The Foundations of the New Era," in Miller, *op. cit.,* 37-38.

49. W.C. Good, *Production and Taxation in Canada* (Toronto, 1919).

50. William Irvine, *The Farmers in Politics* (Toronto, 1920), 22.

51. Salem Bland, *The New Christianity* (Toronto, 1920), 5.

52. Allen, *op. cit.,* 155-56.

53. C.W. Peterson, *Wake Up. Canada* (Toronto, 1919), 355.

54. Stephen Leacock, *The Unsolved Riddle of Social Justice* (New York, London, 1920), 140-41.

55. J.O. Miller, "The Testing of Democracy," *University Magazine,* XV, April 1916, 213.

56. J.S. Woodsworth, "Nation-Building," *University Magazine.* XVI, February 1917, 91.

57. J.T.M. Anderson, *The Education of New Canadians* (Toronto, (1918), 88-89. See also Morris Mott " 'The Foreign Peril': Nativism in Winnipeg" (unpublished M.A. thesis, University of Manitoba, 1970), 78-91. Sir Robert Falconer, "The Education of National Character," in his *Idealism in National Character, op. cit.,* 33-35.

58. P.A.C., Meighen Papers, Calder to Meighen, 24 February 1919. See also Howard Palmer, "Responses to Foreign Immigration: Nativism and Ethnic Tolerance in Alberta, 1880-1920" (unpublished M.A. thesis, University of Alberta, 1971), 216ff.; Rev. (Captain) Wellington Bridgman, *Breaking Prairie Sod* (Toronto, 1920), 261; *Globe,* 3 February 1919.

59. A.M. Willms, "The Brethren Known as Hutterians," *C.J.E.P.S.,* XXIV, 3, 1958, cited 394.

60. Victor Peters, *All Things Common* (New York, 1971), 48-49.

61. *Regina Daily Post,* 18 December 1918. Cited in Huel, *L'Association Catholique Franco-Canadienne de la Saskatchewan, op. cit.,* 137. See also *The Language Question before the Legislative Assembly of Saskatchewan* (Prince Albert, 1918).

62. Charles W. Humphries, "The Banning of a Book in British Columbia," *B.C. Studies,* I, 1, 1968-69, 1-12. The best account of the "alien question" and "nativism" during the war is found in Donald Howard Avery, "Canadian Immigration Policy and the Enemy Alien, 1896-1919: The Anglo-Canadian Perspective" (Ph.D. thesis, University of Western Ontario, 1973), ch. VII-X. This work was completed too late for its conclusions to be incorporated here, though it confirms in detail most of our argument.

63. W.L. Grant, *A Nation of Prophets, of Sages, and of Worthies* (Toronto, 1917), 7.

64. Ajax [A.Y. Jackson], "Dutch Art in Canada: The Last Chapter," *Rebel,* IV, November 1919, 65.

65. Lionel Groulx, "Ce Cinquantenaire," *L'Action française,* I, juillet 1917, 197.

66. A. Savard and W.E. Playfair, *Quebec and Confederation: A Record of the Debate of the Legislative Assembly of Quebec on the Motion Proposed by J.-N. Francoeur* (n.p., 1918).

67. *Ibid.,* 136.

68. P.A.C., Borden Papers, Memoir Notes, Report of Situation in Quebec, April 22, 1918; Elizabeth Armstrong, *The Crisis of Quebec* (New York, 1937), ch. 9; Norman Ward, ed., *A Party Politician: The Memoirs of C.G. Power* (Toronto, 1966), ch. 7; Jean Provencher, *Quebec sous la Loi de Guerre* (Trois-Rivières, 1971).

69. *Le Devoir,* 5 April 1919.

70. Joseph-Papin Archambault, s.j., *La Question sociale et nos Devoirs de Catholiques* (Montreal, 1917), 38.

71. Sister Marie Agnes of Rome Gaudreau, *The Social Thought of French Canada as Reflected in the Semaine Sociale* (Washington, 1946); Lionel Groulx, *Mes Mémoires, 1920-28,* II (Montreal, 1971), 24-26.

72. *Quebec, Sessional Papers #7, 1919-20,* 143. This quotation and some of the information in the preceding paragraph is drawn from the excellent paper by T.J. Copp, "The Condition of the Working Class in Montreal, 1897-1921" (presented to the C.H.A., June 1972).

73. Fernand Dumont, "Histoire du Syndicalisme dans l'industrie de l'amiante," in P.E. Trudeau, ed., *La Grève de l'amiante* (Montreal, 1956), 123-33.

74. *L'action catholique,* 9 novembre 1915.

75. Alfred Charpentier, *Ma Conversion au Syndicalisme Catholique* (Montreal, 1956), 54-57.

76. *Ibid.,* 109.

77. Henri Bourassa, *Syndicats Nationaux ou Internationaux?* (Montreal, 1919), p. 9.

78. Alfred Charpentier, *Dans les Serres de l'Aigle* (Montreal, 1920), 31-32.

79. Michel Têtu, "Les premiers syndicats catholiques canadiens, 1900-21" (unpublished Ph.D. thesis, Laval University, 1961), 200ff.

80. H.A. Logan, *Trade Unions in Canada* (Toronto, 1948), 562; Rumilly, *Histoire, op. cit.,* XXV, 73-75.

81. Stuart Jamieson, *Times of Trouble: Labour Unrest and Industrial Conflict in Canada, 1900-66* (Ottawa, 1968), 158.

82. *Ibid.,* 159-64.

83. Martin Robin, "Registration, Conscription and Independent Labour Politics," *C.H.R.* XLVII, 2, 1966, 101-18.

84. *British Columbia Federationist,* 9 November 1917. Cited in Paul Phillips, *No Power Greater* (Vancouver, 1967), 69.

85. *Ibid.,* 70-77.

86. *The Origin of the One Big Union: A Verbatim Account of the Calgary Conference, 1919* (Winnipeg, n.d.), 11.

87. P.A.C., Borden Papers, White to Borden, 16 April, 1919.

88. *Ibid.,* Borden to White, 29 April 1919. For a discussion of subversive and counter-subversive activities see William Rodney, *Soldiers of the International: A History of the Communist Party of Canada, 1919-1929* (Toronto, 1968), 15-27.

89. James Gray's *The Boy from Winnipeg* presents a charming portrait of Winnipeg in these years. See also Alan F.

Artibise, "An Urban Environment: The Process of Growth in Winnipeg, 1874-1914," (unpublished paper presented to the C.H.A. June 1972); and Morris Mott, "The Foreign Peril: Nativism in Winnipeg, 1916-22" (unpublished M.A. thesis, University of Manitoba, 1971).

90. D.C. Masters, *The Winnipeg General Strike* (Toronto, 1950), 11-14; P.A.M., Rigg Papers, Murray to Rigg, 28 May 1918.

91. Queen's University, Crerar Papers, Crerar to Borden, 31 January 1919; See Mott, *op. cit.*, 23-24.

92. Lionel Orlikow, "A Survey of the Reform Movement in Manitoba, 1910-1920" (unpublished M.A. thesis, University of Manitoba, 1955); David Bercusson, "Liberal Progessivism and 'Union Power' in Manitoba: 1915-1920" (unpublished paper presented to the C.H.A. June 1972).

93. William Irvine, "The Labour Church in Canada," *Nation.* CX, 261, 1 May 1920, 583. See also A.E. Smith, *All My Life* (Toronto, 1949), 42-70.

94. Allen, *op. cit.*, cited 84.

95. Masters, *op. cit.* cited 66.

96. David J. Bercusson, "The Winnipeg General Strike, Collective Bargaining, and the One Big Union Issue," *C.H.R.*, LI, 2, 1970, 175.

97. Borden, *Memoirs*, II, 995; P.A.C., Borden Papers, Private, Diary, 14 June 1919.

98. Vernon Thomas, "Jim Woodsworth," *Statesman*, II, 20, 6 December 1919, cited 9. Norman Cohen has defined millenial movements as "surrogates for the Church–salvationist groups led by miracle working ascetics." The description fits the Labour Church movement while Woodsworth and the other clergymen fit Cohen's category of *prophetae*-"more usually they were intellectuals or half-

intellectuals–the former priest turned free-lance preacher was the commonest type of all." Norman Cohen, *The Pursuit of the Millenium.* (New York, 1970), 283.

99. *Statutes of Canada,* 9-10, George V, ch. 46. S97A.

100. J.E. Rae, "The Politics of Conscience: Winnipeg after the Strike," *C.H.A. Historical Papers,* 1971, 276-88.

101. On the strike, in addition to sources already cited, see K.W. McNaught, *A Prophet in Politics* (Toronto, 1959), ch. 8, especially David J. Bercusson, "Labour in Winnipeg: The Great War and the General Strike" (unpublished Ph.D. thesis, University of Toronto, 1971); and Paul Philips "The National Policy and the Development of the Western Canadian Labour Movement," in Rasporich and Klassen, *op., cit.,* 41-62.

102. Jamieson, *op. cit.,* 185.

103. *Weekly Sun,* 7 March 1917.

104. W.L. Morton, *The Progessive Party in Canada op. cit.,* 43, 48, 58.

105. *Weekly Sun,* 7 March 1917.

106. *C.A.R.,* 1918, 412.

107. P.A.C., Rowell Papers, Nicols to Rowell, cited 22 April 1918.

108. Peter McArthur, "The Farmer's Delegation," *Farmer's Magazine,* 1 June 1918. Cited in W.R. Young, "Conscription, Rural Depopulation and the Farmers of Ontario, 1917-19," *C.H.R.,* LIII, 3, 1972, 312.

109. W.C. Good, "Canada's Rural Problem," *Empire Club Speeches* (Toronto, 1917), 309.

110. W.C. Good, *Production and Taxation in Canada. op. cit.,* 21.

111. *Ibid.,* 132-33. Good's concern for virtuous reform led him to oppose the plans of the manager of the United Farmers' Co-operative Company, who wanted to increase profits by rapid ex-

pansion and centralized control. In 1920, young T.P. Loblaw resigned and Good later commented laconically: "Subsequently he seemed to be very successful in his development of the Loblaw chain of food stores." W.C. Good, *Farmer Citizen* (Toronto, 1958), 106.

112. Irvine, *The Farmers in Politics*, *op. cit.* 53.

113. W.L. Morton, *op. cit.*, Appendix B.

114. *The Farmers' Platform*, Issued by the Canadian Council of Agriculture (Winnipeg, 1917), 1.

115. Henry Wise Wood, "In Defense of Group Politics," *Canadian Forum*, III, 27, December 1922, 74.

116. W.K. Rolph, *Henry Wise Wood of Alberta* (Toronto, 1950), cited 66.

117. *Grain Growers' Guide*, 4 December 1918.

118. Queen's University, Crerar Papers, Crerar to Montgomery, 18 September 1918.

119. Norman Lambert, "The Progressive Party in Canada," *Winnipeg Free Press*, 15 July 1950.

120. W.L. Morton, *op. cit.*, 63.

121. *Canada, House of Commons Debates*, 1919, 540.

122. W.L. Morton, *op. cit.*, 71-72.

123. *Globe*, 27 June 1919.

124. Peter Oliver, "Sir William Hearst and the Collapse of the Ontario Conservative Party," *C.H.R.*, LIII, 1, 1972, 21-50.

125. W.L. Morton, *op. cit.*, 69.

126. Queen's University, Crerar Papers, Crerar to Hudson, 21 June, 1919.

127. P.A.C., Dafoe Papers, Dafoe to Sifton, 24 July 1919.

128. P.A.C., Good Papers, Skelton to Good, 10 January 1919; see also Salem Bland, "Who Will Lead if Not the Churches," *Christian Guardian*, 20 November 1918, 7.

NOTES TO CHAPTER SIXTEEN

1. J.S. Woodsworth, "Nation Building," *University Magazine*, XVI, February 1917, 99.

2. McNaught, *A Prophet in Politics*, *op. cit.*, 75.

3. P.A.C., Dafoe Papers, Dafoe to Sifton, 21 July 1919.

4. P.A.C., Borden Papers, Rowell to Borden, 28 October, 1918.

5. P.C. 3006, October 1917.

6. *C.A.R.*, 1918, 556-57.

7. *Ibid.*, 448-49; see also Hodgetts *et al.*, *The Biography of an Institution*, *op. cit.*, 65-92.

8. *C.A.R.*, 1918, 563-66.

9. *C.A.R.*, 1919, 558-89.

10. *Manitoba Free Press*, 1 May 1919.

11. *C.A.R.*, 1919, 333.

12. *Canada, House of Commons Debates*, 1919, 1518.

13. Robert James McFall, "Regulation of Business in Canada," *Political Science Quarterly*, XXXVII, 2, 1922, 205-10; Tom Traves, "A Short History of the Board of Commerce; A Study in the Relations between Government and Business, 1919-20" (unpublished research paper, York University, 1972).

14. *Labour Gazette*, Supplement, XIX, July 1919.

15. *National Industrial Conference: Official Report of Proceedings and Discussion* (Ottawa, 1919).

16. *Labour Gazette*, *op. cit.*, 1172-81.

17. *Industrial Canada*, October 1919.

18. Michael Bliss, "A Canadian Busi-

nessman and War: The Case of Joseph Flavelle," in J.L. Granatstein and R.D. Cuff, eds., *War and Society in North America* (Toronto, 1971), 20-36.

19. S.D. Clark, *The Canadian Manufacturers Association* (Toronto, 1939), 85-88.

20. *C.A.R.*, 1919, 612; *Report of the Women's Conference Held at the Invitation of the War Committee of the Cabinet, February –March 2, 1918* (Ottawa, 1918), 31-34.

21. Robert M. Stamp, "Technical Education, the National Policy, and Federal Provincial Relations in Canadian Education, 1899-1919," *C.H.R.* LII, 4, 1971, 421-23.

22. J. A. Maxwell, *Federal Subsidies to Provincial Governments in Canada* (Cambridge, Mass., 1937), 214-27.

23. P.A.C., Meighen Papers, Robertson to Meighen, 5 December 1920.

24. *Ibid.*, Meighen to Tom Moore, 11 May 1921. See Christopher Armstrong, "The Politics of Federalism: Ontario's Relations with the Federal Government, 1896-1941" (unpublished Ph.D. thesis, University of Toronto, 1972), 447-56.

25. William M. Drummond, "Financing of Land Settlement in Canada" (unpublished manuscript, University of Toronto Library, n.d.), 310.

26. *Manitoba Free Press*, 18 June 1920.

27. Queen's University, Flavelle Papers, Flavelle to Carnegie, 16 February 1920.

28. Roger Graham, "Meighen and the Montreal Tycoons," *C.H.A.A.R.*, 1957, 71-85.

29. Stevens, *The Canadian National Railways, op. cit.*, II, 483ff.

30. Borden, *Memoirs*, II, 966.

31. P.A.C., Meighen Papers, Meighen to Borden, 17 December 1918.

32. *Ibid.*, Meighen to Borden, 1 February 1919.

33. *Ibid.*, Borden to Reid, 25 January 1919.

34. P.A.C., Borden Papers, Clark to Borden, 26 February 1919.

35. *Ibid.*, Memoir Notes, 340, 2384.

36. *Ibid.*, Memoir Notes, memorandum, 3 May 1918.

37. P.A.C, Borden Papers, Private, Diary, 11 May 1918.

38. P.A.C., Borden Papers, memorandum, 25 July 1919.

39. P.A.C., Borden Papers, Private, Diary, 24 July 1919.

40. P.A.C., Borden Papers, Borden to Rowell, 28 July, 1919.

41. *C.A.R.*, 1919, 603-8.

42. *Farmer's Sun*, 12 August 1919.

43. P.A.C., King Papers, Diary, 5-9, 1919.

44. R. McGregor Dawson, *William Lyon Mackenize King, 1874-1923* (Toronto, 1958), cited 308.

45. *C.A.R.*, 1920, 425.

46. P.A.C., Dafoe Papers, Stevenson to Dafoe, 12 December 1919.

47. P.A.C., Borden Papers, Private, Diary, 2 December 1919.

48. P.A.C., Borden Papers, Foster to Borden, 4 March 1920; Calder to Borden, 11 March 1920; Lougheed to Borden, 9 April 1920.

49. *Ibid.*, Meighen to Borden, 18 April 1920.

50. Graham, *Meighen*, I, 287-99; R.C. Brown, "The Political Ideas of Sir Robert Borden," in Marcel Hamelin, ed., *The Political Ideas of the Prime Ministers of Canada* (Ottawa, 1968), 103-4.

51. P.A.C., Dafoe Papers, Stevenson to Dafoe, 12 December 1919.

52. P.A.C., Meighen Papers, Parsons to Meighen, 19 June 1920.

53. *Ibid.*, Meighen to Clayson, 4 April 1920.

54. *Ibid.*, Meighen to North, 20 January 1920.

55. *C.A.R.* 1920, 416.

56. P.A.C., Willison Papers, Willison to Hearst, 19 February 1919.

57. Anthony MacKenzie, "The Rise and Fall of the Farmer-Labour Party of Nova Scotia" (unpublished M.A. thesis, Dalhousie University, 1969).

58. W.L. Morton, *op. cit.,* cited 116; See Margaret A. Ormsby, "The United Farmers of British Columbia: An Abortive Third-Party Movement," *British Columbia Historical Quarterly.* XVII, 1 and 2 January–April 1953, 57.

59. *Ibid.,* 117.

60. *C.A.R.,* 1920, 433.

61. *Ibid.,* 434.

62. *C.A.R.,* 1921, 454.

63. Graham, *Meighen,* II, 110-12.

64. *C.A.R.,* 1921, 449.

65. *Ibid.,* 458.

66. *Ibid.,* 475.

67. Firmin Letourneau, *l'U.C.C.* (Montreal, 1949), 29-49; Rumilly, *Histoire.* XXV 198-201.

68. *Sydney Post,* 2, 3; 9 November 1921. Cited in Mackenzie, *op. cit.,* 139.

69. P.A.C., King Papers, King to Violet Markham, September 1921. See Margaret Prang, "Mackenzie King Woos Ontario," *Ontario History,* LVIII, 1, 1966, 1-20.

70. Dawson, *King. op. cit.,* 351.

71. C.P. Stacey, *Historical Documents of Canada* (Toronto, 1972), V. 75-76.

72. Margaret Stewart and Doris French, *Ask No Quarter* (Toronto, 1959), cited 60.

73. Howard A. Scarrow, *Canada Votes* (New Orleans, 1962), 34-35.

74. Lionel Groulx, "Notre Doctrine," *L'Action française.* V, janvier 1921, 24-33. See Susan Mann Robertson, "L'Action Française: l'Appel de la Race" (unpublished Ph.D. thesis, Laval University, 1970).

75. Lionel Groulx, "Méditation Patriotique," *Le Devoir.* 24 June 1920. Reprinted in *Dix Ans d'Action française* (Montreal, 1926), 76.

76. Urquhart and Buckley, eds., *Historical Statistics of Canada.* 14.

77. P.A.C., Laurier Papers, Laurier to Gregory, 11 November 1904.

78. P.A.C., Borden Papers, Private, Diary, 11 November 1918.

INDEX

399

THE CANADIAN CENTENARY SERIES

A History of Canada in Nineteen Volumes

The Canadian Centenary Series is a comprehensive history of the peoples and lands which form the Dominion of Canada.

Although the series is designed as a unified whole so that no part of the story is left untold, each volume is complete in itself. Written for the general reader as well as for the scholar, each of the nineteen volumes of *The Canadian Centenary Series* is the work of a leading Canadian historian who is an authority on the period covered in his volume. Their combined efforts have made a new and significant contribution to the understanding of the history of Canada and of Canada today.

W. L. Morton (d. 1980), Vanier Professor of History, Trent University, was the Executive Editor of *The Canadian Centenary Series*. A graduate of the Universities of Manitoba and Oxford, he was the author of *The Kingdom of Canada; Manitoba: A History; The Progressive Party in Canada; The Critical Years: The Union of British North America, 1857-1873;* and other writings. He also edited *The Journal of Alexander Begg and Other Documents Relevant to the Red River Resistance.* Holder of the honorary degrees of LL.D. and D.LITT., he was awarded the Tyrrell Medal of the Royal Society of Canada and the Governor General's Award for Non-Fiction.

D. G. Creighton (d. 1979), former Chairman of the Department of History, University of Toronto, was the Advisory Editor of *The Canadian Centenary Series.* A graduate of the Universities of Toronto and Oxford, he was the author of *John A. Macdonald: The Young Politician; John A. Macdonald: The Old Chieftain; Dominion of the North; The Empire of the St. Lawrence* and many other works. Holder of numerous honorary degrees, LL.D. and D.LITT., he twice won the Governor General's Award for Non-Fiction. He had also been awarded the Tyrrell Medal of the Royal Society of Canada, the University of Alberta National Award in Letters, the University of British Columbia Medal for Popular Biography, and the Molson Prize of the Canada Council.

Ramsay Cook, Professor of History, York University, co-author with R. C. Brown of *Canada, 1896-1921,* volume 14 of the series, is the Executive Editor of *The Canadian Centenary Series,* 1983.